*Connecticut's Indigenous Peoples*

# Connecticut's Indigenous Peoples

*What Archaeology, History, and Oral Traditions Teach Us About Their Communities and Cultures*

Lucianne Lavin
Institute for American Indian Studies

With a contribution to the Introduction by
Paul Grant-Costa, Yale Indian Papers Project

Edited by Rosemary Volpe
Yale Peabody Museum of Natural History

YALE PEABODY MUSEUM OF NATURAL HISTORY

Yale UNIVERSITY PRESS/NEW HAVEN & LONDON

Published with assistance from the Mary Cady Tew Memorial Fund.

Yale University Press books may be purchased in quantity for educational, business, or promotional use. For information, please e-mail sales.press@yale.edu (U.S. office) or sales@yaleup.co.uk (U.K. office).

Designed by Mary Valencia.
Set in Adobe Garamond type by Tseng Information Systems, Inc.
Printed in the United States of America.

*The Library of Congress has cataloged the hardcover edition as follows:*
Lavin, Lucianne
Connecticut's indigenous peoples : what archaeology, history, and oral traditions teach us about their communities and cultures / Lucianne Lavin, Institute of American Indian Studies ; with a contribution by Paul Grant-Costa, Yale Indian Papers Project ; edited by Rosemary Volpe, Yale Peabody Museum of Natural History.
    p.    cm.
Includes bibliographical references and index.
ISBN 978-0-300-18664-2 (alk. paper)
1. Indians of North America—Connecticut—History. 2. Indians of North America—Connecticut—Antiquities. 3. Indians of North America—Connecticut—Folklore. 4. Oral tradition—Connecticut. 5. Connecticut—Antiquities. I. Title.
E78.C7L36 2013
974.6'01—dc23                                                                                          2012044426

ISBN 978-0-300-21258-7 (pbk.)

A catalogue record for this book is available from the British Library.

10 9 8 7 6 5 4 3 2

*publication of this book is enabled by a grant from*

**Jewish Federation of Greater Hartford**

*This book is dedicated to my late mother, Marie Michrina Neff, whose enthusiasm for archaeology and learning in general greatly influenced my life pursuits. Without her gentle guidance, this book might never have been written.*

# Contents

# Foreword

I first met Dr. Lucianne Lavin back in the winter of 1986, when I was a lowly intern at the Yale Peabody Museum of Natural History in New Haven, Connecticut. The institution was preparing to put all of its collections' card catalogue information online—which seemed at the time like a great leap into the future. I was checking the physical inventory of ethnographic materials in collections against the registrar's list and the card catalog. Lucianne was studying these collections for a survey of indigenous pottery shards. We had a brief conversation, then both of us returned to our work. I thought it was brave of her to seek a career in archaeology, a profession that seemed to be overwhelmingly populated by males.

Since then, our paths have kept crossing. Dr. Lavin has instituted and participated in many of the archaeological programs at a variety of scholarly organizations. She has taught archaeological and anthropological courses at Connecticut College, as well as at Adelphi University and Naugatuck Community College, among others. She also owns and operates an archaeological firm and is a consultant on many projects, too. She is the current director of research and collections at the Institute for American Indian Studies, an educational center and museum in Washington, Connecticut, where many programs are offered for both youth and adult education. She is a longtime contributor and editor for the *Bulletin of the Archaeological Society of Connecticut,* and the author of many professional papers on the archaeology and ethnohistory of the Northeast.

As part of the network of professionals in this field, Dr. Lavin has access to the results of the supervised avocational excavations in this region. She has been ideally situated to keep current with recent excavations from around the state. I cannot think of someone better qualified to write a book in this discipline, and I am glad that she has taken time from all of her responsibilities to do so.

The time for this comprehensive book on archaeology and ethnohistory is well past due. Most texts used to teach Connecticut's archaeology in college courses today are thirty or more years out of date, if one judges by the excavations used as examples throughout their text. Professors should be happy to find a chronology of Connecticut from geological time to a more recent era, and a compendium of truncated site reports for the various aspects of Connecticut archaeology between these two covers, as well as a wide-ranging list of references cited to direct their students to more intense documentation.

Beginning with the geology and natural resources of the area, and then the entry of its earliest visitors, the Paleo-Indians, the author uses the environment to explain the lifeways of each of the commonly accepted divisions of pre-contact time, and the reasons for the dissimilar tool kits and patterns of the people who came to Connecticut.

Reports on newer sites as well as materials found at older excavations and never previously analyzed add a new dimension to our studies of the early population of Connecticut. The questions the author raises are provocative, and should lead to further research. I had not known how much new material was available until I read this book.

Also included in this work is information on the history of the Connecticut tribes, from initial contact with their new European neighbors to the most recent federal recognition of some Connecticut tribes. The timeline shows early sporadic contacts between Europeans and these indigenous peoples of New England. The shared past of these tribes, as well as situations unique to each one, both under colonial rule and later, under state government, is based on thorough research, using original documents and secondary sources.

Dr. Lavin serves on the panel of the Native American Heritage Advisory Council, appointed by the president pro tempore of the Senate, along with representatives from the five tribes recognized by the State of Connecticut, which gives her the ability to have an informed discussion of tribal status today and how natives have survived since colonial times—as a people and also as individual groups. She also talks about the native peoples from tribes across the country who make Connecticut their home.

She explains why some tribes appear to have flourished as others struggled to keep their identity. Included is a section on lifeways, the living culture and customs of peoples. A section on myth and folklore shows how native people explained natural phenomena, the cosmos, and their belief systems, as well as how they used these narratives to transmit a code of behavior and manners to the young, much as the Bible, the Torah, and the Koran are used.

I think that the images in this book, many of which have not been published before, are a treasure. Those of us who study the archaeology and history of Connecticut will be satisfied with the extensive bibliography. The scope of information in this book is impressive.

Thank you, Dr. Lucianne Lavin, for dedicating an enormous amount of your time to giving us such an extensive work. This book will be the standard in this field for years to come.

Faith Damon Davison
Elder and Retired Archivist, The Mohegan Tribe
Uncasville, Connecticut

# *Preface*

This book is a greatly expanded and updated version of *Prehistory of Connecticut's Native Americans,* a guide I wrote to accompany an exhibition on the state's Native peoples at Yale University's Peabody Museum of Natural History. The opening of the exhibition in 1984 commemorated the fiftieth anniversary of the Archaeological Society of Connecticut. The project director was Dr. Irving Rouse, Charles J. MacCurdy Professor Emeritus of Anthropology at Yale University and honorary curator of anthropology at the Yale Peabody Museum. I was co-director of the project. The exhibition, a visual presentation of the origin and development of Connecticut's indigenous peoples from earliest times up to European contact, was dedicated to the surviving Native Americans in the state. The guide, popular with teachers, provided a more in-depth discussion of cultural lifeways during the major periods of indigenous history and the techniques of archaeological recovery used in their reconstruction.

Since that time, new and exciting archaeological and historical discoveries have challenged old theories and reshaped traditional interpretations of the histories and cultures of Connecticut's indigenous peoples. These discoveries were the catalyst for revising and updating the original booklet. Recent historical events provided additional incentive—particularly those revolving about the federal recognition status of two colonial and state-recognized tribes, the Schaghticoke and the Historic Eastern Pequot.

Governmental and private appeals by anti-casino groups to the tribes' federal recognition, and the press generated by them, have increased public confusion concerning the history and continuity of American Indian communities in Connecticut. Many people I meet do not know that tribal communities continued to exist in or near their ancient homelands throughout the past four hundred years of Euro-American settlement in Connecticut. Misconceptions abound about "historical" Native Americans. Specifically, they include the erroneous notions that all indigenous peoples moved west to get away from the Europeans or died out from the effects of warfare and disease, and that the occasional nineteenth-century Indians mentioned in local town histories were among a few families left behind when their tribe went west—and who soon died out as well.

It was mainly to eradicate this negative stereotype of the vanishing Connecticut Indian that I added the final two chapters, which discuss Indian communities from European contact to the present. Unlike the detailed, site-specific analyses in the chapters dealing with the previous 10,000-plus years, the post-contact chap-

ters are mainly summaries of major historical events shared by the many indigenous tribal societies after the intrusion of Euro-American explorers and settlers.
They are not meant to be an inclusive discourse on Native American peoples and
events during that time frame—that is another book. Rather, they are intended
merely to *introduce the public* to post-European-contact Indian Country in Connecticut, and the encounters and experiences that affected the cultures and histories of its tribal peoples in general. My aim is to show that tribal communities
continued to live here, interacting with one another and with the Anglo-American
and other, later immigrants, and that several of those communities continue to
exist within our present society.

Connecticut's indigenous peoples have an extremely rich and ancient cultural
heritage. Archaeological studies show that Native Americans settled the lands we
know as Connecticut more than 10,000 years ago. Several American Indian tribal
communities have continuously occupied their homelands from pre-contact times
and throughout the period following European contact. Indigenous communities
were our first governments and, as the reader shall learn, their people were our first
environmental stewards, astronomers, mathematicians, zoologists, botanists, and
geologists. They were extremely knowledgeable of their natural world, which they
perceived—and as many contemporary tribal peoples still do—as fundamentally
linked to the spiritual world. This is expressed in their ancient, complex belief systems, cosmologies, and sacred stories.

I define "community" much the same way as does historian and specialist in
Native American history Dr. Colin Calloway in his preface to his 1995 book *The
American Revolution in Indian Country,* as "a group of people living in face to face
association and occupying a common location, either permanently or seasonally."
Disease, land losses, and the wars of the seventeenth century had so depopulated
and displaced tribal peoples that by the eighteenth century what the English referred to as tribes "were often aggregates of communities; many Indian communities were also multiethnic units rather than members of a single tribe," Calloway
continues. "A community sometimes comprised several villages in a particular area
rather than a single town in a single location. Names of communities should often
be regarded as 'addresses' rather than tribal designations. Native Americans were
accustomed to accommodating a variety of groups and individuals with flexible
bonds and fluid social structures. . . . As Richard White has pointed out, Indian
country was largely a world of villages."

At the time of European contact, many tribal communities populated Connecticut. Although most of these political entities are now extinct, their people
live on in the Connecticut citizens who are their descendants. For example, in her
1986 study of the Wangunk tribe of central Connecticut, published in the journal *Artifacts,* Karen Coody Cooper found that although the tribal organization
is extinct, the people are not. She had discovered more than sixty Wangunk descendants. Five indigenous colony and state-recognized tribes continue to thrive
and dwell in their ancient homelands to this very day. They are the Schaghticokes, with a 400-acre reservation near Kent, the Golden Hill Paugussetts with a

quarter-acre reservation near Trumbull and a 106-acre reservation near Colchester, the Mashantucket Pequots with a 1,640-acre reservation near Ledyard, the Historic Eastern Pequots with a 224-acre reservation near Stonington, and the Mohegans with a 507-acre reservation near Uncasville. There are also several entities who consider themselves descendants of earlier tribes that are not recognized by the State of Connecticut—and sometimes they are also not recognized by other tribal peoples. They include the New England Coastal Schaghticoke Indian Association, The Nehantic Tribe and Nation, the Nipmuc Indian Association, and the Algonquian Confederacy of the Quinnipiac Tribal Council, among others.

Additionally, Connecticut residents include many Native American people who are members of out-of-state tribes. In 2009 the United States Census Bureau reported that there were 3,405,607 persons living in Connecticut, with 0.4 percent (13,622) of these describing themselves as American Indian or Alaska Native persons (http://quickfacts.census.gov/qfd/states/09000.html). Native Americans traditionally have been notoriously underestimated by censuses, however, and also the federal census does not discern the many residents who describe themselves as "white" but trace descent from one or more American Indian ancestors.

All that we know about the pre-contact and early contact history of Connecticut's Native Americans derives from archaeology, from Native American oral histories, and from early accounts by European traders and explorers. Many of these primary accounts were consciously or unconsciously biased by the authors' political agendas, by their ignorance of indigenous societies, and by their Western perspective in general. The later secondary accounts of nineteenth-century local historians are even less reliable. In his dissertation from 1992, archaeologist Dr. John Pfeiffer described these sources.

> With the reduction of Native American populations in Connecticut by 1800, there came a fascination with the inhabitants whom we had nearly eliminated. Much of this was in the form of antiquarian studies . . . primary sources were followed by an interest in local histories of the "Indians in our past." This was manifested in works by De Forest (1852) and Brownell (1859), which were dramatized secondary accounts saying more about how we in the mid 19th century felt about the past than about what had actually happened.

In the late nineteenth and early twentieth centuries, historians wrote of locally extinct Indian tribes even as communities of those tribes struggled to maintain their existence against neglectful, sometimes hostile governments that controlled their reservations and their tribal funds (see, for example, the studies by Jean O'Brien published in 2006 and 2010). Indigenous oral histories, such as those related in the writings of Melissa Fawcett Zobel, Adelphena Logan, and Trudie Lamb Richmond, provide a contrasting perspective to these mainly white, Protestant, male upper-class narratives.

Connecticut archaeology is a relatively new and dynamic field. In the past twenty-five years many exciting discoveries have been made about the history and lifestyles of the state's indigenous people. Yet not many people know of the existence of this body of knowledge. There are few current exhibits, and only two books on New England archaeology for specialists in the field. Dean Snow's *The Archaeology of New England* was published more than thirty years ago, and the other, *Antiquities of the New England Indians* by Charles Willoughby, more than seventy-five years ago. Both are out of print. One popular text on the archaeology of northeastern North America, *The First Peoples of the Northeast* by Esther Braun and David Braun, provides general information on southern New England and does not deal specifically with Connecticut archaeology. Further, it was written more than fifteen years ago. The only popular text dealing with Connecticut archaeology, *The Archaeology of Connecticut* by Kristen and William Keegan, is a small, edited volume more than ten years old on various local archaeological topics, and is outdated by the many important archaeological finds since then.

Connecticut history is a requisite subject in the curriculum of schools in the state. Connecticut Native Americans are often a subject of the social studies curriculum. The more than 10,000 years of pre-European history preceding the 400 years of written history in Connecticut certainly should be an integral part of these curricula. There is a great need in the K-12 curriculum for information on local archaeology. Likewise, the 400 years of colonial and state history should include discussions of our local Native American communities and their significant roles and contributions to the continued growth and welfare of Connecticut.

This book was written to help meet these needs. Its perspective is archaeological and ethnographic. Cultural interpretations are based on an overview of past and current publications and unpublished manuscripts in northeastern North American archaeology and history, public records of the Colony and State of Connecticut, indigenous oral traditions and interviews, and my own ongoing archaeological and documentary research. It was my goal to produce a book that reflects the antiquity, richness, and diversity of Connecticut's indigenous histories to enlighten and stimulate the awareness of educators, students, and the interested public. As written by Aquinnah Wampanoag Linda Coombs, associate director of the Wampanoag Indigenous Program at Plimoth Plantation, "The point of learning about other human beings is not just to collect facts and information, but to use that learning to build respect and understanding."

The book's diverse and often unpublished sources of information, and the interpretations and questions they have engendered, hopefully will promote positive dialogue on these issues among my archaeological and ethnohistorical colleagues as well. Science is cumulative, and it is only through continual accumulation of data and a multi-perspective approach to its interpretation that researchers will be able to construct more accurate local and regional histories.

# Acknowledgments

My deepest thanks go to my many dear friends and colleagues who were generous with time and materials in the preparation of this book. Among them are Dr. Kevin McBride, associate professor at the University of Connecticut Department of Anthropology and director of research at the Mashantucket Pequot Museum and Research Center; Dr. Kenneth Feder, professor of archaeology at Central Connecticut State University; David H. Thompson, president of the Greater New Haven Archaeological Society; Dr. Nicholas Bellantoni, state archaeologist in the Office of Connecticut State Archaeology; Dr. Brian Jones, senior archaeologist at Archaeological and Historical Services, Inc.; Daniel Forrest, staff archaeologist and deputy state historic preservation officer in the Connecticut State Historic Preservation Office; Dr. Barbara Calogero, consultant in geoarchaeology; Dr. Ross Harper, senior archaeologist at Public Archaeology Survey Team, Inc.; Dr. Lucinda McWeeney, consultant in archaeobotany; Dr. Roger Moeller, director of Archaeological Services; Ernie Wiegand, professor of geology and archaeology at Norwalk Community College; Dr. Marc Banks, manager and owner of Marc L. Banks Ph.D. LLC; Dr. Laurie Weinstein, professor of anthropology at Western Connecticut State University; the late Dr. Harold Juli, professor of anthropology at Connecticut College; the late David Cooke, dig chair for the Friends of the State Archaeologist; Marian O'Keefe, curator of the Seymour Historical Society; Timothy Visel, coordinator at the Sound School Regional Vocational Aquaculture Center; ethnobotanist E. Barrie Kavasch; Tim MacSweeney; Doug Currie, head of conservation, and collections manager Meredith Vasta at the Mashantucket Pequot Museum and Research Center.

I especially want to acknowledge the assistance of indigenous elders Trudie Lamb Richmond, Dale Carson, and particularly Faith Damon Davison for her kind words in the foreword to this book, as well as the artists who generously shared their work: David R. Wagner, Gerry Biron, Allan Hazard, Sr., Craig Spears, Sr., Jeanne Morningstar Kent, and Strong Eagle Daly.

Special thanks go to executive director Elizabeth McCormick, assistant director Lisa Piastuch, Ruth and Matt Barr, Ted Swigart, Kimberly Parent, and Lillia McEnaney at the Institute for American Indian Studies for their time and efforts in providing unpublished materials, graphics, and comments on earlier drafts of this book. I am grateful too for the assistance of Andrea Rand, Craig Nelson, and Bruce Kulas of the Litchfield Hills Archaeology Club. My thanks also to the seven reviewers of the manuscript draft; their comments and suggestions enhanced the final product.

At Yale, I would like to thank Dr. Paul Grant-Costa, executive editor of the Yale Indian Papers Project at the Lewis Walpole Library, for his collaboration on the Introduction; senior collections manager Dr. Roger Colten and museum assistant Maureen DaRos at the Yale Peabody Museum's Division of Anthropology; collections manager Dr. Patrick Sweeney in the Peabody Division of Botany/Yale Herbarium and senior collections manager Dr. Christopher Norris of the Peabody Division of Vertebrate Paleontology; Janet Sweeting for her assistance with researching the Peabody anthropology archives; and Joann McIntosh, Armand Morgan, and Diane Lonardelli for their excellent work on updating the charts, illustrations, and photographs used in the book. A very special thank you to Peabody's editor Rosemary Volpe for her outstanding editorial guidance and constant support throughout this multiyear project.

This book reflects the work of the many who have lived the history of archaeology in Connecticut.

# Introduction

## *Archaeology in Connecticut*

Lucianne Lavin and Paul Grant-Costa

The existence of writings from the historic period . . . tempts us to rely on them. . . . But while those writings do add a lot to our understanding, they are scattered, skip over commonplace details that are now lost, and reflect cultural biases of the writers. Archaeology can fill in those gaps, giving us a more complete picture of life in 1620, 1720, 1820, or 1920 than is possible with documents alone.

— Kristen N. Keegan and William F. Keegan, *The Archaeology of Connecticut*, 1999

North America was inhabited by many culturally diverse Native groups thousands of years before its "discovery" in 1492 by Christopher Columbus—who never landed on mainland North America, but explored only as far north as the islands of the Caribbean. Many of these Native American cultures were quite complex, with sociopolitical stratification, intricate mortuary rites, extensive trade networks, and viable economies in balance ecologically with both their physical and social environments.

In Connecticut, the study of Native American history divides into four main stages: Paleo-Indian, Archaic, Woodland, and Post-Contact. These in turn are subdivided into ten major cultural periods:

> Paleo-Indian (about 15,000 to 9000 years ago, or radiocarbon years before the present [RCY B.P.])
> Early Archaic (9000 to 8000 years ago)
> Middle Archaic (8000 to 6000 years ago)
> Late Archaic (6000 to 3800 years ago)
> Terminal Archaic (3800 to 2700 years ago)
> Early Woodland (2700 to 1650 years ago)
> Middle Woodland (1650 to 950 years ago)
> Late Woodland (950 years ago [ca. A.D. 1000] to A.D. 1524)
> Final Woodland (A.D. 1524 to 1633)
> Post-Contact (A.D. 1633 into the twenty-first century)

Traditionally, the Native American cultural periods in Connecticut have been defined mainly by diagnostic artifact styles, usually projectile points and clay pots. More recently, cultural periods have been distinguished by changes in other aspects of culture, such as economic and settlement patterns, trade, and ceremonial practices.[1] Here the year A.D. 1633 marks the beginning of the Post-Contact period in Connecticut, because that is when the first European "town" (Windsor) was created. Obviously, the beginning of the Post-Contact period occurred at different times in different regions, depending on the date of their first European settlements.

How can we make such remarkable statements about long-dead cultures whose people left no written records? The answer is archaeological investigation of their living areas and the objects they left there. The archaeologist fits together bits and pieces of material remains like a jigsaw puzzle to formulate the cohesive life pattern of an ancient culture. Theories are then examined against the evidence of Native oral traditions and an extensive historical record, to be supported or refuted, and to recover possible continuing trends.

The discipline of archaeology in Connecticut is a young and dynamic field. Collections of local Indian artifacts were being assessed by the staff at Yale University's Peabody Museum of Natural History as early as the turn of the twentieth century, and field surveys and excavations were done until the early 1950s, although interest in Native American cultures at Yale University began long before. But at that time ancient artifacts were looked on merely as interesting curiosities, not as the material record of past human behavior and the primary means by which scientists were able to reconstruct the history and lifeways of the earliest settlers of the state—its Native American Indians.[2]

## THE HISTORY OF CONNECTICUT ARCHAEOLOGY

For generations Native American artifacts have been recovered from plowed fields, cellar holes, riverbanks, and rocky ledges throughout Connecticut. These bits and pieces of an earlier time often found their way into informal collections as mere curiosities. Few local collectors had the time, inclination, or formal schooling to study these objects or to propose educated theories about the indigenous peoples who made them. In fact, the science of archaeology as we know it today did not come into being until the middle of the nineteenth century.

From the beginning, the history of archaeology in Connecticut has included many individuals from Yale University who have played crucial roles in developing the scientific study of the state's early Native Americans. Later Yale anthropologists were instrumental in moving the hobby of artifact collecting to a more professional level, or at least in encouraging collectors to adopt scientific methods. Although awkward at first, this relationship with amateur archaeologists developed in time to become a valuable contribution to research in the state.

## The Inquisitive Reverend Stiles

Although the work of Yale College in the eighteenth century included the training of missionaries to preach to the Indians of southern New England, when the ever curious Reverend Ezra Stiles (1727–1795) became its president in 1778, Yale chose someone deeply interested in the region's Native Americans. In this, Stiles—a recognized theologian, scholar, historian, and scientist—was ahead of his time, an exception among those who collected Indian artifacts. For much of his life, Stiles gathered information on New England's Indians: he recorded the memories of the oldest residents, surveyed found artifacts, drew up censuses, and interviewed Indians themselves on their history, customs, myths, and political affairs.

From his discussions, observations, and calculations, Stiles believed, incorrectly however, that Indians and Indian culture in New England were quickly vanishing. This mistaken notion, together with the nineteenth-century romantic idea of the "noble savage," became wildly popular and led to scholar-like, yet inaccurate, pronouncements about Connecticut's Indians well into the twentieth century. "We are increasing with great rapidity," Stiles once wrote, "and the Indians, as well as the million Africans in America, are decreasing as rapidly. Both left to themselves," he continued, "in this way diminishing, may gradually vanish."[3] Despite these errors, modern ethnohistorians nevertheless can be grateful to Stiles for collecting as much information as he did and attempting to make scientific sense out of it.

In the century after Stiles's death no Yale faculty members continued his investigations. The occasional arrowhead or clay pot remained the province of the industrious farmer, the local village historian, and a growing number of collectors who kept and sometimes traded the prettiest, oddest, or most peculiar of their bones, stones, and pottery sherds. These collections, although visually impressive, provided little or no specific information on the context in which the artifacts were found, except perhaps what the collector could remember and was willing to share. Much valuable information was also lost at the death of a collector, as uninterested heirs would often relocate objects to attics, barns, basements, and the occasional trash heap. Although most of these finds were never much publicized, newspapers would nonetheless print news of a discovery every now and then. In 1867 a New Haven paper, *The Columbian Weekly Register,* published the following note.

> —In draining some of the swamp land on the farm of J.D. Alvord, Esq., Old Mill Hill, says the Farmer, several stone axes, arrow heads and other relics of Indian life have been dug up and brought to light. The stone axes have a very keen edge, and must have been very formidable instruments in the hand of a "brave." They will make, even at this remote period of time from their construction, a dent in the toughest piece of steel when it is struck with one.[4]

The *Hartford Daily Courant* in 1871 included this article on archaeological finds from New London County:

EZRA STILES, S.T.D. LL.D.

President of Yale College from 1777 to 1795.

*Ezra Stiles*

Nineteenth-century engraving of Ezra Stiles, a graduate of the Yale College Class of 1746 and president of Yale College from 1778 to 1795.

Asa Fish has in his possession a number of Indian relics which have lately been exhumed upon the Miner farm, now owned by James D. Fish of New York. While digging on the banks of Norwood lake (formerly Williams Cove), the workmen struck a hard substance which proved to be the debris of Indian pottery, and at last a whole pot, lying bottom upward, filled with fresh kept ashes, was struck and carefully laid bare. The spot where these were found, was on a low promontory situated about east of Juniper hill, by the cove or lake, and what is remarkable, they there found a number of fire pits close together, each bearing marks of use. Among other things there exhumed were deers' heads, moose horns, buck horns, quite well preserved, bears' or moose teeth and jaws, only partially decayed, and the bones of various animals, the remains of feasts probably.[5]

During the nineteenth century Yale College made great strides in using its diverse scientific collections for research, teaching, and public exhibition, including establishing the Peabody Museum of Natural History in 1866. Although the museum soon became known more for impressive paleontological, ethnographic, and archaeological collections gathered by expeditions to the American West in the early 1870s, by the beginning of the twentieth century Peabody Museum researchers had made plans for a systematic inventory of information and artifacts from every corner of Connecticut.

## The Attraction of Collecting

The end of the nineteenth century saw an amazing rise of interest in things Indian. The anthropological exhibitions at international fairs like the World's Columbian Exposition of 1893 in Chicago awakened in the public a curiosity for American Indian "antiquities." That same year also witnessed the founding of several scholarly publications in the new science of anthropology, with a similar interest in archaeological discoveries carrying over into the popular press in magazines like *Harper's*. Locally, Native American people in New England, reflecting modern realities, banded together into larger regional confederacies like the New England Indian Council and publicly displayed their culture in summer powwows, in which non-Indians were invited to participate.[6]

This interest produced a demand for Indian objects, creating a thriving market. In the early twentieth century, several of the most prestigious museums in the United States, among them the Heye Foundation's Museum of the American Indian, sent scouts into Connecticut for the sole purpose of purchasing handsome or unique artifacts for display. Bidding wars with astute hobbyists played institutions against each other. As the market grew, so did the propensity for collectors to dig indiscriminately. Sites were pilfered recklessly, and significant amounts of data were lost. Equally disturbing was the introduction of counterfeit artifacts into the stream of commerce. As one editor cautioned,

> Collectors [once] felt safe with what are called eastern or New England specimens — they at least were all genuine, and their ancient appearance caused by long burial in the ground or exposure upon its surface, would always serve to distinguish them. But now deceit has invaded even the land of steady habits. If the Genius of Connecticut surmounting our State Capitol looks sharply she will discover within range of her vision at least two places where Indian relics are now being manufactured for the benefit of an unsuspecting public; while almost beneath her feet she will see these objects mixed with the genuine and offered for sale. . . . Let the collector beware.[7]

Scientists in the new fields of anthropology and archaeology were a definite minority at the start of the twentieth century. In 1899 there were only twenty-eight professional archaeologists in the United States: eleven were researchers at institutions and seventeen were teachers. Many became concerned about the destruction of sites and artifact context. Their systematic recording of all unearthed materials, no matter how small or insignificant, took time and patience, traits that fared poorly in the fast-paced artifact market. Professionals were seen by collectors as "overeducated" competition, and the first steps of archaeologists into the field were met with distrust.

On the national level, in response to the looting occurring throughout the country, the American Association for the Advancement of Science pushed the U.S. Congress to pass the Antiquities Act of 1906, which protected historic and prehistoric Indian sites on federal land.[8] The AAAS also encouraged academic institutions across the country to inventory state archaeological sites.

## Toward an Archaeological Survey of Connecticut

The idea for an archaeological survey of Connecticut was not new. Warren K. Moorehead (1866–1939), who was affiliated with Phillips Academy in Andover, Massachusetts, had already undertaken a preliminary inspection of New England's sites, but his study listed only a few in Connecticut. Knowing that there were significantly more, anthropologists from Yale proposed a comprehensive survey by professionally trained archaeologists, a task that fell to George Grant MacCurdy (1863–1947). A professor of prehistoric Old World archaeology in the recently formed Division of Anthropology at Yale's Peabody Museum of Natural History, Dr. MacCurdy was on the boards of several professional societies, including the American Anthropological Association, and ran the American School of Prehistoric Research in Paris, where each summer archaeologists received training in European excavation methods.

In 1910 Dr. MacCurdy traveled across Connecticut to interview local collectors, historians, and others. The rate at which information was being lost greatly troubled him. At a rock shelter he excavated near New Haven, he witnessed firsthand how collectors had destroyed the context, crucial to the proper interpretation of any archaeological site. Although he attempted some measure of scientific excavation, the rock shelter had been greatly disturbed and subsequently completely demolished by explosives set off by a trap rock company. Despite finding a wealth of information, MacCurdy's published analysis in the *American Journal of Science* in 1914 expressed his remorse at not being able to maintain the appropriate professional standards of his Old World training.[9]

> The noble shelter has completely disappeared, but thanks to the generosity of several local collectors, the Museum possesses the major part of the relics found there. The two-fold regret is that the removal of the deposits could not have been scientifically controlled, and that the shelter itself could not have been spared as a sort of out-door annex to the University Museum. Of the specimens figured all we know is that they came from the Cave. There is absolutely no record as to the relative positions of the various objects in the relic-bearing deposits. . . . American archeology has always been handicapped by the lack of chronological data. These can never be supplied by surface finds. Among the possible sources of such data, caves and rock shelters should rightly be counted. The destruction therefore of a cave record like that at Pine Rock is nothing short of an archeological calamity.[10]

However destructive the collectors, a more pressing concern was the ruinous effect of development, as Connecticut's villages, towns, and cities in the early

George Grant MacCurdy established the Division of Anthropology at the Yale Peabody Museum in 1902, bringing together the museum's archaeological, ethnological, and physical anthropology collections under a single authority.

twentieth century widened roads, put in sewers, and strung power lines across the state. The MacCurdy survey became a salvage operation.

For more than fifteen years Dr. MacCurdy collected newspaper articles, letters of inquiry, and communications from fellow archaeologists, and made copious notes about the collections he saw. While at Yale, he tenaciously pursued this work, scraping together whatever funding he could. In 1927, at the end of his career at the Peabody Museum, Dr. MacCurdy made sure the survey had enough financial support to see it through to completion. It continued under the direction of his successor, Cornelius Osgood (1905–1983), an alumnus from the American School.

In a memo to Yale's Richard Swan Lull, Dr. Osgood emphasized the importance of Connecticut archaeological projects in the Peabody Museum's Division of Anthropology. He proposed a study and organization of its Connecticut archaeology collections and all known information from individuals, collectors, and the academic literature. Taking his lead from Dr. MacCurdy, he also recommended the excavation of Connecticut sites to gain accurate data and material for these collections. This fieldwork gave Yale students the opportunity for the hands-

The rock shelter at the base of the cliff at Pine Rock, New Haven County, Connecticut, circa 1912, photographed by George Grant MacCurdy.

on study of professional archaeological techniques and also provided project directors with a good supply of workers.

Several years later, Dr. Osgood reported on the survey's progress. "The excavation of a large cave-shelter near North Branford has been pushed forward several days of each week," he wrote, "with three to five men actively engaged; three men are registered students in archaeology."[11] These men—Yale College students—worked at the site in coat jackets, white shirts, and ties. Osgood envisioned periodic excavations that would both contribute to the Peabody's knowledge of early Connecticut and be an archaeological training ground for Yale's students.

In 1932 Dr. Osgood welcomed one of these workers as a new assistant, twenty-four-year-old graduate student Froelich G. Rainey (1907–1992). Dr. Rainey's first attempt at archaeology left him unimpressed, but after a summer at MacCurdy's American School in Paris and at a dig in Palestine, he committed himself whole-heartedly back in New Haven working on his graduate assistantship. By the late spring Rainey was in the field getting acquainted with collectors and site diggers throughout the state. His field journal, begun on May 19, 1932, covers a one-year period.

For the rest of the summer he continued to chart the distribution of Indian

Cornelius Osgood was curator of anthropology at Yale University from 1934 to 1973 and may be best known for his research among the Athapaskan-speaking people of interior Alaska.

A Yale excavation of a shoreline site, part of F. G. Rainey's 1932 Connecticut Archaeology Survey (Rainey is at the far right of the photograph).

Froelich G. Rainey at the Melliac excavation site in Haiti, circa 1935.

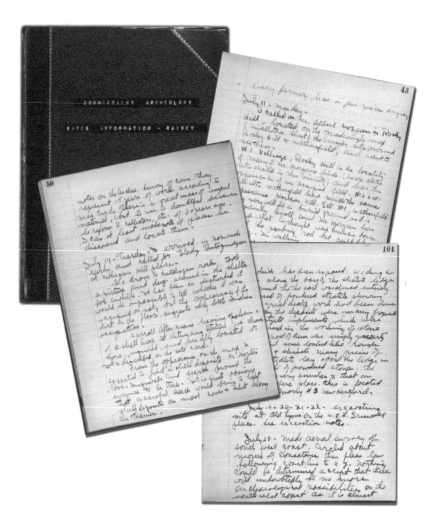

A sampling of pages from F. G. Rainey's "Connecticut Archeology Sites Information" journal. The entry on the page at left mentions a visit by Rainey to Norwich to call on Mohegan medicine woman Gladys Tantaquidgeon.

sites and studied collections not readily available to the public. The original plan was to drive to every town in Connecticut with Dr. MacCurdy's lists and interview town clerks, historians, librarians, museum staff, and artifact collectors knowledgeable about local Indian sites. It proved too simplistic. Dr. MacCurdy's informant list was close to twenty years old. Many people did not care to share their information with him. Even local museum staff turned him away. A little more than a month into the project, Dr. Rainey refined his plan. "I have run across men in different sections who are intelligent enough, interested enough, and have influence enough to act as representative or 'key men' for the museum," he wrote. "If they can be handled right, they could be used as a steady source of information from their region . . . and might even be convinced to do some digging under the direction of the department."[12] He also discovered that several people had been put off by Moorehead and MacCurdy. These tensions between professional archaeologists and amateur collectors would remain a barrier.

The Lovers Leap site, New Milford, as it was in the early 1990s, showing massive destruction of the site by illegal "pot hunting" — indiscriminate digging by collectors that destroyed massive amounts of cultural information.

## Connecticut's Community of Amateur Archaeologists

In reaction to the vast accumulation of uncatalogued and undocumented pre-contact materials in private collections, Dr. Rainey's field notes reveal an urgency to properly record the archaeological record. He was amazed at the size of the collection of Herbert Southmayd of Durham, which had close to 10,000 pieces dug over forty years from forty to fifty rock shelters. Unarguably the largest collection in the state was that of Norris Bull of West Hartford. What Bull did not excavate himself, he either bought or hired others, like William Beebe and his wife, to dig for him. A camp site excavated by Beebe turned up human remains as well as shell and awls. Dr. Rainey became noticeably frustrated. "It is exactly the sort of site that should be excavated in the proper way," he complained. "It is a typical example of archaeological information going to waste. There is no system, no record left, no plan, and complete pot-hunting. It is the richest site Bull ever struck and is rapidly being destroyed."[13]

Despite his frustration, however, Dr. Rainey ultimately understood that Connecticut's early past was in the hands of amateur archaeologists. "I realized that locating every shell heap and camp site no matter of what size is impossible and ridiculous," he mused. "Every valley, every stream and every tide marsh is speckled with shell heap or camp site remains. Also the location of them is to no point. It is necessary to concentrate on the larger or general sites."[14] Although this practical approach found far fewer sites than are now known, the Yale survey and Dr. Rainey's ethnological compilation were significant first steps, and these remain important resources in documenting Connecticut's pre-contact indigenous cultures.

An enduring legacy of the Yale survey's fieldwork was the establishment in 1934 of the Archaeological Society of Connecticut (ASC) under the guidance of Cornelius Osgood, Froelich Rainey and, later, Dr. Irving Rouse. The society sought to create a collaborative bond between archaeologists and collectors, and to promote scientific research methods. It encouraged the exchange of information through meetings and publications such as the *Bulletin of the Archaeological Society of Connecticut.* The society was successful in reaching out to collectors throughout the state, with many of those mentioned in Dr. Rainey's journal listed as members.

The faculty, staff, and students of Yale University have continued to make valuable contributions to professional archaeology in Connecticut. Since it was established in 1937, the Yale Department of Anthropology has been a leading force in educating students in archaeological theory and practice. Among the first of its graduates was Irving "Ben" Rouse (1913–2006), who took over Dr. Rainey's task of cataloguing the Peabody Museum's archaeological collections. Rouse, originally an undergraduate in forestry, shifted to the much younger discipline of anthropology because he saw a more urgent need for classification there. A major figure in the development of archaeological methods, particularly ceramic analysis, typology, and chronology, Dr. Rouse's main contribution to Connecticut archaeology was to organize the collections into categories and chronologies, creating a scientific systematic classification by typology. "As I look back," he later said, "I am impressed by the fact that archaeology by the 1960s had reached the same state of maturity in classification that biology had reached when I was an undergraduate only thirty years earlier."[15] Dr. Rouse used the Connecticut landscape as a teaching resource for his students and, significantly, shared his knowl-

Benjamin Irving Rouse began his career at Yale in 1930 as an undergraduate in forestry and switched to archaeology. He went on to become Charles J. Mac-Curdy Professor of Anthropology and Curator of Anthropology at the Yale Peabody Museum. A pioneer in circum-Caribbean archaeology and a major contributor to the development of archaeological methods, Rouse's interest in the problems of classification was lifelong. His work combined two major themes in archaeological research: the distribution of culture over space and the study of culture change through time.

edge of scientific methods with the wider archaeological audience, going a long way to foster cooperation between amateurs and professionals in the state.

## Bringing Connecticut's Indigenous History to the Museum Visitor

As archaeology developed in the twentieth century into a mature scientific discipline, museums also evolved from "cabinets of curiosities" toward a role in research and teaching. Yale University was a leader in the use of collections in this way. Artifacts from Connecticut's past have been displayed throughout the state at institutions large and small, such as at the Wadsworth Atheneum, the Connecticut Historical Society, and many local libraries and historical societies. Yale's own collections were spread across different departments and in several buildings. Despite substantial geological, paleontological, and archaeological holdings, it was only after World War II that the Peabody Museum first created an exhibition devoted to Connecticut "prehistory" (Native American cultures and communities before European contact). Arranged by museum staff and a Yale graduate student, the exhibition presented lithic materials in groups, supplemented with objects from Iroquoian New York and Labrador. This display was more of a reference collection for visitors to compare objects they had found with those in the cases and lacked any insight into the people who had created the objects.

Some of the cases from the Native American exhibit on display in the 1940s at the Yale Peabody Museum of Natural History.

In time this approach changed. In the early 1970s a display on "historical" (post-contact) Indians was added that incorporated information from recent excavations in the state, especially at the seventeenth-century Mohegan Fort Shantok. Used for teaching by the Peabody's education division, the Connecticut Indian panels became one of the museum's most popular exhibits.

In 1985 a new exhibition brought an interdisciplinary perspective on the region's archaeology and ethnology together. *Connecticut's Native Americans,* directed by Irving Rouse and co-directed by Lucianne Lavin (a recent doctoral graduate from New York University's Department of Anthropology, which was highly active in northeastern archaeological research under the tutelage of professor Bert Salwen from the 1960s until his death in 1988) showed the artifacts as representative of culturally defined periods in the context of developments in anthropological research. The new interpretive exhibition and an accompanying workbook for teachers were designed to inform visitors about local Native American lifeways and culture through local Native American material culture.[16]

Another Yale facility that houses Connecticut archaeological materials is the William Day Museum of Indian Artifacts at the Lewis Walpole Library in Farmington, which owes its existence to Wilmarth Sheldon Lewis and the keen eye of his groundskeeper, Bill Day. It was Day who continually picked up Native American lithic materials from the Lewis backyard, and Lewis had the idea to display Day's finds.

A graduate of the Yale class of 1918, W. S. Lewis corresponded with Dr. Osgood about bringing together other alumni who were collectors and publishing on Yale's general collections in the alumni magazine. By 1938 Lewis was a member of the Yale Corporation, and by the next year was advocating building a new Peabody Museum wing devoted to anthropology. In 1944 he tried to persuade Norris Bull to leave his substantial collection to Yale. Although both endeavors were unsuccessful, in 1946 Lewis published a widely read report with a chapter that included the Peabody Museum's anthropological collections. When Day kept digging up stone artifacts on Lewis's property, Lewis arranged to have an eighteenth-century

Wilmarth S. Lewis and Annie Burr Auchincloss Lewis, circa 1940.

The eighteenth-century house of the Curricomps family that is now the William Day Museum of Indian Artifacts at Yale's Lewis Walpole Library in Farmington, Connecticut.

one-room house (built by or for the Curricomps, a local Tunxis Indian family) moved to his garden to become the William Day Museum of Indian Artifacts.

## Connecticut Archaeology Comes of Age

In 1966, Lewis contacted Dr. Rouse about excavating his garden and fields. Skeptical at first, Rouse quickly agreed once he determined that Day's surface finds were quite old and significant—some material was Paleo-Indian, about 10,000

Graduate students at the Yale Archaeological Field School at the Lewis-Walpole site in Farmington, Connecticut, about 1977.

years old. Their diversity and number convinced Rouse that a systematic excavation of the site was needed.

The discovery of the Lewis-Walpole site occurred at the same time that Yale was considering offering archaeology as an undergraduate major. With Lewis's support and largesse, the Yale Department of Anthropology offered a course in modern field techniques that used his property as a training ground. From 1967 to 1977 many student excavations there, under the watchful eye of Yale faculty (Dr. Michael Coe, Dr. Barbara Stark, and Dr. David Starbuck), added artifacts to both Day and Peabody exhibits. By Lewis's death in 1979, however, the time and expense of transporting students from New Haven to Farmington outweighed the benefits of using the site, and the field school there was discontinued in favor of a historical project a short drive from campus. Field methods classes are still required training, and recent courses have been held at the Henry Whitfield State Museum in Guilford under the auspices of Yale's Council on Archaeological Studies. Yale graduate students continue to use the local landscape in their research, with investigations into local Native American settlements, settlement patterns, vegetation dynamics, and mortuary practices.

A considerable part of our present understanding of Connecticut's archaeological history has also been derived from the ongoing involvement of organizations, such as the Archaeological Society of Connecticut, not only in continuing MacCurdy and Rainey's survey by excavating and reporting sites throughout the state but by promoting the scientific study of cultural relics over the mere collecting of them. Equally important has been their dissemination of proper archaeo-

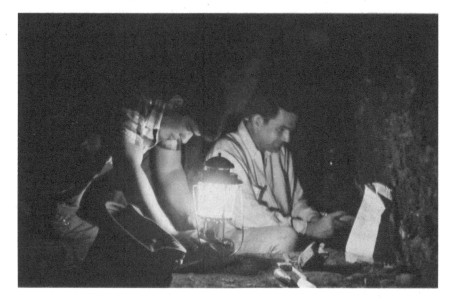

Archaeologist David H. Thompson (left) and Bill O'Connor excavate by lantern light inside the Binette Rock Shelter in Naugatuck, Connecticut. Thompson was president of the Greater New Haven Archaeological Society, a chapter of the Archaeological Society of Connecticut, for many years and also the director of its many site excavations.

logical techniques, ethical practices, and responsible communication of scientific information. Many of these groups—like the Greenwich Archaeology Club and the North East Archaeological Researchers—no longer exist, but the work of their members lives on in many published and unpublished site reports and through the training, advice, and mentorship given to subsequent generations of archaeologists, both professional (among them "Gus" Pope) and avocational. Much would have been lost had it not been for the pursuits of individuals like Eva Butler, Claude Coffin, Lyent Russell, Bernie Powell, Frank Glynn, Dave Cooke, Sid Hessel, and Andy Kowalski, to name only a few.

Whether as informal hobby or as part of an academic program, interest in Connecticut archaeology reached an apogee in the late 1960s and early 1970s, perhaps as incident to a rise in social activism and the civil rights movement. Members of the Shepaug Valley Archaeological Society, formerly the Wappinger Chapter of the Connecticut Archaeological Society, for example, were surprised to find that in one year their membership went from seven to ninety and to four hundred six years later. An interview with one of the society's founding members, Dr. Edmund Swigart, in the first published issue of their periodical, *Artifacts,* revealed the excitement.[17]

> Never in their wildest dreams could the seven stalwart diggers who informally and infrequently met in the summer of 1966 to "learn something about the local Indians" have envisioned what their part-time project has led to in six short years. From that rather minuscule and unpretentious beginning, the little band of hardy and dedicated pioneers has grown to a veritable army of interested persons. Attempting to lead such an organization, Swigart says, "is like sitting on a box of fireworks that are going off in all directions at the same time, and somehow trying to keep some knowledge and control of every spectacular explosion."[18]

*Artifacts* ran for almost twenty years and, like the *Bulletin of the Archaeological Society of Connecticut,* was a useful tool to attract new members, publish results, and share informal news about excavations in the region.

## Beyond Local Interest to a Wider Community

In 1975 the American Indian Archaeological Institute (AIAI) opened its archaeology museum in Washington, Connecticut, boasting the acquisition of the largest private collection of Connecticut Indian artifacts, the Edward H. Rogers Collection (more than 50,000 pieces). Under the direction of Dr. Swigart and Sidney Hessel from the Shepaug Valley Archaeology Society, the AIAI promoted the discipline through many excavations, volunteer "digs, and public programs throughout western Connecticut."[19] After Swigart and Hessel, the archaeology programs at the AIAI (including cultural resource management projects) were directed by professional archaeologists Dr. Russell Handsman and Dr. Roger Moeller during the 1980s and 1990s, followed by Dr. Lucianne Lavin in the twenty-first century. The AIAI changed its name to the Institute for American Indian Studies in 1991, and its museum and educational center continue to celebrate Connecticut archaeology through exhibits, excavation and research, and public programming that includes the Litchfield Hills Archaeology Club, lectures, and an annual Native American-Archaeology Roundtable.

It was also at this time that other educational and archaeological facilities became interested in Connecticut archaeology. Committed to in-the-field training as an essential part of the archaeological program, Dr. Bert Salwen of Columbia University and New York University began a series of archaeology projects in southern New England that included a long-term study of the historic Mohegan village of Fort Shantok and the adjacent pre-contact Shantok Cove site through a series of summer field schools.[20] There he and his associates discovered one of the largest Contact-period assemblages yet recovered in southern New England, which allowed him to persuasively argue that Mohegan and Pequot culture most likely developed "in place" from a common origin in eastern Connecticut.[21]

Around 1962 when Ben Rouse and Donald Clark, president of the Archaeological Society of Connecticut, lobbied in Hartford "to create the position of State Archaeologist," Harvard graduate Dr. Douglas Jordan was appointed to the unpaid post and received an assistant professorship at the University of Connecticut.[22] In 1987 Connecticut established the Office of State Archaeology, and with it the job of state archaeologist, at the Connecticut State Museum of Natural History at the University of Connecticut, to provide the technical assistance for the preservation of local archaeological resources. This led to the creation in 2004 of the Connecticut Archaeology Center, whose mission is to encourage the preservation of Connecticut's archaeological resources through a combination of research, collections conservation, technical assistance, and education. The position of state archaeologist is currently held by Dr. Nicholas Bellantoni, who also serves as an adjunct professor of anthropology at the University of Connecticut and the director of the Connecticut Archaeology Center.

The late Edmund (Ned) Swigart (left) and Sidney Hessel (in the late 1970s or early 1980s), founders of the American Indian Archaeological Institute (now the Institute for American Indian Studies) and the Shepaug Valley Archaeological Society.

With the rise in the last half of the twentieth century of federal and state-mandated oversight into the consequences of local development on historical structures and archaeological sites (such as the National Historic Preservation Act of 1966 and the Archaeological and Historic Preservation Act of 1974), many professionals found employment in the field of cultural resource management (CRM).[23] CRM archaeologists basically conduct archaeological surveys as part of

Left, the 2008 excavations at the Hopkins site by the Litchfield Hills Archaeology Club (Institute for American Indian Studies), in a farm field overlooking Lake Waramaug. Right, students draw a portion of the palisade (dark stain in the ground) during the New York University field school excavations at the Fort Shantok site in Montville, Connecticut, in 1968.

the state and federal permitting process, write technical reports, and advise governmental agencies on both large and small construction projects that may affect cultural resources (archaeology sites and historical structures) in the state.

Dr. Frederick Warner, a professor of anthropology at Central Connecticut State University (CCSU), founded the Connecticut Archaeological Survey (CAS), which worked to obtain government support for salvage archaeology programs for highway construction, bridge work, sewer construction, and commercial development whose subsurface procedures might disturb the state's cultural resources.[24] Dr. Kenneth Feder, a graduate of the University of Connecticut who is now a professor of anthropology at CCSU, created the Farmington River Archaeological Project, which provided a regional archaeology study of the Farmington River valley.[25] Dr. Feder continues to direct summer field schools for CCSU in that area.

In 1976 Kevin McBride and other graduate students at the University of Connecticut established the Public Archaeological Survey Team (P.A.S.T.), what was then a nonprofit CRM organization that conducted many site excavations and important regional studies throughout eastern Connecticut, especially the North-Central Lowlands and Northeastern Highlands Archaeological Projects, and the Lower Connecticut River Valley Project.[26] Today, P.A.S.T. is under the direction of Mary Harper, who also runs a private nonprofit sister organization, Archaeological and Historical Services, Inc. They provide professional CRM consulting

Dr. Bertram B. Salwen (1920–1988), considered by many to be the father of urban archaeology, was professor of anthropology at New York University, where he started an interdisciplinary program in local archaeology and ran field schools for many years.

Dr. Douglas Jordan (top left), Connecticut's first state archaeologist, at the Archaeological Society of Connecticut chapter Albert Morgan Society's dig at the Hollister site, Glastonbury, in the 1960s. Sidney Hessel (top right), co-founder of the American Indian Archaeological Institute (now the Institute for American Indian Studies), excavating inside the Binette Rock Shelter, Naugatuck, during excavations by the Greater New Haven Archaeological Society. Bottom, the Connecticut College field school at the Griswold Point site in Old Lyme, about 1985, with co-directors Dr. Harold Juli (standing, far right) and Dr. Lucianne Lavin (standing, second from left).

Archaeologist David H. Thompson with volunteer Peter Rataic at the Greater New Haven Archaeological Society dig at the Bethany Bog site, late 1990s. Bottom, the crew of the Public Archaeological Survey Team (P.A.S.T.) during the 1981 Lower Connecticut River Valley Survey, East Haddam, including the current state archaeologist, Dr. Nicholas Bellantoni (second row, left), and Dr. Kevin McBride (second row, right), a professor of anthropology at the University of Connecticut and the director of research for the Mashantucket Pequot Museum and Research Center.

services that include archaeological surveys and historic preservation planning for archaeological sites, historic structures, and cultural landscapes. Their research has contributed greatly to understanding the lifeways of Connecticut's many peoples.[27] Meeting the needs of fellow archaeologists to communicate ideas more easily and effectively is still high priority. In 1993, two University of Connecticut archaeologists, Thomas Plunkett and Jonathan Lizee, took advantage of developing technology to create ArchNet, a Web-based "virtual library" of archaeological literature and resources.[28]

## Future Trends in the Study of Connecticut's Past

The explosive development of professionally run CRM projects during the 1970s, 1980s, and 1990s helped promote the development of archaeological theory, site research design, field methodology, and sophisticated analyses of cultural remains. Moreover, several of the graduate students who were part of the field and lab crews during that period are now senior archaeologists working at state educational facilities. Connecticut archaeology has come of age. The University of Connecticut, CCSU, and other schools such as Norwalk Community College and its Archaeology Club, Connecticut College, and Western Connecticut State University have continued their involvement in Connecticut archaeology through field schools, college courses, and public lectures and workshops.[29] Some university programs, such as that of Western Connecticut State University, have initiated working relationships with city and town planners in efforts to mitigate the possible harmful effects of municipal projects on prehistoric and historic sites. Other universities, like Connecticut College and CCSU, offer students laboratory space, coupled with state-of-the-art database, mapping, and GIS (geographic information systems) applications, for paleoanthropological, zooarchaeological, and archaeological lithic analysis.

Extensive archaeological investigation through CRM projects and summer field schools is also conducted by the archaeology department at the Mashantucket Pequot Tribal Nation's Museum and Research Center under the direction

At left, Dr. Frederick Warner (second from left), director of the Connecticut Archaeological Survey, the first cultural resource management agency in Connecticut. With him is Ernest Wiegand, currently professor of anthropology at Norwalk Community College, at the old campus, in 1975. At right, Kenneth Feder, professor of anthropology at Central Connecticut State University, as a University of Connecticut graduate student working the screens at the Woodchuck Knoll site in South Windsor in 1974. Dr. Feder runs CCSU's Farmington River Archaeology Project, a long-term multiyear regional archaeological site survey of the Farmington River valley that he began in 1979.

of Dr. Kevin McBride, a former director of P.A.S.T. The museum's archaeologists have identified more than 250 sites on and off the reservation dating from the Paleo-Indian period (11,000 to 9,000 B.P.) to the present, documenting the long history and presence of the Pequot and southern New England Native people. Visitors to the museum can see many of these artifacts, along with instructive dioramas, videos, and interactive exhibits.

Similar systematic excavations of other Connecticut Indian reservations are also under way. For close to two decades, the Mohegan Archaeological Field School, sponsored by the Mohegan Tribe and the University of Connecticut with Eastern Connecticut State University, has investigated pre-contact and post-contact sites on the Mohegan tribal reservation in Uncasville, including a seventeenth-century fortified village site, and eighteenth- and nineteenth-century Mohegan homesteads. A newer endeavor, the Eastern Pequot Archaeological Field School directed by Dr. Stephen Silliman of the University of Massachusetts, Boston, has run for eight seasons on the reservation in North Stonington as part of the ongoing effort to understand Pequot responses to European colonialism and reservation life.

What these field schools have in common is an opportunity for students to work directly with members of Connecticut's tribal communities in excavating sites in a collaborative process between academics and tribal governments. Often tribal members participate openly in the course as part of the field crew's excavators, screeners, or cultural advisers. Collaborative indigenous archaeology or "covenantal archaeology" is a form of applied archaeology and community-based research, designed to rectify the often discordant relationship between archaeologists and the Native community.[30] Such an approach demonstrates how inclusive research methods and practice "can contribute to contemporary Native communities and encourage trust, responsibility, healing, education, confidence, and pride."[31] As William and Kristen Keegan noted in their book on Connecticut archaeology:

> The fact is not well-known, but there is, has been, and will be a great deal of archaeological work, both public and private, going on in this state. It isn't the stuff of adventure films, but it is part of the unending quest to expand our knowledge about humanity and the world—a quest that many people throughout history and across the world have pursued as their life's work.[32]

During the past few decades Connecticut archaeology has become a rigorous science, using an interdisciplinary approach that combines theoretical modeling with advanced methods and techniques of survey, excavation, and analysis. One of its most important developments is the establishment of a detailed chronology of cultural sequences based on geologic principles of stratigraphy and radiocarbon dating. A second important development is the emphasis on the people behind the aboriginal cultures, and the attempt to reconstruct and understand their lifestyles, their cultural behaviors. Not only do archaeologists want to know "where?" and "when?" but also "how?" and "why?"

## WHAT ARCHAEOLOGISTS DO

Archaeologists study past human behavior by investigating the places, or sites, where people lived and left evidence of their lifeways. Archaeology (Greek *archaeo,* "ancient," and *logos,* "word," "thought," or "discourse") is the study of material culture, the products of past human behavior: artifacts (objects manufactured by human beings, such as pottery and tools, hearths, building structures, and burials) and ecofacts (natural objects used by humans, such as shells, bones, antler, wood, and food remains). Careful study of these objects and their relationships allows researchers to construe the lifeways, or living habits, of cultural groups, especially those communities with no written language, and to gain insights into the dynamics of long-term social processes such as culture change, culture continuity, and adaptation.

Archaeologists begin by scientifically excavating these sites using a grid system of equidistant squares tied to a permanent datum point. The soil in each square is carefully removed and passed through a fine screen to recover as many artifacts and organic remains as possible. The depth and exact location of each find is plotted and catalogued. Excavation follows the natural stratigraphy, or soil layers, of the site; each stratum (or layer) is removed separately. Careful recording of site stratigraphy—the position relative to one another of layers of material—is important in archaeological dating and is based on the geological principle that strata were originally deposited horizontally and continuously, with younger strata at the top overlaying older strata at the bottom.

The checkerboard pattern of the grid system excavation at the Morgan site, Rocky Hill, by the Albert Morgan Archaeological Society, a chapter of the Archaeological Society of Connecticut.

Profile of a Late Woodland stratified pit feature at the Morgan site; bottom, Connecticut College Field School excavation unit at the Griswold Point site, Old Lyme, showing post molds in plan.

If the stratum is thick, or if no strata are visible, the soil is removed in arbitrary levels (for example, 5 centimeters thick). The wall profiles of each square and the plan view of each level are drawn to scale in the field. Scale drawings document all fixed, unportable artifacts, called cultural features, such as hearths, storage pits, and post molds (the dark circular stains that are left when wooden posts rot in the ground). Features, soil profiles, and artifact associations are photographed or drawn to scale.

Why pay such strict attention to these details? By themselves, artifacts and ecofacts are virtually meaningless. It is how they are associated, their relationships to one another, that give them cultural meaning. Stratigraphic and spatial prove-

A field crew from American Cultural Specialists, a CRM firm, excavating shovel test pits along a transit line overlooking the Connecticut River in Haddam, Connecticut. The shovel test units uncovered the Peninsula 1 site.

niences are important, because they allow archaeologists to see those relationships, or the lack of them. In a well-excavated dig, the fieldwork and documentation should be so accurate that every object excavated from the site could theoretically be placed back where it was found. In fact, an archaeological site is very much like a giant jigsaw puzzle (and a constellation of related sites is an even bigger puzzle).

Archaeologists fit together field and laboratory data to try to produce a grand picture of the everyday life of the people that lived, worked, socialized, and worshiped at a site. Because we recover only the broken, used up, lost, mainly non-perishable items left behind by the members of a community (who in all probability carried off most of their belongings when they left), not all of the puzzle pieces are available. Our interpretations are subject to change as new excavations reveal additional pieces of information.

To understand the cultural and social lifeways of a people, archaeologists need to study *undisturbed* living sites. This is why it is so important to preserve such sites or, in the case of imminent destruction, to conduct a professional archaeological investigation. Unfortunately, the information from many sites has often been compromised by subsurface disturbances, both natural (such as floods, hurricanes, and erosion) and cultural (plowing, building, and grading activities).

## After the Dig: The Techniques of Archaeological Investigation

Site excavation is only the beginning. After excavation, artifacts must be cleaned, catalogued, and analyzed. The location of each artifact and ecofact must be mapped, both stratigraphically (vertically) and spatially (horizontally), to discover how they were associated with one another and with cultural features. Are objects and features clustered together in the same soil level (indicating contemporaneity)

Resetting the grid system using a transit during a Connecticut College summer field school at the Griswold Point site; bottom, flags mark each soil stain (potential features) uncovered by American Cultural Specialists at the Larson Farm site in New Milford.

or in a specific area of the site (perhaps indicating a specific activity)? How did the people at the site make each object? How did they use it? What raw materials did they have? Where did these materials originate? What food remains can we identify? Can we determine who occupied the site and what they were doing there? We can answer these questions only through detailed, often interdisciplinary, laboratory analyses in fields as wide ranging as botany, zoology and geology.[33]

## Radiocarbon Dating and Calibration

The absolute radiometric dating technique called radiocarbon dating, developed by W. F. Libby soon after World War II, has enabled archaeologists to accurately

calculate calibrated dates for organic materials as far back as 50,000 years. This technique measures the disintegration of the carbon-14 ($^{14}$C) isotope, which occurs naturally and has a half-life of 5,780 years, in the remains of plants and animals. In other words, when an organism dies, the $^{14}$C in it begins to break down at a regular, measurable rate, with half of the existing carbon disintegrating every 5,780 years.

American Indian Archaeological Institute's (now IAIS) excavation at the Templeton site in Washington, Connecticut, showing troweling technique and the use of baulks as an aid in digging in stratigraphic levels.

The radiocarbon year (RCY) dates reported in this book are uncalibrated, unless otherwise noted. Uncalibrated RCY dates (designated B.P., or Before the Present, which is the radiocarbon present standard of A.D. 1950) are not linked to any system of calendar years and do not correlate with B.C. and A.D. calendar dates. This is because the length of radiocarbon years differs according to variations in the occurrence of carbon-14 through time. Among the factors affecting this variation are changes in the natural production and distribution of atmospheric $^{14}$C and human intervention in the carbon cycle through the burning of fossil fuels and atomic weapons testing. B.P. dates cannot be simply converted to B.C. and A.D. dates, but must be calibrated against another dating method, such as dendrochronology (tree-ring dating), to correlate the age of tested materials to a calendar date. Calibrated dates are labeled cal B.P. (calibrated calendar years before A.D. 1950) or cal B.C. and cal A.D. A related technique uses accelerator mass spectroscopy (AMS) in the dating process.

In the field, charcoal particles are removed with tweezers or other tools that

Careful recovery and measurement of features and artifacts are essential to the recovery of information from an excavation. Top, troweling to identify the outline of a feature at the Schaghticoke Reservation site during a phase 1 survey by Archaeological Research Specialists. Bottom, measurement of artifact at the Shantok Cove site in Uncasville by members of a New York University summer field school in the mid-1960s.

allow the archaeologist to collect the carbon without touching it, to avoid contaminating the sample with additional carbon. The charcoal is put into a packet of aluminum foil for the same reason, and the packet is placed in a plastic bag. This bag has provenience information written on it, such as the site name, unit number, stratum or feature designation, depth, and spatial location within the unit or feature. The sample is later cleaned of dirt and other debris and sent to a radiocarbon laboratory for dating.[34]

In addition to photography, drawing, mapping, and plotting features and artifacts in three dimensions are done on site to capture as much information as possible for later analysis. Top left, Greater New Haven Archaeological Society members drawing in artifacts at the Robillard site, Milford. Top right, bagging artifacts and writing up notes at the Morgan site. Bottom left, screening excavated site soil for the smallest of remains and artifacts for the first phase of an archaeological survey at the Connecticut Army National Guard Camp in Niantic. Bottom right, Lucianne Lavin at the mapping table during Connecticut College summer field school excavations at the Griswold Point (Hillhouse) site in Old Lyme.

## Dendrochronology

Dendrochronology is a dating method that uses annual tree-ring patterns to determine the age of wood and associated artifacts. It was developed in the early 1900s by Andrew E. Douglass at the University of Arizona, who showed the link between the annual growth of trees and climate, as reflected in the width of tree rings. Clark Wissler of the American Museum of Natural History applied this discovery to date wood recovered from archaeological sites. Dendrochronology, which can date wood and therefore any associated materials to an exact year, uses cross-dating, the matching of tree-ring patterns from sample to sample, to build a chronology into the past against which artifacts can be dated.[35]

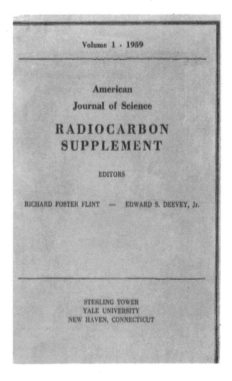

Volume 1 · 1959

American
Journal of Science

RADIOCARBON
SUPPLEMENT

EDITORS

RICHARD FOSTER FLINT — EDWARD S. DEEVEY, Jr.

STERLING TOWER
YALE UNIVERSITY
NEW HAVEN, CONNECTICUT

The first issue of what became the journal *Radiocarbon,* published through Yale University's *American Journal of Science.*

### Thermoluminescence Dating

The technique of thermoluminescence dating measures age by counting the number of electrons released when an artifact that has been subjected to burning, such as pottery, is heated. The high-temperature firing used to make pottery empties the ceramic material of its electrons, which are then replaced through exposure over time to an assumed constant rate of radiation in the environment (from isotopes, radioactive minerals, and cosmic rays). These replacement electrons can be measured when they are released by the application of heat, enabling the dating of the material.[36]

### Geoarchaeology

In the past twenty years or so, geoarchaeologists have applied standard geological techniques to determine the source of the raw materials used to make stone tools. Two of these laboratory techniques—thin-section petrography (analysis of thin slices from an artifact with a petrographic microscope) and neutron activation analysis (measurement of gamma rays from an irradiated specimen to identify its elemental composition)—are particularly useful in determining the sources of the chert, jasper, and other stone used to make tools.[37]

There is a great need to use these techniques to understand how and where Paleo-Indians (and later peoples) obtained their raw materials for tool manufacture, because many of the identifications of lithic sources in the archaeological literature are made only with hand specimen analysis, which is unreliable. For example, chert samples from distinct rock formations in different states can and often do look the same. The mottled brown and gray chert of a point excavated in Connecticut is likely from an Onondaga limestone outcrop in nearby central New York, but there is also the chance that it came from similarly colored cherts in Virginia. Likewise, black, blue-black, greenish black, and gray cherts from the Hudson Valley have identical counterparts from central Maine, the Midwest, and the Mid-Atlantic region.

Complicating the matter are secondary chert sources, which are cherts removed from their original bedrock matrix by glaciers or flooding and rolled into cobbles and pebbles that could be picked up in river valleys or glacial till. Natural forces over thousands of years can produce chemical changes, such as oxidation, that alter the color of the chert from that of its primary source. Some chert pebbles of the Pensauken formation in central New Jersey, for example, are often referred to as jaspers because of their yellowish brown color. Thin-section analysis revealed that these "jaspers" were Onondaga and Helderberg cherts with significantly altered iron oxides and carbonates.[38]

Lithic studies show that it is possible (and relatively inexpensive) to identify the sources of the rocks from which Connecticut artifacts are made through petrographic analysis.[39] In this technique a thin section or slide of a small sample of the artifact's rock material is examined under a microscope. The source can be identified by comparing the rock's traits to a specimen in a reference collection of well-documented materials whose source localities are known.

### Archaeobotany and Palynology

Archaeobotany, also known as paleoethnobotany, is the study of plant remains from archaeology sites. It includes the analysis of macro-remains in the form of preserved plant parts and charcoal, which can be identified through their structures. They are usually recovered during actual site excavation or through flotation. Flotation is a technique whereby water containing excavated soils is agitated so that light archaeological materials float to the top and are scooped off, while a heavier fraction sinks to the bottom of the flotation container. Micro-remains, such as pollen and phytoliths, are also analyzed.

Palynology is the study of living and extinct pollen, spores, dinoflagellates (one-celled aquatic organisms), microfossils, and other palynomorphs (microscopic plant and animal structures that can be extracted from soil samples). This technique, in which prepared samples are examined under a stereoscopic microscope or with a scanning electron microscope (SEM), is used in many fields, from allergy studies to climate change. In archaeology, pollen analysis in particular can yield information on plant species, plant communities, and vegetational succession in pre-contact and post-contact environments, providing important clues about the lifestyles and economies of human communities in the past.

Often called plant "opal," phytoliths are mineral particles, usually siliceous, that form inside living plants. They are fairly indestructible and may be preserved in areas where plant pollens often are not. Because each plant species contains

Photomicrographs of botanical remains, such as this thin section of red oak charcoal, provide information that helps to identify plants, often down to the genus and species level.

distinctively shaped phytoliths, their analysis allows archaeobotanists to identify those plants used by the inhabitants of an archaeology site. By studying pollen grains and other plant remains buried in sediments, scientists are able to identify trees, grasses, and other flora and in what proportion they were present in the local environment.[40]

# 1

## Connecticut's Earliest Settlers

### *The Paleo-Indian Period*

The etymology of the word *Muhheakunnuk,* according to original signifying, is great waters or sea, which are constantly in motion, either flowing or ebbing. Our forefathers asserted that their ancestors were emigrated from west by north of another country; they passed over the great waters, where this and the other country is nearly connected, called *Ukhkokpeck;* it signifies snake water, or water where snakes abounded; and that they lived by [the] side of [a] great water or sea, from whence they derive the name of *Muhheakunnuk* nation.

—Hendrick Aupaumut, Mahikan (Mohican) Grand Sachem, about 1790

For the past million years much of North America was repeatedly covered and uncovered by a series of vast ice sheets. In some areas of New England these glaciers were over a mile thick (2 kilometers). Much of the earth's water was frozen into them. By about 15,000 B.P. sea level had dropped more than 435 feet (135 meters) lower than it is today, leaving much of the continental shelf exposed as dry land.[1]

### THE ARRIVAL OF HUMANS IN NORTH AMERICA

In northwestern North America the lower sea level exposed land along the Bering Strait, connecting Asia and Alaska. Although commonly called the Bering Land Bridge, it was rather a broad plain 1,300 miles (2,100 kilometers) wide. Geological and biological data suggest that this plain was exposed from about 80,000 B.P. to about 35,000 B.P., and that between 35,000 and 11,000 B.P. there were several submergences and re-emergences of the land. The Bering Plain, also called Beringia, was a treeless expanse of marshes, grasslands, and tundra, with low-growing plants capable of supporting large herds of animals.

There are several theories as to how humans came to inhabit North America. The earliest known settlers, the Paleo-Indians, could have easily emigrated from Asia across Beringia to Alaska. Geological evidence shows that there was an ice-free corridor in what are now the Yukon and Mackenzie river valleys.[2] The path into the heart of North America lay along the east side of the Rocky Mountains, down an intermittently ice-free corridor between the Cordilleran ice sheet to the west and the Laurentide ice sheet to the east.

A more recent theory suggests that some Paleo-Indian groups followed the unglaciated coasts southward, possibly by boat, then eastward into the North and South American interiors. Several early sites have been discovered along the west coasts of North and South America.[3] Tools and dietary remains from these sites suggest technologies and subsistence economies very different from those of inland Paleo-Indian sites, which are normally characterized by fluted spear points attributed to Clovis and its related cultural traditions. Radiocarbon-dated sites on islands off the California coast provide proof of Paleo-Indian seafaring.[4] So do the Paleo-Indian boat-building sites on U.S. Department of Defense properties directly along the postulated sea route and along the margins of Glacial Lake Iroquois at Fort Drum, New York.[5] Artifacts—including woodworking tools and an ochre-stained pestle (red ochre was sometimes used to temper the spruce gum used as a sealant for birch-bark canoes)—suggest boat-building activities.[6]

The newest and most controversial theory for human emigration into the Americas suggests a route from Europe across Greenland and Iceland (whose land masses would have been greatly expanded by the dramatic drop in sea level caused by glaciation) into eastern North America.[7] There is yet little evidence to support this theory, although advocates argue that some blade-like tools from the Topper site in South Carolina, which may be 15,000 years old, are reminiscent of European Paleolithic tools.[8] Dr. Frederick Wiseman, an Abenaki Indian who is also a professional archaeologist, confronts western bias by suggesting that it was the Wabanaki (an inclusive term for the Abenaki and other northern New England and adjacent Canadian indigenous peoples), traditionally expert mariners, not Europeans who made the crossing. "Native American voyagers, through accident or design, contacted northwestern Europe and brought back to North America a very few Europeans, one woman of whom bore the X lineage [the genetic X haplogroup present in some Native American groups]."[9]

The exact arrival of human groups in the Americas is heatedly debated. Most Paleo-Indian sites have been dated to between 12,000 and 10,000 B.P.,[10] so a date just before that time has traditionally been given for the arrival of the first humans south of the ice. More and more archaeological studies, however, point to a much earlier date, with sites in both North and South America dated between 37,000 and 15,000 B.P.[11]

One example is the Pendejo Cave site near Orogrande, New Mexico, where soil levels contained artifacts, bones of extinct animals, and human finger and palm prints in baked clay (likely from clay-lined storage pits also at the site). Wood charcoal from the lowest soil level bearing a human print (zone K) provided a series of five radiocarbon dates ranging from 36,920 B.P. to 26,500 B.P. In the activity area where the print was found, archaeologists also unearthed stone artifacts and the toe bone of an extinct species of horse. This bone was pierced by the tip of a bone projectile point or wedge, proving that humans were there at the same time as the extinct animal.[12]

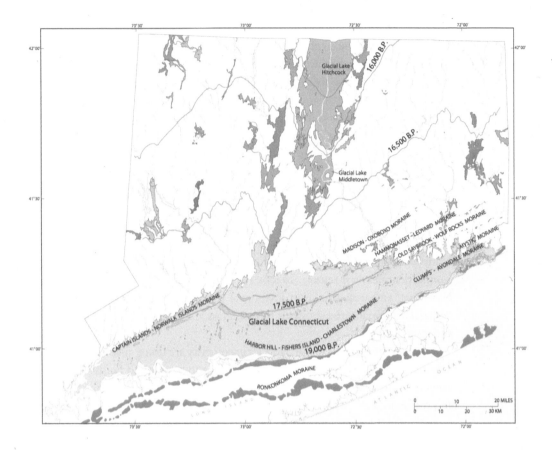

Linguistic studies, and some genetic evidence, suggest that Native American populations diverged from those in Asia around 30,000 to 35,000 years ago. The more than 2,150 indigenous languages spoken in the Americas probably could not have evolved in less than 35,000 years.[13] DNA studies are not that conclusive; those using mitochondrial DNA suggest divergence occurred up to 30,000 years ago while others suggest that divergence had already occurred by 20,000 B.P. Some genetic studies indicate that the early emigrants came from the Lake Baikal region of Russia. However, the skeleton of Kennewick Man, a young man buried over 9,000 years ago in what is now the state of Washington, is more physically similar to South Asian populations.[14] The skeletal evidence supports an earlier DNA study that suggested a population movement from Southeast Asia or Polynesia to North America 6,000 to 10,000 years ago.[15] All this suggests that there were multiple migrations over thousands of years by peoples from multiple Asian localities representing a diversity of cultures.[16]

Receding glaciers deposited moraines on Long Island and in Connecticut (the glacial front was standing at each moraine at the time of the radiocarbon date shown on the map). Long Island and the Atlantic south of it for many miles was dry land surrounding the lake on the south, east, and west. Post-glacial rises in sea level created Glacial Lake Connecticut, separating Long Island from what is now the Connecticut mainland.

## THE FIRST PEOPLE ARRIVE IN CONNECTICUT

As late as 17,500 B.P. the Northeast was covered by glaciers, except for southeastern Connecticut and parts of New York's Long Island, which at that time was attached to Connecticut.[17] There was no Long Island Sound. The Connecticut mainland extended more than 60 miles (100 kilometers) south of Long Island onto the exposed continental shelf. Much of what is now Long Island Sound was covered by a great freshwater lake. As the ice retreated northward, many "glacial lakes" were formed by its moraines.[18] Many smaller lakes, ponds, and swamps were also created by glacial movements throughout the state. Paleobotanical research indicates that a treeless arctic-alpine tundra of mosses, grasses, sedges, and other low-growing plants and small shrubs that included bilberry, dwarf birch, and dwarf willow flourished south of the glacier.[19] Mastodon and mammoth remains recovered from the area show that the region was indeed habitable at the time and could have supported small multifamily communities of Paleo-Indians—the first settlers of New England.[20]

A Paleo-Indian fluted spear point was recovered during dredging more than 900 feet (about 275 meters) from the present shore of Hammonasset Beach in Madison, Connecticut.[21] This was likely an inland site during its occupation by Connecticut's earliest settlers. To look for earlier (pre-17,000 B.P.) humans in the Northeast, archaeologists must investigate the submerged Atlantic shelf, where researchers have located drowned forests, grass and tree pollens, faunal remains, and even artifacts.[22]

Several southern New England archaeologists are doing just that.[23] Underwater archaeological investigations off Block Island have found undisturbed river valleys, terraces, and uplands that would have provided necessary food sources and shelter for early Indian communities.[24] Water, peat, and other favorable conditions unique to submerged sites may have helped to preserve perishable bone, wood, and textiles that would otherwise quickly disappear in the normally acidic soils of terrestrial sites.[25]

## Connecticut's Post-Glacial Environment

By 13,500 B.P. all of Connecticut was ice-free tundra.[26] Meltwater from the retreating glacier created rivers, streams, and brooks whose waters rushed across the countryside into the Atlantic Ocean. The rapidly rising sea level began a chronicle of coastal submergence that continues to this day, albeit at a much slower pace. Rocks and debris dropped by the retreating glacier dammed up some of the meltwater streams, creating many lakes, ponds, and swamps.[27]

The availability of tundra-grazing animals made the area attractive to Paleo-Indian groups. By studying pollen grains and other plant remains buried in sediments, archaeobotanists can tell what kinds of trees, grasses, and other plants were present and in what proportion. Radiocarbon dating enables such materials to be accurately dated as far back as 50,000 years.

Pollen grains and plant parts, such as conifer needles and seeds from aquatic plants found buried in sediments in Connecticut marshes and ponds, indicate that the tundra lasted until about 12,000 B.P. About that time spruce, white pine, fir, and larch began to appear in the tundra.[28] Their number gradually increased until the tundra was almost completely replaced by a mixed conifer-hardwood forest.

This vegetation supported large animals—mastodon, mammoth, horse, giant beaver, giant ground sloth, moose-elk, caribou, musk-ox, and elk.[29] When the deciduous woodlands became established, these animals moved north with the coniferous forest. Mastodon remains have been found in Connecticut, New York, and western Massachusetts in areas that were once ancient lakes and swamps. For example, in 1913 workmen digging a ditch for drinking water found mastodon bones on the Hillstead estate in Farmington in a swampy area near the foot of Talcott Mountain.[30] In the 1970s, mastodon bones were dredged up from Lake Kitchawan in Pound Ridge, New York, just across the Connecticut border. In the early 1980s, a mastodon was excavated from Ivory Pond in the Housatonic River valley of western Massachusetts by archaeologists from the American Indian Archaeological Institute (now the Institute for American Indian Studies) in Washington, Connecticut. This site yielded two radiocarbon dates—one from bone and one from white spruce cones found with the animal—of 11,440 B.P. ±655 years and 11,630 B.P. ±470 years, respectively.[31]

Although radiocarbon dating has established that these animals and Paleo-Indians coexisted, no Connecticut site has the bones of these animals in the same soil levels as Paleo-Indian artifacts. However, only six Paleo-Indian sites have been found in Connecticut to date, and there are sites with animal-human associations in adjacent states: the Hiscock site near Buffalo, New York, with mastodon bones and Paleo-Indian tools; the Whipple site in New Hampshire with caribou and beaver bones; and the possible association of caribou with humans at the Bull Brook site in Massachusetts.[32] These animals may have been part of the diet of Paleo-Indian communities in Connecticut as well.

By at least 10,215 B.P. small pockets of oak trees began to transform the Connecticut landscape into a mosaic of deciduous and evergreen environments, sig-

The evolutionary diversity and striking changes that were transforming the landscape, climate, flora, and fauna of Pleistocene North America at the end of the Ice Age are depicted in this detail from Rudolph F. Zallinger's mural *The Age of Mammals*. Many of the animals shown in the mural would have shared the environment with the early Paleo-Indian communities of the Northeast, such as the forest-dwelling mastodon (behind the mammoth), the woodland musk ox, the giant beaver, the horse, and the ground sloth.

A molar tooth and tooth fragments of a mastodon (*Mammut americanum*) from the Pleistocene of New Haven County, Connecticut. These teeth were collected near Cheshire, Connecticut, in 1827 during the excavation of the Farmington Canal. Scale bar equals 1 centimeter.

naling a warming climate.[33] At the Templeton (6LF21) site, a Paleo-Indian settlement along the Shepaug River in Washington, Connecticut, microscopic studies of charcoal sections were identified as red oak and either juniper or white cedar trees. White oak, or over-cup oak, aspen, and white pine charcoal were also identified from the site.

In Connecticut, the Templeton site provided the earliest radiocarbon dates for Paleo-Indian settlement at 10,215 ±90 years and 10,190 B.P. ±300 years.[34] A radiocarbon date of 10,260 B.P from the Hidden Creek (Power Plant) site overlooking the Great Cedar Swamp, a glacial lake basin at Mashantucket Pequot Reservation near Ledyard, is a bit earlier, but its excavators feel that that date is too early for the site's Late Paleo-Indian "Holcomb-like" unfluted lanceolate points and other artifacts, which better fit the other two radiocarbon dates from Hidden Creek, both calculated to 9160 B.P.[35]

This is not to say that the first human groups arrived in Connecticut on these dates. Archaeological research in Pennsylvania and nearby New York suggests that humans arrived earlier, though not before about 17,500 B.P., because all but southeastern Connecticut was glaciated before then. As noted above, the remains of earlier settlements would be located southward in what is now Long Island Sound and beyond, on the floor of the Atlantic Ocean.

## Paleo-Indian Settlements in Connecticut

We know little about these ancient communities. The stereotype of Paleo-Indian society is one of small groups of widely roaming "big game hunters" whose economy was based on the pursuit of large, migratory herd animals using the highest

## Plant Species Identified from Charcoal Fragments at the Templeton Site

| Species | 45 | 50 | 55 | 60 | 65 | 70 | 75 | 80 | 85 | 90 | 95 | 100 | 105 | 110 | 115 | 120 | 125 | 130 | 135 | 140 |
|---|---|---|---|---|---|---|---|---|---|---|---|---|---|---|---|---|---|---|---|---|
| Maple (*Acer* spp.) | | | | | | | | | ■ | | | | | | | ■ | | ■ | | |
| Hornbeam (*Carpinus/Ostrya* spp.) | | | | ■ | | | | | | | | | | | | | | | | |
| Hickory (*Carya* spp.) | | ■■ | ■ | | ■ | ■ | ■ | | | | | | | | | | | | | |
| Hazelnut (*Corylus* spp.) | | ■ | | | | | | | | | | | | | | | | | | |
| American Beech (*Fagus americana*) | | ■ | | ■ | | | | | | | | | | | | | | | | |
| Butternut (*Juglans* spp.) | | ■ | | | | | | | | | | | | | | | | | | |
| American Sycamore (*Platanus occidentalis*) | | | | | | | | ■■ | | | | | | | | | | | | |
| Quaking Aspen (*Populus tremuloides*) | | | | | | | | | ■ | | | | | | | ■ | | ■ | | |
| Beech Family (Fagaceae [*Quercus/Castanea*]) | | | | ■ ■ | | ■ | | | | | | | | | | | | | | |
| Oaks (*Quercus* spp.) | | ■■ | | ■■■ | | | | ■ | ■■ | | | | | | | | ■ | ■ | | |
| Red Oaks (*Quercus* spp. [*Erythrobalanus*]) | | | ■ | | | | ■ | | | | | | | | | | | | | |
| White Oaks (*Quercus* spp. [*Leucobalanus*]) | ■■■ ■ | ■■■ | ■■■ | ■ ■ | ■■■ | | | | | | | | | ■ | ■ | ■ | | | | |
| Eastern White Pine (*Pinus strobus*) | | | | | | | ■■ | | | | | | | | | | | | | |

Depth below datum in centimeters    45  50  55  60  65  70  75  80  85  90  95  100  105  110  115  120  125  130  135  140

AMS radiocarbon dates (years Before Present) and the depths at which samples were taken

Oak 2765±65 BP     Maple 4835±50 BP    Oak 10,215±90 BP

Plant species identified from charcoal samples taken from Unit N12W1.5 at the Templeton site, Washington, Connecticut. The three AMS radiocarbon dates are from samples selected from the bottom, middle, and top of the excavated unit (the middle date is from an identified maple fragment used to test the early presence of this plant family).

quality stone materials in the manufacture of their weaponry and tool kits. But this traditional image of Paleo-Indian daily life is based on findings from other regions, some of which had very different post-glacial physical environments than Connecticut. Different soils, topography, and vegetation could most certainly promote different kinds of economies and settlements, which could produce divergences in social and political organization, cosmology, spirituality, and other parts of the cultural system.

There are six excavated Paleo-Indian settlements in Connecticut: Templeton in Washington, Hidden Creek near Ledyard, Lovers Leap in New Milford, Liebman in Lebanon, Allen's Meadows in Wilton, and Baldwin Ridge in Groton. By studying these sites we can sketch something about the people who lived there, and the little information we have from them is still enough to refute that stereotype of Connecticut's Paleo-Indian communities.[36]

Although there are only six known encampments, there are more than fifty Paleo-Indian artifact find spots listed in the archaeology site files in Connecticut's Office of State Archaeology.[37] Artifact find spots are represented by a single artifact, often out of its original context, such as a surface find eroded from a hillside or churned up by plowing. Among the most well-known and prevalent of these finds are projectile points, the pointed heads inserted in the wooden shaft or foreshaft of a spear, javelin, dart, or arrow that was used for hunting or defense. Because the normally acidic conditions of our local soils destroy most perishable materials such as wood, all that remains of these implements are their stone tips, so it is often difficult to determine which projectile the point represents.

There are many different point styles, or types. Artifact types are time markers

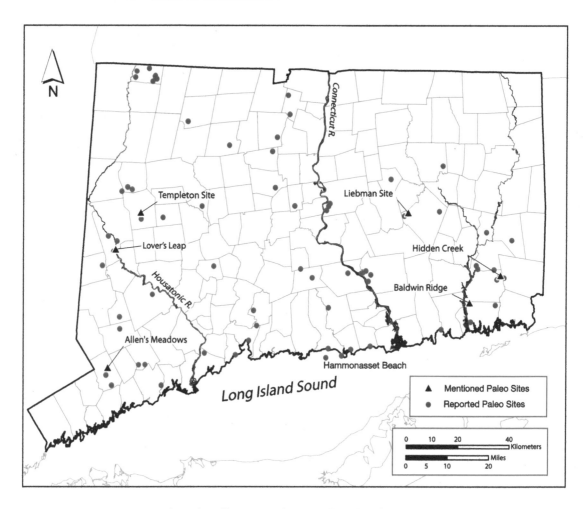

Location of known Paleo-Indian sites on file in the Connecticut Office of State Archaeology along with single fluted projectile point finds in Connecticut.

used to identify a site with a specific cultural period. The material culture of all societies changes through time. We Connecticut folks of European descent no longer wear Pilgrim clothing, shoot muskets, or drive Model T Fords. Similarly, Native American cultural remains changed in style over time. An automobile buff can look at a specific car and tell you the year when it was manufactured. Likewise, archaeologists can identify the age of certain artifact styles, especially for projectile points and clay pottery containers. (These point and pot styles are identified and illustrated in the chapters describing the cultural periods in which they were made and used. The illustrations should help budding archaeologists and amateur collectors identify the age of their collections.)

Native Americans made points and many other tools from stone, bone, antler, and wood, from earliest times right up to contact with European explorers and traders. In northeastern North America indigenous peoples had no knowledge of metallurgy. Metal objects such as copper bead necklaces and some rare copper projectile points were manufactured in later pre-contact periods, but these were cold-hammered from copper nuggets and are relatively soft. A very rare copper axe was found in Essex.[38]

### The Templeton Site

A total of 461 square feet (42.75 square meters) was excavated in the Paleo-Indian component at the Templeton site in Washington, Connecticut.[39] Of the 7,400 artifacts recovered from this area, 7,360 were debitage (waste flakes from the manufacture or maintenance of stone tools). Eleven nonutilized channel flakes (flakes whose removal formed the "flute" of a fluted point) and 72 formal and expedient tools and tool fragments were also found.[40] They included one fluted point and four miniature unfluted points less than an inch (2 centimeters) long.[41] Other formal tools included knives, unfinished bifaces (tools that have been chipped on both their dorsal and ventral surfaces, in contrast to unifacial tools, which have only one worked surface), scrapers, a hammerstone, spokeshaves (a specialized scraper with a concave working edge used for smoothing cylindrical wooden objects), a drill, and gravers and graving spurs as well as expedient tools, unmodified flakes — including some channel flakes — whose naturally sharp edges were used for scraping, cutting, and perforating tasks. There were also retouched flakes, which show no signs of use but whose edges were purposely flaked into shape by the knapper, apparently to enhance their functional ability. These stone tools had a wide range of uses. The indigenous peoples living at Templeton probably used them to butcher animals, whittle and perforate wood, prepare tubers and other plant foods, and process hides.

We know that the Paleo-Indian people who camped at the Templeton site made and maintained stone tools because of the amount of debitage and the many bifacial rejects strewn about the site. Some of these tools were made from locally available stone, such as vein quartz and quartzite cobbles. Several ancient American Indian quartz quarries have been reported in the state.[42] Other tools were manufactured from chert and jasper, but there are no known chert or jasper outcrops in Connecticut. However, locally occurring chert cobbles in the bank of the

The American Indian Archaeological Institute (now the Institute for American Indian Studies) excavation of the Templeton site.

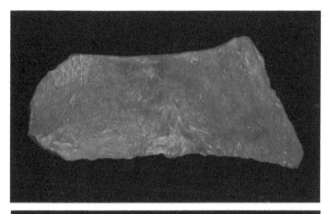

Lithic artifacts from the Templeton site: retouched chert flake; and a chert flake used as a scraper along one edge and as a spoke-shave scraper on the opposite edge.

Shepaug River just 32 feet (10 meters) from the site apparently were broken from outcrops in western Massachusetts and deposited by glacial action in Connecticut Pleistocene rivers. There are glacial boulders that contain jasper in both western Massachusetts and Bethlehem, Connecticut. The origin of these boulder trains might have been the Monkton jasper outcrops in Vermont, although there are also small jasper-like pods in Connecticut's basalt outcrops.[43] These local sources put a kink in the traditional theory that Paleo-Indians migrated far and wide for good toolstone supplies. Dr. Roger Moeller, who directed the excavations at the site, has suggested that Connecticut's Paleo-Indian communities may not have traveled great distances for either food or the raw materials for stone tool manufacture.[44] Rather, they may have followed a much more localized seasonal round for resources and used locally available stone, such as those at the Templeton site.

The small size of the Templeton site, the low weight of the stone remains, the low degree of wear on individual tools, and the similarity of manufacture among artifacts of the same tool type all suggest that the occupation was a single, short-term encampment.[45] Perhaps it was the camp of a small, male hunting party or

## THE FLUTED POINT

The fluted point is found in Northeastern North America on sites reported to date between about 13,000 and 10,000 B.P.[a] It is diagnostic (characteristic) of the Paleo-Indian culture period.

The fluted point's distinctive trait is a narrow vertical channel down the center of each of its two faces. Using a stone hammer the toolmaker, or knapper, chipped a block of stone called a core into a leaf-shaped blank, or preform. This technique, known as direct percussion, created an object chipped on both sides, a bifacial tool, or biface. The flakes removed by this method are called percussion flakes.

Next the base of the biface was struck with a billet or soft hammer of antler, wood, or bone to remove a long, thin flake from one face, producing a channel, or flute. This procedure was repeated for the other face of the blank. The flutes probably made the hafting, or attaching, of the point to a spear or javelin shaft easier. The edges of the biface were then thinned and sharpened by pressure flaking, in which the tip of an antler or bone tool, called a flaker, was pressed against the edge of the biface to remove tiny pressure flakes. The base of the point was ground smooth with a stone to make it easier to haft it onto the spear shaft; if left unground, the sharp edges might have cut and weakened the lashings.

Fluted points have been found in many Connecticut localities, mainly as isolated surface finds or in disturbed contexts such as plowed fields. One fluted point was found in sand dredged from a depth of 16 to 18 feet (about 5 meters) in Long Island Sound,[b] which was once dry land before melting glaciers caused rising seas to swallow it up.

At least eight different styles of fluted points have been identified at eastern North American archaeology sites.[c] The best known is the Clovis style. There is currently a broad consensus among New England Paleo-Indian specialists, however, that no true Clovis cultural *component* has been discovered in the region to date.[d]

Notes

a. Ritchie 1983; Storck 1983; Ellis and Dellar 1997; Curran 1999; Bradley et al. 2008.

b. Glynn 1969.

c. Anderson et al. 1992, table 18, 2009.

d. Bradley et al. 2008.

A Paleo-Indian stone chipper is surrounded by the tools used in the manufacture of fluted points in this diorama at the Yale Peabody Museum of Natural History. Among indigenous peoples men normally made the formal stone tools, such as projectile points and other chipped or ground stone tools.

Paleo-Indian lithic artifacts from the Templeton site. Left, a fluted point, the most characteristic artifact of the Paleo-Indian period, from Washington Depot. Right, top to bottom, miniature points from Washington Depot, graving spurs, and a quartz graver. Miniature points could have been made by an apprentice stone chipper, or for use as charms or for hunting small animals. Scale bars equal 1 centimeter.

a small family group. The limited number of artifacts and types of tools present make it difficult to discern gender-related objects, except for the fluted spear or javelin point, which is traditionally associated with male activities of hunting and defense. The miniature points could have belonged to a child, either a toy made for him or a tool made by the boy himself as an apprentice, a method of learning life skills commonly noted in post-contact Indian societies. In a letter to her young granddaughter, Schaghticoke elder Trudie Lamb Richmond wrote:

> In our way of life it is the elders, the grandparents, who are seen as the bridge to the past, just as the young are the bridge to the future. And both are necessary to complete the circle of life. . . . It is my responsibility as a grandmother to guide you as you are growing up.[46]

However, Moeller believes that the miniature points from Templeton were not made by a knapper's apprentice because they are not fluted and were manufactured in a different way from the fundamental Paleo-Indian weapon, the fluted point.[47] The miniatures could represent hunting magic and would have been carried in medicine bags or buried in a ceremony to ensure a successful hunt. In any case, these artifacts represent the tool kit of a single group of Paleo-Indians at a specific point in time—the earliest known people in Connecticut. (The Templeton artifacts are on display at the Institute for American Indian Studies in Washington, Connecticut.)

### Hidden Creek Site

The Hidden Creek site in Mashantucket, Connecticut, contained about 60 formal and expedient Paleo-Indian tools identified as used in hunting and in rough chopping and scraping tasks.[48] The more than 4,000 waste flakes showed that the people living at Hidden Creek also made and sharpened tools on site, and used chert as well as local quartz and quartzite materials, as at the Templeton site. The relatively new technology of scanning electron microscopy (SEM) identified plant stems, roots, and tubers that are difficult to identify with other techniques. Plant materials recovered from the site included cattail, water plantain, hazelnut, ground nut, Indian cucumber, common yellow cress, fern, clubmoss, possible water lily, and Amaranthaceae[49] (the goosefoot family of plants, which in New England include goosefoot, also known as lamb's quarters, and pigweed, are plants that produce thousands of nutritious small seeds that can be ground into flour or simmered in soups and stews).

Its excavators described Hidden Creek as a small, short-term camp used by a family-sized group of people. Unlike at Templeton, however, they believed the Paleo-Indian peoples at Hidden Creek obtained their gray-green chert from the Hudson River valley, where shale outcrops contain a variety of colored cherts that include green and blue hues. Although the excavators believe that the residents quarried the chert themselves, an alternative interpretation is that they were trading with other Paleo-Indian groups in eastern New York, either directly or through trading partners living in other Connecticut communities.

## FUNCTIONAL TYPES OF STONE TOOLS

Archaeologists determine a tool's function by studying regularities in patterns of wear along the edges and faces of artifacts, such as concentrations of scratches, pitting, polish, or the removal of tiny flakes creating a bite-like appearance.[a] Some wear patterns are easily discernible with the naked eye, but others are seen only with a microscope.

New tool types were developed throughout the later cultural periods. Once introduced, these tools were used by Native peoples until the Contact period.

Note

a. E.g., Semenov 1963; Keeley 1980.

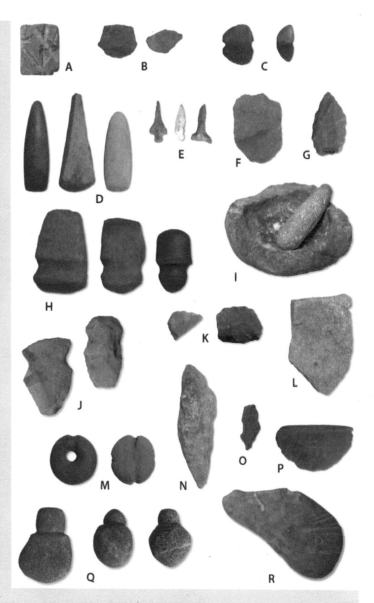

Examples of some functional types of stone tools. A, abrader. B, abrading scrapers (specialized scrapers for smoothing soapstone bowls). C, atlatl weights (previously called bannerstones). D, celts (axes without grooves for hafting). E, drill tips. F, hand gouge. G, knife. H, grooved axes. I, mortar and pestle. J, hoes. K, scrapers. L, spade. M, net or line sinkers. N, pick (tailing breaker). O, spokeshave. P, ulu (specialized slate knife used for processing fish). Q, plummets. R, whetstone. Not to scale.

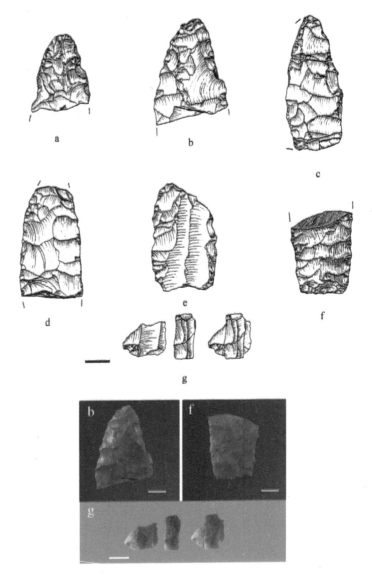

Lithic artifacts from the Hidden Creek site made of gray-green chert from the Hudson River valley south of Albany, New York. Top, illustrated bifaces and fragments recovered from the Hidden Creek site. Bottom, select lithics illustrated above. Left (b), the broken tip of a fluted projectile point that shows the robust flaking technique typical of the Paleo-Indian stone tool tradition. The break at the bottom is probably the end of a channel flake (examples shown below). Right (f), the broken base of a lanceolate parallel flaked point. Below (g), channel flakes removed through subsequent lateral flaking. Image labels correspond to drawings. Scale bars equal 1 centimeter.

This evidence for long-distance transport of stone materials across what is now Connecticut suggests that the historically known Indian paths that cross the state are very ancient indeed. Some are now state highways. Route 7 follows part of the Old Berkshire Path, an Indian pathway that connected inland Native American communities, such as the Mahikan villages in what are today the towns of Sheffield and Stockbridge in Massachusetts, with the Paugussett communities along Long Island Sound near present Stratford and Milford, Connecticut, as well as with other lower Housatonic tribal peoples (the Schaghticoke, Weantinock, and Pootatuck) stretched along the Housatonic River between those two points.[50]

The rock source of the Hidden Creek tools was identified using the geological technique of petrographic analysis.[51] Some researchers use macroscopic or

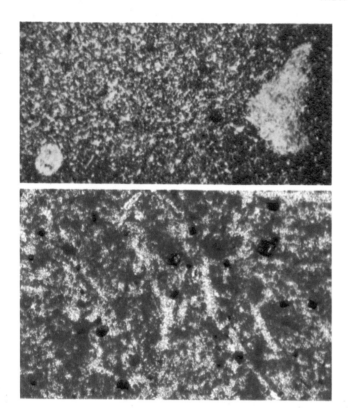

Petrographic thin-section micrographs used to help identify the chert sources of stone tools show how distinctive specific chert types look under a microscope. Top, chert from the dolomitic or limestone Onondaga Formation from the ancient Divers Lake Quarry in western New York state. Bottom, "jasper" from the secondary Pensauken Formation of northern New Jersey, which is actually identified under the microscope by its dolomite and "felty" texture as Eastern Onondaga chert that had been oxidized. Width of bottom image equals 1 millimeter.

hand specimen analysis, an unreliable identification method because of the variability and weathering characteristics of stone types, especially in New England. As lithic sourcing expert Dr. Barbara Luedtke has noted: "Source identifications based solely on this method, sometimes referred to as 'eyeball analysis,' are very common . . . and are often used uncritically by other archaeologists. . . . Eyeball analysis alone is tricky anywhere in the world, but it is especially dangerous in New England because of the particular characteristics of many New England lithic materials."[52] Additionally, many rock sources of the same type—for example, "cherts"—are visually similar if not identical macroscopically.[53] Supplementing this "eyeball analysis" with petrographic and geochemical analyses of lithic tools and possible source outcrops would clarify these macroscopic interpretations.

## Lovers Leap Site

The Lovers Leap site in New Milford, Connecticut, is a well-known collectors' spot that has almost been destroyed by development and unscientific digging. Because it overlooked an important fishing area on the Housatonic River, Native American peoples frequented the site for thousands of years. Excavations on one section of the ridge uncovered two chert points in the lowest stratigraphic level, just above bedrock.[54] According to the author of the site report, both resembled the Clovis type of fluted point except that, like the Templeton specimens, they were smaller. Other artifacts recovered from this level included one Late Archaic Vosburg point, one unidentified biface, an anvil or hammerstone, a pitted stone,

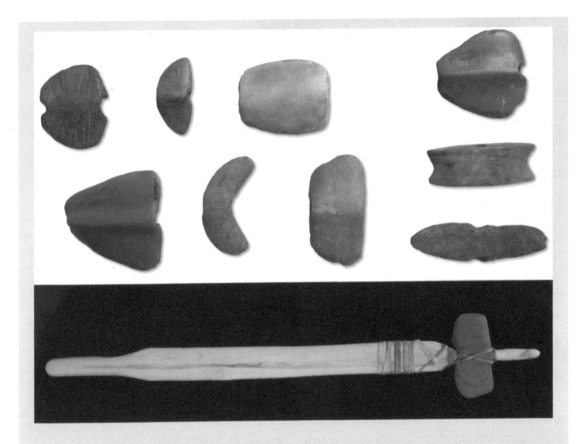

## THE ATLATL

The atlatl was a common tool of early indigenous peoples. Top, a variety of atlatl weights. Bottom, replica of an atlatl made with an atlatl weight and traditional materials, by primitive technologist Jamie Leffler.

The Paleo-Indians most likely mounted their projectile points on a spear thrower, or atlatl, a straight wooden stick with a hook at one end. The name *atlatl* comes from the Aztec words for "water" and "thrower." The Aztecs used the atlatl to spear fish and waterfowl.[a]

Also called a "throwing board,"[b] the atlatl makes a spear go farther and faster, with more power than throwing it directly, improving early man's hunting capabilities. A hunter using an atlatl could achieve a throwing range of more than 300 feet (over 100 meters). Atlatls in northwestern Africa date back more than 25,000 years and were thought to have been introduced to North America from Siberia by at least 12,000 to 10,000 years ago.

It is generally assumed that stone weights were lashed to the atlatl or fitted on the stick through a hole drilled in the center of the stone. "Atlatl weights," or bannerstones, of various sizes and shapes have been found: crescentic, oval, rectangular, cylindrical, and winged; the variety of styles could be a product of different culture groups. Some examples are artistically notched or incised, possibly a way of counting successful kills, or these may be magical or sacred graphics meant to enhance the atlatl's function.

Several primitive technologists question the use of these stones as weights, however, because experiments with them on atlatls fail to show any increased efficiency in the throw.[c] One expert in atlatl throwing notes that most of the "weights" are too heavy, and their drill holes are too small for fitting on the atlatl shaft. He suggests:

> What they all had in common, where the bannerstone was complete enough to detect this, was that they were all balanced as if they were designed to spin. I maintain that it is evident and incontrovertible that bannerstones were balanced around the central hole because they were meant to spin. . . . I believe the bannerstone was used as a spindle weight to make string to tie on fletching and projectile points, and possibly a spindle weight to turn and taper dart shafts. It was not part of the atlatl at all but was carried in a kit, made from bark or leather, with the atlatl.[d]

In his painting *The Spread of the Atlatl*, Connecticut artist David R. Wagner shows an encounter between members of two different Eastern Woodland communities, one of which carries atlatls.

Notes

a. Keddie 2006.

b. Saunders 2004.

c. Jamie Leffler, primitive technologist, personal communication, January 11, 2010.

d. Robert S. Berg, "Bannerstones and How They Relate to the Atlatl," *Thunderbird Atlatl*, November 8, 2007, www .thunderbirdatlatl.com/?p=158 (accessed January 14, 2010).

a round quartz pebble, two scrapers, and part of a winged atlatl weight.[55] A common tool of Late Archaic peoples, atlatl weights are associated with a Middle Archaic burial and Neville points at Annasnappet Pond in Massachusetts, which shows they were also used by earlier hunters.[56] Because of the presence of the later-occurring Vosburg point, except for the fluted points none of these artifacts can be assigned with any certainty to the Paleo-Indian occupation of the site.

### Liebman Site

The Liebman site in Lebanon, Connecticut, is another Paleo-Indian settlement located on a small sandy knoll overlooking a stream. The site contained two concentrations of Paleo-Indian artifacts, a surface collection and a buried component. Cultural finds included one broken fluted point, seventeen steeply angled scraping tools, twelve used flakes, a spurred graver for slotting or engraving hard objects such as wood, bone, or antler, and hundreds of chert flake debitage.[57]

The authors of the site report surmised that the Paleo-Indians living at Liebman obtained their chert supplies from a Hudson Valley source, but do not describe what technique they used to arrive at this conclusion. From the site's small size and the variety of its few artifacts we can infer it was a short-term camp or camps. The fluted point indicates male hunting activities, while many specialized scrapers suggest that some specific but as yet unidentified task was also being performed at the site. The chert debitage shows that there were also tool manufacture and possibly maintenance activities.

### Allen's Meadows Site

The Allen's Meadows site in Wilton, Connecticut, was a few hundred feet from an old meander scar of the Norwalk River. It contained two fluted points, several bifaces, cores, debitage from stone tool manufacture, and more than twenty endscrapers, some with graving spurs. At the time of its occupation it was a small camp, probably overlooking the river, where the occupants engaged in toolmaking and other currently unidentified processing activities.[58] Unfortunately, the site is in a disturbed plow zone, which also contained a Meadowood point and a Late Archaic hearth.

### Baldwin Ridge Site

The Baldwin Ridge site was on a ridge overlooking the Thames River valley in Groton. It contained a fluted point base, endscrapers, and a flake. Its excavators described it as a small, special-purpose site,[59] possibly a game lookout.

All known Paleo-Indian camps in Connecticut are in upland, inland areas that overlooked water sources. None are located in a large river floodplain. This suggests that Paleo-Indian communities relied mainly on the resources of interior lakes and swamps, and not on those of the major river valleys and coastal areas, as did later Indian societies. The cultural evidence is supported by paleoenvironmental reconstructions of the Long Island Sound region. Botanical, faunal, and

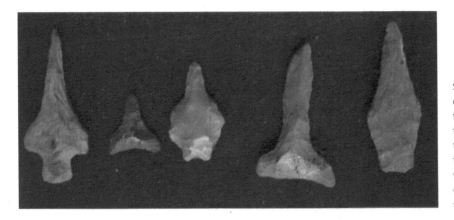

Several styles of undated drills surface collected from the Meadows site in Stratford, Connecticut. Although these are from a later cultural period, Paleo-Indians would have used similar drills to work wood and stone.

climatic information depicts the river valleys and coasts as harsh, relatively barren environments that were distinctly unpleasant for human habitation.[60] The rapidly rising water level prevented the accumulation of sediments necessary for the development of marshes.

Without these great food factories and animal incubators few waterfowl, fishes, and small fur-bearing mammals would thrive as they do along our coasts and rivers today. Instead, the swiftly rising sea would have created barren islands, bars, lagoons, mudflats, and bogs that would have made foot travel along the coast difficult, and the dense insect population would have made it unbearable. Likewise, the dangerous and barren floodplains of fast-flowing rivers, flooded with swirling glacial meltwater, would have none of the biotic diversity characteristic of today's slower, meandering rivers with their marshes, backwater swamps, and oxbow islands teeming with plant and animal life. As archaeologists David George and Brian Jones concluded in their study of the Great Swamp Basin in nearby Rhode Island, "It is becoming clear that [interior] wetlands archaeology is fundamental to reconstructing details of Native American land and resource use in and around swampy areas that have not been systematically examined in traditional archaeological investigations."[61]

However, as Daniel Forrest, staff archaeologist in the Connecticut State Historic Preservation Office, has noted, it is also plausible that the apparent absence of Paleo-Indian sites from the large river valleys may result from the burial or destruction of ancient landforms by the migration of river channels and the aggradation of sediments in response to rising sea levels.[62]

> There are few accessible and intact late Pleistocene terrace settings where any such sites would have a reasonable opportunity to be discovered using traditional archaeological survey methods. This is in many ways comparable to the loss of the former coastal settings beneath Long Island Sound and the Atlantic Ocean.[63]

Fluted points suggest that hunting was important. Botanical evidence such as cattail root, hazelnut shell, and other plant remains recovered by the flotation technique from Hidden Creek, and plant and fish remains from the Shawnee

Flotation was used extensively at both the Templeton and the Hidden Creek sites to recover material from excavated soil. Top, scooping out the light fraction with a fish net. Bottom, recovering the light fraction by floating soil from the Templeton site in the Shepaug River.

Minisink site in northwestern New Jersey,[64] however, show that plant gathering and likely fishing were also part of the Paleo-Indian subsistence strategy.

## INTERPRETATIONS AND QUESTIONS

Until now archaeologists have discovered only one kind of Paleo-Indian settlement in Connecticut—the short-term camp site. These are small sites with relatively little variety among their few artifacts and cultural features. This suggests that only a small group of people lived at each site and that few activities were performed there. The recovery of fluted points and evidence for tool manufacture suggest male hunting camps. However, the few points are always outnumbered by other tool types, particularly general purpose scraping, cutting, and chopping tools. These might have been used by male hunters to prepare their supper, but could just as easily represent women's work of preparing foods and processing plants and skins for clothing, bedding, storage containers, and shelter in a family camp.

Among living Indian groups women also make some kinds of tools, particularly expedient tools, although men make these kinds of tools as well.[65] In the Chipewyan communities of Saskatchewan, women are sometimes hunters. Female hunting groups tended to hunt close to the village, though, while male hunting parties traveled great distances; mixed teams of males and females operated at intermediate distances from the main camp or village. Men often stored their gear at nonvillage "bush settings,"[66] which could explain why so few finished, male-related objects (such as unbroken finished points, other hunting and fishing equipment, and heavy woodworking tools) are found at residential camps through all cultural periods, while female-related objects (such as pottery, food processing tools, awls and other hide-working tools, and hoes) are more common.

Using locally available rock to manufacture stone tools would make it unnecessary—or at least *less* necessary—to travel great distances for high quality chert and jasper. Local rock usage may suggest a less migratory, more localized settlement system for the Templeton and Hidden Creek Paleo-Indian communities. The evidence for an environment that included deciduous trees, with their abundance of edible foodstuffs (such as acorns from the oak at Templeton and hazelnuts at Hidden Creek), and also the edible animal life attracted to these plant foods, suggests that the seasonal collection of locally available food sources so evident during the later Archaic periods may have had its roots in the late Paleo-Indian period. An alternative explanation for the use of local rock sources has been suggested by Forrest.

> The total range of seasonal or even decadal movements is likely shrinking during the period in which these sites were in use, but the people living in these locations may have moved just as frequently as their ancestors. The movements just may have been shorter in distance. The use of local materials in this view would be a means of conserving the high-value cherts, jaspers, etc. that may only be acquired during infrequent trips to lithic sources or during aggregation "events," where large numbers of small groups gather (i.e., Bull Brook [site]).[67]

Many questions remain. How were the Paleo-Indian settlements arranged on the landscape and how were they related to one another? Did the Paleo-Indians have other kinds of settlements or were there only small family groups of mobile hunters and gatherers who traveled from one short-term camp to another? How were their communities organized socially and politically? What was the size of their populations? Did they live in small, egalitarian family groups, as the short-term camps imply, or were those camps only part of a more complicated settlement system that sometimes included larger, seasonal or multiseasonal camps with multifamily or multilineage members? What did they eat? Was hunting the major economic activity? How important were fish and plants to the Connecticut Paleo-Indian economy? Were their cosmological and spiritual beliefs similar to those of later groups? How far and what did they trade, and where were the major trade routes? Only the discovery and careful excavation of additional undisturbed sites will provide answers to these questions. As one study concluded: "Due to the general scarcity of Paleoindian materials, and the comparatively little that is known about these occupations, every effort should be made to increase knowledge of this period, and to preserve the information that remains."[68]

# 2

# Coping with New Environments
## *The Early Archaic Period*

Some call us American Indians. Others call us Native Americans. But we were here long before this continent was renamed "America." Therefore, we claim the right to determine what it means to be indigenous—to maintain our identity and to be respected for who we are. It is important to understand and respect that there are many ways of being human.

—Trudie Lamb Richmond, educator, storyteller, leader
and elder of the Schaghticoke Tribal Nation, 2000

During the Archaic stage the climate continued to warm and sea level continued to rise. At around 10,000 to 8900 B.P. there was a dramatic increase in white pine, yellow and gray birch, and oak trees at the expense of spruce, larch, and firs, showing a continued warming and drying, with July temperatures possibly 8 percent higher than today, although the winters were colder.[1] By 9000 B.P. (8000 cal B.C.) the rising sea had created Long Island Sound, separating Long Island from the Connecticut mainland.[2]

This pine-birch-oak forest could support white-tailed deer, moose, elk, black bear, wolf, fox, lynx, marten, wolverine, turkey, migratory birds, fishes, turtles, and freshwater mussels.[3] By 7500 B.P. the oak-hemlock forest had become the dominant vegetation.[4] These environmental changes stimulated cultural changes in Native American communities and these new lifeways characterize the Archaic cultural stage.

The Archaic has four major cultural periods: Early, Middle, Late, and Terminal. Each of these periods is marked by distinctive projectile point styles, trends toward a greater variety of tool types, generally more and larger settlements, and regionalization of indigenous communities. However, at present there is little archaeological evidence in the form of radiocarbon dates for human activities between 7200 and 5200 B.P.[5] This was a very warm, dry period that caused some water sources to shrink and dry up, which may have triggered population change or movement.

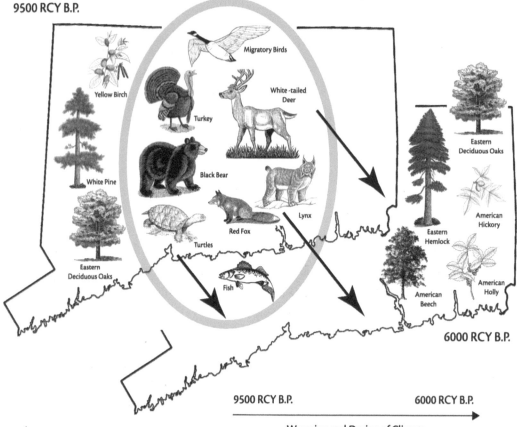

9500 RCY B.P.

Migratory Birds

Yellow Birch

Turkey

White-tailed
Deer

White Pine

Black Bear

Eastern
Deciduous Oaks

American
Hickory

Lynx

Eastern
Hemlock

Red Fox

Turtles

American
Holly

Eastern
Deciduous Oaks

Fish

American
Beech

6000 RCY B.P.

9500 RCY B.P.                    6000 RCY B.P.

Warming and Drying of Climate

Over time southern New England's flora and fauna responded to changes in the post-glacial environment. The spruce-pine woodlands prevalent during much of the Paleo-Indian stage moved toward becoming a mosaic of deciduous-coniferous mixed forests. By 9000 B.P. the rising sea level had separated what is now Long Island from the Connecticut mainland. There was a northerly retreat of spruce woodland and animals, and by 6000 B.P. they had been replaced by temperate deciduous woodland plants and associated animals.

## EARLY ARCHAIC PEOPLES

With few undisturbed sites from this period, we know little about the Early Archaic peoples of the Northeast (about 9000 to 8000 RCY B.P.). The main evidence that these Indian communities existed on the Connecticut landscape are scattered finds of diagnostic corner-notched and stemmed Kirk and Palmer points, bifurcated-base points (stemmed points with notched bases), and points resembling Dalton and Hardaway types (which are undated, and some may be variants of Late Archaic Laurentian types, such as Brewerton Eared Notched and Brewerton Eared Triangle).[6] These point styles were originally identified along the southeastern coast of the United States, but the finds tell us little about the people who used them in Connecticut except that they had southeastern connections.

### The Evidence for Settlement

Excavations of two undisturbed, important settlements, however, uncovered cultural remains with new and exciting implications about the economy and social relationships of local Early Archaic communities.

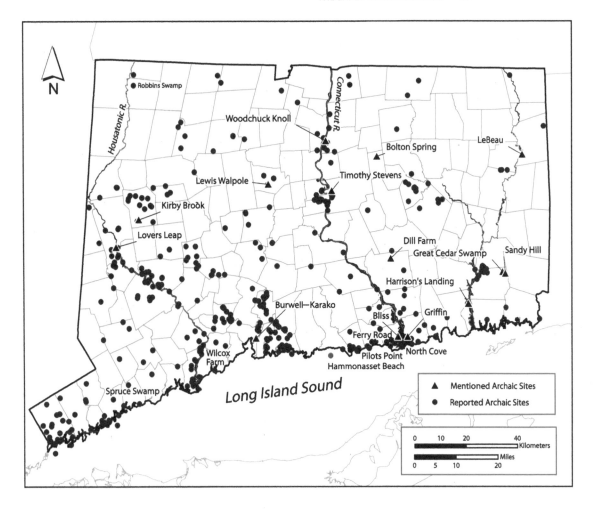

Known Archaic sites and single point finds in Connecticut on file in the Connecticut Office of State Archaeology.

### Dill Farm Site

The Dill Farm site overlooks a large swamp in the uplands of East Haddam, Connecticut. Excavations there unearthed a few tools and cultural features thought to represent short-term camps repeatedly occupied by small groups of people.[7] The artifacts included three bifurcate-base Kanawha-type points, unifacial flake thumbnail-size scrapers, two pieces of worked slate, debitage, and several small features, including a cache of forty quartz crystal quarry blocks and large flakes stored underground in a pit. The cache tells us that the people who made it intended to return to the camp. It suggests the beginnings of the seasonal subsistence round that characterized later Indian communities throughout southern New England.

Charcoal from a hearth that contained debitage and hazelnut and walnut shells produced a radiocarbon date of 8560 B.P. The site also had large amounts of charcoal from burned white oak and white pine. The burned wood confirmed that there was a mixed pine-hardwood forest environment in the lower Connecticut

## The Earliest Definitive Evidence of Some Significant Indigenous Cultural Activities in Connecticut

A chronology of the earliest occurrence of the first definitive archaeological evidence for some significant indigenous cultural activities in Connecticut.

River valley at that time, with deciduous mast trees providing food and cover for animals, particularly white-tailed deer. The nut shells also suggested a late summer–early fall occupation, when the nuts ripen, although nuts can be stored and used at other times of the year.

Dill Farm is similar to the Double P site in the Titicut Basin of neighboring southeastern Massachusetts.[8] Both are part of the Atlantic Slope archaeological tradition, which has a bifacial chipped stone technology represented by southeastern point styles. Significantly, many of the stone tools were made from exotic cherts and rhyolites as well as local quartz, suggesting either long-distance population movements or trading networks. The nearest known chert outcrops are in the Hudson Valley of New York, and the nearest known rhyolite sources are in the Boston Basin and in central New Hampshire.

The Dill Farm and Double P sites reflect the traditional perspective of Early Archaic societies as small groups of mobile hunters and foragers. Yet in Connecticut Early Archaic culture groups were much more diversified, surviving the postglacial changes in climate and environment with a variety of adaptations. There are many cultural ways of accomplishing the same ends, and different cultural behaviors can be successful. A case in point is the Sandy Hill site on the Mashantucket Pequot Reservation in southeastern Connecticut.[9] This Early Archaic complex yielded radiocarbon dates from 9340 to 8470 B.P., making the community at Sandy Hill partly contemporary with the one at Dill Farm.

## Sandy Hill Site

The artifact assemblage, cultural features, and dietary remains from the Sandy Hill site are very different from those at Dill Farm and other sites of the Atlantic Slope tradition. The inhabitants of Sandy Hill did not depend on a bifacial technology for their stone tools, but made frequent use of steeply retouched quartz scrapers and small quartz cores. The cores may have been part of a microlith industry, in which small flakes chipped off the micro-cores were inserted into bone, antler, or wood shafts, handles, or boards and used as multi-pronged projectile points, sickles for harvesting wild plants (as in the Mesolithic Near East), or grater boards (grinding boards for processing roots and tubers as used in South America, the Caribbean, India, and Africa). Huge amounts of small quartz flakes were recovered from the site.[10] Also unlike Dill Farm, over 95 percent of the stone artifacts from Sandy Hill were made from local quartz. Other tools included large chipped stone choppers, and a ground stone gouge and adze for heavy-duty woodworking.

The Sandy Hill unifacial tool and ground stone tool technologies share striking characteristics with those of the Gulf of Maine Archaic tradition.[11] Sandy Hill and two other Early Archaic sites at Mashantucket do contain a few rare bifacially worked, wide-stem, concave Parallel Stem points, a style also found in Maine. These points may reflect deep regional roots with the Late Paleo-Indian communities of New England; such communities thrived in central Maine as late as 6000 B.P.[12]

The Early Archaic Sandy Hill site at Mashantucket (Foxwoods Casino is in the background). Extensive excavations by archaeologists from the Mashantucket Pequot Museum and Research Center at the site show that the Early Archaic peoples there built at least a dozen semi-subterranean residential lodges into the south-facing sandy hillside. The site dates from about 10,000 to 9500 RCY cal B.P. At left, aerial view of the site excavations. Upper right, the partially excavated floor of a pit house, showing the molds of the large post holes that held the supports for the timber-framed structure. Lower right, the first of the structures identified in the hillside, showing the floor of another pit house (the circular splotches are the larger post molds).

Excavation at the Sandy Hill site in 2006 identified other house floors, caches of quartz chunks, and crude gneiss bifaces, or choppers. One showed evidence that the choppers may have been used to dig yellow nutsedge tubers. Used as hand spades, these tools may have also been used to gather cattail tubers. This site provided abundant information on the diet of early Holocene Native people. Plant-food remains included charred fragments of cattail root, bulrush, water plantain, nutsedge, and hazelnuts, among others. Animal-food remains were less common, mostly small game animals. As at Northeast sites of similar age, beaver, muskrat, and turtle from the adjacent Great Cedar Swamp were probably important in the diet of the community at Sandy Hill.

Probably the most important finds at Sandy Hill were its basin-shaped semi-subterranean pit houses filled with dietary remains.[13] "At least a dozen such residential structures" were built into a south-facing sandy hillside.[14] The earliest in New England, these Early Archaic pit houses were 13 feet (4 meters) by more than 19 feet (6 meters) and overlapped, indicating that there were several occupations of the site. Their living floors contained abundant hazelnut shells and a variety of wetland aquatic and terrestrial plant remains from nearby microhabitats. The plants included cattail, bur-reed, water plantain, arrowhead, yellow nutsedge, bulrush, wild calla, Indian cucumber, Solomon's seal, blue flag, and white water-lily. This variety supports what many archaeologists have long thought—that "Early Man the Hunter" is an overstated stereotype and that women with their knowledge of plant lore played a key role in Early Archaic (and probably Paleo-Indian) hunter-gatherer economies. In fact, some ethnographic accounts reported that Native American women also hunted. As we have seen, among the present-day Chipewyan people of Canada both men and women are hunters, differing only in that the male hunting parties range farther into the bush than the women.[15]

The ripening times for the various plant foods show that the Early Archaic Sandy Hill community occupied the pit houses from at least summer through fall. The semi-subterranean construction of the houses—which were built into a hillside—suggests winter occupation as well. According to the excavators, the Sandy Hill site could have been a base camp or village repeatedly occupied by Early Archaic communities for at least five hundred years.

### The Great Cedar Swamp and Robbins Swamp Sites

Isolated finds of bifurcated points have been recovered from terraces overlooking the Great Cedar Swamp on the Mashantucket Pequot Reservation near Ledyard, Connecticut. The points were all made from exotic cherts and rhyolites. They are

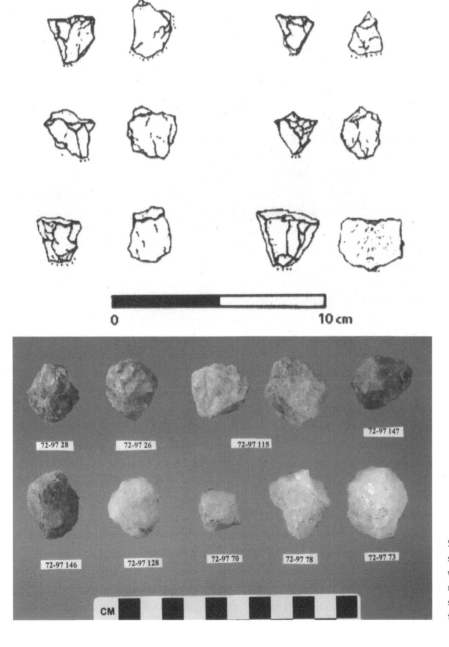

Sandy Hill lithic artifacts: small quartz cores (top) were used to make the micro-flakes found at the site; bottom, quartz scrapers from the Sandy Hill site.

interpreted to show very limited hunting of game at Cedar Swamp by members of an Early Archaic community who lived elsewhere.[16]

An archaeological survey of Robbins Swamp, a large upland wetland covering portions of Canaan, identified thirty-five Early Archaic sites based on the recovery of bifurcated base, Kirk, Palmer, Hardaway, and other diagnostic points.[17] Unlike other Atlantic Slope tradition sites, these were not all interpreted as small, short-term camps. The extensive glacial lake basin mosaic of lake-pond-wetland-forest environments in this part of Connecticut would have provided stable, predictable, highly productive, and diverse food sources able to support larger, less mobile human communities than traditionally envisioned for the Early Archaic.[18] The points and other artifact types occurred in such frequency that excavator Dr. George Nicholas proposed that these sites could represent "affluent" gathering-hunting communities,[19] similar to the historic Indian societies on the Northwest Coast of North America (such as the Haida and Tlinglit), who have social and economic structures more complex than most hunter-gatherer communities.

The Carlson I site in the Robbins Swamp area is in an upland next to springs and the Whiting River, a tributary of the Blackberry River. It contained an Early Archaic point, chert bifaces and flakes, spokeshaves and other scrapers, flake tools, and tool manufacturing workshops. The workshops were strewn with large amounts of jasper cobbles and chunks, many of which had been heated.[20] Hammerstones of different sizes were recovered in and near the workshops. Jasper was extracted from locally available quartzite conglomerate by heating, cooling, and percussion using large hammerstones. "Roasting" jasper "is known to improve the flaking qualities of this raw material," according to Debra Schindler and others who studied the effects of thermal alteration on jasper.[21]

The site shows evidence that the quartzite was heated in large basin-shaped features, which contained jasper debris, quartzite matrix, charcoal, and reddened soil. The discolored soil testifies to the presence of fires hot enough to change the iron oxides in the soil from brown to red. One basin about 3 feet (1 meter) deep returned an unexpectedly late radiocarbon date of 3685 B.P. The workshops may have been associated with later groups rather than the Early Archaic point users, but they could have been used by both peoples. More research on the site is sorely needed.

## CLOTHING AND ORNAMENTATION

The acidic soils and temperate climatic conditions in Connecticut usually allow the recovery of only nonperishable stone items from early indigenous sites. Even so, fragments of hematite and graphite recovered from the Sandy Hill site have wear patterns that suggest that grains were scratched off and mixed with animal fat or plant oil to make red and silver-gray paints. Early post-contact Indians used these and other pigments to paint baskets, mats, clothing, and even their bodies with colorful zoomorphic, floral, and symbolic geometric designs, as noted by European observers in the seventeenth century.[22] These Early Archaic paint stones from Sandy Hill are the earliest known evidence for art and ornamentation in Connecticut.

Some twentieth-century paintings and exhibits continued the nineteenth-century stereotype of pre-contact (and post-contact!) Indian communities as primitive, childlike, simple societies with a rudimentary, undeveloped material culture that included rude skin clothing. There is absolutely no evidence to sup-

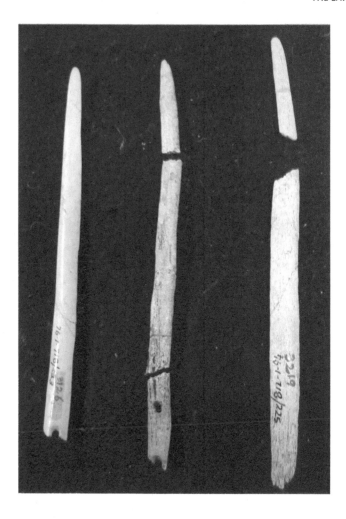

Bone weaving needles
(shuttles) from the Wil-
cox Farm site in Milford,
Connectiut.

port these assumptions. In other areas of the country, particularly the dry regions of the West but also the Northeast, Paleo-Indian and Early Archaic sites have yielded perishable wood and bone articles. Delicate bone needles with drilled eyes are evidence that ancient Indian peoples wore finely tailored clothing,[23] probably very similar to those worn by indigenous peoples at the time of first contact with Europeans. Seventeenth-century European writers reported that both men and women commonly wore breechcloths, leggings, and moccasins of tanned deer hide, often with mantles or "coats" made from deerskin or fur, or feather capes. Men wore tobacco pouches either around their necks or tied to a sash around the waist.[24] The items were so well tanned that they were waterproof. Writing in 1634, Englishman William Wood reported that both men and women had "a longing desire after many kinds of ornaments, wearing pendants in their ears" and on necklaces and belts, carved from stone, shell, and bone into beads and animal forms.[25] Roger Williams, the Puritan minister who founded Providence, Rhode Island, and lived among the Narragansett tribal people in the 1640s, commented on the excellence of their leather-making technology.

Replicated traditional deerskin clothing worn by Ramona Nogic (Mohawk-Shinnecock descent).

Shoes and Stockins they make of their Deere skin worne out, which yet being excellently tann'd by them, is excellent for to travel in wet and snow; for it is so well tempered with oyle, that the water cleane wrings out; and being hang'd up in their chimney, they presently drie without hurt, as my selfe hath often proved.[26]

Thomas Morton, an Englishman who spent a number of years in eastern New England during the 1620s and 1630s, described in detail the indigenous clothing of that period:

Some of these skins they dress with the hair on, and some with the hair off: the hairy side in wintertime they wear next their bodies, and in warm weather they wear the hair outwards. They make likewise some coats of the feathers of turkeys, which they weave together with twine of their own making very prittily. These garments they wear like mantles knit over their shoulders, and put under their arm: they have likewise another sort of mantles, made of moose skins, which beast is a great large deer, so big as a horse. These skins they commonly dress bare, and make them wondrous white, and stripe them with size roundabout the borders, in form like lace set on by a Tailor; and some they stripe with size in works of several fashions very curious, according to the several fantasies of the workmen, wherein they strive to excel one another.

One of the wyues of Wyngyno.

Watercolor illustrations by John White, made from 1585 to 1593 while he was at the English settlement of Roanoke, introduced Europeans to the indigenous peoples, plants, and animals of what is now North Carolina. White's *Indian Woman* shows a Native Algonkian speaker in deerskin clothing and headband, with a beaded ear ornament and beaded necklace. Her body is tattooed or painted on the face, wrists, upper left arm, and calves.

. . . And mantles made of bearskins are a usual wearing, among the Natives that live where the bears do haunt: they make shoes of mooseskin, which is the principal leather used to that purpose; and for want of such leather (which is the strongest) they make shoes of deerskin, very handsomely and commodious. And of such deerskins as they dress bare, they make stockings, that come within their shoes like a stirrup stocking, and is fastened above at their belt which is about their middle.

. . . Every male after he attains unto the age which they call Pubes [puberty] weareth a belt about his middle, and a broad piece of leather that goeth between his legs, and is tuckt up both before and behind under that belt. And this they wear to hide their secrets of nature, which by no means they will suffer to be seen, so much modesty they use in that particular. Those garments they always put on when they go a-hunting to keep their skins from the brush of the shrubs. And when they have their apparel on, they look like Irish in their trousers, the stockings join so to their breeches.

Illustration of two stone "runtee" beads from Farmington, Connecticut.

. . . A good well-grown deerskin is of great account with them, and it must have the tail on, or else they account it defaced, the tail being three times as long as the tails of our English deer, yea four times so long. This when they travel is wrapped round about their body, with a girdle of their making bound round about their middles, to which girdle is fastened a bag in which his instruments be, with which he can strike fire upon any occasion.

Their women have shoes and stockings to wear likewise when they please, such as the men have, but the mantle they use to cover their nakedness is much longer than that which the men use; for as the men have one deerskin, the women have two sewed together at the full length, and it is so large that it trails after them like a great Lady's train. And in time I think they may have their Pages to bear them up. And where the men use but one bearskin for a mantle, the women have two sewed together.[27]

The "Tale of Chahnameed," a four-hundred-year-old Mohegan folktale that tribal elder Fidelia Fielding told to anthropologist Frank Speck in 1902, describes a young Indian woman in a buckskin dress decorated with colored beads, shells, and "fringe"—probably an example of the "size" described by Morton.[28] Local historian Charles H. Townshend cited a 1645 document on the Quinnipiac Indians of New Haven.

This wampum [shell beads] made by the Indians of Connecticut and Long Island was flat and round, measuring about a sixteenth of an inch thick and one-eighth of an inch long, and was strung alternately white and purple on a native hemp thread, and when used for ornamentation was stitched into their buckskin garments by means of a needle made from the sharp bone of a wild fowles leg. It was also stitched to their wampum belts and zigzagged between representations of stars, animals and implements of peace and war.[29]

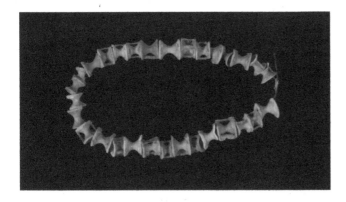

A bracelet made from fish vertebrae beads from Perry's Shell Heap, Truro, Massachusetts.

Wampum beads have been recovered from several archaeology sites (the beads are discussed in later chapters). Three examples of a rare form of bead called a "runtee" were found in an undated grave in Farmington.[30] A runtee is a circular bead with double lines of perforations that run parallel to the flat face of the bead. One face of the bead was engraved or perforated to form a design.

On the islands and coasts, where deer and other fur-bearing animals were relatively scarce, people often wore clothing woven from grasses and other plant materials. In 1605, Samuel de Champlain provided the following description of indigenous inhabitants on Cape Cod:

> All these savages . . . wear neither robes nor furs, except very rarely; moreover, their robes are made of grasses and hemp, scarcely covering the body, and coming down only to their thighs. They have only the sexual parts concealed with a small piece of leather; so likewise the women, with whom it comes down a little lower behind than with the men, all the rest of the body being naked. Whenever the women came to see us they wore robes which were open in front.[31]

## INTERPRETATIONS AND QUESTIONS

The few living sites investigated by local researchers reveal a surprising diversity in the cultural lifeways of Connecticut's Early Archaic communities. The evidence from these sites forces archaeologists to question the traditional model of small, mobile groups of egalitarian foragers and to instead consider that there were multiple models operating simultaneously to explain the presence of these distinct yet contemporary societies. Locally fluctuating microenvironments probably were important factors for the socioeconomic diversity of these Early Archaic communities. Nevertheless, the economies of these societies seem to have been focused on large inland wetlands, where there is evidence of recurring occupations over the years. This strongly suggests that the seeds of regionalism and seasonal subsistence activities seen in late Paleo-Indian sites began to blossom in the Early Archaic period.

We still have many questions about Early Archaic communities in Connecticut. What are the relationships, if any, between the Atlantic Slope tradition settle-

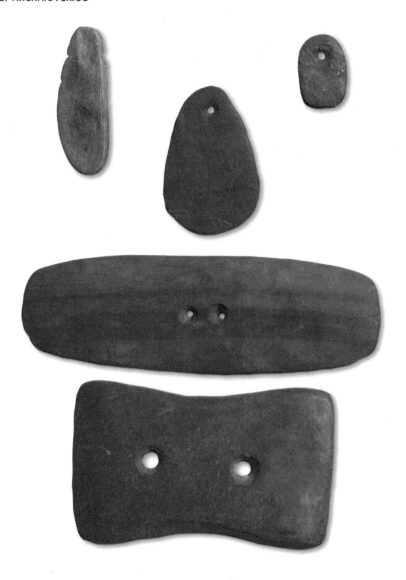

Early indigenous stone jewelry. Top left, effigy pendant carved in the shape of an unidentified animal. Top right, single-hole pendants; these could have been attached to clothing to create sound, perhaps during dances, but can also be interpreted as line weights used in fishing. Below, a two-hole slate gorget from Fairfield County, Connecticut, and a polished gray notched stone pendant, a surface find from near Newington, Connecticut.

ments and those of the Gulf of Maine Archaic in Connecticut? Were they two discrete cultures with distinctive technology and subsistence-settlement systems? Or do they represent two kinds of settlement types within a single subsistence-settlement system? What are the relationships between the Connecticut communities representing these traditions and their counterparts in the Southeast and on the Maine coast, respectively? Are the Early Archaic communities descendants of Paleo-Indian peoples, or were they new migrants to the region?

As with Paleo-Indians, virtually all of the cultural information unearthed by excavations deals with technology, economy, and settlement patterns. We know little about the sociopolitical organizations, belief systems, or recreational activities of these communities. Only scientific excavation of additional undisturbed sites can provide answers.

Possible explanations for the relative lack of Early Archaic materials in New England and upstate New York range from the inability of pine forests to support diverse plant food resources and, therefore, game and people[32] to the submergence of sites by the rising sea.[33] This first theory does not seem to apply to southern New England because studies of charcoal and macro-plant remains show pine-deciduous forests for Connecticut at this time.[34] Perhaps it is not so much a question of *diversity* of those resources as it is their *predictable quantity*.

Diversity without quantity would provide for only small populations of wild game and humans, as the low number of sites may suggest. Alternatively, the plant remains and substantial housing at the Sandy Hill site demonstrate that geographic pockets of productive food sources were present on the Connecticut landscape. More archaeological surveys about inland, upland glacial lake basins are needed to test the idea that early communities were unevenly dispersed and concentrated in those lake basins,[35] which are rarely investigated by archaeologists during cultural resource management projects (the main source of archaeological surveys). Thus, another possible reason for the dearth of Early Archaic sites is that archaeologists just have not been looking in the right places.

That the Atlantic Ocean has been continuously rising since the beginning of post-glacial times supports the submergence theory.[36] On the Connecticut coast, many archaeology sites are now visible only at low tide and some have been completely inundated. Two Early Archaic points were dredged from marsh soils at the Ferry Road site in Old Saybrook.[37] The nearby North Cove site contained submerged cultural materials dating from the Late Archaic through Woodland times.[38] Dredging in 16 feet (5 meters) of water off Hammonasset Beach in Madison uncovered Paleo-Indian, Middle Archaic, Late Archaic, Terminal Archaic, and Woodland artifacts.[39] An inundated portion of the Spruce Swamp site on the East Norwalk coast probably dates to the Late or Terminal Archaic.[40] Several submerged coastal sites in the Pilot's Point section of Westbrook date to Archaic times.[41]

Some of these submerged sites may actually have been inland when Indian communities occupied them thousands of years ago, rather than on the coast, and there likely are sites under the waters of Long Island Sound in undisturbed sediments.[42] In fact, the waters off southern New England do contain undisturbed landscapes below their disturbed "topsoils."[43] Underwater archaeology by several state and private agencies can provide important information on submerged sites.[44] The University of Connecticut now offers a minor in maritime archaeology in the Maritime Studies Program at its Avery Point campus that includes the archaeology of underwater sites.[45]

But the most recent theory for the dearth of Early Archaic sites is a cultural one. It suggests that Gulf of Maine tradition sites might easily be misidentified because of their lack of projectile points and their abundance of local quartz unifacial tools and debitage (the latter trait is common to sites from other cultural periods as well).[46]

# 3

## Surviving in Hot, Dry Homelands

### *The Middle Archaic Period*

Ours is a land culture. In fact, the land is the culture.

—Aurelius Piper (Chief Big Eagle), Golden Hill Paugussett chief, 1989

Radiocarbon dates for Middle Archaic settlements range from about 8000 to 6000 B.P. This was a period of continued warming and drying.[1] Like the Early Archaic period, fluctuations in temperatures did occur, but there is evidence for a hot, dry trend in Connecticut: an expansion of grasslands at the expense of woodlands, a surge of forest fires, and the drying up of wetlands. Botanical studies show a decrease in forest tree pollens except for an increase in warmth-loving oak, more ragweed and herbaceous plants, the first appearance of drought-resistant hickory, and evidence for burning in charcoal particles across large stretches of a soil stratum. The appearance of certain vegetation such as American holly (*Ilex opaca*), whose present range is south of Connecticut,[2] also shows a climate warmer than today. Studies of pollens and plant macrofossils from the Great Cedar Swamp in southeastern Connecticut show that the shrinking and drying up of some wetlands occurred between 7500 and 5000 B.P.[3]

Such dramatic environmental changes surely must have affected the local Indian communities. In fact, there is a cultural gap at Great Cedar Swamp between 7000 and 5000 B.P., during which no Native American settlements were inhabited.[4] Soil corings in the swamp next to the Dill Farm site also suggest this.[5] The shrinking of interior wetland environments and drying up of the smaller ones would have created a domino effect on resources: less water, less vegetation, and fewer fishes, amphibians, and reptiles, along with fewer mammals, including humans. This is probably why many Middle Archaic camps were located in major river valleys, where water sources were less affected than in the drier uplands. Large interior wetlands continued to be exploited as well.

### MIDDLE ARCHAIC PEOPLES

Native American communities of this period are better known than those of the Early Archaic, mainly because of the many sites belonging to the Neville cul-

Middle Archaic projectile points in the Neville (top rows) and Stark (bottom rows) styles, from the Lewis-Walpole site, Farmington, Connecticut.

ture complex. This complex is identified by three point styles: Neville points (medium-bladed with squarish stems); Stark points (medium-bladed with converging stems); and narrower-stemmed Merrimac points.[6] Both Neville and Stark points have been reported from more than one hundred sites in Connecticut.[7] Merrimac points are rarely reported (perhaps they are misidentified as Late Archaic small-stemmed points of the Narrow Point tradition). Originally the three point types were thought to be chronologically consecutive (Neville to Stark to Merrimac). More recently, Dr. John Cross has argued that the Neville and Stark types are contemporary but functionally distinct, with Neville points used for tipping projectiles (such as javelins or darts thrown with atlatls) and Starks having been used as thrusting spear points.[8]

Archaeological surveys showed that in the lower Connecticut River valley,

Ground stone tools used for woodworking. Top left, a polished stone gouge from Granby, Connecticut, likely used to make canoes (length 15.7 centimeters, about 6 inches; collected by H. N. Rust, donated to the Yale Peabody Museum of Natural History by O. C. Marsh). Top right, three gouges used in the manufacture of wooden bowls, ladles, and stirrers for large pots. Bottom, grooved axes. Not to scale.

Neville complex points were associated with bifaces, hammerstones, and ground stone tools.[9] The presence of ground stone tools tells us that Middle Archaic communities were very much involved in heavy woodworking activities. Large axe heads were probably used to fell trees for clearing habitation sites and making dugout canoes, and smaller axe heads to cut saplings for house frames, lean-tos, drying and roasting racks, firewood, and other purposes. Gouges and cutting tools such as adzes were probably used to hollow out canoes, bowls, trays, and other wooden objects.

Gourd rind fragments found on archaeology sites in central Pennsylvania and Maine were directly dated to calibrated dates of about 4225 B.C. and 4545 B.C., respectively (about 6175 B.P. and 6495 B.P.).[10] They indicate that Middle Archaic peoples made and used gourd containers and, possibly, gourd rattles similar to those created by Native New Englanders today.

## THE DUGOUT CANOE

Early-seventeenth-century English accounts reported that the dugout canoe was still the preferred watercraft of post-contact indigenous peoples in southern New England, although in northern New England where birch trees were more com-

These replicated hafted tools are made with traditional modern materials and ground stone tool artifacts from central Connecticut. From left to right, a celt, an axe, and a gouge.

mon the birch-bark canoe prevailed. Dugouts were more sturdy for saltwater "coasting" and for transport across Long Island Sound; colonial documents report dugout canoes with ten or more Native American occupants beyond sight of land.[11] Narragansett dugout canoes were made from pine, oak, or chestnut trees[12] (chestnut was preferred because it was less subject to rot).

Several dugout canoes, most of American chestnut, have been found in Connecticut lakes, including one from Southbury, one 12-foot canoe from the Mountain Pond–East Swamp Aquifer area[13] on the Danbury-Bethel line (in the collections of the Connecticut Museum of Natural History in Storrs),[14] one near Great Pond in Ridgefield, and another from West Hill Pond in Winsted, which was originally given to the Peabody Museum of Natural History at Yale University and later transferred to the Mashantucket Pequot Museum and Research Center, where it has been restored.[15] Coastal Indians in Massachusetts used both stone

Contemporary rattle and containers made by Connecticut artist Jeanne MORNINGSTAR Kent, an enrolled member of the Abenaki Nation, Nulhegan Band, Coosuck-Abenaki of Vermont, from gourds and inspired by traditional designs and motifs. Top, gourd rattle with a Penobscot (Maine) False Lily of the Valley (Canadian Mayflower) floral design; the wavy lines represent water beneath the soil. Bottom left, a Penobscot (Maine) design representing sweet grass. Bottom center, double curve floral and river designs common to Northeastern Woodland indigenous peoples. Bottom right, gourd container with ancient double curve symbol and floral designs. Not to scale.

and shell tools to make canoes, "scraping them smooth with clam shells or oyster shells, cutting their outsides with stone hatchets," according to William Wood.[16]

## Middle Archaic Settlements

### Bolton Spring Site

The Bolton Spring site in Bolton, Connecticut, is a small, temporary camp site of only about 70 square yards (59 square meters). It contained two Neville points, a hearth, charred red oak, and the remains of a meal of muskrat, gray squirrel, and woodchuck. Temporary camp sites may have been typical of the eastern highlands because of the limited range of upland resources, suggesting that the region was used as a "hunting grounds" by Middle Archaic communities living in more sedentary sites in the Connecticut River valley.[17] Excavations at the Dill Farm site,[18] however, suggested that Middle Archaic subsistence settlement systems in the eastern uplands region may have been more diversified.

### Dill Farm Site

The Dill Farm property in East Haddam, Connecticut, also contained a well-known Middle Archaic site.[19] Located in the upland area east of the Connecticut River valley, this site had pits, hearths, and thirty-six Neville points, along with knives, scrapers, thumbnail scrapers, and flake tools. The tools were manufactured from local quartz and nonlocal felsite, quartzite, rhyolite, and a hard reddish brown stone that resembles metamorphized siltstone, which the excavator calls

Manufacturing a canoe was a labor-intensive process of repeated burning and gouging, as depicted in the painting *Making a Dugout Canoe* by David R. Wagner.

ledite. Charcoal from the living floor yielded two radiocarbon dates: 7720 B.P. ±260 years and 7305 B.P. ±280 years. There were also cooked mammal bones broken into small pieces, probably for their marrow or for bone grease. Bone grease was used extensively by post-contact indigenous peoples as a food, an ointment, an insect repellant, and a base for paint.

One early example of this practice is found in the Pilgrims' description of their first meeting with Massasoit, the grand sachem of the Wampanoag tribe of eastern Massachusetts and Rhode Island, on March 22, 1621. The English commented on his lavish use of both grease and pigment on his person.

> In his attire little or nothing differing from the rest of his followers, only in a great chain of white bone beads about his neck [possibly misidentified shell wampum, which high-ranking individuals often wore as a collar], and at it

This 18-foot (5.5 meter) dugout canoe made of American chestnut was recovered in 1989 from West Hill Pond in Winsted, Connecticut. Radiocarbon-dated to A.D. 1670, it was probably deliberately submerged to keep it from drying out and cracking over the winter, to be refloated in the spring. The rock shown in the photograph was found inside the canoe. The canoe was given to the Peabody Museum of Natural History, which donated it to the Mashantucket Pequot Museum and Research Center in 1996, where it has been conserved and put on display.

behind his neck hangs a little bag of tobacco . . . ; his face was painted with a sad [deep] red like murry [mulberry], and oiled both head and face, that he looked greasily. . . . A "great long knife" hanging on a string at his breast was his only weapon.[20]

Other cultural remains from the Dill Farm site included fragments of hazelnut shells, walnut shells, and hickory nut shells, stone cores, thousands of debitage flakes, and a pit with a cache of quartz quarry blocks. This storage pit suggested repeated occupation of the site.

The cultural and organic remains from the site showed that its Middle Archaic inhabitants performed a variety of activities: hunting and processing of game, nut collecting, cooking, bone grease production, stone tool manufacture, pole construction, storage of cached items, and possibly fishing. There were also hundreds of heat-fractured pebbles about two centimeters long (a little less than one inch), possibly the remains of "stone boiling," in which heated stones are dropped into a water-filled container for cooking. The Middle Archaic component at Dill Farm could represent a sizable, long-term settlement repeatedly occupied over time. The suggestion is that the Middle Archaic communities in Connecticut's eastern uplands could have been centered about interior lakes rather than the rivers.[21]

Although the earliest conclusive evidence for fishing presently dates to the Late Archaic in Connecticut, Middle Archaic communities likely participated in this important subsistence activity. Middle Archaic sites in Massachusetts and New Hampshire are near known fish-spawning grounds. Fish bones and a high mercury content in the soil that suggested the presence of fish waste products at these sites most likely mean that fishing was important in those areas.[22] Sites in the lower Hudson River valley dating to this period that have extensive oyster shell deposits (called shell middens or shell heaps) show that shellfish collecting was another Middle Archaic subsistence activity.[23]

About half of the known Middle Archaic sites in Connecticut are in riverine areas,[24] but their lack of evidence for fishing and shellfish exploitation is probably due to acidic soils, which would rapidly destroy bone and antler hooks, gorges, harpoons, and leisters (fish spears), wooden fish traps, and textile nets and line. In addition, rising sea levels probably covered what coastal sites were present. Another explanation, as reported in 1674 by Daniel Gookin, superintendent of Indians in seventeenth-century Massachusetts, would be that fish were dried and later boiled in stews, bones and all.[25] If so, there would be no bones at the fishing camps, because the fish would have been carried back to the base camp or other residential site.

### Lewis-Walpole Site

The Lewis-Walpole site in Farmington in north-central Connecticut overlooks the Pequabuck River and Shade Swamp near the Pequabuck's confluence with the Farmington River.[26] At this multicomponent site most of the later materials were recovered from the thick plow zone (as much as 20 inches, or 50 centimeters, thick). Only Middle Archaic artifacts were recovered from the subsoil (many identified as Neville and Stark styles). Among the artifacts found were points and point fragments, bifaces and preforms, scrapers, perforators, a hammerstone, and a chopper. The heavy chopper could have been used to butcher large animals such as deer.

Functional analysis of several bifaces identified a composite core tool, two or three edges of which had been used as a scraper, and one edge as a denticulate, a specialized toothed scraping tool. A composite flake tool was also identified, with one edge a knife and the other a denticulate. Composite flake tools represent an efficient technological advance because they are light, easy to produce, and easier to carry than separate tools. They would be especially prized in a mobile society.

Experiments using denticulates have shown that this tool efficiently scraped hides, shredded plants, and scaled fish.[27] Denticulates used in plant processing have a gloss on their working edges caused by abrasion from silica phytoliths of grasses and other plant materials. The Lewis-Walpole denticulates do not have any gloss and no fish remains or fishing equipment were recovered from the site. Excavators interpreted the site as a series of deer hunting camps, so the composite tools were probably used to prepare hides. Their cutting and scraping edges may have been used for butchering, while the denticulate edges were used for dressing hides. Although there was no evidence for housing, sixty-six cooking hearths or firepits were excavated, but those that were dated belonged to the site's Late Ar-

Aerial view of the extensive excavations at the Lewis-Walpole (6-HT-15) site in Farmington, Connecticut, about 1977, excavated by Yale University.

chaic component. Hickory nut shells and animal bone were also recovered. Deer bone was present, but most of the several hundred bone fragments were too small to identify and probably represent bone-grease manufacture or the remains of stews.[28]

The entire Middle Archaic complex of tools, hearths, and white-tailed deer bones at Lewis-Walpole represents many recurring seasonal camps where hunting and butchering occurred. The scrapers, drills, and denticulates suggest hideworking and woodworking activities. Hunting and woodworking tools and evidence for bifacial toolmaking activities indicate the presence of adult males, while the evidence for food preparation and hideworking suggests the presence of females. I infer this situation because early English writings describe such a sexual division of labor among early-seventeenth-century Indian communities in New England.[29]

The material remains at the Lewis-Walpole site suggest family hunting camps

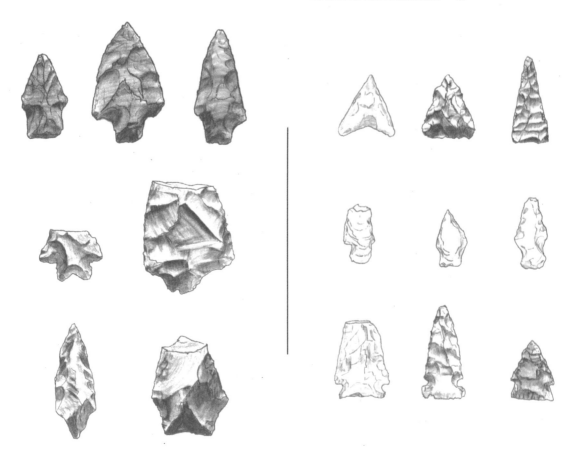

there similar to those of the nineteenth- and early-twentieth-century Innu people of eastern Quebec and Labrador (the Montagnais and the Naskapi), hunter-gatherers who lived in skin tents and hunted caribou, moose, deer, and small game.[30] Like Connecticut's post-contact tribes, their language was part of the Eastern Algonkian language group. The Dill Farm site also has evidence of on-site food processing of nuts and bone-grease production, which are female activities, and its length of occupation suggests a family or multifamily seasonal settlement.

### Great Cedar Swamp

There are sixteen Middle Archaic sites in southeastern Connecticut around the Great Cedar Swamp on the Mashantucket Pequot Reservation near Ledyard.[31] The sites typically contained chipped stone tools, similar to those found at Lewis-Walpole, used in hunting and butchering activities. Most were made from local quartzites and quartz. The sites do not have any of the ground stone tools considered typical of the Neville culture complex. This does not mean that the Middle Archaic community at Mashantucket had no ground stone tool technology; perhaps the community's activities at Great Cedar Swamp did not require ground stone tools.

The small size, lack of cultural features, and dispersed artifact pattern of these

Illustrated projectile points from the Lewis-Walpole site. At upper left: an unidentified stemmed point, a Terminal Archaic Snook Kill point, a Middle Archaic Neville point. At center left: base fragment of an Early Archaic bifurcated point, a Terminal Archaic Broad Spear point fragment. At lower left: a Stark point, an unidentified biface. At upper right: unidentified triangular points. At center right: small quartz points of the Narrow Point tradition. At lower right: a Late Archaic Vosburg point, an Early Woodland Meadowood point, Late Archaic Vosburg point.

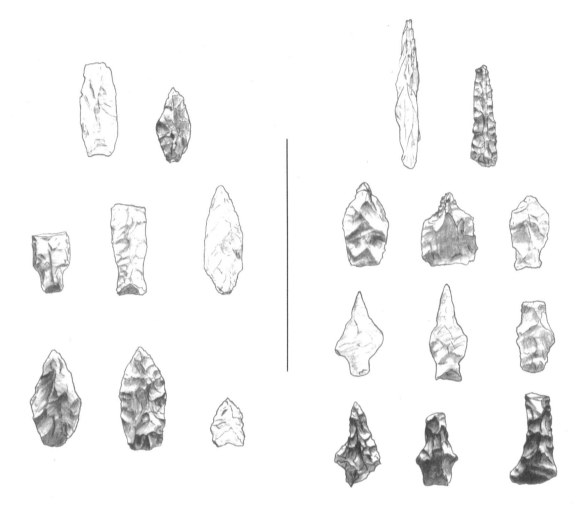

Illustrated points from the Lewis-Walpole site. At top left, two leaf-shaped points; center left, a stemmed point of the Narrow Point tradition, an Orient Fishtail point, and a Stark point; bottom left, unfinished preforms. At right, perforators: top row, two long, narrow drills; second row, short-tipped drills; third row, rounded-shoulder drills; bottom row, sharp-shoulder drills.

sites suggest that Middle Archaic peoples used them repeatedly, but for short periods, to harvest the local resources. No floral or faunal remains have yet been recovered from these sites, but there are hazelnut trees in the area and plenty of frogs, reptiles, and wetland plant foods such as cattail roots. The surrounding pine-oak-shrub forest would have provided good habitat for white-tailed deer and small mammals. The many points at these sites mean that hunting was an important activity. These sites could have been mobile family-size hunting camps,[32] but they could also represent one of several types of settlements in a more complex settlement system of small, short-term hunting and foraging camps centered about a large, more sedentary, residential base camp. Groups from the base camp would move out to the smaller camps at certain times to hunt or collect food and other resources necessary for the survival of the community. The major Middle Archaic residential settlements, or base camps, may have been located in the large river valleys. The community at Mashantucket may have evolved from Early Archaic migrants from the Middle Atlantic region (the Atlantic Slope tradition) whose bifurcate-base projectile points are stylistically similar to the Neville point.[33]

## A CATTAIL RECIPE

The cattail (*Typha latifolia*) was an important source of food for Native Americans and is still eaten by indigenous peoples today. Cattail root fragments have "proved abundant at nearly all prehistoric sites . . . [and the plant] was clearly a very important element of the diet throughout prehistory," as revealed by scanning electron microscopy studies reported in an archaeological survey in Connecticut.[a]

Here is one example of how the plant would be prepared.

### Cattail Pollen Cakes

1 cup of sifted cattail pollen
1 cup of cattail flour (pounded from
    dried roots)
3 teaspoons of finely chopped dried
    spicebush leaves (*Lindera benzoin*)
1 tablespoon of honey
2 eggs, beaten lightly
1 1/2 cups of water or broth
2 tablespoons of sunflower seed oil

Thoroughly blend all ingredients together into a smooth batter. On a very hot greased griddle, ladle the batter out into four large cakes. Cook for 3 to 5 minutes, until bubbles form on the surface, then flip and finish cooking. Serve hot with nut butter and maple syrup. Serves four.

Notes
From *Native Harvests: Recipes and Botanicals of the American Indian* by E. Barrie Kavasch, New York: Vintage Books, 1979, p. 122. Used with permission of the author.

a. Forrest et al. 2006, 37.

This detail of the 35-foot (almost 11 meter) diorama of a location on the Connecticut shoreline in the Yale Peabody Museum of Natural History's Hall of Southern New England shows a salt marsh habitat in Connecticut.

Examples of edible plant species used by indigenous communities: northern spicebush (*Lindera benzoin*), and broadleaf cattail (*Typha latifolia*).

## INTERPRETATIONS AND QUESTIONS

Because archaeologists have studied more Middle Archaic sites than earlier sites, we have more information on the settlement patterns, technology, economy, and diet of Middle Archaic peoples. We know that they relied on local stone materials for making tools and repeatedly occupied sites over time. The greater variety of artifacts suggests people were performing a greater range of subsistence activities, probably because of the increasing diversity and abundance of plant and animal species as the climate warmed. The food staples we find—white-tailed deer (a non-migratory species), various nut species, and anadromous fishes (saltwater species that travel upriver in spring to spawn)—tell us that the subsistence-settlement systems of Middle Archaic communities were probably organized around an annual seasonal subsistence cycle (round) that included spring fishing camps and fall nutting camps. Native communities were more regionalized, calling home a specific territory where they were hunting, fishing, and collecting a broad range of animals and plant foods from the mixed deciduous woodlands and meadows in which they now lived.

More and larger sites than in the Early Archaic suggest that this was a successful economy that nurtured the growth of indigenous populations. The greater number of Middle Archaic archaeology sites has given us insight into the subsistence and settlement systems of Middle Archaic communities, and their ecological relationships to changing physical environments, but we know little beyond their economy and technology. More undisturbed base camps need to be professionally investigated so we can learn more about their sociopolitical organization, their spirituality, art, and beliefs.

# 4

# The Hunter-Gatherer Florescence

## *The Late Archaic Period*

A community within Native cultures is a living circle. Every individual has a place in that circle, where each face is seen, each word is heard, and every hand is held. Each person's view is separate and distinct and is respected as an individual's own.

—Mikki Aganstata, Eastern Cherokee, former Connecticut
Indian Affairs Coordinator and Connecticut resident

The climate continued to become warmer and drier well into the first half of the Late Archaic cultural period (about 6000 to 3800 RCY B.P.). Sea level continued its rapid rise from polar ice melting and post-glacial crustal subsidence, drowning the earlier Archaic coasts.[1] The oxygen isotope content of Greenland ice cores and pollen and plant macrofossil studies show that the climate continued to fluctuate throughout Late Archaic and later Woodland times. Periods cooler and wetter than today—sometimes called "Little Ice Ages"—occurred at about 4330 B.P., 3290 B.P., from 2680 to 2550 B.P., 1550 B.P., 650 B.P. (about A.D. 1300), and from A.D. 1500 to 1850. In contrast, about A.D. 1000, temperature increased one degree Celsius above modern conditions, ushering in the "Little Climatic Warming Period."[2]

Many new and abundant tree and plant species appeared, particularly between 5000 and 4000 B.P., when the climate approached modern conditions: beech, butternut, elm, maple, sassafras, alder, sycamore, aspen, dogwood, bayberry, brambles (blackberry and raspberry), cranberry, partridgeberry, serviceberry, strawberry, swamp currant, wild lettuce, sedges, rushes, and composites such as Joe Pye weed appeared within the established oak-hickory-pine woodlands. Plant diversity normally ensures an abundance of diverse wildlife, and the cooking hearths and refuse pits of Late Archaic communities attest to this fact, containing the bones, teeth, scales, shells, and claws of white-tailed deer, raccoon, rabbit, squirrel, other small mammals, birds (including turkey and waterfowl), freshwater and saltwater fishes, shellfish, and reptiles such as turtles and snakes.[3]

## BROAD-SPECTRUM ECONOMIES AND THE SEASONAL ROUND

Cultural remains from Late Archaic sites reflect not only environmental richness, but also the explosive growth of human settlements, which dramatically increased in number, size, and variety between 5000 and 4000 B.P. The seasonal nature of the indigenous subsistence-settlement systems—only suggested by the material remains from earlier cultural periods—is now obvious in the wealth of dietary, technological, and geographic information from these Late Archaic sites. They show that Late Archaic communities hunted, fished, and gathered a wide range of seasonally available foods through cyclical activities called the seasonal round.

Evidence from Late Archaic settlements across Connecticut suggests that a community's seasonal round was composed of several or all of the activities listed for each season. Of course, this would have depended on geographic location. People living on the coast would exploit saltwater fishes and coastal plants more than would upland and inland communities, who could do so only when visiting friends and relatives living along Long Island Sound.

### The Importance of Wild Plants

Plant foods continued to be an important part of the aboriginal diet. Late Archaic mothers and daughters probably prepared these foods in much the same way as post-contact Native American women did and still do.

Shoots, leaves, and blossoms were steamed, boiled, eaten fresh, or added to gruels and stews. Tubers and bulbs were usually boiled or baked. Some, like those of Jerusalem artichoke, groundnut, arrowhead, cattail, and great bulrush, were dried and ground into flour for breads and flat cakes, or to thicken gruels and stews. Nuts and seeds were eaten fresh, boiled for their oils, or ground into flour. Fruits were eaten fresh or dried and mixed into gruels, stews, breads, and cakes. Flavorings included the natural sugars from the saps of maples, yellow and white birch, black walnut, and butternut trees, and the roots of the great bulrush, a local aquatic plant. Other native flavorings used were black mustard, wild parsley, wild onion and leek and garlic, coltsfoot (which has a very salty taste when dried and burned to ash), catbrier (with a taste like sarsaparilla), wild mint, dried sassafras leaves, dried milkweed blossoms, and the chocolate-flavored roots of purple avens.[4]

These wild plant foods are extremely nourishing—a major reason for the population explosion at this time. For example, a quarter cup of walnut meats has 200 calories and 5 grams of protein, and provides 50 percent of the daily requirement of manganese, 30 percent of fat (mostly polyunsaturated, or "good" fat), 25 percent of copper, 10 percent of magnesium, 10 percent of phosphorus, 8 percent of fiber, 4 percent of potassium, 4 percent of iron, 2 percent of calcium, and 2.5 grams of omega-3 fatty acid,[5] which is known to reduce the risk of heart attacks and lower blood pressure.[6] Certain fish species eaten by Connecticut Indians, such as herring, salmon, mackerel, and lake trout, are also rich in these fatty acids.

Venison is so low in calories, fats, and cholesterol, and such a significant

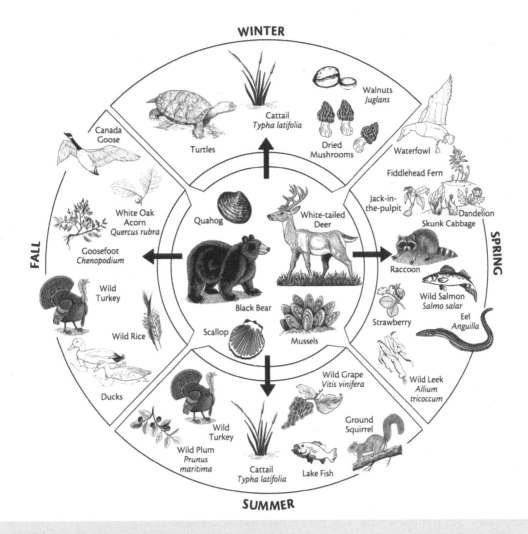

**WINTER**

Canada Goose

Turtles

Cattail
*Typha latifolia*

Walnuts
*Juglans*

Dried Mushrooms

Waterfowl

Fiddlehead Fern

Jack-in-the-pulpit

White Oak Acorn
*Quercus rubra*

Quahog

White-tailed Deer

Dandelion

Skunk Cabbage

**SPRING**

**FALL**

Goosefoot
*Chenopodium*

Raccoon

Wild Turkey

Wild Salmon
*Salmo salar*

Strawberry

Eel
*Anguilla*

Wild Rice

Black Bear

Scallop

Mussels

Ducks

Wild Leek
*Allium tricoccum*

Wild Grape
*Vitis vinifera*

Ground Squirrel

Wild Turkey

Wild Plum
*Prunus maritima*

Cattail
*Typha latifolia*

Lake Fish

**SUMMER**

AN ANNUAL SUBSISTENCE ROUND

*Spring*

Gather early shoots and leaves of plants such as amaranth, black mustard, cattail, catbrier, coltsfoot, fiddleheads of ferns, great bulrush, *Chenopodium* spp. (goosefoot), lamb's quarters, milkweed, mint, plantain, skunk cabbage, thistle, violet, false Solomon's seal, watercress, wild parsley, wild ginger, wild lettuce, wild onion and leek, and wintercress. Collect strawberries and swamp currants.

Collect shellfish.

Fish, especially for anadromous runs of minnows, eels, herring, salmon, and shad, and saltwater fishes such as striped bass, sturgeon, bluefish, cunner, tautog (blackfish), and scup.

Hunt and trap bear and small mammals, deer, reptiles, and birds, especially migratory waterfowl.

Native people exploited food resources in the environments around them according to the availability of animals and plants in different seasons, some of which are shown here. At the center are resources available year round.

*Summer*

Gather most of the leafy plants available in spring, as well as their seeds, and aquatic and terrestrial tubers from plants such as arrowhead, bulrush, cattail, groundnuts, yarrow, false Solomon's seal, and Indian turnip. Gather fruit from cranberry, blueberry, huckleberry, raspberry, blackberry, serviceberry, hackberry, and bayberry bushes, and from grapevines and wild plum and cherry trees. Collect acorns, seeds, or fruit from amaranth, smartweed, sumac, peavine, wax myrtle, dock, viburnum, sassafras, juniper, dogwood, purslane, and Jersey tea.

Collect mushrooms.

Collect shellfish.

Fish for saltwater and freshwater fishes.

Hunt and trap deer, bear, small mammals, reptiles, and birds.

*Fall*

Gather some of the leafy plants that were also available in spring. Collect tubers from bulrush, cattail, Jerusalem artichoke, groundnuts, and yellow pond lily. Collect seeds from amaranth, lamb's quarters, and sunflower. Collect various acorns (red and white oak) and nuts (hickory, walnut, butternut, chestnut, and beech).

Collect mushrooms, and wild rice in some riverine areas.

Fish for saltwater and freshwater fishes.

Collect shellfish.

Hunt and trap deer, bear, small mammals, reptiles, and birds.

*Winter*

Hunt deer and hibernating bear.

Collect shellfish.

Gather plant tubers.

Eat stored nuts, seeds, and dried fruits, tubers, and mushrooms.

Many of these plants and animals have been recovered from Late Archaic sites in Connecticut and at nearby sites in New York, particularly those of the Narrow Point tradition. (To date, Laurentian sites have yielded only nuts, acorns, and goosefoot, a much narrower economy.) Botanical studies suggest that other plants and animals should have been available, as we know from early European accounts of post-contact Indian communities.[a] With more scanning electron microscope studies of carbonized plant tissue, many of these plants likely will be identified in archaeological sites.

Many plants exploited by Late Archaic peoples—such as tannin-filled acorns and plants with minute, hard seeds—required more intensive processing activities for consumption. These foods were available to earlier people, but seem not to have been used with any great intensity. It is likely that increasing population density and constricting territories forced communities to intensify collection of lower-ranked foods.[b]

Notes

a. E.g., Heath 1963; Wood 1634; Williams 1643; Morton 1669; Josselyn 1672.

b. Daniel Forrest, personal communication, January 21, 2011.

Wild plants gathered for both food and medicinal uses: stinging nettle (*Urtica dioica,* collected in Fairfield in 1918), used as a potherb and to soothe the symptoms of rheumatism; Indian cucumber (*Medeola virginiana,* from Hartland, Connecticut, collected in 1929), used as a food. An infusion of leaves and berries was used as a remedy for convulsions in infants.

Eels were an important seasonal food item in the indigenous diet. *Night Harvest of the American Eel,* by David R. Wagner, depicts a spring fishing camp along the Quinnebaug River.

source of vitamins, minerals, and important amino acids, that the American Heart Association recommends it as a good "heart" food.[7] Most traditional hunting and gathering communities, however, prefer high-fat foods because of their greater caloric density. The fat content of deer meat varies greatly with the season and is lowest during the late winter and early spring.[8] This may be one reason why post-European-contact indigenous communities held their communal deer hunts in the fall and early winter.[9]

Clams are also low in calories, fats, and cholesterol, but high in protein, minerals, and vitamins. This nutritious and balanced diet is probably behind the good health and comeliness of New England indigenous people noted by early European explorers and traders. John Brereton, an English explorer in the early seventeenth century, said of the indigenous people of southeastern New England that "they are exceedingly courteous, gentle of disposition, and well-conditioned, excelling and all others that we have seen, so for shape and lovely favor . . . of stature much higher than we."[10]

## Food Processing Technologies

Late Archaic people processed their food in a variety of ways. Archaeologists can reconstruct this technological behavior by analyzing artifacts and cultural features, indigenous oral traditions, and early European documents.

For example, post molds along two sides of a hearth tell us there was probably a spit for roasting meat. Other post-mold patterns suggest racks for drying or smoking fruits, meat, and shellfish. Heat-cracked and reddened stone piles imply that stews and soups were cooked by dropping small hot stones into a skin bag, or that tubers, nuts, acorns, or shellfish were roasted, baked, or steamed atop stone platform hearths or within rock-lined earth ovens—the original New England clambake. The largest reported Native American fish cooking pit (now destroyed) was in Madison, Connecticut, on the grounds of what is now Hammonasset State Park. Uncovered in the 1940s during the construction of a maintenance storage building, it was described as a stone-lined fire pit about 30 feet (9 meters) in diameter and several feet deep, filled with layers of shell, charcoal, ash, fish bones, and artifacts. Its width and depth suggest that the roasting pit was used to feed large numbers of people repeatedly over time, perhaps during public harvest festivals.[11]

Some pitted stones that have a well-formed, evenly rounded depression with smoothed surfaces on one or both faces have been described as nutting stones. They may have been used for cracking nuts (a rather tedious activity whose goal might have been more quickly met by other methods, such as roasting, or crushing in a mortar and then boiling), but more likely many are caps for bow drills. Pitted stones with shallow, irregular pits were probably anvil stones used in the manufacture of stone tools.[12]

A mortar (metate) is a large concave stone where seeds, nuts, and grains were ground into meal with a grinding stone (also called a muller or mano). Tree trunks were also used as mortars, particularly by later peoples for grinding maize. Several

## SEASONALITY STUDIES

Archaeologists use the following kinds of evidence to determine in which season a site was occupied.

### Plant Products

Different plants ripen at specific times and often have distinctive seeds and husks that can be readily identified. Even so, some plant products, such as hickory nuts, can be stored for a long time and therefore may not be reliable indicators of a particular season.

### Fish

Certain fishes, such as salmon, sturgeon, shad, and herring, occur in freshwater streams and rivers only during a specific spawning season, while others, such as bluefish and striped bass, run in coastal waters at certain times of the year. The growth rings of finfish scales and shellfish can show in which season the animal died.

### Hibernating Animals

For animals that hibernate during the winter, finding their remains is thought to indicate that a site was occupied before or after its hibernation period. However, early European documents report that certain species, like the black bear, were collected *during* their winter hibernation as well as in the warmer seasons.

Wild grape (*Vitis aestivalis*) specimen collected in New Haven, Connecticut, in 1900.

### Waterfowl and Other Birds

Certain bird species follow definite seasonal migration cycles and are present in certain regions only during specific times of the year.

### Deer Antlers

White-tailed deer shed their antlers in later winter, so finding antlered deer skulls should indicate a late summer, fall, or early winter occupation, or all three seasons.

### Age at Death

We can use animal remains to infer the season during which a site was occupied by determining how old the animal was when it died. The age of deer can be estimated from tooth eruption and the growth and fusion of bones. Fawns are usually born between April and June.

A Late Archaic platform roasting hearth (top) and earth oven excavated at the Avon Old Farms Brook site.

bedrock mortars have also been found, man-made concavities pecked into a flat bedrock outcrop or the top of a large glacial erratic. These were probably communal mortars, made and used by female work groups collecting plant materials too far from the base camp for the unshelled nuts or seeds to be carried back. Bedrock mortars are normally in upland mast woodlands and can be found throughout the Connecticut countryside.

## TWO TRADITIONS, TWO POPULATIONS

The Late Archaic period is represented by two discrete archaeological traditions: the Laurentian tradition, thought to have originated in southeastern Ontario, southern Quebec, northern New York, and northern New England,[13] and the Narrow Point (or Small Stem) tradition of the southern Atlantic coast.[14] Archaeologists agree that in Connecticut the Narrow Point and Laurentian archaeological traditions represent two distinct Native American populations with differing cultural lifeways.

The two traditions overlap in time; sites of the Laurentian tradition have been radiocarbon-dated to between 4890 and 4180 B.P.[15] Narrow Point sites have been dated to as early as 4610 B.P., but the tradition may have Middle Archaic roots. Two sites excavated by the University of Connecticut—Dill Farm and the Hatheway-Bugbee site in the Farmington River drainage at West Hartford—

Top, the black charcoal stain of a Late Archaic hearth can be seen well below the Woodland–Terminal Archaic shell midden found in the upper levels of the Robillard site. The wall profile shows the base of a later pit feature extending from, and below, the shell midden (center background). Bottom, the 1985 excavations of the Robillard site in Milford by the Greater New Haven Archaeology Society under the direction of David Thompson (far left, facing camera) and Lucianne Lavin (right foreground).

contained narrow, stemmed points in Middle Archaic contexts,[16] as proposed several years earlier for Late Archaic communities in Massachusetts.[17] Artifacts within the Burwell-Karako site overlooking New Haven Harbor clearly showed the continuation of the Narrow Point tradition (represented by more than 1,400 points!) from the Middle Archaic Neville-tradition level through the Terminal Archaic and into the Woodland levels.[18] Radiocarbon dates and site stratigraphy from other Connecticut sites confirm this.[19]

## The Laurentian Tradition

The term "Laurentian," from the French *Laurentien,* refers to the area of the St. Lawrence River in Canada. The noted Dr. William A. Ritchie, New York state archaeologist, first proposed the name for this tradition on the basis of his research of sites in the Lake Champlain region. He believed that the original center of the tradition was the conifer-hardwood forests of eastern Canada.[20]

Top, rock-lined Late Archaic hearth over a pit feature at the Grannis Island site in New Haven, excavated by the Greater New Haven Archaeological Society, a chapter of the Archaeological Society of Connecticut, in the 1950s and 1960s. Bottom, platform hearth at the base of a shell midden, Grannis Island site.

### Laurentian Tools

Archaeologists recognize the Laurentian tradition by its distinctive medium-bladed points with side or corner notches. The earliest and least common is the Otter Creek type, followed by Vosburg, Brewerton Side-notched, Brewerton Eared Notched, and Brewerton Eared Triangle types. Other tools found with Laurentian points include rough stone hammers and grinding stones; bi-pitted stones and net sinkers; chipped stone scrapers, spokeshave scrapers, drills, and knives; chipped and ground stone ulus; and ground stone pestles, gouges, axes, adzes, plummets, and atlatl weights (sometimes called bannerstones). Although local quartz materials were used in tool manufacture, exotic cherts, quartzites, slates, and rhyolites were also used,[21] suggesting that Laurentian peoples main-

Pitted stones from Harwinton, Litchfield County (left), and Rocky Hill, Hartford County, Connecticut.

tained extensive communication networks with other communities to the east, west, and north.

The ulu is a semicircular, usually ground and often polished stone knife normally made from slate. Some specimens were perforated to accommodate a handle. The word "ulu" (*ulo*) is a modern Inuit term for a woman's knife. Among the post-contact indigenous communities of Alaska, the Northwest Coast, and interior Canada women used the ulu to scale and split fish and butcher marine mammals, and to prepare skins for clothing.[22]

Plummets are oval, knobbed, ground stone objects that are commonly thought to have been used in fishing as line sinkers or net sinkers. Interestingly, the Penobscot Indians informed anthropologist Frank Speck during his visit in the early 1900s that plummets were sling-stones (that is, bolas) used in hunting.[23] A copper fish gorge was found in a clam shell at the Meetinghouse Brook site or one nearby in Wallingford, Connecticut. They could be the remains of a 4,500-year-old fish lure, providing more evidence of Laurentian fishing activity.[24]

The prevalence of heavy ground stone axes, adzes, and gouges suggests that Laurentian peoples expended significant energy in cutting trees and working wood, likely in making dugout canoes, given the distribution of Laurentian base camps along rivers and lakes. People of the Narrow Point tradition apparently frequented the same environments but made much less use of these ground stone tool types.[25]

Laurentian men improved their hunting with the atlatl weight, which was a basic part of the Native American tool kit until the introduction of the bow and arrow sometime during the later Middle Woodland period. It is generally thought that this smoothed, ground, and often highly polished stone weight was attached to the wooden atlatl, or spear thrower, to increase the distance and penetrating power of the throw (but see the section "The Atlatl" in Chapter 1 for a differing perspective on the use of these stones). Some of these weights were made from exotic stones, such as green sandstone from central New York and serpentine from as far away as Massachusetts, Vermont, or even southeastern Pennsylvania.[26]

A large bedrock stone mortar from the South Woodstock Village site, Windham County, Connecticut, photographed in 1940.

### Laurentian Settlements

There is some controversy about the pattern of Laurentian settlements on the Connecticut landscape. In the lower Connecticut River valley, for example, some investigators think that Laurentian communities consisted of small, mobile groups of people exploiting many kinds of environments and resources, both riverine and non-riverine. Depending on the seasonal availability of plant and animal foods,

Late Archaic Otter Creek-style projectile points of the Laurentian tool tradition. The larger point was found in 1879 by Jonathan E. Sikes on his land in Suffield, Connecticut.

Late Archaic Vosburg-style projectile points of the Laurentian tool tradition.

they would occupy different sites during different times of the year, often reoccupying these sites year after year.[27]

Others believe that the Laurentian settlement pattern was more complicated and suggest Laurentian peoples frequented three types of sites: (1) large semi-permanent or permanent base camps, like the Bliss-Howard site in Old

A variety of Brewerton projectile point types of the Laurentian tool tradition. Left, Brewerton Eared Notched points. Center, Brewerton Side-notched points. Right, Brewerton Eared Triangle points.

Lyme, near reliable, productive food sources; (2) small temporary special-purpose camps, usually rock shelters (rock overhangs or caves), such as the Ames Rock Shelter in Old Lyme, that probably represent overnight stays for a small group of hunters; and (3) small, multi-activity short-term family open-air camps on high ground overlooking wetlands, such as the Arbucci site in Old Lyme.[28]

*Bliss-Howard Site*   The residential base camp at the Howard site and the associated Bliss Cemetery site provided information on social and spiritual behaviors showing that the Laurentian people were a significant presence in the region. More than a quarter acre (1,000 square meters) in size, the Bliss-Howard archaeological complex overlooked the floodplain near the mouth of the Connecticut River. Post molds revealed the outline of three pole-frame structures. One of these was completely excavated, exposing an oblong house pattern more than 33 feet (10 meters) long and 16 feet (5 meters) wide, with an overlapping entranceway that curved about the structure (like a snail shell), likely to prevent wind from entering the house, and a doorway that faced south to catch the warmth of the sun.[29] The excavator, Dr. John Pfeiffer, associated the structure with the Late Archaic Laurentian occupants of the site.[30] According to Dr. Kevin McBride, however, the site also contained a later Woodland component and it is possible that the houses actually date to much later.[31] In fact, the size and shape of the excavated

Ground stone slate knives, called ulus, are diagnostic for the Laurentian tool tradition.

house is similar to the house pattern from the Middle to Late Woodland Military Academy site in nearby Niantic.

Left, a variety of grooved, notched, and doughnut-shaped line and net sinkers. Right, stone net sinkers from Connecticut's lower Farmington River valley.

The Howard site house had a hearth, a storage pit eventually used as a refuse pit, and a tool workshop area, and contained typical Laurentian tool types as well as quartz cobbles (before this discovery it was thought that Laurentian peoples did not use quartz cobbles). Food remains from the hearths and refuse pits included deer and other mammal bone, bird and fish remains, hickory, acorn, and walnut fragments, and goosefoot (*Chenopodium* spp.), suggesting at least a summer-to-fall occupancy. Food remains from this and other southeastern Connecticut Laurentian sites point to a mixed hunting, fishing, and plant-foraging economy based on white-tailed deer, fish, nuts, and seeds.

*Chenopodium* species such as goosefoot have very small, hard seeds that are rich in fat and protein, but require much time and energy to harvest and process. The shift to harvesting this lower-ranked food could have been caused by population stress and restricted mobility,[32] which may explain the earliest known use and storage of *Chenopodium* among the Laurentian inhabitants of Bliss-Howard.

The Bliss-Howard site was interpreted by its excavator as a multiseasonal residence whose occupants relied on local stone materials. It included a burying ground, suggesting that a small Laurentian band of several family groups was living there year-round within a specific territory.[33] Special work groups would intermittently occupy other sites in this territory to hunt, fish, or forage for food, or collect raw materials for tools, shelter, clothing, and other staples.

*Other Laurentian Settlements*   Laurentian sites have been discovered elsewhere in Connecticut, but have not been studied as intensively or on such a regional scale. Examples of some of the better known sites with Laurentian cultural components include:

Outside view of the Binette Rock Shelter in Connecticut's Naugatuck uplands (top), and the Ames Rock Shelter in Old Lyme, Connecticut.

- the Hammonasset Beach site in Madison along Long Island Sound;[34]
- the Grannis Island site near the mouth of the Quinnipiac River before it empties into New Haven Harbor;[35]
- the Burwell-Karako site on the east side of New Haven Harbor;[36]
- the Binette Rock Shelter in the Naugatuck uplands;[37]
- the Indian Hill site, a fishing camp with net sinkers, ulus, and fish remains on a terrace of the Farmington River in Bloomfield;[38]
- the Fastener site in the Housatonic River estuary in Shelton;[39]
- the Bear Rock Shelter in Stamford and the Perkins-Elmer Rock Shelter in Wilton, overlooking inland wetlands and the Norwalk River floodplain, respectively;[40]

Reconstruction of a Laurentian-tradition dwelling (half-size) from the Bliss-Howard site.

- the Hansel Rock Shelter near Mount Tom in Morris;[41]
- the Lovers Leap site, overlooking the confluence of the Housatonic and Still rivers in New Milford;[42]
- and the Hopkins site, on a terrace between two small streams overlooking the large upland Lake Waramaug in New Preston.[43]

The rock materials, or toolstone, used by Laurentian people at the Fastener and Burwell-Karako sites were mainly local. Locally available quartz was the most popular toolstone for Laurentian points at these sites. Although this supports the concept that indigenous, residential Laurentian communities in south-central coastal Connecticut obtained raw material locally,[44] both Laurentian components were small and do not fit the description of lower Connecticut Valley Laurentian base camps. Most likely they are only one of several site types in the local Laurentian annual settlement system, which in this area is still a mystery. Regional surveys are much needed to answer questions about cultural diversity among Laurentian communities inhabiting different ecological zones.

## Laurentian Spirituality

The burial practices of the Late Archaic period give us the earliest evidence of Native American spirituality in Connecticut. This is not to say that Native American spirituality was nonexistent before then, only that, because of the sparseness of the archaeological record, we have not recovered any earlier evidence. In fact, burials in adjacent Massachusetts have been dated to at least the Middle Archaic period.[45]

The Bliss Cemetery site in Old Lyme, Connecticut, contained twenty-one cremation burials that returned radiocarbon dates between 4775 and 4545 B.P. These burials, the simultaneous cremation of several persons along with a dog or wolf, are associated with Laurentian point types and the material remains of extensive ritual behaviors.[46] Archaeologists can infer spiritual practices not only by interpreting the evidence in burials, but also by making comparisons with behaviors reported in ethnographic studies and written records.

The eyewitness account of death rites among the Huron, an Iroquoian-speaking tribe in central Ontario, Canada, in the late seventeenth century describes how,

> When death overtakes them, they who are more nearly related to the departed person, black their faces, sometimes cut off their hair; they also pierce their arms with knives or arrows. The grief of the females is carried to a still greater excess; they not only cut their hair, cry and howl, but they will sometimes, with the utmost deliberation, employ some sharp instrument to separate the nail from the finger, and then force back the flesh from beyond the first joint, which they immediately amputate. But this extraordinary mark of affection is only displayed on the death of a favorite son, a husband, or a father.[47]

A major Huron ceremony was the Feast of the Dead, which were rites for the final interment of those who had died over a period of time. Major ritual acts in this ceremony included the killing of a dog and burial of personal belongings with the deceased.[48]

The Bliss burials included both dry and green bone cremations. In green bone cremations the bones—and body—are relatively fresh. Dry bone cremations are those in which the bones are not fresh, or green, when they are burned, suggesting that the corpses had been placed in a special location until the bones were free of flesh and could be permanently buried in a communal burying ground.[49] The presence of a burying ground to which a community repeatedly returns to bury its dead provides additional support for the existence of territorial boundaries during this time.[50] The green bone cremations at the site contained only fingers and toes, implying that this skeletal material was not from the deceased, but rather from the mourners, such as those described in the Huron death rites above.

These burials also contained the bones of a *Canis* species (possibly dog) and grave goods, artifacts or food placed in the grave with the deceased. As in the Huron ritual, they could have been the personal belongings of the dead person, or gifts of food and tools thought to be needed in the afterlife. Likely many of the objects were symbolic, with deep spiritual meanings, as was often the case among post-contact indigenous peoples.

We can perhaps learn more about ancient belief systems from accounts like that of the Jesuit priest Gabriel Sagard, who lived among the Huron in the 1620s and explained the philosophy behind their funeral ceremonies. The Huron believed that the souls of the dead continued the same activities in the afterlife that they did in life and continued to have

> the same need of drinking and eating, of clothing themselves and tilling the ground, which they had while still clothed with their mortal bodies. This is

why with the bodies of the dead they bury or enclose bread, oil, skins, toma-hawks, kettles, and other utensils, in order that the souls of their relatives may not remain poor and needy in the other life for lack of such implements. For they imagine and believe that the souls of these kettles, tomahawks, knives, and everything they dedicate to them, especially at the great festival of the dead, depart to the next life to serve the souls of their dead, although the bodies of these skins, tomahawks, kettles, and everything else dedicated and offered remain behind and stay in the graves and coffins among the bones of the deceased.[51]

According to seventeenth-century Europeans, New England Algonkian speakers also believed that the afterlife was a mirror image of the natural world but without the pain, fear, and want associated with the living. Consequently, they too placed everyday objects in graves for use by the deceased in the afterlife.[52]

The Beothuk woman Shawnadithit, speaking of her own demise, said that such materials were needed for her journey after death. These items included small wooden humanoid and bird effigies, canoe models, an axe, bow and quiver of arrows, pyrites, culinary implements, and birchbark dishes.[53]

The Bliss grave offerings included general purpose knives and scrapers as well as tools used in male activities, such as points and atlatl weights (hunting) and axes (woodworking), and those used in female activities, such as pestles (food pro-cessing). Some of the tool fragments from the cremation pits fit those recovered from the Howard residence camp. The people who ate and slept in the Howard houses were the mourners at the Bliss Cemetery. The Bliss burials are the earliest known human graves in Connecticut.

Some of the artifacts at Bliss are highly stylized and perhaps were made spe-cifically to be used in the burial rites. These tools seem to have been ritually bro-ken, or "killed," so that the artifacts' spirits could accompany the deceased on his journey to the spirit world. Offerings of nuts, seeds, and meat were also found with the burial, probably included to sustain the deceased on the way. The burial features were covered in red ochre powder and ground mica. In traditional Na-tive American belief systems, red symbolizes blood and eternal life, and the shiny translucent white of mica had spiritual power. According to Abenaki Dr. Fred-erick Wiseman, ochre also has the power to protect the living from powerful spiri-tual forces within and surrounding burials.

The Mikmaq story "Wsitiplaju" contains important clues to this ancient "red paint" tradition. . . . In the story, red ocher is called *weukuju* and is symboli-cally portrayed as a heart, a metaphor for life represented by blood . . . ochre has a second spiritual property, that of prophylaxis or the protection of mod-ern people from that aspect of the spirit that resides in and around the grave . . . red ochre has the power to encase this spirit below ground and allow it to be at peace with the soil of Aki, the earth mother . . . red ochre seals this power [of the spiritual force] in, thus protecting the living. This is the

Terminal Archaic Broad
Spear artifacts, burned and
ritually killed, from the Bliss
Cemetery site, Old Lyme,
Connecticut.

BLISS
BURIAL COMPLEX

reason why we Wabanakis believe that disinterring the Dead is good neither
for the Dead or the living. The image is analogous to unearthing radioactive
material.[54]

Even the cremation fire likely had spiritual significance. To post-contact Algonkian speakers like the Lenni Lenape (called Delaware by the English), ceremonial fires are "an agent of purification and invigoration. The newly lighted fire
symbolizes a renewal of the pure influences for the life and health of the recipient,
his family, and the participants."[55]

Some of the burials contained quartz crystals and nuggets of iron pyrite.

Pyrites were used to start fires and could have been included as part of a fire-making kit for use by the deceased in the spirit world. Like mica, the quartz, and probably the shiny metal pyrite, had symbolic social meanings. We know that crystals and minerals have spiritual meanings for post-contact Native American societies, and that "there was a strong belief among many historic northeastern Native American groups that through the ritual use of crystals a person could gain power and communicate with the spirit world."[56] A Herkimer diamond (clear quartz crystal) with rounded edges was recovered from the Archaic living floor at the Indian Hill site in Bloomfield, which contained Laurentian and Neville components. According to geologist Dr. Tony Philpotts, the crystal was rounded from having been in a pouch, and not by water.[57] Quartz crystals were recovered at sixteenth- and eighteenth-century A.D. Pequot sites, including from burials, on the Mashantucket Pequot Reservation near Ledyard, Connecticut.[58] Twentieth-century Mohegan culture keeper and medicine woman Gladys Tantaquidgeon was taught by her women elders that quartz brought "good spirits."[59]

Seventeenth-century European accounts and Iroquois, Huron, and Great Lakes Algonkian ethnographies show that among Indian cultures of the Northeast specific colors are metaphors for social values, especially white or clear, black, red, and sky blue or green.[60] White, blue or green, and red assured physical, spiritual, and social well-being. Red, the color of blood, represents life and everlasting life, but also warfare, in which blood is shed and life is lost. Black represents an asocial state with an absence of well-being and harmony, such as death, mourning, and initiations. Likewise, objects with these colors were metaphors for social and spiritual values. For example, traditional members of Great Lakes tribes believe that

> Shell, crystal, and native copper are "other world" substances traditionally obtained . . . through reciprocal exchange with Under(water) World Grandfathers, . . . "charms" which assure and insure long life . . . physical and spiritual well being (the absence of ill-being), and success. . . . Shell is most frequently associated with rituals promotive of the continuity of life in general and the biological and social continuity of human life in particular.[61]

In this context, the Indian interest in European baubles and beads during the Post-Contact period takes on a whole new dimension. The preference for glass beads, copper, red coats and stockings, and blue bolts of cloth[62] was tightly integrated with the complex indigenous ideology, supporting and supported by their social and ritual systems and sacred stories. Significantly, early trading-post account books show that when first introduced to glass beads, indigenous peoples showed a preference for the blue and white beads,[63] symbolic of well-being and such positive values as comfort, security, and happiness.

Our contemporary American culture is also filled with color metaphors: white symbolizes purity and virginity; black denotes sorrow, death, and evil; purple signifies royalty; silver and gold suggest high status and represent twenty-fifth and fiftieth wedding anniversaries; pink is for infant girls and femininity, while blue is for boys and masculinity.

The rituals at Late Archaic Laurentian sites (and later at Terminal Archaic Broad Spear sites) could have been a response to economic stress. Environmental changes such as sea-level rise and climatic warming and drying that shrank the environments on which these communities depended for survival could have intensified the economic competition with nearby communities of the Narrow Point tradition. The occurrence of a "Little Ice Age" around 4330 B.P. likely caused fluctuations in food sources as well. Goosefoot harvesting at the Bliss-Howard site supports the theory that economic stress within Laurentian communities is the reason for more evidence of Laurentian burial rituals. This suggests that group rituals, especially burial rites, were stronger and more complex during the resulting economic and social stress.[64]

### The Narrow Point Tradition

#### *Narrow Point Tools*

Archaeologists identify the Narrow Point tradition by the presence of a variety of small, thick, narrow, stemmed, and notched points. These are classified as the Wading River, Squibnocket Stemmed, Bare Island, Poplar Island, Sylvan stemmed and notched, and Lamoka-like point types. They are associated with a variety of chipped stone scrapers, knives, drills, and choppers; blanks and tool preforms; flake tools for scraping and cutting purposes; and rough stone hammers, anvil stones, and bi-pitted stones. Interestingly, unlike the Laurentian populations, Narrow Point communities had few tools in the larger ground stone categories, such as adzes, axes, gouges, and atlatl weights. This difference could be artificial, created by the nineteenth- and twentieth-century collecting activities of treasure hunters at sites subsequently tested by professional archaeologists.[65] One site with ground stone tools from the Narrow Point tradition, the Long Knoll site in South Glastonbury,[66] suggests this. But would not this also be true for Laurentian sites? An alternative explanation for the basalt ground stone tools at this particular site is Long Knoll's closeness to basalt outcrops and its use as a quarry workshop.

Unlike Laurentian tools, virtually all of the Narrow Point chipped stone implements were manufactured from locally available quartz and quartzite pebbles and cobbles. Chert in tool manufacture was used more (but still in small amounts) among Native American communities in the upper Housatonic River valley, where Indian paths led to chert quarry areas in the nearby Hudson River valley. Researchers also have found chert pebbles in the riverbed of the upper Housatonic and its tributaries.[67]

Sylvan Side-notched projectile points from the Burwell-Karako site in Fair Haven (New Haven), Connecticut.

*Burwell-Karako Site*   People of the Narrow Point tradition once occupied the Burwell-Karako site, a camp site and quartz cobble workshop overlooking New Haven Harbor. The more than 1,400 small stemmed projectile points recovered indicate intensive settlement in repeated occupations over hundreds of years. Beside the points and other tools, the site occupants left many rejects and waste flakes that archaeologists have used to reconstruct the steps in Narrow Point manufacture.[68]

Late Archaic Lamoka-style projectile points from the Burwell-Karako site in Fair Haven.

The toolmaker placed the quartz cobble on a large, flattish anvil stone and struck the cobble with a hammerstone, shattering it into large and small flakes. He chose a flake of proper size (usually half or one-quarter of the cobble) and hammered it along its edges, producing a blank or preform. Using the stone hammer or an antler billet to strike off flakes (or a bone or antler pressure flaking tool to press them off) the toolmaker thinned the blank, created its stem, and sharpened the blade edges to make the point. These steps are known collectively as the quartz cobble reduction technique, which is characteristic of Narrow Point tradition sites (except in eastern Connecticut where quartzite of the Plainfield formation crops out). Cobbles were preferred because any fractures would have been worked out

Points representing the Narrow Point tool tradition from the Burwell-Karako site in Fair Haven: Wading River and Squibnocket Stemmed projectile points; bottom, Squibnocket Triangle projectile points.

Remains of a platform hearth near an axe cache at the Burwell-Karako site in New Haven, excavated by the Greater New Haven Archaeological Society from 1970 to 1976.

by the glacier or water source that created the cobble, making it superior to vein quartz for knapping.[69] Vein (ledge) quartz was also used, however, as demonstrated by several pre-contact quartz quarries in Connecticut. One such quarry was the Eckart site in the Southbury uplands.[70]

### Narrow Point Settlements

The distribution of Narrow Point sites indicates that these communities were highly territorial but mobile, with a somewhat different pattern of settlement than that of the Laurentian communities, which were near river environments. Some important Narrow Point sites include:

- Woodchuck Knoll in South Windsor, Long Knoll in South Glastonbury, and Hubbard Brook in Middletown, all in the Connecticut River valley;[71]
- Harrison's Landing in New London on the eastern coastal slope;[72]
- Sites 270A-4-1, 97-71, and 97-72 in Newtown in the western uplands;[73]
- Cove River in West Haven, likely a freshwater riverine locus on the coastal slope, although because of sea-level rise it is now a saltwater estuary;[74]
- and Rockrimmon Rock Shelter in Stamford, an inland site on the western coastal slope.[75]

Narrow Point camps are located in a variety of micro-environments. These camps include open-air camps, rock shelters, shell middens, and quarry sites for toolstone.[76] Narrow Point communities inhabited central base camps, but some of their members were regularly visiting seasonal camps and temporary or special-purpose sites covering a wide range of environments to exploit seasonally available food and other staple resources. Many of the sites show repeated use over time. A similar situation existed for the north coast of Long Island, just across the sound

THE LATE ARCHAIC PERIOD 109

from Connecticut. The Native Long Islanders early established durable communities and territories. This pattern probably originated with the establishment of modern coastal conditions (as far back as five thousand years ago) and continued fairly unchanged until the seventeenth century.[77]

Some of these micro-environments do not seem to have been used much by earlier peoples. An example is the high ridge top and slopes of West Rock in New Haven. Archaeological sampling of a small portion of West Rock uncovered a variety of Late Archaic Narrow Point site types, possibly suggesting population expansion as a reason why such less readily accessible and somewhat marginal environments were exploited.[78] Do we see in this territoriality and population expansion the seeds of tribalization?

We have seen that base camps are large sites occupied for long periods (multi-seasonal) where community members performed many diverse activities. Narrow Point base camps mainly overlooked interior wetlands. Some were also located in the large river valleys, probably to exploit the spring fish and eel runs during spawning season using fish weirs and nets.[79] Sites near rivers occasionally yield notched or grooved stone net-sinkers, sometimes several together, like at the Baldwin's Station site (6NH47) along the Housatonic River in Milford.[80]

Almost nothing of these nets or other indigenous textiles has survived in the archaeological record. They are described in early European documents as very durable and made from local plant fibers, particularly Indian hemp (dogbane).[81] In 1749 Peter Kalm, a Swedish naturalist who toured New York, Pennsylvania, and New Jersey from 1748 to 1751 studying the native flora, reported how Indian women in the Northeast collected and processed Indian hemp for strings, ropes, and threads that they used to make bags, pouches, quilts, linings, and fishing equipment.

> When the Indians were still living among the Swedes in Pennsylvania and New Jersey, they made ropes of this *Apocynum,* which the Swedes bought and used for bridles and nets. These ropes were stronger and kept longer in water than such as were made of common hemp [normally used by Europeans during this period]. . . . The Indians also make several other articles of their hemp, such as various sizes of bags, pouches, quilts, and linings. On my journey through the country of the Iroquois I saw the women employed in the manufacture of this hemp. They made neither use of spinning wheels nor distaffs, but rolled the filaments upon their bare thighs, and made thread and strings of them, which they dyed red, yellow black, etc. and afterwards worked them into goods with a great deal of ingenuity. . . . Sometimes the fishing equipment of the Indians consists entirely of this hemp.[82]

Wampum band fragments from graves in a late-seventeenth and early-eighteenth-century Pequot cemetery overlooking Long Pond in Ledyard, Connecticut, contained two-ply, Z-twist yarns of Indian hemp that held the quahog shell and copper beads of the deceased's jewelry in place between rows of sinew. At RI-1000, a mid-seventeenth-century Narragansett cemetery in North Kingstown,

Rhode Island, Native-made textiles included close-twined and plaited containers, and mats layered with wool fabric that were used to line the inside of graves.[83] Cordage made from a twisted basswood fiber was recovered from a Late Archaic context at the Long Knoll site in South Glastonbury—the earliest documented in Connecticut. Indirect evidence for indigenous textiles can be found in later clay pottery containers, whose damp surfaces were often impressed with cord, netting, and other fabric.

### Connecticut's Earliest Known Fisheries

Fish weirs are fencelike traps made of wooden poles from saplings pressed into the silty river or lagoon bed and often supported by large stones. Smaller branches and brushwood were woven horizontally between the poles. Fish that swam into the weir at high tide would be trapped as the tide went out. In smaller streams rock walls alone worked as well. In nontidal rivers and streams, V- or W-shaped and diagonal fish weirs were especially effective just below natural obstructions where the fishes' upward progress would have been delayed.[84]

Plan of an early fyke-basket-type Native American brush weir, from about A.D. 1600, that was once located along the coast at South Cove, Old Saybrook, Connecticut.

Brush and stone fish weirs once graced the coves along the state's coastline, where Connecticut's first fishermen trapped salmon, shad, herring, non-anadromous near-shore fish like flounder and smelt, and possibly even seals.[85] A large weir once located at the mouth of the Housatonic River consisted of rows of wooden poles 400 to 500 feet long with a 50-foot trap at its center.[86] Fish were eaten fresh, smoked, or dried, and rendered for their oil. Shad roe was a delicacy; early-seventeenth-century Massachusetts Indians boiled it with acorns.[87] Another delicacy was the head of striped bass, which Roger Williams called "a daintie dish

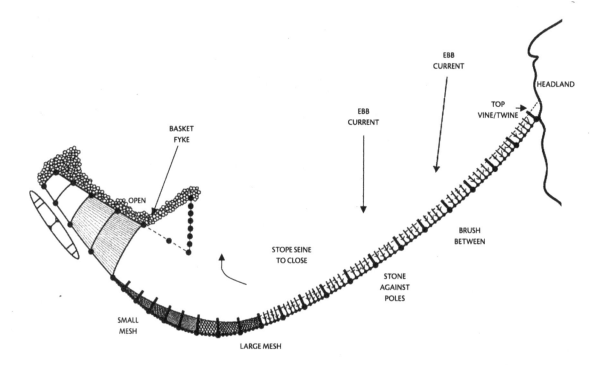

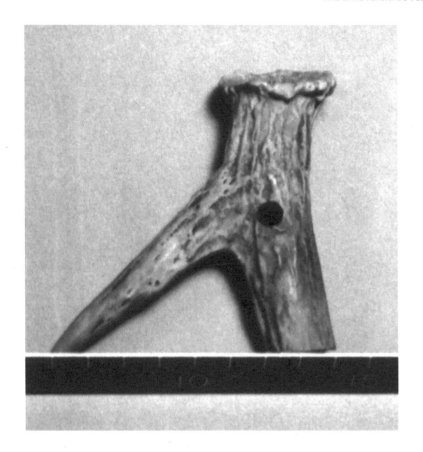

A pipe made from the antler of a white-tailed deer, found in 1982 during a drawdown for dam repairs of Bashan Lake in East Haddam, Connecticut.

... the braines and fat of it being very much, and sweet as marrow."[88] According to fisheries specialist Timothy Visel, among the aquatic resources of Clinton Harbor, Connecticut,

> We can find mounds of shells, of soft shell clams, hard shell clams, oysters and Bay scallops as evidence of these Native American fisheries. But shellfish alone was not the only resource harvested. Examination of shell middens at Hammonasset State Park revealed shad and salmon ear bone otoliths. Hammonasset is one of New England's cold water rivers; its source was the heavy glacial till underground springs, so its outflow was cool and perfect for anadromous fish, shad, salmon and herring such as the alewife. It was one of the few rivers to have salmon runs, and even to the late 1970s contained large numbers of sea run brown trout . . . a brush Indian weir once existed at the southern edge [of Hammonasset Park] near West or "Wheeler Rock" behind a series of boulders off Meigs Point. The "weir rock" now called "west rock" no doubt caught these fish as they returned to spawn. These Indian brush weirs were also found off Westbrook and Old Saybrook . . . the one at Clinton Harbor was the largest.[89]

The remains of several fish weirs had also been reported along the lower Housatonic River[90] and at the inland Bashan Lake site in East Haddam, where net

Remains of the stone fishing weir at the LeBeau site on the Quinebaug River near Killingly, Connecticut.

sinkers for securing the fishnets across the opening of the weir were also found.[91] At least twenty fish weirs have been reported from the Quinebaug drainage in eastern Connecticut; some still exist.[92] One of these, the Dyer Manor fish weir in south Danielson, measures 174 feet (53 meters).

*Lebeau Site*    The Lebeau site was associated with a large stone fish weir that diagonally crossed the Quinebaug River below the village of Danielson, Connecticut.[93] The camp site was directly above the weir. Excavations recovered more than 9,000 artifacts, including points, bifaces, hammerstones, flake tools for cutting and scraping, an unfinished atlatl weight, a steatite bowl fragment, clay pottery sherds, a net sinker, a notched pebble, a piece of possibly worked graphite, stone cores, and thousands of debitage flakes. Almost all the stone material (97 percent) was made from the local Plainfield quartzite. From the variety of point styles, and the steatite and pottery sherds, we know that the site had been used as a fishing camp by Archaic and Woodland peoples for thousands of years.

The Lebeau site contained several large rocks that could have been used as fish processing blocks (similar to our kitchen chopping blocks), or possibly as a windbreak for a hearth. Additionally, the site was near the fish weir and an adjacent stone pile (possibly the base of a work staging area?). Concentrations of artifacts along the bank suggested small camps intensively used by work groups or families. Local fishermen report excellent fishing near the weir because of a deep trough running up the middle of the river in that area. One person noted that spawning suckers ascended nearby Fall Brook predictably about the second week of April every year, followed by larger pickerel and the snapping turtles that fed

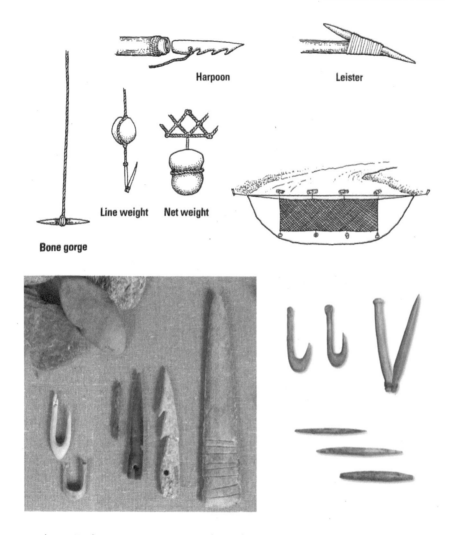

Harpoon

Leister

Line weight

Net weight

Bone gorge

Variety of tools and equipment used for fishing. Bottom left: bone fishhooks from the Tubbs Shell Heap, Niantic, Connecticut; a small fish spear and a bone harpoon from Perry's Shell Heap, Truro, Massachusetts; a bone harpoon from Wilcox Farm/Old Merwin Farm, Milford, Connecticut; and an incised fishing spear or dagger made from a swordfish bill, from Perry's Shell Heap, Truro, Massachusetts. At far right, bone gorges and bone fishhooks, including a rare two-part hook from the Fort Shantok site, the only one found in Connecticut.

on them. Early European accounts show that weirs continued to be an important part of fishing technology for late pre-contact and post-contact New England Native American communities.[94]

We know from descriptions by European settlers that work or task groups based on gender or kinship did many of the economic tasks in Native American communities, although sometimes the entire community was involved (similar to the way Amish communities hold barn raisings). For example, Roger Williams reported that

> When a field is to be broken up, they have a very loving sociable speedy way to dispatch it: All the neighbours men and women forty, fifty, a hundred etc. joyne, and come in to help freely. With friendly joining they breake up their fields, build their Forts, hunt the Woods, stop and kill fish in the Rivers, it being true with them as in all the World in the Affaires of Earth or Heaven: by concord little things grow great, by discord the greatest come to nothing.[95]

Re-creation of indigenous fishing activities by artist David R. Wagner. Left, the difficulty of working a fish weir during spring floods, when anadromous fish normally run. Right, *Fishing on the Quinebaug* shows the processing of fish by women, with girls learning by the traditional apprenticeship method.

*Harrison's Landing Site*   Seasonal camps are smaller sites probably occupied only for a season or so. Temporary or special-purpose camps were used for short stays of less than a day to a few weeks, sometimes for a single activity, such as shellfish or nut collecting. The earliest known shellfish collecting sites in Connecticut date to the Late Archaic period.[96] These are mainly large quantities, or middens, of discarded shells of marine or freshwater mollusks such as Virginia oysters, hard-shell clams (quahogs), soft-shell clams, scallops, and mussels found in a single thick layer over much of the site, in discrete piles, in pit features, or combinations of these deposits.

One example is the Harrison's Landing site at the head of a cove on the Thames River in New London, Connecticut.[97] The shell midden covered about one-tenth of an acre (500 square meters) and was no more than about 10 inches (25 centimeters) thick in some areas. Associated with it were small-stemmed Wading River points and Squibnocket Triangle points of the Narrow Point tradition. The midden consisted mainly of oyster shell with some clam, scallop, and mussel shell. Other food remains included deer, bones of small mammals, and a few fish bones, in all likelihood the dinner of the Indian collectors who shucked and smoked shellfish before gathering the meats into baskets to carry them back to their main camp. Earlier peoples probably collected and ate shellfish too, but those sites are most likely underwater. With an "extraordinary abundance" of oysters on the southern Atlantic Shelf from 12,000 to 5000 B.P., it seems unlikely that such an important food source would be ignored.[98]

## Complex Settlement and Band Society

Narrow Point peoples spent most of their time at their base camp. At different times of the year some would temporarily leave this base to collect resources at one of the many seasonal and temporary camps that dotted the countryside, returning when their task was completed. Men and older boys would form hunting parties, spending days or weeks away hunting deer and bear in the uplands or setting and checking traps for smaller fur-bearing animals. Alternatively, they would scout the major flyways along river valleys and coasts for migratory waterfowl and seabirds. Food remains from these sites also include turkey, grouse, raccoon, and small mammals such as rabbit and squirrel.[99]

A group of males might visit one of the quarry sites to collect toolstone. Women and girls would set off for a day of collecting leafy lakeside plants, or digging tubers, or collecting acorns and nuts in the uplands. Children might spend the afternoon picking berries on a hillside. One or more families might set up a short-term camp to tap maple or birch trees for syrup or collect special woods for making brooms, bowls, spoons, baskets, and even canoes. Community members might visit a sacred site for personal meditation, an initiation rite, or to give thanks and praise to a spirit being.

These sites were connected by a series of well-worn Indian trails that also connected the community with neighbors and with Indian societies located much

A historical (1860?) Wampanoag cane basket fish trap photographed at the Shepaug River in Washington, Connecticut, along with traditional fishing equipment and a waterfowl hunting decoy (at right).

farther away. Many of these trails are now our highways and secondary roads. One prominent example is the Old Berkshire Path, which connected Indian peoples living near Long Island Sound with inland communities northward to present-day Stockbridge, Massachusetts, and possibly as far away as Canada. It is now Route 7. Another is the Great Coastal Path that linked the Connecticut shoreline with indigenous communities on Manhattan Island to the west and at least as far north as what is now the Maine coast. That Indian trail is now Route 1, the Boston Post Road.[100]

Researchers interpret these sites as the settlements of a band society whose kin-related members continuously broke up into smaller family, multifamily, and gender- and age-specific work groups to exploit the seasonally, geographically, and topographically diverse environments of their homeland.[101] The variety of sites, their diverse functions and locations, and the increasing range of tool types and dietary remains add up to an increasing diversity of economic tasks and an ever broadening economy for Narrow Point communities. These Narrow Point band societies continued to thrive throughout the Terminal Archaic and earlier Woodland periods.

### Narrow Point Spirituality

No Narrow Point cemeteries have yet been found in Connecticut. Two burials were recovered from a residential camp at the Long Knoll site in South Glastonbury, Connecticut. Located on a knoll in the floodplain of the Connecticut River, the site was covered with a 4- to 6-inch layer (10 to 15 centimeters) of fire-cracked rock "probably representing the refuse of hundreds of food-processing hearths," according to excavators.[102] Beneath the rock was a series of shell pits, and beneath those was a series of hearths, pits, post molds, and the two cremation burials. One burial was in a deep pit with four stemmed points, juniper berries, nutshell fragments, traces of ochre, and a truly unique find—the twisted basswood fiber mentioned above, the earliest known piece of cordage from a Connecticut site. The juniper berries and nutshell could have been food for the dead. Juniper also has spiritual significance for local post-contact Native Americans, signifying ancestral memories;[103] as an evergreen species, it could also have symbolized everlasting life. As noted previously, red ochre signifies blood and life. To this day indigenous mourners often place evergreen boughs in the coffin or grave with the deceased. This may have also been the case at Long Knoll. The site provided a radiocarbon date of 3995 B.P. ±100 years and contained more than one hundred Narrow Point tradition points, "with examples of Brewerton-eared and Squibnocket Triangles" and a Normanskill point.[104]

One Narrow Point tradition burial has also been reported from nearby eastern Massachusetts. Unlike the Connecticut cremation burials, this burial was of a flexed skeleton in a small pit (with its knees drawn up to its chest in a fetal or seated position). Like the Connecticut burials, it had been sprinkled with ochre and was not accompanied by grave goods. Next to the grave, however, were smaller pits with broken narrow-stemmed points and a broken gouge—possibly ritually killed grave goods. The burial was dated to 4130 B.P. ±225 years.[105] Both sites suggest regional diversity among Narrow Point communities and very different burial rites than practiced by contemporary Laurentian peoples.

Noncremated burials, known as inhumations, provide even more information about indigenous lifestyles. The skeleton itself gives us considerable data on the health, diet, and demography of past indigenous communities. A paper by Connecticut state archaeologist and specialist in skeletal remains Nicholas Bellantoni and his colleagues reports:

> Bones adapt to a variety of factors, including age, diet, physical activity, sex, pregnancy, lactation, disease, infection, injury and deformation. The skeleton records the living history of the individual, thereby providing important insights into past biocultural adaptations. Culture and biology are closely linked in the study of human adaptation. . . . The degree of tooth wear and decay are indicative of cultural practices. For example, Archaic period hunters-gatherers usually exhibit well worn, but relatively sound teeth, which is related to the mastication of foods. Later Woodland period populations show less wear, but more dental decay; this correlates with the intensification of horticulture and dietary changes, such as decreased protein and increased carbohydrates (Larsen 1982). Much attention has focused on skeletal changes associated with the shift from hunting and gathering to agricultural economies. Most researchers believe a decline in general and dental health is associated with the development of sedentary agricultural villages.[106]

## PERSONAL ORNAMENTATION

The Late Archaic is also the earliest period for which we have reliable associations of personal ornamentation. Pre-contact indigenous jewelry usually took the form of beads, pendants, and gorgets (two-holed pendants). Ornaments were manufactured from perishable materials such as bone, shell, antler, claws, seeds, and wood as well as stone, as they were among post-contact peoples. Unfortunately, such items are normally destroyed by New England's acidic soils.

A rare, lovely, polished purple and white shell pendant made from a quahog shell (the raw material of purple wampum) was recovered from the Phillips Rock Shelter in Glastonbury.[107] Another quahog shell pendant and a fish vertebra bead were recovered from the Baldwin's Station site along the Housatonic estuary in Milford.[108] Perforated bear's teeth, worn as beads or pendants, were found at the Eagle Hill site in Milford[109] and the Cedar Ridge site in Shelton.[110] Many incised stone pendants, some in the shape of animals,[111] are surface finds, often from plowed fields, so archaeologists have no way of discovering their age or cultural associations without knowing their original context.[112] Others excavated from stratigraphic levels that contained artifacts characteristic of more than one cultural period are also difficult, if not impossible, to date or associate with a specific culture.

Graphite, reddish yellow "ochre," hematite pigment stones, small cylindrical

## THE PROTECTION OF INDIGENOUS GRAVES

As in all societies, human burials are sacred to Native Americans. In Connecticut, indigenous graves are protected by law. Public Act 89-368 of the Connecticut General Statutes provides that any person who knowingly digs up, damages, or desecrates a Native American grave, or sells, exchanges, transports, receives, or offers to sell human remains or the items associated with them, can be fined as much as $5,000, imprisoned for up to five years, or both.

> (a) Any person who knows or reasonably believes that any human burials or human skeletal remains are being or about to be disturbed, destroyed, defaced, removed or exposed shall immediately notify the Chief Medical Examiner and State Archaeologist of such fact. If human burials or human skeletal remains are encountered during construction or agricultural, archaeological or other activity that might alter, destroy or otherwise impair the integrity of such burials or remains, the activity shall cease and not resume unless authorized by the Chief Medical Examiner and the State Archaeologist. . . .[a]

The importance of avoiding disturbances to graves is made clear in the following passage from a collaborative overview authored by archaeologists and Native Americans:

> Most Native American cultures believe that the body and energy of each individual must be returned to the ecosystem for successive generations to flourish. Thus, the disturbance of one's ancestors threatens the existence of the present generation and the survival of future generations. As a result, great efforts must be taken to restore a disturbed burial to a peaceful rest. This requires returning all elements to their previous state; additional ceremonies must be performed to remove as many physical and spiritual indications of disturbance as possible. Most tribal elders state emphatically that Indian culture and individual lives will remain in disruption until the harmony of and respect for disturbed ancestors are renewed.[b]

Ethical archaeologists will not knowingly excavate Native American burials, but unfortunately indigenous graves are sometimes encountered in archaeological living sites. In such a case state regulations require that the Office of State Archaeology (OSA) be called in to determine whether the burial is Native American and, if so, to contact the Native American Heritage Advisory Council (NAHAC), a state agency that advises the OSA on Native American burials and oversees procedures. NAHAC members include representatives from Connecticut's five state-recognized tribes.

Native peoples prefer that the deceased remain undisturbed in his or her original homeland. If impending land development or vandalism precludes this arrangement, the grave is removed in a large earthen block and the deceased is reburied in a protected Native American burying ground according to traditional customs. The ceremonies are presided over by indigenous spiritual leaders. Referred to as a "shaman" or "religious practitioner" by some anthropologists and as a "holy man," "medicine man," or "spiritual leader" by contemporary tribal people, the leader cleanses the participants and contacts the spirit world with the smoke from burning sacred plants, traditionally tobacco and cedar in New England (sage from the West was incorporated much later, in modern times)—ancient rites that are hundreds, if not thousands, of years old.[c]

Notes

a. Public Act 89-368, Connecticut General Statutes, Chapter 184a, Native American Cultures. Policy Concerning Archaeological Investigations, Sec. 10-388(a), Human Burials (2008), www.cga.ct.gov/.

b. Poirier et al. 1985, 8.

c. E.g., Baxter 1991.

pestles made out of stone or fossil coral, and semicircular "paint pots" for mixing pigments have been recovered from several Late Archaic and Woodland Connecticut sites.[113] These were probably used to produce pigments for painting personal belongings and body painting. Pigments made from tree bark and plants were likely used as well.

## INTERPRETATIONS AND QUESTIONS

The richness of Connecticut's ecozones during the Late Archaic cultural period caused a dramatic growth in Native American communities on the landscape. The increased number, size, and functional diversity of archaeology sites are evidence of the successful exploitation of micro-environments and an extremely broad-spectrum economy, particularly for the peoples of the Narrow Point tradition. Happily, the ensuing population explosion left behind the material remains of many settlements that provide insights into the economy, technology, and social and spiritual lives of Late Archaic peoples. This information is sorely lacking for earlier Indian communities. Still, the excavations have raised important questions about the interrelationships of the two major cultural populations, Laurentian and Narrow Point. Did they relate to each other and in what ways? Were the relations peaceful? Did they barter foodstuffs or tools? Did they intermarry? Did their home territories overlap or were they mutually exclusive, with each population exploiting distinct ecozones?

How large were the Narrow Point and Laurentian settlements, and what size population did an average base camp accommodate? Many known sites were reoccupied repeatedly over time, so isolating discrete settlements within the site is difficult because they often overlap spatially as well as stratigraphically. Was there an "average" base camp or did they differ in size? Perhaps size varied depending on a camp's physical environment or the season when it was occupied. What was the relationship, if any, of Connecticut's Laurentian and Narrow Point populations to the preceding Middle Archaic communities? Did the Late Archaic populations migrate into Connecticut or did some develop from existing Middle Archaic roots?

This grouping of artifacts used for making paints includes: (at left) a paint pot from Fair Haven; (at center) pestles, among them in the middle a small paint pestle from a camp site at Tolland, Connecticut, found sometime from 1890–1915 by Dr. W. N. Simmons; (at right) a triangular piece of graphite with V-shaped groove from the South Woodstock Village Site, Windham County, Connecticut, and a ball of hematite from Fresh Pond, Stratford. Materials like these and most ornaments are often collected at the disturbed surface of a site, and so are undated.

Research in eastern Connecticut has generated questions about intracultural diversity as well. Did Laurentian communities practice different economies because of their occupation of different environmental zones, which in effect generated distinctive socio-settlement systems? Or were the upriver upland sites merely part of a larger settlement system whose base camps are as yet undiscovered but similar to those near the mouth of the Connecticut River? What of the lesser-studied Laurentian communities in the river valleys of western Connecticut and in the upland regions of northwestern and northeastern Connecticut? Do they show a similar diversity in settlement patterning? If so, did the economic differences create distinctions in other aspects of culture such as social organization, politics, art, and spirituality?

Why have we found so little evidence of burial and sacred sites for the Narrow Point tradition peoples? Is the interpretation of environmental stress as the cause of Laurentian ceremonialism correct? If so, is the lack of such stress among Narrow Point societies due to its broad-spectrum economy? Is that the reason for the absence of Narrow Point ceremonialism in Connecticut? Interestingly, almost three-fourths of Narrow Point tradition occupations dated to the Late Archaic period postdate the Little Ice Age of 4330 B.P. (16 of 22, or 73 percent). In contrast, only 3 of 13 Late Archaic Laurentian settlements (23 percent) are later.[114] This suggests that Narrow Point–producing people were much less affected by the environmental changes wrought by the Little Ice Age relative to Laurentian peoples, and that subsequent climatic conditions benefited the Narrow Point economy.

Were Narrow Point dead also cremated, but without grave goods and not in cemeteries, so that their cremation pits have been misidentified as storage pits, hearths, or earth ovens rather than as graves? Were some Narrow Point people merely buried flexed in small simple graves, like the Massachusetts burial described above, as are found in later cultural periods in Connecticut? Narrow-stemmed points from such burials at several sites were not radiocarbon-dated and could not be assigned to a specific cultural period on the basis of their contents.[115]

Where are the Narrow Point houses? Why have we not found any evidence for them? And what of the political organization of the Late Archaic populations? Was the main political unit the base-camp population, composed of related families? Or did the fertile environments promote a larger political unit of several base camps and villages—the beginnings of tribalism? These are but a few of the fascinating questions facing Connecticut archaeologists studying this time period.

# 5

## Environmental Stress and Elaborate Ritual

### *The Terminal Archaic Period*

We, the Iroquois, are not a people who ask or demand anything from the Creator, but instead, we give greeting and thanks for all life. We understand our relationship to all living things and we will always remember the instructions of the Creator and that we have been provided with all things necessary for life. We are to carry love to one another, to show respect for all living things on earth. We will always respect our Mother Earth who gives us life and holds the bones of our past generations, and it is our duty to take great care of these bones and not to poison them.

—Dave Richmond, Connecticut resident and Mohawk, 1985

At the end of Archaic times, known as the Terminal Archaic period (about 3800 to 2700 RCY B.P.), some indigenous communities shifted their base camps from large interior wetlands to the floodplains and first terraces of the large river valleys.[1] Although essentially modern environmental conditions prevailed, the climate continued to fluctuate. During the "Little Ice Age" around 3290 B.P. the weather was wetter and cooler than today. The rise in sea level slowed dramatically because of reduced melting of the polar ice cap, and post-glacial crustal movements (the depressed earth bouncing back after the glacier receded) ceased. The inundation of what was once the coastline during earlier Archaic times continued, but at a slower pace.[2] The slower sea-level rise promoted the development of salt marshes along the coast and mouths of rivers during the late Terminal Archaic and Early Woodland periods.[3]

### TWO DISTINCTIVE ARTIFACT TRADITIONS

Native American communities continued to be characterized by two distinctive artifact traditions. Unlike in the Late Archaic period, however, archaeologists cannot agree that these represent two separate populations. Furthermore, those researchers who believe there were two distinct Terminal Archaic populations express different ideas as to the source of one of those populations.

The continuing Narrow Point tradition and a new Susquehanna, or Broad Spear, tradition define the Terminal Archaic period in Connecticut.

## Narrow Point Tradition Settlements

Narrow Point tradition sites show strong continuity with preceding Late Archaic sites in material objects, food remains, and settlement patterns. Sites such as Woodchuck Knoll in South Windsor, Long Knoll in South Glastonbury, Dibble Creek 1 on Haddam Neck, Cedar Lake in Lyme, Candlewood Hill in Haddam, and Ely's Ferry in Old Lyme leave little doubt that their inhabitants were the descendants of earlier Late Archaic peoples whose successful broad-spectrum economies continued to promote the growth of stable, enduring communities across the Connecticut landscape.[4] The Narrow Point people used the same chipped stone and rough stone tools and continued to inhabit open-air sites, shell middens, rock shelters, and quarry workshops in a series of large multiseasonal base camps, smaller camps of shorter duration, and task-specific temporary camps — often the same camp sites once occupied by their Late Archaic ancestors. And like the residences of their ancestors, researchers have interpreted these settlements as representing a band society whose members continuously broke up into smaller family, multifamily, and gender- and age-specific work groups to exploit the seasonally, geographically, and topographically diverse environments of their homelands.[5]

### Woodchuck Knoll Site

At the Woodchuck Knoll site in South Windsor, in the floodplain of the Connecticut River, a Narrow Point seasonal camp and quartz cobble workshop produced a series of five radiocarbon dates between 3690 and 3220 B.P., with four of the dates occurring between 3690 and 3510 B.P.[6] Tools included chipped stone points, knives, and scrapers; rough stone hammerstones and pitted anvil stones; and a ground stone pestle and three-quarter grooved axe. There were five hearths and two pits that were interpreted as storage pits for goosefoot (*Chenopodium*), from the presence of seeds and from carbonized weevils of the genus *Sitophilous* in the hearths. This weevil feeds on stored grains, so its presence at Woodchuck Knoll suggested that site occupants were not only eating *Chenopodium* seeds, but storing them as well.[7] The relatively larger size of the weevil larvae suggested to other researchers that the residents were also storing acorns.[8]

Unidentified animal bone fragments, and walnut, hickory nut, and hazelnut shell fragments — the latter originally misidentified as *Nelumbo lutea,* or American lotus,[9] were also recovered. The ripening times for the botanical remains show that the community at Woodchuck Knoll was exploiting both the floodplain and the upland environments during the late summer months and possibly into autumn (walnut and hickory trees continue to produce nuts through October and November, respectively). Excavators interpreted the thick cultural deposits as evidence that the people repeatedly returned to the camp site for many years.

In southeastern Connecticut the Narrow Point settlements continued to be concentrated in the uplands. Research in the lower Connecticut River valley shows that, with one exception—Woodchuck Knoll—there were no Narrow Point settlements contemporary with the Broad Spear tradition in riverine areas,[10] suggesting discrete homelands for each cultural group. The Narrow Point Terminal Archaic sites in the lower Connecticut River valley tend to be larger and more numerous than those of the Late Archaic, suggesting continued population increase.[11]

## Susquehanna or Broad Spear Tradition Settlements

Along the Eastern seaboard from Georgia to Maine, the Susquehanna artifact tradition is characterized by broad-bladed "broad spear" and "fishtail" projectile point styles, bowls and other objects made from a soft stone called steatite (soapstone), and an elaborate burial ritual involving cremation ceremonies.[12] In New England, some researchers prefer to call the tradition "Broad Spear" because they believe it may not be the same culture as that discovered in the Susquehanna River valley of Pennsylvania.[13]

In regions outside Connecticut, the point styles are chronologically distinct.[14] From earliest to latest, the point types are:

- broad-bladed, stemmed Atlantic points and Snook Kill points;
- broad-bladed, corner-notched, often round-shouldered Perkiomen points;
- wide-bladed, corner-notched Wayland Notched points, broad-bladed boldly corner-notched concave-base Susquehanna points, broad-bladed pentagonal Mansion Inn blades, and broad-bladed, converging-base Boats blades used as preforms for points or as scrapers and knives;
- medium- to narrow-bladed fishtail Orient points.

The Atlantic point is the earliest in eastern New England. The Snook Kill point type is the earliest broad-bladed point type in New York and western New England. Both occur in Connecticut. Similar in form and technique of manufacture, the two types grade into each other.

In Connecticut, researchers reported that the broad-bladed and fishtail points were found in the same contexts, which suggests that the types were made and used contemporaneously and so cannot be used to date materials within the Broad Spear horizon.[15] The earliest Broad Spear points in Connecticut are from the Museum A site on the Mashantucket Pequot Reservation near Ledyard, dating to 3840 B.P. This is a rare early date for a Broad Spear settlement, however; except for a 3740 B.P. date from the Last site in Bolton, all other Broad Spear settlements are later than 3666 B.P. In the Connecticut Valley, they are no earlier than 3611 B.P.[16] The earliest date for an Orient point is 3600 B.P. from the Horton Farm site in South Glastonbury.[17] The latest date for Broad Spear point styles is 2460 B.P. at the Timothy Stevens site in Glastonbury, where Broad Spear points were associated with steatite bowl fragments.[18]

Stone blades of the Boats
projectile point style.

### Broad Spear Tool Kits

The tool kit associated with Susquehanna broad-bladed points in Connecticut included hammerstones, knives, scrapers, bifacially flaked ceremonial blades, ground wing-shaped atlatl weights, grooved axes, gouges, whetstones, steatite containers, steatite-tempered pottery, shallow mortars (metates) and mullers (manos), cruciform drills, "beveled [sinew] stones," adzes, cylindrical hammers and punches, chisels, cache blades (called "cache" because the blanks were often cached underground), and native copper.[19] Forty-three broad blades from a cache in Newington were manufactured from non-local cherts. One blade was identified through geologic thin-section analysis as Normanskill chert from the mid-Hudson Valley,[20] showing that Terminal Archaic communities in central Connecticut and eastern New York were involved in some form of exchange. The occurrence of mullers and mortars indicates that nuts, acorns, and seeds were ground to make breads and oils and to thicken soups and stews.

Some of the Broad Spear settlements contain the earliest evidence for the use of clay pottery containers alongside soapstone bowls, as at the Timothy Stevens site dated to 2740 B.P., the Lieutenant River site in Old Lyme dated to 2700 B.P.,[21] and the Two Springs site[22] on Fishers Island in Long Island Sound dated to 2785 B.P. Other sites with evidence of early pottery are a shell-midden deposit dated to 2515 B.P. at the Robillard site in Milford,[23] and the possible association with quartz Orient fishtail points at Site 251-4-1 in the uplands of New Milford.[24] A similar association of an Orient point with pottery and steatite fragments was found at Site 294A-AF-21 in Milford, dated to 3530 B.P.[25]

This situation is not unique to Connecticut. Clay pottery had been associated with Broad Spear and Orient points or steatite containers, or both, in other localities of the Northeast and the Middle Atlantic.[26] One Terminal Archaic Narrow Point settlement in Connecticut, the Stavens III site in Bolton, contained a Nar-

Projectile point styles diagnostic of the Susquehanna or Broad Spear artifact tradition. Top to bottom: Susquehanna Broad points; Snook Kill points; Wayland Notched points and a Perkiomen point (at right); Mansion Inn blades; and Atlantic points. Not to scale.

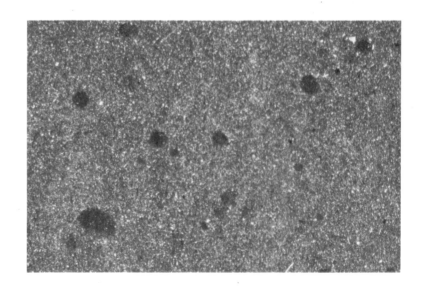

A micrograph of chert from an outcrop of the Normanskill Shale Formation in the Hudson River valley in eastern New York state, identifiable by the radiolaria fossils and the groundmass silt it contains (width of image equals 4 millimeters).

Some Terminal Archaic artifacts from the Grannis Island site: top, Orient points; bottom, pitted stones. Scale bars equal 1 centimeter.

Excavations in 2011 by the Central Connecticut State University field school at the Ragged Mountain Rock Shelter and soapstone quarry in Barkhamsted, Connecticut. The quarry, inside the rock shelter, has a large vein of steatite.

row Point projectile point and pottery dated to 3530 B.P. The small number of clay sherds, however, strongly suggests that clay pots were not important to either the Broad Spear or the Narrow Point economy during the Terminal Archaic period.

Researchers have generally assumed that clay pots were introduced by trade or population movements from outside New England because of their early use in the Midwest and Southeast—as early as 4465 B.P. in South Carolina.[27] Yet recent early dates from sites in Massachusetts and Maine challenge that assumption: 4860 B.P. and 4535 B.P. from the Chassell 2 site in western Massachusetts; 4410 B.P. from the Wamsutta/Signal Hill site in eastern Massachusetts; and 4225 B.P. from the Great Moshier Island A site in Casco Bay.[28]

## Steatite Quarries and Stone Containers

There are several quarries in Connecticut where Native American people carved bowls, platters, cups, and other objects from steatite.[29] One is the Ragged Mountain Quarry and Rock Shelter in Barkhamsted, a large rock shelter whose walls contained veins of steatite.[30]

Small groups, possibly family or male work groups, temporarily inhabited the Ragged Mountain Rock Shelter to quarry the soapstone there and shape it into vessels. The tailings, or quarry waste material, from these activities littered much of the area. The quarry workers broke up these tailings with long, heavy, picklike tools called tailing breakers and removed the tailings with stone spades to dumps on the edge of the habitation area.

### The Demise of Soapstone Bowl Manufacture

Steatite containers have flat bases that exposed less surface to heat than the rounded bases of later Woodland clay pots, making them less efficient for cooking liquids. The nonstick surfaces and fireproof characteristics of metamorphic

## SOAPSTONE

Steatite, a soft metamorphic rock ranging in form from talc to serpentine, is composed of talc, amphibole, chlorite, mica, and pyroxenes. In New England the stone occurs in a variety of colors—grays, greens, bluish grays, and black. It is also called soapstone because of its slippery, soapy feel. In southern New England steatite is found in both outcroppings and glacial boulder fields, both of which were exploited as quarries and workshops by indigenous communities.[a]

There are soapstone outcrops in northern Connecticut, Massachusetts, Rhode Island, and southeastern Pennsylvania. Yet soapstone bowls are found at Terminal Archaic sites throughout Connecticut, suggesting either that Indian communities near outcrops traded soapstone objects to those elsewhere or that members from communities across the state traveled to the quarries, procured soapstone objects, and carried them back to their base camps. Stone quarry tools discovered in a New Haven grave suggest that soapstone was brought back, although trade was probably also a factor.

Note

a. Wall 2003.

These soapstone bowls, completed but never removed, were found in the steatite vein that runs through a newly discovered quarry locus in Barkhamsted.

# Making a Soapstone Bowl

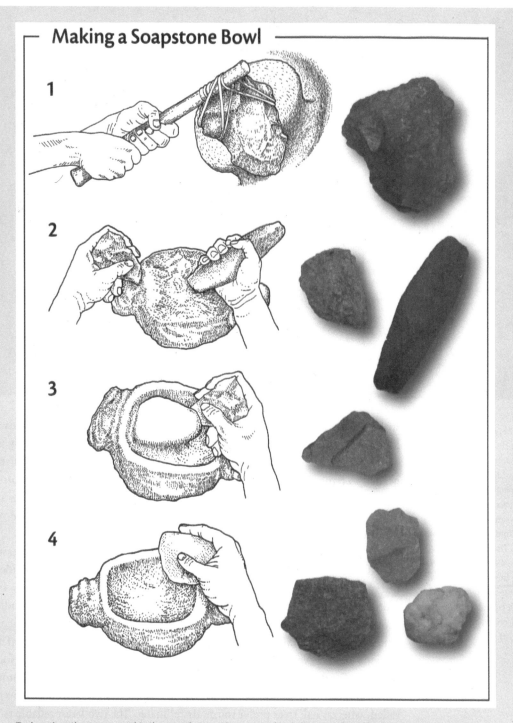

Tools such as these were used in the manufacture of soapstone bowls. *Step 1:* A knoblike preform is pecked out from the quarry wall with an end pick and cut off with a quarry axe or maul. *Step 2:* The handles, or lugs, and outside of the bowl are formed with a pick and chisel. *Step 3:* The interior of the bowl is hollowed out with a pick. *Step 4:* The bowl's surfaces are smoothed with abrading scrapers, shavers, and a hand gouge.

A variety of artifacts made from steatite. Clockwise from left, a tubular atlatl weight from Killingworth, Connecticut, an incised atlatl weight from Milford, a miniature bowl from New Hartford, two elbow pipes from Thamesville and Norwich, three perforated beads (one from Groton and two of unknown provenience), and a pipe bowl from Stratford (center, below the atlatl weight).

steatite made these containers more durable and efficient for cooking solids and for boiling. For these reasons, Dr. James Truncer suggested that they mainly were used to process acorns, because the steatite could withstand the long boiling time needed to remove the bitter tannins from white and especially red oak acorns to make them palatable. Significantly, vessels and quarries are usually found in areas of mast forest. There are no quarries in conifer forests, although there are veins of steatite there.[31]

Fatty-acid analysis of the charred residue on bowls from four Northeastern sites dated to 4910 B.P., 3420 B.P., 3170 B.P., and 310 B.P. revealed unidentified plant material that Truncer interpreted as acidic enough to have come from acorns.[32] If so, then the disuse of steatite bowls among later Early Woodland peoples might have been because they had more efficient ways to prepare acorns, or because they did not collect this lower-ranked food source. Environmental fluctuations could have allowed for more abundant or more easily processed foods, as well as for the decline in acorn harvests. During the "Little Ice Ages" around 3290 B.P. and again around 2680 and 2550 B.P. cooler and wetter conditions prevailed, whereas oak trees prefer warm, dry climates. The two latest reliable radiocarbon dates for the use of steatite vessels in Connecticut are 2515 B.P. from the Robillard site in Milford and 2460 B.P. from Timothy Stevens in Glastonbury,[33] which roughly correlate with the later Little Ice Age.

Technological innovations, such as the introduction of clay pots, could have

A large steatite bowl from Connecticut.

allowed people to increase their consumption of other foods. Clay containers were being used in Connecticut by the middle of the fifth millennium B.P., but did not become common until after 2750 B.P.,[34] around the onset of a Little Ice Age. Low acorn harvests could have caused the Woodland-period peoples to gather more goosefoot, pigweed, wild rice, and other small-seeded plants, aided by the relatively new pottery technology. More research is needed to test these theories.

More improved methods of residue analysis applied to three steatite vessels from one of Truncer's sites—Hunter's Home from central New York, however, specifically identified grass seeds, a wild legume, pine resources, animal meat, and unidentified plants but no acorns.[35] The researchers concluded that although steatite vessels may have been used as specialized mast processing containers in some subregions, this was not the case for Eastern North America as a whole, and that there likely were multiple, subregional causes for steatite manufacture and use[36]—and disuse.

Perhaps these heavy, bulky objects were unsuited to the seasonally mobile lifestyle of Early Woodland peoples. Perhaps they were not as efficient as clay pots for cooking the seeds, rice, maize, and other wild grains on which later Woodland communities depended. Or perhaps the population that made and used stone bowls moved out of the area or became extinct. Perhaps all of these theories have some relevance.

## FROM HEARTHS TO EARLY HOUSING

### Susquehanna–Broad Spear Settlements

We know that the peoples who used artifacts in the Susquehanna–Broad Spear tradition visited estuaries and coastal areas, because they left behind shell middens such as those at Laurel Beach in Milford and the Old Lyme Shell Heap. They took shelter in rock overhangs, including those at Ragged Mountain in Barkhamsted, the Salmon River Rock Shelter in Colchester,[37] Mianus Gorge in Greenwich,[38] and Pine Rock in New Haven.[39] They lived in open-air camps at Broeder Point in Old Lyme,[40] the Murdoch site in Old Lyme,[41] Timothy Stevens in Glastonbury,[42] the Burwell-Karako site in New Haven,[43] and the Kirby Brook site in Washington, Connecticut.[44] Their multiseasonal base camps were consistently located within large river valleys close to floodplain environments.[45] This lack of upland seasonal camps suggests reduced mobility, at least for those communities inhabiting the lower Connecticut Valley.

### Timothy Stevens Site

Broad Spear base settlements were situated in riverine areas, and their small, non-residential sites in the uplands represented short-term gathering trips by groups from the base camp.[46] The Timothy Stevens site, on a terrace overlooking the Connecticut River in Glastonbury, is such a base camp. Estimated at about one-third of an acre (1,500 square meters), the site contained both Broad Spear and Orient Fishtail points, bifaces, drills, one axe, used flakes, unifacial tools, modified cobbles, hammerstones, cores, debitage, steatite bowl fragments, clay pottery sherds, and food remains that included deer, beaver, other unidentified mammals, bird and fish bones, freshwater mussels, hickory, butternut, walnuts, and one charred ragweed seed. The seasonal availability of the nuts and seeds implies that Timothy Stevens was occupied during the late summer and fall.

There were also cooking hearths, trash pits, and a possible storage cache of five complete Orient points in a pit. Two activity areas, each measuring about 15 feet (5 meters) in diameter, had artifact concentrations and post molds that could represent oval house floors.[47] Charcoal from each activity area produced radiocarbon dates of 2740 and 2460 B.P., a very late Terminal Archaic to Early Woodland occupation of the site. Study of Timothy Stevens and other Broad Spear base camps in the Connecticut Valley, such as the Blaschick, Parkos, and Horse Barn sites, showed them to be organized into various work areas, discrete spaces where plants, hides, and wood were processed.[48]

### Kirby Brook Site

The Kirby Brook (6LF2) site in Washington, Connecticut, could have the only known Terminal Archaic housing in western Connecticut. Post molds found at the site could be differentiated from tree roots and rodent burrows by their straight profiles and clean-cut, usually pointed, bases. According to the site's excavator, the post-mold patterns indicated that the people here lived in circular and oblong houses. In the Snook Kill point–bearing level there were six circular

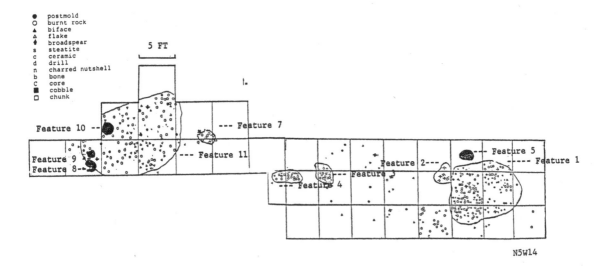

● postmold
O burnt rock
▲ biface
△ flake
♦ broadspear
s steatite
c ceramic
d drill
n charred nutshell
b bone
C core
■ cobble
□ chunk

5 FT

Feature 10 -- 

--- Feature 7

Feature 9
Feature 8 ->

--- Feature 11

Feature 2---

--- Feature 5

---- Feature 1

Feature 3

--- Feature 4

N5W14

houses about 9 feet (3 meters) in diameter, and four oval houses around 12 by 8 feet (about 4 by 2.5 meters) in size. For the later Orient point–bearing level, there were two oblong houses measuring around 16 by 10 feet (about 5 by 3 meters). Each of the Orient houses was divided into two discrete units, each with its own exterior doorway, suggesting that each house was shared by two nuclear families. This rare example of a single occupation yielded household tools that suggested it was an area for women's activities.[49]

Plan of the Timothy Stevens site in Glastonbury, Connecticut, showing activity areas (Features 1 and 10) that may represent house floors. The areas were associated with food remains, food processing tools, trash pits, hearths, and a basin-shaped circular feature (perhaps used for storage).

### Lovers Leap Site

Excavations at the Lovers Leap (6LF70) site in New Milford, which overlooked the Housatonic and Still river valleys, found a Broad Spear component that included stone platform hearths that yielded bone and acorn fragments, and underground stone tool caches.[50] The hearths could have been used to leach acorns and to roast meat. The caches show that the same peoples reoccupied the site. Two hearths each produced radiocarbon dates of 3065 B.P. One had two large, flat, slanted rocks, possibly heat reflectors, with "an arrangement of four post molds forming what might have been a meat- or fish-drying rack."[51]

The Indian name for Lovers Leap is Metichewan ("obstruction" or "turning back"), referring to the 10-foot (more than 3 meter) falls once found on the Housatonic River before a twentieth-century dam created Lake Lillinonah. According to Dr. Edmund Swigart, co-founder of the Institute for American Indian Studies and the Shepaug Valley Archaeological Society, "because the falls stopped the progress of large fish, it was formerly one of the best fishing places for shad and herring in the colony," although this particular part of the site did not yield any fishing equipment or fish bones.[52]

## A Narrow-Spectrum Economy

The food remains at the Griffin site in Old Lyme included hickory nuts, acorns, and hazelnuts; seeds of goosefoot (*Chenopodium*) and pigweed (*Amaranth*); and

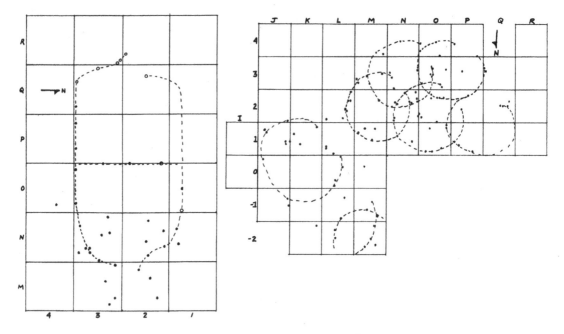

Plan views showing the post-mold patterns for two kinds of structures at the Kirby Brook (6LF2) site in Washington, Connecticut, oblong structures associated with Orient points, and earlier round structures associated with Snook Kill points. Left, Feature 1. Right, Feature 3. Symbol O shows the location of verified post molds. Dashed lines are possible post-mold patterns. All squares are 4 feet (1.2 meters) to a side.

bones from deer, dog, and a rabbit-size mammal.[53] Nut and acorn species were found at other Broad Spear habitation sites in southeastern Connecticut and the lower Connecticut Valley.[54] Acorns, hickory nuts, and *Chenopodium* were also recovered from the Toelles Road site in Wallingford. Acorns from red, white, and black (chinquapin) oak trees, hickory nuts, hazelnuts, and Spotted or Eastern Painted turtle shell fragments (perhaps from a rattle or dish) were identified from the Rye Hill site in Woodbury.[55] These food remnants indicate a narrow-spectrum economy, even more so than for the earlier Late Archaic Laurentian tradition.

Unlike the Laurentian settlements, no shellfish remains, fish bones, or fishing equipment were recovered from any of the Broad Spear sites even though many were near rivers. This absence suggests that the community's economy was based on terrestrial resources, such as deer, nuts, and the small seeds of riverine plants.[56] Riverine locations for camps would have the added advantage of providing efficient transportation by water for procuring the exotic stone materials often used in Broad Spear tool manufacture. The many woodworking tools recovered from Broad Spear sites, which could have been used to construct the dugout canoes, support this interpretation.

The only exception to this scenario is the Timothy Stevens site, which did contain unidentifiable bird bone, freshwater mussel shell, and fish crania. But it is a very late Terminal Archaic site that extended into the Early Woodland period, and perhaps by that time Broad Spear groups needed to broaden their use of resources in the face of dwindling food supplies.

## SPIRITUALITY AND CEREMONIALISM

### Terminal Archaic Cremation Burials

Although we know nothing of Narrow Point spirituality or mortuary practices in the Terminal Archaic period, archaeologists have discovered a great deal about Broad Spear spirituality from the many cremation burial sites of Terminal Archaic Broad Spear communities. Among the several such cremation burial sites in Connecticut are Toelles Road in Wallingford, Rye Hill in Woodbury, Turtle's Back in Bethlehem, Schwartz in South Windsor, Carrier in Glastonbury, and Basto in South Woodstock.[57] As archaeologist David H. Thompson remarked, each one represents "a sacred precinct, at which the collective ritual, the rites of intensification, of band society were performed."[58]

### *The Minor Site*

At the Minor site in New Haven three cremation burials were found four feet (more than a meter) below the surface during the excavation of a drainage ditch in 1916.[59] The decayed bones were apparently too badly damaged to preserve. The stone tool grave goods reportedly from the burials indicated that this Terminal

Artifacts from the Minor site that show evidence of deliberate breakage and burning. Not to scale.

Archaic community engaged in hunting, woodworking, food grinding, and soapstone quarrying activities: Susquehanna Broad, Wayland Notched, Orient, Squibnocket Triangle, and Narrow Point type points; blades; bifaces; blanks; adzes; axes; a chipped celt or ungrooved axe; a polished gouge; ground pestles; a polished stone cobble possibly used as a hammerstone; a soapstone bowl; and three soapstone quarry tools. Several of these artifacts were burned in the crematory fires.

### The Griffin Site

An even more extraordinary cremation cemetery was discovered near the mouth of the Connecticut River in Old Lyme.[60] The Griffin site contained 19 charcoal and ash-laden burial pits with over 1,200 mortuary offerings in a small, concentrated 150-foot (46 meter) area.[61] The mortuary rites indicated by the cultural remains are very similar to those described for the Late Archaic Laurentian people. Some of the pits had red ochre powder.

The offerings included stone bowls, large blades, Susquehanna Broad and Wayland points (but also a few Orient, one Perkiomen, two Turkey Tail, and one possible Narrow Point), blanks and preforms, knives, drills, scrapers, punches, strike-a-lites and iron pyrite for fire-making, chisels, hammerstones, paint pots, grinding pestles, sharpening stones, flake tools, beveled cobbles, food offerings, and more than one hundred heavy woodworking tools (ground gouges, adzes, and axes)—an astonishing number considering that these tools are rarely recovered from sites, probably because, since they took so long to manufacture, they were highly valued. The late Jeff Tottenham, an expert at replicating ground stone tools using the traditional Native American pecking method, told me that he would need to work day and night for four weeks to produce two ground stone axes![62]

Two mortuary pits contained unidentified copper fragments. Except for the copper fish gorge reportedly found at the Laurentian Meetinghouse Brook site in Wallingford, the pieces of copper from Terminal Archaic lower Connecticut Valley sites are the earliest recorded use of the mineral among Connecticut's indigenous peoples. Fragments of stone artifacts from one pit fit artifacts from other features, showing that the burial pits were made at the same time.[63] The Griffin site was radiocarbon dated with charcoal from two of its features to 3535 and 3495 B.P.[64]

## Mortuary Ritual

As in the earlier Late Archaic Laurentian cremations from southeastern Connecticut, many of the objects were stylized. They were manufactured from exotic stone materials and seem to have been made for ritual purposes, such as the large, thin cruciform drills from a cremation burial at Rye Hill.[65] At some sites stylized drills had been deliberately broken, or ritually "killed." Some of the artifacts were not burned and, therefore, had been placed in the burial pits after cremation. Like the Laurentian cremations, they were dry bone cremations[66] and not fresh, or green, when burned, which suggests that the corpses had been in a special location (such as a charnel house) until the bones were free of flesh.[67] The green bones were from fingers and toes, probably amputated by mourners, as in the Laurentian cremations. There were also dry and green bones at the Rye Hill site in western Connecticut.

As with the Laurentian mortuary practices, the cremations and purposeful placement of artifacts in the graves show that Terminal Archaic communities practiced spiritual ceremonialism and obviously believed in an afterlife. The artifacts,

Burned Atlantic Broad Spear points from the Rye Hill cremation site, Woodbury, Connecticut.

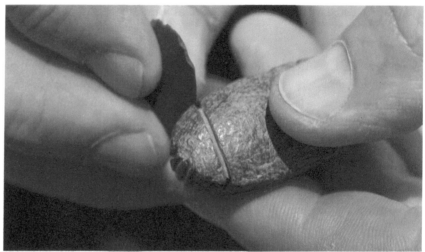

An intricately carved steatite effigy object, possibly depicting a butterfly or moth pupa, from the Rogers site in Lisbon, Connecticut. The site contained at least one cremation burial. The "pupa" may symbolize life after death and the transformation of spirit from life in the natural world to one in the spiritual world. The artifact has no provenience; it was recovered with a bulldozer by pothunters.

used in everyday activities, most likely were placed with the deceased in the belief that he or she would need them for survival in the spirit world.

In the excavator's interpretation of this evidence,

> the body was permitted to decompose, possibly on a scaffold, as was done in post-contact times in the Plains, northern Great Lakes area, the Maritimes, and the Southeast. After some period of time (two or more years) the bones were gathered up and placed on a funeral pyre. On the pyre were also placed food offerings such as dog, deer and rabbit meat, as well as hickory, acorn, and hazel nuts. Complete tool kit offerings were put into the fire. Pits were dug into a slightly hummocked area nearby. Here again, offerings were made. On the bottom of the pits were placed complete ready to use knives, spears, axes, adzes, hones, and stone bowls. Then, after the funeral pyre was burned out, the ashes were collected and poured into one pit after another. As the ash was being poured, still more offerings were made. Finally, the pits which were overflowing with ash, were sprinkled with ocher.[68]

A "killed" (deliberately broken) and burned soapstone bowl from the Laurel Beach site in Milford, Connecticut.

Several small Broad Spear habitation sites near the Griffin burial complex contained similar mortuary artifacts. These suggest a small localized floodplain community of dispersed family and multifamily residential units exploiting a narrow group of resources, which periodically came together for social and spiritual gatherings.[69]

The rising sea level caused by glacial melting slowly but continuously flooded the environments of the Broad Spear communities, literally eating away their economic base.[70] It is possible that such escalating economic stress promoted ceremonial practices expressed as cremation ritual and mortuary offerings. Two archaeo-botanical studies in the Old Lyme area show that freshwater oak-hickory floodplain woodlands had converted to saline grass and marshlands by 2750 to 2600 B.P.[71] If indeed there were two populations on the Connecticut landscape, the presence of the Narrow Point population would have worsened the Broad Spear stress, because the two groups were probably competing for food sources.

## ONE POPULATION OR TWO?

The presence of Narrow Point and Susquehanna points in the same burial pits at the Minor and Griffin sites shows that the two artifact traditions coexisted in southern Connecticut. There is additional evidence for this at sites elsewhere in Connecticut in overlapping radiocarbon dates, association in a cultural feature, and close stratigraphic relationships within a site's soil levels.[72] What does this information tell us about Terminal Archaic communities?

As noted above, some researchers think the points represent two separate social groups that coexisted on the New England landscape.[73] The Susquehanna–Broad Spear peoples may have migrated northward from the Middle Atlantic region, particularly the Susquehanna Valley of Pennsylvania, where their sites were first discovered.[74] Others have suggested that the Susquehanna–Broad Spear artifact complex points to a specialized activity (such as spear fishing) or set of activities (such as burial rites) among the communities of the indigenous Late Archaic tradition,[75] which in Connecticut was represented by the various Narrow Point styles.

American Cultural Specialists' excavations at the Dibble Creek 1 site, in Haddam, Connecticut. Top, a Broad Spear blade cache from the site. Bottom, excavation of a likely Terminal Archaic large platform hearth.

Excavations at the Dibble Creek 1 site, situated on an upland terrace overlooking a small tributary of the Connecticut River on Haddam Neck, provide evidence of social interactions between people from the Narrow Point tradition and the Broad Spear tradition.[76] Dibble Creek 1 has been interpreted as a fall–winter uplands base camp, mainly for Late Archaic through early Middle Woodland communities of the Narrow Point tradition. One of the stone platform hearths produced a Terminal Archaic radiocarbon date of 3600 B.P. ±50 years. Even though less than half a mile from the Salmon River, the site is on a high plateau above and away from the river, and subsistence there emphasized exploitation of the uplands resources of deer, acorns, and nuts; there was no evidence of fishing or collection of riverine plants.

At this site an underground cache of twenty-nine Broad Spear blades was recovered within a domestic living space. They were found neatly stacked in layers separated by sand, probably to protect the blades from fracturing. Unlike the surrounding quartz Narrow Point tools (some were on the same level as, and within inches of, the blade cache), these blades were made from non-local chert, slate, basalt, and hornfels.[77] Most had the asymmetrical form and edge wear of knives, probably used to process deer meat. As part of the Narrow Point tool kit at the site, the cache was probably bartered from a nearby Broad Spear community.

## The Two-Population *in Situ* Theory

Similarities in mortuary ceremonialism, economy, geographic locations, stone technology, and lithic trade patterns suggest that the local Laurentian communities evolved *in situ* (in place, or locally) into the Terminal Archaic Broad Spear users.[78] The distribution of sites from the Narrow Point and Broad Spear traditions points to a geographic division of these populations, with the Narrow Point communities concentrated around the interior wetlands and the Broad Spear communities in the river floodplain.[79]

## The Migration Theory

Artifacts made from non-local materials are somewhat more prevalent during the early Terminal Archaic period.[80] Later sites contained more local materials. This could support the migration theory. Migrating groups usually bring goods local to their home territory with them to new locations. As population movement slowed, so also would the flow of exotic goods. Significantly, geological analyses of tools from the Griffin site indicated source locations in the Mid-Atlantic region. Trace-element analysis of basalt ground stone tools suggests the most likely source is the Watchung Formation of western New Jersey. Scanning electron microscopy of felsite tools identified similarities with the South Mountain felsite quarry in western Maryland. Steatite from the Griffin and Mile Creek sites in Old Lyme has garnet inclusions that, although absent from New England soapstone, are present in a steatite source in eastern Maryland.[81] An alternative explanation would be trade, with a decrease in the number of non-local goods indicating a break in trade relations.

## A Modified Migration Theory

Perhaps both explanations apply. As Mid-Atlantic immigrants and traders moved northward to the Long Island Sound area, they would most likely follow coastal and riverine routes, because heavy stone goods could be most efficiently shipped by water. They would meet the riverine-dwelling Laurentian peoples rather than the more upland Narrow Point population. Additionally, Laurentian communities would be more receptive to the visitors, since their thinner, broader-bladed hunting tools depended on more easily knappable toolstone like the exotic felsites, rhyolites, argillites, and cherts, whereas the thick small-stemmed and notched points of the Narrow Point tradition did not. Unlike the local cobble quartz and quartzites, the exotic toolstones allowed for the easy removal of large flat flakes, so necessary for producing points in the Laurentian and especially the later Susquehanna styles.

## INTERPRETATIONS AND QUESTIONS

Late and Terminal Archaic base settlements in the Mid-Atlantic region exploited estuarine marshlands and major river valleys in the same way as did the later Woodland peoples in southern New England. The intense exploitation of these prolific resources caused population growth. In some areas this led to the splitting off of small populations, but in the central Delmarva peninsula (the Delaware–Maryland–northeastern Virginia coastal region) the limitation of productive zones eventually made this locally impossible.[82] It is plausible that some of these Mid-Atlantic communities emigrated northward as they followed marshlands that began developing in southern New England during late Terminal Archaic and Early Woodland times,[83] eventually joining the resident Laurentian groups yet continuing to remain in contact with their Mid-Atlantic kin. This would explain the presence of the exotic toolstone throughout 1,500 years of the archaeological record.

# 6

## Closure, Continuity, and the Seeds of Change

### *The Early Woodland Period*

I sat in a schoolroom in this town and listened to a teacher say there were no more Pequots in Ledyard because none of them lived through the massacre. But there I was and I was a Pequot living on the reservation. I might have been living on another planet.

—Theresa Bell, Mashantucket Pequot leader and former executive director
of the Mashantucket Pequot Museum and Research Center, 1990

The Archaic stage in southern New England history was followed by the four cultural periods of the Woodland stage: Early Woodland, Middle Woodland, Late Woodland, and Final Woodland. Archaeologists traditionally define each period by its distinct artifact styles and the introduction of new material to the local cultures. During these periods Woodland peoples developed major innovations: the significant use of clay containers (Early Woodland), smoking pipes (Early Woodland), the bow and arrow (late Middle Woodland), and domesticated plant foods (Late Woodland). Recent archaeological, palynological, and geological discoveries show that these cultural periods were also marked by changes in settlement patterns, social relations, and social customs such as burial ceremonies.

There is no consensus on when the Woodland Stage began: proposed dates range from about 3000 to 2500 years ago.[1] This is probably because cultural changes occurred gradually and at different times in different places. In eastern North America in general, the beginning of the Woodland stage is traditionally defined by the introduction of clay pottery.[2] The assumed date for the first *significant* use of clay pottery in the greater New York area is about 3000 B.P.[3] But because of late radiocarbon dates for Broad Spear points and steatite bowl fragments at four different sites in Connecticut—2740 B.P. and 2460 B.P. at Timothy Stevens in Glastonbury, 2740 B.P. at Cooper in Old Lyme, 2700 B.P. at Lieutenant River in Old Lyme, and 2515 B.P. at Robillard in Milford[4]—some eastern Connecticut archaeologists placed the beginnings of the Early Woodland period at around 2700 B.P.[5] Since 1984, new radiocarbon dates and research on environmental, economic, and settlement pattern changes suggest that the beginning of the Woodland stage in southern New England was probably closer to 2700 B.P. than to 3000 B.P., for additional reasons besides the fact that Terminal Archaic Broad Spear point styles continued in use until that time.

A second reason is that clay containers were first introduced during the Terminal Archaic period, but in such small quantities that they obviously were not important to the economy of either the Broad Spear or Narrow Point peoples. Radiocarbon dates clearly showed that clay containers became more common after 2750 B.P.[6]

Third, a major environmental change occurred about 2680 B.P., when there is geophysical and botanical evidence for a "Little Ice Age" in Connecticut. Fir, hemlock, and white pine needles preserved with hickory, butternut, and other species in clay deposits along the Quinnipiac River north of New Haven strongly indicate cool, moist conditions.[7] This climatic change would have been detrimental to the warmth-loving nut-bearing trees that were an economic staple for Archaic peoples. This in turn would have adversely affected two other Archaic food staples, the deer and turkey populations that fed on these trees.

Fourth, by 2450 B.P. soapstone vessels, one function of which may have been to prepare acorns for human consumption, were no longer in use. Their disappearance from the archaeological record could be an indication of chronic nut crop failures.[8] This would have been disastrous for the Broad Spear culture, whose communities depended on a narrow economy of nuts, deer, and other terrestrial resources.

Significantly, between 2900 and 2700 B.P. "all evidence" of the Broad Spear culture disappears in southeastern Connecticut[9] and in other areas of Connecticut as well. Radiocarbon dates from only two Broad Spear sites are later, Robillard in Milford and Timothy Stevens in Glastonbury. By 2450 B.P. the peoples of the Broad Spear culture were gone from Connecticut,[10] having either migrated out of the area, died off, or joined the contemporary Narrow Point peoples, who promptly took over the ecozones once occupied by the Broad Spear communities.

## CULTURAL CONTINUITY AND RESILIENCE: THE NARROW POINT TRADITION

Communities of the Narrow Point tradition continued into the Early Woodland period. Archaeological evidence from settlements at Broeder Point and Great Island in Old Lyme, Cooper site in Lyme, Long Knoll in Glastonbury, Charles Tyler site near Plainfield, Waldo-Hennessey in Branford, Perkins-Elmer in Wilton, and Indian River in Westport[11] showed that the way of life of these peoples was very similar to that of their Archaic ancestors, except for one major difference: there were more riverine and coastal sites.

### A Settlement Shift Along Waterways

Five (63 percent) of eight Early Woodland sites in the Connecticut River valley are in riverine-coastal settings.[12] In southeastern Connecticut all the known Early Woodland period settlements were in the riverine areas once occupied by Broad

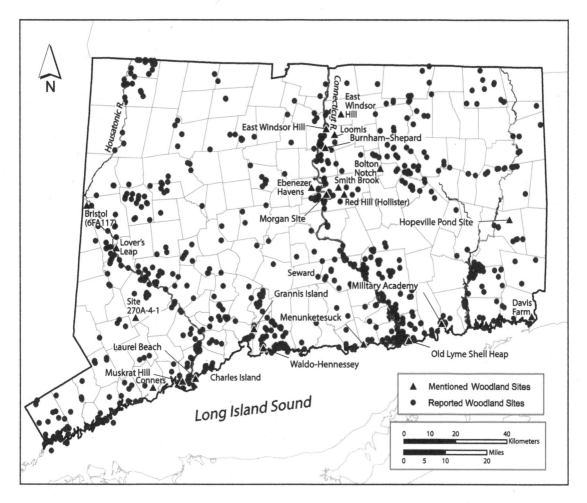

Spear communities.[13] In southwestern Connecticut, with the exception of a few inland rock shelters, Early and Middle Woodland sites are along the coast.[14] The only other Early Woodland sites reported for western Connecticut were both in the floodplain of the Housatonic River in Milford.[15] Research in the 3,500-acre (14 square kilometer) McLean Game Refuge in Simsbury, Granby, and Canton suggested a similar settlement pattern in the north-central uplands of Connecticut.[16] Archaeologists have also reported this settlement shift on Long Island, and in Rhode Island and Massachusetts.[17] Early Woodland Narrow Point sites have been interpreted as mainly seasonal and task-specific camps, with few temporary camps, where populations concentrated along rivers, interior lakes, and interior wetlands and exploited a wide range of environments.[18]

*Known Woodland sites and single point finds in Connecticut on file in the Connecticut Office of State Archaeology.*

## Waldo-Hennessey Site

The Waldo-Hennessey site, along a tidal estuary in Branford, Connecticut, was a series of shell middens occupied for short periods in the fall. The site contained a quartz cobble lithic assemblage, narrow-stemmed, Rossville, and Meadowood points, clay pottery, and more than 250,000 grams of dietary remains. A nearby

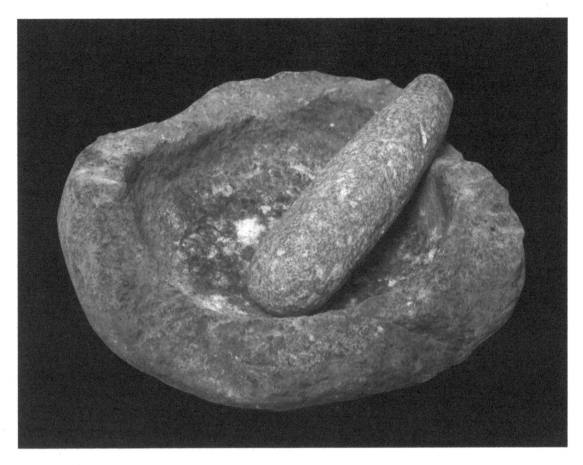

Stone mortar from Somers, Connecticut, and pestle from Wethersfield.

non-shell occupation level was dated to 3550 B.P. ±60 years, but its excavator considers the site Early Woodland, probably because of the presence of Early Woodland Meadowood points.[19]

## Marshland Habitats and Their Ecological Abundance

The settlement change in the archaeological record reflects the growth of marshlands along Connecticut's coasts and river estuaries that began with the slower rise of sea level sometime during the Terminal Archaic period.[20] The slowed currents of meltwater streams allowed fine sediments to sink and build up soil deposits, creating low and high salt marshes of salt-loving grasses that are veritable food factories, nesting areas, and nurseries for a variety of animal life.[21] Southern New England marshes contain more than fifty species of plants and produce huge amounts of edible vegetation. For example, a 12-hectare marsh in Stonington, Connecticut, produces 88 metric tons of plants annually.[22]

The decay of this vegetation releases enormous amounts of nutrients into tidal waters, the basis of a food chain that supports an amazing assortment of wildlife in dense concentrations: one hundred species of birds, thirty species of insects, twenty-five species of fish, twenty species of mammals, eighteen species of mollusks, fifteen species of crustaceans, and ten species of amphibians.[23] New

England marshes are a series of ecozones that provide a great variety of easily accessible seasonal and year-round food supplies: the bay area, lower marsh border (low marsh), high marsh, upper border, and upland.[24]

Salt marsh first began to develop along the coasts and river estuaries. Brackish and freshwater marshes subsequently developed upstream, occurring in the lower Connecticut River sometime after 2600 B.P.[25] Probably caused by a major reduction in sea-level rise during the "Little Ice Age" at the beginning of the Early Woodland period, marsh development accelerated northward, especially after 1800 B.P., when another reduction occurred.[26] The beginning of a brackish tidal marsh at Lord's Cove in Old Lyme was dated to 1515 B.P., while a freshwater tidal marsh farther north at Whalebone Cove in Lyme was dated to as late as 340 B.P.[27] Marsh production continues to this day.[28]

## Ancient Crock Pots

Woodland people continued to make and use fired clay containers. These portable, easy-to-make containers were straight-sided, wide-mouth pots with pointed bases used for slow-cooking gruels and stews in the coals of an open hearth. These pots became even more useful to Early Woodland communities that exploited marsh and riverine environments, particularly the plants that grew in these localities.

Connecticut's indigenous peoples manufactured their pots using the coiling technique. Pottery was probably made by women and girls, as it was in seventeenth-century southern New England,[29] and as suggested by the rare finger imprints found on clay coils and pot fragments.[30] The first step was to prepare the clay by removing pebbles and roots, possibly even pulverizing it into a powder, and kneading it with water and particles of crushed stone called temper into a soft, malleable mass. The temper helped to prevent shrinkage during drying and impeded cracks during firing. In later Woodland times crushed shell was also used as temper. The modified clay was sometimes stored away in underground caches to keep it moist and ready to use. At the Davis Farm site in Stonington, excavated in the 1930s, several clay caches were unearthed at Osbrook Point, some already mixed with fine oyster shell.[31]

The next step was to mold the base of the pot. Bases recovered from this period often have impressions of fabric, which suggests that the clay was placed in a basket or on a woven mat. Short clay coils were then rolled out and wound around the base to make the walls of the pot. The coils were pressed into a solid wall with a wooden paddle wrapped with cord or fabric, which also left impressions on the inner and outer surfaces of the pot. The cord impressions expanded the pot's surface and allowed for more even and quicker heating (a radiator effect). The impressions also made the pot more slip-resistant. The pots were then allowed to dry and, in the last step, were fired over an open hearth.

Pottery with both interior and exterior cord or fabric impressions is called Vinette Interior Cord-marked, or Vinette I, and is characteristic of the Early and early Middle Woodland periods. It is the oldest known pottery type in New England, having been found at Terminal Archaic sites in association with Broad

# Chronology of Major Pottery Types in Connecticut

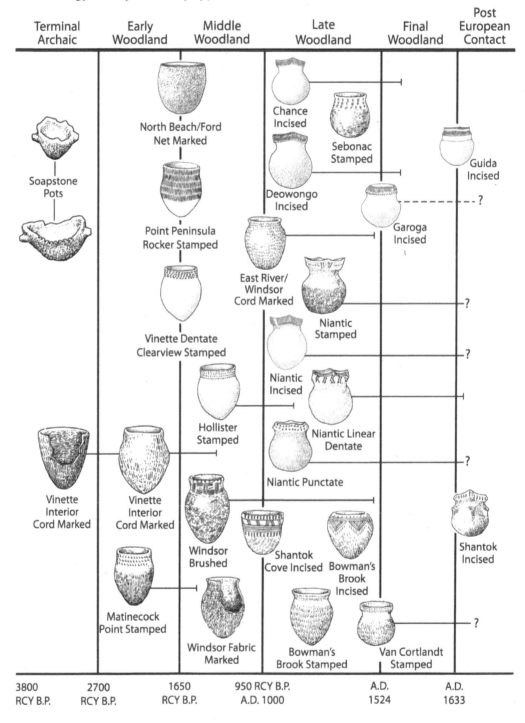

| Terminal Archaic | Early Woodland | Middle Woodland | Late Woodland | Final Woodland | Post European Contact |
|---|---|---|---|---|---|
| 3800 RCY B.P. | 2700 RCY B.P. | 1650 RCY B.P. | 950 RCY B.P. A.D. 1000 | A.D. 1524 | A.D. 1633 |

Soapstone Pots

North Beach/Ford Net Marked

Point Peninsula Rocker Stamped

Vinette Dentate Clearview Stamped

Chance Incised

Sebonac Stamped

Deowongo Incised

Guida Incised

Garoga Incised

East River/ Windsor Cord Marked

Niantic Stamped

Niantic Incised

Niantic Linear Dentate

Hollister Stamped

Niantic Punctate

Vinette Interior Cord Marked

Vinette Interior Cord Marked

Windsor Brushed

Shantok Cove Incised

Bowman's Brook Incised

Shantok Incised

Matinecock Point Stamped

Windsor Fabric Marked

Bowman's Brook Stamped

Van Cortlandt Stamped

A timeline of major diagnostic pottery styles in Connecticut.

Top, Rose Kerstetter (Oneida) demonstrating traditional pottery-making techniques in 1986. Bottom, Jeff Kalin (Cherokee descent) demonstrating how New England indigenous pottery was fired.

Spear, Orient, or Narrow Point points. Vinette I pottery is also found in the Terminal Archaic Susquehanna (Frost Island and Orient phases in New York) and Early Woodland Meadowood cultures of central and western New York.[32] Radiocarbon dates suggest that Vinette I pottery may have occurred several hundred years earlier in New England. Perhaps New England communities introduced the pottery to neighbors in New York and New Jersey through trade.

Pottery styles, their date ranges, and geographic distribution are very important to archaeologists, who use pottery fragments (sherds) to date sites and sometimes identify the people who were there, their cultural affiliations, and their social relations with other communities. Pottery styles can contain symbolic social meaning and reflect social identity. The presence of dentate and net-impressed pottery styles in Early Woodland Connecticut shows that local communities were networking with Indian societies to the south and to the north.

In the later Early Woodland period, Vinette I pottery and Modified Vinette pottery (usually smoothed on either the inside or the outside) was decorated with a rocker or dentate stamp (from the Latin for "toothlike"). Rocker stamping is produced by literally rocking the dentate stamp, or a simple curved stamp (possibly an animal rib bone or a curved bone needle or shuttle used to weave nets and mats), back and forth over the wet clay.

Undecorated net-impressed pottery also made its appearance in late Early Woodland times. The earliest in Connecticut, from Site 270A-4-1 in Newtown, dates to 2130 B.P.[33] This pottery has open-weave, netlike textile impressions produced by applying the textile, an Indian hemp fishnet or open-weave twined container such as a netted bag, directly to the wet clay. Described by early Europeans, some of these bags are still around today in museums and private collections.[34] As the Massachusetts superintendent of Indians Daniel Gookin reported in 1674,

> Several sorts of baskets were made, both great and small. Some . . . are made of rushes, some of bents [coarse grass], others of maize husks, others of a kind of silk grass, others of a kind of wild hemp, and some of the barks of trees, many of them very neat and artificial with portraitures of birds, beast, fishes, and flowers upon them in colors.[35]

Along Long Island Sound this style of pottery is known as North Beach Net-marked.[36] In southern New England, Modified Vinette, dentate-stamped, rocker-stamped, and net-impressed pottery styles all continue into the Middle Woodland period. In the middle Hudson River valley, net-impressed pottery appeared later. Dated to the Middle Woodland period, it is called Ford Net-marked.[37] The difference in names is purely geographic, because the pottery styles in all these areas are virtually identical.[38]

The origins of dentate-stamped pottery lie to the north, as early as 2640 B.P. ±50 years at the Oxbow site in New Brunswick, in Canada, 2619 B.P. ±220 years at the Burley site on Lake Huron, and 2600 B.P. ±220 years at Site 41.40 on Kidder Point in Maine. In the upper Delaware River valley it was dated to 2350 B.P. ±95 years and 2050 B.P. ±135 years at the Fawcett site. Net-impressed pottery, in contrast, has southern and Mid-Atlantic roots. In North Carolina net-marked pottery predates 2750 B.P.[39] In the Delmarva region (Delaware-Maryland-Virginia) it is at least as early as 2450 B.P.,[40] and in the upper Delaware Valley it dates from about 2450 to 2350 B.P.[41]

## Population Decline or Settlement Change?

Because of the relatively fewer Early Woodland sites in southern New England compared with the earlier Terminal Archaic and subsequent Middle Woodland periods, several archaeologists have suggested that there was a population decline—or even a population collapse—during this period.[42] Because the local

Narrow Point tradition extended from the Late Archaic well into the Woodland stage, some archaeologists suggest that some Early Woodland Narrow Point settlements that did not contain pottery were being misinterpreted as Archaic sites. This would have created an inaccurate picture of how many sites there were.[43] However, radiocarbon studies[44] continued to show a decline in Early Woodland sites for southern New England. A more recent study of Connecticut radiocarbon dates[45] also showed a decline beginning about 3000 B.P., and the number of sites remains below the Late Archaic levels until the beginning of the Late Woodland period, around 1000 B.P.

Research on the distribution of sites suggests three plausible scenarios: (1) a population decline occurred during the Early Woodland period; (2) there was a change in settlement pattern, with populations grouped in the most productive ecozones, possibly for longer periods; or (3) both a decline and population grouping occurred. This last scenario seems to best fit the archaeological and environmental data. Environmental factors led to the demise of one of the two Terminal Archaic populations (Broad Spear), which would have resulted in a decline in Early Woodland sites. The opening of their riverine environment to Narrow Point communities around the same time that salt marshes began expanding led to an increase in seasonal camps with satellite task-specific camps, and a decline in temporary camps. In the closely spaced ecozones of a marshland environment, larger groups of people could exploit a variety of food sources quickly while still living at the main, seasonal camp.

## INTERREGIONAL SOCIAL RELATIONSHIPS

Although there may have been a hiatus in major population movements and migrations during the Early Woodland period, interregional social relationships persisted. To understand them we need to look at the big picture of what was happening east of the Mississippi River in general from about 3500 to 1750 B.P. In the Midwest in particular this was a time of momentous religious and sociopolitical change represented by grandiose mortuary rites, the monumental architecture of burial mounds (some several hundred feet in diameter and several stories high), animal effigy and geometric mounds, other earthworks (some with possible astronomical functions), and lavish tombs with mortuary items of exotic materials and artwork.

### Interaction Spheres and Burial Cults

These creations have been attributed to the Adena "culture," the Hopewell "culture," the Hopewellian Interaction Sphere, and the Eastern Burial Cult.[46] Some researchers have named several Eastern Woodlands mortuary complexes that date from Late Archaic to early Middle Woodland times the Eastern Burial Cult. Included were the Red Ocher and Glacial Kame mortuary complexes of the upper Great Lakes area; the mound-building cultures participating in the Adena and Hopewell interaction systems centered in the Midwest; the western New York Middlesex (presently considered part of the Meadowood culture, which is thought to have evolved into the Point Peninsula culture); and the Orient complex on eastern Long Island. These complexes share certain traits: cremation of bone bundles; redeposition of cremated remains; non-cremated skeletal remains; red ochre in burials; caches of leaf-shaped stone blades; ritual killing of artifacts; and finely manufactured grave items.[47]

No such Woodland period burial mounds have been identified in Connecticut, although there are Archaic-period burial mounds with stonework in eastern Canada and northern New England. Interestingly, they seem to be earlier than the more well known mounds to the west.

The Middle Archaic burial mound at the L'Anse Amour site in Labrador was a circular tumulus 3 feet high and 25 feet wide. The Middle Archaic Tumulus II at the Bradon site in Quebec was a burial mound 30 feet wide.[48] The Morrill Point Mound site in Salisbury, Massachusetts, contained a Middle Archaic earthen mound whose cremation burials provided an average radiocarbon date of 7165 B.P., which like the Canadian sites is several thousand years earlier than the New York and Midwest mound sites! The 6-foot-high mound is 180 feet in diameter and is partly enclosed by a three-sided dry-laid stone wall. Grave goods included typical Middle Archaic ground stone tools.[49] The Late Archaic Ketcham's Island site in western Vermont contained a low earthen mound built over the remains of a 15-foot-wide circular dwelling and a red ochre burial.[50]

The shared traits suggest that the peoples who practiced the earlier Late Archaic mortuary ceremonialism of the Great Lakes area passed on their religious ideology to later Adena, Middlesex, and Hopewell communities—popularly known as the "Moundbuilders." This ideology, with its rituals and material objects, was elaborated on by Early Woodland societies in the Ohio Valley and western New York and disseminated over wide areas, including Connecticut. This interaction sphere was probably originally economic, with communication networks following well-known Archaic trade and migration routes. Later interactions involved social and ideological values as well. The rise of these Midwestern religious cults and their accompanying mortuary ceremonialism probably created a need for exotic materials that increased interregional trading relationships. The escalating desire for more non-local, high-status goods led to the creation of an intricate trading network that involved many different Indian societies throughout the Eastern Woodlands and beyond (for example, obsidian objects from sources in Utah, Nevada, California, and Oregon have been found at sites in New England and the Mid-Atlantic).[51]

Ultimately, the Early Woodland and early Middle Woodland Midwestern Interaction Sphere was a trade network that exchanged not only objects, but also ideas. The differences in preparation and contents of graves in Ohio and other areas strongly suggest social stratification and the presence of a political elite (chiefdom or possibly incipient state society) that oversaw the religious ceremonies and controlled the flow of goods. The interaction sphere seems to have fallen apart in the early centuries A.D. No one knows why or how this happened.[52]

### The Exotic and the Enigmatic: "Moundbuilder" Connections

Indigenous southern New England has often been considered a backwater of provincial communities with little or no knowledge of the exciting social dynamics stirring other Eastern Woodland societies. This is not true. Early Woodland New Englanders were quite aware of the economic, social, and spiritual dynamics of their western neighbors. Cultural items such as exotic stone tools and nonlocal projectile point styles from several Early Woodland sites in southern New England and coastal New York imply either direct associations with Midwestern "Moundbuilder" traders or indirect economic trade relationships through contacts with intermediate communities such as the Meadowood-Middlesex communities in west-central New York and those in the Mid-Atlantic region.[53]

### Meadowood Points and Caches

Meadowood points and blades are common to the Meadowood-Middlesex culture of central and western New York, which some researchers associate with the Adena culture.[54] Usually made from Onondaga chert, which derives from a limestone formation that crops out in the heart of the Meadowood-Middlesex homelands,[55] the points and blades are present in relatively low numbers in Connecticut sites. Often they are surface finds or located in disturbed contexts such as plow zones. At the Waldo-Hennessey site in Branford, however, they were found in undisturbed association with Narrow Point types, Rossville points, and Vinette I pottery.[56] At the Lovers Leap 2 site, which overlooked the Housatonic River valley in New Milford, a firepit associated with a Meadowood point gave a radiocarbon date of 2335 B.P.[57]

More dramatic are the underground deposits, or caches, of Meadowood blades unearthed in several Connecticut townships: 31 in the Seward Site Cache in Durham; 125 in the Loomis Cache in South Windsor; more than two hundred in the Ebenezer Havens Cache at Wethersfield; and 499 blades in the Smith Brook Site Cache in a spring in Glastonbury.[58] Meadowood caches have also been reported from central Massachusetts and eastern Long Island.[59] Except for the Smith Brook cache, all are from disturbed or unknown contexts. All were solitary finds with no other cultural remains. All but one of the New England caches were located in the Connecticut River valley. A cache of 160 Meadowood blades was

Meadowood-style projectile points.

Twenty-six of a cache of 129 dolomitic chert Meadowood blades from South Windsor.

Undated cache of blades *in situ*, from the Conners site in Fairfield, Connecticut. Shape and material suggest a Middle Woodland age for these blades, possibly a Fox Creek association.

associated with a cremation burial at the Bristol site (6FA117) in Sherman in the Housatonic drainage.[60]

Meadowood blade caches were found at several sites on Long Island: Rockville Centre in the southwestern portion of the island, and Mattituck, Peconic, and Southold at its far eastern end, the latter situated almost directly across the Sound from the mouth of the Connecticut River. A blade cache on the southwestern shore of Massapequa Lake was associated with a radiocarbon date of 2385 B.P.

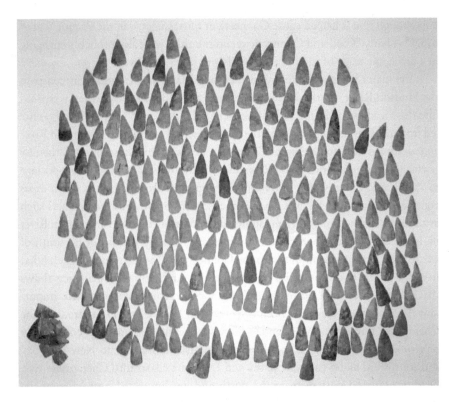

Cache of 499 Meadowood blades found in a spring at the Smith Brook site in Glastonbury.

This Early Woodland Massapequa cache was located at the crossroads of a south-running stream and an east–west Indian footpath mentioned as early as A.D. 1690 in the town records of Oyster Bay.[61] Paths such as these were major trade routes, connecting interior New York and the Mid-Atlantic communities with all of Long Island's settlements to its north coast bays, where dugout canoes could easily run traders—and settlers—back and forth across Long Island Sound to Connecticut's shores. The large river valleys and the sound were the major highways by which Woodland peoples communicated and traded.

### The Early Wampum Trade

But what were the Connecticut people trading for the Meadowood cache blades? Probably steatite[62] and marine shell. Small disk-shaped white and purple marine shell beads, called *wampum* by Native New Englanders and others,[63] have been excavated from upstate New York Meadowood sites in the area that eventually became Iroquois homelands; in that region, shell beads occur as early as 5,500 years ago.[64] Coastal people also produced short, thick, and long (2 inches or more) cylindrical shell beads.[65]

Wampum figured strongly in Native American spirituality as a purifier and protector against evil forces.[66] Deceased tribal members were often dressed in wampum jewelry and wampum-decorated clothing to aid them in their journey to the Creator's house.[67] Considering the extensive wampum trade carried on by post-contact tribes in southern coastal New England—which was important enough that it helped cause Connecticut's first major war, the Pequot War of 1637[68]—Early Woodland Connecticut communities were also probably engaging in a profitable trade of marine shell beads and other jewelry.

The major trade route followed the Long Island and Connecticut coasts to the Hudson River, up the Hudson and onto the Mohawk River, then westward into the Meadowood homelands of west-central New York.[69] Another likely route led from the Connecticut coast up the Connecticut River to the Farmington River and westward into northwestern Connecticut or western Massachusetts, then by portage west to the Housatonic River and northward with another short portage to the Hoosic River, which flows into the upper Hudson River just north of its confluence with the Mohawk River. The discovery of Midwestern artifacts such as a Fulton Turkey Tail point, birdstones, and boatstones in the Farmington River drainage, and Meadowood caches in Connecticut Valley towns not far south of where the Farmington empties into the Connecticut River, strongly suggests that it was a major trade route during this period. Archaeological evidence shows that the trade networks flowed south from Connecticut as well as north. Important Adena-related sites have been discovered in New Jersey, Delaware, and the Chesapeake Bay area of Maryland.[70] From Connecticut, these areas could easily be visited by canoe by traveling through Long Island Sound into New York Bay and southward along the New Jersey and Delaware coasts into Chesapeake Bay. Dentate-stamped pottery from the north and net-impressed pottery from the south—or their techniques of manufacture—most likely were introduced into Connecticut through these networks.

### Adena-Rossville Points

Adena and Rossville points are usually considered two different point types, but are sometimes difficult to distinguish. Rossville points are common to coastal New York and the Mid-Atlantic region. True Adena points are associated with the mound-building Adena culture centered in Ohio. In Connecticut both point types were manufactured from local stone such as quartz as well as exotic cherts. Again, only a few of these points were infrequently found in Connecticut sites of the local Narrow Point tradition. No caches of them have ever been reported.

### Fulton Turkey Tail Points

Another Midwestern point style found on Connecticut sites is the Fulton Turkey Tail, medium- to wide-bladed, corner-notched points with an expanded base shaped like a plucked turkey tail. Found throughout the Southeast and Midwest, from Alabama to the Great Lakes and from eastern Missouri to eastern New York, they have been dated to between 3500 and 2500 B.P. Most Turkey Tail points were made from rock types that crop out in southern Indiana, southern Illinois, and northern Kentucky, signs of an extensive trade network centered in the Ohio River valley.[71] They are rare but present in Connecticut, having been found near the Quinnipiac, Connecticut, Farmington, and Thames rivers—the state's major waterways—like the Meadowood caches.[72] A flint Turkey Tail point

Early Woodland projectile points: top, Fulton Turkey Tail points; bottom, Adena-style and Rossville points.

discovered at the Lovers Leap site in New Milford was seemingly contemporary with a rolled copper bead and Orient points (a style that continued into Early Woodland times).[73] The distribution of Turkey Tail points confirms that the large river valleys and Long Island Sound had become the main trade and communication routes by at least Early Woodland times.

## Ceremonial Mysteries: Pipes, Boatstones, and Birdstones

Other Midwestern artifacts characteristic of the Adena culture that occur sporadically in southern New England are cigar-shaped blocked-end tube pipes, boatstones, and birdstones. Although platform pipes are characteristic of Midwestern cultures participating in the Hopewellian interactions sphere, several have been reported from Connecticut,[74] including an undecorated stone platform pipe found in Durham and a beautifully crafted platform pipe recovered from a site in Milford. A steatite frog effigy pipe found in Norwich is also reminiscent of Hopewellian platform pipes.

### Sacred Smoke

The smoking pipe made its first appearance early in Woodland times. A clay blocked-end tube pipe found in an obvious Adena association is the earliest known smoking pipe in Connecticut. It suggests, tentatively, that smoking was introduced to Connecticut's indigenous peoples by the Midwestern Adena people, possibly as part of a mortuary or sociopolitical ceremony. Eventually, Native Americans introduced smoking to the European traders and explorers, who quickly adopted the custom and took it to Europe as a recreational activity. Pipe smoking, however, had much more important ceremonial and medicinal functions in Native American culture.[75] As Lenape tribal elder Nora "Touching Leaves Woman" Thompson Dean told journalist-historian C. A. Weslager:

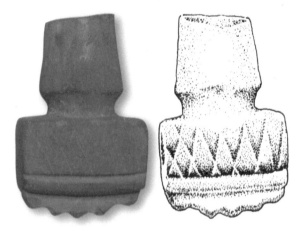

An incised stone platform pipe from Durham, Connecticut, 2.5 inches (6.5 centimeters). The drawing shows the incised decoration on the other side of the pipe.

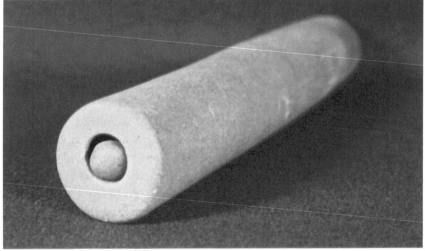

Artifacts from the Hollister (Red Hill) site in Glastonbury. Top, a ground stone "ball" and sphere. Bottom, a blocked-end tube, the earliest known pipe style in Connecticut.

To the Delawares, tobacco was a sacred plant used to aid in diseases or distress, to bring good fortune, to assist those in need, and to allay fear. On this occasion [a naming ceremony] it served to propitiate any evil spirits that might have found their way to the group.[76]

Early European documents describe indigenous pipe smoking as an important part of political, religious, and curative ceremonies.[77] It was thought to drive out evil, conjure up good spirits, and produce good thoughts and friendship, although tobacco was not the only plant smoked (other wild herbs were used as well). The tobacco pouch was an important component of an Indian man's clothing.[78] In 1643 Roger Williams described a typical political meeting among the Narragansetts, in which tobacco smoking played a central part.

> Their manner is upon any tidings to sit round, double or treble, or more, as their numbers be; I have seene neer a thousand in a round, where English could not well neere halfe so many have sitten: Every man hath his pipe of their Tobacco, and a deepe silence they make, and attention give to him that speaketh; and many of them will deliver themselves, either in a relation of news, or in a consultation, with very emphaticall speech and great action, commonly an houre, and sometimes two hours together.[79]

Local tribes still use tobacco in religious ceremonies to purify participants and to contact the Creator or other spiritual beings with sacred smoke rising toward the heavens. I have seen it used this way at weddings, funerals, and public powwows, along with sweet grass, cedar, and sage. The rite is normally performed by a Native American spiritual leader, often accompanied by an assistant. If the ceremony is conducted in a sacred circle, the leader holds the burning plant material in a large shell and wafts its smoke over the body of each individual with a fan made of eagle feathers.

Shells have spiritual significance for indigenous peoples, as do eagle feathers. The eagle is revered as sacred for its strong, courageous, warriorlike character and close relationship to the Creator, because it flies closest to the abode of the spirit world. The eagle is considered an intermediary between the Creator and people, with the ability to convey prayers and messages to the Creator.[80] The Golden Eagle is the most sacred, because it flies at the highest altitudes.[81] A modern eyewitness account of a rare public Native American reburial ceremony at the Morgan site in Rocky Hill around 1990[82] reveals the feeling of deep spirituality and emotional atmosphere that accompanies these and other indigenous ceremonies.

> Soon after the bodies were ready, the Indian spiritual leader reappeared. Carrying a basket of small pieces of dry firewood, a bird feather fan with elaborate beaded handle, and wearing necklaces of bear claws, shell, beads, and with a small white feather thong braided into the hair at the back of his head, he had the air of an archbishop passing down the aisle of a cathedral. . . . He placed an abalone shell filled with cedar, sweet grass, and fragrant materials by his fire. A hot ember set into the shell sent a thin, sweet smoke rising.

The ceremony was like taking communion. Each person waited to be included. First he purified each of us in turn, brushing the smoke from his shell in his hand toward one's head and then whole body. He offered prayer, in English for our benefit, asking that the persons now returned to their proper place be reunited with their spirits.[83]

### Boatstones and Birdstones

Boatstones and birdstones are enigmatic polished ground stone objects made from exotic materials. Unfortunately, in Connecticut most are surface finds or from amateur collections, so we have virtually no information about their associations or use (but see the discussion of the Red Hill site below for the direct association of boatstones with human burials). A boatstone is literally shaped like a small dugout canoe, with two drilled holes in its bottom. Some have a groove carved be-

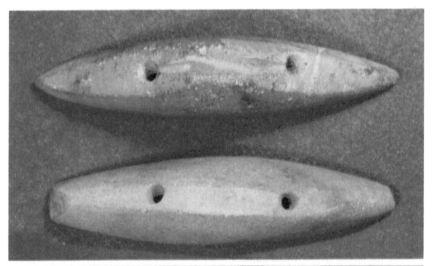

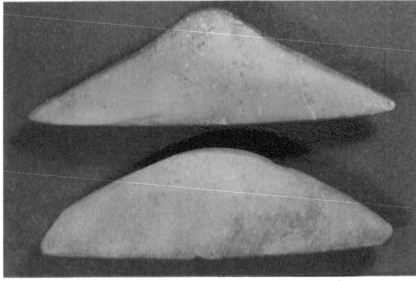

Two carved and polished boatstones found at the Hollister (Red Hill) site in Glastonbury, Connecticut (two sides shown).

A banded slate birdstone from Charles Island, Milford, Connecticut; an incised birdstone from East Granby, Connecticut, and the head of a pop-eyed birdstone from the Housatonic River valley.

tween the two holes, apparently to better guide the tie that attached it to another object. Boatstones were found in Burlington, Farmington, Plainville, Southington, and Glastonbury.[84]

Excavations at the Tremper burial mound on the Scioto River in Ohio uncovered two boat-shaped artifacts filled with quartzite pebbles.[85] Might they have been used as rattles? Or did the pebbles themselves have some spiritual meaning? Northeastern Indian belief systems regarded specific colors and qualities as metaphors for social values. The shiny, white, translucent quality of quartz and quartzite was thought to assure physical, spiritual, and social well-being.[86] Anthropologist George Hamell, who has done extensive research on symbolism among indigenous peoples living in the Northeast, reports:

> Shell, crystal, and native copper were their owner's assurance and insurance of long life (immortality through resuscitation), wellbeing (the absence of ill-being), and success, particularly in the conceptually related activities of hunting and fishing, warfare, and courtship. The archaeological, ethnological, and historical data strongly suggest that at least some of the earliest analogous European trade goods, such as glass and copper/brass wares, were annexed to this value system.[87]

A birdstone is shaped like a perched bird in profile; sometimes it has large, protruding eyes.[88] It also has drill holes in its base. The Institute for American Indian Studies in Washington, Connecticut, houses three birdstones from Connecticut. Two were found in the towns of East Granby and Milford; the provenience of the third, partial birdstone (head only) is the Housatonic River valley.

The location of two birdstones once housed at the Slater Museum in Norwich (one from Colchester and one from near Lebanon) is presently unknown. There are two Connecticut specimens at the American Museum of Natural History in New York City, one from Woodbury and the other of unknown provenience. Two other Connecticut birdstones, one from Hamden and the second of unknown provenience, are at the Museum of the American Indian, Heye Foundation, also in New York City. A soapstone birdstone from Terryville is illustrated in an 1897 report.[89]

Little else is known about these artifacts. Speculation on their use includes as personal ornaments, atlatl weights or handles, clan emblems, and ceremonial objects. Birdstones have been found near Adena burial mounds and in Adena-related graves in western New York,[90] which suggests a spiritual function. So does the shape, because post-contact Native Americans traditionally associate birds with the spirit world, often as intermediaries or spirit guides.[91]

### "Adena" Mortuary Ceremonialism in Connecticut

Of the three "Adena-like" burial sites reported in Connecticut, two are near each other in East Windsor and Glastonbury in the Connecticut River valley. The third site is in the coastal town of Milford. They contained primary, articulated skeletons that are the earliest known inhumations (non-cremated human remains) in the state. They not only included exotic mortuary offerings, but also contained evidence of burial ceremonies characteristic of the Adena culture. These sites help make the case that social relations between Connecticut communities and those of the Ohio River valley and western New York were not merely economic, but ideological as well. An alternate explanation is that the deceased were members of an Adena trading party who, dying far from their Midwestern homeland, were given an Adena burial by their comrades.[92]

### *East Windsor Hill Site*

An "Adena-like" burial at East Windsor Hill, in East Windsor, Connecticut,[93] had been sprinkled with red ochre and contained a flexed skeleton associated with *Olivella* shell beads, shell columella beads, a "mother-of-pearl" bead, and a circular shell bead, probably from a shell necklace. Shells of *Olivella,* a southern genus of marine sea snails from the warm Atlantic waters off the coasts of Florida and the Carolinas, are not found in Long Island Sound. The grave also contained an enigmatic wood fragment with a hole drilled through it, and a blade made from Ohio flint. The flint and the *Olivella* shells strongly suggest local participation in the Adena interaction sphere.

### *Red Hill Site*

The Red Hill (Hollister) site was located on a terrace overlooking the east bank of the Connecticut River in Glastonbury. The information we have from three Adena-like burials found during construction of a condominium complex north of Red Hill in Glastonbury is from salvage excavations. One burial had been completely destroyed by the bulldozer. What remained was the base of the circular burial pit and some copper-stained skull and unidentifiable bone fragments, meaning that the head or neck of the corpse had been decorated with some type of copper ornamentation.[94]

Burial 2 contained the skull and neck of an individual with a necklace of barrel-shaped, rolled copper beads. A reddish boatstone near its wrists was made from a very fine-grained stone, possibly Ohio pipestone (fireclay).[95] A small fragment of wood found in the concavity of the boatstone supports the idea that it had once been attached to a flat wooden object. Possibly the object was held in the hands of the deceased or tied to his wrist, perhaps as a rattle. The skeleton was articulated and a primary burial, not a secondary bundle, with the head pointed east and the face to the south. Although the acidic northeastern soils had destroyed the remainder of the skeleton, fortunately the salts from the necklace had preserved its uppermost portion.[96] Perhaps this is why no inhumations, or non-cremated burials, have been reported for earlier cultural periods.

The third pit was undisturbed. It contained a boatstone of exotic gray banded slate, a rock type usually found in both the Great Lakes region and in the Ohio River valley.[97] Below the boatstone was a quartzite knife and a large flake; below these was a complete miniature clay pot, broken in pieces. It may have collapsed from the pressure of the heavy equipment above it, or it could have been ritually killed. The pot was plain, grit-tempered, with a rounded base and wide mouth. It was 5.5 inches (14 centimeters) high with a diameter of 6 inches (more than 15 centimeters) at the rim. There were calcined bone particles near the pit bottom, and the entire pit had been saturated with red ochre. A blocked-end tube pipe of Ohio fireclay a little over 6 inches long, an egg-shaped stone with wear polish, and a bi-pointed but rounded pecked stone were found near the burials. The pipe contained black charred residue in its tube and a polished pebble with soot on one side. The pebble, used as a check valve, kept the smoker from inhaling the burning plant material producing the smoke.

### Laurel Beach Site

A third Adena-like burial site was investigated in 2004 during construction of a sewer line in the Laurel Beach section of Milford.[98] The grave of a young adult male 21 to 30 years of age was accidentally disturbed by trenching operations. The body was flexed and lying on its right side, facing south, toward Long Island Sound, and heading west-southwest. Only the upper portion of the skeleton remained, stained green and preserved by the leaching of copper salts from jewelry that had once adorned the neck and face. Three chert flakes in direct association with the burial and one Orient-like chalcedony projectile point, one large chert biface, two chert flakes, and two chert endscrapers were also recovered from the dirt backpiles. The site's excavators interpreted the cultural remains as exotic materials carried into Connecticut by Adena traders, one of whom died during the trip.

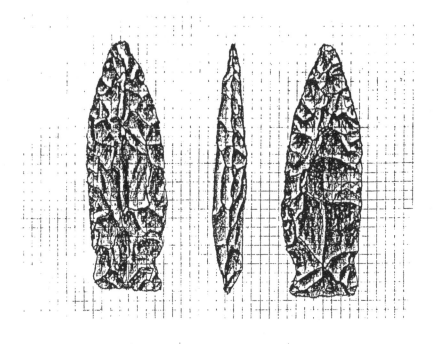

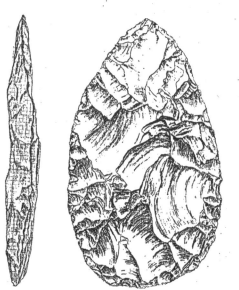

Drawings of an Orient projectile point of an unidentified material (top, length 70 millimeters, width 23 mm, breadth 9 mm) and a chert biface (bottom, length 192 millimeters, width 111 mm, breadth 24 mm) from an Adena-like burial in Laurel Beach, Milford, illustrated from three sides. Striations on this tool suggest that it was used in woodworking activities.

## Other Early Woodland Burial Sites

There are only two other reported examples of Early Woodland graves in Connecticut. The Bristol site (6FA117) on the western side of the state in Sherman in the Housatonic drainage contained a cremation burial associated with a cache of 160 Meadowood points.[99] At the upland and inland Bolton Notch site in eastern Connecticut a single cremation burial was dated to 2650 B.P. ±90 years. Unlike the other contemporary Early Woodland cremation burial site and the earlier

Broad Spear cremations, it had no mortuary artifacts, red ochre, or any other evidence of a ceremony, which suggests that it may be a Narrow Point burial.[100] Why is there no evidence of mortuary ritual like the other Early Woodland burials? Is it because Adena ritual items and the ideology they symbolized only extended to riverine and coastal communities, and inland societies were outside the influence of the interaction sphere? Or did the riverine communities in the sphere control the distribution of its trade goods, and enjoy the benefits of higher status and power, or both? More surveys of inland and upland sites are needed to answer these questions.

### Introduction of the Proto-Algonkian Language

Proto-Eastern Algonkian is the ancestor of the Eastern Algonkian languages spoken by all southern New England tribes post–European contact (and still to this day in some cases). This ancestral language diverged from its parent—Proto-Algonkian, thought to be from a homeland in the Great Lakes region—sometime between 3000 and 2500 B.P.[101] Recent developments in linguistics and archaeology prompted the suggestion that Proto-Eastern Algonkian was introduced by the Eastern Burial Cult societies of the Glacial Kame and Meadowood-Middlesex cultural traditions in Canada and northern New York (supported in the discussion of Meadowood points and caches above).[102]

Artifacts related to the Ohio mound-building Adena culture and the several "Adena-like" burials in Connecticut at the East Windsor Hill, Red Hill, and Laurel Beach sites might be used to support this theory. Interpreting these Adena-like materials as being funneled into Connecticut through Meadowood middlemen can help sustain this hypothesis. Other archaeological evidence provides support for this contention (that is, the evidence for Meadowood socioeconomic connections discussed above). Subsequent associations with the Point Peninsula culture, thought to have evolved from Meadowood (discussed in Chapter 7), would have strengthened the retention and spread of Eastern Algonkian languages among Connecticut's indigenous peoples.

## INTERPRETATIONS AND QUESTIONS

Much of what we know about Early Woodland peoples is economic—where they lived, what they ate, what tools they used, and how important exotic stone was to them. Even that information is scanty. Why do we know so little about these hardy little communities that overcame frustrating climatic fluctuations and participated in a wide-ranging interaction sphere with powerful stratified societies to the west?

Why have so few undisturbed Early Woodland sites been professionally excavated? An intensive archaeological survey of the lower Connecticut River valley in 1984 uncovered only eight.[103] Since then few additional sites have been reported. The extensive archaeological surveys for the Iroquois Gas Pipeline project that ran through much of western Connecticut uncovered only two Early Woodland sites.[104]

One reason is that there are relatively fewer of them than those from earlier and later cultural periods. Second, Woodland-stage occupations in general are usually mixed together in the plow zones throughout Connecticut, where farming has been practiced since European settlement. Plowing churns the soil to about 12 to 18 inches (30 to 45 centimeters) below the surface, muddling *in situ* artifact contexts and destroying cultural features. Luckily, cultural features below the plow zone are normally undisturbed and can be used to interpret activities at a Woodland site even though the actual living floors have been destroyed. Unfortunately, Early Woodland sites tend to have fewer cultural features than the later Middle and Late Woodland sites. Also, the local Early Woodland communities in Connecticut were continuations of Archaic Narrow Point societies, so their material cultures were virtually identical. Without charcoal for radiocarbon dating and without the presence of exotic "Adena" items, Early Woodland settlements cannot be distinguished from those of the earlier Terminal Archaic Narrow Point peoples. This identity problem also extends to other areas of New England.[105]

Where are the Early Woodland houses? How were communities organized socially and politically? Where is the evidence for recreational and children's activities? What of local art and aesthetic traditions? Were they distinct from the art and jewelry dispersed to all corners of the Adena interaction sphere? How involved were local communities in the Adena religio-economic phenomenon? Were all communities equally affected, or only those along the major water routes? And, more importantly, *if* Narrow Point people did adopt Adena mortuary ceremonialism, *why?* Could it be that environmental fluctuations created economic stress that expressed itself through spiritual ceremonies? Undisturbed seasonal and multiseasonal settlements are urgently needed to paint a fuller, clearer picture of the everyday lives of Early Woodland peoples and their participation in the Eastern Burial Cult and Adena and Meadowood interaction spheres.

Woodland communities were infinitely transformed by the consequences of marshland development. The new food sources, dense concentrations of seasonal and year-round foodstuffs, and their location in close and easily accessible ecozones promoted economic recovery from climatic uncertainties, new and more efficient technology, and population concentrations in riverine and coastal areas conducive to interregional social relations and trade. These sociocultural trends show up in the Middle and Late Woodland periods, when economic prosperity, population growth, and semi-sedentary settlement culminated in discrete tribal societies.

# 7

## Prosperity and Population Growth

### *The Middle Woodland Period*

Every adult is a teacher.

> —Chief Harold Tantaquidgeon, Mohegan chief, World War II
> hero, and co-founder of the Tantaquidgeon Museum, 1979

Mohegan oral tradition also requires that we internalize its lessons in order to complete the process of transmitting cultural information. We ritualize words, phrases, and beliefs about people, place, events, and spirit beings as they pass from one generation to the next. This method of cultural transmission promotes deep understanding. My great-uncle, Chief Harold Tantaquidgeon, taught me, *"if you can forget it, you never really knew it."*

> —Melissa Fawcett Zobel, Mohegan leader, tribal historian, and medicine woman, 2000

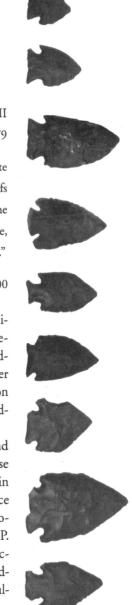

By the Middle Woodland period (about 1650 to 950 RCY B.P.) climatic conditions had stabilized. Paleobotanists, geologists, ecologists, and geophysicists report no evidence for environmental change until the beginning of the Late Woodland period around A.D. 1000.[1] Sea level continued to rise, but at a much slower rate. Marshlands continued to flourish and expand, producing dense vegetation that provided homes, nurseries, and food for more and more animal life, including human communities.

Several major cultural changes occurred between 1650 and 950 B.P., and a major environmental shift at the end of this period likely accelerated those changes. At about 1650 B.P. the influence of the Ohio Adena culture ended in southern New England. Also about this time Mid-Atlantic cultural materials once again began turning up in Connecticut sites, probably from renewed trading associations, another southern population movement, or both. At around 950 B.P. the onset of a "Little Climatic Warming" period, the arrival of maize and its accompanying technology, and the migration of Munsee peoples from the Mid-Atlantic region into Connecticut all marked the onset of the Late Woodland cultural period.

## CULTURAL STABILITY AND A REKINDLING
## OF SOUTHERN CONNECTIONS

In Connecticut, early Middle Woodland peoples continued to live in much the same way as their Early Woodland ancestors, with some notable changes. These changes came gradually. For example, the Second Hill Brook site, a small, mainly Middle Woodland tool manufacturing workshop in Roxbury in the Shepaug River drainage of western Connecticut, contained dentate- and rocker-stamped pottery, narrow-stemmed points, and other tool types typical of the traditional quartz cobble core industry used by local indigenous communities for several thousand years. At this site, 94 percent of the stone artifacts were of quartz, with only 6 percent of other source material present, including chert and argillite.[2] In New Preston, ongoing excavations at the multicomponent Deer Run site have unearthed a similar Middle Woodland complex.[3] On the other side of the state the Middle Woodland assemblage from the Cooper site in Lyme had a similar material culture. Dated to 1490 B.P., it also contained narrow-stemmed points, dentate-stamped pottery, and a quartz cobble industry, with most stone artifacts made from quartz; 15 percent were manufactured from exotic cherts.

In the lower Connecticut River valley, communities continued their seasonal rounds, with increasing dependence on and settlement near expanding tidal marshlands and riverine wetlands.[4] Many seasonal and multiseasonal camp sites with Middle Woodland artifacts, relatively numerous food remains, and cooking and storage features were located along the Connecticut River during this time. The Hamburg Cove site, in Lyme, more than 100 yards (about 100 meters) north of Cooper and also dated to 1490 B.P., was a large seasonal settlement that contained post molds, hearths, and remains of deer, turtle, and small mammals, indicative of a spring–summer occupation. Other seasonal camps contained dietary information that reflected summer and fall occupations.[5]

### Cultural Changes in the Early Middle Woodland Period

The main characteristics that distinguished early Middle Woodland communities in the lower Connecticut River valley from their Early Woodland predecessors were (1) the absence of upland seasonal and base residential settlements (although upland temporary camp sites were common), (2) higher concentrations of people along rivers, and (3) more exotic stone materials (as much as 5 to 10 percent of the lithic assemblage).[6] These settlement changes are probably indicative of increasing sedentism within riverine environments. Geological and botanical evidence from the Hartford area suggests these changes occurred upriver as well. A decrease in tree pollens with a corresponding increase in herbaceous pollens, flooding, and sedimentation at about 1500 B.P. indicate human land-clearing activities along the floodplain.[7]

A study of the few discrete early Middle Woodland components in western Connecticut supported the findings in eastern Connecticut that large settlements were in major riverine localities and only small temporary camps in the uplands.[8]

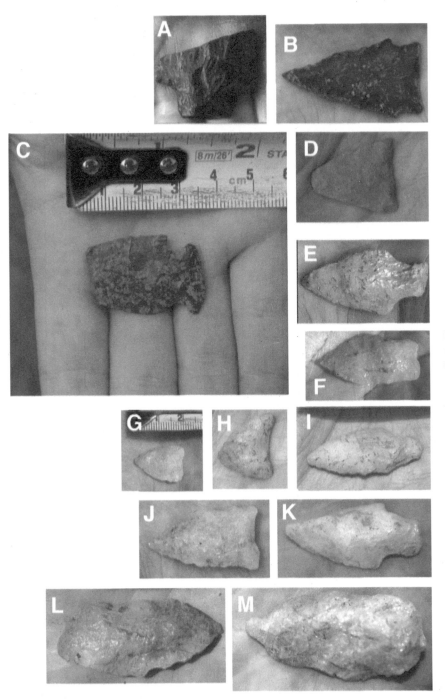

Projectile points from the multicomponent Deer Run site. A, base of a chert Terminal Archaic Snook Kill point. B, chert Late Archaic Vosburg point. C, chert side-notched point. D, quartzite Late Archaic Beekman Triangle point. E, quartz Wading River point of the Narrow Point tradition. F, quartz Middle Woodland Fox Creek Stemmed point. G, H, quartz Late Archaic Squibnocket Triangle points. I, quartz Squibnocket Stemmed point of the Narrow Point tradition. J, quartz Late Archaic Brewerton Eared Triangle point. K, quartz stemmed knife of the Narrow Point tradition. L, leaf-shaped quartz knife. M, quartzite bifacial preform.

Rocker Stamped and Dentate Stamped pottery types are characteristic styles from the early Middle Woodland period. The people who used the two Rocker Stamped and Dentate Stamped vessels represented by these rim sherds from the Deer Run site likely left the Fox Creek point labeled F in the previous figure, as well as some of the many points from the Narrow Point tradition found at the site. Top, exterior of rocker dentate-stamped rim sherds; center, interior of the same sherds, showing rocker-dentate decoration. Bottom, dentate-stamped rim sherd (exterior surface).

The increase in the number and size of storage pits at Middle Woodland sites could be an indication of increasing sedentism.[9] A large seasonal early Middle Woodland component at Site 294-25-2 in the Housatonic floodplain in Milford contained many pit features. Although most of the early Middle Woodland sites in the Connecticut River valley seem to be seasonal camps, they were not "characterized by high densities of lithics, ceramics and features" until after 1200 B.P.[10] The Milford site could be an exception, or it could indicate geographic diversity in economy, settlement system, and even social organization. Perhaps marshes formed earlier at the mouth of the Housatonic River than at the Connecticut River. Studies of marsh corings are urgently needed along the Connecticut coast and river valleys to better reconstruct the local physical environments through time.

### New Point Styles and Toolstone Sources

The small, stemmed and notched points of the Narrow Point tradition "were the everyday point of choice in the Early and Middle Woodland periods of the Housatonic drainage"[11] and in other areas of Connecticut as well. New point styles were introduced from other regions, but were always a very minor element in the local cultures. These included medium-bladed, lanceolate or wide-stemmed, concave base points called Fox Creek[12] and Cony (for *Co*astal *N*ew *York*),[13] or lanceolate Greene points that taper to a rounded or straight base.[14] In a survey of 2,986 points from northwestern Connecticut sites, 50 (1.7 percent) were assigned to the Fox Creek style, no Greene points were identified, and only six Jack's Reef points

Top, Fox Creek-style projectile points. Bottom row, examples of Greene projectile points.

A cache of early Middle Woodland blades for the manufacture of Fox Creek points from the Glazier site in Granby, shown *in situ*. Note the dark circle of the storage pit in which the blades had been cached (see inset).

(0.2 percent) were reported. In contrast, there were 1,438 (49.4 percent) Narrow Point tradition points, 315 (10.5 percent) Laurentian, 210 (7.0 percent) Broad Spears, 138 (4.7 percent) Orient, and 23 (0.8 percent) Meadowood points.[15]

In New York and Massachusetts, site components with Fox Creek and Greene points have been dated to the early Middle Woodland period between 1630 and 1420 B.P.,[16] but by 1100 B.P. these point types had disappeared from the landscape in eastern New York. The only three radiocarbon dates for Fox Creek (Cony) points reported in Connecticut fit into that time range. A cache of what are thought to be thirty blades for manufacturing Fox Creek points discovered at the Glazier site in Granby yielded two radiocarbon dates: 1630 B.P. ±60 years and 1590 B.P. ±80 years.[17] Some of these blades measure 6 inches (over 15 centimeters) in length! The hearth containing a Fox Creek point from Site 6LF115 in New Milford was dated to 1470 B.P. ±200 years.[18] Geological thin-section analysis of one of the Glazier blades identified the material as a dolomitic siltstone not local to Connecticut, suggesting that the blades likely were obtained through a trading network or population movement.[19]

The earliest dates for these point styles are from the Delmarva area. In Delaware they are part of the Carey Complex, dated from A.D. 65 to 455.[20] Researchers in coastal and interior New York and in Massachusetts have excavated discrete Fox Creek (Cony) components characterized by Fox Creek (Cony) points, Greene points, large Petalas-style knife blades, and net-impressed, dentate-stamped,

Jack's Reef-style pentagonal (top row) and corner-
notched (bottom row)
projectile points.

rocker-stamped, and incised pottery.[21] Yet not one discrete Fox Creek (Cony) component has been reported from Connecticut. Is this because their communities were so small and rare, or because the points were merely trade items procured by local Narrow Point communities from their trading partners to the south and west?

In any case, although some of the points were manufactured from local stone materials, many were made from non-local argillites, rhyolites, siltstones, and cherts that reflect the operation of interregional communication networks. The Churchill site in Redding, Connecticut, for example, contained "lanceolate points [that] might be Fox Creek-related" and 78 percent of its stone artifacts were manufactured from non-local rhyolites, jaspers, and cherts.[22] Several geological studies of Middle Woodland artifacts from the Long Island Sound area show the movement of goods or people, or both, from the Mid-Atlantic region. Outcrops in western New Jersey and Bucks County, Pennsylvania, are the source of the argillite of artifacts from the Cony component of the Oakland Lake site on Long Island.[23] The closest source for hornfels artifacts from the Cooper site in Lyme, Connecticut, is the Lockatong formation of north-central New Jersey and Pennsylvania.[24]

Thin, medium-bladed, corner-notched, and pentagonal Jack's Reef points probably made their appearance on Connecticut Woodland sites at or near the end of the Fox Creek time range. Amateur collections suggest concentrations along the Connecticut coast and the Connecticut River valley,[25] but none of the points have been associated with radiocarbon dates. At New York, New Jersey, and Massachusetts sites, however, Jack's Reef points have been dated to the late Middle Woodland period between 1350 and 1040 B.P.[26]

In Connecticut, virtually all the points of this style were made from exotic cherts, mainly jasper.[27] The presence of jasper blanks and blades, and the absence of jasper debitage reflecting the early stages of biface manufacture on Connecticut sites, mean that the Jack's Reef points were being carried in and traded as finished tools and late-stage bifaces. In fact, in southern New England jasper artifacts in general occur mainly in Middle Woodland contexts.[28] Trace element analyses of Massachusetts artifacts identified the source as Pennsylvania Jasper quarries in eastern Pennsylvania.[29] Petrographic thin-section analyses of jasper flakes from a late Middle Woodland–Late Woodland component at the Army National Guard

Examples of the large jasper and chert blades associated with pre-contact hammered copper beads at a gravel pit in Saybrook, Connecticut. Such artifacts indicate the movement of goods and likely populations from the Mid-Atlantic region to southern New England. Scale bar equals 1 centimeter.

Camp site in Niantic, Connecticut, also identified the Hardyston Quartzite formation of eastern Pennsylvania as their source.[30] Material items such as stone tools and cache blades were not the only things traveling along this network. Ideas were moving, too.

> The dissemination of the bow and arrow across North America . . . places the bow in Alaska around 3,000 B.C. However, it was introduced into the western United States around A.D. 200 and reached the Northeast . . . at around A.D. 600. Jack's Reef points . . . mark the first appearance of the bow and arrow in the Northeast.[31]

The presence of small, thin, pressure-flaked Jack's Reef points made from Pennsylvania Jasper strongly suggests that Mid-Atlantic communities introduced the local Connecticut people to the bow and arrow during the late Middle Woodland period. This hunting innovation was an improvement over the spear and atlatl, because it increased the accuracy, distance, and penetrating power of the weapon. Indigenous hunters were still using the bow and arrow when Europeans ventured into their tribal homelands. Martin Pring, an English explorer who investigated the coasts of eastern New England in 1603, described the weaponry of Plymouth Bay warriors that, with the exception of its metal arrow tip, was likely similar if not identical to the late Middle Woodland bow and arrow.

> Their weapons are Bows of five or sixe foote broad of wich-hasell, painted blacke and yellow, the strings of three twists of sinewes, bigger than our Bowstrings. Their arrows are of a yard and an handful long not made of reeds but of a fine light wood, very smooth and round with three long and deepe blacke feathers of some Eagle, Vulture or Kite, as closely fastened with some binding matter as any Fletcher of ours can glue them on. Their quivers are full a yard

Woodland Winter Hunter

An idealized depiction of an Eastern Woodlands hunter in winter clothing, by David R. Wagner.

long, made of long dried Rushes wrought about two handfuls broad above, and one handful beneath with prettie works and compartiments, Diamant wise of red and other colours.[32]

As noted by Englishman James Rosier, a member of the 1605 expedition to Maine under Captain George Weymouth,[33] the arrows of the Maine warriors were made of the same wood as their bows—witch hazel and beech—and also ash. Like Pring, he mentioned three feathers tied to the arrow. He described both arrow and dart point tips made from the shank bone of a deer, the former with prongs "very sharp with two fangs in manner of a harping iron." William Wood, an Englishman who lived in eastern Massachusetts (likely Salem) from 1629 to 1633,[34] also talked about the indigenous bows and arrow of eastern Massachusetts but, unlike Pring, described a two-part arrow, or dart:

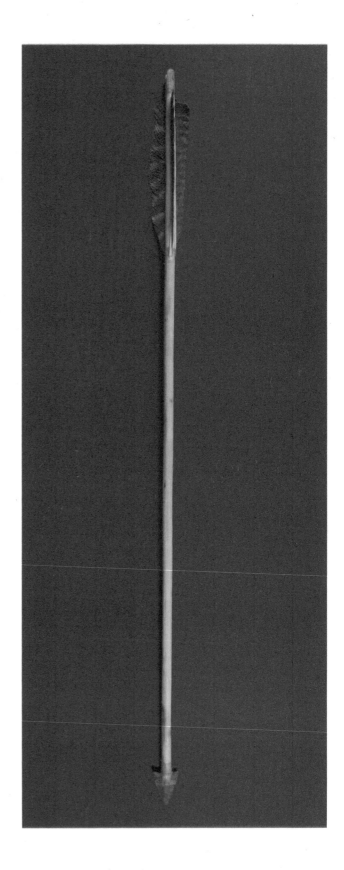

A modern replica of an Eastern Woodlands arrow constructed by the late Jeffrey Tottenham of Seymour, Connecticut, an expert in primitive technology, using traditional materials, including turkey feathers, deer glue, sinew for the bindings, and a Levanna-style projectile point.

Their bows they make of a handsome shape, strung commonly with the sinews of mooses; their arrows are made of young eldern, feathered with feathers of eagles' wings and tails, headed with brass in shape of a heart or triangle, fastened in a slender piece of wood six or eight inches long which is framed to put loose in the pithy eldern that is bound fast for riving.[35]

The Mid-Atlantic communities also likely passed along knowledge of marsh-land plant and animal life and the most efficient technologies for extracting and using them.

### New Pottery Styles

The introduction of new pottery styles at about the same time that the new point styles arrived also supports a Mid-Atlantic connection. In the greater Long Island Sound area these styles are known as North Beach Net-marked, Windsor Brushed, Windsor Fabric-marked, Hollister Stamped, and Shantok Cove Incised. They are part of the Windsor ceramic tradition.[36]

Net-marked pottery was dated to 1690 B.P. ±70 years at Site 270A-4-1 in Newtown[37] and 1310 B.P. ±85 years at the Cobb Island site in Greenwich.[38] Windsor Brushed pottery was dated as early as 1630 B.P. at the Livingston Pond site on western Long Island.[39] Its earliest known appearance on the mainland is dated to 1320 B.P. at the Lieutenant River site in Old Lyme.[40]

Windsor Brushed and other affiliated pottery were found at the Mamacoke Cove site on the Thames River estuary in New London, where a large paved stone roasting pit provided a date of 1280 B.P. ±250 years; another radiocarbon date of 690 B.P. ±60 years indicated that the occupation extended into the Late Woodland period.[41] At the Shantok Cove site in Montville, Windsor Brushed, Windsor Fabric-marked, Hollister Stamped, and Shantok Cove Incised were recovered from a shell midden whose lower and upper levels were dated to 1190 B.P. ±115 years and 1035 B.P. ±150 years, respectively.[42]

Windsor Brushed pottery is named for the shallow parallel grooves on its in-side and outside surfaces, probably scraped with the edge of a scallop or ark shell. Although this pottery was generally undecorated, occasionally motifs were made with the edge of a shell, or possibly with the tines of a bone or antler comb.

The outsides of Windsor Fabric-marked pots have impressions made with a fabric-wrapped paddle (probably twined bags or mats woven from plant fibers, like those made by Native Americans in early post-contact times). The inside surfaces were either brushed or smoothed; the pottery was undecorated.

Hollister Stamped ware is decorated with horizontal rows of shell stamping made by pressing the single flute from a scallop shell into the wet clay.

Shantok Cove Incised pottery also has fabric impressions on its outside surfaces, with the inside brushed or smooth. This pottery was decorated with a band of boldly incised triangles or opposed diagonals, and short, linear depressions called punctates.

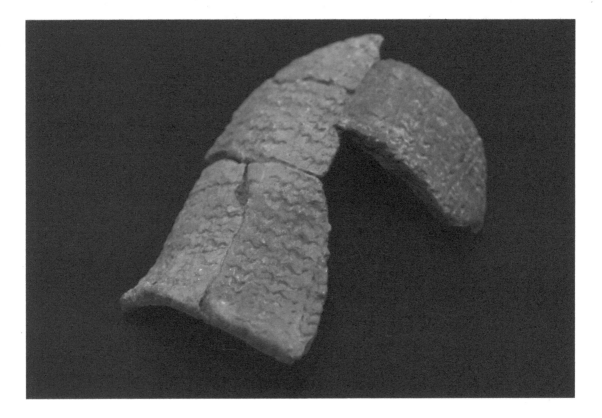

Large rim fragment of a St. Lawrence Pseudo-Scallop Shell vessel (top of vessel toward bottom of photograph) from the Woodruff Cave site, a rock shelter on Lake Waramaug. Since it represents a Canadian and northern New York state pottery style, the pot's presence in Connecticut shows communication with Indian communities in the upper Hudson River valley.

## The Later Middle Woodland Period

Later Middle Woodland settlements continued to increase in frequency and size, particularly in riverine and coastal regions. There are no large seasonal settlements in the uplands. These trends occurred in both western and eastern Connecticut. The extensive archaeological surveys through western Connecticut mandated by construction of the Iroquois Gas Pipeline uncovered intensive occupations by late Middle Woodland and Late Woodland peoples in the Housatonic River estuary at Milford. In contrast, only minor, temporary sites were found in the inland and upland swamps along Cavanaugh Brook and Pootatuck Brook in Newtown.[43] Farther west, at another coastal site, an acorn storage pit recovered from the Middle Woodland occupation at Spruce Swamp in Norwalk showed extended residency.[44]

The large seasonal and multiseasonal camps in the Connecticut River valley contained increasing amounts and kinds of artifacts and dietary remains relative to early Middle Woodland sites, suggesting longer, recurring occupations by larger groups of people.[45] For example, the Mago Point site on Niantic Bay was a large shell midden dated between 1100 and 1040 B.P. and occupied during the spring, summer, and fall.

The later Middle Woodland peoples' repertoire of Windsor ceramic styles had expanded as well. Increasingly higher percentages of non-local toolstone (as much as 30 to 40 percent of the stone assemblage) indicated intensifying trade networks, increased population movements into the region, or both. The Selden Island site, a large multiseasonal (spring–fall) riverine settlement in Lyme, provided radiocarbon dates of 1060 and 1010 B.P. It contained a large and varied stone and pottery assemblage; 50 percent of the toolstone was not local. Because of its size, diverse assemblage, and virtually sedentary nature, it has been called a "village" by its excavator.[46]

## The Village Problem

Several noted New England archaeologists have claimed that there is yet no archaeological evidence for villages.[47] Given the evidence for geographic diversity in earlier cultural periods, village life could be absent from some parts of southern New England, but as Dr. Peter Thorbahn has noted, "the absence of evidence . . . cannot be taken to be evidence of absence."[48] Several explanations have been given for this absence in certain areas: (1) the village locations were also desirable to European settlers, and towns may now sit on the remains of the Native villages; (2) village sites have been erased by hundreds of years of farming, industrial development, and urban sprawl; and (3) New England "villages" may have consisted of a small cluster of houses that left only a faint archaeological footprint.[49]

As archaeologists we must explicitly define what we mean by "village," as did Kevin McBride in his doctoral dissertation. His main criterion for a village site is year-round occupation. Other criteria include the presence of storage, refuse, and cooking features; a spatial extent of about an acre (3,000 to 5,000 square meters or more); and a wide range of stone tool types showing that a variety of activities

In addition to pottery making, this idealized scene of a Woodland village in summer, by David R. Wagner, depicts the multigenerational nature of community activities and the importance of family, cooperation, and the work ethic so often highlighted in indigenous stories for children.

occurred on the site. McBride's definition of "base camp" is almost identical to his definition for a village, except that a base camp was occupied for only two seasons in a year, even though it may have been reoccupied over many years.[50]

One problem with this definition is that it is difficult to know whether a site was occupied in winter because of the lack of seasonal indicators, particularly plants. McBride *assumed* some sites were occupied year-round if there was evidence for three seasons. Second, as for size, sites can become large through long-term use rather than from year-round occupation. Some sites used seasonally for thousands of years can be just as large, or larger, than a probable Late Woodland village. On the other hand, some early post-contact accounts suggest "villages" of dispersed homes, like Samuel de Champlain's description and map of his 1605 visit to Nauset Harbor on Cape Cod depicting small round houses encircled by small gardens and dispersed about the harbor.[51]

For these reasons, a site should meet all of the criteria, not just one or two, to be considered a village. I agree with McBride's criteria for the definition of "village," except I believe that a settlement does not need to be fully sedentary to be a village. For example, the Morgan site in Rocky Hill meets all the requirements for a village and more, yet the site was unoccupied in the late winter and early spring because of frequent flooding by the Connecticut River. Also, the post-contact Mohican and Schaghticoke villages in northwestern Connecticut were inhabited only two seasons out of the year. European documents note that the eighteenth-century communities annually moved from a winter–spring village to a summer–fall village.[52] Under McBride's definition these villages would be considered merely base camps.

### Hopeville Pond Site

Hopeville Pond, on a small knoll overlooking the Pachaug River in Griswold, is one of only two reported single-component Jack's Reef sites in the state, characterized by no other point style than Jack's Reef.[53] Although no pottery was found, it contained one hearth and four charcoal-filled pit features, several Jack's Reef corner-notched and pentagonal points of jasper and black chert, flakes of the same material, a chert steep-edged thumbnail scraper, and at least one flake used as a scraper. Hopeville Pond is also important because it provided dietary information that suggested a late summer–autumn occupation: acorn, hazelnut, and hickory nut fragments, grape seed, possible elderberry, and bone from mammalian and either reptilian or fish species. The second single-component Jack's Reef camp was located on the Salmon River in East Haddam. It contained an assemblage of many used flakes and steep-angled scrapers like the one from Hopeville Pond, along with a dozen or so Jack's Reef points. No other point types were reported from either of these camps. It is possible they represent actual migrants from the Mid-Atlantic.

### Military Academy Site

The only other reported Jack's Reef component is on the U.S. Army National Guard Camp property in the Niantic River valley, in the Niantic section of East

Lyme.[54] This site, uncovered during preparations for the construction of a military academy for the National Guard, had two main pre-contact Native American components: a Late Woodland characterized by collared incised pottery and Levanna points, and a Middle Woodland characterized by Fox Creek and Jack's Reef Corner-notched points (two reworked into a drill and a knife) and uncollared brushed, impressed, and scallop-shell-stamped pottery that represent Middle Woodland Windsor pot types. Use of the uncollared pottery seemed to have extended into the early Late Woodland occupation as well. A single Susquehanna Broad point revealed a very ephemeral Terminal Archaic presence. A single narrow, stemmed point probably belonged to the short-term Early Woodland camp located just to the northeast of the later Woodland settlement.[55]

The site contained a small variety of tools and used flakes reflecting woodworking, food processing, and general purpose pounding and cutting activities. Unfinished bifaces and debitage also suggested tool manufacturing and maintenance activities. The quartz tools were produced by the cobble reduction technique. Although quartz was the most abundant toolstone (62.6 percent of the total stone assemblage), jasper was a surprising second (22.6 percent). Two flakes were identified through thin-section petrography as Pennsylvania Jasper from the Hardyston Quartzite formation; a third jasper flake was identified as a residual material derived from an unknown metamorphic source. A medium-gray flake and a black flake were both identified as chert from the Normanskill Shale formation of eastern New York. Another black flake was identified as chert from the portion of the Onondaga Limestone formation that crops out in eastern New York. The clay pots, several small hearths, and small fragments of calcined bone and shell recovered also denote food preparation and cooking activities. Unfortunately, during the archaeological surveys most faunal remains were recovered from the plow zone, so some or all might have been associated with the post-contact Anglo-American component of the site.

Archaeological monitoring of the Military Academy site during construction activities located an earth oven, a possible storage pit, and several refuse pits filled with shell as well as mammal, bird, and fish bones, seeds, nutshell, and wood charcoal.[56] A large pit 6 feet (almost 2 meters) in diameter, over 2 feet (about 60 centimeters) deep, and filled with charcoal was originally identified as a second earth oven, but subsequent botanical analysis suggested it may have been used as a storage pit. The presence of solid-stem grasses suggests a lining, possibly to prevent mold (see the discussion in Chapter 8 of the use of solid-stem big bluestem grass at the later Burnham-Shepard site), and the intense burning suggested by the huge amount of charcoal may have been done to clear the pit of insects before reuse.

Identifiable faunal remains included those of white-tailed deer, turkey, sand tiger shark, tautog (blackfish), scallop, oyster, soft-shell clam, and a few hard-shell clam (quahog). Tautog live inshore from April through November, while the sand tiger shark is present in New England coastal waters from July to September, indicating a summer-to-fall occupation of the site.[57] Botanical remains included brambles (blackberry, raspberry, or dewberry), huckleberry, black cherry, nuts

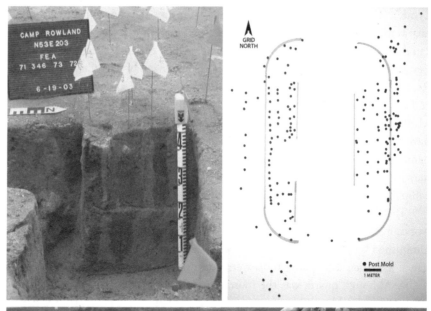

A field crew from American Cultural Specialists unearthing a house structure at the Military Academy site in the Niantic section of East Lyme, Connecticut. The post molds are the remains of the pole framework of an oblong building (outlined in the plan diagram, upper right).

(mainly hickory, but also chestnut), acorns, wild plants (*Chenopodium,* bayberry, and plants in the mint family), grasses, and seventeen maize kernel and cupule specimens. Bayberry and mint were, and still are, used as medicinal plants by Northeastern Indian peoples, and also as seasonings and, in the case of mint, as salad greens. Wood charcoal included more than one species of oak, American chestnut, birch, and conifer, indicating a mixed hardwood-conifer woodland environment. The cupules (cob fragments) show that maize fields were nearby. The different ripening times of the botanical remains support the faunal findings, sug-

A reconstructed circular bark-covered wigwam (weetoo) on exhibit at the Institute for American Indian Studies in Washington, Connecticut, circa 1985 (author's daughter for scale).

gesting that the site was occupied from early summer to midsummer and into the fall.[58]

Among the most exciting finds were the remains of an oblong pole-frame structure 23 feet wide by 38 feet long (7 by 11.5 meters) located between two hearths. Wood charcoal from the hearths generated two radiocarbon dates: 970 B.P. ±110 years and 720 B.P. ±60 years, one or both of which may date the building. Seven additional radiocarbon dates recovered from the pit features discovered during monitoring activities indicate that the site was occupied from the late Middle Woodland period into the early Contact period,[59] a date range of cal A.D. 835–865 to cal A.D. 1610–1660.

The structure had door openings at both ends, and a double line of posts formed the outer walls that would have efficiently held up its outer covering and insulation. About 3 feet (1 meter) in from each of these walls was a parallel row of posts that marked interior platforms for shelving, beds, or seats. If used as beds or seats, the platforms likely would have been covered with deer skins and animal furs, as described in accounts by English explorer and settler Thomas Morton and English minister John Sergeant for early-seventeenth-century and early-eighteenth-century indigenous bedding, respectively.

> Their lodging is made in three places of the house about the fire: they lie upon planks commonly about a foot or 18 inches above the ground, raised upon rails that are borne up upon forks. They lay mats under them, and coats of

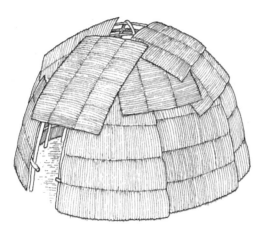 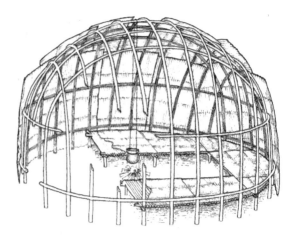

The interior and exterior construction of a wigwam dwelling on the Nehantic reservation in present Niantic. The sapling framework of wigwams was covered with bark, reeds, and seagrasses, or mats made of corn husks, cattails, or other plant fibers, which could be easily dismantled, rolled up, and stored for future use.

deerskin, otters, beavers, raccoons and of bears' hides, all which they have dressed and converted into good leather with the hair on for their coverings. And in this manner they lie as warm as they desire.[60]

According to Reverend Sergeant, winter bedding consisted of a "mattress" of spruce boughs covered with a deerskin and several thick blankets.[61]

Significantly, the middle-eighteenth-century wigwams on the Nehantic (Niantic) Indian reservation just south of the Military Academy site on Black Point[62] had similar storage and rest furniture. The houses, however, were smaller than the structure on that site and oval to round. According to Ezra Stiles, a minister, local historian, and later president of Yale College who visited the reservation in 1761, the houses ranged from about 9 by 14 feet to 12 by 17 feet (3 by 4.7 meters to 4 by 5.8 meters). Families of seven and twelve persons, respectively, lived in each of the two wigwams drawn to scale by Stiles.[63]

Roger Williams described the houses of the Narragansetts, the eastern neighbors of the Niantics, as round wigwams 14 to 16 feet (4 to 6.5 meters) in diameter, with a central firepit, in which two families could live comfortably.[64] On Griswold Point in present-day Old Lyme just west of Niantic, the Griswold Point site also contained the curvilinear post-mold patterns of house structures.[65] Its two radio-carbon dates of 780 ±100 years B.P. and 510 ±110 years B.P. place it in the Late Woodland period and partly contemporary with the Military Academy site. One ovoid house was completely excavated. It was approximately 13 by 17 feet (4 by 5.25 meters) with a firepit near the entrance, a plan remarkably close to descriptions given by Stiles and others, but unlike the structure at the Military Academy site. Morton provided a detailed description of early-seventeenth-century house construction among eastern Massachusetts coastal peoples:

> They gather poles in the woods and put the great end of them in the ground, placing them in form of a circle or circumference; and bending the tops of them in form of an Arch, they bind them together with the bark of Walnut

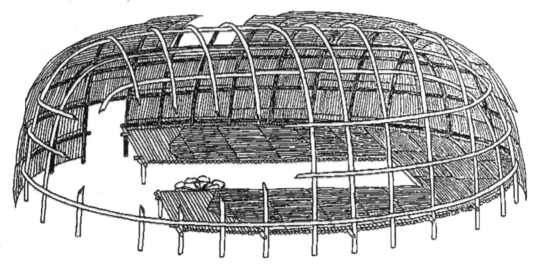

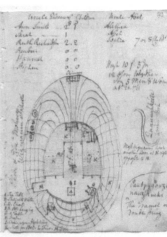

trees, which is wondrous tuffe, so that they make the same round on the top for the smoke of their fire to ascend and pass through. These they cover with mats, some made of reeds and some of long flags, or sedge finely sowed together with needles made of the splinter bones of a Crane's leg, and with threads made of their Indian hemp, which their groweth naturally. Leaving severall places for doors, which are covered with mats which may be rolled up and let down again at their pleasures, they make use of the several doors according as the wind fits. The fire is always made in the middest of the house, with windfalls [tree branches found lying on the ground] commonly: yet sometimes they fell a tree that groweth near the house, and by drawing in the end thereof maintain the fire on both sides, burning the tree by degrees shorter and shorter until it be all consumed; for it burneth night and day.[66]

Illustration of an oval house structure, as described by Ezra Stiles in the mid-1700s (top). Larger than the circular wigwam, it likely housed two or more nuclear families or a large extended family. Below, in these pages from his *Itineraries*, Stiles described and illustrated eighteenth-century indigenous dwellings from the Nehantic (Niantic) reservation in Niantic, Connecticut.

Post-mold pattern at the Griswold Point site in Old Lyme, discovered by members of the Archaeological Society of Southeastern Connecticut, a former chapter of the Archaeological Society of Connecticut; bottom, outlines of house structures uncovered during a Connecticut College summer field school co-directed by Dr. Harold Juli and the author.

The larger dwelling at the Military Academy site suggests a greater number of occupants; perhaps three or more families shared the structure. Lines of post molds near its walls suggested rebuilding and repair, and thus reuse over time. This and the radiocarbon dates tell us that community members continued to return to the settlement for hundreds of years. Other patterns that extended under a paved parking lot may have represented additional structures. Unfortunately, construction activities for the paved lot destroyed all evidence of structures in that area. Smaller post patterns near the house structure could have been wooden racks for roasting and drying foods, and possibly for processing hides into clothing.

## IMMIGRANTS IN A MARSHLAND PARADISE

Although the Windsor tradition was long thought to be the local, indigenous pottery tradition for southern New England and coastal New York,[67] I now believe that this pottery, along with exotic stone materials and a knowledge of marshland technology and ideology, was carried into Long Island and across to mainland New York and southern New England during population movements from the Delmarva region.[68]

The pottery styles characterized by net and fabric impression, brushing, and incising share little in common with the previous Vinette I and dentate-stamped styles. Rather, they are quite similar to several Mid-Atlantic pottery types made and used by people living on Chesapeake Bay and the Delmarva peninsula hundreds of years before their appearance in Connecticut.[69] Archaeological studies in the Delmarva area show that intensive exploitation of coastal and marshland resources began in the Late Archaic period. This created high population densities and increasingly sedentary communities in the riverine and estuarine zones between 2450 and 1950 B.P.,[70] so that small daughter communities developed by at least 1750 B.P.[71] Some of these daughter populations likely migrated northward along the coast, following the developing marshlands in search of sparsely inhabited lands. As previously noted, in Connecticut those marshland environments had been inhabited mainly by Broad Spear communities, who disappear by Early

A cutaway view of a New England shell midden, detail of the salt marsh habitat in the Coastal Region diorama at the Yale Peabody Museum of Natural History's Hall of Southern New England.

Windsor Fabric-marked pottery rim fragment (left); Windsor Brushed pottery fragments from the Tubbs Shell Heap site, Niantic, Connecticut.

Woodland times. The notably sparse Early Woodland communities would have allowed Middle Atlantic emigrants relatively easy access to coastal and riverine marshlands, particularly if they were kin of trading partners.

The easiest way to alleviate overpopulation in such an egalitarian society would be for smaller groups to fission off and follow the northward extension of their familiar marshland environments. The newly established marshlands along Long Island Sound would have been relatively open econiches for them to move into, since the local Point Peninsula[-like pottery-making] populations were adapted largely to an inland wetland environment. Emigrants who were pre-adapted to the marsh environment could move right in. Settlement pattern surveys . . . in the lower Connecticut River Valley and Connecticut side of the Sound support this hypothesis. They show Archaic and Early Woodland groups more oriented to inland and uplands resources.[72]

Middle Woodland components across Connecticut contained pottery styles reminiscent of the Point Peninsula cultural tradition of eastern New York.[73] The presence of Point Peninsula-like pottery in these areas suggests either kin associations between the local peoples and those in the adjacent Hudson River drainage,

A Windsor Cord-marked pot from the east bank of the Connecticut River, South Windsor, Connecticut.

or a continuation of the networking between interior New York and Connecticut communities that was so evident during Early Woodland times, or probably both. The impressed and brushed Windsor pots are concentrated along the coasts and up the major river valleys, particularly along the Connecticut River. Their distribution suggests that the gradual northward movement of the Windsor people onto the Connecticut coast and up the Connecticut River created a wedge that nearly split the older local culture area in two.

The area of Windsor pottery distribution roughly corresponded to the distribution of an Eastern Algonkian language group, the Quiripey-Unquochaug speakers, which included several post-contact indigenous tribal societies in south and central Connecticut: the Quinnipiac, Hammonasset, Niantic, and Wangunk.[74] The Quinnipiac tribal leadership was genealogically related to leaders of the Hammonasset and the Wangunk tribes.[75] Significantly, linguists have commented on the similarities between Quiripey-Unquochaug and Nanticoke, one of the Eastern Algonkian languages spoken in the Delmarva region,[76] and on the close relationship between Nanticoke and the southeastern New England languages of Natick and Narragansett.[77] They suggest that Nanticoke and Natick diverged in 1533 B.P. and Nanticoke and Narragansett in 1412 B.P. These dates fall within the radiocarbon-dated period for the first appearance of Windsor pottery on Long Island and the Connecticut mainland.

The archaeological evidence we have today from Connecticut is too sparse to determine when the influx of Windsor settlers speaking Quiripey-Unquochaug actually began. A long-term study of Middle Woodland sites in New York City and Long Island assigned to the Abbott complex (named for the famous Abbott Zoned pottery from New Jersey and Abbott Farm, its type site near Trenton in the Delaware drainage) suggested that the Mid-Atlantic population movement began sometime during the earlier Middle Woodland Fox Creek–Abbott phase and continued into the late Middle Woodland when Jack's Reef points were in use.[78] A migration of Fox Creek (Cony) point–using people from the Delaware River valley into the Long Island Sound region is plausible, given the distinctive material items found and the associations of pottery style and toolstone with the Delaware drainage. Similar point styles were also used by early Woodland peoples in the Delmarva region. The radiocarbon dates for the Fox Creek–Cony tradition fit well with the dates for the linguistic divergence discussed above.

## INTERPRETATIONS AND QUESTIONS

The problems and questions about Middle Woodland communities are similar to those of the preceding Early Woodland period. Except for the lower Connecticut River valley sites, very few Middle Woodland components have been reported in the archaeological literature. We know they existed in other areas because there are Fox Creek and Jack's Reef points in local amateur surface collections and in the disturbed plow zones of multicomponent site excavations. We should not assume, however, that the trends in settlement change and even material culture change so evident in southeastern Connecticut, such as the proliferation of Windsor pottery styles and increasing amounts of non-local toolstone, also apply to other regions of the state.

We find ourselves asking the same questions as we did about earlier cultures. How were communities organized socially and politically? Where is the evidence for recreational and children's activities? What of their local art and aesthetic traditions? What about Middle Woodland burials? Were they simple cremations, which would make them difficult to locate and identify? Or were they simple burials with little or no grave goods and no copper to preserve the bone? Without red ochre or other ceremonial items to identify them as burials, such graves could be mistaken for storage or refuse pits.

Significantly, the ceremonialism found in Early Woodland sites had disappeared by Middle Woodland times. Was this because the physical environment had become less uncertain and more predictable, with food staples increasingly more productive thanks to the prolific marshlands? Or did the new spiritual ideology driving the ceremonialism require continued support from its Adena source, which then dissolved when the Midwestern interaction networks did? Or perhaps there were no ideological counterparts in Connecticut, just the burials of Adena traders and sporadic exotic trade objects that were status symbols for local leaders. To answer these questions, archaeologists need to discover and study many more undisturbed Middle Woodland sites from a variety of environments.

# 8

## Ecological Abundance and Tribal Homelands

### *The Late Woodland Period*

O Great Creator

Whose voice I always listen for in the winds, Hear me — I am small — part of you — I need wisdom. Let me walk in your beauty, Make my hands respect the things you have made, Keep my ears ever sharp for your voice, Help me to travel a Path of Wisdom, so I may understand all people.

> —Adelphena Logan, Onondaga elder, educator, and former
> Institute for American Indian Studies trustee, from "Onondaga
> Indian Prayer," recited to open and close social gatherings

Several important changes mark the beginning of the Late Woodland cultural period (about 950 RCY B.P. to cal A.D. 1524). One is physical. The "Little Climatic Warming Period" began around 950 B.P. (circa A.D. 1000) and lasted several hundred years.[1] During that time temperature increased by one degree Celsius. This climatic change modified the local vegetation (and probably local animal life, too). Southern tree species have been identified from charred fragments at several local Late Woodland period sites: sourwood at both the Sebonac site on eastern Long Island and the Manakaway site in Greenwich, Connecticut, and black walnut from a refuse pit at the Morgan site in Rocky Hill, Connecticut. This is about the time when maize horticulture was introduced into New England.

The abandonment of horticulture during the fourteenth century A.D. in what is now New York and New England, except for communities near Long Island Sound and in the lower Connecticut River valley below Hartford, suggests a cooling climate at that time.[2] Recent paleoecological data from the Hudson River estuary support this interpretation, indicating increased warming between 1150 and 650 B.P., with cooler and wetter conditions by 550 B.P.[3] A resumption of horticulture in these areas in the subsequent century points to a return of climatic warming. In A.D. 1524, the first documented visit by Europeans to New York and Narragansett bays began cross-cultural relationships that would forever change traditional indigenous lifestyles.[4]

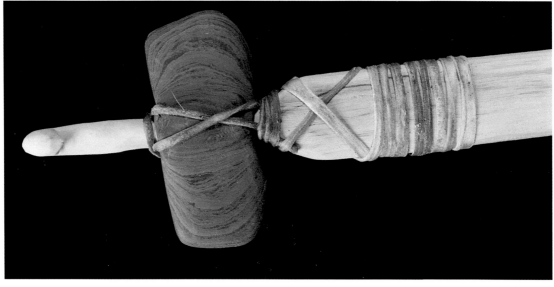

Various styles of atlatl weights, and a detail of an atlatl replica made by primitive technologist Jamie Leffler with traditional materials and an atlatl weight artifact from Litchfield County, Connecticut.

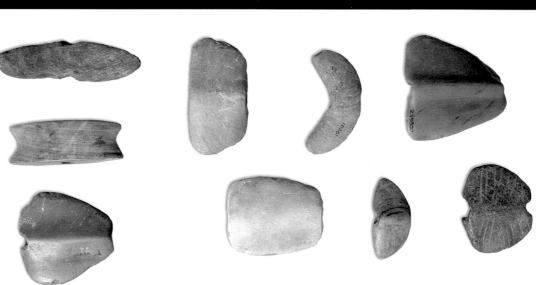

Carved steatite bowl from
Connecticut.

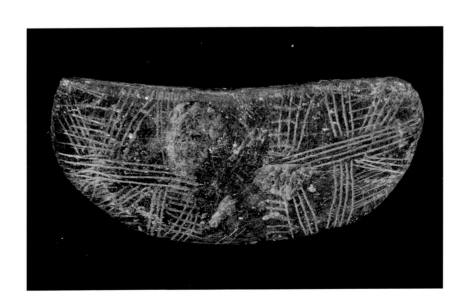

Incised steatite atlatl weight
found at Old Field Lane in
Milford, Connecticut.

Early Late Archaic Otter Creek projectile points. The long spearhead on the right was found in 1879 in Suffield, Connecticut (there is no provenience for the other blade).

Large jasper blades from the Indian Town Gravel Pit site in Saybrook, Connecticut. Scale bar equals 1 centimeter.

A nineteenth-century birch-bark basket with a floral design suggesting leaves of the ash tree, the tree of life in the sacred creation stories of indigenous peoples from northern New England. Maple sugar was stored and traded in containers similar to this one.

Rectangular woodsplint basket with hinged flat lid, wood splints, checkerwork, some splints swabbed red and green, length 5.25 inches (13 centimeters); and a Schaghticoke basket with loop handle from New Milford, Connecticut.

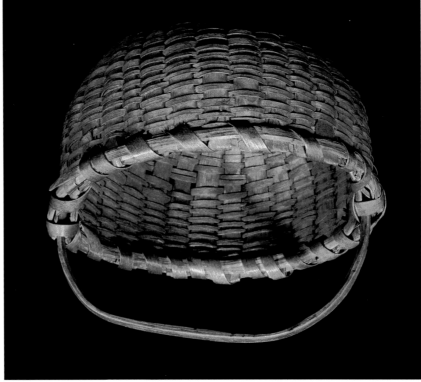

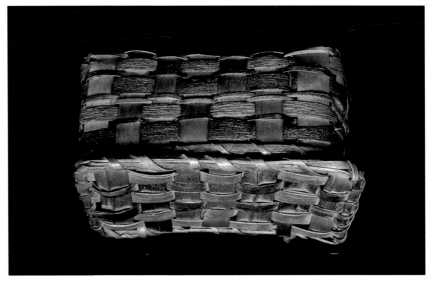

A Mohegan painted wood-
splint basket from Montville,
Connecticut; and an East-
ern Woodlands basket with
rectangular base, an oval
rim, and two loop handles,
checkerwork, and block-
stamp decoration, length 12
inches (30.5 centimeters).

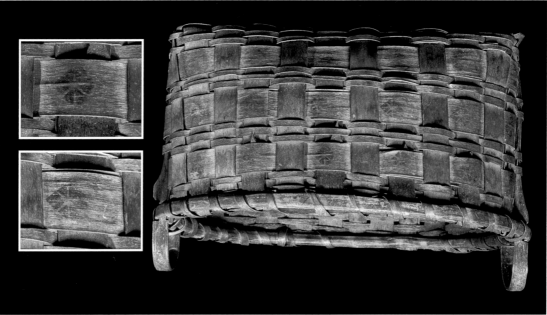

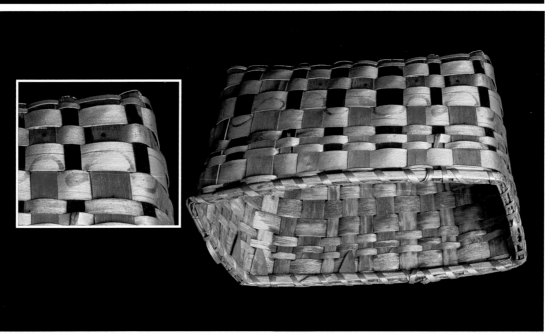

A baby rattle made by
Paugussett basketmaker
Molly Hatchett, circa 1770–
1820, made of ash splints
and filled with dried corn
kernels, height 3 inches
by 2.5 inches wide by
2.5 inches long (7.6 by
6.4 by 6.4 centimeters).

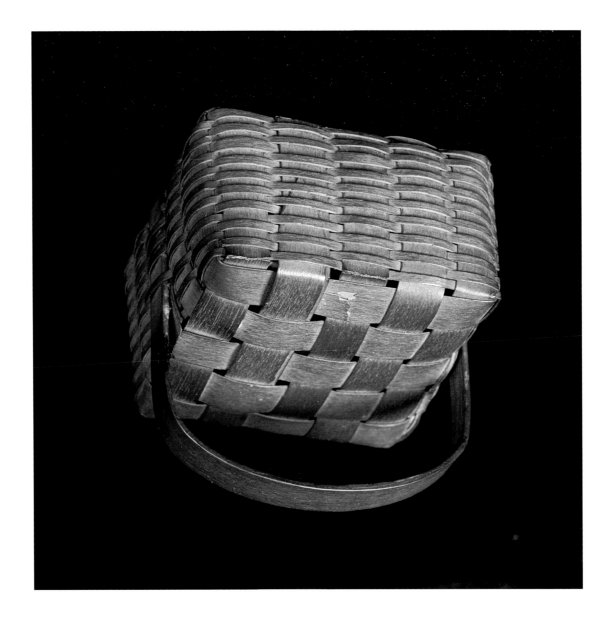

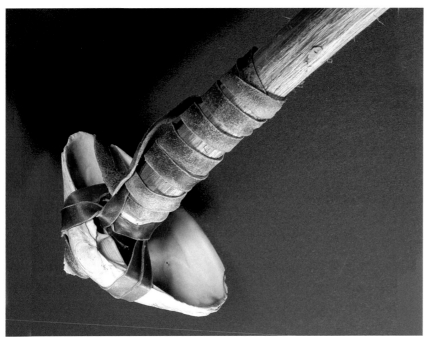

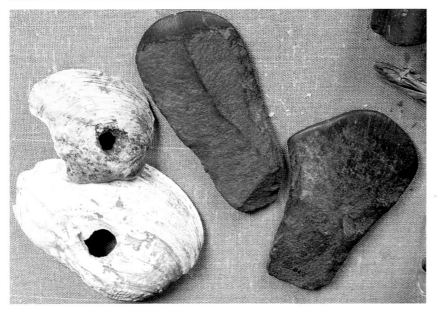

Windsor-style stone hoes from Suffield, Connecticut, and clamshell hoes from West Haven, Connecticut. Bottom, a reconstructed shell hoe made with traditional materials by primitive technologist Jamie Leffler.

Reconstruction of an Eastern Woodlands arrow, made with traditional materials by Connecticut primitive technologist Jeffrey Tottenham. Materials include sinew, deer glue, and turkey feathers, and a Levanna-style projectile point. The wood (traditionally elder, ash, beech, or witch hazel) shows burn marks from the technique used to straighten the arrow shaft. At right, Jack's Reef projectile points thought to be the earliest type used as arrowheads.

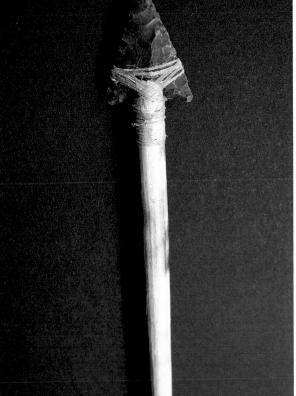

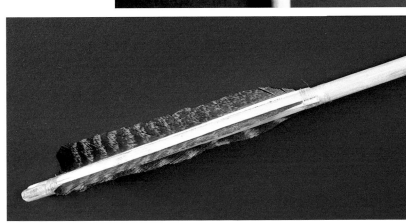

A monolithic axe found
in Branford, Connecticut,
in 1850. It is similar to a
style of stone axe used by
Pequot warriors during the
Pequot War of 1637. Made
from greywacke, a variety
of sandstone local to the
Albany, New York, area, it
is carved with a bird head
effigy and
a human face.

A stone and leather ball
club from the Fort Hill site
in the Weantinock tribal
homelands in New Milford,
Connecticut (center), alongside examples of a smaller
Apache war club with blue
and white beads (above)
and a Plains war club
(below), highlights the
technological and functional
similarities of the weapons.

A face or "maskette," carved from steatite, from the Rogers site, Lisbon, Connecticut. Scale bar equals 1 centimeter.

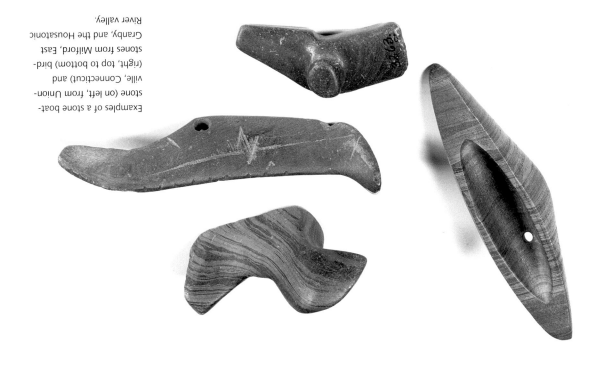

Examples of a stone boat-stone (on left, from Unionville, Connecticut) and (right, top to bottom) bird-stones from Milford, East Granby, and the Housatonic River valley.

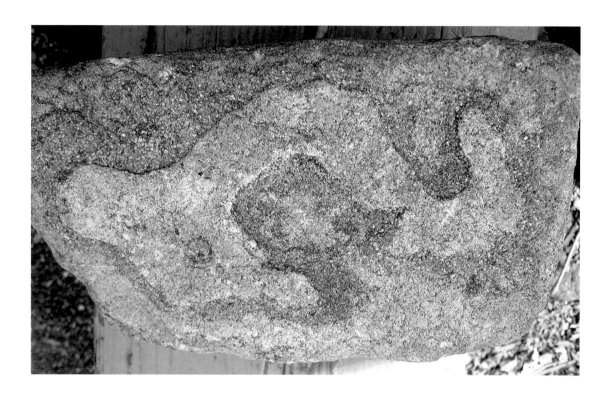

Rock carving found in
Woodbury, Connecticut,
shows an image suggestive
of the feathered or horned
serpent from indigenous
folklore.

A soapstone bowl that has
been deliberately broken
and burned in the crematory
fire. From the Laurel Beach
site in Milford, Connecticut.

Examples of Late Wood-
land to Post-Contact pottery
styles from the Lovers Leap
site, New Milford, Con-
necticut. A, D, G, Garoga
Incised, a typical Hud-
son Valley pottery type,
boldly incised with deep
punctates below the col-
lar, circa A.D. 1500 through
the seventeenth century.
B, Otstungo Notched, an
uncollared pottery style with
incised rims and notching
on the interior and exterior
lip, circa A.D. 1400–1633.
C, E, Chance Incised has
no punctates at the base
of the collar, and a smooth
interior and exterior, circa
A.D. 1100–1500. F, Owasco
Cord-on-cord. H, Garoga-
like sherd.

Examples of pottery from
the Kent Furnace site, Kent,
Connecticut. A, B, Otstungo
Notched. C, G, Chance In-
cised. D, E, I, Garoga-phase
rim sherds from the same
vessel. H, K, L, Garoga-
phase rim sherds. F, J,
Deowongo Incised.

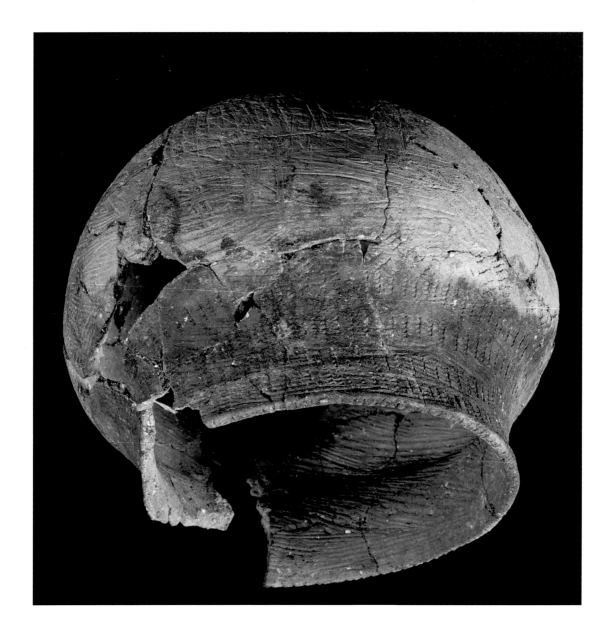

A reconstructed Late Woodland Sebonac pot from the
lower Housatonic River valley (possibly Derby).

A reconstructed North
Beach Net-marked pot
(unknown provenience).

Collared Niantic Stamped pot (right) with scallop shell stamping and cord-impressed body, and a Windsor brushed pot (left) from the Tubbs Shell Heap site, Niantic, Connecticut. Front, a miniature pot, possibly used to mix medicines, from the Wilcox Farm/Old Merwin Farm, Milford, Connecticut.

A Bowman's Brook Incised
pot from Old Merwin Farm,
Milford, Connecticut.

A Niantic Stamped pot from
Niantic, Connecticut.

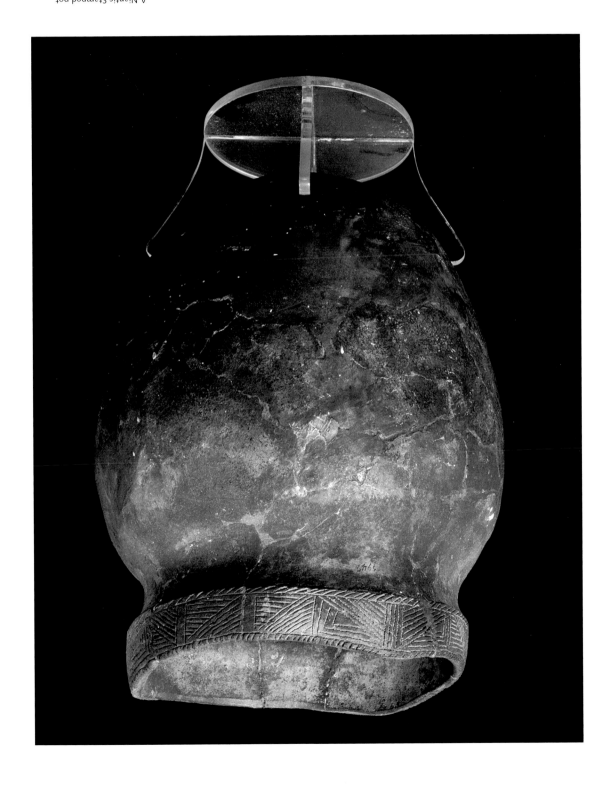

A Niantic Stamped pot
restored from fragments
found in place on the east
bank of the Connecticut
River, South Windsor,
Connecticut.

A pot in the Windsor
Cord-marked style from the
east bank of the Connecticut River, South Windsor,
Connecticut.

A deeply incised herring-
bone pattern on a Bowman's
Brook incised pot from the
Indian Well State Park Rock
Shelter, Shelton, Connecticut, suggesting trade or
intermarriage with the Late
Woodland Munsee-speaking
people living in southwestern Connecticut (women
traditionally made the pots).

Nineteenth-century charcoal baskets made by Schaghti-coke tribal members. The large basket is 36 inches long by 31 inches wide (91 by 79 centimeters); the smaller baskets are (left) 25 inches long by 17 inches wide (63.5 by 43 centimeters) and (right) 18.5 inches long by 15 inches wide (47 by 38 centimeters).

A Mohegan yohícake bag,
circa A.D. 1650, made
from twined hemp cord-
age and false embroidered
with dyed porcupine quills.
It is the oldest known in
Connecticut.

Three of these birchbark containers with embroidered floral designs were made with porcupine quillwork and the fourth (bottom right) with moose hair.

Wabanaki-type beaded bags, inverted keyhole shape (1850s–1880s), made with glass beads, black velvet fabric, and various materials used for the edge binding. The bag in the center is 6.2 inches high (about 16 centimeters) by 5.2 inches wide (13 centimeters). Many of the floral motifs represent medicinal plants, such as the thistle (embroidered on the bag in the lower right corner), which is used to treat a variety of ailments.

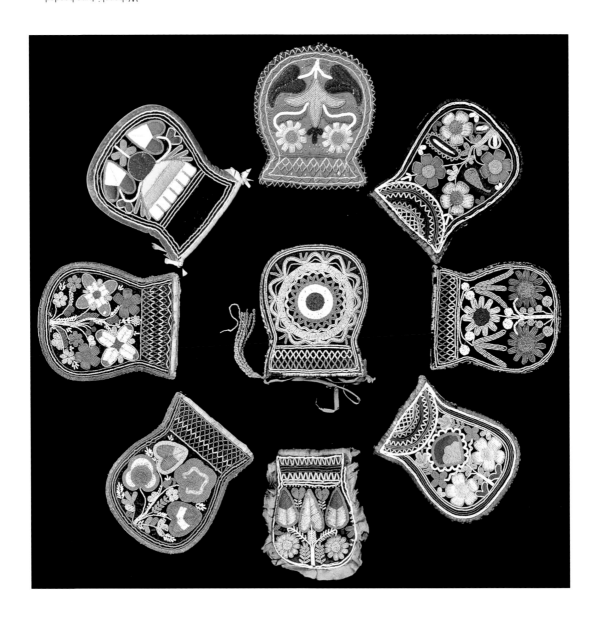

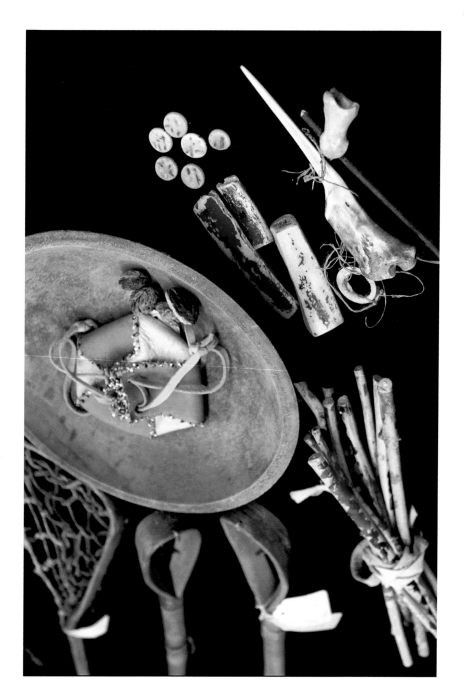

Equipment and pieces used in indigenous games, including sticks, or "strawes," used in a game of chance, a lacrosse stick, pick-up-sticks, a wooden bowl and dice (purple plum pits, round and long red bone pieces) used in a dice game called hubbub, and a cup-and-pin game.

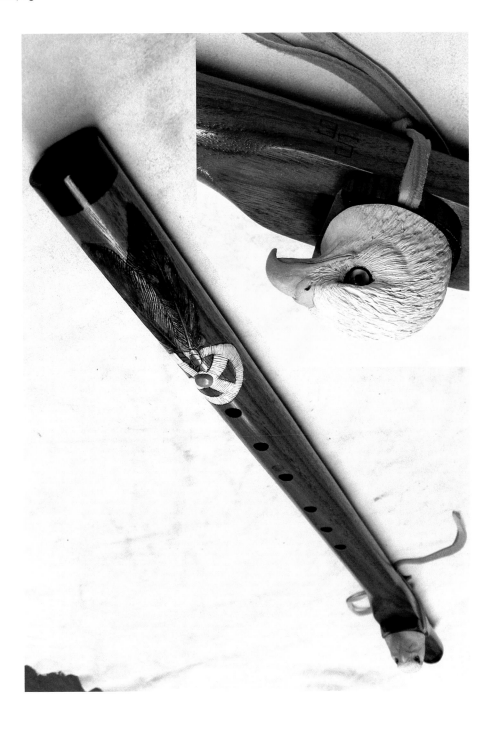

Contemporary hand-carved
and painted wooden flute
made by Strong Eagle Daly
of the Nipmuc Nation.

With skills handed down through many generations, Native American artists Allen Hazard, Sr., and Craig Spears, Sr., of the Narragansett Nation in Rhode Island carry on the tradition of working wampum from quahog shells, imbuing their work with deeply personal, sacred, and cultural meanings. Hazard is well known for handcrafted wampum beads, belts, and items such as the inlaid pipe shown above; Spears, a unique wampum artist, creates masterful carvings of feathers, eagles, and bears.

Dugout canoe of American chestnut on display at the Mashantucket Pequot Museum and Research Center, recovered in 1989 from West Hill Pond in Winsted, Connecticut, with the stone inside it.

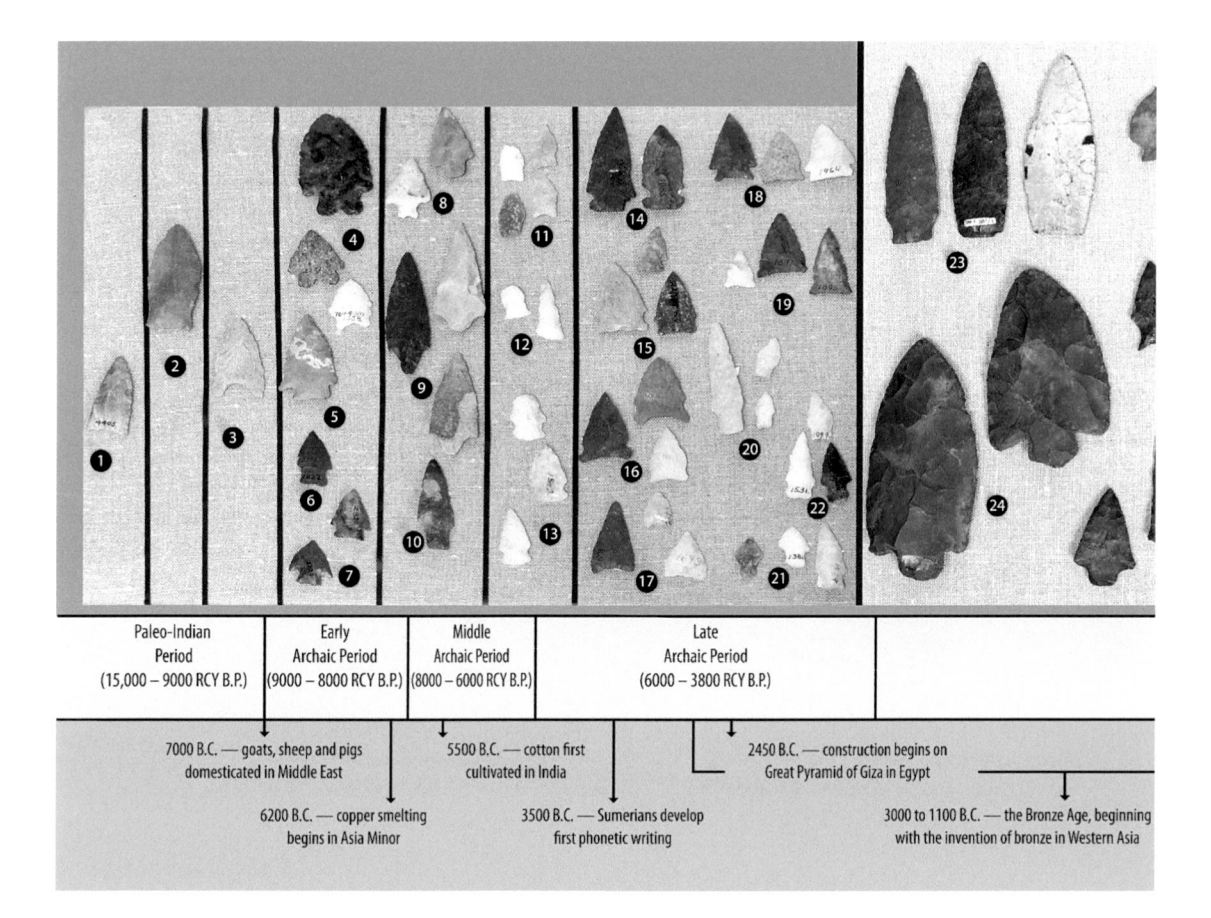

| Paleo-Indian Period (15,000 – 9000 RCY B.P.) | Early Archaic Period (9000 – 8000 RCY B.P.) | Middle Archaic Period (8000 – 6000 RCY B.P.) | Late Archaic Period (6000 – 3800 RCY B.P.) | |

7000 B.C. — goats, sheep and pigs domesticated in Middle East

5500 B.C. — cotton first cultivated in India

2450 B.C. — construction begins on Great Pyramid of Giza in Egypt

6200 B.C. — copper smelting begins in Asia Minor

3500 B.C. — Sumerians develop first phonetic writing

3000 to 1100 B.C. — the Bronze Age, beginning with the invention of bronze in Western Asia

Chronology of major projectile point types in Connecticut (with number of points shown). 1. Fluted (1). 2. Unfluted fluted (1). 3. Dalton (1). 4. Bifurcated (3). 5. Kirk Notched (1). 6. Kirk Stemmed (1). 7. Palmer (2). 8. Neville (2). 9. Stark (3). 10. Merrimack (1). 11. Burwell (4). 12. Karako (12). 13. Sylvan Lake Notched (3). 14. Otter Creek (2). 15. Brewerton Side Notched (3). 16. Brewerton Eared Notched (3). 17. Squibnocket Triangle (3). 18. Vosburg (3). 19. Brewerton Eared Triangle (3). 20. Squibnocket Stemmed (3). 21. Lamoka (3). 22. Wading River (3). 23. Complete blades (3). 24. Lehigh Broad (2). 25. Perkiomen (2).

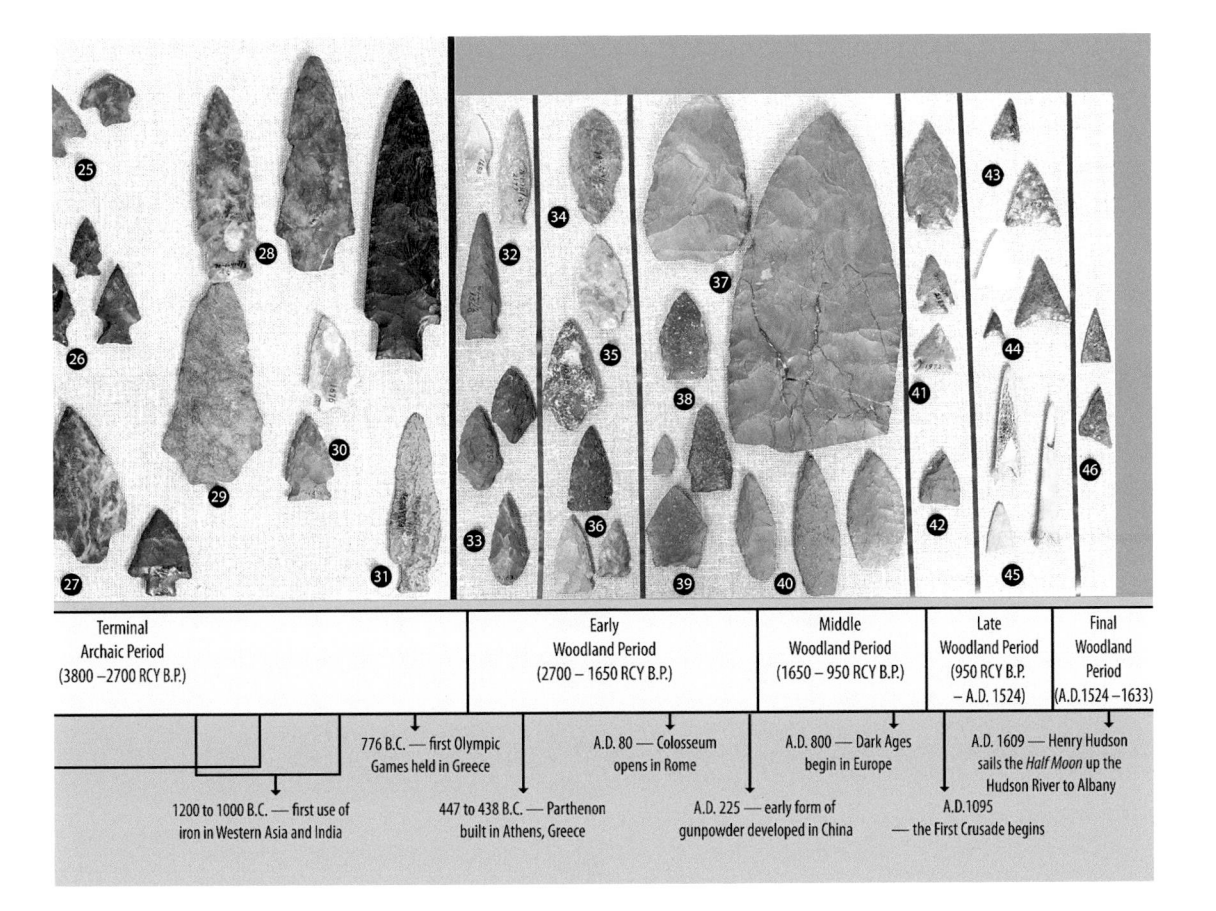

| Terminal Archaic Period (3800 –2700 RCY B.P.) | Early Woodland Period (2700 – 1650 RCY B.P.) | Middle Woodland Period (1650 – 950 RCY B.P.) | Late Woodland Period (950 RCY B.P. – A.D. 1524) | Final Woodland Period (A.D.1524 –1633) |

776 B.C. — first Olympic Games held in Greece

A.D. 80 — Colosseum opens in Rome

A.D. 800 — Dark Ages begin in Europe

A.D. 1609 — Henry Hudson sails the *Half Moon* up the Hudson River to Albany

1200 to 1000 B.C. — first use of iron in Western Asia and India

447 to 438 B.C. — Parthenon built in Athens, Greece

A.D. 225 — early form of gunpowder developed in China

A.D.1095 — the First Crusade begins

26. Susquehanna Broad (3). 27. Snook Kill/Atlantic (3). 28. Genesee (3). 29. Mansion Inn Watertown variety (1). 30. Wayland Notched (2). 31. Hand-pounded copper point (1). 32. Orient Fishtail (3). 33. Rossville (3). 34. Turkey Tail (1). 35. Adena (2). 36. Meadowood (3). 37. Jasper blades (2). 38. Fox Creek Lanceolate (1). 39. Fox Creek Stemmed (3). 40. Greene (3). 41. Jack's Reef (3). 42. Jack's Reef Pentagonal (1). 43. Madison (1). 44. Levanna (4). 45. Bone points (3). 46. Copper Kettle-cut (2).

# Major Chert Sources in the Northeast and Mid-Atlantic Regions

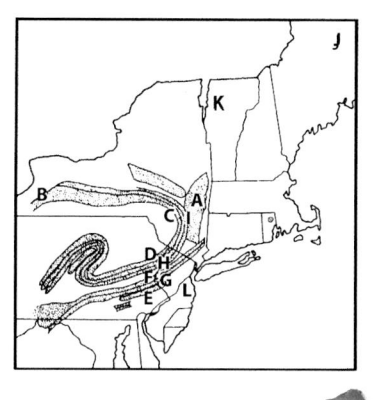

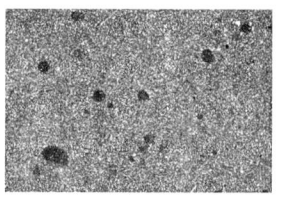

Thin section of a chert fragment from the Normanskill Formation of eastern New York State showing the set of traits that identify the chert source: fossil radiolarians, clay, dolomite, and pyrites.

| | | | |
|---|---|---|---|
| A | Normanskill Chert | | Flint Mine Hill Quarry, eastern New York |
| B | Onondaga Chert | | Divers Lake Quarry, western New York |
| C | Onondaga Chert | | Hudson River Valley, eastern New York |
| D | Onondaga Chert | | Delaware River Valley, northeastern Pennsylvania |
| E | Hardyston Jasper | | Vera Cruz Quarry, Pennsylvania |
| F | Beekmantown Chert | | Epler Formation, northeastern Pennsylvania |
| G | Beekmantown Chert | | Rickenbach Formation, northwestern New Jersey |
| H | Helderberg Chert | | New Scotland Formation, northwestern New Jersey |
| I | Helderberg Chert | | Alsen Formation, eastern New York |
| J | Munsungun Lake Chert | | Northern Maine |
| K | Monkton Jasper | | Vermont |
| L | Pensauken "Pebble" Jasper | | Central New Jersey |

Indigenous peoples obtained stone from a wide variety of sources in the greater Northeast, either by trade, gift exchange, or traveling directly to the quarries. Modern geological analysis can determine the location of these sources, giving insight into the movement of people and materials in the region. Thin-section samples from stone artifacts can be matched to specific quarry sources (top right) using unique identifying characteristics of the stone.

Other new developments of the Late Woodland period are cultural: the proliferation of clay pot and pipe styles, a new point style, minimal burial ceremonialism, bone and antler tools and musical instruments (although these likely show up because they are found in environments that favor preservation, such as shell middens, rather than because they were new to the indigenous material culture), and another southern population movement into the region. None of these changes occurred suddenly (except for the speedy introduction of maize horticulture to most of New England between 950 and 850 B.P.). Rather, they and other cultural developments happened gradually, continuing earlier trends from the Middle Woodland period: larger and more sedentary communities moving into the river valleys and coastal regions, and more exotic toolstone signifying accelerating interregional trade and population movement.[5]

## THE INTRODUCTION OF HORTICULTURE

The warming climate was conducive to an important cultural change that has characterized the Late Woodland — maize horticulture. A single maize pollen was recovered from a pollen sample taken just below a soil horizon dated to 950 B.P. in the Connecticut River floodplain at Hartford.[6] Maize kernels from archaeology sites also begin to occur about this time.

The word *mahiz* comes from the Arawak people of the Caribbean.[7] The earliest maize has been found in Mexican archaeology sites where its ancestor, the wild grass teosinte, grew. It was cultivated by indigenous peoples more than 9,000 years ago.[8] Introduced to the Pueblo peoples in the American Southwest, maize cultivation reached the Southeast by 1775 B.P.[9] In the Mississippi River valley in Illinois, maize has been radiocarbon-dated as early as about cal 45 B.C. (1995 B.P.).[10] Midwestern Ohio peoples were growing maize as early as 1550 B.P.[11] In western New York maize phytoliths, discovered in charred cooking residue on pottery, have been dated by accelerator mass spectrometry (AMS) to around cal A.D. 625 (about 1325 B.P.).[12]

Maize was probably introduced to communities in the Mid-Atlantic and the Northeast along traditional trade routes that had once sustained the Adena and Hopewellian interaction spheres. In Connecticut, maize arrived in indigenous communities around 950 B.P.[13] Horticulture was probably women's work, as English writers noted for seventeenth-century southern New England. One example is Roger Williams's commentary on Narragansett horticulture:

> The Women set or plant, weed, and hill, and gather and barne all the corne, and Fruites of the field. Yet sometimes the man himself, (either out of love to his Wife, or care for his Children, or being an old man) will help the Woman which (by the custome of the Countery) they are not bound to.[14]

According to research by Dr. Tim Ives, seventeenth-century deeds and other historical documents show that in the early Post-Contact period, at least, "women held authority regarding land rights and their transference."[15] (Some researchers believe that this situation may have been changing in seventeenth-century

Connecticut, particularly along the coast, where they suggest hereditary classes were taking the place of matrilineally based kin groups and indigenous societies were becoming reorganized into male-dominated family units.)[16] Because they were matrilineal societies, familial allotments to Native homelands were inherited through the female line. This very likely held true during the Late Woodland period as well—female heads of households governed land use. The only horticultural pursuit that was the sole activity of men was the planting of tobacco,[17] probably because tobacco smoking was associated with male ritual and political ceremony.

In New England, maize was sometimes grown with beans, squash, pumpkins, Jerusalem artichoke, and sunflowers.[18] Charred vegetal remains from a number of archaeology sites across northeastern North America showed that these crops were *not* domesticated together, however, nor were they introduced as a complex.[19] In the Northeast, the earliest domesticates were gourds (introduced into Maine and Pennsylvania around 6,500 and 6,200 years ago, respectively) and squash (introduced into western New York about 3,000 years ago).[20] Beans were the latest domesticates, arriving after 650 B.P., three hundred years after the first maize.[21]

### Early Domesticates in Connecticut

We have yet to recover gourds or squashes from Connecticut sites, although European accounts reported that southern New England Indians were growing pumpkins and squash by the 1600s cal A.D.[22] The Late Woodland inhabitants of the Burnham-Shepard site in South Windsor did cultivate maize, beans, and sunflowers, however. A bean dated to 550 B.P. ±60 postdated the maize at this site by seventy years.[23] The seventeenth-century accounts of English colonists show that the Indians practiced slash-and-burn horticulture, first burning off the planting fields in late spring, which not only cleared the area but added nutrients to the soil, and then planting maize, beans, and squash together in hillocks. The remains of such an early post-contact Indian cornfield, replete with hillocks, were discovered on the Massachusetts coast at the Sandy Point site on Cape Cod.[24] According to Janis Us, "Four Hearts Whispering," a storyteller, artist, and educator of Mohawk-Shinnecock descent,

> Our ancestors always planted corn, beans and squash together in a mound. The corn supported the young bean plants and lifted them up to the sunshine; the beans helped provide important nutrients [nitrogen] to nourish the growing corn; and the large squash leaves protected and shaded the soil, keeping it moist and free of weeds. We call these plants The Three Sisters and even today they remind us that we must always work together, as sisters, if we are to survive and flourish.[25]

Ripe, or "green," corn was eaten in July or early August, and the rest was not harvested until late August and September, when it was husked, dried, and stored. The size and shape of maize kernels recovered from archaeological excavations at

A yohicake bag, the oldest known in Connecticut. It is made of twined hemp cordage and false embroidered with dyed porcupine quills. Mohegan, about 1650.

Burnham-Shepard, Morgan, Tubbs, and other Connecticut sites suggest that indigenous women in those Late Woodland communities were growing northeastern eight-rowed flint corn.[26]

Native women most likely adapted their methods for grinding wild plant seeds and dried tubers to prepare this new food source. Dried maize was normally ground and made into flat bread, corn cakes, or stews and soups cooked with fish, beans, meat, wild plants, or berries. Charred corn cakes recovered from two Connecticut sites, Tubbs in Niantic and Muskrat Hill in Stratford, suggest that grinding corn into meal or flour dates to the Late Woodland period.

Sometimes maize was roasted in the ashes of a cooking fire, sifted, and then ground up for a nutritious traveling food variously called *nocake, nokehick, yokeg, yohicake,* or *yokeag,* depending on the tribal dialect.[27] Roger Williams mentioned its use among the Narragansetts:

> *Nokehick.* Parch'd meal, which is a readie very wholesome food, which they eate with a little water, hot or cold; I have traveled with neere 200 of them at once, neere 100 miles through the woods, every man carrying a little basket of this at his back, and sometimes in a hollow leather Girdle about his middle, sufficient for a man three or four daies.[28]

A beautifully dyed and decorated Mohegan yohicake bag from the middle seventeenth century, one of the earliest in existence, is preserved in the collection of the Connecticut Historical Society. The bag was woven from local Indian hemp (dogbane) and embroidered with dyed porcupine quills.

Beans were baked or boiled directly after harvesting, or dried to be cooked later in gruels and stews. Daniel Gookin, a Virginia Puritan who moved to Massachusetts and was later appointed superintendant of Indians, also mentioned bean cakes used by eastern Massachusetts peoples in the late seventeenth century, and a corn stew known today as succatash.

> Their food is generally boiled maize, or Indian corn, mixed with kidney-beans, or sometimes without. Also, they frequently boil in this pottage fish and flesh of all sorts, either new taken or dried, as shads, eels, alewives or a kind of herring, or any other sort of fish, but they dry mostly those sorts before mentioned.[29]

The sunflowers at Burnham-Shepard were dated between 650 and 500 B.P.[30] The English noted that Virginia Indians used the sunflower mainly for making breads and soup. In New York and Canada, Indian peoples cultivated it primarily for its oil, for health and for ritual purposes, using it to anoint their bodies and hair. One Iroquois claimed that the oil prevented hair loss and color change. The Iroquois also used sunflower oil to anoint the sacred painted and carved wooden masks worn in their False Face healing ceremonies. A dish of roasted, pounded sunflower seeds mixed with roasted white corn and maple sugar was served during the ceremonies. This dish was also used as a cure for coughs.[31] Modern research has confirmed the potential health benefits of sunflower seeds, which are full of vitamin E, a major antioxidant. At Burnham-Shepard sunflowers had been stored in a pit lined with big bluestem grass (*Adropogon gerardii*), also identified as a lining at archaeological sites in upstate New York. This grass resists mold and has been used in the same way by pre- and post-contact Eastern Plains Indians.[32]

So how was horticulture introduced to Connecticut communities and who introduced it? Sites containing maize have been radiocarbon-dated as early as 1100 to 1050 B.P. (at Site 211-1-1 in the Hudson River valley in eastern New York)[33] and 1030 B.P. ±80 years (from the Gnagey site in Pennsylvania),[34] about 100 to 150 years earlier than documented in Connecticut. Using relatively new technologies, New York researchers have recently reported even earlier dates from plant phytoliths "extracted from directly AMS dated cooking residues" on clay pots, which "indicate that maize was being grown in central New York by at least the calibrated first century A.D."[35]

With earlier dates to the west and south, maize was obviously introduced through the established trade routes that had been used to carry exotic stone and other bartered items from these regions into Connecticut for thousands of years. That this trade was as active as ever is made clear by the large percentages of exotic cherts and flints found on Late Woodland sites. At least 80 percent of the lithics from the Late Woodland Burnham-Shepard and Kasheta sites in South Windsor,

## MAIZE SOUP RECIPE

Late Woodland Native peoples would have made a simple maize soup by scraping corn into a clay pot with water and other ingredients, such as pumpkin, beans, or squash added to thicken the soup. Coastal people would have added seafood, fish, or shellfish, an early clam or fish chowder. Each cook undoubtedly had his or her own way of preparing the dish, using any familiar wild herbs, therefore making the flavor of the soup personal. The traditional recipe here lists ingredients that would have been available around A.D. 1000—a really perfect, nutritious food.

### Corn Soup

4 ears of corn, scraped from cob

1 wild onion, diced

6 cups water or broth

1 cup yellow corn meal

1/2 cup of animal fat,diced

1 cup game meat (venison, rabbit or other small game), cut into small pieces

Dash wild pepper and sea salt, or any wild herb

Simmer all for about three hours.

Note

From Abenaki artist, writer, and Connecticut resident Dale Carson, food columnist for the Indian Country Today Media Network and *Indian Life*. Used with permission.

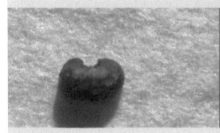 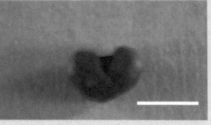

Carbonized maize kernels, from the Morgan site (6-HT-120) in Rocky Hill, and the Indian River site in Milford, Connecticut. Scale bar 1 centimeter.

for example, were of chert and flint.[36] In the Farmington Valley area of central Connecticut, up to 100 percent of the lithic assemblages are exotics.[37] Results of the Iroquois Gas Pipeline archaeological study in western Connecticut show that most chert artifacts are found in late Middle and Late Woodland sites (the study combined these two periods), averaging a little below 50 percent of the total lithic assemblage.[38]

Connecticut peoples most likely received maize from trading partners in the Hudson River valley, the Mid-Atlantic, or both. Several Late Woodland sites in Connecticut show strong associations with Hudson Valley and other New York chert sources. New York pottery sherds from the Owasco and other Late Woodland cultural traditions found at Connecticut sites, such as the Morgan site, are evidence for New York–Connecticut social relationships.[39] Yet jasper artifacts at some sites and Mid-Atlantic pottery styles in southwestern Connecticut show continued southern relations as well. Radiocarbon dates suggest that maize kernels and the information on how to grow them were carried into southern New England along coastal routes and along the major rivers.[40]

In southern New England indigenous societies responded differently to the new food according to each society's specific ecological relations within its homeland. Maize arrived in Connecticut as early as A.D. 1000, according to current evidence, but more recent studies of indigenous coastal communities still showed little pre–A.D. 1500 maize horticulture.[41] Even though they were apparently the first to be introduced to maize, communities on Long Island Sound showed little interest in horticulture until late in the period. There are few examples of maize from pre-contact coastal sites, with most instead dating after European contact, post–A.D. 1500. The marsh and sea ecozones along the coast offered so many food sources that these societies were able to maintain their traditional broad-spectrum economies based on deer hunting, shellfishing and finfishing, and wild plant gathering, supporting large, semi-sedentary villages from the Late Archaic through the Final Woodland period. In contrast, in the inland regions, the food resources were less abundant and more seasonally restricted. It is thought that these distinctive environments promoted different choices in the adoption of maize horticulture. Interior communities needed maize, a reliable, abundant food source that could be stored.[42]

Growing maize is hard work. The clearing, hoeing, planting, and continual weeding and pest control it requires take up lots of time and energy and would have interfered with the traditional seasonal round of foraging activities. Why would indigenous women give up the lucrative foraging technologies of wild plants passed down from mother to daughter over the ages to take on a new, difficult, time-consuming, and potentially risky economic task such as maize horticulture? They apparently did not, if they could avoid it. Indigenous communities were still gathering and consuming wild plants as food well into the early twentieth century.[43] Coastal sites contain little evidence for domesticates and few horticultural tools, unlike the Connecticut River valley sites with their relatively common maize remains and characteristic "Windsor hoes," stone counterparts of the steel cutting ends of modern garden hoes that were first discovered on archaeology sites in Windsor, Connecticut. Archaeological research on Long Island supports this, as archaeologist Dr. David Bernstein noted in his discussion of Native American plant foods there.

> The most interesting question has been whether or not coastal Algonquins were raising and consuming maize in significant quantities prior to the initial European arrival, usually placed at A.D. 1524. For now, the archaeological evidence suggests that the answer to this question is no. The presence of maize, or any other cultigens, at sites in the region, especially those in coastal New York, is very limited, although until many more late (post–A.D. 1000) prehistoric sites are excavated, the issue remains unresolved.[44]

One possible exception could be a Late Woodland community in the Housatonic River estuary reported by Dr. Daniel Cassedy in his summary of the archaeological findings of the Iroquois Gas Pipeline survey. Sites 294A-AF2-1 and 294A-25-2 contained a total of seventy-nine maize remains: fifty-one cupules, thirteen glumes, and fifteen kernels.[45]

### Site 294A-25-2

This large, multicomponent site in the Housatonic estuary at Milford was occupied intensively from the Late Woodland through Post-Contact periods.[46] It contained both Late Woodland artifacts and pit features that provided information on diet and the economic activities performed there. Among the broken clay pots, bifaces, cores, hammerstones, and debitage, not one Late Woodland triangular projectile point was recovered. Because the site was in an old farm field, collectors may have stripped the site of such "treasures." The lower Housatonic River valley

A Sebonac Stamped pot from the lower Housatonic River valley (possibly in Derby).

has been a collector's paradise for well over one hundred years. Still, it may be that hunting was not as important as in earlier periods, possibly taking a back seat to plant and shellfish harvesting and finfishing. Also, we have no idea how important trapping was as an alternative to hunting. Seventeenth-century Europeans noted that their Native American neighbors used a variety of traps and snares.[47]

The main activities at this site were shellfish, plant, and animal processing, and making late-stage biface tools. The calcium-rich mollusk shells in the refuse pits neutralized the acidic soils and preserved deer and fish bones (herring), as well as charred hickory, butternut, and acorn shells, and other plant remains, including maize cobs and kernels. The cobs suggested that the maize fields were close to the settlement—it would be inefficient to carry the cobs any great distance, so they would be shucked and only the kernels transported. Seeds from other edible plants included bindweed, bramble, goosefoot, huckleberry, lady's thumb, pinkweed, pokeweed, ragweed, sumac, and wild legumes. The dietary remains suggested a multiseasonal base camp with occupations from spring through fall.

Four of the six features with maize at Site 294A-25-2 produced five radiocarbon dates: 710 B.P. ±50 years, 690 B.P. ±60 years, 560 B.P. ±70 years, 310 B.P. ±60 years, and 230 B.P. ±60 years.[48] One of the seven maize features at Site 294A-AF2-1, Feature 10, produced two radiocarbon dates, 440 B.P. ±70 years and 430 B.P. ±80 years. This feature also contained six "questionable" bean fragments. Thus, only two of the five dated maize features from the Milford community predate A.D. 1500 (that is, about 450 B.P.).

### Connecticut River Valley Sites

In the lower Connecticut River valley, sites of Late Woodland communities contain relatively large amounts of maize kernels compared with coastal sites, as well as hoes and storage pits.[49] One reason is that the broad, fertile river floodplains are better for large-scale horticulture. Spring flooding continually rejuvenates the soils with fresh nutrients. The area was a breadbasket for English colonists and American Yankees, and continues to produce rich corn and other crops for the few farmers still living in the state. Second, unlike coastal peoples, communities in this part of the valley did not have the dense, rich marsh and marine resources that could be exploited throughout the year.[50]

For the inland indigenous communities, storable maize provided a year-round food source. When the Dutch explorer Adriaen Block sailed up the Connecticut River in 1614 he noted large villages with maize fields between present-day Middletown and Hartford.[51] Some Late Woodland communities farther upriver, such as the residents of the Skitchewaug site in southern Vermont, a large settlement dated to 830 B.P., also practiced maize, bean, and squash horticulture.[52]

Yet it is not certain that maize was important to all Late Woodland Connecticut Valley communities. The sparse presence of maize on four Connecticut Valley sites in Massachusetts—Gill, Indian Crossing, Guida, and Pine Hill—led archaeologist Elizabeth Chilton to conclude that maize was a dietary supplement and not a staple for their inhabitants.[53] Dr. Chilton has also questioned the accuracy

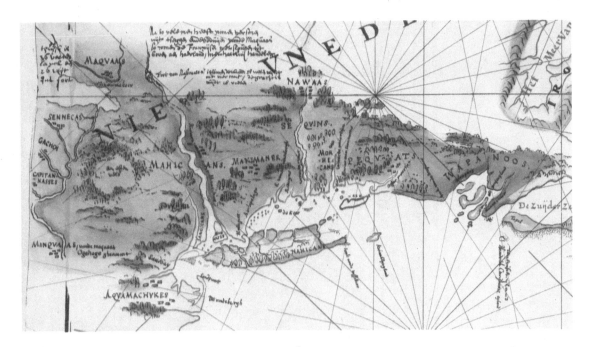

of methods used to determine that cultigens were significant in the Late Woodland economy of inland peoples.[54]

We need more exact measuring to compare the relative importance of cultigens at specific sites and within regions and subregions. One suggestion is to use density studies (kernels per liter of soil) along with complementary studies of technology, settlement patterns, and anthropogenesis (the presence of weeds showing horticultural ground disturbance).[55] Still, 1,500 kernels of maize in 16 features at the inland Burnham-Shepard site,[56] compared with 79 maize specimens from 13 features at the two coastal sites 294A-AF2-1 and 294A-25-2,[57] certainly seems to show the relative significance of horticulture at the inland site.

Moreover, 1,500 kernels can be substantial, even though one cob of Northern Flint corn contains about 240 kernels, once preservation factors are considered. For example, a single plant of goosefoot (genus *Chenopodium*), a wild plant reported from Connecticut sites as early as the late Paleo-Indian period, normally produces tens of thousands of seeds. Yet archaeologists have recovered nowhere near this amount from individual sites. At Burnham-Shepard, a pit feature containing hundreds of maize kernels included only 50 *Chenopodium* seeds. This suggests a preservation bias and that 1,500 kernels really is a substantial amount to recover.

Also, in discussing the practice of substantial maize horticulture, I do not include all inland peoples, but only those who lived in the Connecticut River valley above its estuary to about present-day Hartford. Late Woodland horticulture in this region was considerable, but not intensive, and in no way comparable to the *farming* activities of contemporary Iroquois peoples in central New York or the Pueblo communities in the American Southwest. Maize horticulture was "im-

Detail from a 1616 facsimile of Adriaen Block's map of New Netherland from 1614 showing Native American homelands.

A single plant of lamb's quarters (*Chenopodium album*), a wild plant in the goosefoot family, produces tens of thousands of seeds and is very nutritious. This herbarium specimen was collected in Milford, Connecticut, in 1899.

portant" and "significant" in that it provided a productive, nutritious, storable grain that fed people during the lean winter months, and a "staple" because it was needed to support the expanding, more concentrated Late Woodland populations who lived in large multiseasonal base camps such as the Morgan and Burnham-Shepard sites.

The adoption of maize horticulture does not seem to have affected to any great extent the traditional seasonal round of these communities. Analysis of food remains from Morgan, Burnham-Shepard, and other Late Woodland sites shows that Native Americans continued to collect wild plants in the late spring, summer, and early fall; to process nuts and acorns in late summer and early fall; to harvest anadromous fish species (shad, salmon, rainbow smelt, alewives, blueback herring) in the spring; to hunt migrating waterfowl (ducks and geese) in spring and fall; and to collect shellfish, hunt deer and other mammals (black bear, beaver, squirrel, raccoon, cottontail rabbit, red fox), reptiles (turtles, snakes), and birds (particularly turkey) throughout the year.[58] Planting activities are called "horticulture" rather than "agriculture" in Native Connecticut, because they were only one part of the economy, not its foundation.

The density and variety of artifacts and cultural features found at some Late Woodland sites suggest that the sites were occupied for more than a single season, in contrast to most of the Archaic and earlier Woodland sites.[59] Additionally, in the lower Connecticut Valley at least, the upland sites were only temporary occupations that were often centered around a specific task; for example, a women's nut-collecting and processing camp, or an overnight stay at a rock shelter by travelers, as suggested by the Salmon River Rock Shelter in Colchester[60] and several of the rock shelters in southwestern Connecticut.[61]

### Morgan Site

The Morgan site is a large Late Woodland multiseasonal settlement of over 10 acres (4 hectares) in the floodplain of the Connecticut River in Rocky Hill, about 42 miles (68 kilometers) from Long Island Sound.[62] The site yielded five radiocarbon dates: 885 B.P. ±45 years (directly from a maize kernel), 780 B.P. ±90, 780 B.P. ±70, 630 B.P. ±70, and 590 B.P. ±70 years.[63] The recovery of thousands of artifacts, two human burials, and more than a hundred cooking, refuse, and storage features within a relatively small excavation block of 35.5 by 60 feet, or 2,100 square feet (about 11 by 18 meters, or 195 square meters) shows that the site was intensively occupied.

A major activity at the site was pottery and pipe manufacture, as shown by the recovery of 13,685 sherds, 49 elbow-pipe fragments, 44 pieces of unfired clay coils, a piece of clay whistle or flute, and at least one large, shallow fire-reddened pit feature in which pots may have been fired. The sherds from undisturbed contexts below the plow zone tell us much about the people who lived at this site. A very conservative estimate, based on the rim sherds and distinctive decorative motifs found on body sherds, suggests there were at least 144 pots in a variety of styles. Most were assigned to the Windsor tradition.

The mixture of collared and uncollared styles within the same levels and cultural features suggests gradual material culture replacement rather than the traditional Northeast model of a series of artifact replacements characterizing ceramic stages and cultural phases. Similar diversity occurred in the Late Woodland pottery assemblages from the South Windsor sites of Burnham-Shepard, Kasheta, and Butternut Knolls.[64] The presence of pottery styles from the Point Peninsula and Owasco archaeological traditions of upper New York at the Morgan site indicates social relationships with the Hudson Valley.[65] The increasing presence of these styles through time supports the conclusion drawn from the increased

Ceramic remains from the Morgan site in Rocky Hill, including clay pipe bowls (top left). Scale bar equals 1 centimeter. Top right, a complete collared Niantic Incised pot (illustrated in the pottery chronology chart shown in Chapter 6) found in the pit where it had been stored (Feature 43). Charcoal from four pit features dated from 780 to 590 B.P., although a maize kernel found at the site was directly dated by AMS to 885 B.P. Bottom, a variety of incised and impressed (mainly shell-stamped) rim sherds recovered from the site.

amounts of exotic stone that interregional communications were intensifying. The forty-nine pipe fragments represent at least forty-one different elbow pipes, the largest collection of pipes found on a site in southern New England![66]

The smaller amounts of stone artifacts recovered included chipped, ground, and rough stone tools that represent a variety of economic activities, many gender-related.[67] For example, the recovery of celts, adzes, drills, and some scrapers reflect men's woodworking activities. The triangular Levanna points indicate male hunting or late-stage biface manufacture, or both. The hoes, pestles, and choppers signify women's horticultural and food processing activities. A shallow mortar was used by women to crush stone temper for pottery manufacture.[68] The chipped hand spades were probably used by women to redig the storage pits, since several were cached at the top of the pits. These and the multipurpose hammers, grinding stones, pitted stones, and utilized flakes were the tools and activities typical at village sites.

The virtual absence of cores, primary flakes, and artifacts representing early stages of biface manufacture indicates that the first stages of toolmaking were not part of the community's activities. Most likely this work was done at quarry sites or tool-making workshops that were part of the Morgan community's seasonal round. This kept the residential base camp clean of the sharp debris that experiments replicating this primitive technology show are the by-products of stone knapping.[69]

## Pits, Potage, and Plant Use

The Morgan site had many kinds of cultural features densely packed in the excavated grid area, among them shallow disk-shaped firepits, larger deeper earth ovens, refuse pits, storage pits (one was filled with deer antler—stock for future tool manufacture—another with a complete pot), a shallow deeply reddened pit that may have been used to fire pots, and two burials. The site was deep, over 5.5

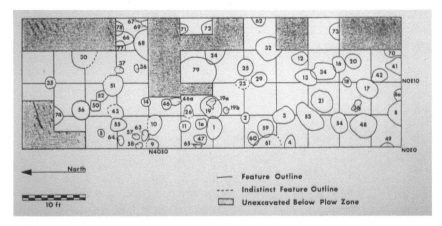

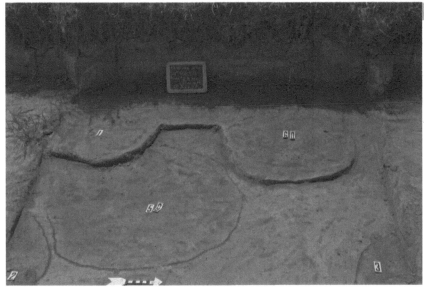

The Morgan site, Rocky Hill, Connecticut: plan of overlapping features (top); and the partly excavated tops of several layered features.

Profiles of earth oven features excavated by Albert Morgan Archaeological Society members at the Morgan site, showing evidence of charcoal, fired rock, and burned earth.

feet (almost 2 meters) in some areas, with features above and below each other and also overlapping. This density in fairly alkaline soils preserved many floral and faunal remains.

Fauna included white-tailed deer (the major meat staple) and a variety of other wildlife: small mammals (wildcat, rabbit, and dog), bird, turtle, fish (yellow perch was the only species identified), and freshwater and saltwater shellfish (mussel, quahog, and soft-shell clam). Morgan is north of marine shellfish beds, which shows that its residents were in contact with coastal communities. Native informants and local histories by Anglo-Americans have mentioned post-contact Indian groups making annual seasonal treks to the coast to fish and returning home with a catch of dried seafood.[70] The Morgan site finds indicate that this aspect of the post-contact inland seasonal round had its roots in the Late Woodland, if not earlier. Thomas Morton, an English colonist at Massachusetts Bay in the early seventeenth century, remarked on the trade between coastal peoples and those living inland: "So likewise, at the season of the year, the savages that live by the seaside . . . trade with the inlanders for fresh water . . . chestnuts and such like useful things as one place affordeth, are sold to the inhabitants of another, where they are a novelty accompted amongst the natives of the land."[71]

Perhaps the Morgan community traded some of its maize for marine resources, or provided it as tribute for the temporary use of a coastal community's homelands for fishing. Marine shell on other inland sites and the small amounts of maize found on some coastal sites before A.D. 1500 suggest exchange and gender dynamics.[72]

Botanical remains from the Morgan site revealed more about the economy, technology, seasonal-settlement system, and medicinal herbalism of its community. Most of the features contained maize kernels or fragments. A radiocarbon date of 885 B.P. ±45 years directly from a maize kernel is one of the earliest dates for maize horticulture in New England.[73] One hearth feature contained a complete pot that seems to have shattered during cooking and been left where it had broken. Its contents included maize and deer bone, probably the remnants of a spilled stew or gruel.

Other floral remains were identified through flotation and microscopic analysis, including butternut or black walnut, hickory, beech or chestnut, mulberry, blueberry, raspberry, *Chenopodium, Plantago* sp. (common plantain or goose-tongue; if the latter, which is a plant that grows in coastal marshes, the remains support the coastal connections discussed above), knotweed, *Gallium* (bedstraw?), *Oxalis* (sorrel), *Gaylussacia* (huckleberry), charred flower parts that resemble *Sparganium* (bur-reed) or *Carex* (sedge), *Portulaca, Potamogeton* (pondweed), *Cerastium, Calandrinia* (redmaids), grasses, and *Brassica* (possibly mustard). A large rectangular piece of burned bark recovered from an area with post molds was identified as elm and could have been from the bark covering of a wigwam, like those described by English colonists.[74]

In 1998, after our excavations had been closed for several years, the property owner ran a 1,600-foot irrigation trench through the original study area northward to the treeline bordering the Connecticut River. Thousands more artifacts and ecofacts were discovered. A total of 173 pit features were located in both walls along the *entire length* of the trench, showing that the Morgan site was much more extensive spatially than originally thought. They included two storage pits with complete pots and three burial pits in addition to the two discovered during our earlier excavations.[75] The trench profile was so complex, it took a field technician thirty-nine consecutive days to draw it.[76]

Soil samples collected from seven of these features identified plant species rarely documented with traditional identification methods, particularly tubers and rice grains.[77] Instead, these plant remains were found with scanning electron microscopy, or SEM, technology. The six most common species (in descending

Some faunal and flora remains from the Morgan site: charred butternut fragments; marine shell recovered from Feature 8; and charred elm bark *in situ*, most likely the remains of a covering from a wigwam. Scale bars equal 1 centimeter.

order) were sedge (some species produce an edible tuber, but sedge also has been used to line storage pits), cattail root, hickory nutshell, water plantain (*Alisma*), wild rice (*Zizania*), and yellow nutsedge. Other plants included *Chenopodium*, maize, medicinal plants such as club moss and members of the mint family, and those prized for their tubers, shoots, pollen, and seeds, such as groundnut, Jerusalem artichoke, iris (flag), rush, Indian cucumber, water lily, arrowhead, bulrush, and bur-reed.

These remains show that the Morgan site was a multiseasonal settlement occupied from late spring through at least fall. Sometime before early spring, the community moved inland because of annual spring flooding in the area, which often left the site a small island in the Connecticut River. The caches of antler raw material for tool manufacture and whole pots, the stored digging tools, and the radiocarbon dates show that the site was used repeatedly for three hundred years as a village in the community's settlement system.

## OF MORTARS AND PESTLES, THE SPIRITUAL, AND MAGIC

Late Woodland women may have used the traditional stone pestle and mortar to grind cattail tubers, nuts, maize, and other plants into meal and flour. The wear on the only stone mortar found at the Morgan site, however, suggests the shallow object was used to grind sandstone into temper rather than to process food.[78] Several complete and broken cylindrical ground stone pestles were also recovered. Made from basalt, they were most likely quarried from outcrops less than a mile west of the site.

### The Green Corn Ceremony

Women at the Morgan site likely used the cylindrical ground stone pestles together with a cylindrical wooden mortar made from a tree trunk, as did post-contact tribal peoples—right up to this day.[79] Antique communal wooden mortars and cylindrical pestles are used by Mohegan women today during the tribe's annual Wigwam Festival, a harvest festival to honor and thank the Creator for the first ripe, or green, corn in August. Schaghticoke elder and educator Trudie Richmond described a Mohegan Wigwam festival she attended:

> While the Mohegan men gathered to build the traditional wigwam shelter of white birch saplings, the women would bring out the large wooden mortars and pestles. These treasured tools, carefully and respectfully passed down for so many generations, had been used by Martha Uncas, Fidelia Fielding, and Mercy Nonesuch [tribal culture keepers]. Mohegan families would gather for the long preparation of yokeg by pounding the corn after roasting and parching the kernels in hot ashes. It was a time of great excitement and joy because families came together for a single purpose: to celebrate Green Corn.[80]

The birch wigwam and corn grinding symbolize Native peoples' close relationship with nature and all living things. As Mohegan tribal historian and medicine woman Melissa J. Fawcett (now Zobel) clearly articulated, the continual use

A Windsor hoe of basalt with a highly polished bit; below, a mortar and grinder from the Morgan site. The only mortar found at the site, it had surface polish similar to mortars used for grinding temper for pottery making.

of the ancient mortars sustains the connections between tribal members, Mother Earth, and the spirit world of their ancestors:

> Cup-shaped carvings at the base of Mohegan mortars reflect the medicine of Grandfather Turtle (on whose back the Great Spirit created the world) and the life-giving powers of Mohegan womanhood. Many mortars and pestles pass from one generation to the next in a sacred chain of remembrance.[81]

The festival and its rituals were, and still are, a graphic reminder to the community — particularly the youngest generation — that they are a part of Nature and must always strive for harmony between the physical and social environment, the mundane and the spiritual worlds, to survive. Many Native American children's stories embrace these themes. Erin Lamb Meeches, a Schaghticoke tribal leader and dancer, explained how the Green Corn festival functioned to help provide the material and psychological balance that indigenous philosophy teaches is so necessary for human survival:

# THE TURTLE IN NATIVE AMERICAN CREATION STORIES

Turtles have spiritual significance among Northeastern Indian peoples. Creation stories credit the turtle with helping to make the world—a bit of soil was brought up from the primordial ocean floor by another animal (usually "brother" muskrat) and placed on the back of "grandfather" turtle to form the earth, or Turtle Island, on which we now live.

For southern New England indigenous peoples, the turtle symbolized earth, motherhood, and fertility.[a] According to some New England sacred stories, the Creator made the first humans of stone. Disliking this creation, he broke them and then made people of wood. From these all people descended.[b] The Lenni Lenape (the Delaware, including the Munsee whose homelands were New Jersey and southern New York) people told a slightly different version, in which the Creator made men grow from the Tree of Life that had sprung up from the turtle's back, as related by anthropologist Dr. Frank Speck:

As early as 1670 the Delaware are recorded as declaring that all things came from the tortoise, that it brought forth the world, that from its back a tree had sprung upon whose branches men had grown, that it had a power and a nature to produce all things such as earth, and the like; that it brought forth what the supreme divinity wished through it to produce.[c]

These stories can be taken either literally or metaphorically, as we do the Judeo-Christian creation story in Genesis.

Notes

a. Bragdon 1996, 214.

b. Bruchac 1987, 2; Williams 1643, 197.

c. Speck 1931, 45.

A turtle-shaped boulder mortar at the edge of wetlands in Torrington, Connecticut.

Traditionally, the Green Corn Celebration in New England heralded the first corn of the season, and brought together members of the community in a celebration to prevent disharmony and famine. It was a time for forgiving and strengthening bonds between families and friends.[82]

According to Dale Carson, a Western Abenaki tribal member and Native American chef and author:

> Corn/maize is referred to in most Native languages as "Mother" or "Life," which indicates its extreme importance. . . . Corn is a "wonder food." So much depends on this beautiful grain, and it is fitting and proper that we celebrate and honor [it].[83]

Carson points out that "almost everything we purchase at the supermarket features corn in some way—from the corn-fed meat we buy and the cornstarch spray . . . to alcoholic beverages, baby food and even makeup."[84]

Green Corn festivals are celebrated annually by tribal peoples throughout New England. These traditional harvest ceremonies have been documented since the seventeenth century,[85] and probably originated in the Late Woodland with the beginnings of maize horticulture. As Trudie Richmond noted,

> It is the indigenous peoples of the Americas who maintain the spiritual and cultural connections with this wondrous plant [maize], which is celebrated in ceremonies, blessings, and in oral traditions. "No matter how much or how little corn your garden gives," my grandmother would say, "always give thanks. Otherwise the Creator may not see fit to give you anything the next year." In southern New England the Green Corn Ceremony was the celebration of the first corn. It was to give thanks and show appreciation for what was being provided. At one time this meant great preparation of corn, songs, dances and special prayers. The early settlers often interpreted this flurry of activity as being a preparation for war because warriors always carried a pouch of *yokeg* (traveling corn) to feed themselves.[86]

Among the Mahikan (now known as Mohican) people, the Green Corn Ceremony was one of the two most important ceremonies in the annual public ceremonial round. Lasting seven days and nights, it included wearing masks, ritual purification, and food offerings to the spirit world. The other important ceremony was the Bear Sacrifice in January, a midwinter religious festival that lasted ten to twelve days. A bear was sacrificed to the Great Bear Spirit and its skull decorated and placed in a tree in hopes that the Great Bear would make game animals plentiful for Mahikan hunters.[87]

## Phallic Pestles

Pestles representing male genitalia have been found on sites in both eastern and western Connecticut, such as on the Dill Farm in East Haddam, in the post-contact grave of an adult male Niantic tribal member accidentally unearthed dur-

## INDIGENOUS STORIES

Native American stories are multilayered. On one level the narratives, legends, and folktales are meant to enter-tain. On another, storylines are tools for teaching tribal members about origins, the natural world, and how to get along with one another and with neighbors, be they one-legged (trees and plants), two-legged (humans), or four-legged (animals). Stories teach tribal cosmology, values, and spirituality. On yet another level they are mnemonic devices for passing down tribal history and other important information to succeeding generations. The Abenaki writer Dale Carson gives these examples:

> Algonquians recounted legends about the origin of corn, beans, squash, cranberries, and other things to their children. One favorite was the tale of Manabozho who, they said, created all living things as well as the earth. There were tales of giants and wee people and stories to explain nature's work—like thunder, lightning, and the wind.[a]

Two of the most famous culture heroes of southeastern New England tribes are Maushop (Weetucks) the giant and his wife Squant (Squannit), leader of the "little people." Writing in 1643, the Puritan minister Roger Williams mentioned the tales of the giant and "Squauanit," the "woman's god," which suggests that the stories are very old. They are still told by modern indigenous peoples.[b]

*(continued)*

Modern storytellers: Janis Us (Mohawk-Shinnecock descent), with her story bag; Trudie Richmond (Schaghticoke), telling a story with animal hand puppets; bottom, Dr. Margaret M. Bruchac (Abenaki), with her husband Justin, using rattles, drum, and song in their storytelling.

Often these stories concern the origin of real localities within indigenous ancestral homelands, linking cultural identity to specific historical and sacred places on the landscape. Ancestral and contemporary indigenous identities are sustained through tribal history, collective memory, and the physical and spiritual landscapes of ancestral homelands.[c] According to one scholarly study: "Landscape is a powerful factor in the operation of memory because of the associations narrators make between the local landscape and the events of the stories they tell. Ancestors and the mythological events often become fixed in a specific landscape and act as timeless reference points."[d]

Notes

a. Carson 1987, 76.

b. As related by Aquinnah Wampanoag Linda Coombs, Associate Director, Wampanoag Indigenous Program at Plimoth Plantation, and cited in Bell 2009; Fawcett 2000; Simmons 1986, 172–246.

c. Bell 2009.

d. Christie 2009, cited in Bell 2009.

An idealized portrait of Granny Squannit, the leader of the "Little People," by David R. Wagner.

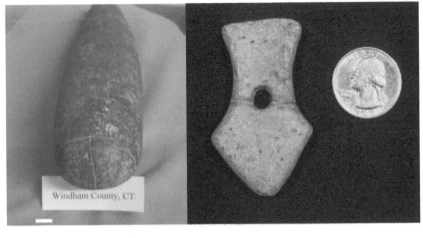

Phallic artifacts: stone pestle from Windham County, Connecticut (scale bar is 1 centimeter); carved stone pendant (top right); large stone pestle found near Norwich, Connecticut (bottom).

ing house construction in a seventeenth-century Niantic tribal cemetery in Old Lyme,[88] and at the small upland Archaic site of Newtown-Hunt.[89] The use of phallic ground stone tools dates back to before European contact.

The symbolism is obvious. Human genitalia produce babies and represent fertility. A phallic pestle used to process food was a charm intended to promote plentiful crops, which were so necessary for the very existence of the toolmaker's community. A phallic stone gouge from Windsor[90] was a magical charm meant to replace and increase the trees cut to form the framework of houses or carved into canoes, bows, arrow shafts, bowls, ladles, flutes, and the many other wooden objects necessary for survival.

## Magic

The form of magic represented by the phallic pestle is described in *The Golden Bough*, the classic study of magic and religion by Scottish anthropologist James Frazer, as sympathetic magic.

> If we analyse the principles of thought on which magic is based, they will probably be found to resolve themselves into two: first, that like produces like, or that an effect resembles its cause; and, second, that things which have once been in contact with each other continue to act on each other at a distance after the physical contact has been severed. The former principle may be called the Law of Similarity, the latter the Law of Contact or Contagion. From the first of these principles, namely the Law of Similarity, the magician infers that he can produce any effect he desires merely by imitating it: from the second he infers that whatever he does to a material object will affect equally the person with whom the object was once in contact, whether it

## MAGICAL POTS AND FERTILE MORTARS

Passive resistance to colonialism was also expressed in indigenous oral traditions, folklore, and material culture.[a] An example is found in the early post-contact Mohegan Shantok Incised clay pots first discovered at the Fort Shantok archaeological site. Archaeologist Dr. Bert Salwen was apparently the first to notice the correlation between the style's decorative designs and female genitalia and breasts.[b]

Some Shantok pots have a molded rim point showing a woman carrying a baby on her back. There is one in the Yale Peabody Museum archaeological collection. The pots were used not only as cooking vessels, but as magical charms for Mohegan-Pequot fertility and food abundance, and they were also potent Mohegan social symbols, as Dr. Russell Handsman explains: "We think 17th century Mohegan pots, with their stylized references to women's bodies and women as mothers, reminded everyone of the need to reproduce and preserve

A wooden (buttonball) Indian mortar, possibly Mohegan, and stone pestle given to the Sherman family of Black Point, Niantic, about 1730 by an Indian, and later (about 1908) given to John C. Booth by the last member of the Sherman family. Mortar height about 10 inches (25 centimeters), breadth at top and bottom about 7.5 inches (19 centimeters); length of pestle about 7 inches (almost 18 centimeters). Right, a Mohegan woman, Harriet Fielding Tantaquidgeon, using a wooden tree trunk mortar in 1937.

native traditions and culture. Mortars also functioned in this way; they shared styles of decoration with the incised and modeled pots."[c]

Large mortars were used to prepare *yokeg*, a corn food, during the Mohegan harvest festival. Also called the Wigwam Festival, it was likely an ancient thanksgiving feast dating back to at least Late Woodland times. Observed in the early twentieth century, it continues to be celebrated by the Mohegans today, who still use the community-owned mortars.[d]

Notes

    a. Handsman 1988.

    b. Douglas Jordan, personal communication.

    c. Handsman 1988, 31.

    d. Fawcett 2000.

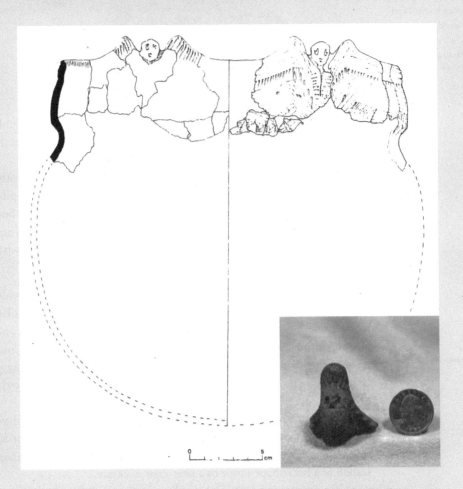

Reconstruction of the pot profile of a Shantok Incised vessel from the Coudert Ledge (75-6) site, a seasonal camp in Lyme, Connecticut, which shows heads emerging from two vagina-like rim points, symbolizing birth. Inset, a Shantok Incised rim point from the Fort Shantok site in Montville, Connecticut, with a face design on one side and a baby on the other.

A stone elbow pipe carved in the form of a seated bird (owl?), from the Spring Brook Farm site in Milford, Connecticut. Birds were often considered intermediaries between humans and the spirit world and the Creator. Owls were associated with death, and often thought to act as guides to the soul.

formed part of his body or not. Charms based on the Law of Similarity may be called Homoeopathic or Imitative Magic. Charms based on the Law of Contact or Contagion may be called Contagious Magic.

But in practice the two branches are often combined; . . . Both branches of magic, the homoeopathic and the contagious, may conveniently be comprehended under the general name of Sympathetic Magic, since both assume that things act on each other at a distance through a secret sympathy, the impulse being transmitted from one to the other by means of what we may conceive as a kind of invisible ether.[91]

The Connecticut pestles and gouge made to look like male genitalia were expected to induce reproduction when they came in contact with plant tubers, maize kernels, or wood. Other artifacts (tools, pipes, basketry) with aesthetically pleasing animal and floral designs in all likelihood held spiritual and magical powers, and the characteristics of that particular animal or plant (bravery, fortitude, hunting prowess, fertility, ability to heal) would be passed on to the object's owner or user.

Bears, for example, were associated with physical and spiritual power and with the spirit world.[92] The Mahikans believed that the Great Bear Spirit controlled all animals.[93] The bear's qualities might be passed on to someone in possession of a bear-shaped pipe or a bear-claw necklace.

Often represented on nineteenth-century woodsplint baskets and beaded bags, the strawberry plant symbolizes cleansing and renewal. Indeed the very clothing worn by indigenous peoples often incorporated magical or spiritual decoration. One example is Native American beadwork, as Mi'kmaq (Micmac)

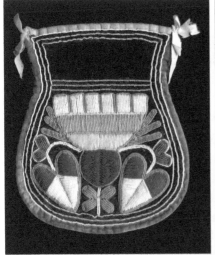
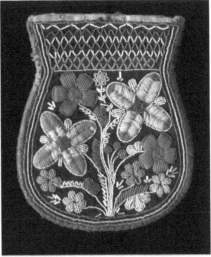
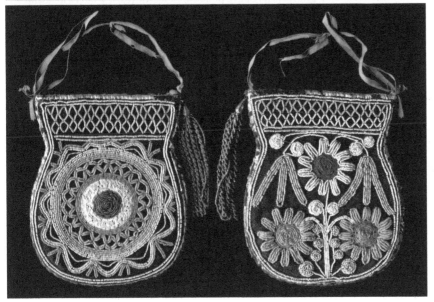

Algonkian Wabanaki-type beaded bags from northern New England, inverted keyhole shape, embroidered with glass beads, in floral designs with deep symbolism, all from the third quarter of the nineteenth century. Top left: With black velvet fabric and brown velvet edge binding, 6.75 inches (17 centimeters) high by 5.75 inches (15 centimeters) wide, with a thistle design and examples of heart-shaped leaves. Thistles are medicinal plants used to cure a variety of ailments, and the thistle design itself may have had preventive properties. Top right: With black velvet fabric, silk ribbon edge binding and cotton lining, 6.2 inches (about 16 centimeters) high by 5.2 inches (13 centimeters) wide. Bottom: With black velvet fabric, silk ribbon edge binding and carrying strap, cotton lining (both sides of the bag are shown), 6.2 inches (16 centimeters) high by 5.2 inches (13 centimeters) wide. The tassel is made entirely of faceted metal beads and may not be original to the bag, but could have been added by the original owner.

descendant and beadwork expert Gerry Biron showed in his traveling exhibit on Northeastern beadwork, *Made of Thunder, Made of Glass*.

> Endowed with sacred values, the design motifs . . . are steeped in the mystical world view of the Northeast Woodland peoples. The Wabanaki in particular believed that there was power and magic in the decorations they placed on their personal attire. An artistic representation of a sacred plant, for instance, had a protective effect upon the wearer that was as powerful as the plant itself.[94]

Among indigenous peoples, art for art's sake was an unfamiliar concept. For them all art had a pragmatic purpose. Magic and reverence of the sacred are two

## INDIGENOUS HEALERS

Called "Indian doctors" by contemporary white neighbors, and "shamans" or "medicine men" by anthropologists, American Indian medical practitioners were chosen by their white clients for the efficacy of their services over those of the local physician. Although most cures were accomplished through the application of medicinal wild plants in the form of teas, poultices, and washes, psychotherapeutical techniques were sometimes used.[a] The Englishman William Wood recounted one of these episodes in 1634.

> He wrapped a piece of cloth about the foot of the lame man [and] upon the wrapping of a beaver skin through which he—laying his mouth to the beaver skin—by his sucking charms he brought out the stump [splinter] which he spat into a tray of water.[b]

Early English witnesses did not understand the psychotherapies of indigenous medicinal and religious practitioners and misinterpreted the meaning and function of the psychiatric performances. Some believed the "powwaws" were in league with the Devil, so in Massachusetts Native healers were prohibited "by English law" from practicing within English jurisdiction under the penalty of five pounds.[c] In recent years, Western medicine has been seriously studying and using both Native American psychiatric practices and herbal remedies. Many of these remedies are sold in health food stores and are prescribed by naturopathic physicians. The root of the black cohosh, for example, is often included in medications that treat premenstrual syndrome. Parts of the echinacea (coneflower) and golden seal plants are used in teas and medicines to alleviate flu symptoms. According to one psychologist:

> For many centuries, Western investigators had little respect or regard for shamanism or for native rituals. In recent years, however, such prominent psychotherapists as Achterberg (1985), Frank and Frank (1991) and Torrey (1986) have found *many native practices to be extremely sophisticated and to contain elements that can be instructive for Western practitioners,* e.g., the use of imagination and altered states of consciousness for health and personal growth . . . rituals are being studied by social scientists from psychoanalytic, linguistic, phenomenological and other perspectives.[d]

Native American healers included women as well as men. Healers were normally taught their craft through an apprenticeship system. Often the teacher was a grandparent or tribal elder. In her book on Eastern Algonquian folk medicine, anthropologist Gladys Tantaquidgeon, herself a Mohegan medicine woman, reported that "beginning in the early 1900s, I accompanied my maternal grandmother, Lydia Fielding, to nearby fields and wooded areas in search of herbs to be gathered and dried for use in making medicine." The elder women would watch the girls and discuss which ones might be suited to learn certain skills, such as plant medicine. Tantaquidgeon listed several of those herbs and their curative functions,[e] and referred to the non-herbal, psychiatric techniques of some medical practitioners as "magic," noting that they

> could effect cures without the use of herbs; others used herbs in addition to their magical practices. . . . [T]his knowledge is regarded as personal property; persons possessed of power to heal the sick, either through magical practices without the use of herbs or through the use of herbs, were held in high esteem by members of the tribe. The fame of certain men and women spread from tribe to tribe, and several informants mentioned itinerant "doctors" within their memory who traveled from place to place healing the sick.[f]

The sweat lodge—a small wigwam-like structure where hot rocks were doused with water to create a steamy atmosphere, something like a modern steam bath—also was used for healing certain illnesses, including joint diseases such as rheumatism, as well as for ritual cleansing.[g] A Native American medicinal plant garden and a trail system at the Institute for American Indian Studies in Washington, Connecticut, have signage that informs visitors about the various healing properties of many native plants and trees.

Notes

a. Moondancer and Strong Woman 1998, 109–110.

b. William Wood 1634, quoted in Bragdon 1996, 201.

c. Gookin 1674, 14.

d. Krippner 1997, 22; emphasis added.

e. Tantaquidgeon 1977, 38–39, 67–80.

f. Ibid., 67–68.

g. Moravian Church Box 114, F1 and Box 115, F. 5; Dally-Starna and Starna 2009, 226.

such purposes. Frank Bergevin, an antiques dealer with a degree in anthropology and an avid collector of Native American beadwork, elaborated on the indigenous attitude toward artwork.

A common thread that runs through much of traditional Native culture is the lack of a concept for art. In fact, the word art is generally not even found in traditional Native vocabularies. The idea that an object could be created for the purpose of producing art is traditionally as foreign to the Native lexicon as the concept that the Earth could be sold. Life is infused with art, and art does not stand alone in contrast to the rest of life. This beadwork that many of us love was not created for the glory of the beadworker, but to revere something beyond the pedestrian.[95]

Melissa Fawcett provided twentieth-century examples of the enduring linkage between craft work and magic in her tribe.

Gladys [Tantaquidgeon]'s uncle, Chief Matahga [Burrill Fielding], knew the power of carving spirit faces onto utensils and animals onto war clubs. Her brother Harold fashioned stone pipes with an X to symbolize the four directions surrounded by four people-dots (representing his esteemed ancestors: Uncas, Sassacus, Occum, and Tantaquidgeon). As they worked, these men spoke of the meaning behind the designs in their work and of the ceremonies related to them.[96]

Belief in magic was also common among European colonists and Connecticut Yankees. In the custom of the "concealment shoe," which goes back to fifteenth-century England and northern Europe, during the construction of a house an old shoe was hidden in the walls or under the floorboards to ward off evil and bring good fortune to the homeowners. English colonists brought the tradition with them and it continued to be practiced into the nineteenth century.[97] The Salem witch trials are a better known example of non-Native New England's belief in magic.

## ADDITIONAL EVIDENCE FOR DIET

## Plant Remains and Food from the Sea

### Burnham-Shepard Site

The Burnham-Shepard site is located in the floodplain of the Connecticut River in South Windsor, north of and across the river from the Morgan site. Discovered in 1978, more intensive excavations were conducted from 1987 through 1990.[98] Burnham-Shepard is a multiseasonal base camp covering about a quarter acre (1,090 square meters), although only about 1,200 square feet (112 square meters) was excavated. Unlike Morgan, it is a multicomponent site. Its major component, however, is Late Woodland, with a small Middle Woodland component. Radiocarbon dates for the Middle Woodland occupations range from 1605 to 1040 B.P. The Late Woodland occupations ranged from 620 to 420 B.P.

As at the Morgan site, cultural features abound and are often overlapping: eighteen hearths, twelve storage pits, three burials, and six unidentified features. One storage pit was about 5 feet by 3 feet (1.5 by 1 meter) in diameter and about a foot (0.33 meter) deep, and lined with big bluestem grass. The pit contained thirty-five sunflower seeds, more than fifty complete and partial *Chenopodium* seeds, and hundreds of maize kernels. One produced a date of 620 B.P., partly contemporary with the later occupation of the Morgan site. Interestingly, the pit was encircled by post molds, suggesting that it may have been enclosed in a structure for protection. These storage pits were similar in size and shape to the underground storage units, or "Indian barnes," used by post-contact New England tribal peoples. Inside, Native American women stored maize in woven bags or baskets capable of holding three to almost eight bushels.[99] In 1637, Thomas Morton described these structures: "Their barnes are holes made in the earth that will hold a hogshead of corne a peece in them. In these . . . they lay their store in great baskets . . . with mats under about the sides and on top: and . . . they cover it with earth."[100]

Although there were so many post molds that patterns were difficult to see, curved configurations and the obvious pairing of several molds indicated the presence of house remains. The excavations also recovered 3,495 stone artifacts, 253 pottery fragments, 2,162 faunal objects, and 17,833 botanical fragments. Unlike Morgan, the relatively small amount of clay sherds suggests that pottery manufacture was not an activity. Like Morgan, the lithic materials did not show early-stage tool manufacture, so those knapping activities were done elsewhere. Only five projectile points were recovered. Exotic chert and flint materials represented 82.4 percent of the total stone assemblage, meaning there was a robust trade for toolstone. Interestingly, 85.6 percent of the earlier Middle Woodland stone assemblage at Burnham-Shepard was made from exotic materials.

More than 70 percent of the faunal remains are highly fragmented, suggesting that women were processing the bone to extract grease, marrow, and the brains and tongue of each animal. Nothing was wasted, in keeping with the respect for nature and the environmental stewardship that figures so prominently in post-contact Native American traditions, art, and folktales. Anything left over from food processing, tool-making, and clothing fabrication was given to the dogs, as seen from the tooth marks on the faunal remains from some sites.[101] Of the identifiable faunal remains, 93 percent were white-tailed deer and medium-sized to large mammals (probably also deer). Those identified simply as mammal accounted for 2.7 percent of the animal remains, while 4.4 percent were identified as beaver, small mammal, bird, turtle, fish (the only identifiable remains were sturgeon), and shellfish (quahog, oyster, and mussel). Like at Morgan, the marine shells show that there was a relationship with coastal communities.

Many of the botanical remains were identical to those recovered at the Morgan site: shells from hickory, butternut, beech nuts, and acorn; seeds of *Chenopodium* sp. (goosefoot, lambsquarters), *Polygonum* sp. (knotweed, smartweed), *Portulaca* sp., *Rubus* sp. (raspberry, blackberry), sumac, cleaver, possible *Viola* sp., grasses, and maize kernels. At Burnham-Shepard, more than 500 whole and 1,000 partial kernels were recovered from 16 features. As noted previously, they closely resemble in size and shape kernels of modern eight-rowed Northeastern Flint corn, the type of corn described as grown by seventeenth-century Indian communities.[102] Additionally, hazelnut shell, wild garlic bulbs, a *Prunus* pit (plum or cherry), and seeds of *Rumex* sp. (dock), *Rosa* sp., wild strawberry, *Vitis* (grape), domesticated sunflower, and domesticated beans were also recovered at Burnham-Shepard. The plant remains suggest a multiseasonal occupation for its Late Woodland community from at least July through October, and possibly longer. (The Middle Woodland occupation was smaller, with less artifact and ecofact content; its plant remains suggested a shorter seasonal duration of September and October.)

The large amount of dietary refuse uncovered at the Burnham-Shepard site shows that, like the Morgan site, the major activities at Burnham-Shepard were food processing and cooking. Discrete activity areas were identified within the site. For example, there were major meat-processing areas located well away from the houses. The community at Burnham-Shepard shared many similarities with that at Morgan: a broad-spectrum economy, relatively significant maize horticulture, multiseasonal occupation with house structures, complex pit technology, simple flexed burials within the residential area, intense food processing and cooking activities, late-stage biface manufacture and maintenance activities, non-anadromous fishing activities, and repeated reuse by the community over time. Some major differences included Morgan's larger size and greater diversity of artifact types (indicating more diverse economic activities), which Dr. Jeffrey Bendremer, a director of excavations at Burnham-Shepard, interpreted to mean that it and Morgan represented two distinct Late Woodland settlement types.[103]

### Another Kind of Settlement: Old Lyme Shell Heap

The Old Lyme Shell Heap was at the confluence of the Connecticut and Blackhall rivers and Long Island Sound in Old Lyme. Also known as the Blackhall site, it is a very different kind of Late Woodland settlement from either Morgan or

# THE EARLIEST KNOWN WOODSPLINT BASKETRY?

Among the unique botanical finds at the Burnham-Shepard site were samples of hickory wood that are suggestive of weaving splints. In her identification of these specimens, archaeobotanist Lucinda McWeeney noted that "these samples appear to have been deliberately separated along the early wood growth ring and the sug-

Stamped and swabbed woodsplint baskets from the Yale Peabody Museum collections: Mohegan basket with a trail design, from Montville, Connecticut; bottom, basket with rectangular base, an oval rim, and two loop handles, checkerwork, and block-stamp decoration, length 12 inches (30.5 centimeters).

gestion of crushing at the margin of the late wood leads me to think they might have been prepared for splints for basket or mat weaving."[a]

Dr. McWeeney identified "shaved" hickory wood samples from the site that she also suggested might be "weaving splints." Archaeologist Jeffrey Bendremer suggested an alternative function, that "these splints were an element of the storage techniques" used in the pit where they were recovered. Both interpretations may be correct, as one seventeenth-century English account of underground Native American "barnes" mentioned using them to store maize in "great baskets."[b] There is an ongoing debate on whether the woodsplint basketry produced by post-contact northeastern Indian peoples was an indigenous tradition or introduced to them by Swedish settlers in New Jersey in the early seventeenth century. The hickory splints from Burnham-Shepard are the first possible evidence for pre-contact basket weaving and support an indigenous origin for woodsplint basketry.

Notes

a. Quoted in Bendremer 1993, 147–148.

b. Morton 1637, 160.

A Nipmuc basket from 1840 with a spiritual medallion motif and a series of Xs, either a trail or path design, or a representation of the four directions, or both. The basket also has a central floral design typical of Nipmuc basketmakers.

Uncovering a rock-lined platform hearth at Yale's excavation at the Old Lyme Shell Heap site in 1940.

Burnham-Shepard. It was a pre-contact shell midden that extended for at least 800 feet (about 250 meters) parallel to the coast, and ranged in width from 8 to 100 feet (2.5 to 30.5 meters). More than 4,000 square feet was excavated in 1939 and 1940 by researchers from Yale University.[104] Much of the remaining site was destroyed during the hurricane of 1955.[105]

The site had two main, seemingly vertically distinct, components. The vertical distinctions were not always clear, as excavations were in arbitrary levels. The components were often spatially distinct, however. The lower shell and junction of midden and subsoil contained a Terminal Archaic component, and the upper shell contained Levanna and Jack's Reef points and collared and uncollared pot fragments of the Windsor style that signify a definite later Woodland presence dating somewhere between 1250 and 450 B.P. Both components were represented in the plowed topsoil.

The Woodland component contained thousands of bone and shell fragments,

and several cultural features that included simple firepits, concentrations of fire-cracked rock, a stone-paved hearth, a shell pit, and a 7-foot double arc of stones that might have been the support for a skin- or mat-covered lean-to. The artifacts included 424 pottery sherds representing a minimum of 33 pots, 31 bone tools, 5 antler tools, and 334 stone artifacts (points, stemmed and notched knives, hammerstones, hammer-grinding stones, an anvil stone, a grinding stone or possible anvil, abrading stones, a hammer or abrading stone, a grooved adze, an adze or axe preform, club head, drills, scraper or gouge, a strike-a-light, a possible chopper, a pebble gouge, denticulates, flake tools for scraping, cutting, and gouging, preforms, debitage, and smoothed ovoid pebbles). Although these could be interpreted as representing a variety of economic behaviors that occurred on site, in truth most of the stone tools are the unfinished products of tool manufacture from local quartz beach cobbles.

*A Shellfish Processing Camp*    The relatively small amount of artifacts recovered from the extensive excavations (0.19 artifacts per square foot) is typical for shell midden sites near Long Island Sound. They were normally fairly temporary, task-specific sites within easy walking distance of a residential base camp where a narrow range of activities occurred.[106] In fact, a residential camp was located about a quarter mile (about 400 meters) from the Old Lyme Shell Heap at Griswold

Pottery fragments from the Old Lyme Shell Heap site showing brushed, fabric-marked, and net-marked surface treatment. Bottom row, second from left, is an example of randomly brushed surface treatment. Third and fourth fragments from left are examples of brushed or combed decoration over fabric-marked surface treatments.

The salt marshes near Old Lyme, Connecticut.

Point. The Griswold Point site contained Late Woodland Windsor pottery, stone tools, and the remains of several oval pole-frame houses (called wigwams or wee-toos), but no shell.[107]

Small groups of people (probably family groups, because both male- and female-related artifacts were found) from the base camp assembled to collect and process shellfish. The meats were carried back to camp and the shell debris was left behind.[108] An estimated 85 percent of the shell at Old Lyme was oyster, 10 percent quahog, and 2 percent scallop.

Roger Williams noted that to collect quahogs, or hard-shell clams, "the Indians wade deepe and dive for [them]." Boats would have been needed to gather the oysters farther out, and seafaring activities traditionally were considered men's work. Community members of all ages might help collect the soft-shell clams in the mudflats, although Williams reported that it was a woman's task among the Narragansetts.

> This is a sweet kind of shellfish, which all Indians generally over the countrey, Winter and Summer delight in; and at low water the women dig for them; this fish, and the naturall liquor of it, they boile, and it makes their broth and their Nasaump (which is a kind of thickened broth) and their bread season-able and savory, in stead of Salt.[109]

The shucking and drying might be a family affair as well, although food processing and cooking were deemed women's work in post-contact times.[110] According to William Wood, an early-seventeenth-century visitor to what is now Massachusetts:

> In the summer these Indian women, when lobsters be in their plenty and prime, they dry them to keep for the winter, erecting scaffolds in the hot

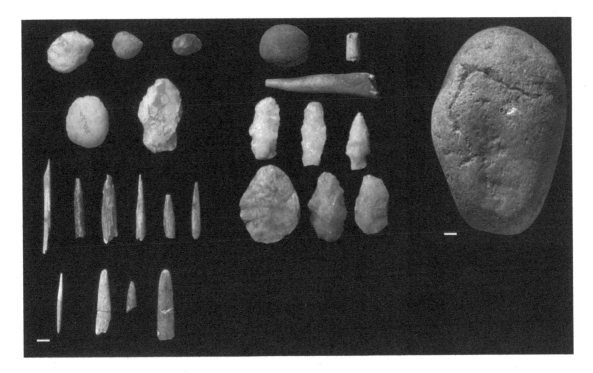

Lithic manufacturing tools—an anvil, hammerstone, and flaker—with a punch and by-products of the quartz cobble reduction technique of stone tool manufacture, from the Old Lyme Shell Heap site. In the lower left corner are bone and antler tools and fragments, including awls, a gorge, and weaving needles/shuttles. Scale bars equal 1 centimeter.

sunshine, making fires likewise underneath them (by whose smoke the flies are expelled) till the substance remain hard and dry. In this manner they dry bass and other fishes without salt, cutting them very thin to dry suddenly before the flies spoilt them or the rain moist them, having a special care to hang them in their smoky houses in the night and dankish weather.[111]

We know that during these shellfishing forays quartz beach cobbles were collected and worked into tool preforms because the sharp and bulky debitage is commonly intermingled with the shell and other organic garbage. Most likely the formal tools were manufactured by the boys or men while they waited for the seafood to finish drying, or for the women to make supper. Women likely made and used expedient (flake) cutting and scraping tools for the tasks at hand: prying open shells, scaling fish, preparing the drying racks, cutting the fish and shellfish into strips for drying or smoking, and processing other foods for daily meals.

The Old Lyme Shell Heap is significant for several reasons. Thousands of faunal remains provided information about diet.[112] Woodland features contained white-tailed deer, Canada geese, mallard duck, shorebirds, wild turkey, box and water turtle, dog or fox, squirrel, muskrat, raccoon, seal, and sturgeon. Mink, snake, *Gadidae* (codfish), and dove or pigeon remains were recovered from non-activity areas.[113] The sturgeon and codfish suggest deep-sea fishing, although at certain seasons, such as spring spawning, sturgeon inhabit near-shore environments, as do some cod species. Pre-contact deep-sea fishing has been confirmed by fauna from other Connecticut sites, such as the Osbrook Point locus on the Davis Farm site, where swordfish vertebrae were found.[114]

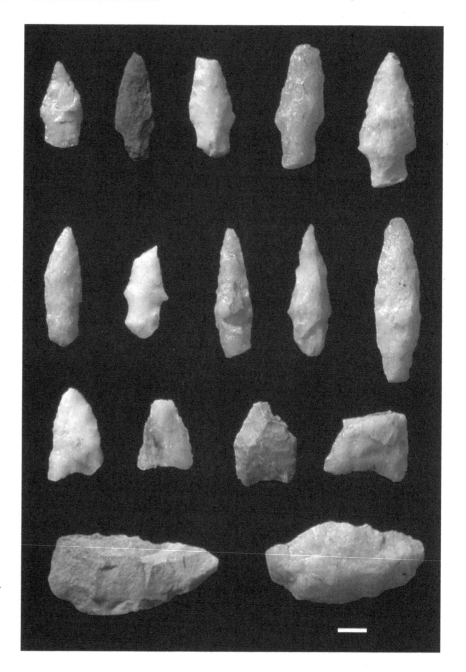

Late Woodland occupation projectile points (except for one Jack's Reef point) and two knives from the Old Lyme Shell Heap. Scale bar equals 1 centimeter.

The waterfowl remains suggest that the site was occupied during seasonal migration cycles, in the early spring or late fall. Although Canada geese are year-round residents today, a hundred years ago they were truly seasonal migrants.[115] This was corroborated 350 years earlier by Roger Williams.

*Sowwanakitauwaw.* They go to the South ward. That is the saying of the Natives, when the Geese and other Fowle at the approach of Winter betake themselves, in admirable Order and discerning their Course even all the night

Connecticut College excavation at the Griswold Point site looking south toward Long Island Sound.

long. *Chepewaukitauog.* They fly Northward. That is when they return in the Spring.[116]

Analysis of wood charcoal from the site identified it as butternut or hickory. Nut trees were growing nearby, but no shells were recovered, lending support to an early spring occupation, at least for this excavated portion of the midden site.

## Bone and Antler Technologies

The preservation of normally perishable bone and antler objects is another significant aspect of the Old Lyme Shell Heap. The Woodland component held thirty-one bone artifacts that included two points, a fishing gorge, two weaving shuttle/needle fragments, twenty-four awls and awl blanks (unfinished awls), an incised flat bone fragment, a carved and incised bird-bone whistle, and five antler tools (two antler preforms, two antler pressure flakers, and a small cylindrical antler punch or pestle fragment, possibly for grinding pigment). Mixed-component deposits yielded fourteen additional awls and an incised bone dagger; four awls were found in Terminal Archaic levels. The alkaline calcium carbonate in the shells lowered the acidity in the soils and helped preserve the bone and antler tools.

Similar perishable tools have most often been discovered in other shell midden contexts, such as at the Indian Field shell midden site on the coast of Greenwich, and at the Manakaway site, another Woodland shell midden in Greenwich. Indian Field also yielded worked antler tines, an antler wedge, a turtle-shell dish, and notched clam shells. Manakaway also contained twenty-five shell scrapers, eleven grooved oyster shells interpreted as possible "sinew frayers," a few worked shells of unknown function, and more than three hundred perforated (drilled and punched) bivalves that the site's excavator thought may have been used as net-sinkers.[117] The Seaside Indian Village site at Fort Trumbull Beach in Milford[118]

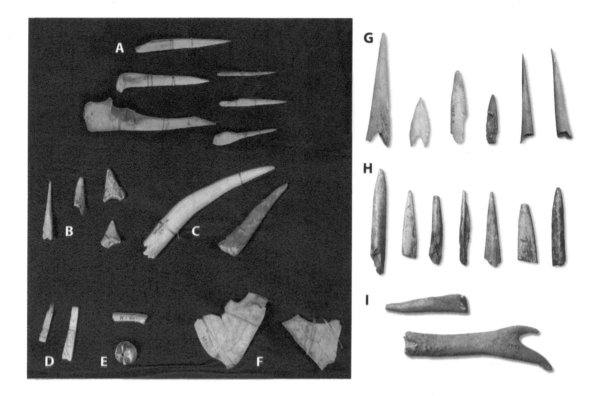

A variety of bone and antler tools. A, bone awls and needles. B, bone arrow points. C, worked antler. D, incised bone fragments. E, bone beads. F, turtle carapace fragments (bowl?). G, bone points. H, bone awls. I, bone flakers. (A–F, from the Tubbs Shell Heap site in Niantic. G, far left and far right, points found together in West Haven; second from left and following, from Stratford; from Indian Cave, Pine Rock, Hamden; worked antler tip from Pine Orchard Swamp, Branford; bird-bone point from Bay View Park, New Haven. H and I, from the Old Lyme Shell Heap, Old Lyme.)

contained bone awls, a "harpoon-like" object, a weaving needle, an antler "plug," fragments of a turtle-shell cup, and "parts of deer antlers" that may have been stock for tools, like the antler cache found at the Morgan site.

Many of the artifacts from the Old Lyme Shell Heap, concentrated in four places, were probably the garbage left by small family groups at different times. Finding certain kinds of artifacts and ecofacts together could mean that there were several other activities occurring besides shellfish processing and stone tool manufacture, such as cooking. The many bird-bone and flat-bone awls and awl fragments in various stages of manufacture, some with polished edges or broken points, may mean that they were being made and used there. Although awls or perforators are usually tools for making holes in tanned hides, they may have also been used as utensils.[119] Another use might be to poke holes in shellfish for stringing and drying.

Flat, ground bone fragments that have one rounded end with a drilled eye are reminiscent of simple weaving shuttles,[120] probably used to weave mats from cattail leaves or rushes that grew in the adjacent salt marsh, or fishing nets or open-weave net bags. The presence of a gorge along with the fish bones indicates finfish fishing; a notched stone net-sinker denotes net fishing. Both of these fishing methods, as well as spear fishing, basket traps, and fish weirs were practices of seventeenth-century Indians in southern New England, as described in early English documents.[121]

Antler from the Morgan site antler cache; bottom, the dark outline of the storage pit and hand spade (for re-opening the pit) found on top of the cache.

## Continuation of the Narrow Point Artifact Tradition

Another important characteristic of the Old Lyme Shell Heap site is the presence of 61 mainly quartz Narrow Point bifaces from the later Woodland levels. Preforms, broken bifaces, and debitage are evidence of bifacial tool manufacture. These suggest, in southeastern Connecticut at least, that later Middle Woodland and Late Woodland knappers continued to make and use biface styles in the Narrow Point tradition. The asymmetrical shapes, sinuous edges, and wear on many of these, however, suggested that they were used as knives and not as projectile points.[122]

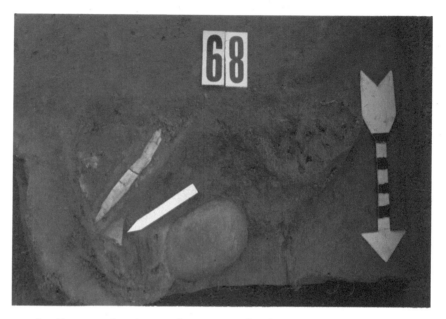

A bone dagger and whetstone for sharpening its blade, found in a small pit at the Morgan site in Rocky Hill.

Small-stemmed points and Late Woodland Levanna points were found in the same levels during excavations in Bashan Lake, East Haddam, during a drawdown.[123] Narrow-stemmed points occurred in pit features at the early post-contact Mohegan Fort Shantok on the Thames River in Uncasville during excavations in an area with no pre-contact levels that could have caused stratigraphic mixing.[124] Across the sound on Long Island, narrow-stemmed points have been radiocarbon-dated to the late Middle Woodland and to the Late Woodland.[125] It would be interesting to know whether any of these "points" had actually functioned as knives.

Two Late Woodland burials were unearthed at Old Lyme Shell Heap. Both were adult males buried with flexed limbs in a fetal position in shallow pits inside the habitation area. The age of a corpse at death can be estimated from tooth eruption, certain bone structures, and the degree of closure of skull sutures. The sex of the skeleton can also often be determined from certain sexually variable bone structures. For example, heavy bony ridges just above the eye sockets are normally a masculine trait. A mandible, or lower jaw, whose ends form an obtuse angle is usually a female trait, whereas the lower jaws of males normally form a right angle. Male chins are usually straight and those of females are generally rounded.

Both Old Lyme burials are fairly unusual because, unlike many later Woodland burials, they contained grave goods. One burial had two quartz knives, two Narrow Point bifaces, and two antler pressure-flaking tools. The second burial had a stone club head and the bird-bone whistle described above. The whistle could have been used in the ceremonial burial rites, or simply as a musical instrument for hunting or recreation, such as during festivals and dances, here provided for the deceased's use in the afterlife.

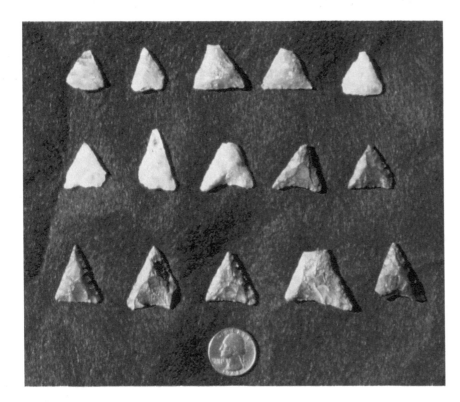

Quartz and hornfels
Levanna points from
the Morgan site.

## NATIVE AMERICAN MUSIC AND DANCE

Seventeenth-century English witnesses tell us that New England Native American social gatherings were nearly always accompanied by singing, dancing, feasting, and games (often sacred in character), similar to the many Indian harvest festivals and "powwows" open to the public today, as this 2007 newspaper account of an Eastern Pequot powwow illustrates.[126]

> The [1675] ban [of powwows by the Colony of Connecticut] didn't stop the tribe from holding pow wows, but they were low-profile affairs. . . . These days, the event takes place on Saturday and Sunday of the fourth weekend in July and includes annual tribal elections on Saturday; a Sunday prayer meeting, which is a traditional meeting with the drum, singers and religious ceremonies led by Eastern Pequot Tribal Nation Chief Roy Sebastian; and a pow wow in the afternoon. The pow wow attracts people from tribes all over the Northeast, attracting between 500 and 1,000 people.[127]

Songs were sometimes accompanied by flute or percussion instruments, as William Wood described for a social gathering in Massachusetts Bay in the early seventeenth century: "While the men play [foot ball], the boys pipe and the women dance and sing trophies of their husband's conquests; all being done, a feast summons their departure."[128]

In 1735 Timothy Woodbridge, the first schoolteacher to the Mahikan community at their village of Stockbridge in western Massachusetts, described the use

Traditional musical instruments: rawhide-covered hand drums; an Onondaga rattle made from the carapace of a snapping turtle, used in curing ceremonies; and a birchbark rattle.

of a pair of 18-inch wooden percussion sticks to accompany singing.[129] Drums were made of wood and rawhide. Some were held in the hand, like the Irish bodhran played in contemporary Celtic bands, and others were larger and rested on the floor. The Iroquois (whose homelands are in upstate New York, although many live in Connecticut today) use a water drum. The amount of water in the drum determines the pitch of its "voice."[130] The drumbeat is the heart of Mother Earth. The drums themselves are symbols of Native American community and history. Twentieth-century Onondaga elder and educator Adelphena Logan emotionally described the deeply personal meanings conveyed by her drum.

> The drum sets a tempo for memories. It is a medium of release for our emotions. . . . A drum reminds us of our lives. My drum is old and full of memories, memories of things learned long ago, of my ancestors and of the ideas and accomplishments of my people and myself. Memories of sweet grass, the closeness of nature, the ancient and beautiful things of the woods. . . . My drum speaks of olden times, for it is a diary of my people. . . . My drum is a mingling of past, present, future. A reassured diary of my people is measured in the beat of my drum.[131]

Rattles were made from bark, turtle shell, gourds, horn, rawhide, and even woodsplint basketry. Most rattles were held in the hand, but some were also tied to the leg, like the turtle shell rattle in a burial from the Morgan site. Some types of rattles were used in all ceremonies, others only in specific rituals. Among the

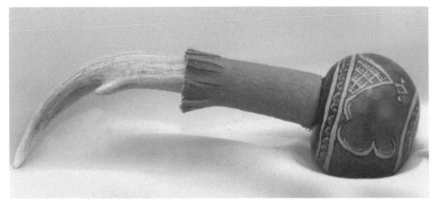

Contemporary gourd rattles with traditional designs and motifs, by Connecticut artist Jeanne MORNINGSTAR Kent, an enrolled member of the Abenaki Nation, Nulhegan Band, Coosuck-Abenaki of Vermont. Vertical zigzag lines are symbolic of a more difficult life, or lightning. Horizontally, these lines are interpreted as mountains. Repeated triangles or pyramids also represent mountains. Top, antler rattle with deer skin. Center, rattle with possibly a Passamaquoddy design that includes an ancient double curve symbol. Bottom, Naskapi design using the ancient double curve motif with a floral design reminiscent of the strawberry leaf, symbol of psychological cleansing and renewal.

Iroquois, for example, turtle-shell rattles are used in the midwinter festival, at longhouse political meetings, and in False Face curing ceremonies.[132] Singing, drumming, and flute playing, sometimes accompanied by specific dances, are still performed during both public powwows and nonpublic religious ceremonies, including naming rituals, weddings, and funerals. Dr. David McAllester, late professor of ethnomusicology at Wesleyan University, reported that most indigenous dance had a spiritual function: "Much of Indian dancing is strictly disciplined physical participation in the music, and in the mythology behind the music, for

Contemporary wooden flute hand-carved and painted by Strong Eagle Daly, Native American-style flute maker, player, and carver of the Nipmuc Nation, from Worcester, Massachusetts.

religious purposes, to bring about a religious result: the curing of a sick person, the bringing of rain, the growing of crops, all sorts of important functions."[133]

Indigenous music and dance are closely related to spirituality, storytelling, and Native American lifeways in general. Dale Carson, the author of several Native American cookbooks and a columnist for *Indian Country Today,* noted that even the most mundane economic activities have a spiritual aspect that is proclaimed in song and dance.

> A bounty of crops, game or fish was never taken for granted. Even the rabbit who gave up his life to feed a hunter's family was thanked. Here music played a part in the food chain. A man would sing his own special song to thank the animal [spirit]. . . . Throughout all of Indian Country . . . song and dance rituals are practiced in honor of food. They may be at planting time

Butch "Sly Fox" Lydem (Schaghticoke elder) wearing his "regalia," a traditional indigenous outfit consisting of deerskin clothing, turkey feather headdress (*gustowah*, the Iroquoian term for this type of head-piece), embroidered deerskin moccasins, and snapping turtle shell rattle.

or harvest. The dancing, patting feet are all at once a kiss, a thank you, and a prayer to our Mother Earth. To this day, some dances are so special that they may not be witnessed by outsiders.[134]

The Eastern Blanket dance symbolizes the rite of passage of a girl into womanhood and marriage. Fourteen-year-old Natasha Gambrell recently explained her interpretation of the dance's meaning for her and other members of the Eastern Pequot tribe.

All my ancestors used to do the Eastern Blanket Dance. Basically, it shows the coming out of the butterfly. The first steps are a woman in a cocoon and as she gets older and matures, she shows her blanket more and is trying to attract a husband, and at the end, she puts her blanket down if they're married, or they cover themselves up, and if you're not married, the person will grab you and I guess it's like, "Will you marry me?"[135]

Unfortunately, little has been written about the specifics of early historical New England Algonkian songs. Musicologist David McAllester knew of only one "'forgotten' record of early Algonkian singing which was made many years ago"[136]—an 1890 recording of the Passamaquoddy Snake Dance Song in Calais, Maine. The words were all vocables, "non-translatable syllables that carry the melody." The song's division into a one-line introduction and a multi-repeated rhythmic part is similar to the Eastern Stomp Dance songs still sung by indigenous musicians.[137] A significant characteristic was that "the vocal timbre is similar to what we hear in New England among Native American singers today, over a hundred years later. The voices are plain, robust, unornamented, without the tense quavers, pulsations, sharp attacks, swoops, and falsetto yodels that are so striking in Plains Indians' powwow singing. The recording suggests that Northeastern native singing has kept the same style for generations."[138]

McAllester compared the 1890 Algonkian song to a 1941 recording of the Seneca (Iroquois-speaking) Quiver Dance song and found that "the two songs support the idea of a general Eastern Woodland musical style with their similarities in rhythm and melody"; their rhythmic structure is bipartite, melodic development is simple, repetitive, and restricted in range, and the dance form is alternating.[139] His earlier analysis of an ancient Seneca song about the passenger pigeon also describes the qualities of this musical style. The song was sung to ensure the continuity of the passenger pigeon, once a major food source for indigenous people until its extinction from overhunting by Euro-American settlers.

The song means something like "The pigeons are dancing," and it begins with a call of the pigeon. Then it goes on with a mixture of meaningful words in the Seneca language and vocables that just carry the tune. It has a complex rhythmic structure. . . . And so you can see another important fact about American Indian songs. Not only are they robust, using vocables as well as English and Indian words; not only are they complex, disciplined and symbolic; and not only are they religious and social, sometimes simultaneously; but they are also a reflection of Indian cultures and lifeways showing traditional beliefs and ideas and the ways in which American Indians have adapted and adjusted to keep pace with change.[140]

### DIVERSE REGIONAL ECONOMIES

There is evidence that there were regional distinctions among Late Woodland communities beyond the relative significance of maize horticulture. A survey of the Route 6/Interstate 84 relocation corridor in the Northeast Hills section of northeastern Connecticut directed by Kevin McBride located 22 Late Woodland sites.[141] Those sites east of the Willimantic River were distinct enough for

Native American people believed that socializing with family, friends, and neighbors was important to community well-being. Individual visiting and group social gatherings were frequent.[a] These social events often included games.

In Native North America, playing games of skill and chance was an important part of everyday life for everyone, whether young or old, male or female. Games strengthened bodies and minds. They taught people how to cooperate. Team games were a way to bring people together and remind them to include each other in their activities. The idea of team sports seems to be more common among Native American peoples than among other cultures anywhere else in the world. Although there were spectator sports in Europe and Asia before contact with North American peoples, these were primarily individual contests such as races on foot, on horseback, or with chariots, as well as wrestling, archery, and boxing. Ball games involving two teams, such as the Native American games of lacrosse and shinny (a form of ice hockey), did not evolve in Europe until the fifteenth century.

Lacrosse was played in all parts of North America and was a test of strength, agility, and endurance. Early games took place on huge fields, some several miles long. The game lasted until one team scored a predetermined number of goals. The ball, made from either wood or deer hide, was carried or thrown with the lacrosse stick to the goal at the opposite end of the field. Women made up a very active cheering section and would often rush out onto the field to urge on their husbands with switches. Tribes often challenged each other to a game of lacrosse to settle disputes.

Although lacrosse was generally played by men, women played a similar game called double ball in which players used a curved stick to toss and catch a ball. Early English documents describe several types of ball games played in Native southern New England, including a kind of football. Some ball games had hundreds of players, sometimes with each team consisting of an entire community.[b]

Snow snake was a popular winter sport played with a smooth maple branch 5 to 9 feet long (1.5 to 2.75 meters), shaped somewhat like a snake and treated with "secret oils." The object of the game was to throw the snow snake the longest distance in the shortest time along a prepared track. The trough, which could be up to a mile long, was made by pressing a log into the snow. To create a slippery surface, the track was watered and allowed to freeze.

The goal of another game, cup and pin, was to get the "pin" (attached to a cuplike object with a string) into the "cup." Another game of skill was played with a bundle of wooden sticks, or "straws," similar to the game known worldwide as "pick-up sticks." This game was mentioned in one of the earliest texts on Connecticut Native Americans, titled *Some Helps for the Indians: A Catechism in the Language of the Quiripi Indians of New Haven Colony,* from 1658, by Abraham Peirson, minister to the Quinnipiac tribe.[c]

Children of all cultures have played with dolls for entertainment and to imitate their mothers and grandmothers caring for younger siblings. The earliest Native American dolls were made from materials found in nature such as corn husks, wood, other plant materials, and animal skin. Just as Native American women carried their babies in cradleboards, allowing mother and child to be together, young girls would learn the important relationship between a mother and child by caring for their dolls in small cradleboards.

Not all dolls were playthings. Some Native American "dolls" have a sacred function, such as the katchina figurines of the western Pueblo people in the American Southwest, which represent spiritual beings in the indigenous cosmology. Northeastern Algonkian speakers had similar sacred figurines that were cared for and honored, even fed, and used in ceremonies and dances.[d] Among the Delawares these spirits or "doll beings" were called "Ohtas." They may have been "house gods," possibly representing spirits concerned with fertility (for crops or humans) or health. Among the Hudson Valley Mahikans and the Lenape (Delaware) people, the Keeper of the Dolls was a female elder. Delaware elder Lynette Perry, herself a Keeper of the Dolls, relates:

> One doll was a man, one a woman. Both were ancient and fragile. Sticks projected from beneath their clothes so they could be carried and held high during ceremonies. It was Grandma's job to keep them in excellent repair and to make new clothes for them before the Doll Dance, which took place each spring. . . . I don't know who made them first or how long ago. I know they were passed, mother to daughter, sister to sister, through a long line of Delaware women of the Turtle clan. . . . The dolls were feasted and feted; they were carried through the swirl of color and noise on the shoulders of the head dancers.[e]

Many Native American games also served a sacred purpose. To play the game well sent a message of thanks to the Creator. The sacred bowl game, for example, was a game of chance with its roots in spiritual ceremonies. "When played during the mid-winter ceremonies, it was to please the plant and animal world and to make the Creator laugh," says Trudie Lamb Richmond. The number and type of dice differed from tribe to tribe. Dice of bone, wood, antler, and even fruit pits were used. The bowl was used to toss the pieces in the air and points were awarded according to how many pieces landed with the "decorated" side up.[f] As summed up by James and Joseph Bruchac, Abenakis: "The joy of playing, the lessons that we learn from playing together with a good heart, the strength of mind and body and spirit that we gain from playing—those things are always more important than winning."[g]

Notes

Adapted from "Harmony in Games," a temporary exhibition at the Institute for American Indian Studies, Washington, Connecticut, based in part on Bruchac and Bruchac 2000.

a. E.g., see Roger Williams 1643, and Moravian Church documents for Schaghticoke (Boxes 114, 115).

b. Bragdon 1996, 120, 224; see also Wood 1634, and Williams 1643.

c. Cited by Philip Rabito in an unpublished and undated manuscript titled "And Play at Strawes," on file at the Institute for American Indian Studies, Washington, Conn.

d. Perry and Skolnick 1999, 27; Thompson 1983, 36.

e. Perry and Skolnick 1999, 27–28.

f. Trudie Lamb Richmond, personal communication.

g. Bruchac and Bruchac 2000, 8.

*(Opposite)* Various types of equipment and game pieces used in indigenous games, including ball sticks, a lacrosse stick, "strawes" or pick-up-sticks, dice (plum pits, bone pieces), and the cup-and-pin game.

their excavators to conclude that the Late Woodland communities in that part of the Northeast Hills were living in and economically exploiting the uplands *year-round*, with settlement patterns quite distinct from those of the North-Central Lowlands communities. The latter had relatively large residential settlements in the broad floodplains of the Connecticut River valley, whose communities were focused on the exploitation of riverine resources and horticulture. Its members visited the Northeast Hills only temporarily, to forage foods that were brought back to their riverine base.[142]

Jeffrey Bendremer's study of Late Woodland subsistence and settlement supported and expanded on this interpretation, concluding that eastern Connecticut was "characterized by a high degree of regional diversity," with local ecology an important factor in the development and maintenance of five distinct settlement systems in the eastern Connecticut region—four on the mainland and one on Block Island.[143] These areas are:

- the Northeast Hills, with no evidence for maize horticulture;[144]
- the North-Central Lowlands;
- the Southeast Hills region, with large semi-sedentary "villages" exploiting the economic resources of the estuaries and tidal marshes of the Connecticut River, and small temporary camps exploiting the uplands;
- the Eastern Coastal Slope, with large, semi-sedentary, and fully sedentary villages geared toward exploitation of marine resources, but also small temporary sites exploiting upland resources;[145]
- Block Island.

Because of the limited and pioneering nature of the archaeological data, regional distinctions focused on economic and settlement patterns.[146] Studies by cultural anthropologists have shown that economy and settlement characteristics may be linked to social and political organization as well as spiritual systems. As our archaeological information accumulates, it would not be surprising to find that the communities inhabiting these geographic regions also differed in other sociocultural ways. The post-contact tribal peoples who lived in them certainly seem to have had such sociopolitical distinctions,[147] as Paulette Crone-Morange and I pointed out in an earlier article, citing the research of Professor Kathleen Bragdon and others.

> Early historic Native American societies of coastal southeastern New England, such as the Mohegan-Pequot and Narragansett, were large, aggregated, fairly sedentary communities . . . typical of chiefdoms. They were characterized by marked social hierarchy; strong centralized leadership; a military elite exemplified by the warrior groups known as pniesesok among the Wampanoag and muckquompauog among the Narragansett; control of environmentally restricted resources and highly desired goods such as furs and wampum; and an ideology stressing the import of the ruling elite. Political leadership was invested in a great sachem, under sachems, the sachem's advisors and

Portrait of an unidentified late-seventeenth-century southern New England sachem, dated by paint analysis to about 1700, originally thought to be the Niantic-Narragansett sachem Ninigret II. On the basis of documentary evidence Dr. Kevin McBride has suggested it is instead the Pequot leader Robin Cassasinomon, who was instrumental in rebuilding the Pequot nation after the devastation of the Pequot War in 1637. *Native American Sachem*, by an unknown artist, depicts the young sachem garbed in traditional deerskin moccasins and loincloth of red tradecloth, wearing a wide headband and necklace of purple and white wampum beads, symbols of his high status. The polished wooden object he holds may be a talking stick, a device used at indigenous political meetings to allow one to speak without interruption.

"principal men" who came from what the English referred to as "noble" families, and a warrior elite. The remainder of the chiefdom was composed of "missinnuok" or "common people" and "obscure or meane" people, a term which may have referred to servants or slaves. Among these coastal societies, sachems were powerful individuals. . . . Contemporary inland societies . . . appear to have contained smaller populations with less complex socio-political systems that were more egalitarian.[148]

Significantly, Bendremer's distinctive regional economic and settlement systems correlated with the homelands of several post-contact tribal peoples: the Northeast Hills with the Nipmucks; the North-Central Lowlands with the large horticultural villages of "Sequins" and "Nawaas" described by Adriaen Block in his 1614 voyage up the Connecticut River (probably villages of the Podunk and Wangunk tribes);[149] the eastern portion of the Southeast Hills and Eastern Coastal settlement systems with the Pequot-Mohegan; Block Island with the Manessis; and the western portion of the Southeast Hills with an unnamed group that exploited the tidal and estuarine regions.[150] This unnamed group fits nicely with the description of the Middle Woodland Windsor-tradition-bearing immigrants and their marsh-oriented economy. The North-Central Lowlands villages of Sequins and Nawaas fit the interpretation of the expansion upriver of these migrant Windsor communities.[151] The economic, settlement, and ceramic information from archaeological investigations show a considerable continuity between later Woodland communities and post-contact (including present-day) tribal peoples.

## Pottery Styles and Tribal Roots

Along much of the Connecticut coast and in the Connecticut River valley at least, Late Woodland women continued to produce pots in the Windsor styles introduced during the late Middle Woodland period. A new style of pipe, the right-angle or obtuse-angle elbow pipe, also appeared during this time. The pipes were made from clay and, more rarely, from stone. A drawdown of Bashan Lake in East Haddam revealed an extremely rare deer-antler pipe that had been preserved in the mud for centuries.[152] The pipes were often decorated using the same techniques applied to clay pots. Although the seventeenth- and eighteenth-century English writers noted that indigenous men were pipe smokers and the caretakers of the tobacco plant, they tell us nothing about whether or not women smoked or who actually made the pipes.

Later in the period women began to manufacture several new pot styles with shell-stamped, incised, fine dentate, or punctate decoration, sometimes with necks decorated by shell stamping or horizontal brushing: Niantic Stamped, Niantic Stamp and Drag, Niantic Incised, Niantic Linear Dentate, Niantic Punctate.[153] All are collared vessels; that is, either the rim was pushed out from the inside (extended or channeled collar) or, more rarely, a strip of clay was applied to the rim (applied collar).

We know little about the pottery styles or their makers in the interior uplands east and west of the Connecticut Valley. There have been few surveys and little published on these areas. West of the Housatonic Valley few Late Woodland sites have been reported, but the ceramic evidence suggests, tentatively, continued associations with Hudson Valley communities.[154] In southwestern Connecticut, a new pottery tradition emerged—the East River tradition.[155]

## The Munsee Migration

Around 950 B.P. women in southwestern Connecticut, adjacent coastal New York, and western Long Island began producing pots in a very different ceramic tradition. Known as the East River tradition, its Bowmans Brook Incised and Bowmans Brook Stamped styles had bold incised decoration and linear cord-wrapped stick or paddle edge designs on smoothed or cord-marked surfaces. Sometime later women potters began to make the collared pot types that archaeologists named Van Cortlandt Stamped, Eastern Incised, and Clason's Point Stamped.

These new East River pottery styles suggest continued population movement into the Long Island Sound area. On the basis of their similarity to pottery styles in New Jersey and on linguistic research in southeastern New York,[156] this movement has been identified as the gradual and peaceful emigration of Munsee

Late to Final Woodland pottery sherds from various Connecticut archaeology sites. Top, collared, shell-stamped pottery representing the Niantic Stamped style, except for the sherd in the lower right corner, from Bridgeport, Connecticut, which is an untyped unique stamped pot with a melon-shaped body form. Bottom, rim sherds representing pots of the Niantic Punctate style.

Lenape (called Delaware by the English) people from northern New Jersey, spilling into southern New York and western Long Island.[157]

Late Woodland Munsee-speaking communities also thrived in southwestern Connecticut. The boundary between these and other indigenous Eastern Algonkian–speaking communities to their east was somewhere between the Housatonic River drainage in Stratford and Milford and the Five Mile River in Norwalk.[158] The boundary most likely fluctuated through time. The Munsee migration began about 950 B.P. and continued for the next three hundred years.[159] The seemingly peaceful nature of this migration (there is no evidence of warfare or violence in the archaeological record to date) was probably because the coastal

Connecticut and Long Island communities with which the Munsee emigrants came into contact had socioeconomic connections, if not ancestral roots in the Mid-Atlantic, as previous discussions of trade and population movements have shown, particularly for the preceding Middle Woodland period. Archaeologist Kenneth Sassaman reported that, in general, many population movements were based on deep-rooted social relationships.

> The folly of older approaches to interpreting such events—and the fodder for processualistic critiques of culture history—was that each of these various "foreign" influences and the indigenes they encountered were imagined to be self-contained internally homogeneous units. In many cases, however, large-scale movements of people were predicated on established social connections that we gloss as "exchange" or "trade."[160]

Also, the East River tradition Clason's Point Stamped pottery style is virtually identical to the Niantic Stamped of the Windsor tradition[161] and may be a single type. If so, it could indicate that there were Windsor pottery-making women in Munsee communities, which would suggest a peaceful assimilation of Munsees into the older Algonkian communities. An alternative explanation would be that Windsor communities were presenting women as brides to Munsee warriors to cement alliances and avoid conflict, a common occurrence in post-European-contact New England. Historian John Menta gave an example of such a marriage that occurred in southern Connecticut.

> Some cases of intermarriage between the two groups [Quinnipiac and Paugussett tribes] occurred; the most notable union was between Nausup, the well-known headman of the Quinnipiac, and Tuckhust, the daughter of Nahuntoway, a Paugussett sachem. The shrewd Nausup, by marrying the daughter of the prestigious Nahuntoway, promoted better relations with the Paugussett proper, who maintained villages in nearby Milford and Derby.[162]

Another possible indication of Munsee relationships are the small stone heads, or "maskettes" (small versions of the larger wooden mask worn during religious and healing ceremonies), found in Branford[163] and at the Rogers site in Lisbon.[164] These are similar to the sacred wooden masks and faces carved on posts and drum sticks used in the "Delaware Big House" ceremony of the Lenni Lenape (Delaware) Indians, that represent the *Mesingwe*, the Masked Being (Living Solid Face, Keeper of the Game) who controls and protects the animal food sources, and other spiritual beings.[165] Elder Adelphena Logan commented on the functions of masks in Onondaga society.

> To my people they [masks] are symbols, reminders of lessons important to the individual's life cycle. . . . The stories symbolized by our masks could be compared to the parables of the Christian Bible.[166]

The stone heads may or may not indicate Munsee relationships. Carvings and maskettes of simple faces have been found throughout New England and

A soapstone maskette found at the Rogers site, Lisbon, Connecticut. Scale bar equals 1 centimeter.

southern New York. In Connecticut, none have been dated or even discovered in undisturbed archaeological contexts to my knowledge. Perhaps they represent deities or revered ancestors. Some may be clan symbols, like the human effigies on pipe bowls among some Northeastern indigenous peoples.[167] Unfortunately, Europeans wrote virtually nothing about social organization among Connecticut's Algonkian speakers.

According to Mohegan elder and medicine woman Gladys Tantaquidgeon, Mohegan masks were made from living trees (like the Iroquois False Face masks). Her brother Harold had made a "crooked-nose mask," which he had worn during the tribe's annual harvest ceremonies "for the general casting out of bad spirits." The tribal historian Melissa Fawcett Zobel relates that the masks also "co-hosted the spirit of their maker and evoked the powerful aid of Gunci Mundo, the Great Spirit."[168]

## The Mississippian Connection?

The Munsee population movement and supposed eastward displacement of earlier Windsor communities was only one of many similar disruptions that were occurring in eastern North America during the Late Woodland period, apparently the result of cultural developments in the Midwest, and likely also the Southeast.[169] By 950 B.P., those regions were peopled by complex societies based on an agricultural economy. Large fortified regional urban centers with a stratified social hierarchy and a ruling priesthood symbolized by huge temple mounds dotted the landscapes of the Midwest and Southeast.[170]

One such center was the 6-square-mile (15.5 square kilometer) town—even city—of Cahokia on the Mississippi River in what is today East St. Louis, Missouri, which is estimated to have had a population of about 20,000 to 30,000 people! At its center was Monk's Mound, a huge flat-topped pyramid ten stories high with a base of about 15 acres (about 6 hectares)—larger than both the Great Pyramid of Giza in Egypt and the Pyramid of the Sun at Teotihuacán in Mexico. Monk's Mound is at the north end of a grand plaza that was the size of forty-five football fields. On its top stood a large temple or palace, from which the community's religious ceremonies were likely directed. These societies were chiefdoms, or even emergent states, supported by an intensive farming economy and characterized by ritual, monumental buildings, extensive trade networks, and craft specialists who made ceremonial and status items for the upper classes.[171]

Some archaeologists believe that these societies, collectively called Mississippian, actually set up colonies in other regions to collect the raw materials and finished products used as status and ritual objects. The presence of Ohio archaeological materials on western Pennsylvania and western New York sites and the ease with which early post-contact canoes could transport bulk cargo argues effectively for such Midwestern intrusions.[172] Travel by canoe from the headwaters of the Allegheny River in western New York to the Late Woodland metropolises in southern Ohio would take only thirteen days. Another thirteen days on the Ohio River would bring you to the Mississippian center of Angel in southern Indiana and others westward along the Wabash River.[173] These infringements on territory would likely have had a domino effect, causing continual displacements of people eastward.[174] They may have been the ultimate cause for the Munsee migration northward and eastward.

## EMBLEMIC STYLES AND SOCIAL IDENTITY

The Windsor pottery styles are what some archaeologists call emblemic styles, emblems of group identity.[175] Distribution of the late Windsor style Niantic Stamped, originally thought to be associated with the Nehantic (Niantic) tribe, showed it was a marker for a more geographically extensive social entity[176]—the Quiripey-Unquochaug language group, whose communities continued to share ideas and traditions, as well as women (the pottery makers) and a common language.[177]

During the very Late Woodland and early Post-Contact periods we begin to see the geographic patterns among other emblemic styles. The few ceramic collections from the upper Housatonic Valley suggest, tentatively, that the late Late Woodland and Final Woodland periods were represented by Garoga-like pottery

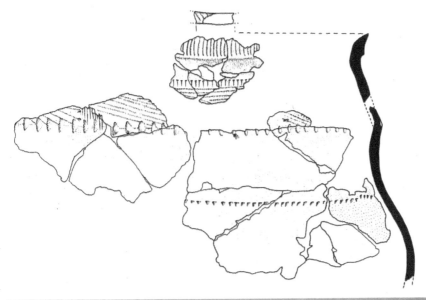

Drawing of profile and rim decoration of a vessel in the Guida Incised style from the Hackney Pond (614-9) site, a seasonal camp in Haddam, Connecticut. The pot was associated with a radiocarbon date of 180 ±40 years B.P. Bottom, pottery rims of the Shantok Incised style excavated at the Fort Shantok site in Montville, Connecticut.

styles characterized by an incised band of interlocking plats along the collar and deep, distinctive punctates along its base.[178] Garoga-style pottery is a common style in adjacent eastern New York as well.[179]

The Guida pottery tradition was first identified in the middle Connecticut Valley of south-central Massachusetts,[180] and later southward in Connecticut.[181] This tradition is characterized by very low collars with no castellations, decorated with a horizontal band of finely incised or stamped, closely spaced lines, with a modeled ring below the collar. Information about Guida pottery at specific Connecticut sites is scant and found mainly in unpublished reports and manuscripts. Because current information shows the pottery occurring in small numbers on geographically dispersed sites, it is difficult to calculate its core geographic distribution (one or two pots on a site could represent trade, gifts, or visits outside its core area). Much more work is needed to determine whether Guida pottery styles are truly emblematic in Connecticut, and whether they are markers for marriage pool distributions or some other social entity.

An example of emblemic style from southeastern Connecticut is the Shantok Incised style,[182] which is very different from the contemporary Niantic styles. It has heavy castellated collars with large punctates and stamp and drag shell designs that look like incising, and globular bodies with applied rings, nodes, and bosses with anthropomorphic and "corn" designs (as noted previously, some also symbolize women's genitalia). Shantok ware may be emblemic of the closely related Mohegan and Pequot tribes.[183] However, the style's distribution extended eastward into the Narragansett and Wampanoag homelands, so one researcher has suggested that Shantok ware could be a symbol of unity among Native American women in southeastern New England, a cry for indigenous alliance in the face of English oppression and aggression.[184] I recently proposed a third interpretation—that the distribution of Shantok Incised pottery represents the core Mohegan-Pequot political sphere, supported by intergroup marriage and kinship ties.

> Another possibility is that Shantok represents an interaction sphere of the various southeastern New England and eastern Long Island ethnic groups created and continued by inter-group marriage and resultant kin networks. . . . [T]he loose form of political alliances forged by seventeenth and eighteenth-century New England Native American societies . . . necessitated other socio-economic relationships such as marriage and kin ties to help stabilize the fragile political relationships. For example, the 1679 genealogy of Uncas, sachem of the Mohegan, showed descent from Pequot, Narragansett, and Long Island Indian societies. . . . Perhaps the distribution of Shantok ware and, ultimately, those ceramic styles characterizing the other regions . . . represent the geographic extent of a Native marriage pool.[185]

The argument that the change to a greater emphasis on maize horticulture along the coast occurred *independently* of European contact[186] lends support to this last interpretation. The increased significance of maize in the diets of late Late Woodland coastal peoples a hundred or more years *before* European settlement in southern New England could have been a response to population growth within increasingly circumscribed tribal homelands, as shown by an increase in small long-term seasonal camps and the increased occurrence of thin-walled globular clay pots,[187] a functional advantage for the extended cooking time required by dried maize kernels.[188]

As Late Woodland populations grew, hunting territories, prime horticultural lands, and good fishing places would have become more prized and protected. This increasing territoriality would lead to a "them versus us" conflict between groups, symbolized by emblemic markers. Additionally, recent research in eastern

New York by Edward Curtin suggests that the climatic warming around A.D. 1050 to 1300 may have caused drought and increased salinity in local rivers.[189] These phenomena would surely have exacerbated any community conflicts caused by population expansions. There is evidence for hostilities at several Late Woodland sites in Niantic, Westbrook, Milford, and Bridgeport. Significantly, all examples are from the coast, a region noted for its high concentration of indigenous populations. One of the earliest descriptions of armed conflict between tribes in Connecticut was discovered in unpublished seventeenth-century documents in the town of Guilford, which mention skirmishes between the Quinnipiac and neighboring Hammonassett tribes over the right to catch alewives in the East River.[190]

## Late Woodland Conflict

A double burial of two flexed males was unearthed in a Niantic shell midden site.[191] One had been shot with fifteen arrows, the other with six. Four arrowheads were quartz triangular points, the remaining seventeen were of bone (one flat triangle and sixteen hollow rounded bird bones with flat points). According to the excavator, the hollow bird-bone points had been found at only one other site—the Mohegan Fort Shantok, suggesting to him that the deaths resulted from a Mohegan raid on a Niantic settlement.

The multicomponent Menunketisuck site in Westbrook yielded a grave with a flexed skeleton that had a bone point lodged in its backbone.[192] The point is a different style—flat, but a narrow isosceles triangle—than either of the bone points from Niantic, suggesting it could be an emblemic style for some other, as yet unidentified Native community.

Multiple burials in Milford and Bridgeport included points embedded in bones.[193] One Milford double burial had skeletons with points in their ribs, and one had a round depression in the skull suggestive of a blow from a ball-headed war club. This type of war club, usually made from a single piece of wood, was popular with local Native American warriors during the Post-Contact period. Another burial in Milford had a single skeleton with a crushed skull and a point embedded in the tibia. The Bridgeport burial contained three male skeletons. One had an arrowhead in its ribs, another had an arrowhead in its skull, and the third had a fractured skull.[194]

## Body Decoration

Body painting and tattooing were common aspects of indigenous beauty. Southern New England Indians painted their clothing and other belongings, and painted and tattooed their bodies in a variety of colors for aesthetic purposes, for a dance, during mourning (when they blackened their faces), for war (red, black, half-red and half-black, half-black and half-white, or multicolored spots were popular), and during team sports and gaming, which often had a sacred nature.[195] Swedish naturalist Peter Kalm described eighteenth-century Indians tattooing themselves while journeying through the Champlain Valley area of Canada:

Two views of the head of a club, with remnants of its leather covering and the original stone, from the Fort Hill site in New Milford, Connecticut.

When they wish to paint some figures on the body, they draw first with a piece of charcoal the design which they desire to have painted. Then they take a needle, made somewhat like a fleam, dip it into the prepared dye and with it prick or puncture the skin along the lines of the design previously made with the charcoal. They dip the needle into the dye between every puncture; thus the color is left between the skin and flesh.[196]

One of the earliest accounts of indigenous southern New England body decoration was given by John Brereton, a crew member on Bartholomew Gosnold's 1602 voyage to Nantucket Sound, in which he described a meeting with a group of Native Americans from the southerly coast of Cape Cod. They had skins for trade, tobacco, and smoking pipes "steeled with copper." One man had "a plate of rich copper, in length a foot, in breadth half a foot, for a breastplate, the ears of all the rest had pendants of copper. Also one of them had his face painted over and head stuck with feathers in manner of a turkey cock's train."[197]

William Wood's description from eastern New England in the seventeenth

At left: *Indian in Body Paint*, watercolor by John White from the late sixteenth century recording the artist's observations on a visit to the English colony of Roanoke, including a handwritten note: "The manner of their attire and painting themselues when they goe to their generall huntings, or at theire Solemne feasts." At right: portrait of the Mahikan grand sachem Etowaucum or Etow Oh Koam (also known as Nicholas), painted by John Verelst in 1710 when the sachem traveled to England. Because birds signify a spiritual connection, the bird designs on his face and his bird feather earrings make it likely that he was a healer or holy man; Europeans claimed that he was a "sorcerer" or shaman as well as grand sachem. The turtle at his feet shows that he was a member of the Mahikan turtle clan, and the silk cape and long shirt of European cloth, sword, and scabbard were probably gifts from the English monarch. The wooden ball club indicates his authority and high status; the embroidered soft-sole moccasins (with either beading or porcupine quillwork) were typical of northeastern indigenous peoples.

century suggests that some body decorations indicated social status, group membership, spirit guides or guardians, or even a form of imitative magic.

> Many of the better sort [bear] upon their cheeks certain portraitures of beasts, as bears, deers, mooses, wolves, etc.; some of fowls, as of eagles, hawks, etc . . . whether they be foils to illustrate their unparalleled beauty (as they deem it) or arms to blazon their antique gentility, I cannot easily determine.[198]

Among the Algonkian-speaking Lenape people, whose homelands were New Jersey and southern New York, some geometric face decorations mimicked the patterns found on the faces of rattlesnakes and turtles, animals associated with the supernatural and imbued with spiritual powers among many indigenous societies. Black paint was used to summon the spirits.[199] Kalm noted that popular colors among the Canadian Indians were red from "cinnabar" and black from charcoal; motifs included snakes.[200] Roger Williams noted that the Narragansett people painted their clothing and themselves with colors, particularly white, black, red, yellow, green, and blue. According to Williams, the most popular was red pigment (which they called "wunnam"), obtained from both plant and mineral sources.

> They paint their Garments, etc. The men paint their Faces in Warre. Both men and Women for pride, etc. . . . Wunnam their red painting which they most delight in, and is both the Barke of the Pine, as also a red Earth.[201]

## THE EVIDENCE FOR INDIGENOUS SPIRITUALITY

### Human Mortuary Rites

The greatest archaeological information on indigenous spirituality comes from burials. Although most professional archaeologists will not excavate known grave sites (and in Connecticut it is illegal to do so), sometimes graves are unexpectedly located within camp and village sites. These were likely winter burials in the unfrozen storage pits of living areas.

Late Woodland burials were usually simple inhumations in shallow pits with few or no grave goods. The individual was normally flexed or semi-flexed and lying on his or her side. Most were interred with their heads to the east.[202] This may not have been the body's original position during burial, however, as non-Christian indigenous corpses were often described as being buried in a seated position.[203]

### Menunketisuck Site

The Menunketisuck site burial in Westbrook (discussed above) was dug into a hillside overlooking the river. The almost six-foot-tall flexed skeleton was laid on his right side with his head pointed to the southwest. The southwest direction had great spiritual meaning for Native Americans in southern New England, who believed that the Creator had his house there, where all good men and women went to live after death, while the souls of evildoers "wander restless abroad."[204] Other evidence of ritual was the placement of a *Canis* jawbone (dog or wolf) and a fragment of a child's jaw near the back of the adult.[205]

### Burnham-Shepard Site

Three graves in the residential Burnham-Shepard site in South Windsor were in empty storage pits, as at the Morgan site.[206] Likely the individuals died during cold weather, when the ground was frozen. Of the three, an adult male and female were buried on their left sides facing west-southwest, toward the Connecticut River. The third, a child, was buried on its right side facing northeast, away from the river. Was that position accidental or did it have some meaning? None of the burials contained grave goods. The food (including maize and beans) and broken pottery found in some of the grave fill were probably part of the previous camp debris.[207]

### Morgan Site

At the Morgan site in Rocky Hill two separate pit features contained flexed individuals, an adult male and a child. In contrast to the deceased at Burnham-Shepard, both faced east and toward the river. It may be that the preference was not the direction itself, but that the corpses faced toward the water, which has spiritual connotations for indigenous peoples.[208] Late Woodland and post-contact burials do often overlook bodies of water. The Pequot burials overlooking Long Pond, the three Schaghticoke burying grounds along the Housatonic River on the tribe's reservation in Kent, the Mohegan burying ground at Fort Shantok

Remnants of a leather pouch and hammered copper beads that predate European contact, both associated with large jasper and chert biface blades found at Indian Town Gravel Pit site in Saybrook, Connecticut.

above the Thames River, and the Niantic burying ground at Crescent Beach in East Lyme are a few examples. In fact, sacred sites in general often overlook or are associated with water (see Chapter 9 under "Mortuary Ceremonies and Indigenous Spirituality" for a discussion of the relationship of water and Native American spirituality, and the section "Stone Piles, Farm Clearing, and Sacred Places" for a discussion of other, non-burial, sacred localities).

The child lay on his or her left side. The grave was distinguished by a dark lining in the pit, possibly bark, grasses, or matting, such as were found in seventeenth-century Pequot graves. The pattern of tooth eruption showed that the child had died at five or six years of age.[209] (Sex cannot be determined in children because the identifying skeletal traits do not appear until adulthood.)

The burial included a triangular quartz Levanna projectile point at the bottom of the pit, the upper jaw of a white-tailed deer, and a complete box turtle shell (the latter two both faced the child). X-ray photographs taken of the turtle carapace revealed a deer knucklebone inside it and a quartz artifact plugged into the neck opening, forming a rattle. (The quartz items likely were included for their symbolic, spiritual meaning as well as their functional uses.) The turtle shell was near the child's leg, so the rattle may have been worn on the thigh or lower leg. A nineteenth-century Cree rattle (at the Institute for American Indian Studies in Washington, Connecticut) made of small turtle shell rattles tied together with a leather thong was also worn in this way.

The size and shape of certain features on the skull and pelvis clearly identified the second individual as an adult male between forty and fifty years old at death and about 6 feet, 1 inch tall (155 centimeters).[210] Unlike the child, he lay on his right side, with his head toward the south. There were no grave goods, but near the foot of the grave was a small pit with a bone dagger and an abrading stone. Although these could have been a ceremonial offering for the deceased, the storage pit may have been unrelated.

Skeletal characteristics also provide information on health. For the Morgan adult, missing back molars and bone loss in the upper jaw suggest periodontal disease. He had a slight case of osteoarthritis in his lower back, indicated by lipping on the vertebrae. His major cause of anguish, however, was osteomyelitis, an infection of the bone caused by a deep, unhealed wound in his lower left leg down to his ankle joint that left him with a badly deformed left foot and, if he could walk at all, with a profound limp.[211]

This condition has been identified in two other Late Woodland adult male skeletons from Connecticut, suggesting that osteomyelitis could be a response to the shift from more mobile hunting and gathering societies to more sedentary horticultural societies. A study of six adult male burials from three late pre-contact Milford sites (Merwin Farm, Wilcox Farm, and Laurel Beach) also showed the presence of osteoarthritis in two cases and dental disease (periodontal infection, caries, wear, and tartar buildup) in all.[212] These health problems, especially those relating to oral health, have also been correlated "with the intensification of horticulture and resulting dietary changes, namely less protein and more carbohydrates."[213]

### The Dog in Native American Community Life

The dog was the earliest domesticated animal and the only one domesticated worldwide. In North America dogs have been dated to Paleo-Indian times, about 10,000 years ago, with at least four distinct breeds identified: the large, wide-muzzled Eskimo dog; the smaller Spitz-type long-haired "wool dog" of the Northwest Coast, whose fur was sheared off with mussel shell knives and woven into ceremonial blankets; a medium-sized "dingo-like" dog; and a small, terrier-like dog that occurred as both a short-faced variety and one with a long, narrow muzzle.[214] DNA studies suggest that dogs may have been domesticated much earlier—100,000 years ago or more—but definitive dog bones appeared in Old World archaeology sites only about 14,000 years ago. This conflict in age could be because the earlier animals were tamed wolves, or "dogs-in-process." Wolf bones have indeed been associated with early humans for more than 100,000 years.[215]

Ethnographic accounts and the archaeological record show that among Eastern Woodlands peoples, dogs were important members of the community and figured significantly in sacred stories and ritual, as summarized by New York avocational archaeologist Edward Kaeser.[216]

The dog provided protection, companionship, hunting assistance, kept humans warm, cleaned up camp, served as emergency food and as on the North American Plains, possibly used as a beast of burden prior to the adoption of the horse. In ritual context, the animal appears centrally in meals

## Conflict over Dogs and Livestock in Colonial New Haven

In 1657, the English colonists living at Quinnipiac (now New Haven, Connecticut) offered to give back tribal land and shellfish beds on Oyster Point to the Quinnipiac tribe, provided the tribal members agreed to several conditions, included killing all their dogs.

Indian dogs were a nuisance to the English because they attacked livestock, which the English allowed to wander freely, particularly hogs. For their part, the Indians despised the livestock, because the animals trampled planting fields and destroyed important shellfish beds.

The Quinnipiacs agreed to all of the colonists' conditions, except the dog kill, and so negotiations ended. A few years earlier the magistrates of New Haven Colony had demanded that the Quinnipiacs either make payment for several hogs killed by Indian dogs, or kill all the Indian dogs. When they tried to force the sachem Momauguin to reveal the owners of the "mischievous dogs yet alive," the sachem refused, because he feared he might be poisoned by his own people for helping to bring about the death of their beloved dogs.[a]

## The Carolina Dog

Today, in the isolated swamps and forests of the Carolinas, there still live some short-haired, foxlike feral dogs that archaeological studies suggest may be the descendants of dogs that came to the eastern woodlands with early indigenous peoples. With reddish yellow to ginger-colored fur, locally they are called "pariah" or "yaller" dogs, otherwise known as the Carolina dog. Genetic research shows that these animals are related to the Australian dingo and to the New Guinea singing dog. Bred in captivity since the 1980s, these dogs have shown some unique behaviors, but have proved to be suitable as domesticated pets. The Carolina dog has been recognized as a registered breed by both the American Rare Breed Association and the United Kennel Club.[b]

Notes

a. Menta 2003, 108–114.

b. Buckland 2002, 93–96. See also "Primitive Dogs of the Southeast," fact sheet (updated April 13, 2001), Savannah River Ecology Laboratory, University of Georgia, archived at http://web.archive.org/web/2007 0614135050/http://www.uga.edu/srel/dogs .html (accessed August 31, 2012); Scott Weidensaul, "Tracking America's First Dogs," March 1999, www.smithsonianmag.com/sci ence-nature/Tracking-Americas-First-Dogs .html (accessed August 31, 2012).

The Carolina dog.

and as sacrifices, interred as grave goods, and demonstrating that dogs enjoyed the affection of their owners, buried as humans in bundle or articulated fashion.[217]

In his article on Late Woodland dog ceremonialism on Long Island, historian John A. Strong discussed the dog's importance in post-contact Native American spirituality: "The role of the dog as an intermediator, messenger, or guide between this world and the spirit world has been frequently documented by early European explorers and settlers."[218]

Writing in 1634, William Wood noted that the southern New England Algonkian speakers believed a great dog guarded the entrance to the afterlife, allowing only worthy individuals to enter.[219] Among the Mohegans of southeastern Connecticut, the dog was the animal totem (that is, the spiritual animal) for one of the tribe's clans.[220] In south-central Connecticut, dogs were such an important part of Quinnipiac tribal life that in 1657 impoverished tribal members chose them over more planting lands, even though they did not have enough land to support their families. According to his reading of early colonial documents, John Menta described the situation and provided background information that led up to the event.

> The English occupation of the surrounding area made it increasingly difficult for the Indians to live by their traditional means of farming, fishing, hunting and gathering. No longer did the Indians have unimpeded access to the food sources along the shoreline; the colonists built dams on the rivers that altered Indian fishing sites. The English farmers clearcut the forest and transformed much of the Quinnipiac country into an Old World pastoral community. . . . These changes in the physical environment made traditional subsistence activities less convenient for the Indians. . . . Momauguin and his council had previously informed the governor that since they did not have enough land for planting they desired to "hire some English" lands on the west shore at a place called Oyster Point. . . . The townspeople finally agreed to consider the matter if the following conditions were honored by the Quinnipiac: . . . that they kill all their dogs who had done mischief already.[221]

### Dog Burials in Connecticut and Southern New York

What could be the earliest dog burial in Connecticut is the Late Archaic cremation discovered at the Bliss site in Old Lyme. These few remains were identified to genus only as *Canis* and could be either dog or wolf. Burials positively identified as those of dog date from the late Middle Woodland and Late Woodland periods. They are an important part of Native American spirituality. In southern New York and New England, deceased dogs were often treated in much the same way as their human counterparts—flexed or bundled, and buried in small pits or in graves with humans.

Often these burials contained evidence of other ritual behavior, such as a

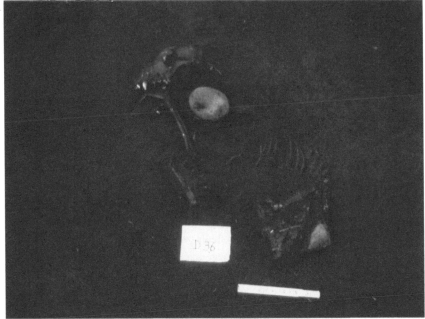

Late Woodland dog burials from the Grannis Island site, New Haven. The dog burials are virtually identical to the flexed, small-pit human Late Woodland burials.

hearth and food above or adjacent to the grave, perhaps the remains of a ceremonial feast. The inclusion of complete shells in a burial pit otherwise devoid of midden material has been reported from several Late Woodland sites in the Long Island Sound area.[222] At least one researcher has suggested that the dogs were ceremonially killed and purposely buried near hearths—the center of family life—to fulfill their role as spirit guardians "to protect the household from danger."[223]

There are several examples of dog burials and accompanying remains of ritualized behavior.

*College Point Site*   College Point overlooks Flushing Bay and the East River in the borough of Queens, New York. At this site a small dog was found lying on its right side in a pit with three unmodified stones in a row between its legs, and three unhinged shell valves (oyster, clam, and scallop) near its backbone. The dog's skeleton was missing its head, tail, and a few ribs; near where its head should have been the excavators found a fragment of its lower jaw, charred by fire. Also in the grave near the dog was the skeleton of a young fisher (a fisher cat, a member of the weasel family), also decapitated. Directly above the grave were the remains of a hearth, indicating a ceremonial fire. Four large stones at the periphery of the grave marked the four directions, each usually associated with a spirit being and laden with spiritual meaning. The excavators suggested that the heads and one of the dog's organs were ritually eaten (the removal of the ribs might have made the removal of the canine heart easier).[224]

Another possible reason for the decapitations may have been the ritual use of the dog in warfare, as discussed by Alvin H. Morrison in an unpublished paper presented at a meeting of the Canadian Ethnology Society.

> The Wabanaki [peoples of northern New England] held a Dog Feast in preparation for warfare. They believed that the flesh of the dog would give the warriors courage. The head of one of the dogs was removed and singed in the fire. Then it was taken in the hands of the war chief who sang to it, telling the dog spirit who and where the war party would attack. He passed the skull to each of his fellow warriors. Those who accepted the skull and sang to it signified that they would join the attack.[225]

*Grannis Island Site*   Five flexed dog burials, four adult animals and one juvenile, were discovered at the Grannis Island site in New Haven.[226] Buried with care in pits and in a formal ceremonial fetal position, they represent a pre-contact Quinnipiac ritual, likely to ensure eternal life in the spirit world for a beloved animal companion—or to evoke the aid of dog spirits in some social or political matter. Like in the College Point find, some shells were recovered from these burials, although it is possible that they may have been accidently introduced from the shell midden at the Grannis Island site.

*Muskrat Hill Site and Nearby Coastal Sites*   Several other dog burials at Connecticut coastal sites suggest additional complex ritual meaning.[227] In an unidentified "Indian village" site a "small dog" was found buried on its stomach with its head pointed to the southwest and feet and tail missing; another dog burial was "cremated" (possible food remains?). At the Muskrat Hill site in Stratford, three dogs were arranged in a triangle, with the largest at the point of the triangle and the other two at its base. Small and collie-like, the dogs were buried at a depth of 30 inches (76 centimeters) lying on their stomachs with their heads facing east. A whelk shell was buried with them. The top of the grave was covered with oyster shell. The dog grave was similar to human burials excavated in Southport and Stratford. The Southport graves were 18 inches to 2 feet deep (about 45 to 60 centimeters) on a slope overlooking the Pequot Swamp. The bodies were flexed and facing east. Over each grave was a layer of oyster shell and charcoal. The flexed burial at the Fresh Pond site in Stratford had its head to the east and was buried at a depth of 3 feet (about 90 centimeters).

## Shell as Spiritual Metaphor in Indigenous Belief Systems

The ritualistic, spiritual nature of the dog burials is highlighted by the inclusion of shell. According to the research of anthropologist George Hamell, the color white had symbolic significance among the post-contact northern Iroquois and Algonkian-speaking peoples of the Great Lakes region.[228] As one of the two main colors of wampum, it represented the "traditional concept of wealth as physical, spiritual and social well-being." Among the Iroquois, at least, a shell bead is "a metaphor for light and life, for the continuity of life in general and for the social continuity of human life in particular . . . light, bright, and white things, including white shell beads, are 'good to think' and serve as visible and tangible metaphors of revered cultural values. Fusing aesthetic and ideational interests within the context of ritual, white shell beads metaphorically communicate culturally valued states of physical, spiritual, and social well-being."[229]

Among the Mohegans of southeastern Connecticut, medicine woman Melissa Fawcett Zobel reports white wampum beads sewn onto black backgrounds symbolize stars and extraordinary souls: "The tiny white beads on black velvet . . . depict both people and stars in the dark of night. Stars are the advanced form taken by Indian people with extraordinary gifts of the spirit after they pass into the spirit world."[230]

Likely the white shells in the dog burials were significant mortuary items.[231] Shells have symbolic as well as economic significance among other contemporary New England tribal peoples. Native American artisans still produce wampum jewelry from quahog shells, which tribal peoples wear with and without their regalia (traditional ceremonial clothing). Wampum jewelry is often worn by mourners at Native American funerals and burial services. In discussing the traditional serving of clam chowder at the Eastern Pequot Tribal Nation's annual powwow, former tribal chairwoman Marcia Flowers commented: "We are known for our quahogs. They were a big commodity for us historically. They were used as money exchange as well as a food product, and we used every part of the quahog, and that's a tradition we've kept up."[232]

## Effigy Objects

Effigy objects carved or molded in the shape of animals or humans have been recovered from several Connecticut sites.[233] Unfortunately, because they were found in disturbed contexts or multicomponent sites with stratigraphically overlapping occupations, many cannot be assigned to a specific cultural period. Happily, some can be identified even though they have no known provenience, because either the tool or its style was popular at a particular time. One example is a clay elbow pipe (a pipe style appearing in Late Woodland times) with a bowl

A variety of carved beads (shell or bone) from the Kent Furnace site, Kent, Connecticut.

shaped like a seated bird, possibly an eagle or crow, collected in the Connecticut River valley above Cromwell (now in the Rogers Collection of the Institute of American Indian Studies). In Native North America birds are often linked to tobacco and smoking pipes, and tobacco and smoking are, as a rule, linked to the spirit world.[234] Anthropologist Dr. Kathleen Bragdon reported that "in much of the Northeast, beings endowed with Manitou are thought to be 'addicted' to tobacco, and smoking thus attracts and appeases them (Von Gernet and Timmons 1987:40). Shamans often relied on Manitou who took the form of birds [that is, a bird spirit guide]."[235]

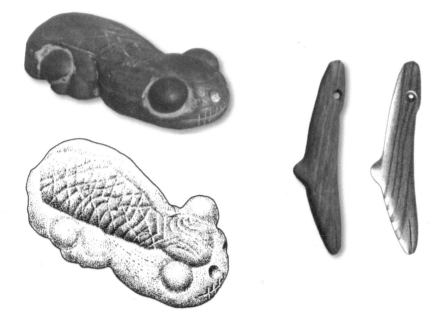

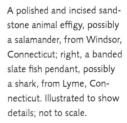

A polished and incised sand-stone animal effigy, possibly a salamander, from Windsor, Connecticut; right, a banded slate fish pendant, possibly a shark, from Lyme, Connecticut. Illustrated to show details; not to scale.

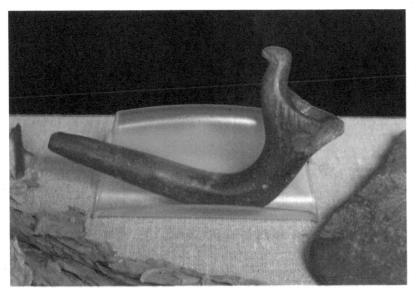

A seated bird effigy stone elbow pipe from Cromwell, Connecticut. The pipe, which burns sacred plants like tobacco, is particularly potent with its spiritual bird, which helps to carry the smoker's message heavenward to the Creator.

Birds, especially eagles, owls, and crows, were often considered spirit helpers, conduits between the spirit world and humans. In some indigenous societies religious practitioners and those on a vision quest were thought to be able to transform themselves into birds.[236] Southern New England Native Americans believed that the crow was an important spirit helper of the Creator.[237] It has been suggested that the animal effigies on smoking pipes may have been the "personal totems" of their owners.[238] The pipe is normally shaped so that the animal faces its user, suggesting an intimate relationship, such as with a clan symbol or with a

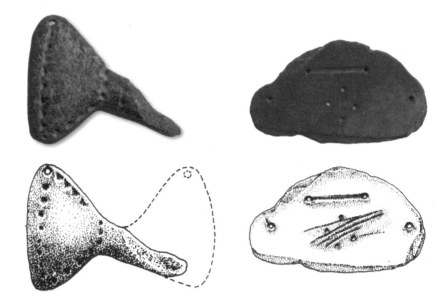

A broken pendant, possibly a winged animal effigy, with reconstruction; the dots recall marks on pottery and basketry that symbolize the "path of life" or "beautiful path," which the soul followed through the Milky Way to reach the Creator's house. Right, an incised pendant with dots and lines, possibly in the shape of a turtle. Illustrated to show details; not to scale.

spiritual guardian acquired during puberty rites, dreams, or solitary fasting and meditation. As archaeologist Michael Volmar noted:

> All Northeastern Algonquian speakers had spiritual guardians. While many guardians were spirit beings, inanimate objects, or even ghosts, most were animals (Kraft 1986:178). . . . Once a guardian spirit was recognized and accepted, the recipient might make an amulet or fetish made of bird or animal claws or teeth. . . . Bear effigies, claws, and teeth have been found in several archaeological sites, and are good examples of these kinds of spiritual objects.[239]

## INTERPRETATIONS AND QUESTIONS

The importance of maize horticulture and the existence of "villages" are major questions in the study of Late Woodland communities. These are slowly being resolved as more Late Woodland sites are excavated, particularly wide horizontal expanses of sites, so that cultural features—especially the small, easily missed post molds—can be located and house patterns and dietary information identified. Large, complex sites such as these take time to excavate. Unfortunately, time is money, and cultural resource management surveys do not lend themselves to lengthy excavations.

One approach to this problem is to use heavy machinery to peel off most of the topsoil (which in Connecticut is almost always disturbed plow zone, particularly in the riverine and coastal areas) over large portions of a site. The remaining few inches of topsoil can then be shaved by hand with a shovel down to the light-colored undisturbed subsoil, revealing the cultural features. This technique was used with much success at Sites 294A-AF2-1 and 294A-25-2 in Milford during the Iroquois Gas Pipeline archaeological survey,[240] at the Larson Farm site in New Milford before construction of the new high school,[241] and at the Military

## PUBERTY RITES

Edward Winslow, a Pilgrim leader on the *Mayflower* and governor of Plymouth Colony in Massachusetts in the 1630s and 1640s, briefly referred to the rituals by which adolescent boys formally became men in indigenous societies, a rite of passage comparable to, but much more physically strenuous than, the Jewish bar mitzvah. Both can be described as puberty ceremonies wherein a person passes from childhood to adulthood. Winslow commented, "A man is not accounted a man till he do some notable act or show forth such courage and resolution as becometh his place."[a]

Yet it was a Dutchman, Isaac de Rasieres, who provided the only specific description of a southern New England Native American puberty rite, after his visit to Plymouth Colony. In about 1628, in a letter to Samuel Bloomaert, de Rasieres reported that a boy is left in the wilderness all winter to fend for himself. He returns to his village in the spring, when he is forced to eat "bitter herbs" (possibly the "black drink" made from yaupon holly, used in Southeastern rituals). If he holds it down he is brought before all the members of the community, who decide whether he is ready for manhood. If he seems healthy and well-nourished, he is deemed a man and presented with a wife.[b] According to one historian:

As a result of such training young Algonquians learned not only how to survive but also how to develop the capacities to withstand the severest physical and psychological trials. The result was the Indian personality type that Euro-Americans came to characterize as stoic, the supreme manifestation of which was the absolute expressionlessness of prisoners under torture.[c]

Girls also underwent a form of puberty rite, but we have no description of one. Likely it was similarly designed to prepare them for the rigors of wilderness life and motherhood. On achieving adult status, both males and females received a new name. Hair styles, clothing, and jewelry were also markers of age-related (and also social) status.[d]

Notes

a. Winslow 1634, *Good News from New England,* cited in Salisbury 1981, 229.

b. de Rasieres 1628, cited in Salisbury 1981, 229.

c. Salisbury 1981, 230.

d. Bragdon 1996, 170.

Academy site in Niantic during phase 3 investigations as part of the permitting process before construction of an Army National Guard academy.[242] At all three sites this method revealed many hearths, pits, and post-mold features without holding up those projects and at less expense than manual excavation alone would have required.

Current information on the significance of horticulture in Late Woodland Connecticut, and the factors involved in its acceptance, practice, and importance, suggest that the situation is more complicated than once thought. Although the data still indicate that along the coast cultigens were of only minor importance for most of the Late Woodland period, the Housatonic estuary may have been an exception. There may have been greater subregional diversity than we have originally assumed, which remains yet undiscovered. We have virtually no published

Excavation at the Larson Farm site in New Milford by American Cultural Specialists in the late 1990s. After heavy equipment removes the upper portion of the plow zone (below), crew members shovel-shave the base of the plow zone to the subsoil in search of features.

information on subsistence-settlement systems from many portions of northeastern and western Connecticut, and central Connecticut outside the Connecticut River valley (such as inland between the Connecticut and Housatonic drainages). More archaeological surveys are desperately needed in those areas to help resolve this controversy.

More critical is the relative lack of interpretive data on the social and political organizations of Late Woodland communities, and their identification with post-contact tribal peoples. Again, this is mainly because of the few undisturbed Late Woodland residential sites located by modern archaeologists. Many such sites were excavated by amateurs in the nineteenth and early twentieth centuries, well before the introduction of radiocarbon dating, flotation analysis, petrographic microscopy, use-wear analysis, archaeobotany, and the realization of the importance of cultural feature configurations and their artifact and ecofact associations. These early diggers were often interested only in the unbroken artifacts and not in what the associated "garbage" might tell us about the lifeways of the people who made them. By the 1970s most of these sites had been destroyed by development.

We need to find more undisturbed residential sites to study and compare those cultural remains — particularly houses and their contents — that could enable sociopolitical interpretations. While excavating the Hatchery West site in Illinois in 1963, the eminent archaeologist Dr. Lewis Binford and others made the discovery that the location of house structures and other cultural features were not necessarily correlative with the density of artifacts.[243] Recent field studies in the Northeast echo those findings, showing that pre-contact indigenous housing may be located in areas of low artifact scatter rather than in those of high artifact density, where excavations are normally concentrated.[244] The findings suggest that traditional archaeological methodology should be changed to include intensive excavations also in areas of low artifact density.

We also need more study of the artwork from this period. There is probably a wealth of data on artistic symbolism and correlations to post-contact sacred stories, folktales, plant medicine, and indigenous belief systems awaiting anyone who has the patience to mine it from early documents, amateur collections, and Native American oral traditions.

# 9

## Beaver Skins for Iron Axes

### *The Final Woodland Period*

Brothers, we must be one as the English are, or we shall all be destroyed. You know our fathers had plenty of deer and skins and our plains were full of game and turkeys, and our coves and rivers were full of fish. But, brothers, since these Englishmen have seized our country, they have cut down the grass with scythes, and the trees with axes. Their cows and horses eat up the grass, and their hogs spoil our bed of clams; and finally we shall starve to death.

> —Miantunnomoh, Narragansett grand sachem, from a 1642 speech to Long Island Indians under the sachem Waindance at Meaticut

Archaeological evidence has proved that Scandinavian explorers known as the Vikings, or Norsemen, were the first Europeans to make landfall in North America, which researchers believe was the "Vinland" referred to in Norse sagas.[1] A Viking settlement dating to about A.D. 1000 was excavated at the L'Anse Aux Meadows site in Newfoundland, Canada.[2] Because of its archaeological importance, the site was named a World Heritage Site by the United Nations Educational, Scientific, and Cultural Organization in 1978.[3]

Our earliest definitive documentary evidence for specific European contacts with indigenous communities of northeastern North America dates to around the beginning of the sixteenth century, when European explorers and fishermen began frequenting the Canadian Grand Banks and New England. In 1497 John Cabot explored the coast of Newfoundland, where the codfish were so populous his men caught them in baskets.[4] Almost immediately thereafter and throughout the 1500s English, Portuguese, and particularly French mariners plied the waters off eastern Canada and New England, making landfall for freshwater and other supplies, and to trade for furs with the local Native Americans. Canadian archaeologists have located some of these early European camp sites.[5]

The earliest record of Europeans in Long Island Sound is the voyage of Giovanni da Verrazzano, an Italian explorer working for the French, who in 1524

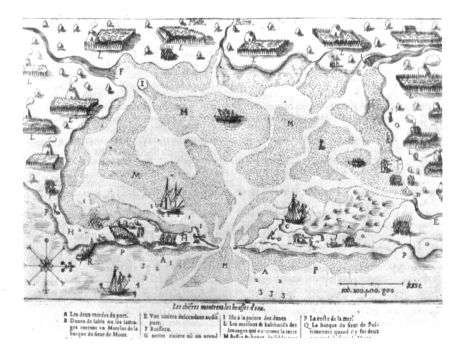

Samuel de Champlain's 1605 map of Malle Barre (Nauset Harbor, Eastham, Cape Cod) shows a Native American village consisting of dispersed circular wigwams and associated gardens.

sailed up the Atlantic coast into New York Harbor, then eastward along Long Island's southern coast and into Narragansett Bay.[6] In 1525 Estevan Gomez, a Spaniard sailing for France, explored coasts from Nova Scotia to Cape Cod and Nantucket, and in 1542 Jehan Alphonsce, a Frenchman, explored coasts from Cape Breton to Massachusetts Bay.[7]

The next documented explorations of southern New England came sixty years later, by several Englishmen—Bartholomew Gosnold in 1602, Martin Pring in 1603, and George Weymouth in 1605—followed by Frenchman Samuel de Champlain, who visited Canada and New England as far as Cape Cod from 1604 to 1606.[8]

In 1609 Henry Hudson, an Englishman sailing for the Dutch, explored New York Harbor and the river that now bears his name. Seeking a northwest passage to the Orient, Hudson met with local indigenous leaders and opened up the area for a near trading monopoly by the Dutch East India Company. The hospitality of the Mahikan (now Mohican) Indians, whose homelands stretched across both sides of the upper Hudson River valley, and the rich trade in furs persuaded the Dutch to establish settlements on both sides of Long Island Sound and along the Hudson River from Manhattan Island to north of Albany. Soon after Hudson's return to Holland, Dutch traders such as Adriaen Block (for whom Block Island is named), Hendrick Christiaensz, Cornelius May, and others began plying Connecticut waters, exchanging goods with local Indians.[9] There were Dutch settlements on Long Island, up the Connecticut River, and along the Connecticut coast, including at Branford and possibly Old Saybrook. Dutch farmers moved east from the Hudson Valley to settle in what is now western Massachusetts and northwestern Connecticut.

A little known fact is that present-day Connecticut was once part of Dutch New Netherland, which originally extended from Cape Cod to the Delaware River![10] (And no, Christopher Columbus never made landfall on the North American continent, let alone New England, having sailed no farther north than the Caribbean Islands.) The English also stepped up exploration and trading activities. John Smith of Pocahontas fame sailed from Virginia to New England in 1614, and Thomas Dermer crossed the Atlantic in 1619.[11]

The year 1633 marked the first documented European settlement in Connecticut—the trading House of (Good) Hope built by the Dutch at Hartford—and the beginning of the end of the pre-contact Woodland lifestyle. During the Final Woodland period (A.D. 1524 to 1633) European contacts were increasingly frequent, bringing changes in the Woodland way of life that eventually led to the rapid transitions and fracturing of traditional Native American cultures in the Northeast.

## EARLY POST-CONTACT LIFESTYLES

When these early Europeans sailed into Long Island Sound and up the major rivers in what is now the state of Connecticut, they were met by American Indian peoples whose lifestyle was much the same as it had been for the previous five hundred years. As in the Late Woodland period, the practice of horticulture did not greatly affect traditional hunting, fishing, and wild plant gathering activities. Gardening and fruit orchards introduced by Europeans apparently were substituted for some of the latter endeavors. The Native Americans of early post-contact times cultivated maize, beans, squash, tobacco, Jerusalem artichokes, and sunflowers with edible tubers. They fished in freshwater and saltwater areas throughout the year, collected shellfish in the summer and winter, fruits and plants in the spring and summer, nuts in the fall, and gathered roots and tubers in the fall and winter. Large hunting parties of men hunted deer in the fall and early winter. William Wood[12] and Roger Williams[13] both attested to the continued importance of white-tailed deer to the early post-contact indigenous diet. In fact, early English documents note that Native Americans hunted a wide range of animals, although they did not pinpoint in what seasons.

### The First Environmental Stewards

To ensure plentiful game and other foods for the future, indigenous communities practiced environmental management.[14] They selectively burned off forested areas to create "edge habitats" that were optimal environments for important food sources in the Indian diet, such as deer, wild turkey, seed-bearing plants, and berries.[15] The Europeans marveled at these parklike areas, which also made it easier for hunting parties and others to travel through the "greenwood."

Ezra Stiles reported that the Quinnipiacs burned tracts at the top of West Rock, one of the two highest promontories in New Haven, to provide a clear view when hunting deer.[16] Indigenous societies also used fire to control game movements, funneling the animals toward the hunters, and to enhance their physical environment. Many of the hills in Litchfield were cleared by Indian hunters setting them on fire; Potucko, one of the signers of the first land deed to present-day Waterbury, was said to have made "a fire in the form of a large ring around a hill" near the current Waterbury-Wolcott border while hunting deer.[17] Adrian Van der Donck, who lived in New Netherlands along the Hudson River from 1641 to 1649, described these annual burnings by the local Indians:

> The Indians have a yearly custom (which some of our Christians have also adopted) of burning the woods, plains and meadows in the fall of the year, when the leaves have fallen, and when the grass and vegetable substances are dry. . . . This practice is named by us and the Indians, "bush-burning," which is done for several reasons: First, to render hunting easier, as the bush and vegetable growth rends the walking difficult for the hunter, and the crackling of the dry substances betrays him and frightens away the game. Secondly, to thin out and clear the woods of all dead substances and grass, which grow better the ensuing spring. Thirdly, to circumscribe and enclose the game within the lines of the fire, when it is more easily taken, and also, because the game is more easily tracked over the burned parts of the woods.[18]

The significance of controlled burning as a powerful environmental management tool is forcefully demonstrated by the Connecticut Department of Energy and Environmental Protection's recent reintroduction of "prescribed fires" to Connecticut state lands as an "ecological management measure." In effect, the DEEP is using the Native American technique of controlled burning to sustain and stabilize the state's endangered grassland habitats (and their endangered animal residents), and "to offset the loss of early successional habitat [such as oak savannas and pitchpine–scrub oak forests] to development and forest succession."[19] Native peoples managed the local plant and animal populations in other ways as well. Gladys Tantaquidgeon reported that when collecting wild plants, Mohegans did not pick the first plant they saw (since at least one would be needed for reseeding the area for future plants) but picked only what they needed, leaving "some in reserve. The Indian practiced conservation in its true meaning."[20]

Indigenous hunters did not kill female animals with young. They thanked the animal spirits with prayers and offerings. Hunting territories were clearly defined, avoiding an imbalance in nature from overhunting.[21] The Algonkian children's story "Gluscabi and the Game Animals" teaches the importance of harmony in Nature and the place of humans as relatives of animals as part of the natural world. Such stories illustrate that any imbalances in that world will ultimately bring disaster to human society, a central theme in the indigenous worldview, as Schaghticoke elder Trudie Richmond compellingly explained in an open letter to her granddaughter Wunneanatsu.

> As time passed Indian people multiplied and walked in four directions of this great Turtle Island, speaking different languages, living in different ways,

dressing differently. They even differed in their explanation of our Creation. Yet certain facts did not differ, and that is our respect for Mother Earth and an awareness and respect for all living things because we are all relatives. . . . All societies have a particular way of viewing the world around them and it is reflected in their lifeways and culture. Native American people have a special way of viewing the universe, believing that one must live in harmony with all living things. To us, maintaining that balance of nature is critical to survival. We are taught that the land does not belong to the people, but rather the people belong to the land.[22]

## House and Home

European descriptions of Final Woodland and early post-contact indigenous housing show that at that time Native Americans in southern New England used several types of structures: a round wigwam, or "weetoo," a longer rectangular house, and an oval house. The wigwam was big enough to fit a single or extended family, while the longer houses could accommodate several family groups. Some communities lived in the smaller wigwams in the summer when families dispersed and larger 50- or 60-foot (15 to 18 meter) multifamily structures in the winter.[23] Houses were usually covered with bark or mats made from rushes, cattails, or corn husks. The mats could easily be rolled up for storage and moved from one site to another during the seasonal round. On the islands and along the coast where large trees were scarce, houses were often covered with the plentiful sea grasses or corn husks.

Ezra Stiles studied the layout of several wigwams during a visit to the Nehantic (Niantic) Indian reservation in East Lyme. According to his notes and illustrations, a mid-eighteenth-century Nehantic house contained a central hearth with a cooking pot hung over it. Low wooden platforms built along the walls of the house provided sleeping and storage space.[24] There are accounts of similar housing in adjacent eastern Massachusetts and Rhode Island in the writings of earlier European settlers. The Pilgrim author of *Mourt's Relation* (1622), thought to be Edward Winslow, a passenger on the *Mayflower* and leader of Plimoth Plantation, provided a detailed description of a wigwam of the Massachusett tribe in the area of present-day Plymouth, which the Pilgrims came across shortly after landing on the Massachusetts mainland in 1620:

> The houses were made with long young sapling trees, bended and both ends stuck into the ground. They were made round, like unto an arbor, and covered down to the ground with thick and well wrought mats, and the doors as not over a yard high, made of a mat to open. The chimney was a wide open hole in the top, for which they had a mat to cover it closed when they pleased. One might stand and go upright in them. In the midst of them were four little trunches [stakes], knocked into the ground, and small sticks laid over, on which they hung their pots, and what they had to seeth [simmer, boil]. Round about the fire they lay on mats, which are their beds. The houses were

## GLUSCABI AND THE GAME ANIMALS

Storytelling was and still is an integral part of the Native American tradition dating back to earliest memory. Native societies are based on oral tradition. It is what breathes life into the culture. The season for telling stories begins with the first frost, a time of great excitement when the *Hageota* (Storyteller) travels from village to village, from home to home. Everyone gathers around to share in this wonderful time, to hear what it was like when the world was new. Stories are an important method of teaching the young, of passing down culture from one generation to the next. They hold many lessons, teach us the values of our culture, and show us how to live in our world. They often describe unacceptable behavior and express, enhance, and enforce the morals and norms of tribal society.[a]

The following New England story about the Abenaki culture hero Gluscabi (also spelled Glooscap or Gluskabe, among other spellings) teaches how misuse of environmental resources can throw the natural world out of balance and harm human society.

Long ago Gluscabi went hunting, but all the animals decided to hide from him. His Grandmother Woodchuck wove a magical game bag for him to use. Taking the bag, Gluscabi walked to a large clearing and called out, "All you animals, listen to me. A terrible thing is going to happen. The sun is going to go out and the world is going to end." Frightened, the animals asked Gluscabi how they would survive. "My friends," he said, "just climb into my game bag and you will be safe." Soon all the animals in the world were in his bag. Gluscabi laughed and went home proudly to his grandmother.

"Why must you always do things this way," she said. "You cannot keep all of the animals in a bag. They will sicken and die. There will be none left for our children and our children's children. It is also right that it should be difficult to hunt them. Then you will grow stronger trying to find them. And the animals will also grow stronger and wiser trying to avoid being caught. Then things will be in the right balance."[b]

Notes

a. Text adapted from "Annual Storytelling Celebration for November, 2009," Institute for American Indian Studies, Washington, Connecticut.

b. Recounted in Richmond 1989, 29.

double matted, for as they were matted without, so were they within, with newer and fairer mats. In the houses we found wooden bowls, trays and dishes, earthen pots, handbaskets made of crabshells wrought together, also an English pail or bucket. . . . There was also baskets of sundry sorts, bigger and some lesser, finer and some coarser, some were curiously wrought with black and white in pretty works [wampum beads?], and sundry other of their household stuff. We found also two or three deer's heads, one whereof had been newly killed, for it was still fresh. There was also a company of deer's feet stuck up in the houses, harts' horns, and eagles' claws, and sundry such like things there was, also two or three baskets filled with parched acorns, pieces of fish, and a piece of broiled herring. We found also a little silk grass, and a little tobacco seed, with some other seeds which we knew not. Without was sundry bundles of flags, and sedge, bulrushes and other things.[25]

In 1643 Roger Williams wrote about a Narragansett house: "Two Families will live comfortably and lovingly in a little round house of some fourteen or sixteen feet over, and so more and more families in proportion."[26] In his journey along the northern New England coast from 1604 to 1607, the French explorer Samuel de Champlain described some of the reed-, corn husk-, and grass-covered houses he saw while visiting an indigenous coastal village on Cape Cod.

> Their dwellings are separate from each other, according to the land which each one occupies. They are large, of a circular shape, and covered with thatch made of grasses or the husks of Indian corn. They are furnished only with a bed or two, raised a foot from the ground, made of a number of little pieces of wood pressed against each other, on which they arrange a reed mat, after the Spanish style, which is a kind of matting two or three fingers thick on these they sleep.[27]

Men cut and fixed the poles of these structures, but it was the women who built, dismantled, and carried them on their backs from one camp to the next.[28]

The sachem's house was larger than that of other tribal members, since meetings were often held in it.[29] Reverend Daniel Boardman from New Milford remarked on the size of the house of Weramaug, a grand sachem of the Weantinock tribe of west-central Connecticut in the early eighteenth century, and commented on the beautiful mats that covered the inside bark walls, artfully covered with animal and other paintings.[30] Roger Williams also mentioned that in southeastern New England a sachem's house was different from those of other tribal peoples in its size and the quality of mats.[31] He described decorated mats for the interiors of Narragansett houses as "embroydered," possibly with moose hair or porcupine quillwork (traditional for needlework before the introduction of European glass beads).[32]

The early descriptions portray Indian wigwams and weetoos as well-made, comfortable, functional structures with plenty of storage for foodstuffs and natural resources for the repair and maintenance of household objects. Roger Williams also mentioned three other types of housing: hunting houses, menstrual huts, and sweat lodges.

> Small fall hunting houses were occupied in the bush by a hunter often accompanied by his wife and children, ". . . little hunting houses of Barks and Rushes (not comparable to their dwelling houses)."[33]

Among many of the world's peoples, menstrual blood is considered a powerful agent and harmful to men. In Native New England, women were often separated from others during their monthly cycles, and menstrual huts were built specifically for that purpose.[34]

> A little house; which their women and maids live apart in, foure, five, or six days, in the time of their monethly sicknesse, which custome in all parts of the countery they strictly observe, and no Male may come into that house.[35]

The third structure, called *pesuponck* or "hot house" by the Narragansetts, was a sweat lodge, used by Indian peoples throughout North America in curing and spiritual cleansing ceremonies.

> This Hot-house is a kind of little Cell or Cave, six or eight foot over, round, made on the side of a hill (commonly by some Rivulet or Brooke) into this frequently the men enter after they have exceedingly heated it with store of wood, laid upon an heape of stones in the middle. When they have taken out the fire, the stones keepe still a great heat: Ten twelve, twenty, or more or lesse, enter at once starke naked, leaving their coats, small breeches (aprons) at the doore, with one to keepe all: here doe they sit round these hot stones an houre or more, taking Tobacco, discoursing, and sweating together; which seating they use for two ends: First, to cleanse their skin: Secondly, to purge their bodies, which doubtlesse is a great means of preserving them, and recovering them from diseases especially from the French disease [syphilis], which by seating and some potions, they perfectly and speedily cure: when they come forth (which is matter of admiration) I have seene them runne (Summer and Winter) into the Brooks to coole them, without the least hurt.[36]

The records of the Moravian missionaries for the Schaghticoke Reservation in Kent, Connecticut, frequently mentioned the separate use of a sweat lodge by groups of men and women. Functions included ritual cleansing and the reduction of joint pain.[37]

## INDIGENOUS PHILOSOPHY

As in the Late Woodland period, Native New England in the Contact period was a culturally diverse region of many independent indigenous societies. They not only had different economic and settlement systems, but early European documents tell us they also had separate histories, spoke different but apparently mutually understandable dialects of the Eastern Algonkian language, and had different social and political organizations. Inland groups seem to have been smaller and more egalitarian, with decision-making based on consensus. The larger coastal communities displayed some social stratification, with grand sachems and sub-sachems wielding relatively more power than upland leaders.[38]

### Land, Nature, and World Order

These societies did, however, share similar value systems, bodies of natural knowledge, and a general worldview. They saw (and still do see) themselves as a part of the natural world, related to all of nature, with a duty to always harmonize with and maintain the natural world order. There is a spiritual reverence for land and all its resources. Everything—animals (including humans), plants, rocks, rivers, and the rest of the natural world—contains, to different degrees, the spiritual essence commonly referred to as *manitou*. Homelands are a gift of the Creator shared by all tribal members, sustaining them, their ancestors, and spirits.

Trudie Lamb Richmond forcefully describes this ideology:

Walking in harmony with the cycles of the seasons was a vital concept evolving from a specific way of life amongst Native American peoples of North America. They believed that they were a part of the universe and all living things were their relatives. They believed that it was important to maintain the balance of nature . . . sustaining that balance meant survival. Holding special ceremonies at specific times was one way of ensuring that harmony. Not only did ceremonies reflect respect but they were part of the annual cycle. The ceremonies, songs, and dances were an integral part of the seasonal changes and assisted in keeping the balance of those life-giving forces.[39]

## Spiritual Omnipresence and Symbolic Social Meanings

Spirituality, therefore, pervades all parts of the indigenous culture system. Ritual and spiritual symbols are used not only in religious rites, but also in economic, social, and political activities, in the arts, and in music. It is reflected in, and sustained by, sacred stories and children's tales about Grandmother Woodchuck, Father Bear, Mother Earth, and the Three Sisters (maize, beans, and squash) that explain the common origins and connectedness among all living things.

Europeans who lived among indigenous peoples commented on their generous use of metaphors. The Jesuit priest Jean de BreBeuf in the early seventeenth century seems to have better understood their deeper meanings than the Moravian missionary John Heckewelder in the early nineteenth century. "Metaphor is largely in use among these Peoples; unless you accustom yourself to it, you will understand nothing in their councils, where they speak almost entirely in metaphors."[40] But in Heckewelder's view: "Indians are fond of metaphors. They are to their discourse what feathers and beads are to their persons, a gaudy but tasteless ornament."[41]

Animals, plants, colors, metals, crystals, beads, and other objects were imbued with symbolic social meanings. For the Schaghticoke people, for example, the rattlesnake is a spiritual guardian the Creator placed on Schaghticoke Mountain to protect the medicinal plants that grow there.[42] Tribal administrator and elder Paulette Crone-Morange, of the Mauwee-Harris lineage, descends from a long line of Schaghticoke rattlesnake handlers:

Mashantuckets have their symbol, or their spiritual animal [the fox], for guidance. . . . Ours is the rattlesnake. And I know that we do have a rich history of the rattlesnakes on the reservation . . . my grandfather and great grandfather would capture them and they would put them in a bag and take them to . . . Yale Hospital—there where they used to do a lot of studying. And they would remove the venom . . . and send them back up to the reservation because rattlesnakes reproduce their own venom.[43]

Designs on clothing and crafts often included spiritual symbols,[44] such as the symbolic decorative motifs of woodsplint baskets, beadwork, and an ancient Mohegan belt that features motifs representing the Tree of Life, the Trail of Life, and

Northeastern Woodland birchbark boxes embroidered with traditional materials in floral motifs. Three are decorated with porcupine quillwork and the fourth (bottom right) with dyed moose hair.

the spiritual force often called *manitou*. Mohegan historian and medicine woman Melissa Fawcett Zobel provided the following interpretation of its design:

> Four semicircular symbols of earth domes, representing the four directions and the concentrated spiritual force of the universe, adorn the belt. On either side of the domes is a beaded trail beside the Tree of Life. Fidelia taught Gladys that the sacred tree grows from the earth to the sky, reaching out from Mother Earth to the celestial beings.[45]

Symbols that suggest the spirits of the four directions, essentially a map of the indigenous world, were often incised or impressed on Late Woodland and Contact-period clay pots, usually below the rim points. The pots often include linear rows of impressed dots (punctates) that may represent the Trail of Life, also called the Beautiful Path or the Path of the Sun by some indigenous peoples. Zobel explains its significance:

> For it follows life's circle from birth and sunrise (in the east) to death and passage into the spirit world (in the west) — then on again to rebirth and the dawn of the next generation. *Gizaxk* (Father Sun) and *Doyup* (Grandfather Turtle) oversee this journey. When Father Sun rises and sets each day, he travels over and under the rounded back of Grandfather Turtle.[46]

Archaeologists have long believed that certain incised and modeled decoration on seventeenth-century Mohegan-Pequot clay pots represented female

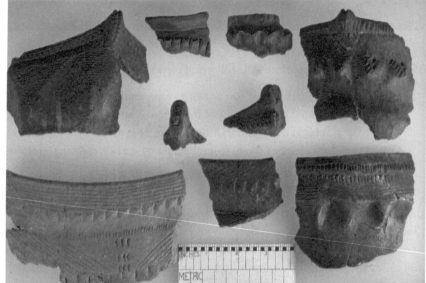

An unusual Niantic Stamped pot from the Tubbs Shell Heap with the spiritual symbol for six directions of the world under each rim point (north, south, east, west, heaven, and the underworld). Typically only four directions are symbolized. Below, Shantok Incised pottery rim fragments from the Fort Shantok site, Montville, Connecticut, including two "Janus" rim points (center) showing a woman with a child on her back. Of these two rim points, the one on the left shows a child in a cradle board; the one on the right shows a stylized face with a vagina symbol below.

breasts and genitalia.[47] The Janus-like figures on the rim points of vessels from Fort Shantok, a major Mohegan village from 1636 until 1682 and the home of its greatest sachem, Uncas,[48] support this theory (such as two in the collections of the Peabody Museum of Natural History at Yale University that show an Indian woman on one side and a baby on the other). Another Mohegan-Pequot pot recovered from the Coudert Ledge site in Lyme, dated to A.D. 1520 on the basis of trade goods from the site, has a molded face in a V-shaped rim point just above the typical genitalia symbol, as if the face were springing forth from it as in childbirth.[49] The pots, almost all used for cooking gruels and stews, symbolically called for the increased fertility of Native foods and the Native community at a time when both were being rapidly depleted by European aggression, diseases, and land acquisition. This is another example of the use of imitative and sympathetic magic.

## Mortuary Ceremonies and Indigenous Spirituality

Burial ceremonies were a continuation of Late Woodland ritual, simple inhumations with the deceased placed on his or her side in a flexed position in a small pit with few or no grave goods. One example is the grave of a 45-year-old male located below a shell midden at the College Soccer Field site at the Connecticut Arboretum in New London, on the western shore of the Thames River.[50] Accidentally disturbed during construction activities, the skeleton, flexed and lying on its right side, was unaccompanied by any grave goods save for a broken sandstone blade near the knee. A radiocarbon date on the bone placed the burial at 330 B.P. ±70 years. The body was placed with its head toward the southwest and faced the river. As we have seen, the southwest direction was significant in New England indigenous spirituality. The Narragansetts told Roger Williams that the Creator dwelled in the Southwest, and all good things came from there.

> Lastly, it is famous that the Sowwest (Sowaniu) is the great Subject of their discourse. From thence their Traditions. There they say (at the South-west) is the court of their great God Cautantouwit: At the South-west they goe themselves when they dye; From the South-west came their Corne, and Beanes out of their Great God Cautantowwits field: And indeed the further Northward and Westward from us their Corne will not grow, but to the Southward better and better.[51]
>
> They believe that the soules of Men and Women goe to the Sou-west, their great and good men and Women to Cautantouwit his House, where they have hopes (as the Turkes have) of carnall Joyes: Murtherers thieves and Lyers, their Soules (say they) wander restless abroad.[52]

That the body at the College Soccer Field site faced the river was also probably of spiritual importance. As previously noted, water held spiritual significance for indigenous peoples. The corpses in Late Woodland burials tend to face rivers and swamps, and post-contact indigenous cemeteries often overlook bodies of water in general. Roger Williams reported that one of the many gods worshiped by the Narragansetts was Paumpagussit, the Sea God.[53] Professor Kathleen Bragdon recounted other Native New England spiritual entities associated with water.

> Water, serpents, and their associations with the underworld, were also closely tied to Abbomocho or Chepi [a powerful spiritual being in local indigenous cosmology], and thus were sources of great power. Substances derived from water or water-dwellers, particularly shell, were likewise symbolically significant. . . . The connection between shamanism, serpents, and shell was so compelling as to survive in southern New England folklore well into the nine-

teenth century. A tradition recorded on Nantucket recounts that the body of a malicious sorcerer would not stay buried until a whelk shell was placed in each of its hands.[54]

Seventeenth-century Pequot burying grounds in Ledyard, where some graves were disturbed by vandals or construction activities, reflect traditional Late Woodland mortuary ritual, with flexed skeletons and grave goods.[55] Construction of a house cellar recently uncovered a large seventeenth-century Pequot burying ground overlooking Long Pond in Ledyard. The graves contained both Native matting for grave linings and European textiles for shrouds. A protein matrix on the surfaces of two matting fragments could mean that skins or furs had been placed on top of the grave lining. Wampum band fragments on the deceased suggested shell headbands, sashes, and bracelets, sometimes accompanied by copper beads.[56] Some of the necklaces and headbands incorporated shell and brass animal effigies (salamanders, turtles, ducks, claws, or crescents) that were so similar to those from other Northeast sites of the late seventeenth and early eighteenth centuries that they could be evidence of an exchange system that extended from Wisconsin to southern New England.[57]

The Pilgrims discovered a Native American burying ground while exploring the area around present Wellfleet on Cape Cod in 1620. It was "encompassed with a large palisade, like a church-yard with young spires four or five yards long, set as close one by another as they could, two or three foot in the ground. Within, it was full of graves, some bigger, some less. Some were also piled about. And others had like an Indian house made over them, but not matted."[58]

Other indigenous graves on Cape Cod were mounded over with sand or soil; one was covered with mats and one with mats and boards. The former had a wooden mortar atop it and a clay pot set in a hole at one end. Both contained grave goods.[59] Edward Winslow noted that southeastern Massachusetts Native Americans "sew up the corpse in a mat" before burial.

> If the party be a sachem, they cover him with many curious mats and bury all his riches with him, and enclose the grave with a pale. If it be a child, the father will also put his own most special jewels and ornaments in the earth with it; also will cut his hair, and disfigure himself very much in token of sorrow. If it be the man or woman of the house, they will pull down the mats and leave the frame standing, and bury them in or near the same, and either remove their dwelling or give over housekeeping.[60]

Roger Williams witnessed several southern New England burial ceremonies. Although he did not mention grave linings, he did write of the use of matting and grave shrouds (a special individual called *Mockuttasuit* performed this function, "commonly some wise, grave, and well descended man hath that office") and sometimes a few grave goods among certain tribal peoples.[61]

> When they come to the Grave, they lay the dead by the Grave's mouth, and then all sit downe and lament, that I have seen teares run downe the cheeks of

stoutest Captaines, as well as little children in abundance: and after the dead is laid in Grave, and sometimes (in some parts) some goods cast in with them, They have then a second great lamentation, and upon the Grave is spread the Mat that the party died on, the Dish he eat in; and sometimes a faire Coat of skin hung upon the next tree to the Grave, which none will touch.[62]

Williams noted that after the ceremony the dead were never mentioned by name, and that sometimes the wigwam where the person died was abandoned. In one instance, the father of the deceased burned his own house with all of its contents.[63] Lenni Lenape (Delaware) elder Nora "Touching Leaves Woman" Thompson Dean explained the reason for avoiding mention of the real name of the deceased (as opposed to the several nicknames or "aliases" of individual Indians often mentioned by historical sources) to anthropologist C. A. Weslager:

The *real* name which every male and female bore was not intended to facilitate interpersonal communication, as names are used in modern American society. The real name was the identification by which the Creator, *Kee-shay-lum-moo-kawng,* and the Spirit Forces, the *Manitowuk,* knew the individual, and by which the individual recognized himself as a physical and spiritual entity different from other persons. Many of the Delawares were reluctant to disclose their real names beyond the immediate family hearth because they believed that knowledge of a person's real name by a conjuror, or others capable of purveying evil, could have serious consequences. They believed that the powers of witchcraft (turned against another) were reinforced and intensified if the victim's real name was known. To the Delawares, a person and his real name were indivisible, the name being, in fact, the person. . . . Only under extremely unusual circumstances was the name of a deceased man or woman ever spoken aloud by those who knew his real name. For them to do so would have disturbed the dead person, causing his spirit to want to return to earth; and since this was not possible he would suffer misery.[64]

In addition to the Creator Cautantouwit, the Narragansetts supplied Roger Williams with the names of thirty-six other gods. Many of the deities were worshiped by specific groups in the tribe, or for specific reasons, such as Squauanit, the Woman's God (a reference to Granny Squannit, leader of the little people); Muckquachuckquand, the Children's God; Wetuomanit, the House God; and Yotaanit, the Fire God, among others. Williams likened indigenous worship to Catholicism, with its many saints and martyrs who are often associated with specific protections.[65] In reality, Native spirituality has little in common with Catholicism. In general, Native belief systems are far more ancient, polytheistic, and animistic—all objects contain spiritual matter or *manitou* (similar to our concept of the soul), including animals, plants, rivers, and rocks—and are closely affiliated with the natural world. The hereafter was, and is, thought to be a continuance of the material world, but without its sorrows and problems. Traditional belief systems also included several types of supernatural beings quite foreign to

Catholicism, some of which were listed by archaeologist Froelich Rainey in his compilation of ethnographic data on southern New England Indians.

> Surviving among the Mohegan of Connecticut was the memory of beliefs in "Makiawisag" "little people" of the forest and river, in the "gachatcang," "will-o-the-wisp," or spirits traveling at night with lights, and in "Jibal" ghosts or wandering spirits who made terrifying noises.[66]

A series of thanksgiving festivals was held annually to express gratitude for bountiful food harvests. Williams and other English sources described these, some of which are still practiced by indigenous peoples today. The Maple Sugaring Festival "foretold winter's end with the gathering of their most important seasoning and sweetening." Shad fishing in early spring led to "one of many fishing and shellfishing rites."[67] Thomas Morton described such a festival among eastern Massachusetts communities: "Salvages [*sic*] meete 500 or 1000 at the place where lobsters come in with the tyde, to eate, and save dried for store, abiding in that place, feasting and sporting a moneth or 6 weeks together."[68]

Planting seeds in late spring and picking strawberries in June initiated festivals during the midsummer growing season. The Green Corn Ceremony "offered early thanks for the summer harvests." Corn, bean, and squash harvesting festivals "meant the end of the growing season . . . for all but the wild botanicals."[69] Other feasts and dances were held in times of need, such as famine, drought, war, or sickness. These were both public and private. Many involved gifting rituals, in which the host would give away food and items to guests.[70] Roger Williams described gift–giving ceremonies, called Nickommos, that he had attended among the Narragansetts.

> He or she that makes this Nickommo Feast or Dance, besides the Feasting of sometimes twenty, fifty, an hundredth, yea I have seene neere a thousand persons at one of these Feasts, they give I say a great quantity of money, and all sort of their goods (according to and sometimes beyond their Estate) in several small parcels of goods, or money, to the value of eighteen pence, two Shillings, or thereabouts to one person; and that person that receives this Gift, upon the receiving of it goes out, and hollowes thrice for the health and prosperity of the Party that gave it, the Mr. or Mistris of the Feast.[71]

Roger Williams misunderstood the sociopolitical importance of these give-aways, seeing them as selfish, materialistic consumerisms. In reality, they were strategies for redistributing wealth among all tribal members and cementing social and political alliances (described further in Chapter 10).

### Indigenous Scientists

Indigenous peoples were our first naturalists, zoologists, botanists, and geologists. They were extremely knowledgeable about the character and habits of the animals and plant life surrounding them. William Wood reported that "as these Indians be good marksmen, so are they well experienced where the very life of every crea-

## CULTURAL INFORMATION FROM SKELETAL REMAINS

Human skeletal remains can provide interesting information on the health, diet, and economic activities of a community, information that cannot be retrieved elsewhere. The teeth of the individual from the burial discovered at the College Soccer Field site in New London, for example, were in very poor shape, with severe tooth decay and heavy wear.[a] More than half of them had been lost before he died. The tooth wear indicates a coarse diet, while the decay suggests the effect of the sugars from eating maize. Deep grooves in his right lower canine and lateral incisor "are typical of dental task activity such as cordage-making."[b] He had been 5 feet 10 inches tall (178 centimeters)—taller than the average European he may have encountered during his lifetime.

Additionally, several bones show that this individual had suffered from chronic diseases. His vertebrae showed extensive spinal degeneration, or *spondylosis deformans*, a condition that progresses with age and is often associated with a "physically arduous lifestyle." The internal surfaces of the maxillary sinuses of his face had signs of chronic sinusitis. Lesions on several of his ribs are characteristic of chronic pulmonary tuberculosis, one of the many lethal diseases that Europeans transmitted to Native American populations.

Notes

a. Juli and Kelley 1991.
b. Ibid., 9.

ture lieth, and know where to smite him to make him die presently."[72] Likewise, they were also aware of the properties of rock types and minerals and their locations on the landscape.

New England Indians were accomplished mathematicians and astronomers as well. The Indians of southern New England had words for the numbers one through one million. According to Roger Williams, they were skillful at "Europes" arithmetic, using kernels of maize as counters.[73] Archaeological finds in the Western Hemisphere have confirmed that indigenous peoples were knowledgeable astronomers who charted the heavens to keep time, plant crops, and even make war. New England's Native peoples were no exception.

That indigenous people had a good understanding of astronomy is clear from their knowledge of the constellations and the movements of celestial bodies.[74] They had names for constellations—the Great Bear, the Brood-Hen, the Golden Metewand, the Morning Star—and sacred stories about them. Roger Williams confirmed that the Narragansetts kept time by the heavenly bodies: "And then they point with the hand to the Sunne, by whose highth they keepe account of the day, and by the Moone and Stars by night, as wee does by clocks and dialls, etc."[75]

## Stone Piles, Farm Clearing, and Sacred Places

There has been much controversy and some acrimony over the meaning of certain stone piles and other artificial rock formations. Archaeologists often see these features as either natural or the result of Anglo-American land clearing practices.[76] In contrast, many Native Americans believe them to be cultural features imbued

## AN AGAWAM LUNAR CALENDAR

John Pynchon, a prominent merchant and trader in the Connecticut River valley and resident of Springfield, in about 1648 provided an early historic example of a Native New England lunar calendar used by the Agawams, a tribal people whose homelands were in south-central Massachusetts. It was reproduced by archaeologist Peter Thomas.[a] The calendar was based mainly on major economic activities, the months being named for the beginning of anadromous fish runs, planting, weeding, harvesting, and other activities. As cited by Pynchon, it reveals the importance of horticulture in the Connecticut Valley by that time.[b]

1. *Squannikesos* (part of April & May) — when they set Indian corne
2. *msonesqua nimock kesos* (part of May & June) — when ye women weed their corne
3. *Tow wa kesos* (part of June & July) — when they hill Ind corne
4. *matterl la naw kesos* — when squashes are ripe & Ind beans begin to be eatable.
5. *mi cheen mee kesos* — when Ind corne is eatable
6. *pa[s] qui taqunk kesos* — ye middle between harvest & eating Ind corne
7. *pe pe narr — bec.* Of white frost on ye grass & g[round]
8. *qunnikesos*
9. *pap sap qhoho* (about January 6th), *Lonatanassick* — they account it ye middle of winter
10. *Squo chee kesos* — because ye sun hath [not] strength to thaw
11. *Wapicummilcom* (part of February and March) — bec. Ye ice in ye River is all gone
12. *Namossack kesos* (part of March & April) — bec. of catching fish.

Notes

    a. Thomas 1978, 17–18.

    b. See also Bendremer 1999, 147.

with spiritual meaning.[77] Gladys Tantaquidgeon told Melissa Fawcett Zobel, her grand-niece:

> In the Mohegan language, the spirit of rocks is acknowledged in the names for our leaders: a male leader is called *sachem* (which means rock man) and a woman leader is referred to as *sunqsquaw* (which translates as rock woman).[78]

Several English sources in early New York and New England noted the presence of Native American sacred sites on the landscape, particularly stone monuments they usually described as "stone piles," which they believed marked the burial of a sachem or the place where an important Native event had occurred.

### Stone and Brush Monuments

Reverend John Sergeant, the first minister to the Mahikans (today known as the Mohican Nation, Stockbridge Munsee Band, with a reservation in Wisconsin), and several European contemporaries reported a huge stone pile in Great Barrington, Massachusetts, near the base of present-day Monument Mountain (named for the stone monument) just west of a major Indian trail, the Old Berkshire Path (now Route 7). Indian people would regularly add a stone to the pile each

Ezra Stiles's sketch of the large and well-documented stone monument that gave its name to Monument Mountain in Great Barrington, Massachusetts.

time they passed the location. The local Natives were unwilling to explain to their Christian minister what obviously was an indigenous spiritual tradition.

> There is a large heap of stones, I suppose ten cart-loads, in the Way to Wnahtukook [present Stockbridge], which the Indians have thrown together as they have passed by the place; for it used to be their custom, every time any one pass'd by, to throw a stone upon it. But what was the end of it they cannot tell, only they say their fathers us'd to do so, and they do it because it was the custom of their fathers.[79]

John Sergeant's Indian interpreter Ebenezer (Poo-poo-nuck) supposed the stone monument was a gesture of gratitude to the Creator, "that he had preserved them [those who added a stone to the structure when passing] to see the place again."[80] Mahikan leader John Konkapot, a contemporary of Sergeant, reported that the stone pile originally marked the burial of an early sachem, but later was also used as a boundary marker.[81] This function was also noted by Chief Yocum, who in 1754 reported that it and another stone pile at the confluence of the Green River and the Housatonic River in Great Barrington marked the boundaries between the Mahikans of Stockbridge and those centered at the village of Weatoque

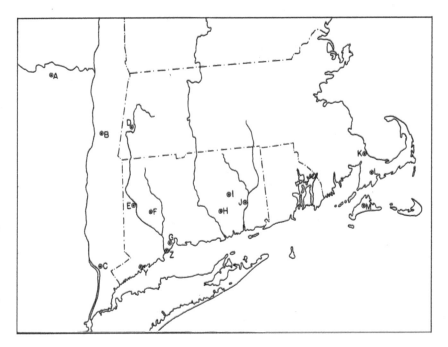

This 1946 map by Eva Butler locates historically documented memorial stone heaps in southern New England and eastern New York state (A-M), the site of Naramake's Village (Y), and the Eagle Hill site (Z).

in present-day Salisbury, Connecticut. Jehoiakim Van Valkenburgh, a local Dutch settler who spoke Mahikan, claimed that when the Indians added a stone to the monument, "they said 'Grandfather I recover you.'"[82]

Similar stone and "brush" (wood) monuments were located throughout southern New England and eastern New York,[83] including one that stood along the New Haven–Milford road three miles out of Milford. Like the sacred structure at the foot of Monument Mountain, many were historically documented by seventeenth- and eighteenth-century Euro-Americans as having been created by the local indigenous peoples.

Avocational archaeologist Frank Glynn actually excavated two stone mounds at the Pilot's Point site in Westbrook in the early 1950s.[84] The mounds were oval heaps of stone about 2 feet high (about 60 centimeters). Stone Heap 1 was about 12 feet wide by 21 feet long (more than 3 by 6 meters), with the long axis aligned east–west. It had a well-defined stone wall at its base, inside which was a 3-inch (almost 8 centimeter) layer of black clay overlaid by a stone pavement. There were hearths, pit features, and post molds beneath the stone pavement. Above the pavement was a layer of burned stones and charcoal, also with hearths and post molds. The mound contained indigenous items in and below the pavement. Glynn described the projectile points as "stemmed and barbed," and referred to the stone items as a "Late Archaic stone inventory," although he also noted the presence of early Middle Woodland rocker-stamped pottery. At its eastern end was a large pit 5 feet deep and about 5 feet wide (about 1.5 by 1.5 meters), with its mouth outlined by a ring of stone. The soil at the bottom was "fire-scorched."

Stone Heap 2 was a circular mound 9 feet (2.75 meters) in diameter. The only culturally diagnostic artifact was a sherd of Vinette Interior Cord-marked pottery

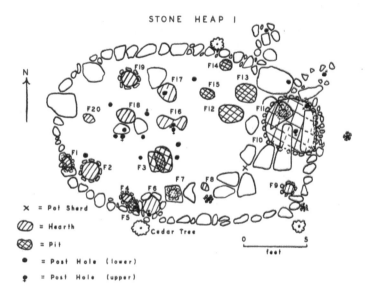

STONE HEAP 1

N

F19  F14
F17  F13
F15
F20  F18  F16  F12  F11
F10
F1
F2  F3
F4  F6  F7  F8  F9
F5

X = Pot Sherd
◲ = Hearth
▨ = Pit
● = Post Hole (lower)
♀ = Post Hole (upper)

Cedar Tree

0                    5
feet

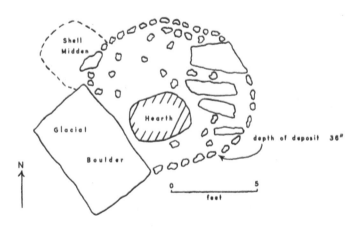

STONE HEAP 2

Shell
Midden

Hearth

Glacial

Boulder

depth of deposit  36"

N

0                    5
feet

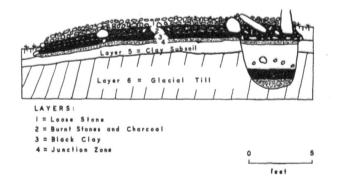

Layer 5 = Clay Subsoil

Layer 6 = Glacial Till

LAYERS:
1 = Loose Stone
2 = Burnt Stones and Charcoal
3 = Black Clay
4 = Junction Zone

0                    5
feet

Drawings of the two stone
heaps at the Pilot's Point
site in Westbrook: plan of
Stone Heap 1; plan of Stone
Heap 2; and profile of Stone
Heap 1.

near the base of the heap, suggesting a possible Terminal Archaic, Early Woodland, or early Middle Woodland date for the structure. No skeletal material was discovered at the site, but Glynn did not rule out the possibility that Stone Heap 1 marked a crematory. "The pavement might be interpreted as either a cremation floor, a parching floor, or a hut floor, or perhaps a combination of these. The immediate sealing-off of fires by either covering them with stones or rolling a large stone into them was evident."[85]

For the most part, Native Americans refused to explain the significance of their actions to their white neighbors. The few explanations that were given fell into six categories: (1) the pile marked the grave of a sachem or (2) the location of an important tribal event; (3) it was a boundary marker; (4) a stone was placed on the pile to bring "blessings" or (5) success in hunting (and if the ritual were not performed, then the opposite would occur, such as failure or misfortune); and (6) the stone was a symbol of thanksgiving to the Creator or some unknown deity.[86]

Stone monuments continue to figure in modern tribal stories and folktales. Twentieth-century Mohegans told anthropologist Frank Speck that their seventeenth-century ancestors had built a stone pile above the road leading from Norwich to Hartford to mark the northern boundary of their great leader Uncas's sachemdom, with tribal members adding a stone to the pile each time they passed. At another stone pile several feet high on the Schaghticoke Reservation in Kent, tribal members explained to Speck that they still added a stone as they passed because they thought the ghost of a murdered Schaghticoke resided there. Some Schaghticokes would also pour a "swallow or two of the whiskey" down a nearby rock crevice as a sacrifice to the ghost.[87]

Archaeologist Dr. Patricia Rubertone's in-depth study of the archaeology of Roger Williams and the Narragansett Indians concluded that stone monuments were the culmination of basic ritual acts that were personally meaningful experiences connecting an individual with the supernatural world of spirits and ancestors.

> Through simple ceremonial acts, the living made contact with ancestors, much as the stones they heaped on the pile touched and mixed with those placed there by earlier generations of Narragansetts. In the ongoing creation of these monuments, the living kept in touch with the dead and honored them by impressing on the monuments their own meanings, histories, and memories.[88]

### Other Native American Stone-Related Sites

One earthen mound in Salisbury, Massachusetts, of Middle Archaic age was partly enclosed by a dry-laid stone wall.[89] Native American oral traditions recount significant and sacred places in caves, near large boulders and other rock formations, and on hilltops.[90] Roger Williams reported that the Narragansetts had "great and important meetings from all parts at one high place, to supplicate their gods, and to beg rain."[91]

Rock carving found in Woodbury, Connecticut, suggestive of the feathered or horned serpent, a supernatural being found in indigenous sacred stories from New England and throughout the Western Hemisphere.

Native peoples used and still do use simple boulder monuments.[92] As late as 1836, Quinnipiac people regularly returned to their lost homeland to conduct harvest thanksgiving ceremonies at a large basalt boulder known locally as the Quinnipiac Thanksgiving Rock and the powwow stone of Cautantowit, or Kiehtan (Algonkian names for the Creator). The ceremony included feasting, singing, and dancing. Food was placed atop the rock for the Creator in gratitude for his generosity. In 1836, after a Native American died on the property during the festival, the Anglo-American owner of the property ordered the Indians to stop holding powwows at the boulder.[93]

Carvings on boulders, cobbles, and rock outcrops attributed to Native Americans have been reported throughout New England.[94] They include a variety of anthropomorphic, animal, and geometric images, including mythical beings such as the horned serpent engraved on a rock in Long Island and one from Woodbury, Connecticut. Some engravings are unidentifiable. Such "pictographic art" has been interpreted as reflections of "shamanic practice and experience."[95] Some researchers have suggested that the carvings are a record of "shamanic" visions. Kathleen Bragdon, however, has suggested that they have a more complicated role in indigenous societies.

> If pictographic images were indeed associated with shamanic activities, they communicate something of the complexity of cosmological beliefs and the embodiment of those beliefs in the social world. Powwaws [religious practitioners, or shamans] served their communities as advocates and champions in relations with the supernatural. . . . Pictographs are not so much a "record" of their role and function as they are a "conversation" to which other-than-

human powers, the powwaws as intermediaries, and those who "read" the pictographic signs, all contributed.[96]

Of the two on a hilltop overlooking the Housatonic River valley in Kent, across the river from the Schaghticoke Reservation, one is the famous Molly Fisher Rock, with incised characters that have yet to be identified.[97] A similar outcrop I visited, less than a mile from the Molly Fisher Rock, also has carvings. The rocks' locations and characteristics strongly indicate a connection to the indigenous Weantinock-Schaghticoke historical and spiritual landscape.

Another rock carving is the Blaschick Petroglyph overlooking Salmon River in East Haddam. The rock has "three 't' shaped components with additional markings" incised in its mica schist. Similar symbols were reported in Ontario, Canada, and along the Susquehanna River in Pennsylvania. Some American Indian groups used "cruciform figures" to indicate trade and direction, the four winds, mosquito hawks, and dragonflies, and as part of "shamanistic" ritual.[98] The Portsmouth, Rhode Island, pictographs also include several incised "t"s.[99]

Carved stone anthropomorphic images have also been found throughout southern New England, as in the small stone faces or "maskettes" described earlier. Full figurines and "busts" were also found, apparently originally *in situ* but sometimes later removed by Anglo-American colonists and placed into their stone fences. Ezra Stiles said he had "found about or above twenty" images of such Native American stone "gods" or "idols," as he called them, "in diff. Places from Boston to Hudsons River, & part[l]y between New Milf[or]d on W. and Medfield, Mass. on East."[100]

Stiles provided descriptions for some, which suggests that they were relatively large. One stone sculpture from East Hartford was 3 feet 6 inches long (about a meter) and 6 to 12 inches (15 to 30 centimeters) thick. Stiles estimated another sculpture from East Guilford weighed about one and a half tons.[101] Of the three images for which he gives an *in situ* description, two were located near the edge of a swamp and a spring, respectively. As we have seen, in the Northeastern Native worldview bodies of water are often associated with spirits and the underworld. Springs, particularly, "are considered portals to the underworld."[102] The third image was described as originally standing in a now cleared farm field from which many projectile points and "Hatchets" were recovered.[103] Stiles described other "stone gods":

12 May 1780

At East Hartford or 5 m. from Connect. River saw an Indian Idol of Stone. It was found about 1775 by Mr. Silas Spencer who shewed it to me & gave me the acco[unt] of it. He was born 1705, aet. 75. He says he cleared up the Land about 25 y. ago & it looks like new Ground now, the ind. Name of the place is Wyketeassick. It stood in the Ground a little declining— the place about it somewhat cleared—& abundance of Indian Hatchets & Arrows found in that Ground. He gave it to Yale College. It has something

## THE "OLD INDIAN GOD."

### Further Facts Concerning the Relic Recently Unearthed.

NEW-HAVEN, Conn., Sept. 23.—Traditions of the Pequot Indians, whose early home along the Sound, centuries ago, is frequently recalled by the discovery of new relics, are revived by the "Old Indian God," unearthed at Madison last week. The oldest inhabitant barely remembers seeing it and hearing it mentioned as a familiar sight about Tuli's Pond, but for nearly seventy-five years it has existed only in memory.

In Smith's History of Guilford and other reminiscent sketches of the locality references to it are frequent. Its whereabouts were thought to be permanently unknown till it was dug up by a gang of workmen a week ago.

The village antiquarian, R. B. Maynard, took it in charge, and finally sold it to A. T. Bushnell, who has placed it in front of his residence. It is a colossal brownstone rock, about 3½ feet

high, with a broad base and tapering head. On the front are the distinct features of a man, with a rudely-carved necklace hollowed in the stone.

Indications point to an Indian origin, from the appearance of the carving. This is not, however, certain, and will not be settled till some of the Yale professors pass judgment on the rude attempt at sculpture. Theories have been advanced that it antedates the time of the Indians' abode in America, but this is uncertain.

Prof. Townsend of New-Haven has visited Mr. Bushnell, the owner, since its discovery, and made him a handsome offer for it, for the new Historical Society Building in this city, but his overtures were declined. Mr. Bushnell is anxious to learn just what his treasure is before he parts company with it.

In his writings, Ezra Stiles noted that he had seen or visited twenty images of Native American "stone gods," like the one from Madison, Connecticut, illustrated in this 1893 article from the *New York Times*. The drawing of the "god" resembles the upper portion of a turtle and may represent the indigenous sacred creation story of the world being formed on the back of a giant turtle.

of a human Appearance being a cut or carved Stone perhaps three foot long & ½ foot to a foot thick. No tradition about it. The Indians tho' once numerous at Hartfd ever concealed it.[104]

29 January 1789

At E. Guilford 28th I visited an Indian Stone God which lay in a Fence about half a Mile East of Mr. Todd's Meetghouse . . . Mr. Phineas Meigs died about 1781, aet. 73 cir. He told Rev. Jona[than] Todd (born 1713) that he removed this stone God from the Bottom of the Hill at the Edge of the Swamp, and put it into the fence. It was removed about twenty Rods. I judge it a Ton & half weight.[105]

Mr. Benja[min] Teal gave me an account of a Fort or Inclosure by Earthern Walls about 2½ M. N.W. from the Image, 30 or 40 Rds. Long, two Rds. Wide Trench, Wall ten feet high Inside next a Swamp & five feet next to the Hill, being on a Declivity.[106]

18/19 May 1789

Rode to Springfield Mr. Lothrops & lodged there. View an Indian Stone God there, similar to ours in the College Library.[107]

22 May 1789

Rode to Middleto[wn], dined at Major Otis's. Visited Rev. Mr. Huntington who went & showed me another Indian stone Gd. About a half mile East of his Meetghouse. . . .[108]

24 March 1790

Capt. Peter Pond of Milfd spent this Aft. & Eveng with me. He left Milfd April 1773 & spent almost 17 years in the Indian Trade Countries N.W. of Mischlimakinak & Lake Superior . . . He gave me much Information.[109]

. . . The Ratio of Indian Popula. & Sachemdoms in the interior Parts over to the Pacific Ocean & Asia much the same as this side L. Superior. The same sort of People—almost beardless—Above twenty Factories or Indian Tradg. Houses for fur Trade beyond L. Sup. & almost over to the Ocean. . . . the Name of the evil spirit Manito or Manit or Manit-to as among all the Indian Nations across the Continent Eastwd to Narraganset & the Atlantic—Paint Rocks & stones & offer Tobacco &c to them as Manitoos or Semblances or Symbols of evil spirits. Believe in a good spirit but have little to do with him—are great Dealers with familiar Spirits and Spectres from whom they receive oracular Responses & prophecies. . . .[110]

8 June 1790

. . . Sent by Rev. Mr. Mansfield of Exeter, my Acco[unt] of the Inscriptions on Rocks in Kent, & the Draw[in]g of the Indian God in our College Museum [Yale] to Gov. Bowdoin Presidt Acady at Boston.[111]

22 September 1790

Rode with Mr. Whit[in]g & viewed the singular pond on the Summit of a Rock on Symsb[ur]y Mount[ai]n in the N.W. Corner of Northington. Rode to Symsb[ur]y & dined at Col. Humphreys. Visited an Indian God & lodged at Sq[ui]r[e] Danl Humpreys.[112]

23 September 1790

Rode 13 m. to Southwick. Viewed & copied a Stone Sculpture or Indian God.[113]

22 October 1793

Aged Deacon Avery of Groton Pockatunnek tells me that the Mohegan Indians once had Idols: that in the Great Reforma[tion] of 1741 as he called it those Indians brot in & gave up to the English a number of stone & wooden Idols; & have had & worshipped none since.[114]

19 September 1794

Spring on the northern Declivity of a Hill on Captain Newtons farm in Amity about seven Miles from the center of New Haven.[115]

. . . The spring runs NE 6 or 8 R.[ods] & looses itself on the Ground. On the side of the stream & a few feet from the fountain I spied a carved or wro't stone, which I knew to be one of the Indian Gods, of which I have found about or above twenty in diff. Places from Boston to Hudsons River, & part[l]y between New Milf[or]d on W. and Medfield, Mass. on East.[116]

A stone with a human head and neck roughly carved, formerly lying in a fence half a mile northeast of Madison meeting-house, is supposed to have been used by them as an idol.' When the railroad was built, this stone was removed and built into a wall, where it was found in the summer of 1895. It is now in the yard of Mr. Nathan Bushnell of Madison.[117]

Several archaeoastronomy sites have been postulated for the Northeast, mainly by persons who are neither local professional archaeologists nor anthropologists (described in the *NEARA Journal* of the New England Antiquities Research Association). One proposed site is an area of wetlands and caves in Sharon, Massachusetts, known as King Philip's Cave and King Philip's Rocks. (Local tradition claims that it was one of the headquarters of Metacomet, called King Philip by the English, a seventeenth-century leader of the Wampanoag tribe and principal leader in the conflict known as King Philip's War, in 1675–1676.) Some have used astronomical theory, coupled with the use of global positioning and geographic information systems, in attempts to make the case that such rock clusters and caves form sight lines in the direction of important solar events, such as summer and winter solstices,[118] usually around June 21 and December 21, marking the longest and shortest days of the year.

In contrast Onkwe Tasi, a Native American and longtime resident of Dracut, Massachusetts, reported that "indigenous New Englanders did not construct stone structures to calculate celestial, solar or lunar change. Instead they relied upon the variety of predicative faunal, floral, and climatic cues marking transitions between seasons."[119] Tasi claimed his ancestors had no need for elaborate stone calendars, and that he knew of no contemporary Native groups using sites with stone piles, stone walls, outcrops, or boulders for ceremonial purposes.[120] Trudie Lamb Richmond has echoed Tasi's comments regarding local indigenous use of natural phenomena rather than stone calendars.[121] The Agawam calendar supports this claim, and many professional researchers agree. Still, this does not negate the fact that some stone formations reflect the spirituality and ideology of local First Nations. And there is always the possibility that in the distant (and now forgotten) past some indigenous peoples did use stone sight lines to mark important celestial events. Patricia Rubertone refers to these cultural stone monuments as "memory keeping places," mnemonic devices that link tribal members to their ancestral history and to each other:

Recently, archaeologists have begun to pay closer attention to the traces of purposeful placemaking and memory keeping lurking under the surface or lying on top of it, though perhaps not as prominently or widely-recognized as landmarks from the perspective of the colonial or dominant society. Despite the often masking presence of Europeans, researchers have noted "special attention" places ranging from marked locales or natural features that serve as mechanisms for creating and re-creating linkages between past and present, and setting precedents for the future in Indigenous cultures.[122] Such memory keeping places may include stone cairns, deposits of offerings, or engraved or painted rock art, as well as caves, mountains, springs, swamps, rivers, rock outcrops, and a host of other landscape features that are revered and revisited. Alternatively, some have also observed that special places of memory might be intangible or not marked in any particular way. The suggestion that memory-work might not require a physically—or materially—marked place does not undermine the premise of the importance of a "sense of place" to cultural and social identities, experiences, and values.[123]

I have encountered stone walls and rock piles during archaeological surveys. In my limited experience, those particular stone walls marked European-American land boundaries or farm fields. During one survey we tested some stone piles located in a wooded area in North Stonington and found that they were usually atop bedrock outcrops. We found nothing inside, below, or between them except one nail, which strongly suggested that the piles were indeed the result of post-contact field-clearing activities. In support of this, a descendant of the nineteenth-century farm family on whose land we were digging confirmed that the area was used as a woodlot because the outcroppings made it unsuitable for agriculture. The pragmatic Yankee farmers apparently had carted stones from their agricultural fields and dumped them atop the natural outcrops where nothing was able to grow anyway.

Certainly not all rock piles and formations are Anglo-American in origin. Unfortunately, colonial Anglo-American land use has masked that of earlier indigenous peoples,[124] and white histories of the region often rather effectively omit any memories of indigenous practices (detailed further in Chapter 10). It is possible, for example, that not all the stone piles in North Stonington described above were Euro-American in origin. Perhaps the presence of older indigenous stone piles led the white farmer to dump the contents of his stone sled in the same area. The origins of most artificial stone formations were not documented by early historical sources, and they are otherwise difficult if not impossible to date.

Archaeologists have a good idea of the diagnostic characteristics of stone piles and stone walls related to European farming. We now need to get a handle on the distinctive traits of indigenous sacred rock sites. This may prove difficult, because "sacred" is sometimes equated with "secret." Also, the presence of quartz cobbles in a stone pile is often cited as evidence that the pile is of indigenous origin. Some spiritual elements, however, such as the use of quartz as a conduit to the

Stone features (cairns) in Harwinton, Connecticut. Top, about a dozen carefully piled stone features such as these line a ridge overlooking a wetland and vernal pool; they are so carefully built that one can see through them. A stone wall begins at the top of the ridge and ends at the wetland below (bottom right). Two semicircular stone features are located near the base of the ridge (one of these is shown in the bottom left photograph).

supernatural, are found in other cultures beside those of local indigenous peoples. Celtic quartz is still mined for its energetic healing value.[125] It is not unthinkable that early Anglo-American farmers with Celtic roots may have produced some of the stonework that NEARA authors once attributed to Irish monks.

Continuing dialogue between the archaeological community and Native elders and spiritual leaders is greatly needed to resolve this dilemma and preserve traditional sacred spaces. Also, many sacred sites are not stone-related. They are, however, often identified in indigenous sacred stories and folktales involving the physical landscape of homelands[126]—another important reason for dialogue.

## INDIGENOUS CONFLICT

There is both archaeological evidence and historical documentation of fortified Indian settlements during this period, particularly along the coasts and navigable waterways where major villages and most of the indigenous populations were located. In the seventeenth century European explorers and settlers reported palisaded Native American "forts" along the Thames, Mystic, and Connecticut rivers, as well as in other areas of coastal Long Island Sound and southern New England.[127] Archaeologists have investigated several of them, many of which are now listed on the National Register of Historic Places; some are National Historic Landmarks.[128] The Dutch trader Adriaen Block reported seeing an Indian fort among the Sequins (Nawaas) tribal people in the lower Connecticut River valley near present-day South Windsor as early as 1614. "The natives there plant maize, and in the year 1614 they had a village resembling a fort for protection against the attacks of their enemies."[129]

The Western Niantic tribe had forts on Black's Point and at the head of the

Niantic River in present Niantic.[130] In 1789 Ezra Stiles described the remains of an Indian fort in East Guilford as "30 or 40 Rds. Long, two Rds. Wide Trench, Wall ten feet high Inside next a Swamp & five feet next to the Hill, being on a Declivity."[131] The Paugussett tribe had two documented seventeenth-century forts in Milford, one at Wepawaug at the mouth of the Housatonic River, and one on Turkey Hill "with flankers."[132]

Boulder monuments mark the locations of two additional seventeenth-century Paugussett forts, one overlooking the Housatonic River in Derby, along what is now Route 34, and the other near the present-day Derby-Ansonia town line near the intersection of Division Street and Seymour Avenue. The presence of indigenous forts in many other areas of the state is suggested by the "fort" names of roads and geographic areas, such as Fort Hill in Shelton, where a stone boulder marks the general location of a Pootatuck fort above the Housatonic River built in 1673, and Fort Hill in New Milford, where a palisaded Weantinock fort stood overlooking the tribe's planting fields in the Housatonic floodplain.[133]

It is unclear whether all of these forts were a post-contact phenomenon. Some may have been built as a consequence of power plays among indigenous communities over land, tribute, or other natural resources such as good fishing grounds, wampum, and furs,[134] rather than as a result of conflict with European explorers or settlers. Some could have been trading stations where wampum was manufactured and bartered, along with furs, to European traders.[135]

Conflict among indigenous groups was present during the preceding Late Woodland period, when a great deal of population movement in the eastern Woodlands[136] may have been due to warfare. We have an inkling of this from Mohawk elders who told French Jesuit priests in 1659 about wars with the Algonkian-speaking groups in the late sixteenth century that nearly decimated the Iroquois-speaking Mohawks. A few years later the Algonkians were defeated by the Mohawks. Soon after, they waged a ten-year war with a tribe they called the Andastogehronnons (the Minquaas of the Susquehanna River valley), who overthrew the Mohawks just about the time of contact with the Dutch, from 1609 to 1614.[137]

Later European documents mention Iroquois forays into New England and the fear instilled by the Mohawk tribe among local Indians.[138] Archaeologist Ralph Solecki's detailed review of seventeenth-century indigenous fortified structures in the Long Island Sound region showed that, out of the nine forts studied, only three could be considered stations for wampum making and trade—Fort Shantok in Connecticut, Fort Ninigret in Rhode Island, and Fort Massapeag on Long Island.[139] Dr. Solecki concluded: "The building of forts by local coastal Indians appears to have been well under way before the Europeans arrived. The conclusion from this is that they were built as defensive measures against hostile neighbors."[140]

## Wars with the Iroquois

The original Iroquois Confederacy was a group of five Native American tribes in New York—the Seneca, Cayuga, Onondaga, Oneida, and Mohawk. Before the 1620s, the Mohawks inhabited upper eastern New York west of the Hudson River valley, adjacent to the Algonkian-speaking Mahikan tribe, whose homelands extended along both sides of the upper Hudson Valley and eastward into western Massachusetts and northwestern Connecticut. Stockbridge, Massachusetts, was a major Mahikan town in the eighteenth century.[141]

During the early 1600s the Iroquois were busy expanding their political control south and east into Pennsylvania and New England.[142] Dutch records describe the wars over the Dutch trade between the Mohawk and the Mahikan nations from 1624 to 1628,[143] and again in the 1660s, with New England Algonkian groups joining the Mahikans.[144] The latter hostilities may have been over the English trade. The papers of seventeenth-century Dutch patroon Kiliaen van Rensselaer[145] show that by 1640 the Dutch were complaining that the Mahikans and Mohawks were trading with the English on the Fresh River, the Dutch name for the Connecticut River.[146] It is about this time that the Mohawks obtained guns and ammunition from both English and Dutch traders and became greatly feared by other Native nations.[147] It caused them "to be respected by the surrounding Indians even as far as the sea coast, who must generally pay them tribute, whereas, on the contrary, they were formerly obliged to contribute to those."[148]

The Mohawks' original name for themselves, Kanienkehaka or Kanien'Kahake, means "People of the Flint" in the Iroquoian language, reflecting the important chert (flint) quarries located in their homelands. The term "Mohawk" means "eaters of men."[149] It was applied to them by Algonkian-speaking peoples because of their cannibalistic behavior in war (which probably had more to do with a magical belief among some non-western peoples about consuming the power of an enemy, rather than with any fondness for human flesh).

In 1660 the Mohawks were at war with the Abenakis in Maine. In 1662 they were warring with the Sokokis of New Hampshire.[150] The Mahikans allied themselves with some of the New England tribes around 1663.[151] By the mid-1660s another war was in full swing between the Mohawk and the Mahikan tribes and their New England Algonkian allies. It lasted until 1671.[152] Historical incidents, particularly the wars with the Iroquois, forced the Mahikans to leave their lands on the west side of the Hudson River and move northward and eastward.[153] The Pocumtuc war with the Iroquois in 1664 caused the Pocumtuc to sell their Connecticut Valley lands to the English.[154]

After the Algonkian defeats, some New England and eastern New York communities paid tribute to the Mohawks.[155] This suggests that political pressure from the Mohawks and the threat of warfare along Connecticut's northwestern borders may have caused temporary population movements southward and eastward and the fortification of settlements in those areas. Protection from Mohawk domination was one of the reasons indigenous communities welcomed English settlement.

## Symbiotic Trade Relations

Early relations between Europeans and indigenous peoples were relatively cordial, based as they were on mutually satisfying trade arrangements. The Dutch and English received animal furs—a hot status item in Europe at the time—while Indians received metal tools and utensils, woven blankets, and bolts of cloth (improvements over their stone implements and hide clothing), as well as ideational items (in particular, colored glass and metal beads).

When fur-bearing animals became scarce, the prized purple and white wampum beads made by coastal Indians from locally available hard-shell clam and conch shells replaced furs in the trading network. Several coastal Connecticut sites contained evidence of shell bead manufacture.[156] Indian communities in upstate New York and inland Pennsylvania eagerly exchanged fur pelts for strings of wampum, which they used not only as jewelry, but also as symbols and mnemonic devices in their social and political relationships.[157] They used fathoms of wampum and wampum belts to record political events and forge alliances.[158] The papers of Sir William Johnson, British superintendent of Indian affairs for the northern colonies from 1756 to 1774, are filled with descriptions of meetings with Iroquois tribal leaders and the Algonkian-speaking Mahikans in which wampum strings and belts were used in these ways.[159] The Moravian ministers also described similar wampum exchanges among the Mahikan and Delaware people.[160]

Wampum was valued for its spiritual associations. The shell beads were a metaphor for light and life, particularly "the biological and social continuity of human life."[161] Wampum jewelry adorned loved ones who had died and whose souls would be journeying to a new life in the Creator's house.[162] Wampum strings and belts symbolized social events or proposed actions and could be "read" by Native scholars, who remembered the event and could recite its historical meaning verbatim. Dutch traders quickly picked up on its ritual importance and began manufacturing their own wampum.

Friction was often the result of cultural misunderstanding. Instances of unscrupulous European traders cheating and abducting Indians[163] may have been the exception rather than the rule. Apparently based on amicable trading relations, some communities actually welcomed the early European presence, inviting the newcomers to settle among them. Their motives were obviously economic and political: easy and continual access to European goods would enhance economic efficiency and social status and make them middlemen in the European market, thus promoting their political status among neighboring tribes. A European presence, with its larger populations and advanced weaponry, would also keep them independent and safe from politically dominant tribes such as the Mohawks and Pequots, whom European sources mention often forced subordinate tribes to accede to their demands and pay tribute.[164]

As early as 1631, for example, Wahginnacut, the sachem of a Wangunk community on the Connecticut River, offered the Massachusetts Bay Colony corn and beaver skins if they would settle in his homelands.[165] Likewise, in 1638 the

# A WAMPUM MARCH IN 1720

This account of the journey of two wampum belts from the Mid-Atlantic through Connecticut and New York in 1720 illustrates the use of these items as political symbols and mnemonic devices by local Native Americans. The story also reveals the intricacies of indigenous politics, a widely ranging social network, and the ease of communication among participating communities.

> To the hon'ble Gen'l Assembly Sitting at New haven
> May it Please the hon'ble the Gen'l Assembly
> Oct. 1720
>
> Pursuant to Ord'r of this assembly signed by Mr. Secretary Willis, We underwritten journeyed to Bedford [New York] to here from Mr. Jos. Seely of Bedford, we had the acco't that followeth vis
>
> That about six weeks since, an horsneck [early name for Greenwich, Connecticut] Indian named Moses told me at my house he was going to Ridgefield & after His absence one night & two days, return'd to my house & as to his business, told me he was sent by tapaunanawk an horseneck Indian to make payment to an Indian Chickens [Warrups, also known as Sam Mohawk, a leader of the indigenous community at Redding] for ye Death of sd Chickens sisters husband a great Sagamore over the Indians about Hudsons River, but without seeing Chickens was returned Back again.
>
> This for saith Jos. Seely.

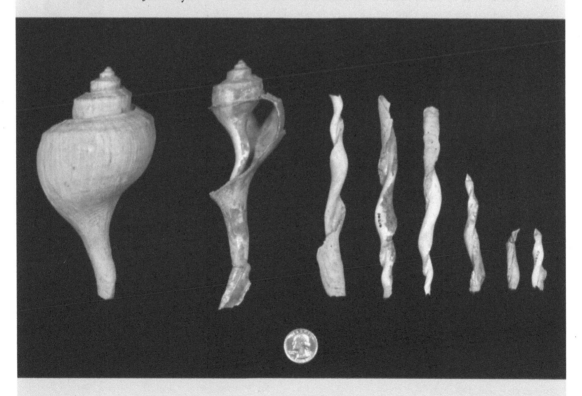

Steps in making white wampum beads from a conch shell.

From Bedford we moved for Tapaunanawk in the Evening & slept at horse-neck; whence this morning We moved with Rev'd Mr. Sacket & Timothy Knap of horseneck, & all of us came to sd Tapaunanawk's wigwam & had this account of the two Belts of Wampam sent to Chickens. The Wampam came from an Ind'n place called Towattoway, being a great way southward, and a great people of Indians, sent thence first to Ammawawgs on East side of hudson's river a little below the highlands—thence to bear ridge about Rye [New York]—thence to Byfield in horseneck bounds by Rauriquoss, who thence delivered it to tapauna-nawk telling him, the Wampam was sent in token the Indians of Towattowaus would joy'd Indians to Sett to the English or Indians in those parts. Ordering it to be sent to Chickens—thence to Chickens or mohawk at Lonetown [the manor of John Read] by Moses an Indian sent by Tapaunanawkoo as ordr'ed—thence to Potatuck [the village of Pootatuck in what is now Southbury]—thence to Wyantinuck [Weantinock, the village in New Milford] w'ch is the End of the wampum March.

Then the Belts to be returned to Ammawawgs & then to Towattowaw.

Tapaunanawkoo saith further that the Belts going to the places afores'd & returned back to the first place is an Argument of the Consent & Expectation of Each s'd places that Captive Indians be here brought to be sold.

This is the Account from Tapaunanawkoo.

Stamf. Oct. 18, 1720

. . . . . . . The Whole account of the other side & this given

Before us Jos. Bishhop Justice

Samuel Couch

Note

"A 1720 Wampum March." Connecticut Archives, *Indian Papers* Series 1:92a–b. Transcribed by Kathleen von Jena, October 18, 2010. Transcription provided by Dr. Stewart Reeve.

An Eastern Woodlands wampum belt dated to the eighteenth or nineteenth century. Made from white and purple marine shell beads, hide, and plant fiber (8.8 by 82 centimeters; about 3.5 by 32 inches).

sachem Momauguin and other leaders of the Quinnipiac tribe invited the English to come and live among them. From his research of colonial documents, historian John Menta reported:

> The Quinnipiac sachems then addressed what was for them the main issue: their desire for English military protection from their Indian enemies. The sachems acknowledged that the threat they felt from the Pequot, Mohawk and others had forced the Quinnipiac to seek refuge close to the English towns on the Connecticut River. While in temporary residence in the vicinity of the river towns, the Quinnipiac had observed that their associates, the River Indians, benefited from the "safety and ease" of having the English nearby. Now that the Davenport-Eaton settlers had established a town in their homeland, the Quinnipiac refugees on the Connecticut River returned to their country.[166]

Unfortunately, the indigenous peoples had little knowledge of the vast European populations that would soon immigrate to their continent, or of the European economic practices (among them overhunting, farming techniques that destroyed animal habitats, industrial water pollution, and dam construction that devastated fishing), customs (such as single proprietorship), and laws that would forever change indigenous physical and social environments.[167]

## Positive Early Relations

In contrast to the negative stereotypes of later historians, early European descriptions of Indian character and social relations were positive. Writing in 1524, Giovanni da Verrazzano commented on the comeliness and civility of a southern New England indigenous people he encountered.

> These people are the most beautiful and have the most civil customs that we have found on this voyage. They are taller than we are; they are a bronze color, some tending more towards whiteness, others to a tawny color; the face is clearcut; the hair is long and black and they take great pain to decorate it; the eyes are black and alter, and their manner is sweet and gentle.[168]

In 1609 Henry Hudson wrote favorably about his encounters with the indigenous Mahikan communities along the Hudson River.

> On our coming near the house, two mats were spread to sit upon and immediately some food was served in well-made bowls; two men were also dispatched at once with bows and arrows in quest of game, who soon after brought a pair of pigeons which they had shot. . . . The natives were good people, for when they saw I would not remain, they supposed I was afraid of their bows and arrows, and taking the arrows they broke them into pieces and threw them into the fire.[169]

# SOME EARLY NATIVE AMERICAN CONTRIBUTIONS TO AMERICAN CULTURE

The late Irving "Ben" Rouse, professor of anthropology at Yale University, noted that the word "transculturation" was used by Caribbean archaeologists "to indicate that, especially in the beginning, customs flowed in both directions, from the Native to the Pilgrims and vice versa."[a]

Rouse also mentioned the "Columbian exchange," a term coined by historian Alfred W. Crosby, Jr., in 1972 to refer to both the biological and cultural consequences of Columbus's discovery of the Caribbean Islands and South America in the 1490s. This exchange included the movement of genes, diseases, crops, customs, and words.[b] A similar exchange process occurred in New England.

The examples of indigenous words and objects listed here attest to the influence of Native Americans in the success of European communities. These goods did not necessarily originate in Connecticut, but were introduced in the state to the immigrant European settlers.

## Clothing, Tools, and Utensils

Gourd containers
Moccasins
Smoking pipes

## Cultivated Plants

Corn
Beans
Gourds
Pumpkins
Squash
Sunflowers
Tobacco

## Prepared Foods

Hominy
Johnnycakes
Pemmican
Popcorn
Succotash

## Wild Foods

Groundnuts
Herbal medicines
Jerusalem artichokes
Maple syrup

## Transportation

Dugout canoes
Indian pathways
    (which became our toll roads,
    highways, and railroad lines)
Snowshoes
Toboggans

## New Words

Caribou
Caucus
Chipmunk
Cohosh
Hickory
Hominy
Hubbub
Mackinaw
Moose
Mugwump
Muskellunge
Muskrat
Opossum
Papoose
Powwow
Punk
Quahog
Quonset

*New Words (continued)*

Raccoon

Sachem

Sagamore

Skunk

Squash

Squaw

Tamarack

Tautog

Terrapin

Tomahawk

Totem

Wampum

Woodchuck

*Place Names*

Many states, towns, rivers, lakes, brooks, ponds, recreation areas, public structures and schools, private businesses, and streets have names of local indigenous origin. Here are a few:

Aspetuck

Bantam

Connecticut

Hammonasset

Higganum

Housatonic

Massachusetts

Menunkatesuck

Mianus
   (River, Greenwich)

Mystic

Naugatuck

Niantic

Noank

Norwalk

Paugassett
   (Hook & Ladder Company
   No. 4, East Derby)

Pawcatuck

Pocotopaug

Pomperaug

Quassapaug

Quinnipiac

Quinebaug

Rowayton

Saugatuck

Schaghticoke
   (Middle School, New Milford)

Shepaug

Waramaug

Weekapeenee

Wepawaug

Willimantic

Wyantenock
   (State Forest, Litchfield County)

Notes
   a. Rouse 1984, 152.
   b. Ibid.

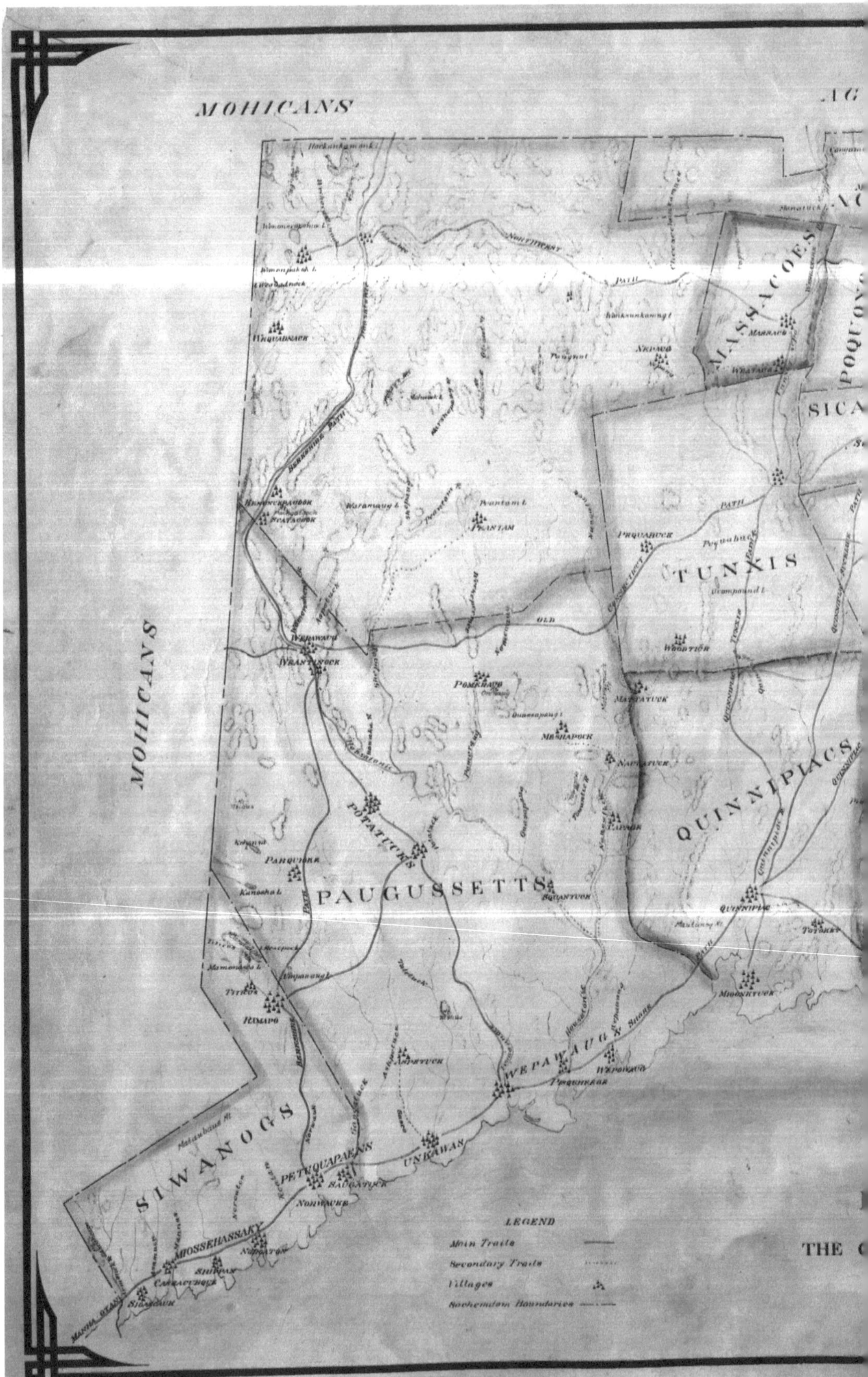

MOHICANS

AG

MOHICANS

MASSACOES

SICA

POOTOTO

TUNXIS

QUINNIPIACS

PAUGUSSETTS

POTATUCK

WEPAWAUGS

UNKAWAS

SIWANOGS

THE

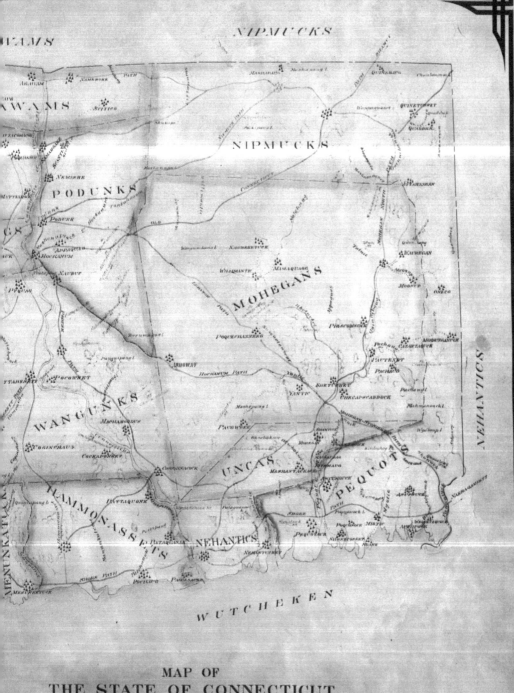

# MAP OF
## THE STATE OF CONNECTICUT
### SHOWING
# INDIAN TRAILS, VILLAGES, & SACHEMDOMS
#### MADE FOR
### CONNECTICUT SOCIETY OF THE COLONIAL DAMES OF AMERICA

| INFORMATION COMPILED BY | DRAWN BY | PRESENTED BY |
|---|---|---|
| MATHIAS SPIESS | HAYDEN L. GRISWOLD C.E. | MRS. MARY PIERSON CHENEY |
|  | A.D. 1930 | Ⓒ |

Writing in 1622, "Mourt" (likely Edward Winslow of Plimoth Plantation) described the honest and friendly manner of the eastern Massachusetts Indian communities toward the immigrant Pilgrims.

> We have found the Indians very faithful in their covenant of peace with us, very loving and ready to pleasure us. We often go to them, and they come to us; some of us have been fifty miles by land in the country with them.[170]

Likewise in 1643, Roger Williams commented on the generous, loving spirit and high moral fiber of the Narragansett tribal people he lived with for several years: "I have knowne them leave their House and Mat [bed] to lodge a Friend or stranger, When Jewes and Christians oft have sent Christ Jesus to the Manger."[171]

> There are no beggars amongst them, nor fatherlesse children unprovided for. . . .
> Their affections, especially to their children, are very strong; so that I have knowne a Father take so grievously the losse of his childe, that hee hath cut and stab'd himselfe with grief and rage.[172]

Having spent six weeks in 1736 at two Mahikan communities in western Massachusetts, Reverend John Sergeant reported: "I was treated very well while I was with them . . . they are very modest and the women and children bashful. They are kind one to another, and make everybody welcome, in their way, that comes to their houses."[173]

### Indigenous Trading Networks and Trade Goods

Indigenous peoples were well accustomed to trade relations, having participated in such dealings with other Native communities for thousands of years before the arrival of the Europeans. Narrow pathways, inland rivers, and coastal sea routes connected Connecticut's Indian communities to Native societies hundreds, possibly even thousands, of miles distant. As a result, local Indians were experts in the art of bartering, as confirmed by Roger Williams.

> They are marvailous subtle in their Bargaines to save a penny: And very suspicious that English men labour to deceive them: Therefore they will beate all markets and try all places, and runne twenty thirty, yea forty mile, and more, and lodge in the Woods, to save six pence.[174]

The archaeological record in Connecticut details trade in shell and toolstone dating back thousands of years. Early European documentary sources also described inter-indigenous trade in many perishable goods, such as carved wooden items, hides, mats, clay pots, clothing, fishnets, hemp (that is, dogbane fibers, from which indigenous nets, rope, string, and other items were made), tobacco, chestnuts, maize, venison, fish, and other foodstuffs.[175] Roger Williams reported: "Amongst themselves they trade their Corne, skins, Coates, Venison, Fish, &c. and sometimes come ten or twenty in a Company to trade amongst the English."[176]

The only things new about the European trade were the trade goods. In con-

Previous page:
The location of major
Indian paths, trails, villages,
and nineteen sachemdoms
in Connecticut, circa
A.D. 1625.

trast to the disparaging stereotype of Indians trading valuable furs and land for trifles such as glass beads, the most valued goods were functional items that increased Native American economic and technological efficiency, such as iron tools and bolts of cloth. Stone tools worked as well as metal ones, but wore out much faster. Woolen cloth was much easier to clean than deerskins and furs, and did not attract fleas and other vermin. Roger Williams commented that English cloth was lighter in weight than the aboriginal skin and fur clothing.[177] He also remarked that Indians wore English clothing only in the presence of the English. "While they are amongst the English they keep on the English apparell, but pull off all, as soone as they come againe into their owne Houses, and Company."[178]

Unfortunately, the virtual extinction of deer, bear, and other fur-bearing animals from English overhunting and farming practices eventually forced Indians to wear English clothing year-round. The introduction of European trade goods brought changes to Native American crafts and art forms. European metal kettles and earthenware began to displace clay pots. With the popularity of the more durable sheet-metal arrow points and iron tools, stone toolmaking declined. European trade cloth and clothing replaced skin clothing, and glass beads and brass were often substituted for porcupine quillwork, moose hair embroidery, and other traditional ornaments and crafts.

These changes did not signal Indian assimilation or acculturation into white society, but rather adaptation of European goods into the traditional indigenous cultural frameworks[179]—complex sociocultural organizations in balance with the surrounding natural and social environments. As seventeenth-century Europeans

This idealized "Eastern Woodland Village Scene" in winter, by David R. Wagner, shows what was likely the typical winter clothing of Native Woodlands peoples. The sachem is wearing a turkey-feather cape like that mentioned by Roger Williams.

themselves noted, these indigenous societies were functioning successfully in environments where European technology and economies were not always suitable and sometimes downright inferior. As historian Dr. Karen Kupperman reported:

> Some colonists were anxious to describe Indian religion and social organization, stressing that though these were different from European models, they were recognizable as performing the same essential functions. Many wrote with admiration about the reciprocal and respectful relations of young to old, high and low, women and men, as well as praising the lack of covetousness, a prime Christian quality, in Indian life. . . . English people in America were equally enthusiastic, however, when they described Indian technology. The picture that emerged was very much of people who were so well-suited to their environment that they could succeed where English technology could not.[180]

## INDIGENOUS ECONOMIC CHANGES

Some trade items were accepted because they were pretty, innovative, and ideational; others, like cloth and iron goods, because they increased economic efficiency. European guns and farming practices were rapidly destroying the main source of hide clothing, the white-tailed deer, as well as other local animal populations. As early as 1698 the Connecticut Court passed an act restricting deer hunting. The law was reinstated several times during the early 1700s, and a deer protection act was passed in 1756, but to little avail.[181] By 1800 there were virtually no deer in Connecticut, and no wild turkeys either, as historian, minister, and Yale College president Timothy Dwight sadly noted in his *Travels in New England and New York:* "We have hardly any wild animals remaining besides a few small species of no consequence except for their fur. . . . Bears, wolves, catamounts and deer are scarcely known below the forty-fourth degree of north latitude [middle of Vermont and New Hampshire]."[182]

Besides their being a major food source, turkeys provided for lovely feather cloaks, coats, and blankets that were highly esteemed by New England indigenous peoples. Roger Williams claimed that these turkey feather garments, called *Neyhommauashunck* by the Narragansetts, "is with them as velvet with us."[183] They were probably status items worn during political meetings and socioceremonial gatherings.

The wild turkeys we see today are descendants of New York birds reintroduced in the 1960s. Secreted in a rural area of northwestern Connecticut, the flock increased and birds were removed to populate other areas of the state. The passenger pigeon, another indigenous food source, was overhunted to extinction by the Anglo-American settlers.

The European fur and wampum trade also began to affect the traditional Native American subsistence-settlement patterns. The increased time spent in hunting fur-bearing mammals and making wampum beads from conch and clam shells was time taken away from traditional subsistence tasks. It is also possible

Artifacts from the Pine Orchard Swamp site in Branford, Connecticut: an iron arrow point (top right), and Levanna points made from quartz, chert, and possibly basalt.

that this increased involvement resulted in larger and longer habitations in coastal areas, which were most easily accessible to the European traders. Karen Coody Cooper, a Cherokee educator and the former director of education at the Institute for American Indian Studies in Washington, Connecticut, reported:

> Indigenous peoples had long been trading goods with each other, but the establishment of the business of trade [with Europeans] caused hunters to spend more time looking for pelts than for meat, to waste parts of animals (which spiritual leaders spoke against) and, on Long Island Sound, to increase wampum production (used as "money" to facilitate trade exchanges). A way of life was being transformed in subtle ways and one can only guess at the ripple effect upon other corporations within the society.[184]

An archaeological example of this amalgamation of old and new cultural lifeways was found at the Pine Orchard Swamp site in Branford, dated by its excavator to A.D. 1635–1660.[185] The people inhabiting this early-Contact-period Quinnipiac site used both traditional stone triangular points and clay pottery with sheet-metal points and other metal objects obtained from European traders (similar mixing was found at the Pootatuck Wigwam site in Southbury, discussed in Chapter 10).

## Transculturation in Early Connecticut

The combined use of English and indigenous material goods does not necessarily show assimilation into white society, but rather adaptation, accommodation, and transculturation. Tribal peoples adapted European items into their traditional lifeways and accommodated white colonists as a survival strategy. Early post-contact Native American communities in Connecticut also contributed much to early American society.

Native peoples introduced Europeans to indigenous plants and animals, and taught them the most efficient ways to hunt, collect, and cook them. They showed them which plants were suitable for local horticulture and how to grow them. Indian healers used medicinal plants to cure a variety of ills. Indians guided Euro-

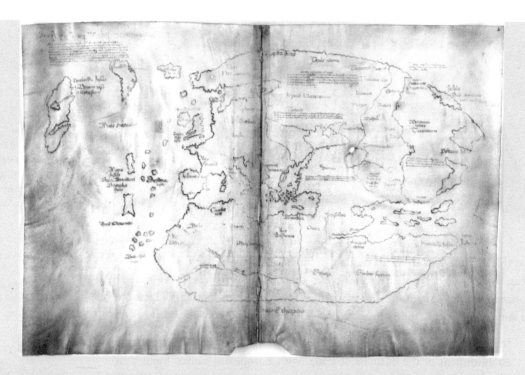

The Vinland Map, dated to the mid-fifteenth century, showing land labeled "Vinland" (far left) to the west of Greenland. The authenticity of the map has been considerably debated.

## BEFORE THE PILGRIMS

Documentation in the form of ships' logs, letters, and other written records shows that hundreds of Europeans visited northeastern North America many years before the Pilgrims landed in 1620 in what is now eastern Massachusetts. In the course of vandalizing indigenous villages and burying grounds, they opened a grave containing the body of a man with red hair wearing European clothing. It is no wonder that the tribes European colonists met in the early 1600s were already crippled societies, much diminished in population by introduced diseases.[a]

1003–1015    Vinland sagas and the archaeology site L'Anse Aux Meadows show that Scandinavian Vikings were on the Canadian coast and possibly even farther south in New England.

1497    John Cabot, an Italian sailing for the English, explores Cape Breton (Nova Scotia).

1498    John and Sebastian Cabot, sailing for the English, explore coasts from Nova Scotia to Cape Hatteras in North Carolina.

1500–1501    Gaspar Cortereal, Portuguese noble, explores Labrador and Newfoundland, possibly as far south as Massachusetts; his ship is lost at sea, and another returns to Lisbon with seven kidnapped Indians, the first documented abduction of indigenous people.

1502    Miguel Cortereal, Gaspar's brother, sails from Newfoundland southward and is also lost at sea; immediately after his voyage the Portuguese Fishing Company is formed to exploit cod fishing in Newfoundland.

1502    Denis of Honfleur, a Frenchman, sails into the Bay of St. Lawrence.

1504    Breton, Norman, and Basque ships fish at Cape Breton.

1504–1508    Thomas Aubert, a Frenchman, sails in the Gulf of St. Lawrence and returns to Dieppe with several Indians.

| | |
|---|---|
| 1509 | Norman ship captains kidnap seven Indians, steal a canoe, and take them to Rouen. |
| 1517 | Fifty Spanish, French, and Portuguese ships are reported fishing off the Grand Banks in Newfoundland. |
| 1518 | First French attempt to found a colony in Canada, on Sable Island off Nova Scotia. |
| 1524 | Giovanni da Verrazano, an Italian employed by the French, sails northward along the Carolina coast and explores New York Harbor, southern Long Island, and Narragansett Bay to Maine. |
| 1525 | Estevan Gomez, a Spaniard sailing for France, explores coasts from Nova Scotia to Cape Cod and Nantucket, then down the coast to Cuba; Gomez kidnaps several Indians while in the Gulf of Maine. |
| 1525 | Portuguese attempt to found a colony at Cape Breton. |
| 1527 | John Rut, an Englishman, sails from Newfoundland to the West Indies. |
| 1534–1541 | Frenchman Jacques Cartier explores the St. Lawrence River, attempting to found a French colony above Quebec in 1541; he also brought to France kidnapped Indians, including the chiefs of the Quebec village. |
| 1541 | Diego Maldonado, sailing for the Spanish, explores the coasts from Florida to Newfoundland. |
| 1541–1542 | French merchants send at least sixty boats to the Canadian coast to fish for cod. |
| 1542 | Jehan Alphonsce, a Frenchman, explores coasts from Cape Breton to Massachusetts Bay. |
| 1543–1545 | French ships fish off Canada; an average of two ships leave France every day during January and February. |
| 1556 | French traveler Andre Thevet sails from Florida to Penobscot Bay with Huguenot Admiral Coligny. |
| 1565 | Englishman John Hawkins sails along the coast from Florida to Newfoundland. |
| 1568 | Englishman David Ingram, a crewman on John Hawkins's disastrous voyage to Mexico where his ship was disabled by the Spanish, walks from Mexico to New Brunswick, Canada. |
| 1578 | One hundred Spanish, fifty English, one hundred fifty French, and fifty Portuguese ships are reported fishing at Newfoundland's Grand Banks. |
| 1579 | Simon Ferdinando, a Portuguese sailor in the service of the English Earl of Walsingham, voyages to an unidentified part of the New England coast. |
| 1580 | John Wallace, an Englishman in the service of Sir Humphrey Gilbert, sails to Penobscot Bay (Maine). |
| 1583 | Englishman Stephen Bellinger sails to Cape Breton and along coastlines to the south. |
| 1584 | Sir Walter Raleigh commissions captains Amadas and Barlowe to explore the Carolina coasts. |
| 1585–1590 | Raleigh attempts to found an English colony at Roanoke, North Carolina. |
| 1593 | Englishmen Richard Fisher and Richard Strong sail southwest of Cape Breton to latitude 44 degrees (Maine) and encounter other trading vessels along these coasts. |
| 1602 | Englishman Bartholomew Gosnold explores the coasts from southern Maine to Martha's Vineyard. |
| 1603 | Englishman Martin Pring sails the coasts from Casco Bay to Plymouth. |
| 1604–1606 | Samuel de Champlain, sailing for the French, explores the coasts from Penobscot Bay to Cape Cod. |
| 1606 | English captain George Waymouth explores Monhegan Island and St. Georges River (Maine), kidnapping five Indians and stealing their canoes and bows and arrows. |
| 1606 | Englishmen Thomas Hanham and Martin Pring explore the Maine coast. |
| 1607–1608 | Englishmen attempt to start a colony on the Sagadahoc River in Maine under George Popham and Raleigh Gilbert. |

| 1609 | Henry Hudson, sailing for the Dutch East India Company, explores the coast from Maine to Cape Cod; to avoid the Nantucket shoals, he puts out to sea and does not see land until around the latitude of Delaware, where sailing north he explores the Hudson River. |
| --- | --- |
| 1610 | English captain Samuel Argall, affiliated with the Jamestown colony, explores Penobscot Bay to Cape Cod; his fishing was so successful that Jamestown regularly sent fishing boats to New England every year. |
| 1611 | Jesuit Pierre Biard and Monsieur de Biencourt visit Maine and explore several rivers, including the Kennebec, St. John, St. Croix, and Penobscot. |
| 1611 | Englishman Edward Harlow sails the coast from Monhegan to Cape Cod, where he kidnaps five Indians, including the famous Epenow. |
| 1611 | The Frenchman Captain Plastrier sails from Passamaquoddy to Monhegan. |
| 1613 | French colonies at Penobscot Bay and the Bay of Fundy are destroyed by Samuel Argall, as commissioned by the governor of Virginia. |
| 1614 | Dutchman Adriaen Block trades along the New York and southern New England coasts from Manhattan to Massachusetts. |
| 1614 | Englishman John Smith explores the New England coasts from Penobscot Bay to Martha's Vineyard. |
| 1614 | Englishman Sir Francis Popham sends ships to Maine to trade and fish. |
| 1614 | French traders reported in Boston Harbor. |
| 1614 | Englishman Thomas Hunt explores Monhegan, Plymouth, and Eastham (Cape Cod); abducts Indians to sell as slaves, including the famous Squanto. |
| 1614 | Englishman Nicholas Hobson sails to Martha's Vineyard. |
| 1614 | Englishman Humphrey Damerill visits Damariscove. |
| 1615 | Englishman Richard Hawkins fishes at Monhegan. |
| 1615 | Englishman Michael Cooper fishes at Monhegan. |
| 1615 | Englishman Thomas Dermer explores the New England coast. |
| 1615 | Englishman Richard Vines fishes and trades at Saco Bay. |
| 1616 | Englishman Edward Brande fishes at Monhegan. |
| 1616 | A French ship is burned at Peddocks Island in Boston Harbor. |
| 1618 | French traders are reported at Monhegan. |
| 1619 | Captain Thomas Dermer trades at Monhegan, Cape Cod, Buzzards Bay, and Long Island Sound. |
| 1619 | Englishman Sampson from Virginia is reported at Monhegan. |
| 1620 | Thomas Dermer explores the Delaware and Hudson rivers; he and his crew are attacked by Indians under Epenow at Martha's Vineyard and all but one are killed (Dermer dies of his wounds in Virginia). |
| 1633 | The first documented settlement in Connecticut is founded, at Windsor. |

Note

a. Adapted from Howe 1969. Information on the Viking explorations from Ingstad and Ingstad 2001, and from "The Archaeology of the Earliest Viking Settlers of Iceland" by John Steinberg, 2011, paper presented at the Massachusetts Archaeological Society and Archaeological Society of Connecticut co-sponsored spring meeting, Old Sturbridge, Massachusetts, May 21, 2011. The Pilgrims digging up Native American graves is from *Mourt's Relation* (Heath 1963).

pean travelers through unknown lands, and Native interpreters helped them to communicate with indigenous leaders and traders. In sum, Indian peoples showed Europeans how to survive and thrive in an unfamiliar landscape very different from what they had known.

No one has ever suggested that those European colonists who grew Indian corn, paddled dugout canoes, used wampum, and consulted Indian doctors had assimilated into Native American society. So why is it that many professionals who studied post-contact Native Americans often considered those who built houses with nails and windows and ate foods from red earthenware and stoneware containers to have assimilated into white society? Such an ethnic double standard has little value in scientific approaches to material culture studies, as archaeologist Dr. Stephen Silliman is demonstrating in his ongoing study of Eastern Pequot reservation life:

> Whereas redware, a common artifact found on Eastern Pequot sites from the early eighteenth to the mid-nineteenth century, was once a European/Euro-American artifact, newly introduced and adopted into Native American material practices, it could not remain so. Eastern Pequot children raised in households with redware who then purchased and used it themselves as adults in households with their own children transformed these into objects that transmitted their own meanings and cultural practices. . . . When used on the reservation and in Native American community life, *these items became Eastern Pequot objects* . . . shifting their originally colonial meanings to function and convey meaning in Eastern Pequot cultural traditions and material worlds. . . .
>
> Where are the archaeological and historical interpretations that consider Euro-Americans in the early decades of U.S. Nationhood as becoming more Chinese because they had Cantonese or Nanking porcelain in their houses? The same standards applied to Native American culture change and continuity are clearly not directed to non-Native American households and for good reason. Most see these European/Euro-American households as using the increasingly global market as a resource for persisting. What should be apparent is that the Eastern Pequot case discussed reveals the same outcome.[186]

## Trading in Death

Unfortunately, European trade also included alcohol, often to give the white traders the upper hand in bartering. Indigenous peoples in New England had no knowledge of fermented beverages and their subsequent effects on one's body and mind. Addiction led to impoverishment and death for many Indians.

Native peoples had no immunity to the European diseases transmitted by traders, sailors, and—later—settlers. They were vulnerable to smallpox, plague, cholera, tuberculosis, syphilis, whooping cough, and even childhood diseases such as measles, and they died in great numbers.[187] Among the dead were often the community's political and spiritual leaders.

An epidemic of European origin in eastern Massachusetts decimated the local Indian communities from 1616 to 1619.[188] The geographic extent of the epidemic suggests that it was spread along traditional indigenous communication and trade routes.[189] In 1633 William Bradford, leader of the Plimoth Colony, reported a "plague" among the Indian community around what is now Windsor, Connecticut, that spread up the Connecticut River to other communities. Dutch traders reported more than 900 out of 1,000 Indians had perished—over 90 percent of the community! This plague was followed in 1634 by a smallpox epidemic among Connecticut Valley Indian communities. In that epidemic entire villages were wiped out, with no one left to bury the dead. Bradford reported:

> They dye like rotten sheep . . . they were (in the end) not able to help one another; no, not to make a fire, nor to fetch a little water to drinke, nor any to burie the dead. . . . The cheefe Sachem himself now dyed, & almost all his friend & kindred.[190]

John Winthrop, Jr., eldest son of the first governor of the Massachusetts Bay Colony and an assistant to the colony at that time (twenty-three years later he became governor of the Colony of Connecticut), confirmed this dire news, and possibly more deaths west of the valley. So many Indian leaders and influential tribal members were dead or disabled that the disease literally stopped all trading activity.

> Hall and the two others, who went to Connecticut, . . . informed us, that the small pox was gone as far as any Indian plantation was known to the west, and most people dead of it, by reason whereof they could have no trade.[191]

The indigenous tribes in western Connecticut did not escape unscathed. The epidemic spread southwestward to the Quinnipiac villages in what is today New Haven and Branford.[192] As the younger Winthrop pointed out, smallpox reached the westernmost known Indian village (likely Weantinock in New Milford), where a trading post was established by men from New Haven in 1646.[193] Smallpox epidemics also raged in the Hudson Valley a few miles west of Connecticut, so that an estimated 90 percent of the indigenous population had perished of the disease by 1656.[194]

Some researchers have estimated that as much as 90 percent of the Native American population in New England had been lost by 1650.[195] The few estimates we have of pre-epidemic populations are of questionable reliability, however,[196] particularly for interior groups that the early Europeans knew little about, as seen by the inaccuracy of their maps. Twentieth- and twenty-first-century scholarly population estimates differ widely, depending on which historical and archaeological data are used: recent estimates for the pre-European population of North America range from 2.4 million to 18 million.[197] Given the scanty evidence, archaeologist Dr. Dean Snow's estimate of a 77 percent general population decrease for southeastern Connecticut and eastern Long Island is plausible.[198]

The demise of political and spiritual leaders and elders was a loss not only of leadership, but also of tribal experience and traditional lore, as these were the culture keepers, medical practitioners, and craft specialists of the tribe. Just imagine what life would be like if the swine flu suddenly reached epidemic proportions and 77 to 90 percent of our families, friends, and countrymen died—including police, military and medical staff, scientists, craftsmen, educators, bankers, pilots and train conductors, farmers, truckers who transport food and other staples to our grocery stores, and so on. Our society would be economically, socially, and politically damaged, and our normal ways of doing things changed forever. This is what happened to the tribal peoples of southern New England. Their communities were already sorely depopulated and badly crippled before the arrival of many European settlers, setting the stage for the major sociopolitical upheavals and cataclysmic economic devastation created and fueled by relentless Anglo-American colonialism.

## INTERPRETATIONS AND QUESTIONS

The Final Woodland period was a dynamic time in American history, with rapid cultural and social change sparked by intensifying Native–European, Native–Native, and European–European relations. Much of what we know about this period comes from European documents. The sixteenth and early seventeenth centuries saw increasing European exploration and trading activities on Long Island Sound and along its affiliated river systems. Relations between the traders and indigenous peoples were usually mutually satisfying, although conflict did occur because of cultural misunderstandings and some unscrupulous traders cheating and abducting Indians, often to sell as slaves in Europe.[199] European accounts often provided descriptions of indigenous peoples, their lifeways, and intertribal relations, such as the "beaver wars" with the Iroquois. Final Woodland sites are rare, but much needed to supplement and test the reality of the archival information.

As history proceeded, Native American communities continued to contribute to the growth and success of the colony and state of Connecticut—and still do. The next chapter touches on the history and adaptive changes of indigenous communities during the later Post-Contact period, called the "historic period" by many, because only after the Europeans arrived were written records produced in North America. Indigenous peoples are often offended by this dichotomy between prehistoric and historic, because they had been preserving and passing down their oral traditions for thousands of years. Oral traditions are histories. For this reason, I use the term "pre-contact" to refer to the time before European arrival, and "post-contact" for the document-driven, "historical" period since then.

# 10

## Surviving European-American Colonialism

### *A.D. 1633 into the Twenty-first Century*

Oh, why does the white man follow my path
Like the hounds on the tiger's track?
Does the flush on my dark cheek
Waken his wrath?
Does he court the bow at my back?
Go back, go back from the red man's track
For the hunter's eyes grow dim,
To find that the white man wrongs the one
Who never did harm to him.

> —"The Indian Hunter Song," sung by Mohegan Eliphalet Peegee Fielding to his granddaughter Gladys Tantaquidgeon (b. 1899) when she was a child

Following closely on the heels of the explorers and traders, English settlers came in droves, seeking land and natural resources denied to them in England, and religious freedom for themselves—although not for others, sadly. Indigenous people, the first residents of the United States, were not allowed to practice their traditional religions until 1978, when the United States Congress finally passed the American Indian Religious Freedom Act.[1] They became United States citizens only in 1924, when the Snyder Act gave tribal peoples the right to vote.[2]

Problems between the English and the continent's First Nations multiplied during the settlement period, particularly after the demise of the fur fad in Europe and the colonists' replacement of wampum with coin currency. With this, indigenous people lost their status as equal trading partners with the English. Not only were Indian communities no longer necessary for a profitable English economy, they were perceived as an obstacle to that economy.

## NEGATIVE STEREOTYPES AND CONTINUAL DISCRIMINATION

Consequently, European-American leaders began a series of dehumanizing social and political assaults on local Indian peoples, a prelude to the exploitation and oppression that has continued to this day. Erroneously portraying tribal members as lazy, wanton, wicked, devil-worshiping savages provided a plausible excuse for taking their lands and destroying their homes. In 1625, Anglican minister William Morrell wrote:

> They're wondrous, cruell, strangely base and vile, / Quickly displeased, and hardly reconciled.[3]

In 1852, Connecticut historian John W. De Forest wrote:

> We have now examined the social condition of the aborigines of Connecticut, and have seen that, while they possessed some pleasing traits of character, and some few sources of comfort and pleasure, they were still a people purely barbarous, whose nature was unsoftened by a single trait of civilization. Had they remained unmolested and unvisited by Europeans till the present day, they would now have been as rude, as poor, as warlike, as disdainful of labor, as fond of torturing their enemies, and, in every way, as uncivilized, as when Adriaen Block first explored the Connecticut River.[4]

In 1903, Connecticut historian Alexander Johnston wrote:

> All these [Connecticut] tribes were alike unclean in their habits, shiftless in their mode of life, and much addicted to powwowing, devil-worship, and darker immoralities. . . .[5]

In 1946, Connecticut historian Chard P. Smith wrote:

> The first human beings to inhabit the [Housatonic] valley were the heathen of the Mohican family of the great Algonkin race . . . an unwarlike, submissive and pessimistic people. Their solution of emotional problems was suicide, normally by leaping from a cliff into the arms of the Great Spirit, after singing a hymn to apprise him of their approach. . . . [T]he chief concern of the river Indians during their bodily lives was with Hobbamocko, the Evil Spirit who they believed would ultimately destroy their world. Their principal festivals were horrid orgies to propitiate him, during which the frenzied powwows or medicine men threw their possessions and sometimes their children into the flames. . . . [I]t can hardly be supposed that individual colonists, who were sharp enough in dealing with one another, would have any reticence about driving sharp bargains with the filthy savages.[6]

In 2004, Nancy Johnson, then a United States representative from Connecticut, proclaimed:

> There are people I represent who have owned their property and tilled their soil for 200 years and now we're going to tell them that because of a

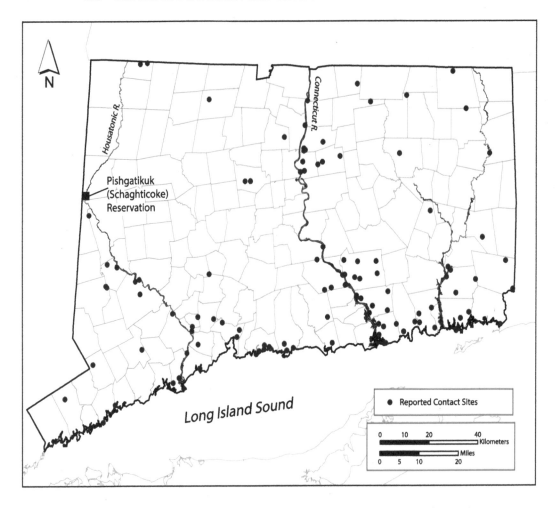

Location of known Indian sites during the Post-Contact period in Connecticut on file in the Connecticut Office of State Archaeology.

rag-tag group that has not been around until money and gambling came on the scene we're going to take their property rights?[7]

English colonial governments passed several unfair acts that denied or restricted the rights of local Indians to ancient traditions, including access to ancient tribal hunting and fishing grounds, freedom to bear arms for hunting and protection, freedom to practice their indigenous religion, the ability to trade maize with individual colonists, the wearing of body paint, participation in traditional social activities such as powwows and dances, even denying them the right to enter an English town.[8] English-run Indian missions and schools forbade children to wear traditional dress and speak their native language. English colonists unashamedly admitted to stealing from their Indian neighbors.[9] John Winthrop, the governor of Massachusetts Bay Colony, reported that when local Indians refused to sell corn to the settlement at Saybrook, colonists trespassed into the Indian fields and stole it.

The twenty men of Saybrook . . . went to fetch some of the Indians' corn; and having fetched every man one sackful to their boat, they returned for more, and having loaded themselves, the Indians set upon them. So they laid down their corn and gave fire upon them, and the Indians shot arrows at them.[10]

## EARLY LAND TRANSACTIONS

Indigenous people were also erroneously portrayed as simple and primitive. This negative stereotype was furthered by the early land transactions, wherein large tracts of Native American homelands were purportedly "sold" for a few trinkets and relatively minute amounts of money. The most famous example is the indigenous "sale" of *Manna-hata,* "the island of many hills" in the Lenape dialect[11] now known as Manhattan Island, to the Dutch for about $24 worth of items, including glass beads and alcohol, about which people today wonder and laugh.[12]

Before European settlement, indigenous New Englanders had no concept of private ownership of land. Land was considered a gift from the Creator and an inheritance from the ancestors, owned by the tribe and shared in common by its members.[13] The tribal community inhabited an intensely spiritual landscape filled with collective memories continually sharpened by objects marking the location of historical events, folktales and sacred stories, and holy precincts where funerals, burials, puberty rites, vision quests, and other spiritual ceremonies occurred.[14] Hence their continual opposition to selling or leaving their homelands, despite poverty, discrimination, and threat of force, as shown by their many petitions in the Public Records of the Colony and State of Connecticut.

### The Tunxis Case

One particularly persistent petition concerns the Tunxis tribe, whose entire homelands in the Farmington River valley were "sold" to the English in 1640 by Sequassen, the chief sachem of the neighboring Sukiog people, whose homelands lay east of the Tunxis along the Connecticut River. The Tunxis leadership disputed the legality of this deed and for 127 years continued to petition the Connecticut General Court for justice. The last petition, presented in 1767, produced no satisfactory result from the General Court, and Tunxis leaders reluctantly accepted its judgment. Thirteen years later most of the tribe (but not all) joined the Brothertown movement of Christian Indians and accepted the invitation of the Oneida tribe to live at Oneida, and removed to western New York.[15]

The spiritual connection was so strong that even after losing their homelands tribal peoples continued to return. The Quinnipiacs came back annually to hold ceremonies at a sacred boulder site. Niantics who had followed the Brothertown movement to upstate New York and Wisconsin made repeated visits back to their homeland in the 1800s,[16] writing "long letters" to "claim their share in the Reservation" lands. The Stockbridge Mahikans, who also were forced westward to Wisconsin in the 1820s, continued to make pilgrimages to their old homeland throughout the nineteenth and twentieth centuries, and still do today.[17]

In early transactions, Native Americans and Europeans had very different ideas of what a "deed" signified. For the English and Dutch a deed was a permanent transfer of land, proof of sole proprietorship of a piece of real estate and all its resources. For the indigenous locals, it was a formal acknowledgment of a temporary sharing of resources, not a land sale. They considered the payment received from the Europeans a "gift" cementing the friendship and alliance between the two societies.

Among non-western societies, survival often depended on loose socioeconomic alliances with neighboring groups, which were supported and strengthened by reciprocity in the form of gift exchange.[18] In essence, indigenous leaders were attempting to deal with these new foreigners in the same way that their ancestors had dealt with indigenous neighbors for thousands of years. Gifts were obligations that bound indigenous individuals and groups through a continual reciprocal relationship of giving and taking.[19] As museum professional Lynne Williamson (Mohawk-Mississauga descent) noted:

> Gifts of food and ceremonies in which household objects and clothing are given are also ways in which Algonkian people construct a web of mutual obligation, responsibility, and trust. . . . Seen through the eyes of Algonkian peoples, exchange was not simply a matter of private property or profit; economic activity could not be separated from traditions of sharing and reciprocity or kinship relations of alliance and support. Undoubtedly this perspective was a constant source of misunderstanding (and thus tension) as Indian New England was colonized. Even the astute and somewhat sympathetic seventeenth-century observer Roger Williams would condemn Narragansett people for never paying debts, while praising their generosity and kindness. Where he saw different and unrelated "customs," Native Americans see a continuous history of giving and receiving gifts.[20]

## The Quinnipiac Case

This was the case in the early land transactions between the English and leaders of the Quinnipiac tribe, whose homelands extended along the Connecticut coast from New Haven on the west to Madison on the east, and as far north as Meriden.[21] The English–Quinnipiac land negotiations of 1638 and 1639 marked some of the earliest indigenous meetings with European colonists (rather than traders) in the state. At that time each group knew very little about the other's culture and expectations, and approached such transactions from their own culturally distinct viewpoints. As John Menta observed, although "the whites were concerned primarily with gaining title to Menunkatuck by buying the land from the Quinnipiac, . . . the Indians . . . viewed the goods as 'gifts of goodwill'" and not as payment for a land sale.[22] This was obviously the real reason why Shaumpishuh, the sister of the Quinnipiac sachem Momaugin and the sunksquaw (female leader), or squaw sachem, of a Quinnipiac band at Menunkatuck (now in Guilford), accepted only two "looking glasses" (mirrors) for all that property, not because she was "vain," as one local historian described the event.[23]

Indigenous history was traditionally orally transmitted. Quinnipiac leaders had not yet learned to read or write in these early colonial times, so they left no documents of their negotiations with the English. As historian Richard Carlson has pointed out, we have only the English version of the agreements, which was likely quite different from the Quinnipiac understanding of them.

> The records of these councils exist only as written by and for Englishmen, whose perspective was that they were giving the Indians, a subordinate group, certain rights and privileges in exchange for exclusive ownership of carefully defined parcels of land. It is safe to assume, however, that the Quinnipiacs entered into these agreements with greatly different ideas of what was being negotiated. While they may have interpreted English protection—even submission to specific laws regulating contact between the two groups—in the familiar terms of their previous tributary status to the Pequots, there is no suggestion in the treaties that the Indians believed they were relinquishing sovereignty over themselves. Indeed, as a sovereign people, they most likely understood that, in negotiating as equals and as the original occupants of the area, they were giving the English certain rights and privileges in the lands the two people now shared, most importantly the right to occupy and use the land in specific ways. The provision in the first treaty respecting English rights to resources within the Quinnipiac reservation appears to support this conclusion. For the Quinnipiacs, the treaties represented agreements to share uses of the land, not agreements for exclusive ownership of the land itself.[24]

Native American leaders quickly perceived the cultural misconceptions and were careful to demand larger sums and many more useful goods, such as metal tools, cloth, and guns, for later deeds, which were transacted nearly always "under economic and cultural duress."[25] As discussed by archaeologist Russell Handsman and Trudie Lamb Richmond, they also insisted on the inclusion of specific language allowing tribal members access to important resources and localities.

> In reality, the documents the colonists (and later historians) referred to as deeds were often carefully worded agreements to share the use of homelands and resources. In them native people consistently reserved for themselves the rights to collect firewood, hunt and fish, use their planting fields, and even build wigwams on the colonists' common pastures.[26]

## The Mahikan Case

By the late eighteenth century many tribes had been separated from their homelands through war, poverty, and especially questionable land transactions—the legality of which was often contested by Indian leaders in the Connecticut General Assembly or General Court—and outright encroachment by the English. The many petitions and complaints in the Connecticut Public Records, Court documents, and town records dating from the 1600s to today are ample evidence that Anglo-Americans often ignored and violated the agreements in those transactions.[27] A typical example is a 1742 petition of the Mahikan Indian community in Sharon to the Connecticut General Court about fraudulent deeds. Several townspeople supported the petition and asked that the land be returned to the Indians as long as the white proprietors would be reimbursed by the Connecticut government. This never happened, and the Sharon Mahikans lost their home-lands.

> To the Honorable, the General Assembly of the colony of Connecticut, in General Court assembled, at Hartford, in said Colony, on the second Thurs-day in May, A.D. 1742. The memorial of Peter Pratt [minister of Sharon], Nathaniel Skinner and Jonathan Dunham, agents of said town, and Stephen Nequitimaugh Nanhoon, and others of the Indian nations, residing in said Sharon, humbly showeth — "that Nanhoon and other Indians sold lands to Thomas Lamb of Salisbury . . ." and that he, the said Lamb, in negotiating the said purchases of said Indians, did take advantage of their ignorance, and as they have since understood, *did obtain a deed or deeds from them or some of them for more of said land than ever they sold or intended to sell* to said Lamb, and particularly the place at the northwest corner of said Sharon, *where the said Indians live and improve, and always designed to reserve to themselves for a settlement, besides several other parcels that have never been sold to the English;* that the Government's Committee have obtained the rights purchased of said Lamb of the Indians, and have sold all the lands in the townships of Salisbury and Sharon to the proprietors of said Towns, who are now improving and are entering on the said lands still claimed by the said Indians, which has aroused a great deal of uneasiness among the Indians, *they are looking upon themselves defrauded of their right.*[28]

Archaeologist and Old Lyme town historian John Pfeiffer supplied an ex-ample in which the court actually provided a legal mechanism for encroachment of Indian land at Niantic:

> Other approaches to the acquisition of Nehantic lands were recorded in the daily journal of Moses Warren (1789). An entry in the journal illustrates the encroachment upon the Reservation. On July 1st Moses Warren, acting as a surveyor for the court, was assigned to "straighten the line" between Joseph Smith, George Jeffrey, and Isaac Piunko. The net affect of this survey was to grant Joseph Smith part of the lands owned by George Jeffrey and Isaac Piunko. Jeffrey and Piunko were Nehantics.[29]

### The Mohegan Case

Tribal peoples soon realized the potential advantage — or need — for individual land ownership like under the English system as a means of staving off encroach-ment.[30] By the mid-1700s, many indigenous peoples held property in severalty on their reservation lands, including the Wangunks, whose reservation overlooked the Connecticut River in what is now Portland.[31] In 1789 the Mohegans, long re-sistant to accepting English ways, petitioned the Connecticut General Assembly to divide up their reservation lands into individual allotments held in severalty.

For in Times past, our Fore Fathers lived in Peace, Love, and great harmony, and had everything in Great plenty. . . . And they no Contention about their Lands. It lay in Common to them all, and they had but one large Dish, and they Cou'd all eat together, in Peace and Love. But alas, it is not So now, all our Fishing Hunting and Fowling is entirely gone, And now we have now begun to work on our Land, keep Cattle horses and Hogs: and Wee Build Houses and fence in Lots, And now Wee plainly See, that one dish and one Fire will not do any Longer for us. Some few there are, that are Stronger than others, and they will keep off the poor wealth, the daft and the Blind, and will take the Dish to themselves, Now, they will rather Call the White People and Molattoes to eat with them out of your Dish; and poor Widows and Orphans must be pushed one [side] and there they must Set so Laying, Starveing and die. And so Wee are now Come to our Good Brethren of this Assembly, With Hearts full of Sorrow and Grey; for Immediate help. And therefore are most humble and Earnest Request and Petition that our Dish of Succhuttash may be equally divided among us, that every one may have his own little Dish by himself, that he may eat Quietly, and do with his Dish as he pleases and let everyone have his own Fire.[32]

In 1790 the United States Congress passed the Indian Intercourse Act, which forbade the sale or purchase of Indian lands without the consent of Congress. Yet many Indian homelands were nevertheless subsequently sold off by the white overseers appointed by the state, as shown by the dates of land transactions and the landsuits brought by extant tribes against the government in the later twentieth century. In the 1980s the Mohegans initiated legal action to reclaim Mohegan homelands and also applied to the U.S. Bureau of Indian Affairs for the federal recognition that would help them recover their lands.[33] They were able to regain lost homelands through federal recognition by the BIA; the Mashantucket Pequots received recognition by the U.S. Congress.[34] Only through such recognition were these tribes able to reclaim tribal lands, because only *federally* recognized tribes have been able to win suits to regain control over reservation resources. The Schaghticoke tribe filed three suits between 1936 and 1975 for hundreds of acres that had been illegally sold. Realizing the need for federal recognition, in the 1980s they began actively working toward that end.[35] The Paugussetts and the Eastern Pequot Tribal Nation have also sought redress through federal recognition. Mohegan traditionalist and culture keeper Fidelia Fielding penned these words (in the Mohegan language) in her diary many years before the federal recognition process was initiated:

White men think [they] know all things. Half [the things they are] saying not are so. Poor white men. Many want all this earth. It can not be for another person [to] have anything to eat, because white men want the money. They can not carry it when they die.[36]

Burrill Fielding, chief of the Mohegans in the early twentieth century, and his daughter Myrtice Fielding, dressed in traditional indigenous clothing. Chief Fielding is wearing a typical New England upright feathered headdress in a crown around his head.

## THE SEVENTEENTH-CENTURY INDIAN WARS

The two great Indian wars of the seventeenth century in Connecticut exacerbated the indigenous population decline and poverty caused by disease, land losses, and destruction of their economies. Both Indian-Anglo wars — the Pequot War of 1637 and King Philip's War of 1675 to 1676 — ended in defeat for indigenous peoples. In the first it was mainly the Pequot tribe that suffered loss. In King Philip's War, however, even the Christianized Native American communities and tribal societies that had remained neutral did not escape the calamitous consequences. In 1675, English-friendly and Christianized Nipmucks from the Praying Indian towns of Natick and Marlborough, Massachusetts, were forced from their homes and imprisoned on barren Deer Island in Boston Harbor — the first concentration camp in North America. Despite the English government's promise to feed and clothe the prisoners, hundreds died, including women and children. Indigenous people still visit the island annually to honor those who lost their lives there.[37] King Philip's War intensified the downward spiral of land losses, political dependency, impoverishment, disease, and discrimination among New England's indigenous communities that continued well into the twentieth century.

We have several perspectives on these wars, from the seventeenth-century Englishmen who fought in them, from later white historians, from the oral traditions of the tribal peoples whose ancestors were directly involved in the conflicts, and most recently from archaeology.[38] As the philosophy of science suggests, we can never know truth, but can only get closer to it as we continue to observe and learn. This is especially the case in the social sciences, so it is important to acknowledge and understand the perspectives of all groups involved in intercultural events.[39]

## The Pequot War of 1637

A series of confrontations between Native Americans and English traders and settlers led up to the main conflict that was the Pequot War of 1637, but the spark that ignited this simmering discord was the murder in 1636 of the "notorious" and "turbulent" English trader John Oldham by Indians on Block Island.[40] The English accused the Pequots of involvement in the crime and of sheltering the murderers. Marching into Pequot homelands, they demanded that the killers be turned over along with 1,000 fathoms of wampum (a length of 5,000 to 5,500 feet) and some Pequot children as hostages.[41] Even though Oldham was disliked by the people of Massachusetts Bay and was probably killed by the Narragansetts, enemies of the Pequots, English leaders used his death as the reason for an attack on the main Pequot village at Mystic. Scholars debate about the ulterior motive behind the English attack. One possible motive was to remove the powerful Pequots as middlemen in the fur and wampum trade with the Dutch and English. Several Native American tribes supported the colonists, while others remained neutral, because they chafed under Pequot demands and dominance, or hoped to replace the Pequots as the premier power broker in the region. According to Kevin McBride, who is overseeing a study of the Pequot War battlefields, the war was a series of skirmishes and encounters that occurred before and after the Mystic attack, and lasted almost a year.

> The Pequot War is often portrayed as a conflict between the English and Pequot, and the attack on the Pequot fortified village at Mystic as the only action of the war, resulting in the immediate collapse and defeat of the Pequot. In fact, the Pequot War was as much a conflict between the Pequot confederacy and their Native enemies as it was a war against the English. The Mystic Massacre was . . . but one of dozens of battles and actions fought between the Pequot confederacy and the English and their Native allies. These actions took place over a period of almost one year and within . . . the present states of Rhode Island, Connecticut and eastern New York.[42]

The attack on the Mystic village occurred while many of the Pequot warriors were away. A force of Englishmen and their Indian allies—Narragansetts, Niantics, and Mohegans led by the sachem Uncas—burned the fortified village to the ground. Any Pequot who attempted to escape was shot. English estimates of the death toll ranged from three hundred to seven hundred, mostly women and children.[43] A large group of Pequots was pursued westward. Some were killed or captured at a battle in a swamp at Southport; others escaped northward, finding sanctuary in Indian villages on the northwestern Connecticut frontier, of which Englishmen then knew little.[44]

The Pequot grand sachem Sassacus and other leaders and members of their families continued northwestward up the Housatonic River valley to seek pro-

A 1638 engraving, based on eyewitness accounts, of the colonial attack on the Pequot fort overlooking the Mystic River during the Pequot War of 1637, during which an estimated four hundred to seven hundred Pequots—mostly women and children—were slaughtered in a surprise attack while most of their warriors were away. The engraving shows a round wooden stockade enclosing round pole-frame wigwams, surrounded by English soldiers firing guns at the Indians inside. Behind the colonial line is a second line of their Indian allies (shown with bows and arrows)—the Narragansetts, Niantics, and the Mohegans led by their sachem Uncas. The English captain John Mason ordered the fort burned with everyone in it and any escaping Pequots were shot.

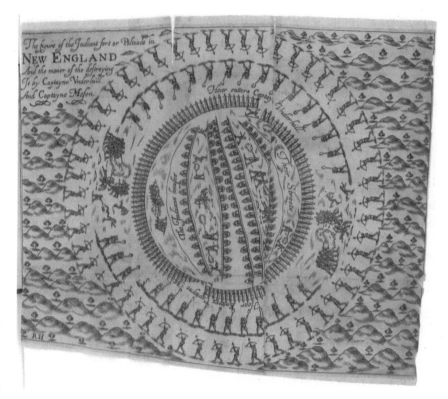

tection and support from the Mohawks. According to recent research in the unpublished Pynchon papers (1640–1647) housed at the Massachusetts Archives by staff of the Mashantucket Pequot Museum and Research Center, somewhere near Poquiatog (possibly west of present-day Danbury, Connecticut),[45] a group of Mohawk and apparently Mohegan warriors caught up with Sassacus, approximately six sachems, and fifteen warriors, surprising them as they slept in their wigwams. Sassacus was killed immediately, and several other sachems escaped, only to be killed shortly after. A Mohawk informant stated that the Pequot sachems were killed two days' journey east of the Hudson at Pequaug chiefly by "Moeagans," adding, "and the Mohawks had the least hand" in it. Sassacus and several others are purported to have been beheaded at Woquitog, and their heads sent back to the English.[46] Those Pequots remaining in their homeland were put to death, enslaved, or dispersed throughout the countryside.[47] These events must have been unsettling and foreboding to other tribal peoples, as Cherokee author and educator Karen Coody Cooper maintained in her article on the Wangunk Indians of Wethersfield.

> The River Indians [living along the Connecticut River] had seen the high cost of war borne by the Pequot. Undoubtedly, their villages buzzed with debate on how to handle their perilous situation. They were outgunned, the European populations seemed limitless and overbearing and now their form of government, rule by consensus, worked against them. Who could agree on

Inscribed stone marking
the former location of a
pre-1654 Paugussett fort
in the area of what is now
State Route 34 in Derby,
Connecticut.

one course of action against such an unpredictable situation: Too much had
happened too fast. Too much was unknown. And all of it was disheartening.

The English were in a new unknown land, but they brought with them
the comfortable trappings of Old World life. Conversely, the Indians were
still in their homeland, but found their way of life altered uncomfortably.[48]

It was not until several decades later that the Pequots, under the leadership
of sachem Robin Cassacinamon, were given a 500-acre reservation, in Groton in
1651.[49] This land was taken away seventy years later, probably because of its choice
location near good fishing areas on Long Island Sound. In 1666, the English set
aside a 3,000-acre reservation at Mashantucket for these Western Pequots. In
1683, 500 acres on Long Pond in North Stonington was reserved for the use of
the Eastern, or Paucatuck, Pequots led by the sachem Wequash. Continuous non-
Indian encroachment on these reservation lands decreased the acreage at a time
when shrinking population caused by poverty, disease, and the absence or death
of Pequot men in seafaring and military service for the English and American
governments in various colonial wars was having a debilitating effect on Pequot
society.

In 1856, the Connecticut legislature reduced the Mashantucket reservation
to a mere 214 acres through a law ironically called "An act relating to the Ledyard
Pequot Indians, and the preservation of their property." Mashantucket is located
in a rocky uplands region with "thin and poorly drained" soils surrounding the
large Cedar Swamp. The area was never conducive to agriculture and the reduced
acreage could sustain only a few Pequots. Most tribal members were forced to
move off the reservation to find work to support their families. The Pequots never
gave up their reservation, which was on part of their original homelands and re-
tained much social and spiritual meaning for them. In 1976, the Mashantucket
Pequot tribe sued for the return of those lost reserved lands. In 1983, the U.S.
Congress responded by passing the Connecticut Land Claims Settlement Act,
which recognized the Mashantucket Pequot tribe and provided for the acquisition of 2,270 acres of the original 1666 reservation, to be held in trust for the tribe

## INDIGENOUS WEAPONRY

Over the course of thousands of years, the indigenous peoples of North America developed highly functional and often elaborately decorated weapons for use in warfare and related ceremonies. In addition to gaining status from victory in battle, a warrior could improve his standing by expertly crafting his weapons. Young boys learned early the ways of war. Design elements that could provide spiritual protection were often given the same consideration as pragmatic details, such as which species of tree should be used to make an arrow's shaft.

The bow and arrow continued to be a mainstay of Native American warfare until European traders provided guns to their indigenous trading partners. The bow and arrows were carved from wood. Early English accounts list the use of elder, witchhazel, beech, and ash for arrow shafts.[a] The shaft was fletched with wing and tail feathers, usually from an eagle or turkey. Arrowheads, usually triangular, were made from stone, bone, or brass. Bows were made from ash, oak, witchhazel, beech, and hickory, and bowstrings from animal sinew. Early New England bows were 5 to 6 feet (less than 2 meters) in length, much longer than those of Western and Plains Indians. Of different shapes, some were

A monolithic axe unearthed from a "charcoal pit" in Branford in 1850. The axe is 11.4 inches (29 centimeters) long with a bird head effigy at one end and the butt end carved into a human face. When originally dug up, the axe had discs or ellipses of pearly shell inlaid in a series of ten "pits" (some are visible in this photograph).

colored, these distinctive characteristics likely indicating cultural distinctions.[b] The bow sheath and arrow quiver were crafted from animal hide, bark, or wood, stitched with sinew, and sometimes decorated with beadwork and fringe. Skill with a bow and arrow was acquired early, as related by William Wood: "They are trained up to their bows even from their childhood; little boys with bows made of little sticks and arrows of great bents will smite down a piece of tobacco pipe, every shoot a good way off."[c]

Also popular was the war club, one of the earliest types of weapon. Warriors in southern New England used several kinds. One was a small round stone covered with rawhide and stitched with sinew, attached to a wooden stick. An example was recovered from an archaeology site on Fort Hill in New Milford. The stone with its leather covering is missing its wooden handle, which had dissolved in the acidic subsoil.

Wooden ball-headed war clubs were carved from a single piece of wood and polished. They were often inlaid with spiritually meaningful items, sometimes those announcing the high status of their owners, such as wampum shell and copper beads.

A third type of war club was the "monolithic axe," a stone hatchet carved from a single block of stone that was ground and polished. Edward Johnson in 1654 described such an axe as one of the weapons used by the Pequots in the Pequot War.[d] Johnson wrote that the axe was inlaid with shell and contained "vermilion," both symbolic of the spirit world, suggesting that the Pequots purposely decorated the weapon to empower it with spiritual energies. A monolithic axe dug up in Branford in the early 1800s has a handle that terminates in a bird-head effigy; on the poll end is a carved human face. The axe was originally inlaid with a series of ten shell disks.[e] According to geologist Dr. Tony Philpotts, the axe was made from a greywacke local to the area of Albany, New York.[f] Dr. Kevin McBride, director of research at the Mashantucket Pequot Museum and Research Center, believes that the axe dates to the seventeenth century.[g]

Notes

Adapted from "Ways of War," a 2007 exhibit at the Institute for American Indian Studies in Washington, Connecticut.

a. William Wood, quoted in Bragdon 1995, 103; James Rosier, quoted in Karr 1999, 93.

b. Wilbur 1978, 54–55.

c. William Wood 1634, 97–98, 101, as cited in Karr 1999, 93.

d. Kevin McBride, "The Fairfield Swamp Fight," paper presented at the spring meeting of the Archaeological Society of Connecticut at Western Connecticut State University, April 24, 2010, Danbury, Conn.; McBride, personal communication, 2010, citing Johnson.

e. Bellantoni 2008.

f. Kevin McBride, personal communication, March 25, 2011.

g. McBride, "The Fairfield Swamp Fight"; McBride, personal communication, December 30, 2011.

by the U.S. secretary of the interior as a federal Indian reservation. In 1992, over 1,245 acres of the reservation, with its more than 70 archaeological sites covering over 9,000 years of indigenous history, was designated a National Historic Landmark.[50]

## King Philip's War

The great population losses and other devastation caused by disease and war helped the ever-increasing tide of English settlers to overrun and engulf precious Indian homelands, creating a situation of escalating negative feedback. King Philip's War

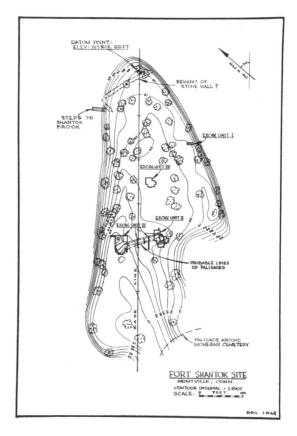

Plan of the New York University excavations at Fort Shantok site in Montville, Connecticut.

was the Indian response.[51] Metacomet, known as Philip to the colonists, was a son of Massasoit, the early-seventeenth-century Wampanoag grand sachem. Ironically, it was Massasoit who had aided the small English colony at Plimoth in its early years and provided the banquet for their Thanksgiving ceremony (actually a traditional Native American harvest festival). The Wampanoags' thanks were disease, social disintegration, and despair. Philip thought that the only remedy was for the New England Indian tribes to join together to drive out the English while their settlements were still relatively small and far apart.

Unfortunately, not all tribal peoples agreed. Some remained neutral and some even sided with the English.[52] Their leaders may have thought this was in the best interests of their respective tribes. For some, the choice may have been forced on them by the colonists. To insure that the Connecticut River communities remained loyal to the English, for example, in 1675 the Connecticut Court (forerunner of the General Assembly) demanded hostages. The court also tried to force the Wangunk tribe to live under the political control of Owaneco, the son of Mohegan sachem Uncas, a known ally of the English.[53] Karen Coody Cooper portrayed the Wangunks' dilemma:

> We can only imagine what the Indians of the Connecticut River were thinking. Devastated by disease and seeing a continuous influx of settlers arriving with destructive free-roaming livestock, erecting substantial settlements, pos-

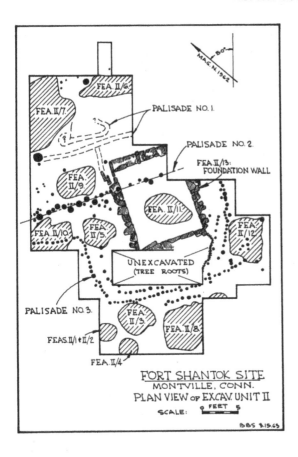

Plan view of Excavation Unit II at the Fort Shantok site, showing three lines of palisades, a building foundation, and many pit features.

sessing cannons and muskets, traveling in large sailed ships, dazzling the eye with varied possessions, acting in unpredictable ways, what were the Connecticut River Indians to do? With loss of population and a changing environment, their most immediate concern was survival. Thus, what they could do was garden, hunt, seek protected areas, and try to engage in positive political alliances, which included seeking ties not only with each other, but with the ever-growing foreign presence.[54]

The Pequots had remained neutral during King Philip's War, but English threats and attacks on neutral groups such as the Wangunks, Nipmucks, and others were likely common knowledge. To protect themselves against any such attack, around 1675 the Pequots built a defensive fort adjacent to their great cedar swamp. Its remains were accidentally discovered by Mashantucket Pequot Museum and Research archaeologists in 1992. Subsequent excavations revealed the square shape and European-like bastions of its palisade, seventeenth-century artifacts, and interior features including a large storage pit and a forge for manufacturing iron items and lead musket balls.[55]

Philip was killed in 1676, and his followers were hunted down and killed or enslaved. Never again would southern New England tribal peoples declare war on the English. Native leaders quickly surmised that the best survival strategy was

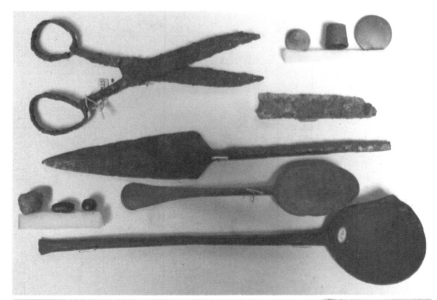

European trade goods from Connecticut sites. Top, iron scissors from Laurel Beach Shell Heap, Milford; metal bell, thimble, and button from Tubbs Shell Heap, Niantic; iron knife blade from Laurel Beach Shell Heap, Milford; iron fish spear point from Salmon Beach, East Haddam; glass trade beads from Middlefield, Derby (Pickets Pond), and Stratford (The Meadows); pewter spoon from Costelote Point, Stratford; iron trade spoon from North Guilford. Bottom, copper bracelet from Essex; copper projectile points from Tubbs Shell Heap, Niantic and Thompson, Connecticut; steatite button mold from The Meadows, Stratford; flint nodule carved into a duck from New Milford; restrung copper beads from Essex; steatite brooch mold from Laurel Beach Shell Heap, Milford; steatite bullet mold from Thamesville; perforated stone disc from Hadlyme.

diplomacy coupled with a working knowledge of English language, law, and customs. The Schaghticoke tribe, for example, continually acted and reacted peaceably to colonial and federal attempts to control tribal lands and destroy their tribal community.[56] Since the mid–eighteenth century, the Schaghticoke leadership accomplished this mainly through Anglo-American law and its court system—as did other successful tribal governments in the state.[57] As Schaghticoke leader Paulette Crone-Morange and I concluded in our article on her tribe's history,

> In summary, the lessons taught by the seventeenth century Indian wars and the eighteenth century Moravian missionaries induced the Schaghticoke and neighboring tribes to alleviate conflict and survive amid the dominant white

society by working peaceably within the Anglo-American legal structure. The numerous tribal petitions, memorials, and letters to the Connecticut legislature and courts throughout the eighteenth, nineteenth and twentieth centuries demonstrate that from earliest historic times the Schaghticoke Tribe established a survival strategy of negotiation and cooperation based on English law that has successfully conserved tribal resources and tribal community while maintaining the Tribe's distinct identity as a separate entity from that of their non-Schaghticoke neighbors. They managed this through education, Anglo intermediaries, and direct tribal participation in the English Court system. The efficacy of this political strategy is demonstrated by the fact that the Tribe and part of its original Homelands at Schaghticoke Reservation have survived to this day in a world dominated by Anglo-American society, while neighboring tribal governments emigrated west or dissolved.[58]

To avoid English reprisals, many Native peoples relocated during and after the war, either northward to Canada, or westward to Native refuges in swamps or uplands along disputed state borders,[59] where Native communities were often safe. The hilly, rocky, often snake-infested topography was not attractive to English families, and the intergovernmental quarreling over colonial borders made it risky for whites to buy land there.[60] Some moved even farther, into western New York and beyond. Others continued in their tribal communities, determined to maintain or regain the sacred homelands of their ancestors. In his discussion of the Moravian mission at Schaghticoke, Harold Bradshaw commented on the persistence of tribal members to remain on their reservation despite the intolerance of white neighbors after the demise of an active mission and loss of resident missionaries: "The [Moravian] mission at Pachgatgoch [Schaghticoke] in Connecticut was not abandoned entirely until 1770, the Brethren making regular visits *to those remnants that preferred persecution to exile.*"[61] More than two hundred years later, Schaghticoke people still have a strong spiritual attachment to their reservation homelands, as demonstrated by this quote from Trudie Lamb Richmond's article on her tribe's history of resistance and survival:

> Historical silences have largely contributed to the invisibility of the indigenous peoples of southern New England. Local histories have reduced our existence to a few short paragraphs in their writings. We are often discussed in the past tense and seldom in the present. But we have endured and survived, in spite of being fragmented, factionalized, Christianized and Americanized. Our tenacity, our resilience, our stubbornness, and our beliefs enable us to continue and work toward rebuilding who we are: the indigenous people of this land.[62]

## Indian Slaves

When most Americans hear the word "slavery," they think of the African slave trade and the antebellum South. Although some research on the local history of slaves has been published,[63] it is only recently that the general public has been reintroduced to white New Englanders' participation in the slave trade.[64] This included not only the better known purchase and sale of slaves from Africa by northern ship captains in the Triangle Trade (African slaves to Caribbean sugar to New England rum), but also the use of slaves on New England farms and in New England homes. It is not well known that many of these farm and house slaves were American Indians.[65] Writing in the *Connecticut Magazine* in 1899, Frederick C. Norton reported:

> Contrary to the usual notion the first slaves in Connecticut were not chiefly negroes, but Indians taken in battle and afterwards distributed among the settlers. The first Pequot War, for instance, furnished a large number, even a superfluity of servants of this character. There is, however, reason to believe that the two institutions of Indian and Negro slavery co-existed for a period: for in the famous "Articles of Confederation" of 1643 provision was made for the distribution among the inhabitants of "persons, as well as lands and goods, taken in the spoils of war."[66]

Captured Pequot warriors, as well as their wives and children, were sold as slaves locally and to planters in the Caribbean. Historical records show that after both the Pequot War and King Philip's War, Indian men, women, and children were sold into slavery. Pequots and others thought to be sympathetic to them and to King Philip and the Wampanoag tribe were shipped off to the Caribbean to spend the rest of their lives toiling in sugarcane fields.[67] Some were also put to work building boats and fishing or as house slaves to local Connecticut citizens.[68] The journal of Puritan governor John Winthrop described the disposal of Pequot captives:

> The remaining captives, consisting of about 80 women and children, were divided. Some were given to the soldiers, whether *gratis* or for pay does not appear. Thirty were given to the Narragansett who were allies of the English, 48 were sent to Massachusetts and the remainder were assigned to Connecticut. The women and girls of the Massachusetts captives were distributed among the towns. . . . The boys were ordered to be sent to Bermuda but instead sold on the island of Providence.[69]

The English settlers branded their Pequot slaves on the shoulder with a branding iron.[70]

Many Native Americans were held in virtual slavery through the practice known as indenture. Indentured servants bound themselves out, or were bound out by their parents, to work for an individual for a certain number of years to pay off a debt or as payment for some service provided by the holder of the indenture. As a group, indigenous people were one of the most impoverished and indebted in colonial and early federal Connecticut, and easy targets for those seeking long-term laborers for little cost.

Many prominent Connecticut families owned slaves that were part Indian or were Indian indentured servants. The Mumford family of Salem owned Nehantic Indian slaves, whom they eventually freed but kept as servants. Seven-year-old Aaron Waukeet, a Nehantic Indian, was bound out for fourteen years to Ezra Stiles, president of Yale University. In return Stiles promised to teach the boy to read the Bible and provide him with a suit of clothes. Another Nehantic child, Mercy Ann Nonesuch, was indentured to the Ethelinda Griswold family of Lyme in 1829 for seventeen years.[71] Native American debtors and those found guilty of petty crimes were also "bound out" as servants by the court for relatively lengthy periods. A Quinnipiac Indian named Anthony, for a debt of three pounds and seventeen shillings, was bound out to an Englishman for nine and a half months. An Indian woman named Hannah, convicted of stealing thirteen pounds from an Englishman, was sentenced to five years of servitude to him.[72] John Pfeiffer states that:

> Toward the end of the eighteenth century and beginning of the nineteenth there is apparently an increase in Native American indenture. Part of this was due to criticism leveled by English loyalists pointing out the hypocrisy of American colonists proclaiming their independence from England while simultaneously maintaining slaves. The use of indentured Native Americans instead of enslaved African Americans served to lessen the basis for faultfinding and reoriented the approach to "contractual" labor of a group of people who were treated by governmental policy as non-persons.[73]

## EIGHTEENTH- AND NINETEENTH-CENTURY INDIGENOUS COMMUNITIES

### Military Service

Indigenous people have always been loyal patriots, serving in all of America's wars in relatively large numbers, from the French and Indian Wars to Vietnam and the Iraqi and Afghanistan conflicts.[74] In the American Revolution, the Christian Indian community at Stockbridge, Massachusetts, formed an entirely Native American company of about forty men known as the "Indian Company."[75] Several of them were Connecticut Indians, including Schaghticoke tribal members Peter Mauwehew (Mauwee, misspelled on the Connecticut militia list as Warwehew), Daniel Succanox, and Thomas Warrups.[76] The Stockbridge Indian Company fought at the battles of Bunker Hill, Bennington, and White Plains, and were with Washington's army during the Philadelphia campaign.

Led by Wappinger tribal leader Captain Daniel Nimham, the Indian Company served as "elite shock troops engaged in scouting, skirmishing, spearheading assaults, and generally striking at the enemy at the best opportunity."[77] For this reason, Nimham and fourteen of his troops were ambushed and killed by the British at the Battle of Kingsbridge in the Bronx, New York, in 1778.[78]

So far 220 Connecticut Indians have been identified as serving in the colonial forces, likely a conservative number as research is ongoing, according to David Naumec.[79]

## INDIGENOUS PATRIOTS: THE STOCKBRIDGE INDIAN COMPANY

The Stockbridge militia, drawn from the local Native American communities of western Massachusetts and including Schaghticokes from Connecticut, fought on the side of the colonists in the American Revolution. While on patrol in New York the unit was ambushed by the British in what came to be known as the Stockbridge Massacre, told in this description of the battle based on a contemporary account.

*On August 1778, while serving on patrol in the Bronx, the Indian company lay in ambush for the enemy and very nearly captured Colonel Simcoe, the British commander. In retaliation, Simcoe set out to ambush the Indians and posted his men along a road near the lines. Some forty Indians from Stockbridge and other tribes under Captain Abraham Nimham fell into the trap on August 31. The ensuing fight was a bloody affair and the Indians fought bravely to the death, with Captain Nimham and fourteen of his warriors killed in hand to hand combat. Following the engagement, Captain Johann von Ewald of the Hessian (German) Jager Corps walked the field and observed the bodies of the Indians lying on the ground. In his journal he noted:*

"I was struck with astonishment over their sinewy and muscular bodies. Their strong, well-built, and healthy bodies were strikingly distinguished among the Europeans, with whom they lay mingled on the ground, and one could see by their faces that they had perished with resolution. . . . Their costume was a shirt of coarse linen down to the knees, long trousers also of linen down to the feet, on which they wore shoes of deerskin, and the head was covered with a hat made of bast [plant fiber]. Their weapons were a rifle or musket, a quiver with some twenty arrows, and a short battle-axe which they know how to throw very skillfully. Through the nose and in the ears they wore rings, and on their heads only the hair of the crown remained standing in a circle the size of a dollar piece, the remainder being shaved off bare. They pull out with pincers all the hairs of the beard, as well as those on all other parts of the body."*

A 1778 sketch of a member of the Stockbridge Indian Company, from the diary of Hessian soldier Johann von Ewald.

From this battlefield experience, the Hessian officer von Ewald later produced a watercolor of a member of the Indian Company. A stone monument in Van Cortlandt Park in the Bronx, New York, commemorates the valor and patriotism of the members of the Stockbridge Indian Company.

Note

a. Miles 2009, 51–52, citing the diary of Captain Johann von Ewald.

Connecticut's Indian veterans served in the militia, with state troops, and in the Continental line. They were represented in nearly every military service branch: Army Infantry, Dragoons (Cavalry), Navy, and Marine Corps. These men served in every major military engagement in which Connecticut troops were present, from Lexington to the siege at Yorktown. . . . Indian men served in front-line combat units, on land and at sea, and were listed among Connecticut's casualties in some of the most trying campaigns and fierce battles of the war.[80]

Even non-military tribal members aided the American war effort. Stockbridge Mohican Ken Mynter revealed:

During the bitter winter of 1777–78 at Valley Forge, the faithful Stockbridge and Oneidas had not forsaken their friends, as they delivered over 300 bushels of corn by snowshoe and packbasket through snow-clad forests when it was needed the most. This unselfish act is but another little noted fact in the history of the Revolution, left out of history books—too unimportant to mention![81]

The census of 2010 counted about 5.2 million Native Americans and Alaskans living in the United States, of which 153,000 were military veterans. That is 2.9 percent of the entire indigenous population![82]

## Economic and Social Survival Strategies

To escape the continual poverty, racism, and pressures to assimilate into white society, some Native Americans moved out of their tribes and assimilated into the African American or white cultures. Others chose to keep their tribal relationships, living in or near their tribal homelands—which whites continued to encroach on and sell illegally.[83] Even reservation lands shrank as white overseers illegally sold tribal lands. Of the 3,000-acre reserve granted to the western (Mashantucket) Pequot tribe in 1666, by 1856 this reservation had been reduced to only 213 acres.[84]

Indian people continued to adapt and peaceably resist the devastating changes the introduction of white farming and industry created in their natural and social environments.[85] Men often worked as farmhands for local white farmers. Both

Schaghticoke tribal member William H. Cogswell from Cornwall enlisted in the U.S. Army 5th Connecticut Volunteer Infantry at the onset of the Civil War at the age of 22. During his extraordinary military career he commanded and led white soldiers, reaching the rank of second lieutenant. The 5th Connecticut skirmished with Confederate forces throughout 1861 and 1862. Cogswell was captured behind enemy lines at Harrisonburg, Virginia, but was eventually released. Although official records state he was discharged on May 21, 1862, Cogswell was present with the 5th Connecticut in Virginia at the battles of Winchester on May 25 and Cedar Mountain on August 9. Cogswell immediately reenlisted in the 19th Connecticut Volunteer Infantry, known as the Litchfield County Regiment, and was promoted to first sergeant, a rank that gave him authority over four other sergeants, eight corporals, and nearly seventy enlisted men. He served in what became known as the Wilderness Campaign and by March 1864 was promoted to second lieutenant. Cogswell was with his company as the regiment participated in operations throughout the Shenandoah Valley and fought at the Battle of Cedar Creek, Virginia. In September in action near Winchester he received a leg wound, which required amputation, and he died on October 7, 1864. Cogswell was so well respected locally that residents purchased a large obelisk monument in his memory for his gravesite in North Cornwall.

men and women were basketmakers, selling baskets and other traditional wooden items to local farmers and storekeepers. An article in the *New Milford Times* in 1939 described a group of Schaghticoke basketmakers peddling their wares.

> It was a common thing to see a group of older Indians going along the road . . . loaded down with baskets of all descriptions, from strong oak bushel baskets, which the farmers like to own when picking corn or digging potatoes, to nice little ones made from very fine black ash splints.[86]

When farming (and thus commercial basketmaking) collapsed at the end of the nineteenth century, many Native people who still had reservations were forced to move to nearby cities to work in factories, in foundries, and on the docks. To support their families, Indian men joined the crews of whaling and fishing vessels, or became colliers and day laborers to white merchants and industrialists. Indian women served as laundresses and servants in white homes.[87] Yet they returned

John and Thomas Hamilton were Mohegan enlistees in World War I. Here they are shown with family members in front of the Hamilton home in New London, Connecticut, about December 1917. Bottom row, Lillia Mae Hamilton Crappo, Helen (Tom Hamilton's wife), Thomas Hamilton, Marion Ethel Hamilton. Second row, Alice Melinda Story Hamilton, her mother, Mary Tracy Fielding Story. Third row, Irving Labensky, Beatrice Harriet Hamilton Sword. Top row, John Ernest Hamilton. All are Mohegan except Tom's wife Helen and Labensky, who was married to a Mohegan woman.

regularly to the reservation community to visit kin, attend weddings, funerals, and powwows, and elect tribal leaders at political meetings.

## The Value of Christianity

Many Native Americans converted to Christianity as a survival strategy.[88] Becoming a Christian often had little to do with religion. Ministers sometimes paid Native Americans to attend church service; otherwise, the gospel societies in Europe who had hired them to convert Indians might withdraw their patronage. Those societies often provided goods such as blankets and clothing to indigenous parishioners. White ministers were authority figures who could protect their Indian congregation from discrimination and the illegal activities of their white neighbors. Ministers often formed schools where Christian Indians learned the English language and English law, enabling them to read deeds and other documents to better avoid becoming victims of fraud or paying a hefty fine for breaking a law about which they had no knowledge (such as working on Sunday). It was this education in the English language and law that allowed indigenous people to apply to the Connecticut General Assembly and courts for redress of illegal actions by whites, which they did frequently. The Public Records of Connecticut are full of petitions and memorials by Native American leaders on behalf of their communities, as well as by indigenous individuals acting on their own behalf.

Likely it was for these reasons that Schaghticoke and Mahikan leaders allowed their main villages—in Kent for the Schaghticoke (Pishgatikuk, which in Eastern Algonkian means at "the meeting of the waters,"[89] but mispronounced by the English as Scaticook or Schaghticoke), and in Sharon (Wechquadnach) for the Mahikans—to become Moravian mission villages in the early 1740s. Schaghticoke and Mahikan leaders thought English education an important survival strategy and strove to acquire village schools for adults and children. The Schaghticoke sachem Mawehue (Christianized Gideon Mauwee) and the Mahikan sachems Aaron Umpachenee and John Konkapot sent their sons to live with Englishmen to learn English language and convention.[90]

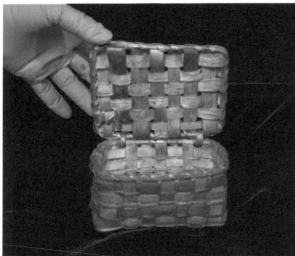

# NATIVE AMERICAN HEIRLOOMS

Lovely examples of Native American material culture have been passed down as heirlooms by both indigenous and white families. Many of these heirlooms, beautifully and artistically decorated, ended up in museum collections, such as at the Peabody Museum of Natural History at Yale University and at the Institute for American Indian Studies.

Such pieces include intricately beaded and embroidered buckskin clothing and pouches; polished wooden succotash bowls, often with carved animals for handles; a carved wooden doll; a carved wooden pipe; a carved wooden ball-head war club; and swabbed, painted, or stamped woodsplint baskets. Other perishable items recovered from Final Woodland and early post-contact contexts include incised and carved animal effigy combs; incised metal jewelry; pouches, moccasins, and clothing embroidered with dyed porcupine quills and moosehair; an incised antler knife handle; a wooden war club inlaid with wampum.

The polished wooden succotash bowl now at the Yale Peabody Museum of Natural History belonged to Anne Walkhead, a leader of the Niantic Indians whose homelands were centered about the Niantic River valley and adjacent coastlands of southeastern Connecticut. Another succotash bowl in the Yale collection, inlaid with white shell wampum beads, belonged to Lucy Tantaquidgeon, sister of Reverend Samson Occom.

Top, a baby rattle of ash splints filled with dried corn kernels, made by Paugussett basketmaker Molly Hatchett, circa 1770–1820, 3 inches high by 2.5 inches wide by 2.5 inches long (7.6 by 6.4 by 6.4 centimeters). Center, rectangular basket with hinged flat lid, wood splints, checkerwork, some splints swabbed red and green, length 5.25 inches (13 centimeters). Below, basket with loop handle, made by "Scatacoke" Indians living in New Milford, Connecticut.

Mercy Nonesuch Mathews (Niantic), holding one of the glass beaded pouches she made for the Anglo-American trade, in 1912; Henry Harris, a well-known basketmaker, gunsmith, and tinsmith. Harris married Schaghticoke Abigail Mauwee and resided on the Schaghticoke reservation in Kent, Connecticut.

Because white society equated Christianity with civilization, Christian Indian communities in the Northeast believed that they would therefore be exempt from white prejudice and governmental injustices such as President Andrew Jackson's racist anti-Indian removal policies of the 1830s, which forced thousands of Indian people from their ancient homelands in the East to relocate to marginal lands west of the Mississippi River.[91] According to Melissa Fawcett Zobel, it was not by chance that the Mohegan tribe concentrated in Uncasville built the Mohegan Church there in 1831. "Mohegans resisted Federal relocation by claiming to be already 'civilized' and 'christianized.' To support that claim, they founded a Christian church and school on their reservation in 1831."[92]

Reverend Eleazar Wheelock was a New Light evangelical minister who became the headmaster of Moore's Indian Charity School in Lebanon Crank (present-day Columbia, Connecticut) around 1754, where he taught Indian children.[93] At the urging of Wheelock, his former student Reverend Samson Occom, a Christian minister and eighteenth-century leader of the Mohegan Indians of eastern Connecticut, toured England to raise funds for the local Indian school.[94] Between February 16, 1766, and July 22, 1767, Occom presented over 300 sermons and raised over 12,000 pounds for Wheelock's Indian school, a huge sum in those days. Sadly, Wheelock broke his promise and used the money instead to establish Dartmouth College in New Hampshire. Wheelock had also promised to look after Occom's wife and seven children, but Occom returned from England to find them neglected and impoverished.[95]

These discouraging experiences led Occom to conclude that Indians were better off without white neighbors, so he founded the Christian Indian settlement of Brothertown in central New York.[96] The Oneida tribe provided the community

## AURELIUS PIPER OF THE GOLDEN HILL PAUGUSSETTS

Aurelius H. Piper, Sr. (1916–2008), was the hereditary chief of the Golden Hill Tribe of the Paugussett Indian Nation. The tribe retains a quarter-acre of its original 1659 reservation in Trumbull, Connecticut, as well as a 106-acre reservation in Colchester, provided by the state as recompense for the unlawful sale of the tribe's homeland by its government-appointed white overseers.

Also known as Chief Big Eagle, Piper was named chief in 1959 by his mother Ethel Sherman Piper (Chieftess Rising Star), the clan mother of the tribe. A World War II veteran of both the U.S. Navy and U.S. Army, Piper traveled extensively as an activist for Native American and minority rights, serving on many boards and commissions of advocate organizations, including the Minority Advisory Council of the Department of Aging. He visited Russia as part of a delegation of indigenous leaders and was a foreign correspondent for the De Kiva Society, an organization based in Belgium and The Netherlands that presents Indian rights cases before the International Human Rights Council. A traditional cultural leader, he was a founding member of the Native American Prison Project and served as spiritual adviser to Native Americans in prison. He founded and was a consultant and instructor in the Indian education program for the Bridgeport elementary schools. For his work Piper was named Chief of the Century by the Florida chapter of the White Buffalo Society.

Note
From "Aurelius Piper, Chief of Connecticut Tribe," Associated Press/Boston Globe, August 6, 2008; Smith 1985.

Chief Aurelius Piper of the Golden Hill Paugussetts, portrait painted by David R. Wagner in 1994.

## THE SCHAGHTICOKE RATTLESNAKE CLUB

Edson Charles Harris belonged to the Schaghticoke Rattlesnake Club, a group of tribal members and local non-Indian men that met each year to hunt snakes on the Schaghticoke reservation. Tribal members of the club would catch rattlesnakes and store them in pillowcases during the week before the annual club meeting, when the white members would come to the reservation to catch the snakes. On the day of the meet, the handlers would let loose the snakes at the top of Schaghticoke Mountain ahead of the others, ensuring an easy hunt that would guarantee a return hunt each year.

A survival strategy dating to the late nineteenth and early twentieth centuries, Rattlesnake Club activities helped the local indigenous economy (Indian women kept what was left of the food the whites brought for them to cook, and the Indians sold the visitors "souvenir" baskets) and enhanced political ties with important white men, especially newspapermen and politicians who made up most of the club's membership.

This reproduction of a postcard from 1908 shows Edson Charles Harris, eldest son of Schaghticoke leader James Harris, handling a live rattlesnake.

Schaghticoke basketmakers Rachel Mauwee and her sister Abigail Mauwee holding woodsplint baskets on the Schaghticoke reservation, about 1890-1894. With them are Abigail's son James Harris—a basketmaker, rattlesnake handler, minister, and the postman for Gaylordsville—and tribal leader Value Kilson, listed in the U.S. census as a collier.

with land, and the Mohegans were joined by members of several southern New England Indian tribes, including the Pequots, Nehantics (Niantics), Narragansetts, Mashpees, Tunxis, Wangunks, and Long Island Montauks.[97]

The Brothertowners were eventually forced out by whites who lusted for the improved lands of the hard-working Christian Indians. New York State took their land and gave it to Revolutionary War veterans as "bounty land" for their service. The new federal government removed the indigenous people in the area of Green Bay, Wisconsin, to settle the Brothertowners on their lands. It was not until the early twentieth century that the tribe received payment for its New York lands.[98] Today most of the 3,000 members of the Brothertown Indian Nation continue to reside in Wisconsin.

### The Inaccuracy of Local Town Histories

Local historians in the nineteenth and early twentieth centuries misrepresented or ignored the Indian communities around them, instead persuading the public that their Indian neighbors were extinct.[99] Local writers portrayed the colonial period as one of continued economic and social disintegration for Native societies. Tribal members were dismissed as the few ignorant, barbaric, alcoholic, and lazy individuals who were left behind when the rest of their tribe either moved west or died out, to eventually fade into oblivion, leaving the township to its industrious and courageous white citizens who brought civilization to New England. To support their false assumptions, these writers used the then popular notion of "racial purity" to brand their contemporary indigenous counterparts of mixed blood as no longer Indian. The Native American survival strategy of adaptation was de-

At left, one of John Elwell's daughters, possibly Mary Matilda ("Til") Elwell Merril, of the Lighthouse community, photographed early in the twentieth century. Til was born in 1849 or 1850 at the Lighthouse and died in Burlington in 1929; in her later years she described herself as "the last of the Lighthouse tribe." Her father and grandfather (Joseph Elwell) were listed as basketmakers on the 1850 U.S. census. At right is Ray Ellis (in 1991), a seventh-generation descendant of Narragansett Indian James Chaugham (founder and leader of the original Lighthouse community) and his white wife, Molly Barber.

scribed as assimilation and the "adaptees" as non-Indian as well.[100] Ironically, indigenous people traditionally had no concept of blood quota; it was a white concept. Foreign Native Americans as well as non-Indians were frequently adopted into indigenous communities. Russell Handsman and Trudie Lamb Richmond wrote:

> That Native Americans sometimes consciously decided to continue living in their ancestral homelands is a fact seldom mentioned in town histories or in the writings of colonial historians today. . . . Yet even as . . . homelands were appropriated, surveyed, divided, and fenced, some native people resisted by making themselves less visible, resettling their families and communities beyond the fringes of colonial settlements. . . . The existence of such historic communities cannot be documented with any certainty from the records and maps of the colonialists. Similarly material signs of their presence are either unrecognized or misinterpreted today by those who continue to assume that Native Americans were not an integral part of New England's social landscape after the early 1700s. Yet archaeological sites representing just such . . . settlement have already been excavated and can be used to aid in the recognition of further evidence.[101]

## POOTATUCK WIGWAM SITE AND OTHER EIGHTEENTH- AND NINETEENTH-CENTURY INDIGENOUS COMMUNITIES

One such site was the Pootatuck Wigwam site in Southbury, which was the locus of a seventeenth- and eighteenth-century Pootatuck tribal community. It contained indigenous clay pottery fragments and stone tools as well as European lead-glazed red earthenware and salt-glazed stoneware, European gunflints, and brass and copper kettles that had been cut into pendants.[102] Made from high quality European flints, the gunflints may have been reworked as scrapers by the Indians.

The reworked gunflints and kettle pendants are good examples of indigenous recycling of European items into traditional Native economic activities and aesthetic objects, and show active Indian participation in local Anglo social relations. It was the same among Pequot communities in Ledyard.[103] The historic Oliver Ellsworth site in Bloomfield also contained indigenous tools made by chipping European glass and European flint, another example of Native American presence and adaptation of European items to improve indigenous technology and economy.[104]

Archaeological excavations of Mohegan sites in Uncasville from the late eighteenth and nineteenth centuries show that although most artifacts were imports to North America, tribal consumers chose those whose design elements resembled traditional Mohegan cultural symbols. For example, they chose European ceramics whose hand-painted designs resembled traditional Mohegan basketry and pottery motifs that held cultural meaning for community members. Additionally, these items were being used in a uniquely Mohegan habitation setting.[105]

Post-contact Indians were not merely passive recipients in relationships with whites. They acted and reacted to events—adapting, accommodating, and sometimes resisting—rather than assimilating. Recent ethnohistorical research also has uncovered oral and archival evidence for a continued and widespread Native American presence in nineteenth-century southern New England. According to archaeologists Edward Bell and Dr. Brona Simon, these new discoveries

> disclose the colonialist reproductions of the mythic trope of the "disappeared Indians" that concealed genocidal eradication, the appropriation of land by force, fraud, and economic machinations, and which are responsible for planting and reproducing romantic notions of the "noble savage" and other and racist, ethnocentric inaccuracies about historical and contemporary Native American people and their cultures.[106]

Many indigenous communities continued to exist throughout the nineteenth century—some through to the present—on-reservation and off-reservation. Often these were refuges for people of color in general—including families from different tribes as well as free black families—who banded together to survive in a racist, class-conscious world that treated them all like foreigners and second-class citizens. (Connecticut State Statutes, for example, discussed its Native American residents in a section entitled "Aliens and Indians," which was not changed until the last quarter of the twentieth century.) Among the off-reservation communities are the Lighthouse community in what is today Peoples' State Forest in Barkhamsted;[107] the mainly Schaghticoke community centered about Second Hill Street in New Milford; the Danbury Indian communities around Beaver Brook Mountain and Great Plain, Neversink Pond, Joe's Hill, and Mill Plain Pond (now called Lake Kenosia);[108] the Paugussett-Schaghticoke community of Chusetown

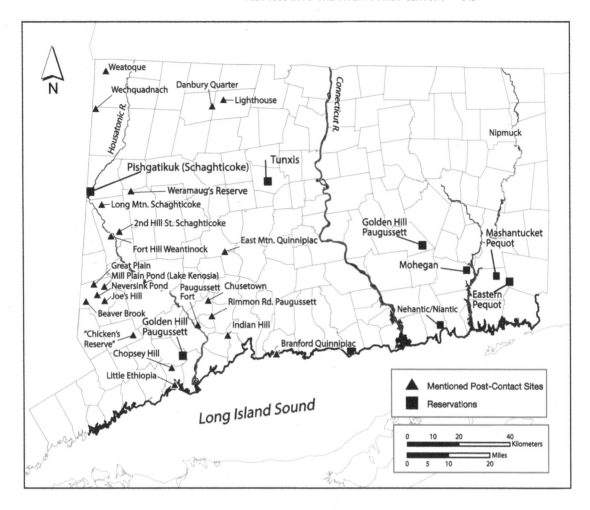

near the Tingue Dam falls in downtown Seymour; the Paugussett "Indian Settlement" off Rimmon Road, now northern Ansonia, and the Potatuck-Paugussett "Chickens Reserve" in Redding near John Read's Lonetown Manor;[109] the community on Indian Hill in Orange, supposedly formed by Kent Schaghticoke tribal members in 1776;[110] and the mainly Paugussett Little Ethiopia (Liberia) near the Bridgeport docks.[111]

Despite the efforts of archaeologists and social historians, the public tends to believe inaccurate portrayals of Native histories. Few people have any conception of the continuity of local Native communities, Native preservation of cultural traditions and group identities, and the longtime resistance of Native people to the intensive, continuous discrimination and detribalization efforts of local and federal governments and non-Native individuals. This book aims to change all that. As Cree-Salish-Kootenai author D'Arcy McNickle wrote: "Only the Indians seemed unwilling to accept oblivion as an appropriate final act in the New World drama. . . . They lost, but were never defeated."[112]

Known post-contact archaeology sites and major eighteenth- and nineteenth-century non-reservation indigenous communities mentioned in the text, along with present-day reservations. Many more early communities are only beginning to be discovered.

Structure 1 at the Lighthouse site excavation, one of the house foundations at the settlement. It has no cellar and the floor was supported by stone piers (shown in the photograph). Dr. Kenneth Feder describes these houses as stone-lined, small, and irregular, and a few had only small cellar holes of a few square meters with no stone lining. These remains are quite distinct from those of neighboring white farmers in size, shape, and construction. They are good examples of contemporary differences in material culture among groups of different ethnicity and socioeconomic status. Bottom, map of the Central Connecticut State University field school excavations at the Lighthouse site, where a mixed community of Native Americans, blacks, and a few lower-class whites supported themselves with basketmaking, charcoal manufacture, and subsistence farming.

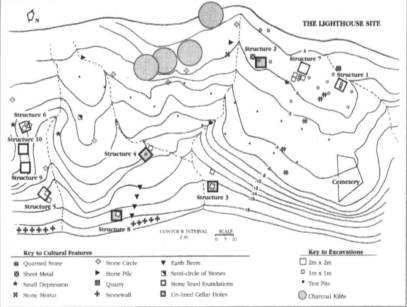

THE LIGHTHOUSE SITE

Structure 2
Structure 7
Structure 1
Structure 6
Structure 10
Structure 4
Structure 9
Structure 3
Cemetery
Structure 5
Structure 8

CONTOUR INTERVAL
2 m

SCALE
0 5 10

**Key to Cultural Features**

| | | |
|---|---|---|
| # Quarried Stone | Stone Circle | ▼ Earth Berm |
| Sheet Metal | ▶ Stone Pile | Semi-circle of Stones |
| ★ Small Depression | Quarry | Stone lined foundations |
| ✷ Stone Mortar | + Stonewall | Un-lined Cellar Holes |

**Key to Excavations**

□ 2m x 2m
1m x 1m
• Test Pits
Charcoal Kilns

## NATIVE CONNECTICUT IN THE TWENTIETH AND TWENTY-FIRST CENTURIES

Things did not get better for Connecticut Indian communities during the twentieth century. Like other Connecticut residents, they felt the debilitating effects of the two world wars and the Great Depression. White antipathy from the Indian wars and skirmishes in the American West and Southwest in the late 1800s, exacerbated by local newspaper accounts of massacres that reinforced negative Indian stereotypes, continued to hound New England Native people.[113]

Their state-appointed overseers continued to usurp the authority of tribal leaders, exerting control over reservation resources and residents. Government continued its efforts to assimilate them by banning indigenous cultural traditions. Melissa Fawcett Zobel described the situation at Mohegan in the early 1900s.

> Children in school were expected to learn English and forget all about their Indian cultural background. If some of the older women . . . were speaking and some of the children appeared, they would cease talking because they didn't want the children to be punished for learning the Mohegan language.[114]

About this time, Connecticut began to replace the individual overseers with an institutional one, the state's Park and Forest Commission, with the idea of turning the reservations into state parks. In its discussion of the Schaghticoke reservation in Kent, the 1926 Report of the State Park and Forest Commission noted that it "is not of course a State park, but could apparently be made so by an act of the Assembly."[115] This intention was expressed in a poem penned by Fred Lane, Schaghticoke overseer from 1905 to 1914:

> They saw their weakness resigned to the fate
> gave up their struggle and applied to the state . . .
> Thus my friends they will leave their mark
> The reservation will become a State Park.[116]

### Detribalization and Discrimination as Usual

Reservation houses were allowed to deteriorate.[117] Many lacked running water and electricity. When a tribal member died or left the reservation the house was pulled down. Tribal members seeking to return were told there was no available housing. Reservation visitors had to be authorized by the overseer and had to be off the reservation by nightfall. Any meetings or festivities also had to be approved by the overseer. No economic endeavors could be undertaken except farming, which could not have been very profitable given the marginal nature of reservation lands in Connecticut. The state attempted to force tribal members to pay for hunting and fishing licenses.[118] When tribal members refused to leave reservation lands, despite poverty and stringent government restrictions, in 1941 the Park and Forest Commission was replaced as overseer by the Welfare Department. In her genealogical report on the Schaghticoke tribe, Kathleen April relates:

The one hundredth birthday celebration in 1900 of "Aunt Icy," a member of the Indian community at Indian Hill in Orange, Connecticut. According to local history, around 1776 members of the Scaticook tribe moved from Kent to Orange. Icy, who lived to be 102, may have had a Niantic mother and a Paugussett father. Left to right, standing, Mrs. Dora Shillinglaw, Frank Peck, Minnie Clark, Theron Alling, Henry Oviatt, John Oviatt, a grandson, William Russell, Dwight Alling, Elizur Russell. Seated, Mrs. Fields Andrew, little Fields, Elias Clark, Edith Edmundson, Billy Sharpe (grandson), Mrs. Sharpe, Mrs. Brien Oviatt (Aunt Icy), Polly Jackson (daughter), Mrs. William Russell, Mrs. Elizur Russell, Mrs. Dwight Alling, Mrs. Wade, Mrs. Luke Clark. On the ground, Mrs. Leonard Andrew, Beulah Russell, Ruby Russell, Inez Russell, Lottie Peck.

Tribal elders and chiefs found repeated obstructions first by the Park and Forest Commission, and then the Welfare Department to keep them from returning to live on the Reservation. . . . Eventually, this uncomfortable relationship under the Welfare Department was named a "hand out, palm up" attitude that was abhorrent. . . . Authority over the reservation lands had to change in the eyes of the [Schaghticoke] leadership and the Tribe.[119]

Welfare's authority over tribal reservations was a great stigma, because it gave the impression that Native people were receiving handouts from the state. They were not. Each of the five tribes had had individual tribal funds since at least the early 1800s, money earned from rented or sold tribal lands or reservation resources such as cordwood and charcoal.[120] These funds, controlled by the overseer, were used to care for the elderly and sick.

Healthy tribal members supported themselves and their families. Often this was not possible with the meager reservation resources and the scarcity of local job opportunities after the demise of farming. Most men had to move to the cities where factory and foundry work, or coastal employment at the docks or on ships, was available. This is why there were only a few elderly people living on Connecticut's reservations by the middle of the twentieth century, not because there were no Indians. There is plentiful documentation to show that the many off-reservation tribal members continued contacts with those living on the reservation and regularly returned for social gatherings, political meetings, weddings, and funerals. In other words, they remained in tribal relations.

The Connecticut Welfare Department continued state efforts to terminate its Indian tribes and take their remaining homelands with its support in 1953

for Senate Bill 502, "An Act Concerning Indians," which attempted to sell tribal homelands.[121] In a Senate hearing, indigenous people heard themselves characterized as "a problem" and "a burden to the Welfare Department."[122] Native American leaders lobbied against the bill, which would not only turn their ancient reservations into parcels of individual proprietorship, identical to their non-Native neighbors, but also undermine traditional beliefs and leadership. The *New Haven Register* reported: "State welfare authorities had asked the lawmakers to order such a sale. But the 31 Indians living on those lands, aided by friendly legislators, bitterly attacked the measure at a public hearing."[123]

Dr. Russell Handsman, former director of research at the Institute for American Indian Studies, clearly articulated the anti-tribal, anti-Indian basis for the bill.

> The real intent of the bill's architects was more obvious to others who attended the public hearing at the state capitol in March 1953. If passed and signed into law, it would disperse communally-owned lands reserved long ago for native peoples; some would be sold at public auction while others would be incorporated into state forests and parks. The cultural assimilation of indigenous Native Americans would thus be hastened. As the hearing ended, the bill's supporters remained seated. The 25 or so in opposition stood, joining the Schaghticoke, Golden Hill Paugussett, and Mashantucket Pequot peoples at the rear of the room. They had listened silently as others dismissed their heritage, declaring their presence on ancestral lands was no longer relevant, affordable, or meaningful. Word arrows heard yet again.[124]

The bill was voted down. Eastern Pequot Marcia Jones Flowers referred to the infamous Senate Bill 502 when she made the following statement; she was tribal chairwoman at the time.

> The Eastern Pequot Tribal Nation never detribalized, unlike other tribes who are now federally recognized. Even . . . though the state tried to detribalize

Frank Cogswell, chief of the Schaghticoke tribe from the 1930s until his death in 1954, wearing his regalia during one of the tribe's powwows. His headdress was given to him by western Indian members of a pan-Indian organization. The blanket, featuring Woodland white-tailed deer, was likely made by his older brother William Cogswell, a former chief of the tribe and a basketmaker and weaver. His staff features locally obtained turkey tail feathers. At right, the Cogswell family house on the Schaghticoke reservation circa 1950. The enlarged section of the porch in the inset shows that woodsplint baskets were still in use.

Traditional powwows, such as this one held about 1939 or 1940 on the Schaghticoke reservation, were often co-sponsored by pan-Indian movements after passage of the Indian Reorganization Act of 1934. Governor Raymond Baldwin of Connecticut spoke at the 1939 powwow, which was held in honor of American Indian Day in Connecticut. The event was sponsored by the Eastern Algonquian Indian Federation. Indigenous leaders, dancers, and craftspeople from all over the United States attended, including those from the Plains tribes, who camped in their teepees (as they do at powwows today). Their teepees and Plains-style headdresses are not traditional to southern New England, although Western Indians sometimes gave portions of their regalia to Native New Englanders.

us as recently as 1953 . . . we resisted. *How can the state of Connecticut claim a tribe isn't a tribe when they were attempting to detribalize it?*[125]

That is a very good question.

By the 1960s, change was in the air. The atmosphere created by public opposition to the Vietnam War began to stir social sympathy for tribal peoples. Native American leadership took advantage of the situation, promoting pan-Indian alliances, and the national Red Power movement emerged in the 1970s. Red Power also came to Connecticut.

In the late 1960s, Schaghticoke Chief Irving "Ernie" Harris united the local tribes in a concentrated lobbying effort aimed at state politicians. This effort resulted in 1973 legislation that removed the Welfare Department as tribal overseer and created a Connecticut Indian Affairs Council to supervise indigenous concerns within the state. Members included government appointees and representatives from each of the five state-recognized tribes. The Connecticut Department of Environmental Protection became the new institutional overseer, however, so state-recognized tribes still do not have complete control over their reservations and resources (PA 73-660, SHB 9191). In that same year the state legislature required an "Indian" to have at least one-eighth Indian blood from one of the five state-recognized tribes (CGS 47-63).[126]

## Federal Recognition and Casinos

Incredibly, even though state tribes have been consistently recognized by the Colony and State of Connecticut for more than 350 years, only two—the Mohegan and Mashantucket Pequot—are eligible to receive federal grants for health

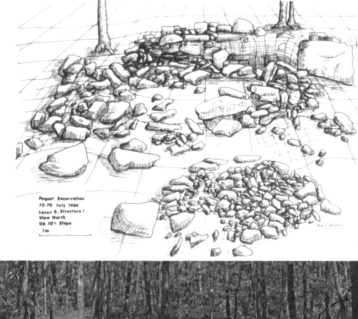

Dry-laid foundation of an eighteenth-century Pequot house at the Mashantucket Ledyard site 72-70. Above, scale drawing of the house remains.

programs for their members, higher education for their children, or housing for their elders, because those grants require federal recognition. These are the reasons tribes want federal recognition, not casinos.

Casinos are a white man's institution. To produce a federal recognition petition meeting the rigid requirements of the U.S. Bureau of Indian Affairs, a tribe must spend millions of dollars to fund the professional genealogists, historians, anthropologists, office staff, and lawyers necessary to gather and prepare the proper documents proving indigenous genealogy, community, and political leadership from initial European settlement in the tribal homelands to the present—an awesome requirement to fulfill, particularly for a nation whose history has been preserved mainly through oral transmission!

To accomplish this a tribe needs wealthy white backers, and it is the backers

Several members of the Schaghticoke tribe in front of the Value Kilson house along Schaghticoke Road on their reservation early in the twentieth century. Tribal leader Value Kilson is standing in the center background next to his grandson Earl Kilson. In the left foreground is Bertha Kilson Riley (holding a child) and Mary Kilson. Bottom left, Value Kilson attempting to remove graves from the second Schaghticoke burying ground before it was flooded by construction of the dam at Bull's Bridge. Bottom right, the later razing of the Kilson reservation home.

who seek the casino as debt payment. Of course, if a tribal casino is successful enough the tribe can eventually buy out its backer and become sole reaper of its profits. Such is the history of the Mohegan Sun casino and the Mashantucket Pequot casino complex Foxwoods. Their successful casinos provide economic opportunities for tribal members previously forced to move off the reservation to find work to support their families. Off-reservation members are now able to return to their homelands, strengthen community ties, promote tribal history, and preserve cultural identity. As the Mohegan tribe notes on its Web site, the casino "has allowed a number of Tribal members who have had to move away the chance to come home. The casino has provided a stable economic foundation for the future. Moreover, it has helped our efforts to preserve our culture, to strengthen our identity, to educate our members and launch new business initiatives."[127]

The tribe also reported that "gaming tribes within the state contribute *25% of all slot revenues to the state, making them the second largest contributor to Connecticut's revenue after the federal government.* In 2005, this amounted to $217,193,576. Since inception the Tribe has contributed $1,479,277,026 to the state of Connecticut."[128]

An ironic situation, because the anti-federal recognition activities of some

Steve Kelley © 1994—*San Diego Union Tribune*, Copley News Service.

governmental leaders is supposedly due to their anti-gambling—and, therefore, anti-casino—stance. Is not the state lottery a form of gambling?

Fifty-eight years after the demise of Senate Bill 502, Connecticut's tribes find themselves in a similar situation, with some politicians and private individuals once again promoting anti-tribal measures that include denouncement of tribal identity, requests for tribal termination, and appeals to positive findings for federal recognition.[129] Is the federal recognition process merely a tool for achieving the political extinction of tribes? Dr. Margaret Bruchac, an anthropologist and Abenaki, asks:

> Why is federal recognition now the marker of authenticity for Native communities? Why is it that so many western tribes, having been removed to reservations, have had such an easy time being recognized by the descendants of those who removed them, while so many eastern tribes have had to fight for their reputations as Indians? . . . . Why is it that towns and state officials in Connecticut flipped out at the prospect that the Schaghticoke and eastern Pequot might be recognized as sovereign tribes within that state? How can the American public and government officials find it so terrifying to acknowledge the persistence of Native tribes east of the Mississippi? I would suggest that federal recognition, in its current structural form, has little to do with Native authenticity in a deep indigenous sense, and everything to do

with federal power and selective constructions of the history of marginalized ethnic peoples. For generations, white historians have been busily scripting heroic narratives of their forefathers' wars with the Indians, while hoping that the Indians would eventually disappear, or be assimilated. In the modern world, that disappearance can also be accomplished bloodlessly by recourse to a single set of fixed federal criteria, heavily reliant upon paper documentation written and archived by non-Native observers. The delays in federal recognition cases (with an average waiting period of 14 years), and the denials based on spotty documentation, are achieving a de-tribalization akin to that practiced in the mid-twentieth century.[130]

## Enduring Traditions

The very brief synopsis here of the past 400 years of indigenous history does little justice to specific tribal histories. To document the many social injustices, economic travails, and political obstacles heaped on post-contact indigenous communities, and their members' often courageous actions to continue tribal relations and keep alive their traditions, would require another entire book. After 375 years of continual and intensive governmental attempts at detribalization and cultural assimilation, five of the many tribal communities that once peopled colonial Connecticut still exist today, continuously recognized, first by the Connecticut Colony and then the State of Connecticut, as sovereign, independent nations: the Schaghticoke tribe, with a reservation in Kent; the Golden Hill Paugussetts, with reservations in Trumbull and Colchester (the latter given by the state to make up for lands illegally taken from the former); the Mohegan tribe near Uncasville; the Mashantucket Pequots near Ledyard; and the Eastern Pequot Tribal Nation in North Stonington. The Mashantucket and Mohegan tribes are also recognized by the U.S. government. (There are, however, several other extant tribal entities in Connecticut that are not recognized by either the state or federal government.)

In 1989 the state legislature adopted Public Act 80-368, which recognized these five tribes as self-governing tribal entities with powers and duties to their members and reservations.[131] In a 1993 response to anonymous questions on Indian land claims, the then senior attorney in Connecticut's Office of Legislative Research admitted that state statutes recognized these five Indian tribes.

> State statutes recognize the state's indigenous tribes as self-governing entities possessing powers and duties over tribal members and reservations. The law specifies the power to: (1) determine tribal membership and residency on reservation land; (2) determine the tribal form of government; (3) regulate trade and commerce on the reservation; (4) make contracts, and (5) determine tribal leadership in accordance with tribal practice and usage. The tribes are the Schaghticoke, Paucatuck Eastern Pequot, Mashantucket Pequot, Mohegan, and Golden Hill Paugussett (Connecticut General Statutes Sec. 47-59A).[132]

In November 1996 the governor issued an official statement designating November Native American Month in the state of Connecticut. That statement

## INDIGENOUS WOMEN

American Indian women had a much better quality of life than their colonial and early federalist white counterparts. They could participate in political meetings and hold political office. English records mention several New England "squa" sachems like Shaumpishuh, *sunksquaw* (female leader) of a Quinnipiac band living at Menunkatuck in present Guilford.[a] Anglo-American women in the United States could not vote before passage of the 36th Amendment in 1920.

A few of the many women leaders and activists among Connecticut's indigenous communities. Clockwise from upper left: Educator and author Trudie Lamb Richmond, former chair of the Schaghticoke Tribal Nation; Theresa Bell, former executive director of the Mashantucket Pequot Museum and Research Center; author and Schaghticoke tribal administrator Paulette Crone-Morange (1943–2004), the first female chair of the Connecticut Indian Affairs Council; Dale Carson (Abenaki, in traditional dress), museum consultant and a food columnist for the Indian Country Today Media Network and *Indian Life;* Mohegan medicine woman, scholar, and author Gladys Iola Tantaquidgeon (1899–2005), whose many honors include honorary doctorates and the National Organization for Women Harriet Tubman Award; and Schaghticoke storyteller Erin Lamb Meeches, a highly regarded traditional dancer.

An indigenous woman could also pursue "careers" such as medical practitioner, trader, and merchant (peddling baskets, carved wooden goods, and beadwork to storekeepers and throughout the countryside). She owned property and could inherit. In fact, all of a family's material goods, except for the husband's clothing and hunting and fishing equipment, belonged to the wife. The indigenous woman also had complete control of her children, who belonged to their mother's lineage and clan. In neighboring Anglo-American communities the husband owned and controlled everything in the home, including his wife and children.

Native American women could divorce their husbands, and frequently did so. Anglo-American women could not, and if they tried they would find themselves socially dead and economically impoverished (which would likely lead to physical death, because they had never learned how to be self-supporting outside of wifely duties). John Sergeant, the first minister to the Stockbridge Mahikans in the mid-1700s, reported:

> The parting of man and wife (saith he [an indigenous man]) is a very common thing among them. In-deed it us'd rarely to happen that a married couple live together till they are old. And as they use but little ceremony in the business of marriage, so they make a less thing of parting. In such a case 'tis their law that the children and all the household stuff belong to the woman; and indeed everything else but the gun, for that is the man's livelihood. The man, according to their custom, has no right to the children, any more than any other person whatever.[b]

Indigenous women were highly regarded as important contributing members to the economic, sociopolitical, and spiritual well-being of their tribal societies. They were always welcomed into a community. In the words of another European, from the 1600s: "If a woman have a bad husband, or cannot affect him, and there be war or opposition between that and any other people, she will run away from him to the contrary party and there live, where they never come unwelcome, *for where are most women there be greatest plenty.*"[c]

Notes

a. Menta 1988; also, Sachem Shaumpishuh is mentioned frequently in Menta's 2003 book on the Quinnipiac tribe.

b. Sergeant 1735, quoted in Hopkins 1753, 45.

c. Winslow 1623, 364, quoted in Karr 1999, 58; emphasis added.

recognized the five remaining tribes by name as individual political bodies with authority over their respective peoples and reservations.

> Whereas, Connecticut further recognizes that the indigenous tribes, the Schaghticoke, the Paucatuck Eastern Pequot, the Mashantucket Pequot, the Mohegan and the Golden Hill Paugussett are self governing entities possessing powers and duties over tribal members and reservations.[133]

These official statements from the state's legislative and executive branches are less than twenty years old, yet some of the state's politicians have apparently already forgotten them. Nevertheless, Connecticut's tribal peoples continue to endure as they have for thousands of years, as their leaders continue to fight for justice and the right to dwell in and control their sacred homelands.

The oldest reservation house on the Mashantucket Pequot reservation, where the Plouffe family resided. A typical southeastern Connecticut reservation home, the original one-room house on the left is from the early eighteenth century, with a later two-story addition attached.

## SOME FINAL THOUGHTS

Connecticut's Native American tribal peoples have a long, rich, and sophisticated cultural heritage. Their ancestors had important, complex industries in stone, bone, antler, clay, leather, fur, plant materials, and wood, and their everyday lives were—and still are—entwined in a rich cultural fabric of artistic creativity, comprehensive oral literature, and sophisticated spirituality. Archaeological findings depict Connecticut's indigenous communities as much more diversified than once thought. This diversity occurred in all time periods and in various segments of their cultures—particularly in their economy, technology and settlement organization, which are particularly prominent because of the material remains in the archaeological record. But there are distinctions in other cultural subsystems as well.

Throughout their lengthy history, the state's American Indian peoples had, and continue to have, strong, viable cultures intensely articulated with the natural environment. Their long-term cultural continuance, as shown by the archaeological remains, as well as their tribal folklore and sacred stories, reflects their harmonious relationships with nature. These cultures were not static, however. The archaeological record shows stylistic changes and technological improvements. Yet the economic-technological-ecological framework on which their physical survival depended remained basically the same until it was disrupted by European colonization.

This continuity was not for lack of outside contacts. The presence of Adena and Hopewell material from the Midwest, and exotic raw materials and items whose sources lay in the Mid-Atlantic, interior New York, Boston Basin, and points north show that southern New England groups were not isolated from outside influences. Conversely, goods produced by Connecticut's Native Americans, such as shell beads, were traded throughout northeastern North America.

## WHAT DOES A NATIVE AMERICAN LOOK LIKE?

It is impossible to describe what a Native American looks like. Today's Native Americans are descended from more than three hundred distinct nations (also known as tribes) from across the North American continent. Just as the appearance of someone from a southern European nation can be very different from that of a northern European individual, so too are Native Americans different. A person with Eastern Woodland heritage will have different physical characteristics than people from the Plains, Southwest, or Northwest Coast regions.

Indigenous peoples living along the Atlantic coast were the first to feel the ill effects of European colonialism, hundreds of years before the Plains Indians ever saw a white man. By the nineteenth century, eastern populations were so depleted by the consequences of European war, disease, and poverty caused by land losses and the destruction of their traditional economy that for a tribe to survive, many of its members were forced to marry outside their communities.

The first choice in such marriages was to take a spouse from another Indian tribe, but these too had been dangerously depopulated. Intermarriage with non-American Indians became common, and many of today's Native Americans therefore may have African, European, or Asian features. Many persons of mixed ancestry left their tribes and joined the non-Native communities of their spouses, but many did not, remaining in tribal relations. Their descendants continue their indigenous traditions and beliefs even as United States citizens and participants in the greater American society today.

Note

Adapted from the brochure "What Does a Native American Look Like?" Institute for American Indian Studies, 2011.

Having achieved balance with nature, local Native Americans simply had little need for major change. Ecologically stable societies flourished undisturbed until the traumatic effects of European contact eroded, and in many cases destroyed, the ancient equilibrium between Native Americans and their environments.

Yet even the deleterious effects of disease, discrimination, and economic practices failed to extinguish the indigenous presence. Thousands of Native American descendants live in Connecticut, and many belong to one of the five state-recognized tribes whose roots extend deep into the time before Europeans arrived. This book was written to introduce the non-indigenous public to the rich histories and congruent sociocultural concepts that helped maintain social, economic, and political balance in indigenous communities. Lauding the ethics and cultural practices of southern New England's indigenous peoples, who referred to themselves as the Ninnimissinuok, a southern New England indigenous term meaning "people,"[134] archaeologist Edward Bell urges us to consider these social strategies as we seek ways to reduce "human-induced, catastrophic impacts" plaguing our contemporary societies.

Ninnimissinuok social mechanisms and ethical principles to reduce social tensions, resolve conflicts and restore losses, including the eventual full social integration of captives through adoption; ascribing honored social roles to experienced elders and power rather than disdain to "otherness"; agreeing to authority by earned or ascribed rank; leadership by consent and decision-making by consensus; enforcing humility through embarrassment and hu-mor; social obligation networks created through reciprocity and marital resi-dence patterns; the material reflections and embodiments of their personal and cultural identities, cosmology and ritual; "language and intimate posses-sion," "the phenomenology of usufruct" and, their "open, political and social boundaries" all bear attention.[135]

# Notes

INTRODUCTION: ARCHAEOLOGY IN CONNECTICUT

Epigraph: Keegan and Keegan 1999, ii–iii.

1. Cassedy 1992, 1998; McBride 1984a; McBride, Dewar, and Wadleigh 1979, 1980; McBride and Soulsby 1989.

2. Lavin 1985a.

3. Stiles 1783, 411–412.

4. *Colombian Weekly Register,* New Haven, Conn., November 2, 1867.

5. "State Items, New London County," *Hartford Daily Courant,* Hartford, Conn., August 28, 1871.

6. McMullen 1994, 123–150.

7. *The Connecticut Magazine,* vol. 5, 1899, 588.

8. An Act for the Preservation of American Antiquities (34 Stat. 225, 16 U.S.C. 431–433).

9. MacCurdy 1914.

10. Ibid. 518–519, 522.

11. Cornelius Osgood to Richard S. Lull, October 30, 1931, Peabody Museum of Natural History Records, Yale University, ca. 1873–1959, RU 471, YRG: 33-A, Series II, Box 7, Folder 93. Manuscripts and Archives, Yale University Library.

12. Rainey 1932–1933.

13. Ibid.

14. Ibid.

15. Quoted in Reid 2006.

16. Lavin 1985b.

17. Although an amateur archaeologist, Dr. Swigart, a graduate of Yale University (1954), received a master of science degree from the Yale Conservation School and earned a doctorate in Conservation and Education from Columbia Pacific University.

18. "From 7 to 400 in Seven Years," 1972.

19. Swigart 1974.

20. Salwen 1966, 1970, 1978; Salwen and Ottesen 1972; Salwen and Mayer 1978; Lavin and Salwen 1983; Rothschild and Wall 1991–1992.

21. Salwen 1969.

22. Kra 1984, 3.

23. An Act to Establish a Program for the Preservation of Additional Historic Properties Throughout the Nation, and for Other Purposes (P.L. 89–665; 80 Stat. 915; 16 U.S.C. 470); Archaeological and Historic Preservation Act (P.L. 93-291 [amends P.L. 86-523]; 16 USC 469–469c).

24. Kra 1984, 3.

25. Feder 1981.

26. McBride, Dewar, and Wadleigh 1979, 1980; McBride and Dewar 1981; McBride 1984a, 1984b.

27. See, for example, Harper, Clouette, and Harper 1999.

28. ArchNet, WWW Virtual Library, Archaeology, Archaeological Research Institute, Arizona State University, http://archnet.asu.edu.

29. Juli 1981, 1992; Weinstein 2011.

30. Silliman 2008.

31. Mohegan Archaeological Field School 2011, brochure, www.sha.org/documents/Mohegan2011.pdf.

32. Keegan and Keegan 1999, i.

33. Feathers 2008.

34. R. E. Taylor, "Radiocarbon Dating," AccessScience, 2008, © McGraw-Hill Companies, www.accessscience.com; Reimer 2009; Michael Balter, 2010 January 15, "Radiocarbon Daters Tune Up Their Time Machine," *ScienceNOW Daily News,* http://sciencenow.sciencemag.org/cgi/content/full/2010/115/3; Daniel Forrest, personal communication, January 21, 2011; Radiocarbon Dating, University of Oxford School of Archaeology, www.arch.ox.ac.uk/C.html.

35. Henri D. Grissino-Mayer, "Dendrochronology," AccessScience, 2008, © McGraw-Hill Companies, www.accessscience.com.

36. James H. Schulman, "Thermoluminescence," AccessScience, 2008, © McGraw-Hill Companies, www.accessscience.com; "Luminescence Dating," 2010, University of Oxford School of Archaeology, www.arch.ox.ac.uk/L.html; "Luminescence Dating, How It Works," 2010, University of Oxford School of Archaeology, www.arch.ox.ac.uk/how-L.html.

37. Lavin 1983; Lavin and Prothero 1987; Luedtke 1987, 1993; Prothero and Lavin 1990; Calogero 2002; Boulanger 2006.

38. Prothero and Lavin 1990; Lavin and Prothero 1992.

39. E.g., Prothero and Lavin 1990; Calogero 1991; Calogero and Philpotts 1995, 2006.

40. Jeffrey M. Osborn, "Palynology," AccessScience, 2008, © McGraw-Hill Companies, www.accessscience.com.

## 1. CONNECTICUT'S EARLIEST SETTLERS

Epigraph: Aupaumut 1987, 28–29.

1. Fairbridge 1977, 90.

2. Butzer 1971, 492; Lemonick and Dorfman 2006.

3. Johnstone 1980; Englebrecht and Seyfert 1994; Erlandson et al. 2011; Christopher Joyce, "In Ancient Ore. Dump, Clues to the First Americans?" July 12, 2012, www.npr.org/2012/07/13/156685336/in-ancient-ore-dump-clues-to-the-first-americans (accessed July 14, 2012).

4. Cassidy, Raab, and Kononenko 2004; Fagan 2004.

5. Cassidy, Raab, and Kononenko 2004; Laurie W. Rush and Jim Cassidy, "Testing the Paleo Maritime Hypothesis for Glacial Lake Iroquois, Fort Drum, New York," poster presented at the 70th Annual Meeting of the Society for American Archaeology, March 30–April 3, 2005, Salt Lake City, Utah.

6. Rush and Cassidy, "Testing the Paleo Maritime Hypothesis"; Margaret Schulz, Laurie Rush, and Amy Wood, "Fossi Islands—A Potential Maritime Context in the Northeast," paper presented at the 71st Annual Meeting of the Society for American Archaeology, April 26–30, 2006, San Juan, Puerto Rico.

7. E.g., Bradley and Stanford 2004, as cited in Toner 2006, 44–45, and in Zax 2007.

8. Chandler 2001; Lemonick and Dorfman 2006.

9. Wiseman 2005, 120.

10. David G. Anderson, David S. Brose, Dena F. Dincauze, Michael J. Shott, Robert S. Grumet, and Richard C. Waldbauer, "Introduction," in *The Earliest Americans: Theme Study for*

*the Eastern United States,* Section E, Statement of Historic Contexts [updated September 13, 2007]. National Park Service, Archeology Program, United States Department of the Interior, Washington, D.C., www.nps.gov/archeology/pubs/nhleam/E-Introduction.htm.

11. Irwin-Williams 1968; MacNeish 1973; Adovasio et al. 1975; Dillehay 1989, 1999; Chandler 2001; Marsha Walton and Michael Coren, "Scientist: Man in Americas Earlier Than Thought; Archaeologists Put Humans in North American 50,000 Years Ago," November 17, 2004, www.CNN.com (accessed March 3, 2007); Lemonick and Dorfman 2006; Tom Pertierra, "The Topper Site: Intriguing Evidence of Ice Age Man in South Carolina," paper presented at the Norwalk Community College Archaeology Club Meeting, December 10, 2009, Norwalk Community College, Norwalk, Conn.

12. Chrisman et al. 1996.

13. Largent 2004.

14. Lemonick and Dorfman 2006.

15. Bishop 1993.

16. The most recent study of variations in DNA sequences among Native Americans not only posits at least three major migrations from Asia to the Americas, but also shows back-migrations from the Americas to Asia, and from South America to North America and back. Further, the findings indicate that the initial route from Asia followed the American coast southward. David Reich, Nick Patterson, Desmond Campbell, Arti Tandon, Stéphane Mazieres, et al., "Reconstructing Native American Population History," *Nature* 488 (July 11, 2012): 370–374, doi:10.1038/nature11258.

17. Stone et al. 2005, 8–9.

18. Ibid., 7–11.

19. McWeeney 1994, 1999, 6; Stone et al. 2005, 13.

20. Edwards and Merrill 1977, 9–11.

21. Bourn 1977.

22. Bell 2009, 19–21.

23. E.g., Daria E. Merwin, "Submerged Evidence of Early Human Occupation in the New York Bight," abstract, paper presented at the annual meeting of the Conference on New England Archaeology, May 28, 2011, University of Massachusetts, Amherst; Merwin, Lynch, and Robinson 2003, 46–52; Kevin A. McBride, "The Archaeological Potential of the Continental Shelf," paper presented at the Maritime Archaeology thematic annual fall meeting of the Archaeological Society of Connecticut, Oct. 21, 2006, Connecticut College, New London, Conn.

24. McBride, "The Archaeological Potential of the Continental Shelf."

25. Jordan 1975, 71.

26. Ogden 1977, 24; McWeeney 1999, 6.

27. Stone et al. 2005.

28. McWeeney 1999, 7.

29. Flint 1930, 260; Salwen 1975, 44.

30. Cook 1978.

31. Moeller 1983, 1984b.

32. Laub 2000; Ellis, Tomenchuk, and Holland 2003; Curran 1984; Spiess, Curran, and Grimes 1985.

33. McWeeney 1994, 1999, 7–9.

34. Moeller 1980; McWeeney 1999, 7.

35. Brian D. Jones, "The Powerplant Site: A Late Paleo-Indian Site in Ledyard, Connecticut," paper presented at the fall meeting of the Archaeological Society of Connecticut, October 8, 1994, Enfield, Conn.; Jones 1997; Jones and Forrest 2003; Brian Jones, personal communication, January 14, 2010.

36. See Moeller 1999.

37. Nicholas Bellantoni, Connecticut State Archaeologist, personal communication.

38. Shepard 1893, 330.

39. Moeller 1980, 4.

40. Ibid., 126.

41. Moeller 1980, 126; 1984c; 1999.

42. E.g., Jostand 1970; Powell 1981, 76; Ernest A. Wiegand, "Phase 1 Cultural Resources Survey of the Proposed Rosenstiel Subdivision, Greenwich, Connecticut," manuscript prepared for S. E. Minor Co., Greenwich, Conn., 1987, pp. 15–18.

43. Calogero 1991.

44. Moeller 1999.

45. Moeller 1980, 1984c, 1999.

46. Richmond 1987a, 7. The quote is from an open letter to Richmond's granddaughter Wunneanatsu (One Who Is Beautiful or Good Inside).

47. Roger W. Moeller, "The Templeton Site: 10,000 Year Old Secrets Revealed," paper presented March 13, 2011, at the Institute for American Indian Studies, Washington, Conn., Litchfield Hills Archaeology Club Lecture Series.

48. Jones, "The Powerplant Site"; Jones 1999b; Jones and Forrest 2003.

49. Molecular phylogenetic studies have led to the reclassification of the *Chenopodium* genus into the *Amaranthaceae* family (Reveal and Chase 2011). See also P. F. Stevens, 2001 onward, "Angiosperm Phylogeny Website," Version 9, June 2008 (and updated more or less continuously since), www.mobot.org/MOBOT/research/APweb/.

50. Spiess and Griswold 1930.

51. Daniel Forrest, personal communication, January 21, 2011, citing the work of Dr. Don Hermes.

52. Luedtke 1993, 56.

53. Lavin 1983.

54. Edmund K. Swigart, n.d., "The Lovers Leap Site," unpublished manuscript available from the Institute for American Indian Studies, Washington, Conn.

55. Ibid., 30–39.

56. Cross 1999.

57. "Liebman Paleo-Indian Site" 1994; Parkos 1994, "The Liebman Paleo-Indian Site," paper presented at the Albert Morgan Archaeological Society, November 13, 1994, Wood Memorial Library, Windsor, Conn.; Moeller 1999, 72, citing a personal communication from John Pfeiffer.

58. Ernest A. Wiegand, personal communication.

59. Graves and Mair 2006, 30, citing McBride 1984b and Soulsby, Gradie, and McBride 1981.

60. Edwards and Emery 1977, 252; Newman 1977; Lavin 1988a, 103–104.

61. George and Jones 1997, 44.

62. Daniel Forrest, personal communication, January 21, 2011; e.g., Forrest et al. 2006.

63. Daniel Forrest, personal communication, January 21, 2011.

64. Kauffman and Dent 1982.

65. Rieth and Johnson 2011, 49.

66. Jarvenpa and Brumbach 1995; Brumbach and Jarvenpa 1997.

67. Daniel Forrest, personal communication, January 21, 2011.

68. Anderson, Brose, et al., "Introduction," in *The Earliest Americans*.

## 2. COPING WITH NEW ENVIRONMENTS

Epigraph: Richmond 2000.

1. McWeeney 1999, 8–9.

2. Dincauze and Mulholland 1977, fig. 7; Stone et al. 2005.

3. Fagan 1978, 80.

4. Davis 1969; see also McWeeney 1999, 10.

5. Reeve and Forgacs 1999, 20.

6. Moeller 1984c, 49–50; Pfeiffer 1983b, 6–9; Nicholas 1987b, 1988; unpublished collections at the Institute for American Indian Studies.

7. Pfeiffer 1986.

8. Forrest 1999, 80–83.

9. Ibid., 1999, 83–97; Jones and Forrest 2003, 79–84.

10. Daniel Forrest, personal communication, December 6, 2010; Brian Jones, personal communication, December 7, 2010.

11. Forrest 1999, 83–85, 90.

12. Jones 1999a, 119.

13. Forrest 1999, 85–90, 94.

14. Mashantucket Pequot Museum and Research Center: The Sandy Hill Site, www.pequotmuseum.org/Home/ResearchCollections/ARCHAEOLOGY/ArchaeologicalResearch/TheSandyHillSite.htm (accessed December 20, 2011).

15. Brumbach and Jarvenpa 1997.

16. Jones 1999a, 119.

17. Nicholas 1985, 1987b, 1988; George P. Nicholas and Russell G. Handsman, "The Carlson I Site, Preliminary Report of Field Investigations: 1984–1986, A Technical Report of the Robbins Swamp Project, American Indian Archaeological Institute," 1987, CHPC no. 1194, unpublished report prepared for the Connecticut Historical Commission, State Historic Preservation Office, Hartford, Conn.

18. Nicholas 1988, 265–276.

19. Ibid., 288.

20. Nicholas 1987a.

21. Ibid., 18, citing Schindler et al. 1982.

22. Karr 1999.

23. E.g., Alexander 1963; Lindsay 1992; Wiseman 2005.

24. Young 1841, 365; Wood 1634, 72–74; Williams 1643, 185–187.

25. Wood 1634, 72–74.

26. Williams 1643, 186.

27. Morton 1637, 24–26.

28. Fawcett 2000, 48.

29. Townshend 1893, 176, as cited in Kavasch 1983, 5.

30. Shepard 1893, 329, 331–332.

31. Champlain, cited in Karr 1999, 44.

32. Ritchie and Funk 1971, 46.

33. Salwen 1975, 47.

34. McWeeney 1994.

35. Nicholas 1988, 281–284.

36. Lavin 1988a.

37. Bourn 1995.

38. Bourn 1972.

39. Bourn 1977.

40. Powell 1965.

41. Glynn 1953.

42. E.g., Kevin A. McBride, "The Archaeological Potential of the Continental Shelf," paper presented at the Maritime Archaeology thematic annual fall meeting of the Archaeological Society of Connecticut, October 21, 2006, Connecticut College, New London, Conn.

43. David S. Robinson, "Maritime Archaeology at the University of Connecticut," paper presented at the Maritime Archaeology thematic annual fall meeting of the Archaeological Society of Connecticut, October 21, 2006, Connecticut College, New London, Conn.

44. Merwin, Lynch, and Robinson 2003; Poirier and Bellantoni 2003; Daria E. Merwin, "Submerged Evidence of Early Human Occupation in the New York Bight," abstract of paper presented at the annual meeting of the Conference on New England Archaeology, May 28, 2011, University of Massachusetts, Amherst; David S. Robinson, "Nipmuc Nation's Project Mishoon (2001–2011): A Status Report," abstract, paper presented at the annual meeting of the Conference on New England Archaeology, May 28, 2011, University of Massachusetts, Amherst.

45. Rozwadowski 2006, 6.

46. Forrest 1999, 96–97.

## 3. SURVIVING IN HOT, DRY HOMELANDS

Epigraph: Aurelius Piper, as quoted in the exhibition *As We Tell Our Stories,* Institute for American Indian Studies, Washington, Conn., 1989.

1. McWeeney 1999, 9–10.

2. Ibid.; Burns and Honkala 1990, Silvics of North America, *Ilex opaca* Ait. American holly Web page, www.na.fs.fed.us/spfo/pubs/silvics_manual/volume_2/ilex/opaca.htm (accessed February 27, 2011).

3. McWeeney 1999, 9.

4. Forrest 1999, 85.

5. Pfeiffer 1986, 24–25.

6. Lavin 1984; McBride 1984a.

7. Jones, 1999a, 102–103.

8. Cross 1999.

9. McBride 1984a, 1984b.

10. Hart 2011, 102.

11. Faith Damon Davison, retired Mohegan archivist, personal communication, April 28, 2010.

12. Williams 1643, 176.

13. Nicholas Bellantoni, personal communication.

14. Stuart A. Reeve, David Silverglade, and Kathleen Von Jena, "Historical and Archeological Assessment Survey of Easton, Connecticut," unpublished report prepared for the Town of Easton Planning and Zoning Commission and the Connecticut Trust for Historic Preservation, May 2009, p. 72; Norris Bull Collection, Connecticut Archaeology Center, www.cac.uconn.edu/bullcollection.html (accessed January 1, 2012).

15. Maureen DaRos, Division of Anthropology, Peabody Museum of Natural History, Yale University, personal communication, June 7, 2010.

16. Wood 1634, 109.

17. McBride and Soulsby 1989.

18. Pfeiffer 1986.

19. Ibid.

20. Vaughan 1965, 72.

21. Pfeiffer 1986.

22. Dincauze and Mulholland 1977.

23. Brennan 1974.

24. McBride 1984a, 56.

25. Gookin 1792, 15, as cited in Little 1988, 79.

26. Starbuck 1980, 1992.

27. Howard W. Winters, manuscript on the Lawes Farm Site, Montgomery County, Illinois, on file at the Center for American Archaeology, Kampsville, Ill.

28. Starbuck 1980, 1992.

29. Williams 1643; Wood 1634.

30. Armitage 1991.

31. Jones 1999a, 104–118.

32. Jones 1999a.

33. Ibid.

## 4. THE HUNTER-GATHERER FLORESCENCE

Epigraph: Aganstata 1988.

1. Bloom and Stuiver 1963; Oldale 1986.

2. McWeeney 1999, 10–11.

3. Cassedy 1998, 1999; Forrest et al. 2006, 32; Juli 1992, 3–7; Lavin 1984, 13–14; Little 1988, 79; McBride 1984b; McBride and Dewar 1987; Pfeiffer 1984, 74–76; Powell 1981; Swigart 1974, 13–14, 32–33; Wiegand 1978, 1980, 24–27, 1983, 49, 92–106, 150, 162.

4. Kavasch 1979.

5. Mariani Nut Company, nutrition facts on bag of chopped walnuts, Winters, Calif., 2007.

6. American Heart Association 2002.

7. American Heart Association, "Meat, Poultry, and Fish," Dallas, Texas: AHA, Inc., 2011, www.heart.org/HEARTORG/GettingHealthy/NutritionCenter/Meat-Poultry-and-Fish _UCM_306002_Article.jsp, updated May 20, 2010 (accessed December 2, 2011).

8. Daniel Forrest, personal communication, January 21, 2011.

9. E.g., Williams 1643; Wood 1634.

10. Brereton 1602, 40.

11. Timothy C. Visel, October 31, 1986, letter to Diane Mayerfield, Natural Resources Center, Connecticut Department of Environmental Protection; Visel 2006b, 7–8; Visel et al. 2009, 11.

12. Barber 2001.

13. Ritchie 1969b, 79.

14. Ritchie 1969a, 219; Dincauze 1975; Snow 1980; Custer 2001, 85–107.

15. Reeve and Forgacs 1999, 20–21.

16. McBride 1984a, 56. Some of the points may represent the Stark type, first identified in Middle Archaic contexts in Massachusetts sites.

17. Dincauze 1975, 25.

18. Lavin and Russell 1985, table 1.

19. Cuzzone and Hartenberger 2009; Lavin 1984, 16; Lavin and Salwen 1983; McBride 1984b; Swigart 1974, addendum; Funk and Pfeiffer 1988, 80.

20. Ritchie 1969b.

21. Pfeiffer 1984, 1992; Swigart 1974, 11–12.

22. Marc L. Banks, "A Study of Ground-Slate Knives from Connecticut," paper presented at the annual meeting of the Northeastern Anthropological Association, State University of New York, Geneseo, 1994, http://archnet.asu.edu/archives/lithic/ulu/ulus.html.

23. Speck 1940, cited in Wiseman 2005, 145.

24. David Thompson, personal communication, July 11, 2007.

25. Cassedy 1999; Pfeiffer 1992, 153.

26. Swigart 1974, 11–12.

27. McBride 1984a; McBride and Dewar 1981, 48; McBride and Soulsby 1989, 144.

28. Pfeiffer 1984, 1992, 144–148, 153–155.

29. Pfeiffer 1984, 1992.

30. Pfeiffer 1984, 1992.

31. Kevin McBride, personal communication.

32. Forrest et al. 2006, 35.

33. Pfeiffer 1984, 1992.

34. Bourn 1977.

35. E.g., Sargent 1952.

36. Lavin and Russell 1985.

37. Thompson 1969.

38. Banks 2000; Marc Banks, "Recollections of Dr. Douglas Jordan and the 1991 UCONN Field School," paper presented at the fall meeting of the Archaeological Society of Connecticut, October 16, 2010, South Windsor.

39. Lavin and Salwen 1983.

40. Wiegand 1983.

41. Thompson 1975.

42. Swigart 1974.

43. Rand 2010; Swigart 1974.

44. Lavin and Russell 1985, 51–52.

45. Cross 1999; Robinson 1996; Wiseman 2005, 206.

46. Pfeiffer 1984, 1992, 137–139, 159–163.

47. MacKenzie 1801, 148–149, as cited in Pfeiffer 1992, 162.

48. Heidenreich 1978, 374.

49. Pfeiffer 1980, 10–12, 58.

50. Daniel Forrest, personal communication, January 21, 2011.

51. Wrong 1939, 172. The similarities between the Bliss rituals and those of the Huron do not necessarily mean that the two communities were related, only that the ritual acts represented by the material remains at Bliss were practiced among post-contact people living in what is thought to be the original homelands of the Laurentian population.

52. Winslow 1624, 362–363, and Wood 1634, 104–105, cited in Karr 1999, 134–135; Wiseman 2005, 83–84.

53. Marshall 1996, 384, 398, cited in Wiseman 2005, 84.

54. Wiseman 2005, 93.

55. Weslager 1974, 4.

56. Pfeiffer 1992, 163.

57. Banks, "Recollections of Dr. Douglas Jordan."

58. McBride and Grumet 1996, 17–18, 22.

59. Fawcett 2000, 39–40.

60. Hamell 1987.

61. Hamell 1983, 6.

62. E.g., Gookin 1792, 17; Ordonez and Welters 2004, 172.

63. Gerry Biron, unpublished review of "Iroquois Beadwork: A Haudenosaunee Tradition and Art" by Dolores Elliott, which was published in 2010 in *Preserving Tradition and Understanding the Past: Papers from the Conference on Iroquois Research, 2001–2005,* ed. Christine Sternberg Patrick, *New York State Museum Record* 1:35–48, submitted to the New York State Museum in Albany, November 2010.

64. Pfeiffer 1984, 84–86. Of course, there are other causes for ritual and ceremonialism besides social stress and hard times. In fact, the opposite situation—good times—could lead to rituals that give thanks to the responsible deity. But this is a case study, and the deteriorating physical environment, coupled with the increasingly populated social environment as indicated by the number of Narrow Point sites on the landscape, strongly suggest that the creators of the Late Archaic Bliss cemetery were living in stressful times.

65. Pfeiffer 1992, 112–113.

66. Forrest et al. 2006, 32.

67. Cassedy 1999, 134–135; Lavin and Salwen 1983; McBride 1984a, 59; Pfeiffer 1980, 61–63; Roger W. Moeller, "The Templeton Site: 10,000 Year Old Secrets Revealed," paper presented to the Litchfield Hills Archaeology Club, March 13, 2011, at the Institute for American Indian Studies, Washington, Conn.; Swigart 1974, 14, 31–33; Wiegand 1983.

68. Lavin and Russell 1985.

69. Luedtke 1981, 71.

70. Jostand 1970.

71. McBride 1978, 1984b; Forrest et al. 2006.

72. Juli 1992.

73. Jones et al. 1997.

74. Cuzzone and Hartenberger 2009.

75. Wiegand 1987.

76. Keener 1965; Jostand 1970; Swigart 1974; Pfeiffer 1980, 61–63; Feder 1981; Wadleigh 1981; McBride 1984a, 1984b; McBride and Dewar 1981; McBride and Soulsby 1989; Lavin 1988a; Cassedy 1992, 1998, 1999; Jones, Forrest, and Binzen 1997; Cuzzone and Hartenberger 2009.

77. Bernstein 2002, 40.

78. Sgarlata 2006.

79. E.g., McBride 1984b; McBride and Soulsby 1989; Lavin and Banks 2007, 2010.

80. Lavin and Kania 2001c, photograph 17.

81. Williams 1643, 180.

82. Kalm 1770, 277–278.

83. Ordonez and Welters 2004, 171–172.

84. Banks 1990, 2000.

85. Visel 2006a, 2006b; Visel et al. 2006; Visel and Visel 2008.

86. Coffin 1947, 37, cited in Menta 2003, 46.

87. Visel et al. 2006, 8.

88. Williams 1643, 182.

89. Visel 2006a; Timothy C. Visel, "Clinton's Fish and Shellfish Resources: An Ecological Review," Clinton Harbor presentation to the Clinton Lions Club, Clinton, Connecticut, February 2, 2006.

90. Coffin 1947.

91. Pfeiffer 1983c; 1992, 113.

92. Russo 1994, 48.

93. Lavin and Banks 2003, 2008.

94. Heath 1963; Meader 1869; Potter 1856; Wood 1634.

95. Williams 1643, 170.

96. McBride 1984b, 263; Juli 1992, 2–7.

97. Juli 1992, 2–7.

98. Edwards and Emory 1977, 252.

99. McBride 1984b, 266–268, 274; Pfeiffer 1980, 62; Swigart 1974, 13–14; Wiegand 1978, 1980, 1983.

100. Spiess and Griswold 1930.

101. McBride 1984b, 372; Pfeiffer 1992, 180.

102. Forrest et al. 2006, 32.

103. Edward Sarabia, personal communication.

104. McBride 1984b, 111.

105. Dincauze 1975.

106. Poirier, Bellantoni, and Aganstata 1985, 4.

107. Keener 1965, 33.

108. Coffin 1963.

109. Coffin 1937, 18.

110. Coffin 1938, 10.

111. E.g., Keener 1965, fig. 19; Lavin 1984.

112. E.g., Russell 1995, 3–4.

113. E.g., Glynn 1973, 82; Jostand 1970, 9; Juli 1992, 6; Parkos 1991b, 81; Edmund K. Swigart, n.d., "The Lovers Leap Site," unpublished manuscript on file at the Institute for American Indian Studies, Washington, Conn., 12, 30; Swigart 1974, 14.

114. Reeve and Forgacs 1999, 21–22.

115. Pfeiffer 1992, 114.

## 5. ENVIRONMENTAL STRESS AND ELABORATE RITUAL

Epigraph: Richmond 1985, 15.

1. McBride 1984b, 280, 370; Pfeiffer 1984; Lavin 1988a, 105; Pagoulatos 1988, 1990; Cassedy 1998, 200–201.

2. Bloom and Stuiver 1963, 334; Kaye and Barghoorn 1964; Gordon 1983; Oldale 1986.

3. McBride 1984b, 22, 228; Lavin 1988a, 107–108.

4. E.g., see McBride 1978, 1984b, 123–124, 132, 1984a; Funk 1984; Lavin and Russell 1985; Pagoulatos 1988; Pfeiffer 1992, 217e, 234–238; Cassedy 1999; Lavin and Banks 2005a, 2010).

5. McBride 1984a, 71; Pfeiffer 1992, 180.

6. Forrest et al. 2006, 34.

7. McBride 1978.

8. George and Dewar 1999, 122–123.

9. Later correctly identified by Tonya Largy, personal communication.

10. McBride 1984b, 124.

11. McBride and Dewar 1981, 48.

12. Ritchie 1969b, 150–178; Snow 1980, 235; Witthoft 1953.

13. E.g., see Pagoulatos 1983.

14. Ritchie 1969a, 1969b; Dincauze 1972; Kraft 1972.

15. Lavin 1984, 16.

16. Reeve and Forgacs 1999, 22–25.

17. Cooke 2006, 5.

18. Reeve and Forgacs 1999, 25.

19. Pagoulatos 1988, 1990; Pfeiffer 1992, 208–210.

20. Calogero and Philpotts 2006, 61.

21. Reeve and Forgacs 1999, 22–25.

22. Funk and Pfeiffer 1988, 80.

23. Reeve and Forgacs 1999, 25.

24. Cassedy 1998, 199.

25. Reeve and Forgacs 1999, 25.

26. E.g., Ritchie 1969b, 155–156, 163; Kinsey 1972, 451; Hoffman 1998.

27. Stoltman 1966, 57.

28. Hoffman 1998, 50.

29. Truncer 2004a, 489.

30. Fowler 1951.

31. Truncer 2004a, 507, fig. 1; 2004b, 104.

32. Truncer 2004b, 98–104.

33. Reeve and Forgacs 1999, 25.

34. Ibid., 24.

35. Hart et al. 2008.

36. Ibid., 739–740.

37. Gudrian 1991.

38. Wiegand 1983, 164.

39. MacCurdy 1962.

40. McBride 1984b; Pfeiffer 1992, 120, 194–195.

41. Pfeiffer 1992, 196–197.

42. Pagoulatos 1988.

43. Lavin and Russell 1985.

44. Swigart 1974.

45. McBride 1984b, 370; Pagoulatos 1988, 1990; Pfeiffer 1992; Cassedy 1998, 200–201.

46. Pagoulatos 1990.

47. Forrest et al. 2006, 35.

48. Pagoulatos 1990.

49. Swigart 1974.

50. Swigart 1975, 5–7.

51. Ibid., 6.

52. Ibid., 7.

53. Pfeiffer 1980, 9–11; 1992, 92.

54. Pfeiffer 1992, 196–198, 290–307; Pagoulatos 1988, 81.

55. Thompson 1989, 22–25.

56. Pfeiffer 1992, 92–94, 119.

57. Pfeiffer 1980, 1984, 1992; Pagoulatos 1988; Kline 1995; Thompson 1989.

58. Thompson 1989, 40.

59. Lavin 1984, 15–16; 1988a.

60. Pfeiffer 1980, 1984.

61. Pfeiffer 1984, 79.

62. Jeffrey Tottenham, personal communication.

63. Pfeiffer 1980, 14–15.

64. Ibid., 59.

65. Thompson 1989, figs. 2, 3.

66. Ziac and Pfeiffer 1989.

67. Pfeiffer 1980, 10–12, 58.

68. Ibid., 11–12.

69. Pfeiffer 1992, 193–200.

70. Pfeiffer 1984, 1986.

71. Pfeiffer 1992, 202.

72. McBride 1984b, 131; Lavin and Russell 1985; Cassedy 1999; Reeve and Forgacs 1999, 22–23; Lavin and Banks 2007.

73. E.g., Swigart 1974, 33–34; McBride 1984b, 61–63; Pfeiffer 1984, 1992; Cassedy 1999, 129, 136.

74. E.g., Dincauze 1974, 49; 1975, 27; Ritchie 1969b, 219; Witthoft 1953.

75. Cook 1976, 350–353; Pagoulatos 1983, 57; Snow 1980, 247–248.

76. Lavin and Banks 2005a, 2007, 2010.

77. Lavin and Banks 2005a, 243; Calogero and Philpotts 2006, 70–71.

78. Pfeiffer 1984, 1986, 1992.

79. Pfeiffer 1992, 219, 225.

80. Pfeiffer 1994, 121–124.

81. Pfeiffer 1992, 203.

82. Custer 1988, 125–129.

83. McBride 1984b, 27–28; Lavin 1988a, 106–110.

## 6. CLOSURE, CONTINUITY, AND THE SEEDS OF CHANGE

Epigraph: Theresa Bell, as quoted in the exhibition *As We Tell Our Stories,* Institute for American Indian Studies, Washington, Conn., citing the *Hartford Courant,* 1990.

1. E.g., Ritchie 1969a, 1969b; Swigart 1974; McBride 1984b; Luedtke 1985; Pfeiffer 1992.

2. E.g., "Report on the First Archaeological Conference" 1943; Willey and Phillips 1958; Ritchie 1965; Sanger 1986, 139; Chapdelaine 1990, 125.

3. E.g., Funk 1976; Lavin 1984; Cassedy 1992.

4. Pfeiffer 1984, 86; Reeve and Forgacs 1999, 24–25.

5. E.g., McBride 1984b; Pfeiffer 1984.

6. Reeve and Forgacs 1999, 24–26.

7. McWeeney 1999, 10–11.

8. Truncer 2004a, 2004b.

9. Pfeiffer 1992, 227.

10. Swigart 1974; Reeve and Forgacs 1999, 24–25.

11. Pope 1952; Wiegand 1978, 1983, 96–97; McBride 1984b, 130–133, 294–300, 370–371; Juli and McBride 1984; Pfeiffer 1992, 339–344; Juli 1999; Pagoulatos 2002, 36–37.

12. McBride 1984b, 302, 304–305.

13. Pfeiffer 1992.

14. Wiegand 1983, 165.

15. Cassedy 1998, 151–154, 203.

16. Feder and Banks 1996, 49.

17. E.g., Smith 1950; Dincauze 1974; Hoffman 1985; George and Jones 1997.

18. McBride 1984b; Pagoulatos 2002, 37.

19. McBride 1984b, 132, 296–297, 325.

20. Lavin 1988a, 106–108.

21. Sanders and Ellis 1961, 17; Strahler 1966, 65–67.

22. Steever 1972.

23. Barske 1961; Roberts 1971, 2–3.

24. Lavin 1988a, 108–109.

25. McBride 1984b, 27.

26. Gordon 1983.

27. McBride 1984b, 27–29.

28. E.g., Gordon 1983, 69.

29. Williams 1643, 215.

30. E.g., Lavin 1988a, 13.

31. John L. Davis, as cited in "An Older Culture" 2006, 7.

32. E.g., Ritchie 1969b, 155–156, 163, 180, 194; Cantwell and Wall 2001, 73–75.

33. Cassedy 1998, 204.

34. Drooker and Hamell 2004.

35. Gookin 1792 [1970], cited in Willoughby 1935, 250.

36. Smith 1950.

37. Funk 1976, 314.

38. Lavin 2002, 157–159.

39. Kostiw 1995.

40. Wright 1973; Maryland Archaeological Conservation Lab (MAC Lab), 2007, *Diagnostic Artifacts in Maryland,* "Ware Description—Prehistoric," Maryland Department of Planning, Maryland Historical Trust, Jefferson Patterson Park and Museum, Baltimore, www.jefpat.org /diagnostic/Prehistoric_Ceramic_Web_Page/Prehistoric_Ware%20Description.htm.

41. Kostiw 1995.

42. E.g, Braun 1974; Dincauze 1974; Swigart 1974; Fiedel 2001.

43. Lavin and Salwen 1983; Juli and McBride 1984; McBride 1984a.

44. Hoffman 1985, 1998.

45. Reeve and Forgacs 1999, 59.

46. Webb 1952; Struever and Houart 1972; Dancy 2005.

47. Ritchie 1955, 1969b, 175, 179, 196–205; Dragoo 1963; Granger 1978.

48. Robinson 1996; Robinson, Petersen, and Robinson 1992; Wiseman 2005, 105–106, 109–110.

49. Wiseman 2005, 206.

50. Ibid., 146.

51. The sources were identified through geological analyses of the specimens that were compared with mineral compositions of known obsidian source localities. See Bello and Cresson 1998; Boulanger et al. 2007; Dillian, Bello, and Shackley 2010. Archaeologist Matthew Boulanger of the Archaeometry Laboratory at the University of Missouri Research Reactor in Columbia, however, has questioned the authenticity of the obsidian artifacts from Mid-Atlantic sites: "Results of more than 50 years of analyses suggest that the most frequently encountered compositional profiles of obsidian recovered from *bona fide* archaeological deposits in the eastern Woodlands are attributable to large obsidian sources in or near modern-day Yellowstone National Park. These include Obsidian Cliff (Wyoming) and Bear Gulch (Idaho). Several recent papers have suggested that artifacts from less extensive obsidian sources may have made their way prehistorically into the Middle Atlantic region (e.g., Bello and Cresson 1998; Dillian et al. 2007). However, Boulanger et al. (2007) point out that in all such instances, there are reasons to doubt the validity of these specimens as representative of prehistoric exchange patterns." (Matthew T. Boulanger, "Provenance Analysis by X-ray Fluorescence of Obsidian Artifacts Attributed to Woodruff Rockshelter (6LF216), Washington, Litchfield County, Connecticut," report prepared for Lucianne Lavin, August 8, 2012, p. 3). The Woodruff Rock Shelter in Washington, Connecticut, contained obsidian flakes. X-ray fluorescence analysis by Boulanger showed that the flakes came from one of three lava flows in far western Mexico. But Boulanger makes a good case that their location in pre-contact levels at Woodruff is suspect. His reasons include that the site excavator does not mention them in his site report; there is not one other instance of obsidian east of the Mississippi River attributed to Mexico; the tags on the artifacts

note they were recovered in 1977, but site excavations had ended by 1976, after which the site report noted that the site had been vandalized to a minor extent (ibid., 2–4).

52. Dancy 2005.

53. E.g., Swigart 1974, 22–25; McBride 1984b; Lavin and Russell 1985, 60; Cassedy 1998, 203; Pagoulatos 2002, 36.

54. Ritchie 1969a, 180–204; Granger 1978; Snow 1980, 264.

55. Lavin 1983.

56. McBride 1984a, 1984b, 132.

57. Swigart 1974, 25.

58. Bourn 2002.

59. Ibid.

60. Cassedy 1992, 103.

61. Kaplan 1976.

62. Granger 1978, fig. 6.

63. Although in the Post-Contact period, seventeenth-century Europeans and some present-day archaeologists used this term solely to refer to a cylindrical shell bead about one-quarter inch long and one-eighth inch wide, drilled with an iron awl called a mux, or muxe.

64. Ritchie 1969a, 191; Ceci 1989; Pendergast 1989. The Iroquois-speaking tribes inhabiting what is now upstate New York and Canada used strings and belts of wampum in their political functions and were major importers of coastal wampum beads during the Post-Contact period (see, for example, Hayes 1989 and Becker 2006).

65. E.g., Boyle 1911, figs. 28747, 28748, 28750.

66. C. A. Weslager 1974, 6.

67. Ordonez and Welters 2004, 171–172, discussion of the contents of Pequot graves at Long Pond in Ledyard, Connecticut; John Pfeiffer, personal communication, regarding his unpublished investigation of disturbed burials from the circa seventeenth-century Nehantic burying ground in Niantic, Connecticut.

68. E.g., see Becker 2006, 79, 91.

69. Granger 1978, fig. 6.

70. Ritchie 1969a, 201–204.

71. Justice 1987, 179, map 74, cited by Thompson 1995, 74–75.

72. Thompson 1995.

73. Edmund K. Swigart, n.d., "The Lovers Leap Site," pp. 11–12, unpublished manuscript on file at the Institute for American Indian Studies, Washington, Conn.

74. Willoughby 1935; Dincauze 1974, 51; Keegan and Keegan 1999, I; Lavin 2006. See also the "Connecticut Archaeology" exhibit at the Peabody Museum of Natural History, Yale University, New Haven, and the main exhibition at the Institute for American Indian Studies, Washington, Conn.

75. Logan 1979:35.

76. Tribal elder Nora "Touching Leaves Woman" Thompson Dean, as told to C. A. Weslager (C. A. Weslager 1974, 5).

77. See Bragdon 1996, 220.

78. Bragdon 1996, 107; Vaughan 1965, 72.

79. Williams 1643, 134.

80. Harris 1987; Logan 1979, 49.

81. Connecticut Indian Affairs Coordinator and Tlingit holy man Edward Sarabia, personal communication to author.

82. Cooke 1990.

83. Baxter 1991, 22.

84. Shepard 1893, 337; Williams 1897, 412; Cook 1989.

85. Cooke 1989, 13.

86. Hamell 1983, 1987.

87. Hamell 1983, 25.

88. Becker 2010.

89. Williams 1897, 411. See Becker 2010 for a discussion of these eleven birdstones.

90. Ritchie 1969a, 181–182, 200–203.

91. Volmar 1996, 40; Gerry Biron, "Made of Thunder, Made of Glass," traveling exhibit on northeastern beadwork, appearing at the Institute for American Indian Studies, Washington, Conn., January–June 2009; Edward Sarabia, personal communication.

92. See Nadeau and Bellantoni 2004, and the description of the Laurel Beach site burial, below.

93. Cooke and Jordan 1972.

94. Cooke 1989.

95. Ibid., 8.

96. Ibid., 9.

97. Granger 1978.

98. Nadeau and Bellantoni 2004.

99. Cassedy 1992, 103.

100. McBride 1984b, 132.

101. Goddard 1978a, 1978b; Denny 2003.

102. Denny 2003, 6, 10–11.

103. McBride 1984b, 301–302.

104. Cassedy 1998, 208.

105. E.g., Russo 1994.

## 7. PROSPERITY AND POPULATION GROWTH

Epigraphs: Tantaquidgeon, as quoted in "More than a Museum," 1979; Fawcett 2000, xv.

1. McWeeney 1999, 10, 11.

2. Goodwin 2006.

3. The Deer Run site dig is sponsored by the Institute for American Indian Studies' Litchfield Hills Archaeology Club, an affiliate of the Archaeological Society of Connecticut.

4. McBride 1984b, 135–137.

5. Jones, Forrest, and Binzen 1997, 22.

6. McBride 1984b, 137, 306, 311–312, 374–375; Juli and McBride 1984. But see the survey by Lavin and Banks (2007) of the Connecticut Yankee Atomic Power Company property on lower Haddam Neck, which located two multiseasonal base camps overlooking interior wetlands with multi-components that included dentate-stamped pottery assigned to the early Middle Woodland period (the Dibble Creek 1 and Dibble Creek 2 sites). Because these are multiple component sites of the Narrow Point archaeological tradition, it is difficult to assign the tradition's many small-stemmed points—not to mention the large numbers of nondiagnostic artifacts—to a specific cultural period. Most of the features, however, seem to date to the Late Archaic and Terminal Archaic periods. Possibly the function of the sites had changed by Woodland times to a more temporary, albeit repeatedly used, camp. More research at the Dibble Creek sites would clarify the chronological extent of their use as base camps.

7. Forrest et al. 2006; Forrest, Jones, and Thorson 2008.

8. Cassedy 1998, 206.

9. Snow 1980, 287.

10. McBride 1984b, 138.

11. Cassedy 1998, 176.

12. Funk 1968; 1976, 287–294.

13. Kaeser 1968, 2006.

14. Ritchie 1961, 50–52, 122.

15. Swigart 1974, 23.

16. Moore 1997; Funk 1976, 290–293.

17. Reeve and Forgacs 1999, 26; Feder 2004.

18. Reeve and Forgacs 1999, 26.

19. Calogero and Philpotts 2006, 57.

20. Custer 1984, 131, 181–182.

21. Funk 1976, 120; Moore 1997; Kaeser 2006.

22. Stuart A. Reeve, David Silverglade, and Kathleen Von Jena, "The Archaeology and Ethnohistory of Frontiers and Cultural Brokers, Examples from Easton and Redding, Connecticut," paper presented at the spring meeting of the Archaeological Society of Connecticut, April 24, 2010, Danbury, Conn.

23. Kaeser 2006, 45.

24. Tryon and Philpotts 1997.

25. Pfeiffer 1993, 104; Moore 1997, fig. 4.

26. Ritchie 1961, 26–28; Ritchie and Funk 1973, 155; Kostiw 1995, 40.

27. Strauss 1992; Pfeiffer 1993; Joseph Parkos, personal communication, 1992; Henry Golet, personal communication, 1997; and my own perusal of Woodland-period collections at the Peabody Museum of Natural History at Yale University, and at the Institute for American Indian Studies.

28. Ritchie 1969a, 226.

29. Luedtke 1987.

30. Lavin and Banks 2002, 36, 52.

31. Kostiw 1995, 40.

32. Pring 1603, cited in Howe 1969, 71.

33. Quoted in Karr 1999, 93.

34. As discussed in Vaughan 1977.

35. Wood, quoted in Bragdon 1996, 105.

36. Smith 1950; Lavin 1980, 1983, 1987; McBride 1984b.

37. Tracy Millis, Daniel F. Cassedy, Heather Millis, Paul A. Webb, and Nancy Asch Sidell, "Iroquois Gas Transmission System Phase III Archaeological Data Recovery Report," vol. 3, "The Connecticut Sites," unpublished report submitted by Garrow & Associates, Inc., of Atlanta to the Iroquois Gas Transmission system, Shelton, Conn., 1995.

38. Reeve and Forgacs 1999, 26.

39. Truex 1983.

40. McBride 1984b, 137.

41. Juli 1992, 9–13.

42. Salwen and Ottesen 1972.

43. Cassedy 1998, 216.

44. Ernest A. Wiegand, "Phase 1 Cultural Resources Survey of the Proposed Rosenstiel Subdivision, Greenwich, Connecticut," manuscript prepared for S. E. Minor Co., Greenwich, 1987, p. 6.

45. McBride 1984b.

46. Ibid., 139–141, 228–229, 322–332.

47. E.g., Kerber 1988; Luedtke 1988; Thornbahn 1988; see also Becker 2006.

48. Thorbahn 1988, 55.

49. Binzen 2009, 10.

50. McBride 1984b, 228–233.

51. Champlain 1613.

52. Binzen 1997; Crone-Morange and Lavin 2004, 134–135.

53. Pfeiffer 1993.

54. Lavin and Banks 2006.

55. Ibid.

56. Lavin and Banks 2011.

57. Petruzelli 2011.

58. Largy 2011.

59. The seven radiocarbon dates from the site are 1205 B.P. ±15 years, 1080 B.P. ±40 years, 910 B.P. ±50 years, 830 B.P. ±40 years, 700 B.P. ±40 years, 540 B.P. ±40 years, and 290 B.P. ±30 years (Lavin and Banks 2011).

60. Morton 1637, 21–22.

61. For the western Massachusetts Mohicans, at least, as noted by Sergeant in 1736 and cited in Miles 2009, 20.

62. Pfeiffer 1996, 71.

63. Juli and Lavin 1996, 87, citing Sturtevant's (1975) reconstruction of Niantic wigwams based on Stiles's measured sketches.

64. Juli and Lavin 1996, 86, citing Roger Williams's 1643 manuscript.

65. Juli and Lavin 1996.

66. Morton 1637, 21.

67. Rouse 1947; Smith 1950; Lavin 1980, 1987; McBride 1984b.

68. Lavin 1998.

69. E.g. Custer 1982, 1984; Egloff and Potter 1982, 99; Gardner 1982, 67; Griffith 1982, 52–53; Stewart 1982, 74; R. Michael Stewart, "Prehistoric Ceramics of the Lower and Middle Delaware River Valley," paper presented at the 1985 annual meeting of the Society for American Archaeology, Denver, Colorado.

70. Jay F. Custer and R. Michael Stewart, "Maritime Adaptations in the Middle Atlantic Region of Eastern North America," paper presented at the New World Maritime Adaptations meeting of the Society for American Archaeology, Pittsburgh, Pa., April 1983; Gardner 1982.

71. Custer 1988, 13.

72. Lavin 1998, 12.

73. Wilcox 1967, 17; Lavin 1984, 20; 1997b; Lavin and Miroff 1992; McBride 1984b; Cassedy 1992; Cassedy and Lavin 2007.

74. Goddard 1978b.

75. Menta 2003, 52–54.

76. Stuart J. Fiedel, personal communication, September 25, 1996; Carl Mastay, personal communication, March 4, 1996.

77. See Lavin 1998.

78. Kaeser 2006.

## 8. ECOLOGICAL ABUNDANCE AND TRIBAL HOMELANDS

Epigraph: Logan 1975.

1. McWeeney 1999, 10–11.

2. Bendremer and Dewar 1994.

3. Pederson et al. 2005.

4. Verrazzano 1970.

5. E.g., Feder 1980–1981, 1984; McBride 1984b; Bendremer 1993.

6. Forrest et al. 2006.

7. Richmond 1979, 1.

8. Piperno et al. 2009; Zarillo et al. 2008.

9. Chapman and Crites 1987.

10. Riley et al. 1994.

11. Wymer 1987, 1992, cited in Kostiw 1995, 42.

12. Hart 2011, 102.

13. Bendremer 1993, 374; Forrest et al. 2006.

14. Williams 1643, 170.

15. Timothy H. Ives, "Expressions of Community: Reconstructing Native Identity in Seventeenth Century Central Connecticut Through Land Deed Analysis," paper presented at the Fifth Annual Algonquian Peoples' Conference, March 14, 2004, Albany; see also the early Mohican land transactions listed in Dunn 1994b, many of which were signed by women.

16. See Bragdon 1996, 50–51, 152–153.

17. Ibid., 103.

18. Rainey 1933, 16–17, citing seventeenth-century Dutch, English, and French sources.

19. Hart 1999, 63, 65; 2000, 4; 2011, 102.

20. See Hart 2011, 102.

21. Ibid.

22. E.g. Pring 1603 and Champlain 1632, cited in Howe 1969, 72–73, 101; Williams 1643, 172.

23. Reeve and Forgacs 1999, 29.

24. Mrozowski 1994.

25. Janis Us, "Four Hearts Whispering," quoted in the Institute for American Indian Studies Main Exhibit, Washington, Conn., 2009.

26. Bendremer, Kellogg, and Largy, 1991, 336.

27. Bendremer 1999, 147–148.

28. Williams 1643, 100.

29. Gookin 1792 [1970], 150, cited in Bragdon 1996, 104.

30. Bendremer and Dewar 1994.

31. Bodner 1999, 30–31. The health benefits of maple syrup and maple sugar are similar to those of berries, red wine, and tea; the syrup contains antioxidant compounds that act as anti-cancer and anti-inflammatory agents. Initial laboratory studies suggest that the polyphenols in the syrup may inhibit enzymes relevant to Type 2 diabetes. Jonathan Kantrowitz, "Maple Syrup's Health Benefits," *Health News Report,* April 2, 2011, http://healthnewsreport.blogspot.com/2011/04/maple-syrups-health-benefits.html (accessed March 6, 2012).

32. Bendremer, Kellogg, and Largy 1991.

33. Cassedy 1998, 215; Cassedy and Webb 1999.

34. Blake and Cutler 1983.

35. Hart and Brumbach 2005, 3–4.

36. Bendremer 1993, 263–264.

37. Feder 1980–1981. The Farmington River was a major conduit to the chert quarries in the Hudson and Mohawk valleys. Its headwaters in southwestern Massachusetts are a short portage to the Housatonic River; from there another short portage to the Hoosic River will lead into the Hudson just north of its confluence with the Mohawk River, the gateway to the Onondaga quarries in western New York and to the Midwest.

38. Cassedy 1992, 218–221.

39. Lavin, Gudrian, and Miroff 1992–1993, 1993.

40. Bendremer 1993, 377–378.

41. E.g., Bernstein 1999; George 1997, 1999; Juli and Lavin 1996; Lavin and Banks 2011; Mrozowski 1994; Reeve and Forgacs 1999.

42. Lavin 1988a, 113.

43. Tantaquidgeon 1977, 83.

44. Bernstein 1999, 111.

45. Cassedy 1992, 191–192; Cassedy and Webb 1999, 88.

46. Cassedy 1998, 147–152, 218–219.

47. E.g., Morton 1637, 70; Williams 1643; Wood 1634.

48. Cassedy and Webb 1999, 91.

49. E.g, Bendremer 1993; Bendremer, Kellog, and Largy 1991; Lavin 1988b.

50. Andrews 1986; Little 1986.

51. De Laet 1909.

52. Heckenberger, Petersen, and Asch-Sidell 1992.

53. Chilton 1999, 167–171.

54. Ibid., 157–158.

55. Crawford 1999.

56. Bendremer 1999.

57. Cassedy and Webb 1999.

58. Bendremer 1993; Lavin 1988b; McBride 1984b.

59. McBride 1984b, 326, 374–75.

60. Gudrian 1991.

61. Wiegand 1983.

62. Cooke 1988; Gudrian 1995; Lavin 1988b; Lavin, Gudrian, and Miroff 1992–1993.

63. Lavin 1988b; McWeeney 1994; Reeve and Forgacs 1999, 27–29.

64. Bendremer 1993, 248.

65. Lavin, Gudrian, and Miroff 1992–1993.

66. Gudrian 1995.

67. Lavin 1988b.

68. Robert Karalus, primitive technologist, personal communication.

69. Jeff Kalin and Jeffrey Tottenham, primitive technologists, personal communications.

70. E.g., Speck 1903; 1909b, 205–206.

71. Morton 1637, 157–169, quoted in Karr 1999, 100.

72. Williams and Bendremer 1995.

73. Reeve and Forgacs 1999, 26, citing Dr. Lucinda McWeeney.

74. Williams 1643, 118.

75. Bruce Greene, archaeologist and dig chair of the Friends of the State Archaeologist, personal communication, February 2011.

76. Nicholas F. Bellantoni, "David G. Cooke and Harold D. Juli: Contributions to Connecticut Archaeology," paper presented at the fall meeting of the Archaeological Society of Connecticut, October 16, 2010, South Windsor.

77. Forrest et al. 2006, 37–38.

78. Bruce Karalus, primitive technologist, personal communication, about 1990.

79. Bragdon 1996, 103; Fawcett 2000, 47–52.

80. Richmond 1989, 25.

81. Fawcett 2000, 50.

82. Quoted in Ferris 2010.

83. Ibid.

84. Ferris 2010.

85. Richmond 1989.

86. Ibid., 24.

87. Stephen Comer, Mohican tribal member and anthropologist, personal communication, 2007.

88. John Pfeiffer, Old Lyme town historian, personal communication.

89. Lavin and Kania 2001a.

90. David Cooke, personal communication.

91. Frazer 1922, 12, 13.

92. Volmar 1996, 39; Simmons 1986, 51, 132.

93. Stephen Comer, "Cultural Beliefs and Ceremonial Practices of the Early Historic Mohican Tribe," paper presented at the annual Algonquian Peoples Seminar at the New York State Museum in Albany, March 24, 2007.

94. Biron 2009.

95. Frank Bergevin, unpublished review of "Iroquois Beadwork: A Haudenosaunee Tradition and Art," by Dolores Elliott, which was published in 2010 in *Preserving Tradition and Understanding the Past: Papers from the Conference on Iroquois Research, 2001–2005*, ed. Christine Sternberg Patrick, *New York State Museum Record* 1:35–48, submitted to the New York State Museum in Albany, November 2010.

96. Fawcett 2000, 15–16.

97. Cruson 2005; Vara 2008; West 2005.

98. Bendremer 1993, 74–106, 131–284.

99. Bendremer 1999, 146–147.

100. Morton 1637, 160.

101. See also Menta 2000, 109–110, for examples of the abundance and importance of dogs among seventeenth-century indigenous communities.

102. The Winthrop Papers 1678, 136.

103. Bendremer 1993, 298, 304.

104. Praus 1942.

105. Lavin 1991.

106. Ibid.

107. Juli and Lavin 1996.

108. Kerber 1985; Lightfoot et al. 1985, 75; Lavin and Kra 1994; Lavin 1991, 83–84; Juli and Lavin 1996; Lucianne Lavin and David H. Thompson, "New Discoveries in Connecticut Archaeology: The Robillard Site, Milford, Connecticut," paper presented at a meeting of the Milford Land Preservation Trust, May 27, 1986, Milford, Conn.

109. Williams 1643, 182.

110. E.g., see Williams 1643 and Wood 1634.

111. Wood 1634, cited in Howlett 2004, 72.

112. Amorosi 1991.

113. For a wonderfully detailed description of the variety of fin- and shellfish collected by Native Americans, and the ways in which they were prepared and eaten, see the article by fishery specialist Timothy Visel, coordinator of the Sound School Regional Vocational Aquaculture Center, "What Coastal Native Americans Fished For; The Sound School Heritage Day 2008," Part II, Appendix II, in publication MH/SF-24, Hammonassett Beach Native American Cultural Center Adult Education and Outreach Education Program, Hammonassett Beach Native American Fisheries, reprinted for the Bauer Lecture Series, February 21, 2009, www.soundschool.com/hammonassett.pdf.

114. "An Older Culture," 2006, 7.

115. Fred Sibley, Chief Museum Preparator of Vertebrate Zoology at the Peabody Museum of Natural History at Yale University, personal communication, March 21, 1984.

116. Williams 1643, 165.

117. Suggs 1958.

118. Coffin 1963.

119. Cantwell 1980, 25–26.

120. E.g., Winters 1969, plate 26.

121. E.g., Heath 1963; Williams 1643; Wood 1634.

122. Lavin 1991.

123. Pfeiffer 1983a, 50.

124. Williams 1972.

125. Wyatt 1977, 404, 406.

126. E.g., see Bragdon 1996, 217–228, and Karr 1999, 103–107.

127. Toensing 2007.

128. William Wood (1634) describing a social gathering in Massachusetts Bay, cited in Karr 1999, 104.

129. Hopkins 1753, 36.

130. Logan 1979, 18.

131. Adelphena Logan, Onondaga elder and educator (1979, 17).

132. Logan 1979, 44.

133. Dr. David McAllester, Professor of Ethnomusicology at Wesleyan University ("David McAllester Speaks" 1976, 9).

134. Carson 1987, 76.

135. Natasha Gambrell, a 14-year-old Eastern Pequot who has been dancing at powwows since she was 7 years old, quoted in Toensing 2007.

136. McAllester 2009, 98.

137. McAllester 1987, 40.

138. McAllester 2009, 99.

139. Ibid., 100.

140. "David McAllester Speaks" 1976, 7, 9.

141. McBride and Soulsby 1989.

142. McBride 1992.

143. Bendremer 1993, 347–350.

144. Bendremer 1999, 148.

145. Bendremer 1993, 1999.

146. McBride 1992; Bendremer 1993, 1999.

147. E.g., Bragdon 1996; Crone-Morange and Lavin 2004.

148. Crone-Morange and Lavin 2004, 143, citing Bragdon 1996, unpublished eighteenth-century accounts, and various archaeological and anthropological articles.

149. De Laet 1909.

150. Bendremer 1999, 388.

151. Lavin 1998.

152. Parkos 1991a.

153. Lavin 1987.

154. Cassedy 1998; Cassedy and Lavin 2007; Lavin 2010, 2011a.

155. Smith 1950.

156. Goddard 1978b.

157. Snow 1980, 330, 307.

158. Lavin 1984, 23; Ernest A. Wiegand, "Phase 1 Cultural Resources Survey of the Proposed Rosenstiel Subdivision, Greenwich, Connecticut," manuscript prepared for S. E. Minor Co., Greenwich, 1987.

159. Salwen 1968.

160. Sassaman 2008, 7.

161. See Smith 1950.

162. Menta 1988, 58.

163. David Thompson, personal communication, 1983.

164. Nicholas Bellantoni, personal communication, 2007.

165. Harrington 1921, fig. 11; Speck 1931; Grumet 2002.

166. Adelphena Logan, Onondaga elder and educator (1979, 60–62).

167. Logan 1979, 37.

168. Fawcett 2000, 136.

169. E.g., Dincauze and Hasenstab 1989; Hasenstab 1987; Lavin, Gudrian, and Miroff 1992–1993; Niemczycki 1986, 1987.

170. For information on Mississippian cultures see Cole 1951; Cox and Dye 1990; Griffin 1978; Holt 2009; O'Connor 1995; Stoltman 1991; and Adams 2010.

171. Adams 2010; Hodges 2011; Milner 2006; Pauketat 1994, 2004; Young and Fowler 1999.

172. Hasenstab 1987.

173. Little 1987.

174. Lavin, Gudrian, and Miroff 1992–1993, 58–60.

175. Goodby 2002; Pretola 2002.

176. Puniello 1993.

177. Lavin 1998, 2002.

178. Lavin 2002, 2010.

179. Funk 1976; Ritchie 1969b.

180. Byers and Rouse 1960.

181. McBride 1984b.

182. Williams 1972.

183. Rouse 1947, 22–23; Smith 1950, 109–110; McBride 1984b, 159; 1990, 99.

184. Goodby 2002.

185. Lavin 2002, 168.

186. McBride and Bellantoni 1982.

187. Ibid.

188. Bendremer 1999.

189. Curtin 2011.

190. Timothy Visel and Abigail Visel, "Alewives: Once the Fish to War Over," unpublished paper presented at the Hammonasset Festival, Hammonasset Beach, Madison, Connecticut, October 1–2, 2011, pp. 1–2.

191. Rogers 1935.

192. Russell 1942.

193. Coffin 1963.

194. Coffin 1963, 62. Coffin does not describe the arrowheads found in specific burials. He does mention the greater penetrating power of narrow, smooth bone arrowheads, suggesting that at least some of the points may have been of the hollow birdbone variety.

195. Morton 1637, 44; Williams 1643, 219, 240–41, 247; Wood 1634, 103, 104.

196. Kalm 1770, 578.

197. Brereton 1602, cited in Howe 1969, 59.

198. Wood 1634, 85.

199. Speck 1931, 71–72.

200. Kalm 1770, 577–578.

201. Williams 1643, 240.

202. Bellantoni 1991; Bendremer 1993, 213–214.

203. E.g., unpublished notes of local historian Frances Manwarring Caulkins on the Niantic tribal cemetery at Crescent Beach, ca. 1845, cited in Kevin A. McBride, "Phase II Intensive Archaeological Survey, Crescent Beach Cemetery Sanitary Sewer System Project, East Lyme, Connecticut," unpublished report prepared for Consulting Environmental Engineers, October 1989, on file with the author, p. 5.

204. Williams 1643, 86, 194; see also Morton 1637, 43, and Karr 1999, 123, citing Winslow 1624, 355–357.

205. Russell 1942.

206. Lavin 1988b; Bellantoni 1991.

207. Bendremer 1993, 213–214.

208. Ibid., 214.

209. Bellantoni 1991.

210. Ibid.

211. Ibid., 18.

212. Bellantoni et al. 1986.

213. Ibid., 50.

214. Johnson 2002, 33–36.

215. Vila et al. 1997.

216. E.g., Flannery 1939; Henry 1809; Butler and Hadlock 1949, as cited in Kaeser 2004, 53; Lopez and Wisniewski 1958; Strong 1985. In particular, dogs and wolves figured prominently in ceremonies involving war and conflict, and were often associated with members of warrior and "soldier" sodalities. See Cook 2012.

217. Kaeser 2004, 59–60.

218. Strong 1985, 33.

219. Cited in Menta 2003, 109.

220. Speck 1909a, 193.

221. Menta 2003, 111–112.

222. Coffin 1963, 64; Kaeser 2004; Kerber 1990; Strong 1985, 35–36.

223. Strong 1985, 36.

224. Lopez and Wisniewski 1958.

225. Alvin H. Morrison, "Dawnland Dog Feast: Wabnaki Warfare and Slavery," unpublished paper presented at the Canadian Ethnology Society annual meeting, May 8–11, 1982, Vancouver, British Columbia, Canada, cited in Strong 1985, 36.

226. David Thompson, personal communication, July 11, 2007.

227. Coffin 1963, 63–64.

228. Hamell 1987, 66; George R. Hamell, "Immortal Shell: Wampum as a Light and Life Metaphor," abstract, paper presented at the 11th annual Algonquian Peoples Seminar, April 30, 2011, New York State Museum, Albany, N.Y.

229. Hamell 1983, 205.

230. Fawcett 2000, 4.

231. Kerber 2002, 18.

232. Toensing 2007.

233. E.g., Lavin 1984, fig. 4a, d, e; Rand 2010, 101.

234. Bragdon 1996, 204.

235. Bragdon 1996, 204.

236. Ibid., 204, 207.

237. Simmons 1970, 61.

238. McMullen 1985, 10.

239. Volmar 1996, 40.

240. Cassedy and Webb 1999, 89.

241. Lavin, Dumas, and Kania 1999.

242. Lavin and Banks 2005b.

243. Binford et al. 1970.

244. E.g., Craig S. Chartier, "Home and Homelot Archaeology at the Lot Harding House, Truro, Massachusetts: What Can Be Learned from Focused, Low Impact Testing in Disturbed Areas," paper presented at the joint spring meeting of the Archaeological Society of Connecticut and the Massachusetts Archaeological Society, May 3, 2008, Storrs, Connecticut; Lavin, Dumas, and Kania 1999.

9. BEAVER SKINS FOR IRON AXES

Epigraph: Armstrong 1972, 3.

1. John Steinberg, "The Archaeology of the Earliest Viking Settlers of Iceland," paper presented at the co-sponsored spring meeting of the Massachusetts Archaeological Society and Archaeological Society of Connecticut, May 21, 2011, Old Sturbridge, Massachusetts.

2. Ingstad and Ingstad 2001.

3. UNESCO World Heritage Centre—World Heritage List, http://whc.unesco.org/en/list/ (accessed April 22, 2011).

4. Howe 1969, 6–10.

5. Crompton and Irwin 2007; Pope 2007; Turgeon 1998.

6. Verrazzano 1970.

7. Howe 1969, 2, 23.

8. Brereton 1602; Pring 1603; Rosier 1605; Champlain 1613.

9. McBride 1990.

10. McBride 2006b, 255.

11. Smith 1624; Dermer 1619.

12. Wood 1634.

13. Williams 1643.

14. Wood 1634, 17; Morton 1637, 45.

15. Morton 1637, 45; Cronon 1983, 50–51; Patterson and Sassaman 1988, 115–116.

16. Ezra Stiles, cited in Menta 2003, 44.

17. Orcutt and Beardsley 1880, xxi, xcvi.

18. Van der Donck as quoted in Axtell 1974, 34–35.

19. Gluck 2011, 6–7.

20. Tantaquidgeon 1977, 69.

21. Joseph Bruchac, an Abenaki storyteller and writer (Bruchac 1987, 5).

22. Trudie Lamb Richmond, open letter to her granddaughter, Wunneanatsu (Richmond 1987, 7).

23. Wood 1634, 105–106.

24. Sturtevant 1975, citing Ezra Stiles, who visited the Niantic reservation in 1761 (Stiles Papers).

25. Cited in Buckland 2002, 161.

26. Williams 1643, 118, see also 117.

27. Champlain 1613, 95–96.

28. Wood 1634, 105–106; Williams 1643, 60–67.

29. Johnson 1654, 162.

30. Handsman 1989, 21.

31. Williams 1643, 201.

32. Ibid., 117.

33. Ibid., 224.

34. Hopkins 1753, 63–64, citing Rev. John Sergeant.

35. Williams 1643, 116.

36. Ibid., 244. There was no real standard for the spelling of English words until Samuel Johnson's *Dictionary of the English Language* in 1755. Seventeenth-century English documents were written phonetically, so there are often several different spellings for the same word. This was particularly true in the recording of unfamiliar Algonkian place names and proper names. This is the main reason the names of many Native Americans show so much variation in land transactions, petitions, and early Anglo-American literature. Jack Lynch, "How Johnson's *Dictionary* Became the First Dictionary," paper presented at the Johnson and the English Language conference, August 25, 2005, Birmingham, England, http://andromeda.rutgers.edu/~jlynch /Papers/firstdict.html (accessed January 4, 2012).

37. Moravian Church Archives 1743–1769; Dally-Starna and Starna 2009, 226.

38. Bragdon 1996; Crone-Morange and Lavin 2004.

39. Richmond 1979, 1.

40. Reverend Father Jean de BreBeuf, New France (1636), cited in Thwaites 1897 (10), 219.

41. John Heckewelder 1876, 137.

42. Richmond 1987a, 6.

43. Unpublished interview with Schaghticoke tribal administrator and historian Paulette Crone-Morange, October 10, 1996, 10–11.

44. E.g., Tantaquidgeon and Fawcett 1987; Speck 1915.

45. Fawcett 2000, 32.

46. Fawcett 2000, 4.

47. According to the late Connecticut state archaeologist Dr. Douglas Jordan, the first archaeologist to expound this theory was the late Professor Bert Salwen from the Department of Anthropology at New York University (Douglas Jordan, personal communication to Lucianne Lavin). Dr. Salwen directed excavations at Fort Shantok and the adjacent pre-contact Shantok Cove site in Uncasville from 1962 to 1965 while at Columbia University, and from 1966 to 1968 and in 1970 during his time at NYU (Williams, McBride, and Grumet 1997, 29).

48. Williams, McBride, and Grumet 1997, 29.

49. McBride and Bellantoni 1982, fig. 1.

50. Juli 1992, 16–20; Juli and Kelley 1991.

51. Williams 1643, 86.

52. Ibid., 194.

53. Ibid., 190.

54. Bragdon 1996, 207, citing Jenks 1827, Little 1986, 51, and Simmons 1986.

55. McBride and Grumet 1996, 19–21.

56. Ordonez and Welters 2004, 172.

57. McBride 1991, 70.

58. *Mourt's Relation,* 1622, cited in Howe 1969, 301.

59. Ibid., 295, 298.

60. Young 1841, 362–363, cited in Karr 1999, 134.

61. Williams 1643, 248–249.

62. Ibid.

63. Ibid., 95, 128.

64. Weslager 1974, 2–3.

65. Ibid., 190–191.

66. Rainey 1933, 105, citing Speck 1909a, 201.

67. Kavasch 1978, 1–2.

68. Morton 1637, cited in Rainey 1933, 24.

69. Kavasch 1978.

70. Hopkins 1753, 25; Williams 1643, 191–193.

71. Williams 1643, 193.

72. Wood 1634, 101, quoted in Karr 1999, 93.

73. Williams 1643, 112.

74. Ibid., 119, 141–142, 155–156; Young 1841, 365–366, as quoted in Karr 1999, 138.

75. Williams 1643, 119.

76. E.g., Moeller 1987.

77. E.g., Troy Phillips, "Preserving Sacred Sites," paper presented at the Annual Algonquian Peoples Seminar, March 24, 2007, at the New York State Museum in Albany. (Phillips is a Nipmuck tribal member.)

78. Gladys Tantaquidgeon, quoted in Fawcett 2000, 21.

79. Rev. John Sergeant 1734, cited in Hopkins 1753, 24.

80. Ibid., 24–25.

81. "Native American Profile" 1866, cited in Drew 2009, 42.

82. Cited in Miles 2006, 4.

83. Butler 1946; Crosby 1991; Handsman 2008; Lavin 2011; Rubertone 2001, 166–167; Simmons 1986, 252–254; Stiles 1916.

84. Glynn 1973.

85. Ibid., 80.

86. Hopkins 1753, 24–25; "Sunday in Great Barrington" 1866, cited in Drew 2009, 42; Speck 1945, 19, 22; Butler 1946; Miles 2006.

87. Speck 1945, 19, 22.

88. Rubertone 2001, 167.

89. Wiseman 2005, 106.

90. E.g., Fawcett 1995, 48–53; 2000, 21–24.

91. Williams 1643, 145.

92. E.g., Fawcett 1995, 48–53; 2000, 21–24; Rubertone 2008b.

93. McLoughlin 2010; Menta 2003, 197.

94. Lenik 2002.

95. Bragdon 1996, 208–214.

96. Ibid., 214.

97. Clifford C. Spooner, *The Story of Molly Fisher and the Molly Fisher Rock,* 1930, reprinted from *Kent Tales* on www.skyweb.net/~channy/SpoonerMF.html.

98. Calogero 1983.

99. Bragdon 1996, fig. 19.

100. Dexter 1901(3), 538 iii.

101. Ibid., 339 iii. Faith Damon Davison kindly provided this and the following Stiles citations regarding Indian "stone gods."

102. Smith 2011, 13.

103. Dexter 1901(2), 424n ii; 1901(3), 340 iii, 538 iii.

104. Dexter 1901(2), 424n ii.

105. Dexter 1901(3), 339 iii.

106. Ibid., 340 iii.

107. Ibid., 354 iii.

108. Ibid.

109. Ibid., 385 iii.

110. Ibid., 386 iii.

111. Ibid., 396 iii.

112. Ibid., 403 iii.

113. Ibid.

114. Ibid., 508 iii.

115. Ibid., 537 iii.

116. Ibid., 538 iii.

117. Steiner 1897, 71.

118. E.g., Martin and Martin 2004.

119. Cited in Leveillee 1997, 26.

120. Ibid., 27.

121. Personal communication to author; see also Gladys Tantaquidgeon's remarks about the use of natural phenomena to determine the times of planting activities in Fawcett 2000, 47.

122. E.g., Carmichael et al. 1994; Morphy 1995; Simmons 1986.

123. Rubertone 2008a, 13–14.

124. Rubertone 2008a.

125. E.g., see the Web site "Kacha Stones" for a discussion of the healing abilities of Welsh and Irish quartz: www.kacha-stones.com/celtic_quartz.htm.

126. E.g., Bell 2009; Simmons 1986.

127. E.g., De Laet 1909, 43; Timothy H. Ives, "Expressions of Community: Reconstructing Native Identity in Seventeenth Century Central Connecticut Through Land Deed Analysis," paper presented at the Fifth Annual Algonquian Peoples' Conference, March 14, 2004, Albany; Salwen 1978; Shepard 1893, 329.

128. E.g., McBride 1991, 1994, 2006b, 2006a; Solecki 1950, 1992–1993, 2006; Salwen 1966; Salwen and Mayer 1978; Taylor 2006; Williams 1972.

129. Adriaen Block, cited in Howe 1969, 221–222.

130. Smith 1916, 1.

131. Dexter 1901(3), 340 iii.

132. Woodruff 1949, 9–11.

133. Cavallaro 2008, 25, 137; Marion O'Keefe, local Seymour and Derby historian, personal communication.

134. E.g., McBride 2006b, 260–261; see below for some examples.

135. Ceci 1980, cited by Solecki 1992–1993; Taylor 2006, 282.

136. Custer 1996, 307; Stewart, Hummer, and Custer 1986.

137. Dunn 1994b, 4.

138. E.g., Bruchac and Thomas 2006; Menta 2003, 60–61, 80, 124; Orcutt and Beardsley 1880, lxxv–lxxvi.

139. Solecki 1992–1993.

140. Ibid., 76.

141. Dunn 1994b.

142. Menta 2003, 59–61; O'Callahan 1855(1), 223.

143. Dunn 1994b, 96–100; Trigger 1971.

144. Dunn 1994b, 117–121.

145. Van Laer 1908, 484.

146. Dunn 1992, 10.

147. Dunn 1994a, citing Jameson 1909, 274, 344, 369.

148. Shirley W. Dunn, "Effects of the Mahican–Mohawk Wars on the Transfer of Mahi-

can Land," 11, paper presented at the 1992 People to People Conference, Rochester, New York, quoting a seventeenth-century source in Jameson 1909, 274. See also Dunn 1994a.

149. Whipple 1974, 27.

150. Dunn, "Effects of the Mahican–Mohawk Wars," 15, citing Trelease 1960, 129. See also Dunn 1994a.

151. Ibid., 15, citing seventeenth-century Dutchman Jeremias Van Rensselaer. See also Dunn 1994a.

152. Ibid., 14, 16; see also Dunn 1994a; Menta 2003, 61; see also Bruchac and Thomas 2006.

153. Dunn, "Effects of the Mahican–Mohawk Wars," 18. See also Dunn 1994a.

154. Bruchac and Thomas 2006, part 2.

155. Dunn 1994b, 107–108; Menta 2003, 60.

156. E.g., Lawrence and Rowe 1953, 33.

157. Ceci 1988; Pendergast 1988; Sempowski 1988.

158. Becker 2006.

159. Hamilton 1957.

160. Moravian Church Archives, box 119, folder 1, April 5, 1753, cited in Richard S. Walling, "The Delawares and Mohicans: A Lasting Covenant," paper presented at the annual Algonquian Peoples Seminar on March 24, 2007, New York State Museum in Albany, N.Y. Similar meetings among Algonquian speakers in the lower Hudson and Housatonic river drainages of New York and Connecticut are described in "A Wampum March in 1720," in this chapter.

161. George R. Hamell, "Immortal Shell: Wampum as a Light and Life Metaphor," abstract, paper presented at the 11th annual Algonquian Peoples Seminar, April 30, 2011, New York State Museum, Albany, N.Y.

162. McBride 1993, 70; Ordonez and Welters 2004. McBride's excavations at the seventeenth-century Mohantic fort at Mashantucket located artifacts related to the manufacture of brass objects, wampum, and lead shot, as well as for the maintenance and repair of firearms; McBride 1993, 68–70.

163. Salisbury 1981, 229, 233–235; Howe 1969, 172, 185–186, 274–277.

164. E.g., Juliano 2006; McBride 2006b, 260.

165. Winthrop 1908, 61.

166. Menta 2003, 86.

167. For a cogent account of the deleterious effect of Anglo practices on indigenous homelands and their traditional lifeways, see William Cronon's 1983 book *Changes in the Land: Indians, Colonists, and the Ecology of New England.*

168. Verrazzano, cited in Wroth 1970, 38.

169. Henry Hudson, quoted in Armstrong 1972, 1.

170. Karen Coody Cooper (1986, 6), former education director at the Institute for American Indian Studies and enrolled tribal member of the Cherokee Nation of Oklahoma, citing Edward Winslow of Plymouth Colony in *Mourt's Relation,* published in London in 1622; Heath 1963. Winslow is thought to be the main author of that book, which was published without identifying its writer(s).

171. Williams 1643, 108.

172. Ibid., 115, 115–116.

173. Sergeant, cited in Hopkins 1753, 63.

174. Williams 1643, 217–218.

175. Morton 1637, 35; Wright 1967.

176. Williams 1643, 215.

177. Ibid., 216.

178. Ibid., 187.

179. E.g., Rubertone 1989.

180. Kupperman 1980, 10.

181. Harper 2008, 10.

182. Dwight, quoted in Harper 2008, 17.

183. Williams 1643, cited by Butler 1953, 41–42.

184. Cooper 1985, 4.

185. Vescelius 1952; Menta 2003, 44.

186. Silliman 2009, 225, 227.

187. Spiess and Spiess 1987.

188. Bragdon 1996, 27.

189. Salisbury 1981, 236.

190. Bradford 1650, 176.

191. Winthrop 1908, 118.

192. Menta 2003, 103.

193. Ibid., 105.

194. Miles 2009, 8.

195. Bragdon 1996, 26–28.

196. See, e.g., Milner and Chaplin 2010, 708.

197. Ibid., 707.

198. Snow 1980.

199. Salisbury 1981, 234–239; Silverman 2005, 1.

## 10. SURVIVING EUROPEAN-AMERICAN COLONIALISM

Epigraph: Fawcett 2000.

1. Public Law No. 95-341, 92 Stat. 469 (Aug. 11, 1978), U.S.C., Title 42, Chapter 21, Subchapter I, §1996, Protection and Preservation of Traditional Religions of Native Americans.

2. Indian Citizenship Act of 1924, 43 U.S. Stats. at Large, ch. 233, p. 253 (1924).

3. Rev. William Morrell, 1625, quoted in Vaughan 1965, 45. See also Morrell 1895.

4. De Forest 1852, 43.

5. Johnston 1903, 26–29.

6. Smith 1946.

7. Nancy Johnson, former U.S. representative from Connecticut, referring to the Schaghticoke tribe, quoted in Toensing 2004. The Public Records of Connecticut show that the Schaghticokes were granted their Kent reservation by the Connecticut General Assembly and have lived there since at least 1736, before the Town of Kent was even founded in 1739—and it was founded on the east side of the Housatonic, not the west side where the Schaghticoke Reservation is located, as the original 1739 proprietors' map for Kent clearly showed (Crone-Morange and Lavin 2004, 133).

8. E.g., Cooper 1986, 5–6; Flowers 2005; Connecticut (Colony) 1872, 551–552; Menta 2003, 106, 123, 136; Toensing 2007; Trumbull 1852, 574–576; Trumbull and Hoadley 1881, 11.

9. Bendremer 1999, 146.

10. Winthrop 1908, 191.

11. J. Kēhaulani Kauanui, *2011 Audio Archives: Indigenous Politics: From Native New England and Beyond,* radio program, WESU, Middletown, Conn., October 24, 2011, www.indigenouspolitics.com/?p=27.

12. The sale for sixty Dutch guilders was first mentioned by Pieter Schaghen, representative of the States General in the Assembly of the Nineteen of the West Indian Company, in a November 7, 1626, letter to the company's directors. At that time, sixty guilders would have

equated to twenty-four American dollars. The letter and its translation are available online from the New Netherland Institute (www.nnp.org/nnp/documents/schagen_main.html).

13. See Bragdon 1996.

14. Bell 2009; Fawcett 2000; Handsman 2008; Rubertone 2008a, 2008b.

15. Feder 1982. The Oneida invitation was to leaders of the Brothertown movement, a Christian Indian movement led by Mohegan leader and Presbyterian minister Reverend Samson Occom, with his son-in-law Joseph Johnson and Occom's brother-in-law Montauk David Fowler. Disgusted with the shameful treatment indigenous peoples regularly received at the hands of Anglo-Americans, even those who were educated and Christian, they concluded that Native American communities could live successfully and peacefully only by separating themselves from white communities. Joined by members from several southern New England and Long Island tribes that included the Tunxis, in 1785 the group began moving to Oneida country near present-day Waterville, New York, where the original Brothertown settlement was located. Pressures from the white government and neighbors forced them to leave New York for Wisconsin in the 1830s, where their descendants—members of the Brothertown Indian Nation—still live today. For a history of the Brothertown tribe, see Caroline K. Andler, n.d., "Brothertown Indian Nation, Brief History," www.brothertownindians.org/History.htm; Commuck 1859 (also online at http://library.wisc.edu/etext/wireader/WER0439.html); Love 2000; Silverman 2011. See also "The Value of Christianity" in this chapter for a brief discussion of the Brothertown movement.

16. Smith 1916, 12.

17. Lavin 2011.

18. E.g., see Marcel Mauss (1925), a French sociologist whose classic work *The Gift* explained the structure and significance of this social convention among non-Western peoples.

19. Wright 1967.

20. Lynne Williamson, Mohawk-Mississauga descent, museum professional and former curator at the Institute for American Indian Studies (1989, 13).

21. Carlson 1987; Menta 1988, 2003.

22. Menta 1988.

23. Watrous 1939.

24. Carlson 1987, 26.

25. Bell 2009, 22.

26. Handsman and Richmond 1995, 101.

27. E.g., Binzen 1997; Timothy L. Binzen, "Weataug and Wechquadnach: Native American Settlements of the Upper Housatonic," paper presented at Mohican Seminar 2000: The Continuance—An Algonquian Peoples Seminar, April 15, 2000, New York State Museum, Albany, N.Y.; Campisi 1990; Crone-Morange and Lavin 2004; Den Ouden 2005; Feder 1982; Lavin 1997a; Crone-Morange and Lavin 2003; Michael Lawson, "Historical Report Supplementing the Petition of the Schaghticoke Tribal Nation of Kent, Connecticut, for Federal Acknowledgment," unpublished report prepared for the Schaghticoke Tribal Nation of Kent, Conn., 1997; Menta 2003, 142–146; Smith 1916, 2–3; Smith 1985.

28. Sedgwick 1877, 32; emphasis added.

29. Pfeiffer 1996, 72.

30. Silverman 2003.

31. Ives 2011, 8, 13–14.

32. Connecticut Archives, Record Group 001:010, Early General Records, 1629–1820, *Indians*, ser. I, vol. II, 1789, 330a-330b.

33. Williamson and Richmond 1991, 7.

34. Campisi 1990, 140.

35. Crone-Morange and Lavin 2003.

36. Fidelia Fielding, Mohegan culture keeper and last of the speakers and writers of the Mohegan-Pequot dialect, writing in her diary on May 23, 1904.

37. Troy Phillips, "Preserving Sacred Sites," paper presented at the Annual Algonquian Peoples Seminar, on March 24, 2007, New York State Museum in Albany.

38. From seventeenth-century Englishmen: e.g., Mason 1637; Underhill 1638. From archaeology: McBride 2010; Kevin McBride and David Naumec, "Battlefields of the Pequot War," paper presented at the fall meeting of the Archaeological Society of Connecticut, October 17, 2009, Mashantucket Pequot Museum and Research Center, Mashantucket, Conn. The Mashantucket Pequot Museum and Research Center received a multi-year grant from the National Endowment for the Humanities to research the battlefields of the Pequot War. Research in the form of archival studies and archaeological surveys under the direction of Dr. Kevin McBride, director of research at the museum, is ongoing.

39. I urge the reader to look at indigenous versions of American history and to visit the Mashantucket Pequot Museum and Research Center in Ledyard, Connecticut, for a more balanced view of factors leading to and culminating in the Pequot War.

40. Whipple 1974, 90.

41. Washburn 1978, 90; Hauptman 1990, 71.

42. McBride and Naumec 2010, 6.

43. Washburn 1978, 90; Hauptman 1990, 72–76.

44. Barzillai Slosson, *History of Kent,* 1812, photocopy of manuscript on file at the Connecticut State Library, Hartford, www.consuls.org/record=b3038595-S1.

45. Local folklore and histories suggest that Sassacus may have been killed in the area of present-day Dover Plains, New York.

46. Kevin McBride, personal communication, February 23, 2011; McBride and Naumec 2010, 6–7.

47. Hauptman 1990, 76–77.

48. Karen Coody Cooper, Cherokee, museum professional, author, poet, finger weaver, and former director of education at the Institute for American Indian Studies (1985, 7).

49. McBride 1990.

50. McBride and Grumet 1996, 15–16.

51. Washburn 1978, 92–94; Bourne 1990.

52. Menta 2003, 61–62; Smith 1916, 2.

53. Cooper 1986, 5.

54. Cooper 1985, 6.

55. McBride 2006a; Mashantucket Pequot Museum and Research Center, Archaeology at Mashantucket Web page, www.pequotmuseum.org/Home/ResearchCollections/ARCHAE OLOGY/ArchaeologyatMashantucket.htm (accessed December 29, 2011).

56. Crone-Morange and Lavin 2004.

57. E.g., see Kawashima 2004; Campisi 1990; Den Ouden 2005.

58. Crone-Morange and Lavin 2004, 153.

59. Grumet 1992, 81; McBride and Grumet 1996, 22; Weinstein and Heme 2005; Wojciechowski 1985.

60. Binzen, "Weataug and Wechquadnach"; Crone-Morange and Lavin 2004.

61. Bradshaw 1935, 50; emphasis added.

62. Richmond 1994, 104.

63. E.g., Norton 1899; Brown and Rose 1980.

64. The Editors of *Northeast Magazine,* "Complicity: How Connecticut Chained Itself to the Slave Trade," *Hartford Courant* Special Report, September 29, 2002, www.courant.com /news/specials/hc-slavery,0,1421221.special; Farrow et al. 2005.

65. Lauber 1979; Newell 2003. Europeans had been kidnapping indigenous people for over a hundred years prior to the Pequot War. The first documented kidnapping was of seven Indians by Gaspar Cortereal of Portugal in 1500–1501. A number of these abducted Indians were sold as slaves in Europe; Howe 1969.

66. Norton 1899.

67. And likely also the Caribbean salt mines, where many African slaves ended their days. Philip Wyppensenwah Rabito, a Shawnee affiliated with the American Indian Archaeological Institute in the late 1970s, where he initiated a study of Bermuda's Native American slaves, noted that in 1664 the Dutch governor of New York shipped a group of Mahikan war captives to the islands as slaves; Rabito 1977, 3.

68. Boissevain 1981; Orcutt and Beardsley 1880, lvii–lxii.

69. Lauber 1979, 123–124.

70. Speck 1947, 2.

71. Pfeiffer 1996, 75–76.

72. Menta 2003, 159.

73. Pfeiffer 1996, 74–75.

74. Steven Edwin Conliff, "Revolutionary Traditions of the Munsees, Mohicans, and Oneidas: We Always Heard We Helped . . . and You'd Remember," paper presented at the 5th Annual Seminar, March 2004, Native American Institute and the New York State Museum, Albany, N.Y.; Fawcett 1995, 19; Gaines 1930, 47–48; Mancini and Naumec 2005; Mynter 1987; Moravian Church Archives, 1760, box 115, folder 6 (May 6, 7, 10, 19), folder 9 (January 15), folder 10 (December 8); David J. Naumec, "From Mashantucket to Appomattox: The Native American Veterans of Connecticut's Volunteer Regiments and the Union Navy," paper presented at Insiders and Outsiders: Ethnicity, Immigration, and Status in Connecticut, conference of the Association for the Study of Connecticut History, November 2006, Manchester Community College, Manchester, Conn.; Naumec 2008a; Smith 1916, 2; Laurie Weinstein, Bethany Morrison, and Cosimo Sgarlata, "Archaeological Investigations at Redding's Middle Encampment," paper presented at the annual meeting of the Archaeological Society of Connecticut, October 17, 2009, Mashantucket Pequot Museum, Ledyard, Conn.; Linda Gray, Schaghticoke tribal genealogist, personal communication.

75. Miles 2009, 51.

76. Lion Miles, personal communication, September 3, 2010.

77. Naumec 2008a, 196.

78. Almeida 1975; Calloway 1995; Walling 1999; Richard S. Walling, "Nimham's Indian Company of 1778: The Events Leading Up to the Stockbridge Massacre of August 31, 1778," paper presented at the Mohican Seminar 2000: The Continuance—An Algonquian Peoples Seminar, April 15, 2000, New York State Museum, Albany, N.Y., available from Americanrevolution.org.

79. Naumec 2008a, 182.

80. Ibid., 185.

81. Mynter 1987, 32.

82. See 2010 Census Brief: Overview of Race and Hispanic Origin (www.census.gov/prod /cen2010/briefs/c2010br-02.pdf) and 2009 American Community Survey (http://factfinder .census.gov/servlet/DatasetMainPageServlet?_program=ACS&_submenuId=&_lang=en& _ts=). The Institute for American Indian Studies hosts an annual Native American Veterans Day program in November, during which a local indigenous veteran is honored.

83. Conkey, Bolissevian, and Goddard 1978; Fowler 1953; Pfeiffer and Malcarne 1989; Naumec 2008a, 204; Smith 1916, 2–12.

84. "Archaeology at Mashantucket," Mashantucket Pequot Museum and Research Center, www.pequotmuseum.org/Home/ResearchCollections/ARCHAEOLOGY/Archaeologyat Mashantucket.htm.

85. April 1997; Butler 1947; Campisi 1990; Crone-Morange and Lavin 2004; Den Ouden 2005; Fawcett 1995, 2000; Johnson 1996; Crone-Morange and Lavin 2003; Jason R. Mancini, "Land, Race, and Ethnic Formation: Reassessing the Social History and Geography of Minorities in Eighteenth-Century Connecticut," paper presented at the Association for the Study of Connecticut History (ASCH) conference "Insiders and Outsiders: Ethnicity, Immigration, and Status in Connecticut," November 4, 2006, Manchester Community College, Manchester, Conn.; Mancini 2009; Menta 2003; McBride 1990, 1991, 1993; McBride and Grumet 1996; Richmond 1987b, 1989; Wojciechowski 1985.

86. *New Milford Times,* October 26, 1939.

87. Brilvitch 2007; Crone-Morange and Lavin 2004; Feder 1993; Russell G. Handsman, "Some Middle-Range Theory for Archaeological Studies of Wampanoag Indian Whaling," abstract, paper presented at Emerging Challenges to Coastal and Maritime Archaeology, annual meeting of the Conference on New England Archaeology, May 28, 2011, University of Massachusetts, Amherst; McBride 1991; Jason Mancini, "Beyond Reservation: Indians, Maritime Labor, and Communities of Color from Eastern Long Island Sound, 1713–1861," paper presented at the fall meeting of the Archaeological Society of Connecticut, October 18, 2008, Fairfield Museum and History Center, Fairfield, Conn.

88. Fawcett 1995, 20–21; Lavin 2001.

89. Lossing 1871, 574.

90. Frazer 1992, 23; Hopkins 1753, 30–31; Lucianne Lavin, 1997a, "Anthropological Report Supplementing the Petition of the Schaghticoke Tribal Nation of Kent, Connecticut, for Federal Acknowledgment," unpublished report prepared for the Schaghticoke Tribal Nation of Kent, Conn.; Lavin 2001, 2011; Lossing 1871.

91. E.g., Satz 2002, Wallace 1993.

92. Fawcett 1995, 21.

93. Naumec 2008a, 188.

94. Weinstein 1994.

95. Love 2000, 146, 147, 152, 153.

96. See Caroline K. Andler, n.d., "Brothertown Indian Nation, Brief History," www.brothertownindians.org/History.htm.

97. Menta 2003, 181–193.

98. Faith Davison, personal communication, April 28, 2010, citing Love 2000.

99. O'Brien 2006; Jean M. O'Brien, "New England Local Histories as Replacement Narratives," paper presented at Yale University, February 27, 2006, New Haven, Conn.

100. O'Brien 2010.

101. Handsman and Richmond 1995, 103–104.

102. Kevin A. McBride, "Pootatuck Wigwams: Overview of Its Historic Significance and Archaeological Values," nomination form for the National Register of Historic Places, prepared for the Connecticut Historical Commission, Hartford.

103. McBride and Grumet 1996, 22.

104. Marc Banks, "Recollections of Dr. Douglas Jordan and the 1991 UCONN Field School," paper presented at the fall meeting of the Archaeological Society of Connecticut, October 16, 2010, South Windsor.

105. Jeffrey Bendremer, Elaine Thomas, Stephanie Fielding, and Faith Davison, "Yo Nik (This Is My Home): Vernacular Architecture and Changing Indigenous Domestic Spaces on the Mohegan Reservation," paper presented at the Society for American Archaeology, Atlanta, Ga., April 22–26, 2009, and "Historic Native American Communities in Southern New England: What Local Town Histories Never Told Us," the 4th Annual Native American-Archaeology Roundtable at the Institute for American Indian Studies, Washington, Conn., Sept. 27, 2009.

106. Bell and Simon 2007, 3.

107. Feder 1993.

108. Weinstein 2011.

109. Orcutt and Beardsley 1880, xlii–xliv, liv–lv. See Brent M. Colley, The History of Redding, "The Early Settlement of Redding From Charles Burr Todd's History of Redding," www.historyofredding.com/HRearlysettlers.htm.

110. Woodruff 1949, 11–12.

111. Brilvitch 2007.

112. D'Arcy McNickle, a Cree-Salish-Kootenai writer (1973).

113. E.g., "Indian Tragedy" 1893; Darwin 1903.

114. Fawcett 2000, 34.

115. Connecticut State Park and Forest Commission 1926, 42.

116. Fred Lane, n.d., "The Schaghticoke Trail," unpublished manuscript, available from the Schaghticoke Tribal Office, Derby, Conn.

117. Campisi 1990; Lucianne Lavin, "Anthropological Report Supplementing the Petition of the Schaghticoke Tribal Nation of Kent, Connecticut for Federal Acknowledgment," unpublished report prepared for the Schaghticoke Tribal Nation of Kent, Conn., 1997; Flowers 2005.

118. Francis Sugrue, ca. 1951, news clipping from the New York Herald Tribune entitled "They Need Licenses Numbers: Connecticut Ends Indians' Free Hunting," on file at the Schaghticoke Tribal Office, Derby, Conn.

119. April 1997, 109.

120. In the early twentieth century, the state, which held tribal lands in trust and was responsible for the land and buildings, provided biannual appropriations for each reservation. Judith A. Shapiro, "Rebuttal of Schaghticoke Tribal Nation to Legal Authorities Submitted by the State of Connecticut et al.," unpublished report submitted to the United States Department of the Interior, September 29, 2003, pp. 17–23.

121. Albert Hoover, "Statement in Favor of Senate Bill 502," 1953, Connecticut State Welfare Department, Public Welfare Council, Connecticut Archives, Connecticut State Library, Hartford.

122. Fowler 1953.

123. "State Decides Against Selling Indian Reserves," New Haven Register, March 22, 1953.

124. Handsman 1991, 3.

125. Marcia Jones Flowers, chairwoman of the Eastern Pequot Tribal Nation (2005), emphasis added.

126. Reinhart 2002. This blood requirement was rescinded sometime before 2002 (ibid.).

127. The Mohegan Tribe: Frequently Asked Questions Web page, www.mohegan.nsn.us/pressroom/faq.aspx.

128. Ibid., emphasis added.

129. E.g., Benedict 2000; Toensing 2005, 2006, 2011; Zielbauer 2001, 2002.

130. Bruchac 2006.

131. Christopher Reinhart, "OLR Research Report, Questions About State Recognition of Indian Tribes," 2002-R-0072, January 23, 2002, www.cga.ct.gov/2002/rpt/2002-R-0072.htm.

132. David K. Leff, "Memorandum," June 25, 1993, Office of Legislative Research, Hartford, Conn., p. 5.

133. Official Statement by John G. Rowland, Governor of Connecticut, designating November 1996 as Native American Month in the State of Connecticut, referencing Connecticut Public Law 368, Sec. 16, 1989.

134. Bragdon 1996, xi.

135. Bell 2009, 33–34.

# References

Achterberg, Jeanne. 1985. *Imagery in Healing: Shamanism and Modern Medicine.* Boston: Shambhala.

Adams, James R. 2010. "Cahokia 101, A Primer on a Hidden Past: What You Never Learned in School About a 12th Century Indian Metropolis." *National Museum of the American Indian* 11:12–21.

Adovasio, J. M., Joel D. Gunn, J. Donahue, and R. Stuckenrath. 1975. "Excavations at Meadowcroft Rockshelter, 1973–1974: A Progress Report." *Pennsylvania Archaeologist* 45(3):1–30.

Aganstata, Mikki. 1988. "The Women Within a Circle." *Artifacts* 16(3–4):38–39.

Alexander, Herbert L., Jr. 1963. "The Levi Site: A Paleo-Indian Campsite in Central Texas." *American Antiquity* 28(4):510–528.

Almeida, D. 1975. "The Stockbridge Indian in the American Revolution." *Historical Journal of Western Massachusetts* 4:34–39.

American Heart Association. 2002. "AHA Scientific Statement: Fish Consumption, Fish Oil, Omega-3 Fatty Acids, and Cardiovascular Disease, #71–024." *Circulation* 106:2747–2757.

———. 2010. Meat, Poultry and Fish. Dallas, Tex.: AHA, Inc.; www.heart.org/HEARTORG/GettingHealthy/NutritionCenter/Meat-Poultry-and-Fish_UCM_306002_Article.jsp (updated 20 May 2010; accessed 2 December 2011).

Amorosi, Thomas. 1991. "Vertebrate Archaeofauna from the Old Lyme Shell Heap." In *The Archaeology and Ethnohistory of the Lower Hudson Valley and Neighboring Regions: Essays in Honor of Louis A. Brennan,* ed. Herbert C. Kraft, pp. 95–124. New York State Archaeological Association 11. Bethlehem, Conn.: Archaeological Services.

Andrews, J. Clinton. 1986. "Indian Fish and Fishing Off Coastal Massachusetts." *Massachusetts Archaeological Society Bulletin* 47(2):42–46; www.nha.org/history/hn/HN-fall94-andrews.htm.

Armitage, Peter. 1991. *The Innu (The Montagnais Naskapi).* New York: Chelsea House.

Armstrong, Virginia I. 1972. *I Have Spoken: American History Through the Voices of the Indians.* New York: Pocket.

Aupaumut, Hendrick. 1987. Mahican Subsistence. (Excerpted from "Extract from an Indian History" in the 1804 publication of his circa-1790 narrative in *Massachusetts Historical Society Collections* ser. 1, vol. 9, 99–102, Boston: Hall and Hiller.) In *Rooted Like the Ash Trees: New England Indians and the Land,* ed. Richard G. Carlson, rev. ed., pp. 28–29. Naugatuck, Conn.: Eagle Wing.

Axtell, James. 1974. *America Perceived: A View from Abroad in the 17th Century.* New Haven: Pendulum.

Banks, Marc. 1990. Aboriginal Weirs in Southern New England. *Bulletin of the Archaeological Society of Connecticut* 53:73–83.

———. 2000. "Anadromous Fish and Prehistoric Site Selection in the Farmington Valley of Connecticut." Ph.D. diss., University of Connecticut. Ann Arbor, Mich.: University Microfilm.

Barber, John W. 1838. *Connecticut Historical Collections.* New Haven, Conn.: Durrie and Peck and J. W. Barber.

Barber, Michael B. 2001. "Pitted Hammerstone: Form and Function." *Quarterly Bulletin of the Archaeological Society of Virginia* 56(2):60–67.

Barske, Philip. 1961. "Wildlife of the Coastal Marshes." *The Connecticut Arboretum Bulletin* 12:13–15.

Baxter, Elizabeth S. 1991. "Retrospective on Respect." *Bulletin of the Archaeological Society of Connecticut* 54:21–22.

Becker, Marshall. 2005. "Penobscot Wampum Belt Use During the 1722–1727 Conflict in Maine." In *Papers of the Thirty-sixth Algonquian Conference,* ed. H. C. Wolfart, pp. 23–51. Winnipeg: University of Manitoba.

———. 2006. "Foragers in Southern New England: Correlating Social Systems, Maize Production, and Wampum." *Bulletin of the Archaeological Society of Connecticut* 68:75–107.

———. 2010. "Birdstones: Insights from a New Inventory in New England." *Bulletin of the Archaeological Society of Connecticut* 72:5–61.

Bell, Edward L. 2009. "Opinion: Eligibility for National Register of Historic Places, Nantucket Sound Wampanoag Traditional Cultural Property." Massachusetts Historical Commission, Office of the Massachusetts State Historic Preservation Officer, Boston.

Bell, Edward L., and Brona Simon. 2007. "MHC Opinion: Eligibility for National Register. Fieldstone Wall and Rock Piles, Turners Falls Airport." On file at the Massachusetts Historical Commission, Boston.

Bellantoni, Nicholas F. 1987. "Faunal Resource Availability and Prehistoric Cultural Selection on Block Island, Rhode Island." Ph.D. diss., University of Connecticut, Storrs.

———. 1991. "Two Prehistoric Human Skeletal Remains from the Morgan Site, Rocky Hill, Connecticut." *Bulletin of the Archaeological Society of Connecticut* 54:13–20.

———. 1999. "Precontact Archaeology in Connecticut: An Overview of 11,000 Years of Cultural Adaptation." In *The Archaeology of Connecticut,* ed. Kristen N. Keegan and William F. Keegan, pp. 1–6. Storrs, Conn.: Bibliopola.

———. 2008. "Norris L. Bull's 'Monolithic Ax.'" *Bulletin of the Archaeological Society of Connecticut* 70:101–102.

Bellantoni, Nicholas F., Lucianne Lavin, and Peter H. Buschang. 1986. "Comparative Analysis of Prehistoric Human Osteological Materials." *Bulletin of the Archaeological Society of Connecticut* 49:37–52.

Bello, C. A., and J. H. Cresson. 1998. "An Obsidian Biface from the Lower Delaware Valley." *Bulletin of the Archaeological Society of New Jersey* 53:127–128.

Bendremer, Jeffrey C. 1993. "Late Woodland Settlement and Subsistence in Eastern Connecticut." Ph.D. diss., University of Connecticut, Storrs.

———. 1999. "Changing Strategies in the Pre- and Post-Contact Subsistence Systems of
Southern New England: Archaeological and Ethnohistorical Evidence." In *Current
Northeast Paleoethnobotany,* ed. John P. Hart, pp. 133–155. Bulletin 494. Albany: New
York State Museum.

Bendremer, Jeffrey C., and Robert Dewar. 1994. "Advent of Maize Horticulture in New
England." In *Corn and Culture in the Prehistoric New World,* ed. Sissel Johannessen
and Christine Hastorf, pp. 369–393. University of Minnesota Publications in Anthropology 3. Boulder, Colo.: Westview.

Bendremer, Jeffrey C., E. Kellogg, and T. Largy. 1991. "A Grass-Lined Storage Pit and
Early Maize Horticulture in Central Connecticut." *North American Archaeologist*
12:325–349.

Benedict, Jeff. 2000. *Without Reservation.* New York: HarperCollins.

Benson, Adolph B., ed. 1964. *Peter Kalm's Travels in North America: The English Version of
1770.* New York: Dover.

Bernstein, David. 1999. "Prehistoric Use of Plant Foods on Long Island." In *Current Northeast Paleoethnobotany,* ed. John P. Hart, pp. 101–119. Bulletin 494. Albany: New York
State Museum.

———. 2002. "Late Woodland Use of Coastal Resources at Mount Sinai Harbor, Long
Island, New York." In *A Lasting Impression: Coastal, Lithic, and Ceramic Research in
New England Archaeology,* ed. Jordan E. Kerber, pp. 27–40. Westport, Conn.: Praeger.

Binford, Lewis R., Sally R. Binford, Robert Whallon, and M. A. Hardin. 1970. "The Archaeology at Hatchery West." *American Antiquity Memoirs* 24.

Binzen, Timothy L. 1997. "Mohican Lands and Colonial Corners: Weataug, Wechquadnach, and the Connecticut Colony, 1675–1750." Master's thesis, University of Connecticut, Storrs.

———. 2009. "The River Beyond the Mountains: Native American Settlements of the
Upper Housatonic During the Woodland Period." In *Mohican Seminar 2, The Chal-
lenge—An Algonquian Peoples Seminar,* ed. Shirley W. Dunn, pp. 7–17. New York State
Museum Bulletin 506. Albany: University of the State of New York, New York State
Educational Department.

Birket-Smith, Kaj. 1959. *The Eskimos.* London: Methuen.

Bishop, Jerry E. 1993. "Strands of Time, Variations in Fragments Hint Some American
Natives May Hail from Polynesia." *Wall Street Journal,* September 3, 1993.

Blake, Leonard, and Hugh C. Cutler. 1983. "Plant Remains from the Gnagey Site." *Pennsylvania Archaeologist* 53:83–88.

Blitz, John H. 1988. "Adoption of the Bow in Prehistoric North America." *North American
Archaeologist* 9(2):123–145.

Bloom, Arthur L., and Minze Stuiver. 1963. "Submergence of the Connecticut Coast."
*Science* 139(3552):332–334.

Bodner, Connie Cox. 1999. "Sunflower in the Seneca Iroquois Region of Western New
York." In *Current Northeast Paleoethnobotany,* ed. John P. Hart, pp. 27–45. Bulletin
494. Albany: New York State Museum.

Boissevain, Ethel. 1981. "Whatever Became of the New England Indians Shipped to Bermuda to Be Sold as Slaves?" *Man in the Northeast* 21:103–114.

Boulanger, Mathew T., Thomas R. Jamison, Craig Skinner, and Michael D. Glascock. 2007. "Analysis of an Obsidian Biface Reportedly Found in the Connecticut River Valley of Vermont." *Archaeology of Eastern North America* 35:81–92.

Bourn, Richard Q., Jr. 1972. "New Submerged Sites of Coastal Connecticut." *Bulletin of the Archaeological Society of Connecticut* 37:5–16.

———. 1977. "The Hammonasset Beach Site (6 NH 35)." *Bulletin of the Archaeological Society of Connecticut* 40:14–39.

———. 1995. "The Ferry Road Site (6-MD-96)." *Bulletin of the Archaeological Society of Connecticut* 58:31–66.

———. 2002. "The Smith Brook Site (6-HT-23)." *Bulletin of the Archaeological Society of Connecticut* 64:3–22.

Bourne, Russell. 1990. *The Red King's Rebellion: Racial Politics in New England, 1675–1678.* New York: Atheneum, Macmillan.

Boyle, David. 1911. *Annual Archaeological Report.* Ontario Archaeology Museum (Toronto), Toronto Ontario Provincial Museum. Toronto: L. K. Cameron, Printer to the King's Most Excellent Majesty.

Bradford, William. 1650. *Of Plymouth Plantation,* ed. Harvey Wish. New York: Capricorn, 1962.

Bradley, Bruce, and Dennis Stanford. 2004. "The North Atlantic Ice-Edge Corridor: A Possible Palaeolithic Route to the New World." Special Issue: Debates in World Archaeology, *World Archaeology* 36(4):459–478.

Bradley, James W., Arthur E. Spiess, Richard A. Boisvert, and Jeff Boudreau. 2008. "What's the Point? Modal Forms and Attributes of Paleo-Indian Bifaces in the New England-Maritime Region." *Archaeology of Eastern North America* 36:119–172.

Bradshaw, Harold C. 1935. *The Indians of Connecticut, the Effects of English Colonization and of Missionary Activity on Indian Life in Connecticut.* Deep River, Conn.: New Era.

Bragdon, Kathleen J. 1996. *Native People of Southern New England, 1500–1650.* Norman: University of Oklahoma Press.

Braun, David P. 1974. "Explanatory Models for the Evolution of Coastal Adaptation in Prehistoric New England." *American Antiquity* 39:582–596.

Braun, Esther K., and David P. Braun. 1994. *The First Peoples of the Northeast.* Lincoln, Mass.: Lincoln Historical Society.

BreBeuf, Jean de. 1636. "Relation of What Occurred in the Country of the Hurons in the Year 1636." Sent to Quebec to Reverend Father Paul le Jeune, Superior of the Mission of the Society of Jesus, in New France, July 16, 1636. In *The Jesuit Relations and Allied Documents: Travels and Explorations of the Jesuit Missionaries in New France, 1610–1791,* ed. Reuben Gold Thwaites, vol. 10, Hurons: 1636, pp. 5–317. Cleveland: Burrows Bros., 1897.

Brennan, Louis A. 1974. "The Lower Hudson: A Decade of Shell Middens." *Archaeology of Eastern North America* 2(1):81–93.

Brereton, John. 1602. "A Briefe and True Relation of the Discoverie of the North Part of

Virginia." Reprinted in *Sailors' Narratives of the Voyages Along the New England Coast, 1524–1624,* ed. George P. Winship. New York: B. Franklin, 1968.

Brilvitch, Charles 2007. *A History of Connecticut's Golden Hill Paugussett Tribe.* Charleston, London: History Press.

Brown, Barbara, and James Rose. 1980. *Black Roots in Southeastern Connecticut, 1650–1900.* Detroit: Gale Research.

Brownell, Charles De Wolf. 1859. *Indian Races of North and South America.* New York: American Subscription Publishing House.

Bruchac, James, and Joseph Bruchac. 2000. *Native American Games and Stories.* Golden, Colo.: Fulcrum.

Bruchac, Joseph. 1987. "Rooted Like the Ash Trees: Abenaki People and the Land. In *Rooted Like the Ash Trees: New England Indians and the Land,* ed. Richard G. Carlson, pp. 2–5. Naugatuck, Conn.: Eagle Wing.

Bruchac, Margaret, and Peter Thomas. 2006. "Locating Wissatinnewag." *Historical Journal of Massachusetts* 34(1):56–82.

Brumbach, Hetty Jo, and Robert Jarvenpa. 1997. "Woman the Hunter; Ethnoarchaeological Lessons from Chipewyan Life-Cycle Dynamics." In *Women in Prehistory: North America and Mesoamerica,* ed. Cheryl Claassen and Rosemary A. Joyce, pp. 17–32. Philadelphia: University of Pennsylvania Press.

Buckland, John A. 2002. *The Wiechquaeskeck Indians of Southwestern Connecticut in the Seventeenth Century.* Bowie, Md.: Heritage.

Burns, Russell M., and Barbara H. Honkala, tech. coords. 1990. *Silvics of North America.* Volume 2, Hardwoods. Agriculture Handbook 654. Washington, D.C.: U.S. Department of Agriculture, Forest Service; www.na.fs.fed.us/pubs/silvics_manual/table_of_contents.shtm.

Butler, Eva L. 1946. "The Brush or Stone Memorial Heaps of Southern New England." *Bulletin of the Archaeological Society of Connecticut* 19:2–12.

———. 1947. "Addendum: Some Early Indian Basket Makers of Southern New England." In *Eastern Algonkian Block-Stamp Decoration: A New World Original or An Acculturated Art,* ed. Frank G. Speck. Trenton: Archaeological Society of New Jersey.

———. 1953. "Notes on Indian Ethnology and History." *Bulletin of the Archaeological Society of Connecticut* 27:35–47.

Butler, Eva M., and Wendel S. Hadlock. 1949. "Dogs of the Northeastern Woodland Indians." *Massachusetts Archaeological Society Bulletin* 10(2):17–35.

Butzer, Karl W. 1971. *Environment and Archaeology: An Ecological Approach to Prehistory.* 2nd ed. Chicago: Aldine.

Byers, Douglas S. 1959. "The Eastern Archaic: Some Problems and Hypotheses." *American Antiquity* 24(3):242.

Byers, Douglas S., and Irving Rouse. 1960. "A Re-Examination of the Guida Farm." *Bulletin of the Archaeological Society of Connecticut* 30:3–66.

Calloway, Colin G. 1995. *The American Revolution in Indian Country.* New York: Cambridge University Press.

Calogero, Barbara L. 1983. "Rock Art of New England." *Bulletin of the Archaeological Society of Connecticut* 46:1–13.

———. 1991. "Macroscopic and Petrographic Identification of the Rock Types Used for Stone Tools in Connecticut." Ph.D. diss., University of Connecticut, Storrs.

———. 2002. "A Petrographic Assessment of Stone Tool Materials in New England." In *A Lasting Impression,* ed. Jordan E. Kerber, pp. 89–103. Westport: Praeger.

Calogero, Barbara L., and Anthony R. Philpotts. 1995. "Rocks and Minerals Used by Tool Knappers in New England." *Northeast Anthropology* 59:1–17.

———. 2006. "Human Behavior as Reflected in Stone Cache Blades." *Bulletin of the Archaeological Society of Connecticut* 68:55–74.

Campisi, Jack. 1990. "The Emergence of the Mashantucket Pequot Tribe, 1637–1975." In *The Pequots in Southern New England: The Fall and Rise of an American Indian Nation,* ed. Laurence M. Hauptman and James D. Wherry, pp. 117–140. Norman: University of Oklahoma Press.

Cantwell, Anne-Marie. 1980. "Dickson Camp and Pond: Two Sites of the Havana Tradition in the Central Illinois Valley, Illinois State Museum." *Reports of Investigation* No. 36. Springfield, Ill.: Dickinson Mounds Museum Anthropological Studies.

Cantwell, Anne-Marie, and Diana diZerega Wall. 2001. *Unearthing Gotham.* New Haven: Yale University Press.

Carlson, Richard G. 1987. "The Quinnipiac Reservation: Land and Tribal Identity." In *Rooted Like the Ash Trees: New England Indians and the Land,* ed. Richard G. Carlson, pp. 25–27. Naugatuck, Conn.: Eagle Wing.

Carmichael, David L., Jane Hubert, Brian Reeves, and Audhild Schanche, eds. 1994. *Sacred Sites, Sacred Places.* One World Archaeology Series 23. London: Routledge.

Carson, Dale. 1987. "Native New England Cooking." In *Rooted Like the Ash Trees: New England Indians and the Land,* ed. Richard G. Carlson, pp. 76–78. Naugatuck, Conn.: Eagle Wing.

Cassedy, Daniel F. 1992. "Native American Interaction Patterns and Lithic Acquisition Strategies in Eastern New York and Southern New England." Ph.D. diss., State University of New York, Binghamton.

———. 1998. "From the Erie Canal to Long Island Sound: Technical Synthesis of the Iroquois Pipeline Project, 1989–1993." Report submitted to the Iroquois Gas Transmission System, L.P., Shelton, Conn., Atlanta, Ga.: Garrow and Associates.

———. 1999. "The Archaic Florescence: The Late Archaic and Terminal Archaic Periods of Connecticut as Seen from the Iroquois Pipeline." *Bulletin of the Archaeological Society of Connecticut* 62:125–140.

Cassedy, Daniel F., and Lucianne Lavin. 2007. "Prehistoric Interaction Between Eastern New York and Southern New England." *Bulletin of the Archaeological Society of Connecticut* 69:103–121.

Cassedy, Daniel F., and Paul Webb. 1999. "New Data on the Chronology of Maize Horticulture in Eastern New York and Southern New England." In *Current Northeast Paleoethnobotany,* ed. John P. Hart, pp. 85–99. Bulletin 494. Albany: New York State Museum.

Cassedy, Daniel F., Paul A. Webb, and James Bradley. 1996. "The Vanderweken Site: A Protohistoric Iroquois Occupation on Schoharie Creek." *The Bulletin of the New York State Archaeological Association* 111–112:21–34.

Cassidy, Jim, L. Mark Raab, and Nina A. Kononenko. 2004. "Boats, Bones, and Biface Bias: The Early Holocene Mariners of Eel Point, San Clemente Island, California." *American Antiquity* 69(1):109–130.

Cavallaro, Michael-John. 2008. *Tales of Old New Milford, the History, Legend and Lore of a Connecticut Frontier Town.* New Milford, Conn.: Arkett Publishing.

Ceci, Lynn. 1977. "The Effect of European Contact and Trade on the Settlement Pattern of Indians in Coastal New York, 1534–1665: The Archaeological and Documentary Evidence." Ph.D. diss., City University of New York. Ann Arbor, Mich.: University Microfilms.

———. 1980. "The First Fiscal Crisis in New York." *Economic Development and Cultural Change* 28(4):839–847.

———. 1989. "Tracing Wampum's Origins: Shell Bead Evidence from Archaeological Sites in Western and Coastal New York." In *Proceedings of the 1986 Shell Bead Conference: Selected Papers,* gen. ed. Charles F. Hayes III, pp. 63–80. Research Records No. 20. Rochester, N.Y.: Research Division, Rochester Museum and Science Center.

Champlain, Samuel de. 1613. *Voyages of Samuel de Champlain, 1604–1618.* New York: Barnes and Noble, 1946.

———. 1632. *The Voyages and Explorations of Samuel de Champlain, 1604–1616.* Narrated by himself, trans. Annie Nettleton Bourne, together with "The Voyage of 1603," reprinted from *Purchas his Pilgrimes,* ed. with introduction and notes by Edward Gaylord Bourne. New York: Allerton, 1922. [New York, AMS, 1973].

Chandler, James M. 2001. "The Topper Site: Beyond Clovis at Allendale." *Mammoth Trumpet* 16(4):1–5.

Chapdelaine, Claude. 1990. "Le Concept de Sylvicole ou l'hegemonie de la poterie." *Recherches Amerindiennes au Quebec* 20(1):2–4.

Chapman, Jefferson, and Gary D. Crites. 1987. "Evidence for Early Maize (*Zea mays*) from the Icehouse Bottom Sites, Tennessee." *American Antiquity* 52(2):352–354.

Chilton, Elizabeth S. 1999. "Mobile Farmers of Pre-Contact Southern New England: The Archaeological and Ethnohistorical Evidence." In *Current Northeast Paleoethnobotany,* ed. by John P. Hart, pp. 157–176. Bulletin 494. Albany: New York State Museum.

Chrisman, Donald, Richard S. MacNeish, Jamshed Mavalwala, and Howard Savage. 1996. "Late Pleistocene Human Friction Skin Prints from Pendejo Cave, New Mexico." *American Antiquity* 61(2):357–376.

Christie, Jessica J., ed. 2009. *Landscapes of Origin in the Americas: Creation Narratives Linking Ancient Places and Present Communities.* Tuscaloosa: University of Alabama Press.

Clouette, Bruce, and Matthew Roth. 1991. "National Register of Historic Places Inventory-Nomination: Danielson Main Street Historic District." National Park Service. Prepared for the Connecticut Historical Commission, Hartford; http://pdfhost.focus.nps.gov/docs/NRHP/Text/92000265.pdf.

Coffin, Claude C. 1937. "A Prehistoric Shell Heap at the Mouth of the Housatonic." *Bulletin of the Archaeological Society of Connecticut* 5:10–19.

———. 1938. "An Indian Village Site at Cedar Ridge, Upper White Hills, Shelton, Connecticut." *Bulletin of the Archaeological Society of Connecticut* 7:9–11.

————. 1947. "Ancient Fish Weirs Along the Housatonic River." *Bulletin of the Archaeological Society of Connecticut* 21:35–38.

————. 1963. "Connecticut Indian Burials." *Bulletin of the Archaeological Society of Connecticut* 32:61–64.

Cole, Fay-Cooper. 1951. *Kincaid: A Prehistoric Illinois Metropolis.* Chicago: University of Chicago Press.

Commuck, Thomas. 1859. "Sketch of the Brothertown Indians." *Wisconsin Historical Collections* 4:291–298; http://library.wisc.edu/etext/wireader/WER0439.html.

Conkey, Laura E., Ethel Bolissevian, and Ives Goddard. 1978. "Indians of Southern New England and Long Island: Late Period." In *Handbook of North American Indians,* vol. 15, *Northeast,* ed. Bruce G. Trigger, pp. 177–189. Washington, D.C.: Smithsonian Institution.

Connecticut Archives, Connecticut State Library, State Archives, Hartford; www.cslib.org/archives/.

Connecticut (Colony). 1872. *The Public Records of the Colony of Connecticut from May, 1717, to October, 1725,* ed. Charles H. Hoadley. Vol. 6. Hartford: Press of Case, Lockwood and Brainard; www.colonialct.uconn.edu/.

Connecticut State Park and Forest Commission. 1926. *Report of the State Park and Forest Commission to the Governor.* Public Document 60. Hartford: State of Connecticut.

Cook, Frederick B. 1978. "The Finding of the Farmington Valley Mastodon." *Artifacts* 7(2):8–10.

Cook, Robert A. 2012. "Dogs of War: Potential Social Institutions of Conflict, Healing, and Death in a Fort Ancient Village." *American Antiquity* 77(3):498–523.

Cook, Thomas A. 1933. *Geology of Connecticut.* Hartford: Bond.

Cook, Thomas G. 1976. "Broadpoint: Culture, Phase, Horizon, Tradition, or Knife?" *Journal of Anthropological Research* 32(4):337–357.

Cooke, David G. 1988. "The Morgan Site: The Beginning." *Bulletin of the Archaeological Society of Connecticut* 51:3–6.

————. 1989. "Adena Related Burials: Glastonbury, Connecticut." *Bulletin of the Archaeological Society of Connecticut* 62:7–15.

————. 1990. "Morgan Site: Closure and Reburial." *Newsletter of the Archaeological Society of Connecticut* 170:2.

————. 2006. "Radiocarbon Dating." *ASC News* 212:5.

Cooke, David G., and Barbara Jordan. 1972. "An Adena-Like Burial at East Windsor Hill." *Archaeological Society of Connecticut Bulletin* 37:47–51.

Coombs, Linda. 2002. "Holistic History: Including the Wampanoag in an Exhibit at Plimoth Plantation." *Plimoth Life* 1(2):12–15.

Cooper, Karen Coody. 1985. "They Have Seized Upon Our Country: The Wangunk of Wethersfield." *Artifacts* 14(2):4–8.

————. 1986. "The Complete Thanksgiving." *Artifacts* 15(1):6–7.

Cox, Cheryl Anne, and David H. Dye, eds. 1990. *Towns and Temples Along the Mississippi.* Tuscaloosa: University of Alabama Press.

Crawford, Gary W. 1999. "Northeastern Paleoethnobotany: How Are We Doing?" In *Cur-*

*rent Northeast Paleoethnobotany,* ed. John P. Hart, pp. 225–234. Bulletin 494. Albany: New York State Museum.

Crompton, Amanda, and John Irwin. 2007. "French Island Tickle (EaBa-19)." *Council for Northeastern Historical Archaeology Newsletter* 66:24–25.

Crone-Morange, Paulette, and Lucianne Lavin. 2003. "Schaghticoke Time Line for Community and Political Authority." Unpublished report submitted to the Schaghticoke Tribal Nation of Kent, Connecticut. On file at the Schaghticoke tribal office in Derby, Connecticut, and with the Bureau of Indian Affairs, Branch of Acknowledgment and Recognition (BAR), Washington, D.C.

———. 2004. "The Schaghticoke Tribe and English Law: A Study of Community Survival." *Connecticut History* 43(2):132–162.

Cronon, William. 1983. *Changes in the Land: Indians, Colonists, and the Ecology of New England.* New York: Hill and Wang.

Crosby, Constance A. 1991. "The Algonkin Spiritual Landscape." In *Algonkians of New England Past and Present,* ed. Peter Benes, pp. 35–41. Amherst: Boston University.

Cross, John R. 1999. "Typology in the Northeast." In *The Archaeological Northeast,* ed. Mary Ann Levine, Kenneth E. Sassaman, and Michael S. Nassaney, pp. 57–73. Westport, Conn.: Bergin & Garvey.

Cruson, Daniel. 1994. *Newtown's Slaves: A Case Study in Early Connecticut Rural Black History.* Newtown, Conn.: Newtown Historical Society.

———. 2005. "More About Concealment Shoes." *ASC News* 208:1.

Curran, Mary Lou. 1984. "The Whipple Site and Paleo-Indian Tool Assemblage Variation: A Comparison of Intrasite Structuring." *Archaeology of Eastern North America* 12:5–40.

———. 1999. "Exploration, Colonization, and Settling In: The Bull Brook Phase, Antecedents, and Descendants." In *The Archaeological Northeast,* ed. Mary Ann Levine, Kenneth E. Sassaman, and Michael S. Nassaney, pp. 3–24. Westport, Conn.: Greenwood.

Curran, Mary Lou, and Dena F. Dincauze. 1977. "Paleo-Indians and Paleo-Lakes: New Data from the Connecticut Drainage." In *Amerinds and Their Paleoenvironments in Northeastern North America,* ed. Walter S. Newman and Bert Salwen, pp. 333–348. Annals of the New York Academy of Sciences 288. New York: New York Academy of Sciences.

Curtin, Edward V. 2011. "A Small Site in Coxsackie, Circa A.D. 1200: Some Ecological Issues Concerning Its Age and Location." In *Current Research in New York Archaeology: A.D. 700–1300,* ed. Christina B. Rieth and John P. Hart, pp. 53–76. New York State Museum Record 2. Albany: University of the State of New York, State Education Department.

Custer, Jay F. 1982. "A Reconsideration of the Middle Woodland Cultures of the Upper Delmarva Peninsula. In *Practicing Environmental Archaeology: Methods and Interpretations,* ed. Roger W. Moeller, pp. 29–38. Occasional Papers of the American Indian Archaeological Institute 3. Washington, Conn.: American Indian Archaeological Institute.

———. 1984. *Delaware Prehistoric Archaeology: An Ecological Approach.* Newark: University of Delaware Press.

———. 1988. "Coastal Adaptations in the Middle Atlantic Region." *Archaeology of Eastern North America* 16:121–135.

———. 1996. *Prehistoric Cultures of Eastern Pennsylvania.* Harrisburg: Pennsylvania Historical and Museum Commission, Commonwealth of Pennsylvania.

———. 2001. *Classification Guide for Arrowheads and Spearpoints of Eastern Pennsylvania and the Central Middle Atlantic.* Harrisburg: Pennsylvania Historical and Museum Commission, Commonwealth of Pennsylvania.

Cuzzone, Holly, and Britt Hartenberger. 2009. "Late Archaic and Late Woodland Occupations at Cove River, West Haven: New Data on Subsistence and the Narrow Point Tradition." *Bulletin of the Archaeological Society of Connecticut* 71:17–40.

Dally-Starna, Corinna, and William A. Starna, trans. and ed. 2009. *Gideon's People.* Vols. 1 and 2. Lincoln: University of Nebraska Press.

Dancy, William. 2005. "The Enigmatic Hopewell of the Eastern Woodlands." In *North American Archaeology,* ed. Timothy R. Pauketat and Diana DiPaolo Loren, pp. 108–137. Malden, Mass.: Blackwell.

Darwin, R. James. 1903. "Leasing of Indian Lands." Letter, *New York Times,* Dec. 21, 2003. On file at the Schaghticoke Tribal Office, Derby, Conn.

"David McAllester Speaks on American Indian Music and Dance to Gathering at AIAI Annual Meeting." 1976. *Artifacts* 4(4):1, 7, 9.

Davis, Margaret Bryan. 1969. "Palynological and Environmental History During the Quaternary Period." *American Scientist* 57(3):317–322.

———. 1983. "Holocene Vegetational History of the Eastern United States." In *Late-Quaternary Environments of the United States,* vol. 2, *The Holocene,* ed. H. E. Wright Jr., pp. 166–181. Minneapolis: University of Minnesota Press.

De Forest, John W. 1852. *History of the Indians of Connecticut from the Earliest Period to 1850.* Hartford: Wm. Jas. Hamersley.

De Laet, Johannes. 1909. "Extracts from the New World." In *Narratives of New Netherlands,* ed. J. Franklin Jameson. New York: Charles Scribner's Sons.

Denny, Peter. 1989. "Algonquian Connections to Salishan and Northeastern Archaeology." In *Papers of the Twentieth Algonquian Conference,* ed. by William Cowan, pp. 86–107. Ottawa: Carleton University.

———. 2003. "Archaeological Signs of Eastern Algonquian." In *Essays in Algonquian, Catawban, and Siouan Linguistics in Memory of Frank T. Siebert Jr.,* ed. David Costa and Blair Rudes, pp. 1–25. Winnipeg: University of Manitoba Press.

Den Ouden, Amy E. 2005. *Beyond Conquest: Native Peoples and the Struggle for History in New England.* Lincoln: University of Nebraska Press.

Dermer, Thomas. 1619. "To His Worshipfull Friend M. Samuel Purchas, Preacher of the Word, at the Church a Little Within Ludgate, London." Reprinted in *Sailors' Narratives of the Voyages Along the New England Coast, 1524–1624,* ed. George P. Winship. New York: B. Franklin, 1968.

Dexter, Franklin Bowditch, ed. 1901. *The Literary Diary of Ezra Stiles, D.D., L.L.D.* 3 vols. New York: Charles Scribner's Sons.

Dillehay, Tom D. 1989. *Monte Verde: A Late Pleistocene Settlement in Chile*. Washington, D.C.: Smithsonian Institution Press.

———. 1999. "The Late Pleistocene Cultures of South America." *Evolutionary Anthropology* 7(6):206–216.

Dillian, Carolyn D., Charles A. Bello, and M. Steven Shackley. 2007. "Crossing the Delaware: Documenting Super-Long Distance Obsidian Exchange in the Mid-Atlantic." *Archaeology of Eastern North America* 35:93–104.

———. 2010. "Long-Distance Exchange of Obsidian in the Mid-Atlantic United States." In *Trade and Exchange: Archaeological Studies from History and Prehistory*, ed. Carolyn D. Dillian and Carolyn L. White, pp. 17–36. New York: Springer.

Dincauze, Dena F. 1972. "The Atlantic Phase: A Late Archaic Culture in Massachusetts." *Man in the Northeast* 4:40–61.

———. 1974. "An Introduction to Archaeology in the Greater Boston Area. *Archaeology of Eastern North America* 2(1):39–67.

———. 1975. "The Late Archaic Period in Southern New England." *Arctic Anthropology* 12(2):23–24.

———. 1976. *The Neville Site: 8,000 Years at Amoskeag*. Peabody Monographs 4. Cambridge, Mass.: Peabody Museum of Archaeology and Ethnology, Harvard University.

Dincauze, Dena F., and Robert J. Hasenstab. 1989. "Explaining the Iroquois: Tribalization on a Prehistoric Periphery." In *Centre and Periphery: Comparative Studies in Archaeology*, ed. Timothy C. Champion, pp. 67–87. Boston: Unwin Hyman.

Dincauze, Dena F., and Mitchell T. Mulholland. 1977. "Early and Middle Archaic Site Distributions and Habitats in Southern New England." In *Amerinds and Their Paleoenvironments in Northeastern North America*, ed. Walter S. Newman and Bert Salwen, pp. 439–456. Annals of the New York Academy of Sciences 288. New York: New York Academy of Sciences.

Dowhan, Joseph J., and R. Craig. 1976. "Rare and Endangered Species of Connecticut and Their Habitats." *Geological and Natural History Survey of Connecticut, Report of Investigations* 6:1–137.

Dragoo, Don. 1963. *Mounds for the Dead*. Annals of the Carnegie Museum 37. Pittsburgh: Carnegie Museum.

Drew, Bernard A. 2009. *Faded Tracks on Monument Mountain*. Great Barrington, Mass.: Attic Revivals.

Drooker, Penelope B., and George R. Hamell. 2004. "Susannah Swan's 'Wampum Bag.'" In *Perishable Material Culture in the Northeast*, ed. Penelope Ballard Drooker, pp. 197–216. New York State Museum Bulletin 500. Albany: New York State Education Department.

Dunn, Shirley W. 1994a. "Effects of the Mahican–Mohawk Wars on the Transfer of Mahican Land." In *Proceedings of the 1992 People to People Conference, Selected Papers*, gen. ed. Charles F. Hayes III, assoc. eds. Connie Cox Bodner, Lorraine P. Saunders, pp. 85–103. Research Record No. 23. Rochester, N.Y.: Research Division of the Rochester Museum and Science Center.

———. 1994b. *The Mohicans and Their Land, 1609–1730*. Fleischmanns, N.Y.: Purple Mountain.

Edwards, Robert L., and K. O. Emery. 1977. "Man on the Continental Shelf." In *Amerinds and Their Paleoenvironments in Northeastern North America,* ed. Walter S. Newman and Bert Salwen, pp. 245–256. Annals of the New York Academy of Sciences 288. New York: New York Academy of Sciences.

Edwards, Robert L., and Arthur S. Merrill. 1977. "A Reconstruction of the Continental Shelf Areas of Eastern North America for the Times 9,500 BP and 12,500 BP." *Archaeology of Eastern North America* 5:1–42.

Egloff, Keith T., and Stephen R. Potter. 1982. "Prehistoric Ceramics from Coastal Plain Virginia." *Archaeology of Eastern North America* 10:95–117.

Ellis, Christopher J. 1994. "Miniature Early Paleo-Indian Stone Artifacts from the Parkhill, Ontario Site." *North American Archaeologist* 15:253–267.

Ellis, Christopher J., and D. Brian Deller. 1997. "Variability in the Archaeological Record of Northeastern Early Paleoindians: A View from Southern Ontario." *Archaeology of Eastern North America* 25:1–30.

Ellis, Christopher J., John Tomenchuk, and John D. Holland. 2003. "Typology, Use and Sourcing of the Late Pleistocene Lithic Artifacts from the Hiscock Site." In *The Hiscock Site: Late Pleistocene and Early Holocene Paleoecology and Archaeology of Western New York State,* ed. Richard Laub, pp. 221–237. Proceedings of the Second Smith Symposium, October 14–15, 2001, Buffalo Museum of Science. Bulletin of the Buffalo Society of Natural Sciences 37. Buffalo, N.Y.: Buffalo Society of Natural Sciences.

Englebrecht, William E., and Carl K. Seyfert. 1994. "Paleoindian Watercraft: Evidence and Implications." *North American Archaeologist* 15(3):221–234.

Erlandson, Jon, Torben C. Rick, Todd J. Braje, Molly Casperson, Brendan Culleton, Brian Fulfrost, Tracy Garcia, Daniel A. Guthrie, Nicholas Jew, Douglas J. Kennett, Madonna L. Moss, Leslie Reeder, Craig Skinner, Jack Watts, and Lauren Willis. 2011. "Paleoindian Seafaring, Maritime Technologies and Coastal Foraging on California's Channel Islands." *Science* 331(6021):1181–1185.

Fagan, Brian. 2004. "The House of the Sea: An Essay on the Antiquity of Planked Canoes in Southern California." *American Antiquity* 69(1):7–16.

Fagan, Lisa A. 1978. "A Vegetational and Cultural Sequence for Southern New England, 15000 BP to 7000 BP." *Man in the Northeast* 15–16:70–92.

Fairbridge, Rhodes W. 1977. "Discussion Paper: Late Quaternary Environments in Northeastern Coastal North America." In *Amerinds and Their Paleoenvironments in Northeastern North America,* ed. Walter S. Newman and Bert Salwen, pp. 90–92. Annals of the New York Academy of Sciences 288. New York: New York Academy of Sciences.

Farrow, Anne, Joel Lang, and Jenifer Frank, with Cheryl Magazine. 2005. *Complicity: How the North Promoted, Prolonged, and Profited from Slavery.* New York: Ballantine.

Fawcett, Melissa J. 1995. *The Lasting of the Mohegans,* part 1, *The Story of the Wolf People.* Uncasville, Conn.: The Mohegan Tribe.

———. 2000. *Medicine Trail: The Life and Lessons of Gladys Tantaquidgeon.* Tucson: University of Arizona Press.

Feder, Kenneth L. 1980–1981. "Waste Not, Want Not: Differential Lithic Utilization and Efficiency of Use." *North American Archaeologist* 2(3):198–206.

———. 1981. "The Farmington Archaeology Project: Focus on a Small River Valley." *Man in the Northeast* 22:131–146.

———. 1982. "'The Avaricious Humour of Designing Englishmen': The Ethnohistory of Land Transactions in the Farmington Valley." *Bulletin of the Archaeological Society of Connecticut* 45:29–40.

———. 1984. "Pots, Plants, and People: The Late Woodland Period of Connecticut." *Bulletin of the Archaeological Society of Connecticut* 47:99–111.

———. 1993. *A Village of Outcasts: Historical Archaeology and Documentary Research at the Lighthouse Site.* New York: McGraw-Hill.

———. 1995. *The Past in Perspective: An Introduction in Human Prehistory.* Mountain View, Calif.: Mayfield.

———. 2004. "The Glazier Blade Cache: 30 Remarkable Blades Found in Granby, Connecticut." *Bulletin of the Archaeological Society of Connecticut* 66:101–113.

Feder, Kenneth L., and Marc Banks. 1996. "Archaeological Survey of the McLean Game Refuge, Granby and Simsbury, Connecticut." *Bulletin of the Archaeological Society of Connecticut* 59:39–51.

Ferris, Jaime. 2010. "The Wampanoag Dancers and Singers Will Perform Saturday at the Fourth Annual Green Corn Festival at the Institute for American Indian Studies in Washington." *Housatonic Times,* August 5, 2010; housatonictimes.com/articles/2010/08/05/entertainment/doc4c5ad265704b4980421761.txt.

Fiedel, Stuart J. 1990. "Middle Woodland Algonquian Expansion: A Refined Model." *North American Archaeologist* 11(3):209–230.

———. 2001. "What Happened in the Early Woodland?" *Archaeology of Eastern North America* 29:101–142.

Filios, Elena. 1989. "The End of the Beginning, or the Beginning of the End: The Third Millennium B.P. in Southern New England." *Man in the Northeast* 38:79–93.

Flannery, Regina. 1939. *Analysis of Coastal Algonquin Culture.* Washington, D.C.: Catholic University of America Press.

Flint, Richard Foster. 1930. *The Glacial Geology of Connecticut.* Hartford: Connecticut State Geological and Natural History Survey.

Flowers, Marcia Jones. 2005. "Surviving Termination: The Eastern Pequots, Then and Now." *Indian Country Today,* July 28, 2005.

Forrest, Daniel T. 1999. "Beyond Presence and Absence: Establishing Diversity in Connecticut's Early Holocene Archaeological Record." *Bulletin of the Archaeological Society of Connecticut* 62:79–99.

Forrest, Daniel T., Brian D. Jones, and Robert M. Thorson. 2008. The Adriaen's Landing Project and the Development of the Connecticut River Floodplain at Hartford. *Bulletin of the Archaeological Society of Connecticut* 70:5–16.

Forrest, Daniel T., Michael S. Raber, Brian D. Jones, and Robert M. Thorson. 2006. "Archaeological and Historical Resource Study, Adriaen's Landing Project, Hartford, Connecticut." Report prepared for the Connecticut Office of Policy and Management. Storrs, Conn.: Archaeological and Historical Services, Inc., CHPC no. 1489.

Fowler, William David H. 1953. "Indians Make Last Fight—for Survival." *Hartford Courant.* On file at the Schaghticoke Tribal Office in Derby, Connecticut.

Fowler, William S. 1951. "Soapstone Bowl Making as Practiced at the Westfield Quarry." *Massachusetts Archaeological Society Bulletin* 4(3):39–41.

Fragola, Patricia, and David K. Schaefer. 1999. "Phase 2 Intensive Survey, Supplemental Phase 2 Survey, Nathaniel Sillick Site. Reconstruction of Route US 7, State Project 34-260-SUP, On-call Service Agreement No. 7.19-04 (96), Ridgefield and Danbury, Connecticut." Pawtucket, R.I.: Public Archaeology Laboratory, Inc. Submitted to State of Connecticut Department of Transportation, Newington. Original dated 1997; revised 1999.

Frank, J. D., and J. B. Frank. 1991. *Persuasion and Healing.* Baltimore: Johns Hopkins University Press.

Frazer, James G. 1922. *The Golden Bough.* New York: Macmillan.

"From 7 to 400 in Seven Years." 1972 September. *Artifacts* 1(1):1. Shepaug Valley Archaeological Society, Washington, Conn.; www.iaismuseum.org/artifacts.shtml.

Funk, Robert E. 1968. "A New Middle Woodland Complex in Eastern New York." *New York State Archaeological Association Bulletin* 44:1–7.

———. 1972. "Early Man in the Northeast and the Late Glacial Environment." *Man in the Northeast* 4:7–39.

———. 1976. *Recent Contributions to Hudson Valley Prehistory.* New York State Museum Memoir 22. Albany: State Education Department, University of the State of New York.

———. 1984. "Recent Advances in Connecticut Archaeology: The View from New York." *Bulletin of the Archaeological Society of Connecticut* 47:129–143.

Funk, Robert E., D. W. Fischer, and E. Reilly. 1969. "A Radiocarbon Date for Early Man from the Dutchess Quarry Cave." *New York Archaeological Association Bulletin* 46:19–21.

Funk, Robert E., and John Pfeiffer. 1988. "Archaeological and Paleoenvironmental Investigations on Fishers Island, New York: A Preliminary Report." *Bulletin of the Archaeological Society of Connecticut* 51:69–110.

Furman, Gabriel. 1875. *Antiquities of Long Island,* ed. Frank Moore. New York: J. W. Bouton.

Gaines, Ruth. 1930. "The Stockbridge Conversion." Museum of the American Indian, Heye Foundation. *Indian Notes* 7(1):39–52.

Gardner, William. 1982. "Early and Middle Woodland in the Middle Atlantic: An Overview." In *Practicing Environmental Archaeology: Methods and Interpretations,* ed. R. W. Moeller, pp. 53–86. American Indian Archaeological Institute Occasional Papers. Washington, Conn.: American Indian Archaeological Institute.

George, David R. 1997. "Late Prehistoric Archaeobotany of Connecticut: Providing a Context for the Transition to Maize Horticulture." *Bulletin of the Archaeological Society of Connecticut* 60:13–28.

———. 1999. "Native American Subsistence Methods." In *The Archaeology of Connecticut,* ed. Kristen N. and William F. Keegan, pp. 16–20. Storrs, Conn.: Bibliopola.

George, David, Nicholas Bellantoni, William Keegan, S. Douglas Dumas, and Kristen Noble Keegan. 1998. "Historical and Cultural Reconnaissance Survey, Cultural Resource Management Plan, Connecticut National Guard Properties, Camp Rowland,

Camp Hartell, and Stone's Ranch." CHPC no. 783. On file at the Office of State Archaeology, Storrs, Conn.

George, David R., and Robert E. Dewar. 1999. "Chenopodium in Connecticut Prehistory: Wild, Weedy, Cultivated or Domesticated?" In *Current Northeast Paleoethnobotany*, ed. John P. Hart, pp. 121–132. Bulletin 494. Albany: New York State Museum.

George, David R., and Brian D. Jones. 1997. "Prehistoric Archaeology of the Great Swamp Basin, South Kingston, Rhode Island." *Bulletin of the Massachusetts Archaeological Society* 58(2):44–56.

Gluck, Emery. 2011. "Prescribed Burning on State Lands in Connecticut." *Connecticut Wildlife* 31(3):6–7.

Glynn, Frank. 1953. "The Pilots Point Submerged Sites." *Bulletin of the Archaeological Society of Connecticut* 27:11–29.

———. 1969. "Connecticut Indian Origins in the Light of the Submerged Sites." In *An Introduction to the Archaeology and History of the Connecticut Valley Indian*, ed. William Young, pp. 68–73. Springfield, Mass.: Springfield Museum of Science.

———. 1973. "Excavation of the Pilot's Point Stone Heaps." Introduction by Richard Q. Bourn, Jr. *Bulletin of the Archaeological Society of Connecticut* 38:77–89.

Goddard, Ives. 1978a. "Delaware." In *Handbook of North American Indians*, vol. 15, *The Northeast*, ed. Bruce G. Trigger, pp. 213–239. Washington, D.C.: Smithsonian Institution.

———.1978b. "Eastern Algonquian Languages." In *Handbook of North American Indians*, vol. 15, *The Northeast*, ed. Bruce G. Trigger, pp. 70–77. Washington, D.C.: Smithsonian Institution.

Golet, Henry. 1983. "Connecticut Paleo Points." *ASSEC News* 1:7.

Goodby, Robert. 2002. "Reconsidering the Shantok Tradition." In *A Lasting Impression: Coastal, Lithic, and Ceramic Research in New England Archaeology.* ed. Jordan E. Kerber, pp. 141–154. Westport, Conn.: Praeger.

Goodwin, Matt F. 2006. "The Second Hill Brook Site, Roxbury, Connecticut." *Bulletin of the Archaeological Society of Connecticut* 68:29–41.

Gookin, Daniel. 1792. *Historical Collection of the Indians in New England.* Boston: Massachusetts Historical Society, 1970.

Gordon, Robert B. 1983. "History of Sea Level Changes Along the Connecticut Shore." In *Connecticut Archaeology Past, Present, and Future*, ed. R. E. Dewar, K. L. Feder, and D. A. Poirier, pp. 61–78. Occasional Papers in Anthropology. Storrs: University of Connecticut.

Gramly, Richard M. 1982. "The Vail Site: A Paleo-Indian Encampment in Maine." *Bulletin of the Buffalo Society of Natural Sciences* 30.

Granger, Joseph E., Jr. 1978. "Cache Blades, Chert, and Communication: A Reappraisal of Certain Aspects of Meadowood Phase and the Concept of a Burial Cult in the Northeast." In *Essays in Northeastern Anthropology in Memory of Marian E. White*, ed. William E. Englebrecht and Donald K. Grayson, pp. 96–122. Occasional Publications in Northeastern Anthropology 5. Rindge, N.H.: Department of Anthropology, Franklin Pierce College.

Graves, Anna K., and A. Peter Mair II. 2006. "Archaeological Assessment Survey CONN-

DOT Project No. 174–309, Short-Term Improvements, I-84 Interchanges 17 and 18, Middlebury/Waterbury, Connecticut." Public Archaeological Laboratory (PAL) Report No. 1846. Submitted to Connecticut Dept. of Transportation, Newington, Conn., by PAL, Pawtucket, R.I., April 2006.

Gray, O. W. 1869. *Atlas of Windham and Tolland Counties.* Hartford, Conn.: C. G. Keeney, 1976.

Griffin, James B. 1978. "Late Prehistory of the Ohio Valley." In *Handbook of North American Indians,* vol. 15, *The Northeast,* ed. Bruce G. Trigger, pp. 547–559. Washington, D.C.: Smithsonian Institution.

Griffith, Daniel R. 1982. "Prehistoric Ceramics in Delaware (An Overview)." *Archaeology of Eastern North America* 10:46–68.

Grumet, Robert S. 1992. *Historic Contact: Early Relations Between Indian People and Colonists in Northeastern North America, 1524–1783.* National Historic Landmark Theme Study. Washington, D.C.: United States Department of the Interior, National Parks Service, National Register Programs Division, Mid-Atlantic Region; www.cr.nps.gov /history/online_books/nhl/grumet.pdf.

———. 2002. *Voices from the Delaware Big House Ceremony.* Norman: University of Oklahoma Press.

Gudrian, Fred W. 1991. "The Salmon River Rock Shelter." *Bulletin of the Archaeological Society of Connecticut* 54:57–64.

———. 1995. "An Examination of Late Woodland Ceramic Pipe Fragments from the Morgan Site in Rocky Hill, Connecticut." *Bulletin of the Archaeological Society of Connecticut* 58:13–29.

———. 2001. "An Analysis of Lithic Artifacts from the Morgan Site in Rocky Hill, Connecticut." *Bulletin of the Archaeological Society of Connecticut* 63:3–24.

Guzy, Dan. 1999. "Fish Weirs in the Upper Potomac River." *Maryland Archeology* 35(1):1–24.

Hamell, George R. 1983. "Trading in Metaphors: The Magic of Beads." In *Proceedings of the 1982 Glass Trade Bead Conference,* ed. Charles F. Hayes III, pp. 5–28. Rochester Museum and Science Center Research Records 16. Rochester, N.Y.: Research Divison, Rochester Museum and Science Center.

———. 1987. "Mythical Realities and European Contact in the Northeast During the Sixteenth and Seventeenth Centuries." *Man in the Northeast* 33:63–87.

Hamilton, Milton W., preparer. 1957. *The Papers of Sir William Johnson.* Vol. 12. Albany: University of the State of New York.

Handsman, Russell G. 1988. "Algonkian Women Resist Colonialism." *Artifacts* 16(3–4): 29–31.

———. 1989. "Algonkian Wigwams: An Invisible Presence, Political Spaces." *Artifacts* 17(4):19–23.

———. 1991. "What Happened to the Heritage of the Weantinock People." *Artifacts* 19(1):3–9.

———. 2008. "Landscapes of Memory in Wampanoag Country—and the Monuments upon Them. In *Archaeologies of Placemaking: Monuments, Memories, and Engagement in Native North America,* ed. Patricia E. Rubertone, pp. 161–193. Walnut Creek, Calif.: Left Coast.

Handsman, Russell G., and Trudie Lamb Richmond. 1995. "Confronting Colonialism: The Mahican and Schaghticoke Peoples and Us." In *Making Alternative Histories: The Practice of Archaeology and History in Non-Western Settings,* ed. Peter. R. Schmidt and Thomas C. Patterson, pp. 87–117. Santa Fe, N.M.: School of American Research Press.

Harper, Mary G., Bruce Clouette, and Ross Harper. 1999. "The Rochambeau Project: Historical and Archaeological Documentation of the French Army's Marches Through Connecticut in 1781 and 1782." CHPC no. 1784. Public Archaeology Survey Team, Inc. [Hartford: Connecticut State Historic Preservation Office.] Archives & Special Collections, Thomas J. Dodd Research Center, University of Connecticut Libraries, Storrs, Conn.

Harper, Ross K. 2008. "Hunting, Trapping, and Fowling in 18th-Century Connecticut." *Museum of the Fur Trade Quarterly* 44(3):2–19.

Harrington, M. R. 1921. *Religion and Ceremonies of the Lenape.* Indian Notes and Monographs 19. New York: Museum of the American Indian, Heye Foundation.

Harris, Richard. 1987. "The Spirit of the Eagle." In *Rooted Like the Ash Trees: New England Indians and the Land,* ed. Richard G. Carlson, pp. 72–73. Naugatuck, Conn.: Eagle Wing.

Hart, John P. 1999. "Dating Roundtop's Domesticates: Implications for Northeast Late Prehistory." In *Current Northeast Paleoethnobotany,* ed. John P. Hart, pp. 47–68. Bulletin 494. Albany: New York State Museum.

———. 2000. "Squash Down, Beans Up." *Newsletter of the Massachusetts Archaeological Society* 26(1):4. Reprinted from *Archaeology,* January–February 2000.

———. 2011. "The Death of Owasco—Redux." In *Current Research in New York Archaeology, A.D. 700–1300,* ed. Christina B. Rieth and John P. Hart, pp. 95–107. New York State Museum Record 2. Albany: New York State Education Department.

Hart, John P., and Hetty Jo Brumbach. 2005. "Cooking Residues, AMS Dates, and the Middle-to-Late-Woodland Transition in Central New York." *Northeast Anthropology* 69:1–34.

Hart, John P., Eleanora A. Reber, Robert G. Thompson, and Robert Lusteck. 2008. "Taking Variation Seriously: Testing the Steatite Mast-Processing Hypothesis with Microbotanical Data from the Hunters Home Site, New York." *American Antiquity* 73(4):729–741.

Hasenstab, Robert J. 1987. "Canoes, Caches, and Carrying Places: Territorial Boundaries and Tribalization in Late Woodland Western New York." *Bulletin of the New York State Archaeological Association* 95:39–49.

Hauptman, Laurence M. 1990. "The Pequot War and Its Legacies." In *The Pequots in Southern New England: The Fall and Rise of an American Indian Nation,* ed. Laurence M. Hauptman and James D. Wherry, pp. 69–80. Norman: University of Oklahoma Press.

Hayes, Charles F., III, ed. 1989. *Proceedings of the 1982 Glass Trade Bead Conference.* Rochester, N.Y.: Research Division, Rochester Museum and Science Center.

Heath, Dwight B., ed. 1963. *A Journal of the Pilgrims at Plymouth [Mourt's Relation].* New York: Corinth. (Originally published in 1622.)

Heckenberger, Michael J., James Petersen, and Nancy Asch-Sidell. 1992. "Early Evidence of Maize Agriculture in the Connecticut River Valley of Vermont." *Archaeology of Eastern North America* 20:125–149.

Heckenberger, Michael J., James B. Petersen, Ellen R. Cowie, Arthur E. Spiess, Louise A. Basa, and Robert E. Stuckenrath. 1990. "Early Woodland Mortuary Ceremonialism in the Far Northeast: A View from the Boucher Cemetery." *Archaeology of Eastern North America* 18:109–144.

Heckewelder, John. 1876. *Account of the History, Manners, and Customs of the Indian Nations Who Once Inhabited Pennsylvania and the Neighbouring Province.* Philadelphia: Historical Society of Pennsylvania. (Originally published in 1818.)

Heidenreich, Conrad E. 1978. "Huron." In *Handbook of North American Indians,* vol. 15, *The Northeast,* ed. Bruce G. Trigger, pp. 368–388. Washington, D.C.: Smithsonian Institution.

Henry, Alexander. 1809. *Travels and Adventures in Canada and in the Indian Territories Between the Years 1760 and 1776.* New York: Riley. Reprint, ed. James Bain, New York: M. G. Hurtig, 1964.

Higgeson, Reverend J. 1629. "New-England's Plantation." In *Collections of the Massachusetts Historical Society for the Year 1792.* Vol. 1, pp. 117–124. Reprint, New York: Johnson Reprint Corporation, 1968.

Hodges, Glenn. 2011. "Cahokia, America's Forgotten City." *National Geographic,* January 2011, 219(1):126–145.

Hoffman, Curtiss. 1985. "Revising the Late Archaic Period in Southern New England." *Archaeology of Eastern North America* 13:58–78.

———. 1998. "Pottery and Steatite in the Northeast: A Reconsideration of Origins." *Northeast Anthropology* 56:43–68.

Holt, Julie Zimmermann. 2009. "Rethinking the Ramey State: Was Cahokia the Center of a Theater State?" *American Antiquity* 74(2):231–254.

Hopkins, Reverend Samuel. 1753. *Historical Memoirs Relating to the Housatonic Indians.* Boston: S. Kneeland. Reprint, New York: William Abbatt, 1911.

Howard, James H. 1968. *The Southeastern Ceremonial Complex and Its Interpretation.* Missouri Archaeological Society Memoir 6. Columbia: Missouri Archaeological Society.

Howe, Henry F. 1969. *Prologue to New England.* Port Washington, N.Y.: Kennikat. (Originally published in 1943.)

Howlett, Katherine. 2004. "Gendered Practices: Ethnohistoric and Archaeological Evidence of Native American Social Divisions of Labor." *Bulletin of the Archaeological Society of Connecticut* 66:65–83.

Hudson, Charles. 1976. *The Southeastern Indians.* Knoxville: University of Tennessee Press.

"An Indian Tragedy—The Work of Bloodthirsty Indians Quickly Avenged." *Danbury Evening News,* May 15, 1893, p. 6.

Ingstad, Helge, and Anne Stine Ingstad. 2001. *The Viking Discovery of America: The Excavation of a Norse Settlement in L'Anse aux Meadows, Newfoundland.* New York: Checkmark.

Irwin-Williams, Cynthia C. 1968. "Archaeological Evidence on Early Man in Mexico." *Contributions in Anthropology* 1(4):39–41.

Ives, Timothy H. 2007. "Data Recovery at Preston Plains, Preston." *Conference on New England Archaeology Newsletter* 26:5.

———. 2011. "Reconstructing the Wangunk Reservation Land System: A Case Study of Native and Colonial Likeness in Central Connecticut." *Ethnohistory* 58(1):65–89.

Jameson, J. Franklin, ed. 1909. *Narratives of New Netherland, 1609–1664*. New York: Charles Scribner's Sons. Early Encounters in North America; www.alexanderstreet2 .com/eenalive/index.html.

Jarvenpa, Robert, and Hetty Jo Brumbach. 1995. "Ethnoarchaeology and Gender: Chipewyan Women as Hunters." *Research in Economic Anthropology* 16:39–82.

Jenks, Samuel. 1827. "The Tradition of the Taumkhods." *New England Galaxy* 10(486), February 2.

Johnson, Dennis. 2002. "Dogs Throughout Time." *American Archaeology* 6(3):32–37.

Johnson, Edward. 1654. *Johnson's Wonder-Working Providence, 1628–1651*, ed. J. Franklin Jameson. Reprint, New York: Charles Scribner's Sons, 1910.

Johnson, Eric S. 1993. "'Some by Flatteries and Others by Threatenings': Political Strategies Among Native Americans of Seventeenth-Century Southern New England." Ph.D. diss., Ann Arbor, Mich.: University Microfilms International.

Johnson, Frederick. 1942. *The Boylston Street Fishweir*. Papers of the Robert S. Peabody Foundation for Archaeology 2. Andover, Mass.: Phillips Academy, The Foundation.

Johnston, Alexander. 1903. *American Commonwealths. Connecticut—A Study of a Commonwealth-Democracy*. Boston: Houghton Mifflin.

Johnstone, Paul. 1980. *The Sea-Craft of Prehistory*. Cambridge, Mass.: Harvard University Press.

Jones, Brian D. 1997. "The Late Paleoindian Hidden Creek Site in Southeastern Connecticut." *Archaeology of Eastern North America* 25:45–80.

———. 1998. "Human Adaptation to the Changing Northeastern Environment at the End of the Pleistocene: Implications for the Archaeological Record." Ph.D. diss., University of Connecticut, Storrs.

———. 1999a. "The Middle Archaic Period in Connecticut: The View from Mashantucket." *Bulletin of the Archaeological Society of Connecticut* 62:101–124.

———. 1999b. "The Paleo Period." In *The Archaeology of Connecticut*, ed. Kristen N. Keegan and William F. Keegan, pp. 8–14. Storrs, Conn.: Bibliopola.

Jones, Brian, and Daniel Forrest. 2003. "Life in a Postglacial Landscape: Settlement-Subsistence Change During the Pleistocene-Holocene Transition in Southern New England." In *Geoarchaeology of Landscapes in the Glaciated Northeast*, ed. D. L. Cremeens and J. P. Hart, pp. 75–90. New York State Museum Bulletin 497. Albany: University of the State of New York, State Education Department.

Jones, Brian, Daniel Forrest, and Timothy Binzen. 1997. "Phase III Archaeological Data Recovery Excavation, Newtown Sewer System Project, Newtown, Connecticut." Vol. 1. Prepared for Fuss and O'Neill, Inc. CHCP #758. Special Collections Dodd Center, Storrs, Conn.

Jordan, Douglas F. 1975. "Factors Affecting New England Archaeology." *Man in the Northeast* 10:71–74.

Josselyn, John. 1672. *New England's Rarities, Discovered in Birds, Beasts, Fishes, Serpents, and Plants of that Country.* Reprint, Boston: Press of John Wilson and Son, 1865.

Jostand, Theodore H. 1970. "The Eckhart Site, Southbury, Connecticut." *Bulletin of the Archaeological Society of Connecticut* 36:7–11.

Juli, Harold. 1992. "Archaeology in the Connecticut College Arboretum." *The Connecticut College Arboretum Bulletin* 33:1–48.

———. 1999. "Current Perspectives on Early and Middle Woodland Archaeology in Connecticut." *Bulletin of the Archaeological Society of Connecticut* 62:141–153.

Juli, Harold D., and Marc A. Kelley. 1991. "The Excavation of a Human Burial Along the Thames River, Southeastern Connecticut." *Bulletin of the Archaeological Society of Connecticut* 54:3–11.

Juli, Harold, and Lucianne Lavin. 1996. "Aboriginal Architecture in Southern New England and Coastal New York." *Northeast Anthropology* 51:83–99.

Juli, Harold, and Kevin A. McBride. 1984. "Early and Middle Woodland Periods of Connecticut Prehistory: Focus on the Lower Connecticut River Valley." *Bulletin of the Archaeological Society of Connecticut* 47:89–110.

Juliano, Frank. 2006. "Digging Up Ancient History in Milford." *Connecticut Post Online*, November 19, 2006; www.connpost.com/.

———. 2010. "Unknown Graves Remain Underfoot." *Connecticut Post*, November 21, 2010, p. A3.

Justice, Noel D. 1987. *Stone Age Spear and Arrow Points of the Midcontinental and Eastern United States: A Modern Survey and Reference.* Bloomington: Indiana University Press.

Kaeser, Edward J. 1968. "The Middle Woodland Placement of Steubenville-like Projectile Points in Coastal New York's Abbott Complex." *Bulletin of the New York State Archaeological Association* 44:8–26.

———. 2004. "The Bartow Lagoon Site, Pelham Bay Park, Bronx County, New York." *Bulletin of the Archaeological Society of Connecticut* 66:51–64.

———. 2006. "The Abbott Complex of Coastal New York." *Bulletin of the Archaeological Society of Connecticut* 68:43–53.

Kalm, Pehr. 1770. *Peter Kalm's Travels in North America: The America of 1750; The English Version of 1770*, rev. from the original Swedish and edited by Adolph B. Benson, with a translation of new material from Kalm's diary notes. Originally published 1937; New York: Dover, 1987.

Kaplan, Daniel H. 1976. "The Massapequa Lake Blade Cache." *Bulletin of the New York State Archaeological Association* 66:18–31.

Karr, Ronald Dale, ed. 1999. *Indian New England, 1524–1674.* Pepperell, Mass.: Branch Line.

Kauffman, Barbara E., and R. Joseph Dent. 1982. "Preliminary Floral and Faunal Recovery and Analysis at the Shawnee-Minisink Site (36MR43)." In *Practicing Environmental Archaeology: Methods and Interpretations*, ed. R. Moeller, pp. 7–12. Occasional Papers of the American Indian Archaeological Institute 3. Washington, Conn.: American Indian Archaeological Institute.

Kavasch, E. Barrie. 1978. "A View from the Wild." *Artifacts* 6(4):1–2.

———. 1979. *Native Harvests: Recipes and Botanicals of the American Indian.* New York: Vintage.

———. 1983. "Herbaria. Dogbanes: Common Fiber, Food, and Medicinal Plants of the American Indians." *Artifacts* 11(4):5–7.

Kawashima, Yasuhide. 2004. "Uncas's Struggle for Survival: The Mohegans and Connecticut Law in the Seventeenth Century." *Connecticut History* 43(2):119–131.

Kaye, Clifford A., and Elso S. Barghoorn. 1964. "Late Quaternary Sea-Level Change and Crustal Rise at Boston, Massachusetts, with Notes on Auto-Compaction of Peat." *Bulletin of the Geological Society of America* 75(2):63–80.

Keegan, Kristen N., and William F. Keegan. 1999. "Introduction." In *The Archaeology of Connecticut,* ed. Kristen N. Keegan and William F. Keegan, pp. i–iv. Storrs, Conn.: Bibliopola.

Keeley, L. 1980. *Experimental Determination of Stone Tool Uses: A Microwear Analysis.* Chicago: University of Chicago Press.

Keener, Roger L. 1965. "The Phillips Site Excavation." *Bulletin of the Archaeological Society of Connecticut* 33:13–44.

Kenefick, James. 1973. "More Facts of Indian History." *The Windham County Transcript,* 125th Anniversary Edition, March 8, 1973, p. 13.

Kerber, Jordan E. 1985. "Digging for Clams: Shell Midden Analysis in New England." *North American Archaeologist* 6(2):97–113.

———. 1988. "Where Are All the Late Woodland Villages in the Narragansett Bay Region?" *Bulletin of the Massachusetts Archaeological Society* 49(2):66–71.

———. 1990. "Saving Endangered Sites in Southern New England: Public Archaeology at Lambert Farm, Warwick, Rhode Island." *Bulletin of the Connecticut Archaeological Society* 53:17–24.

———. 2002. "Interpreting Diverse Marine Shell Deposits of the Woodland Period in New England and New York: Interrelationships Among Subsistence, Symbolism, and Ceremonialism." In *A Lasting Impression: Coastal, Lithic, and Ceramic Research in New England Archaeology,* ed. Jordan E. Kerber, pp. 13–26. Westport, Conn.: Praeger.

Kinsey, W. Fred, III. 1972. *Archaeology in the Upper Delaware Valley* (with contributions by Herbert C. Kraft, Patricia Marchiando, and David J. Werner). Anthropological Series 2. Harrisburg: Pennsylvania Historical and Museum Commission.

Kline, R. M. Philip. 1995. "The Land Remembers: A Contextual Approach to the Abbey of Regina Laudis Archaeological Project." Ph.D. diss., Union Institute, Cincinnati, Ohio.

Kostiw, Scott F. 1995. "A Fresh Look at the Middle Woodland Period in Northeastern North America." *Bulletin of the New York Archaeological Association* 110:38–45.

Kra, Renee. 1984. "Preface: Fifty Years of the Archaeological Society of Connecticut." *Bulletin of the Archaeological Society of Connecticut* 47:1–4.

Kraft, Herbert C. 1970. *The Miller Field Site, Warren County, New Jersey,* part 1, *The Archaic and Transitional Stages.* South Orange, N.J.: Archaeological Research Center, Seton Hall University Museum.

———. 1972. "The Miller Field Site." In *Archaeology of the Upper Delaware Valley,* ed. Fred Kinsey, pp. 1–54. Harrisburg: Pennsylvania Historical and Museum Commission.

———. 1986. *The Lenape: Archaeology, History, and Ethnography.* Collections of the New Jersey Historical Society Vol. 21. Newark: New Jersey Historical Society.

Kraft, John C. 1977. "Late Quaternary Paleogeographic Changes in the Coastal Environments of Delaware, Middle Atlantic Bight, Related to Archaeological Settings." *Annals of the New York Academy of Sciences* 288:35–69.

Krause, Aurel. 1956. *The Tlingit Indians.* Seattle: American Ethnological Society and University of Washington Press.

Krippner, Stanley. 1997. "The Role Played by Mandalas in Navajo and Tibetan Rituals." *Anthropology of Consciousness* 8(1):22–31.

Kris-Etherton, Penny M., William S. Harris, and Lawrence J. Appel, for the Nutrition Committee, American Heart Association. 2002. "Fish Consumption, Fish Oil, Omega-3 Fatty Acids and Cardiovascular Disease." *Circulation* 106:2747–2757. Reprint no. 71-0241.

Kupperman, Karen O. 1980. "The Meeting of English and Indian Technology. *Artifacts* 9(1):10–11, 17.

Langton, H. H., and W. F. Ganong, trans. 1922. *The Works of Samuel de Champlain . . . ,* Volume 1. Gen. ed. H. P. Biggar. Toronto: Champlain Society.

Largent, Floyd B., Jr. 2004. "Yana River, Siberia: Implications for the Peopling of the Americas." *Mammoth Trumpet* 19(3):2–4, 13.

Largy, Tonya. 2011. "Archaeobotanical Recoveries from the Military Academy Site, Niantic, New London County, Connecticut." Appendix 1 in Lucianne Lavin and Marc Banks, "Archeological Monitoring of the Military Academy Site at Camp Rell, the Army National Guard Camp in Niantic, Connecticut." Unpublished report for Skanska USA Building, Inc., New Haven, Conn. On file at the Homer Babbidge Library, Special Collections, University of Connecticut, Storrs.

Larson, C. S. 1982. "The Anthropology of St. Catherine's Island. 3. Prehistoric Human Biological Adaptation." *Anthropological Papers of the American Museum of Natural History* 57 (pt. 3):157–276.

Laub, Richard S. 2000. "A Second Dated Mastodon Bone Artifact from Pleistocene Deposits at the Hiscock Site (Western New York State)." *Archaeology of Eastern North America* 28:141–154.

Lauber, Almon W. 1979. *Indian Slavery in Colonial Times Within the Present Limits of the United States.* Williamstown, Mass.: Corner House.

Lavin, Lucianne. 1980. "Analysis of Ceramic Vessels from the Ben Hollister Site, Glastonbury, Connecticut." *Bulletin of the Archaeological Society of Connecticut* 43:3–41.

———. 1983. *Patterns of Chert Acquisition Among Woodland Groups Within the Delaware River Valley: A Lithologic Approach.* Ann Arbor, Mich.: University Microfilms International.

———. 1984. "Connecticut Prehistory: A Synthesis of Current Archaeological Investigations." *Bulletin of the Archaeological Society of Connecticut* 47:5–40.

———. 1985a. "Peabody Museum Exhibit Documents New Discoveries in Connecticut Archaeology." *Discover* 18(2):16–19.

———. 1985b. *Prehistory of Connecticut's Native Americans.* New Haven: Peabody Museum of Natural History, Yale University.

———. 1986. "Pottery Classification and Cultural Models in Southern New England Prehistory." *North American Archaeologist* 7(1):1–14.

———. 1987. "The Windsor Ceramic Tradition in Southern New England." *North American Archaeologist* 8(1):23–40.

———. 1988a. Coastal Adaptations in Southern New England and Southern New York." *Archaeology of Eastern North America* 16:101–120.

———. 1988b. "The Morgan Site in Rocky Hill, Connecticut: A Late Woodland Community in the Connecticut River Valley." *Bulletin of the Archaeological Society of Connecticut* 51:7–21.

———. 1991. "Re-examination of the Old Lyme Shell Heap: A Look at Shell Midden Form and Function Along the Long Island Sound." In *The Archaeology and Ethnohistory of the Lower Hudson Valley: Essays in Honor of Louis A. Brennan,* ed. H. Kraft, pp. 69–94. New York State Archaeological Association 11. Bethlehem, Conn.: Archaeological Services.

———. 1997. "Diversity in Southern New England Ceramics: Three Case Studies." *Bulletin of the Archaeological Society of Connecticut* 60:63–81.

———. 1998. "The Windsor Tradition: Pottery Production and Popular Identity in Southern New England." *Northeast Anthropologist* 56:1–17.

———. 2001. "The Schaghticoke Nation and the Moravian Movement." In *Archaeology of the Appalachian Highlands,* ed. L. P. Sullivan and S. C. Prezzano, pp. 252–263. Knoxville: University of Tennessee Press.

———. 2002. "Those Puzzling Late Woodland Pottery Styles: A Hypothesis." In *A Lasting Impression: Coastal, Lithic, and Ceramic Research in New England Archaeology,* ed. Jordan E. Kerber, pp. 155–178. Westport, Conn.: Praeger.

———. 2006. "Museum Showcase: Three Birdstones from Connecticut." *Bulletin of the Archaeological Society of Connecticut* 68:131–132.

———. 2007. "Connecticut Connections: The Places That Teach Us About Historical Archaeology." *Connecticut History* 46(2):294–308.

———. 2010. "Pre-Contact Native American Jewelry from the Kent Furnace Site." *Bulletin of the Archaeological Society of Connecticut* 72:129–131.

———. 2011. "Archaeology and Ethnohistory in Connecticut's Northwest Corner: The Mohican Connection." *Bulletin of the Archaeological Society of Connecticut* 73:109–129.

Lavin, Lucianne, and Marc Banks. 2002. "Phase 1 and Phase 2 Archaeological Investigations of the Proposed Military Academy Site at Camp Rowland in East Lyme, Connecticut." Unpublished report prepared for Kaestle Boos Associates, Inc., New Britain, Conn., June 2002. On file at the Homer Babbidge Library, Special Collections, University of Connecticut, Storrs.

———. 2003. "Phase 1 and Phase 2 Archaeological Surveys of the Quinebaug Multi-Purpose River Trail Project in Killingly, Conn. (Project No. QC-024)." Unpublished report prepared for Fay, Spofford & Thorndike, Inc., Burlington, Mass., December

2003. On file at the Homer Babbidge Library, Special Collections, University of Connecticut, Storrs.

———. 2005a. "Phase 1 and Phase 2 Archaeological Investigations of the Connecticut Yankee Atomic Power Company Property in Haddam Neck, Connecticut." Prepared for CYAPCO, Haddam Neck, Conn., November 2005. On file at the Homer Babbidge Library, Special Collections, University of Connecticut, Storrs.

———. 2005b. "Phase 3 Archaeological Investigations of the Proposed Military Academy Site at Camp Rell/Rowland in the Niantic Section of East Lyme, Connecticut." Unpublished manuscript prepared for Kaestle Boos Associates, Inc., New Britain, Conn. On file at the Homer Babbidge Library, Special Collections, University of Connecticut, Storrs.

———. 2007. "Phase I and Phase 2 Archaeological Investigations of the Connecticut Yankee Atomic Power Company Property in Haddam Neck, Connecticut. The 2005–2006 Field Seasons, with a Synopsis of the 2002–2004 Field Seasons and an Overview of the Entire 7-year Archaeological Study, Vols. 1–3." Prepared for CYAPCO, Haddam Neck, Conn., August 2007. On file at the Homer Babbidge Library, Special Collections, University of Connecticut, Storrs.

———. 2008. *Connecticut's First Fishermen: LeBeau Fishing Camp and Weir.* State Archaeological Preserve Booklet. Centerbrook, Conn.: Essex Printing.

———. 2010. "Dibble Creek 1 Site (#61-124): A Seasonal Camp and Blade Cache in Haddam, Connecticut." *Bulletin of the Archaeological Society of Connecticut* 72:83–98.

———. 2011. "Archaeological Monitoring and Discovery Report, the Military Academy Site (45-64) at Camp Rell, the Army National Guard Camp in Niantic, Connecticut." Unpublished report for Skanska USA Building, Inc., New Haven, Conn. On file at the Homer Babbidge Library, Special Collections, University of Connecticut, Storrs.

Lavin, Lucianne, S. Douglas Dumas, and Cynthia Kania. 1998. "Phase I and II Archaeological Surveys of the Proposed Sanitary Sewer Facilities Project Area at Camp Rowland in Niantic, Connecticut." Prepared for United International Corp., 821 N. Main St. Ext., Wallingford, Conn., and the Connecticut Dept. of Public Works. On file at the Homer Babbidge Library, Special Collections, University of Connecticut, Storrs.

———. 1999. "Phase 3 Archaeological Data Recovery Program for the Larson Site (6LF123) West-Central Locus in New Milford, Connecticut." Unpublished report prepared for Fletcher-Thompson, Inc., and the New Milford High School Building Committee, New Milford, August 1999. On file at the Homer Babbidge Library, Special Collections, University of Connecticut, Storrs.

Lavin, Lucianne, Fred Gudrian, and Laurie Miroff. 1992–1993. "Pottery Production and Cultural Process: Prehistoric Ceramics from the Morgan Site." In *From Prehistory to the Present: Studies in Northeastern Archaeology in Honor of Bert Salwen,* ed. N. A. Rothschild and D. Wall. Special issue, *Northeast Historical Archaeology* 21–22:44–63.

———. 1993. "Prehistoric Pottery from the Morgan Site, Rocky Hill, Connecticut." *Bulletin of the Archaeological Society of Connecticut* 56:63–100.

Lavin, Lucianne, and Cynthia Kania. 2001a. "Final Report: Phase 1 Archaeological Reconnaissance Survey and Phase 2 Intensive Survey of a Proposed 21-Lot Residential Subdivision in the Hawleyville Section of Newtown Connecticut, The Newtown-Hunt Site." Unpublished report prepared for Toll Brothers, Inc., of Armonk, New York, August 2001. On file at the Homer Babbidge Library, Special Collections, University of Connecticut, Storrs.

————. 2001b. "Final Report: Phase II Intensive Survey of Site 69-2, Within the Confines of the Proposed Industrial Park Expansion in Killingly, Connecticut." On file at the Homer Babbidge Library, Special Collections, University of Connecticut, Storrs.

————. 2001c. "Final Report: Extended Phase 2 Archaeological Investigation of a Proposed Residential Subdivision at the Baldwin's Station Site (6NH47, Southwestern Locus) in Milford, Connecticut." Unpublished report prepared for Baldwin's Station LLC, Bridgeport, Conn., August 2001. On file at the Homer Babbidge Library, Special Collections, University of Connecticut, Storrs.

Lavin, Lucianne, and Renee Kra. 1994. "Prehistoric Pottery Assemblages from Southern Connecticut: A Fresh Look at Ceramic Classification in Southern New England." *Bulletin of the Archaeological Society of Connecticut* 57:35–51.

————. 1996. "Prehistory Pottery Assemblages from Southern Connecticut: A Fresh Look at Ceramic Classification in New England." *Bulletin of the Archaeological Society of Connecticut* 57:35–51.

Lavin, Lucianne, and Laurie Miroff. 1992. "Aboriginal Pottery from the Indian Ridge Site, New Milford, Connecticut." *Bulletin of the Archaeological Society of Connecticut* 55:39–61.

Lavin, Lucianne, and Marina E. Mozzi. 1996. "Historic Preservation in Connecticut," vol. 1, "Western Coastal Slope: Overview of Prehistoric and Historic Archaeology and Management Guide." Unpublished manuscript prepared for the Connecticut Historical Commission, State Historic Preservation Office, 59 South Prospect Street, Hartford, Conn.

Lavin, Lucianne, and Donald R. Prothero. 1987. "Identification of Jasper Sources in Parts of the Northeast and Mid-Atlantic Regions." *Bulletin of the New Jersey Archaeological Society* 42:11–23.

————. 1992. "Prehistoric Procurement of Secondary Sources: The Case for Characterization." *North American Archaeologist* 13(2):97–113.

Lavin, Lucianne, and Lyent W. Russell. 1985. "Excavation of the Burwell-Karako Site: New Data on Cultural Sequences and Artifact Typologies in Southern New England." *Bulletin of the Archaeological Society of Connecticut* 48:45–87.

Lavin, Lucianne, and Bert Salwen. 1983. "The Fastener Site: A New Look at the Archaic-Woodland Transition in the Lower Housatonic Valley." *Bulletin of the Archaeological Society of Connecticut* 46:15–43.

Lawrence, Julia F., and H. Gordon Rowe. 1953. "Indian Sites in and Near Pine Orchard." *Bulletin of the Archaeological Society of Connecticut* 27:30–34.

Lemonick, Michael D., and Andrea Dorfman. 2006. "Who Were the First Americans?" *Time,* March 13, 2006, 45–52.

Lenik, Edward. 2002. *Picture Rocks: American Indian Rock Art in the Northeast Woodlands.* Lebanon, N.H.: University Press of New England.

Leveillee, Alan. 1997. "When Worlds Collide: Archaeology in the New Age—The Conant Parcel Stone Piles." *Bulletin of the Massachusetts Archaeological Society* 58(1):24–30.

"The Liebman Paleo-Indian Site 4/18–5/3." 1994. *Archaeological Society of Southeastern Connecticut Newsletter* 2:2.

Lightfoot, Dent, Robert Kalin, Owen Lindauer, and Linda Wicks. 1985. "Coastal New York Settlement Patterns: A Perspective from Shelter Island." *Man in the Northeast* 30:59–82.

Lindsay, Sylvia. 1992. "Forensic Methods Focus on Paleoindian." *Mammoth Trumpet* 7(3):1–3.

Little, Elizabeth A. 1986. "Observations on Methods of Collection, Use, and Seasonality of Shellfish on the Coasts of Massachusetts." *Massachusetts Archaeological Society Bulletin* 47(2):46–59.

———. 1987. "Inland Waterways in the Northeast." *Midcontinental Journal of Archaeology* 12(1):55–76.

———. 1988. "Where Are the Woodland Villages on Cape Cod and the Islands?" *Massachusetts Archaeological Society Bulletin* 49(2):72–82.

Logan, Adelphena. 1975. "An Onondaga Indian Prayer, Recited by Adelphena Logan." *Artifacts* 3(4):8.

———. 1979. *Memories of Sweet Grass.* Washington, Conn.: American Indian Archaeological Institute.

Lopez, Julius, and Stanley Wisniewski. 1958. "Discovery of a Possible Ceremonial Dog Burial in the City of Greater New York." *Bulletin of the Archaeological Society of Connecticut* 29:14–19.

———. 1978. "The Ryder Pond Site, Kings County, New York." In The *Coastal Archaeology Reader: Selections from the New York State Archaeological Association Bulletin, 1954–1977.* Readings in Long Island Archaeology and Ethnohistory 2, ed. G. S. Levine, pp. 208–227. Stony Brook, N.Y.: Suffolk County Archaeological Association.

Lossing, Benson. 1871. "The Last of the Pequods." *Scribner's Monthly* II-37:573–577.

Love, W. DeLoss, with an introduction by Margaret Connell Szasz. 2000. *Samsom Occum and the Christian Indians of New England.* Ithaca, N.Y.: Syracuse University Press. (Originally published in 1899, Boston: Pilgrim.)

Luckenbach, A. H., W. E. Clark, and R. S. Levy. 1987. "Rethinking Cultural Stability in Eastern North American Prehistory: Linguistic Evidence from Eastern Algonquian." *Journal of Middle Atlantic Archaeology* 3:1–33.

Luedtke, Barbara E. 1981. "Quartz Technology on Patience and Prudence Islands, Rhode Island." In *Quartz Technology in Prehistoric Southern New England,* ed. R. Barber, pp. 63–76. Cambridge, U.K.: Institute for Conservation Archaeology.

———. 1985. "The Camp at the Bend in the River: Prehistory at the Shattuck Farm Site." *Occasional Publications in Archaeology and History* no. 4. Boston: Massachusetts Historical Commission.

———. 1987. "The Pennsylvania Connection: Jasper at Massachusetts Sites." *Bulletin of the Massachusetts Archaeological Society* 48(2):37–47.

———. 1988. "Where Are All the Late Woodland Villages in Eastern Massachusetts?" *Bulletin of the Massachusetts Archaeological Society* 49(2):58–65.

————. 1992. *An Archaeologist's Guide to Chert and Flint*. Archaeological Research Tools 7. Los Angeles: Institute of Archaeology, University of California.

————. 1993. "Lithic Source Analysis in New England." *Bulletin of the Massachusetts Archaeological Society* 54(2):56–60.

MacCurdy, George Grant. 1914. "The Passing of a Connecticut Rock Shelter." *American Journal of Science* (December Series 4) 38:511–522.

————. 1962. "The Passing of a Connecticut Rock Shelter." *Bulletin of the Archaeological Society of Connecticut* 31:9–18.

MacKenzie, Alexander. 1801. *Voyages from Montreal on the River St. Laurence Through the Continent of North America to the Frozen and Pacific Oceans in the Years 1789 and 1793, with a Preliminary Account of the Rise, Progress, and Present State of the Fur Trade in that Country.* London: Noble and Baily.

MacNeish, Richard S. 1973. "Early Man in the Andes." In *Early Man in America,* ed. R. S. MacNeish, pp. 69–79. San Francisco: W. H. Freeman.

Mancini, Jason R. 2009. "New London's Indian Mariners." *Hog River Journal* 7(2):22–25.

Mancini, Jason R., and David J. Naumec. 2005. *Connecticut's African & Native American Revolutionary War Enlistments: 1775–1783.* Mashantucket, Conn.: Mashantucket Pequot Museum and Research Center.

Mangelsdorf, Paul C. 1974. *Corn: Its Origin, Evolution, and Improvement.* Cambridge, Mass.: Belknap Press of Harvard University Press.

Marshall, Ingborg. 1996. *A History and Ethnography of the Beothuk.* Montreal: McGill-Queens University Press.

Martin, F. W., and E. F. Martin. 2006. "A Midsummer Sunbeam Site in New England." In *Viewing the Sky Through Past and Present Cultures,* ed. Todd W. Bostwick and Bryan Bates. Proceedings of the Oxford VII International Conference on Archaeoastronomy. Pueblo Grande Museum Anthropological Papers No. 15. Phoenix, Ariz.: City of Phoenix Parks and Recreation Department.

Mason, John. 1637. *A Brief History of the Pequot War: Especially of the Memorable Taking of Their Fort at Mistick in Connecticut in 1637.* Reprint, Boston: Kneeland and T. Green, 1736.

Mauss, Marcel. 1925. *The Gift: The Form and Reason for Exchange in Archaic Societies.* London: Routledge. (Translated by W. D. Halls in 1990.)

McAllester, David P. 1987. "New England Indian Music." In *Rooted Like the Ash Trees: New England Indians and the Land,* ed. Richard G. Carlson, p. 40. Naugatuck, Conn.: Eagle Wing.

————. 2009. "Mohican Music, Past and Present." In *Mohican Seminar 2, The Challenge—An Algonquian Peoples Seminar,* ed. Shirley W. Dunn, pp. 97–101. New York State Museum Bulletin 506. Albany: University of the State of New York, New York State Educational Department.

McBride, Kevin A. 1978. "Archaic Subsistence in the Lower Connecticut River Valley: Evidence from Woodchuck Knoll." *Man in the Northeast* 15–16 (1978):124–132.

————. 1984a. "The Middle and Late Archaic Periods in the Connecticut River Valley: A Re-examination." *Bulletin of the Archaeological Society of Connecticut* 47:55–72.

————. 1984b. *The Prehistory of the Lower Connecticut Valley.* Ann Arbor, Mich.: University Microfilms International. *Dissertations Collection for the University of Connecticut*, Paper AAI8509510; http://digitalcommons.uconn.edu/dissertations/AAI8509510.

———. 1990. "The Historical Archaeology of the Mashantucket Pequots, 1637–1900: A Preliminary Analysis." In *The Pequots in Southern New England: The Fall and Rise of an American Indian Nation*, ed. Laurence M. Hauptman and James D. Wherry, pp. 96–116. Norman: University of Oklahoma Press.

———. 1992. "Prehistoric and Historic Patterns of Wetland Use in Eastern Connecticut." *Man in the Northeast* 43:10–23.

———. 1993. "'Ancient and Crazie' Pequot Lifeways During the Historic Period." In *Algonkians of New England: Past and Present*, ed. Peter Benes, pp. 63–75. Proceedings of the annual Dublin Seminar for New England Folklife 1991. Boston: Boston University.

———. 1994. "The Source and Mother of the Fur Trade: Native Dutch Relations in Eastern New Netherlands." In *Enduring Traditions: The Native Peoples of New England*, ed. Laurie Weinstein, pp. 31–51. Westport, Conn.: Bergin and Garvey.

———. 2006a. "Fort Island: Conflict and Trade in Long Island Sound." In *The Native Forts of Long Island Sound Area*, ed. Gaynell Stone, pp. 255–266. Volume 8. Stony Brook, N.Y.: Suffolk County Archaeological Association.

———. 2006b. "Monhantic Fort: The Pequot in King Phillip's War." In *The Native Forts of Long Island Sound Area*, ed. Gaynell Stone, pp. 323–336. Vol. 8. Stony Brook, N.Y.: Suffolk County Archaeological Association.

———. 2010. "Preserving the Battlefields of the Pequot War." *Connecticut Preservation News* 33(6):6–7, 12.

McBride, Kevin A., and Nicholas F. Bellantoni. 1982. "The Utility of Ethnohistoric Models for Understanding Late Woodland-Contact Change in Southern New England." *Bulletin of the Archaeological Society of Connecticut* 45:51–64.

McBride, Kevin A., and R. Dewar. 1981. "Prehistoric Settlement in the Lower Connecticut River Valley." *Man in the Northeast* 22:37–66.

———. 1987. "Agriculture and Cultural Evolution: Causes and Effects in the Lower Connecticut River Valley." In *Emergent Horticultural Economies in the Eastern Woodlands*, ed. W. Keegan, pp. 305–328. Occasional Papers 7. Carbondale, Ill.: Center for Archaeological Investigations, Southern Illinois University.

McBride, Kevin A., R. Dewar, and W. Wadleigh. 1979. "The North-Central Lowlands Archaeological Survey, South Windsor, Connecticut." Archaeology Research Monograph 1. On file at the Public Archaeology Survey Team, Inc., Storrs, Conn.

McBride, Kevin A., and Robert S. Grumet. 1996. "The Mashantucket Pequot Indian Archaeological District: A National Historic Landmark." *Bulletin of the Archaeological Society of Connecticut* 59:15–26.

McBride, Kevin A., and Mary G. Soulsby. 1989. "Prehistory of Connecticut Phase 1, 2, and 3 Archaeological Surveys—Relocation of Route 6/I-84 Project." Unpublished report submitted to the Connecticut Department of Transportation, Hartford.

McBride, Kevin A., W. Wadleigh, R. Dewar, and M. Soulsby. 1980. "Prehistoric Settlement in Eastern Connecticut: The North-Central Lowlands and Northeastern Highlands Surveys, 1979." Archaeology Research Monograph 15. On file at the Public Archaeology Survey Team, Inc., Storrs, Conn.

McLoughlin, Pamela. 2010. "Modern-Day Explorer Rediscovers Rock." *New Haven Register,* December 17, 2010. Newspaper clipping provided by New Haven historian Deb Townshend to author.

McMullen, Ann. 1985. "'Stories Archaeologists Tell' Opening Mid-March." *Artifacts* 14(2):10.

McNett, C. W., Jr. 1985. *Shawnee Minisink: A Stratified Paleo Indian-Archaic Site in the Upper Delaware Valley of Pennsylvania.* New York: Academic.

McNickle, D'Arcy. 1973. *Native American Tribalism: Indian Survivals and Renewal.* Oxford: Oxford University Press.

McWeeney, Lucinda. 1994. "Archaeological Settlement Patterns and Vegetation Dynamics in Southern New England in the Late Quaternary." Ph.D. diss., Yale University, New Haven, Conn.

———. 1999. "A Review of Late Pleistocene and Holocene Climatic Changes in Southern New England." *Bulletin of the Archaeological Society of Connecticut* 62:3–18.

Meader, J. W. 1869. *The Merrimack River: Its Source and Its Tributaries.* Boston: B. B. Russell.

Menta, John. 1988. "Shaumpishuh, 'Squaw Sachem' of the Quinnipiac Indians." *Artifacts* 16(3–4):32–37.

———. 2003. *The Quinnipiac: Cultural Conflict in Southern New England.* Yale University Publications in Anthropology 86. New Haven: Peabody Museum of Natural History, Yale University.

Merrell, James H. 1989. "Some Thoughts on Colonial Historians and American Indians." *William and Mary Quarterly* 46(1):94–119.

Merwin, Daria E., Daniel P. Lynch, and David S. Robinson. 2003. "Submerged Prehistoric Sites in Southern New England: Past Research and Future Directions." *Bulletin of the Archaeological Society of Connecticut* 65:41–56.

Miles, Lion. 2006. "The Mystery of the Monument Mountain Stone Heap." *The Advocate Weekly,* April 6, 2006.

———. 2009. *A Life of John Konkapot: The Mohican Chief Who Sold His Berkshire (Massachusetts) Hunting Grounds to Puritan Settlers Hoping that Their Faith and Example Would Benefit His People.* Troy, N.Y.: The Troy Bookmakers.

Mills, William C. 1917. *Certain Mounds and Village Sites in Ohio.* Volume 2. Columbus, Ohio: F. J. Heer.

Milner, George R. 2006. *The Cahokia Chiefdom: The Archaeology of a Mississippian Society.* Washington, D.C.: Smithsonian Institution Press.

Milner, George R., and George Chaplin. 2010. "Eastern North American Population at ca. A.D. 1500." *American Antiquity* 75(4): 707–726.

Moeller, Roger W. 1980. *6LF21: A Paleo-Indian Site in Western Connecticut.* Washington, Conn.: American Indian Archaeological Institute.

———. 1983. "Mastodon Date." *Artifacts* 11(3):21.

———. 1984a. *Guide to Indian Artifacts of the Northeast.* Blaine, Wash.: Hancock House.

————. 1984b. "The Ivory Pond Mastodon Project." *North American Archaeologist* 5(1): 1–12.

————. 1984c. "Paleo-Indian and Early Archaic Occupations in Connecticut." *Bulletin of the Archaeological Society of Connecticut* 47:41–54.

————. 1987. "Stone Walls, Stone Lines, and Supposed Indian Graves." *Bulletin of the Archaeological Society of Connecticut* 50:17–22.

————. 1999. "A View of Paleo-Indian Studies in Connecticut." *Bulletin of the Archaeological Society of Connecticut* 62:67–78.

Moondancer and Strong Woman. 1998. *A Cultural History of the Native Peoples of Southern New England: Voices from the Past and Present.* Newport, R.I.: Aquidneck Tribal Council.

Moore, Susan T. 1997. "History of the Fox Creek Phase and Its Manifestations in Massachusetts." *Bulletin of the Massachusetts Archaeological Society* 58(1):2–19.

Moravian Church Archives. 1743–1769. Bethlehem, Pa. Also available on microfilm at Sterling Library, Yale University, New Haven, Conn.

"More than a Museum." 1979. *Artifacts* 7(4):9.

Morphy, Howard. 1995. "Landscape and the Reproduction of the Ancestral Past." In *The Anthropology of Landscape: Perspectives on Place and Space,* ed. Eric Hirsch and Michael O'Hanlon, pp. 184–209. Oxford: Oxford University Press.

Morrell, William. 1895. "Morrell's Poem on New England." *Massachusetts Historical Society Collections* 1 (ser. 1):125–139. Facsimile of the original edition of 1625.

Morton, N. 1669. *New England's Memoriall.* Reprint, ed. H. J. Hall, New York: Scholars Facsimiles and Reprints, 1937.

Morton, Thomas. 1637. *The Essential New English Canaan.* Reprint, ed. Jack Dempsey, Scituate, Mass.: Digital Scanning, 2000.

Mrozowski, Stephen A. 1994. "The Discovery of a Native American Cornfield on Cape Cod." *Archaeology of Eastern North America* 22:47–62.

Mynter, Ken. 1987. "Leaving New England: The Stockbridge Indians." In *Rooted Like the Ash Trees: New England Indians and the Land,* ed. Richard G. Carlson, pp. 30–32. Naugatuck, Conn.: Eagle Wing.

Nadeau, Jaclyn, and Nicholas F. Bellantoni. 2004. "Lithic Artifact and Bio-Archaeological Analyses of a Possible Adena Burial Site (CT84–51) in Milford, Connecticut." *Bulletin of the Archaeological Society of Connecticut* 66:3–15.

"Native American Profile, Karen Coody Cooper—Cherokee." 1986. *Artifacts* 15(2):6.

Naumec, David J. 2008a. "Connecticut Indians in the War of Independence." *Connecticut History* 47(2):181–218.

————. 2008b. "From Mashantucket to Appomattox: The Native American Veterans of Connecticut's Volunteer Regiments and the Union Navy." *New England Quarterly* 81(4):596–635; doi:10.1162/tneq.2008.81.4.596.

Newell, Margaret E. 2003. "The Changing Nature of Indian Slavery in New England, 1670–1720." In *Reinterpreting New England Indians and the Colonial Experience,* ed. Colin G. Calloway and Neal Salisbury, pp. 106–136. Boston: Colonial Society of Massachusetts.

Newman, Walter S. 1977. "Late Quaternary Paleoenvironmental Reconstruction: Some Contradictions from Northwestern Long Island, New York." *Annals of the New York Academy of Sciences* 288(1):545–570.

Nicholas, George P. 1985. "Overview of the 1984 Field Season Around Robbins Swamp." *Artifacts* 13(1):1–5.

———. 1987a. "Hunter-Gatherer Society and the Prehistoric Use of Jasper." *Artifacts* 15(4):16–19.

———. 1987b. "Rethinking the Early Archaic." *Archaeology of Eastern North America* 15:99–124.

———. 1988. "Ecological Leveling: The Archaeology and Environmental Dynamics of Early Postglacial Land Use." In *Holocene Human Ecology in Northeastern North America,* ed. G. Nicholas, pp. 257–296. New York: Plenum.

———. 1991. "Putting Wetlands into Perspective." *Man in the Northeast* 42:29–38.

Niemczycki, Mary Ann Palmer. 1986. "The Genesee Connection: The Origin of Iroquois Culture in West-Central New York." *North American Archaeologist* 7(1):15–44.

———. 1987. "Late Woodland Settlement in the Genesee." *Bulletin of the New York State Archaeological Association* 95:32–38.

Norton, Frederick C. 1899. "Negro Slavery in Connecticut." *Connecticut Magazine* 5(6). Connecticut American History and Geneaology Project; www.rootsweb.ancestry.com/~ctahgp/history/slavery.htm.

Oakes, Jill E. 1987. *Factors Influencing Kamik Production in Arctic Bay, Northwest Territories.* Ottawa: National Museums of Canada.

———. 1991. *Copper and Caribou Inuit Skin Clothing Production.* Canadian Ethnology Service, Mercury Series Paper 118. Hull, Quebec: Canadian Museum of Civilization.

O'Brien, Jean M. 2006. "'Vanishing' Indians in Nineteenth-Century New England: Local Historians' Erasure of Still-Present Indian Peoples." In *New Perspectives on Native North American Cultures, Histories, and Representations,* ed. Sergei A. Kan and Pauline T. Strong, pp. 414–432. Lincoln: University of Nebraska Press.

———. 2010. *Firsting and Lasting: Writing Indians Out of Existence in New England.* Minneapolis: University of Minnesota Press.

O'Callahan, Edmund B. 1855. *History of New Netherland, or, New York Under the Dutch.* 2d ed., vols. 1 and 2. New York: D. Appleton.

O'Connor, Mallory McCane. 1995. *Lost Cities of the Ancient Southeast.* Gainesville: University Press of Florida.

Office of the State Archaeologist. n.d. Connecticut archaeological site inventory forms (site files) and accompanying maps. Office of State Archaeology, Storrs, Conn.

Ogden, J. Gordon. 1977. "The Late Quaternary Paleoenvironmental Record of Northeastern North America." In *Amerinds and Their Paleoenvironments in Northeastern North America,* ed. Walter S. Newman and Bert Salwen. Annals of the New York Academy of Sciences 288. New York: New York Academy of Sciences.

Oldale, Robert N. 1986. "Late-Glacial and Postglacial Sea-Level History of New England: A Review of Available Sea-Level Curves." *Archaeology of Eastern North America* 14:89–99.

"An Older Culture Survives on the Davis Farm." 2006. *Historical Footnotes,* May 2006, pp. 6–7. (Originally published in John L. Davis, 1986, *The Davis Homestead,* ed. Emily H. Lynch, Stonington, Conn.: Stonington Historical Society.)

Orcutt, Samuel, and Ambrose Beardsley. 1880. *The History of the Old Town of Derby, Connecticut, 1642–1880, with Biographies and Genealogies.* Springfield, Mass.: Press of Springfield Printing Company.

Ordonez, Margaret T., and Linda Welters. 2004. "Textiles and Leather in Southeastern New England Archaeological Sites." In *Perishable Material Culture in the Northeast,* ed. Penelope Ballard Drooker, pp. 169–184. New York State Museum Bulletin 500. Albany: New York State Education Department.

"Orient Data at Boulder Site." 1972. *Artifacts* 1(2):4.

Osgood, Cornelius. 1940. *Ingalik Material Culture.* New Haven: Yale University Press.

Pagoulatos, Peter. 1983. "Terminal Archaic Settlement-Subsistence Patterns in the Lower Connecticut River Valley: A Series of Testable Hypotheses." *Bulletin of the Archaeological Society of Connecticut* 46:55–62.

———. 1986. "Terminal Archaic Settlement and Subsistence in the Connecticut River Valley." Ph.D. diss., University of Connecticut, Storrs.

———. 1988. "Terminal Archaic Settlement and Subsistence in the Connecticut River Valley." *Man in the Northeast* 35:71–93.

———. 1990. "Terminal Archaic 'Living Areas' in the Connecticut River Valley." *Bulletin of the Archaeological Society of Connecticut* 53:59–72.

———. 2002. "Early Woodland Settlement Patterns: A View from the State of New Jersey." *Bulletin of the Archaeological Society of Connecticut* 64:23–42.

Parkos, Joseph. 1991a. "A Deer Antler Pipe from Eastern Connecticut." *Bulletin of the Archaeological Society of Connecticut* 54:55.

———. 1991b. "The M.R. Site, A Preliminary Report." *Bulletin of the Archaeological Society of Connecticut* 54:77–86.

Patterson, William A., III, and Kenneth E. Sassaman. 1988. "Indian Fires in the Prehistory of New England." In *Holocene Human Ecology in Northeastern North America,* ed. George P. Nicholas, pp. 107–135. New York: Plenum.

Pauketat, Timothy R. 1994. *The Ascent of Chiefs: Cahokia and Mississippian Politics in Native North America.* Tuscaloosa: University of Alabama Press.

———. 2004. *Ancient Cahokia and the Mississippians.* New York: Cambridge University Press.

Pederson, Dee Cabaniss, Dorothy M. Peteet, Dorothy Kurdyla, and Tom Guilderson. 2005. "Medieval Warming, Little Ice Age, and European Impact on the Environment During the Last Millennium in the Lower Hudson Valley, New York, USA." *Quaternary Research* 63(3):238–249.

Pendergast, James F. 1989. "The Significance of Some Marine Shell Excavated on Iroquoian Archaeological Sites in Ontario." In *Proceedings of the 1986 Shell Bead Conference: Selected Papers,* gen. ed. Charles F. Hayes III, Research records 20, pp. 97–112. Rochester, N.Y.: Research Division, Rochester Museum and Science Center.

Perry, Lynette, and Manny Skolnick. 1999. *Keeper of the Delaware Dolls.* Lincoln: University of Nebraska Press.

Petersen, James B. 1991. "Archaeological Testing at the Sharrow Site: A Deeply Stratified Early to Late Holocene Cultural Sequence in Central Maine." Manuscript on file at the University of Maine at Farmington Archaeological Research Center, Farmington.

Petersen, J. B., N. D. Hamilton, D. E. Putnam, A. E. Spiess, R. Stuckenrath, C. A. Thayer, and J. A. Wolford. 1986. "The Piscataquis Archaeological Project: A Late Pleistocene and Holocene Occupational Sequence in Northern New England." *Archaeology of Eastern North America* 14:1–18.

Petruzelli, Renee. 2011. Appendix 2 in Lucianne Lavin and Marc Banks, "Archaeological Monitoring of the Military Academy Site at Camp Rell, the Army National Guard Camp in Niantic, Connecticut." Unpublished report for Skanska USA Building, Inc., New Haven, Conn. On file at the Homer Babbidge Library, Special Collections, University of Connecticut, Storrs.

Pfeiffer, John E. 1980. "The Griffin Site: A Susquehanna Cremation Burial in Southern Connecticut." *Man in the Northeast* 19:129–133.

———. 1983a. "Bashan Lake: 4500 Years of Prehistory." *Bulletin of the Archaeological Society of Connecticut* 46:45–53.

———. 1983b. "The Early Archaic 10,000–8,000 B.P." *ASSEC News* 2:5–9.

———. 1983c. "The Middle Archaic 8,000–6,000 B.P." *ASSEC News* 4:6–8.

———. 1984. "The Late and Terminal Archaic Periods in Connecticut Prehistory." *Bulletin of the Archaeological Society of Connecticut* 47:73–88.

———. 1986. "Dill Farm Locus I: Early and Middle Archaic Components in Southern Connecticut." *Bulletin of the Archaeological Society of Connecticut* 49:19–35.

———. 1990. "The Late and Terminal Archaic Periods in Connecticut: A Model of Continuity." In *Experiments and Observations on the Terminal Archaic of the Middle Atlantic Region*, ed. R. Moeller, pp. 85–104. Bethlehem, Conn.: Archaeological Services.

———. 1992. "Late and Terminal Archaic Cultural Adaptations of the Lowest Connecticut Valley." Ph.D. diss., State University of New York, Albany.

———. 1993. "Hopeville Pond: Archaeological Evidence of a Middle Woodland Jacks Reef Point Component in Eastern Connecticut." *Bulletin of the Archaeological Society of Connecticut* 56:101–114.

———. 1994. "The Archaeological Rescue of the Spencer Site in Westbrook, Connecticut." *Bulletin of the Archaeological Society of Connecticut* 57:27–34.

———. 1996. "Post-Contact Populations on the Nehantic Reservation of Lyme, Connecticut." *Bulletin of the Archaeological Society of Connecticut* 59:67–78.

Pfeiffer, J. E., and D. Malcarne. 1989. "An Investigation into the Ancient Burial Ground at Crescent Beach, Niantic, Connecticut." *Bulletin of the Archaeological Society of Connecticut* 52:61–69.

Pfeiffer, John E., and Robert Stuckenrath. 1989. "Radiometric Dates from Two Cremation Burial Sites in Southern New England." *Bulletin of the Archaeological Society of Connecticut* 52:51–54.

Pierson, Abraham, trans. 1658. *Some Helps for the Indians: A Catechism in the Language of the Quiripi Indians of New Haven Colony.* Cambridge: Samuel Green. Reprinted from the original edition, with an introduction by J. Hammond Trumbull. From the Collections of the Connecticut Historical Society, vol. 3. Hartford: M.H. Mallory, 1873.

Piperno, Dolores R., Anthony J. Ranere, Irene Holst, José Iriarte, and Ruth Dickau. 2009. "Starch Grain and Phytolith Evidence for Early Ninth Millennium B.P. Maize from the Central Balsas River Valley, Mexico." *Proceedings of the National Academy of Sciences* 106(13):5019–5024.

Poirier, David A. 1981. Southern New England Archaeological Surveys: A Preservation Planning Perspective." *Man in the Northeast* 22:153–158.

———. 1984. "Conservation Archaeology: The Perspective of Historical Archaeology in Connecticut." Ph.D. diss., University of Connecticut, Storrs.

Poirier, David A., and Nicholas F. Bellantoni. 2003. "Landlubbers in a Wet World: Administrative Perspectives on Connecticut's Underwater Heritage." *Bulletin of the Archaeological Society of Connecticut* 65:57–66.

Poirier, David A., Nicholas F. Bellantoni, and Mikki Aganstata. 1985. "Native American Burials in Connecticut: The Ethical, Scientific, and Bureaucratic Matrix." *Bulletin of the Archaeological Society of Connecticut* 48:3–12.

Pope, G. D., Jr. 1952. "Excavation at the Charles Tyler Site." *Bulletin of the Archaeological Society of Connecticut* 26:3–29.

Pope, Peter. 2007. "Archaeology of the Petit Nord." *Council for Northeastern Historical Archaeology Newsletter* 66:22–23.

Potter, C. E. 1856. *History of Manchester.* Manchester, N.H.: C. E. Potter.

Powell, Bernard W. 1958. "Preliminary Report on a Southwestern Connecticut Site." *Bulletin of the Archaeological Society of Connecticut* 28:12–29.

———. 1965. Spruce Swamp: A Partially Drowned Coastal Midden Site in Connecticut." *American Antiquity* 30(4):460–469.

———. 1981. "Carbonized Seed Remains from Prehistoric Sites in Connecticut." *Man in the Northeast* 21:75–85.

Praus, A. A. 1942. "Excavations at the Old Lyme Shellheap." *Bulletin of the Archaeological Society of Connecticut* 13:3–66.

Pretola, John P. 1985. "The Springfield Fort Hill Site: A New Look." *Bulletin of the Archaeological Society of Connecticut* 48:35–44.

———. 2002. "An Optical Mineralogy Approach to Northeastern Ceramic Diversity." In *A Lasting Impression: Coastal Lithic and Ceramic Research in New England Archaeology,* ed. Jordan E. Kerber, pp. 179–205. Westport, Conn.: Praeger.

Pring, Martin. 1603. "A Voyage Set Out from the Citie of Bristoll with a Small Ship and a Barke for the Discoverie of the North Part of Virginia." In *Early English and French Voyages Chiefly from Hakluyt 1534–1608,* ed. Henry S. Burrage, pp. 341–352. New York: Charles Scribner's Sons, 1906.

Prothero, Donald R., and Lucianne Lavin. 1990. "Determination of Prehistoric Acquisition Patterns by Petrographic Analysis of Chert Artifacts." In *The Archaeological Geology of North America,* ed. N. Nasca and J. Donahue, pp. 561–584. Boulder, Colo.: Geological Society of America.

Public Archaeology Laboratory, Inc. 1991. "Phase 1 Archaeological Reconnaissance Survey of the Algonquin Gas Transmission Company Proposed 6.7-mile, 36-inch Pipeline Loop, Berlin, Middletown, and Cromwell, Connecticut." Pawtucket, R.I.: Public Archaeology Laboratory.

Puniello, Anthony. 1993. "Evidence of the Niantic Indians in the Archaeological Record." In *From Prehistory to the Present: Studies in Northeastern Archaeology in Honor of Bert Salwen,* ed. N. A. Rothschild and D. Wall. Special issue, *Northeast Historical Archaeology* 21:79–95.

Rabito, Philip Wyppensenwah. 1977. "The Missing Native Americans." *Artifacts* 6(1):3–4.

Rainey, Froelich G. 1932–1933. *Journal of the Archaeological Survey of Connecticut,* May 19, 1932, to July 29, 1933. Yale Indian Papers Project Transcriptions, Division of Anthropology Archives, Peabody Museum of Natural History, Yale University.

———. 1933. "A Compilation of Historical Data Contributing to the Ethnography of Connecticut and Southern New England Indians." Master's thesis, Yale University, New Haven.

———. 1936. "A Compilation of Historical Data Contributing to the Ethnography of Connecticut and Southern New England Indians." *Bulletin of the Archaeological Society of Connecticut* 3:1–89.

Raisieres, Isaack de. 1628. "Letter of Isaack de Raisieres to Samuel Blonmaert, 1628 (?)." In *Narratives of New Netherland, 1609–1664,* ed. J. Franklin Jameson, pp. 102–115. New York: Charles Scribner's Sons, 1909.

Rand, Andrea. 2010. "The Hopkins Site: 6LF1 Revisited." *Bulletin of the Archaeological Society of Connecticut* 72:99–127.

Reeve, Stuart A., and Katharine Forgacs. 1999. "Connecticut Radiocarbon Dates: A Study of Prehistoric Cultural Chronologies and Population Trends." *Bulletin of the Archaeological Society of Connecticut* 62:19–66.

Reid, Basil. 2006. "Passing of a Pioneer Researcher in Caribbean Archaeology." *UWI Today,* March 12. Office of the Campus Principal, University of the West Indies, St. Augustine, Trinidad, West Indies.

Reimer, P. J., M. G. L. Baillie, E. Bard, A. Bayliss, J. W. Beck, P. G. Blackwell, C. B. Ramsey, C. E. Buck, G. S. Burr, R. L. Edwards, et al. 2009. "IntCal09 and Marine09 Radiocarbon Age Calibration Curves, 0–50,000 Years cal BP." *Radiocarbon* 51(4):1111–1115.

"Report on the First Archaeological Conference on the Woodland Pattern." 1943. *American Antiquity* 8(4):393–400.

Reveal, James L., and Mark W. Chase. 2011. "APG III: Bibliographical Information and Synonymy of Magnoliidae." *Phytotaxa* 19:71–134.

Richmond, Dave. 1985. "Midwinter." *Artifacts* 13:14–15.

Richmond, Trudie Lamb. 1979. "Out of the Earth I Sing: The Story of Corn." *Artifacts* 8(2):1, 7, 13.

———. 1987a. "Algonquian Women and the Land: A Legacy." In *Rooted Like the Ash Trees: New England Indians and the Land,* ed. Richard G. Carlson, pp. 6–8. Naugatuck, Conn.: Eagle Wing.

———. 1987b. "Spirituality and Survival in Schaghticoke Basket-Making." In *A Key into the Language of Woodsplint Baskets,* ed. Ann McMullen and Russell G. Handsman, pp. 126–143. Washington, Conn.: American Indian Archaeological Institute.

———. 1989. "'Put Your Ear to the Ground and Listen.' The Wigwam Festival Is the Green Corn Ceremony." *Artifacts* 17(4):24–39.

———. 1994. "A Native Perspective of History: The Schaghticoke Nation: Resistance and Survival." In *Enduring Traditions: The Native Peoples of New England*, ed. Laurie Weinstein, pp. 103–112. Westport, Conn.: Bergin and Harvey.

———. 2000. "This Is Who We Are." In *The Native Americans of Connecticut, Holding On and Moving Forward*, ed. Kathleen A. Hunter. Teacher Resource Guide. Hartford, Conn.: State Department of Education.

Rieth, Christina B., and L. Lewis Johnson. 2011. "Trace Element Analysis of Lithic Artifacts from the Trapps Gap Site." In *Current Research in New York Archaeology: A.D. 700–1300*, ed. by Christina B. Rieth and John P. Hart, pp. 41–52. New York State Museum Record 2. Albany: University of the State of New York, State Education Department.

Riley, T. J., G. R. Waltz, C. J. Bareis, A. C. Fortier, and K. E. Parker. 1994. "Accelerator Mass Spectrometry (AMS) Dates Confirm Early *Zea mays* in the Mississippi River Valley." *American Antiquity* 59:490–497.

Ritchie, William A. 1955. *Recent Discoveries Suggesting an Early Woodland Burial Cult in the Northeast.* Albany: New York State Museum and Science Service Circular 40.

———. 1961. *A Typology and Nomenclature for New York Projectile Points.* Albany: New York State Museum and Science Service Bulletin 384.

———. 1965. *The Archaeology of New York State.* Garden City, N.Y.: Natural History.

———. 1969a. *The Archaeology of Martha's Vineyard.* Garden City, N.Y.: Natural History.

———. 1969b. *The Archaeology of New York State,* revised ed. Garden City, N.Y.: Natural History.

———. 1983. "The Mystery of Things Paleo-Indian." *Archaeology of Eastern North America* 11:30–33.

Ritchie, W. A., and R. E. Funk. 1971. "Evidence of Early Archaic Occupations on Staten Island." *Pennsylvania Archaeologist* 41(3):45–49.

———. 1973. *Aboriginal Settlement Patterns in the Northeast.* Albany: New York State Museum and Science Service Memoir 20.

Roberts, Mervin F. 1971. *Tidal Marshes of Connecticut: A Primer of Wetland Plants.* Reprint series 1. New London: Connecticut Arboretum.

Robinson, Brian S. 1996. "Archaic Period Burial Patterning in Northeastern North America." Special issue: *Contributions to the Archaeology of Northeastern North America,* ed. B. S. Robinson. *The Review of Archaeology* 17(1): 33–44.

Robinson, B. S., J. P. Petersen, and A. K. Robinson, eds. 1992. *Early Holocene Occupation in Northern New England.* Occasional Publications of Maine Archaeology Volume 9. Augusta: Maine Historic Preservation Commission.

Rogers, Edward H. 1935. "A Double Burial from Niantic." *Bulletin of the Archaeological Society of Connecticut* 1:1–2.

Rogers, John. 1985. *Bedrock Geological Map of Connecticut.* Hartford, Conn.: Connecticut Geological and Natural History Survey.

Rooth, Anna B. 1971. *The Alaska Expedition, 1966: Myths, Customs, and Beliefs Among the Athabascan Indians and the Eskimos of Northern Alaska.* Lund, Sweden: C. W. K. Gleerup.

Rosier, James. 1605. "A True Relation of the Voyage of Captaine George Waymouth."

Reprinted in *Early English and French Voyages Chiefly from Hakluyt 1534-1608,* ed. Henry S. Burrage, pp. 353–394. New York: Charles Scribner's Sons, 1906.

Rothschild Nan A., and Diana diZerega Wall. 1992–1993. "Introduction." In *From Prehistory to the Present: Studies in Northeastern Archaeology in Honor of Bert Salwen,* ed. Nan A. Rothschild and Diana diZerega Wall, Northeast Historical Archaeology 21–22, pp. 1–6. [n.p.]: Council for Northeast Historical Archaeology.

Rouse, Irving. 1947. "Ceramic Traditions and Sequences in Connecticut." *Bulletin of the Massachusetts Archaeological Society* 21:10–25.

———. 1984. "The Exhibits of Connecticut Archaeology and Ethnology in the Peabody Museum of Natural History: Past, Present, and Future." *Bulletin of the Archaeological Society of Connecticut* 47:144–156.

Rozwadowski, Helen. 2006. "Maritime Archaeology Minor." *ASC News* 212:6–7.

Rubertone, Patricia E. 1989. "Archaeology, Colonialism, and 17th Century Native America: Towards an Alternative Interpretation." In *Conflict in the Archaeology of Living Traditions,* ed. R. Layton, pp. 32–45. One World Archaeology Series. London: Unwin Hyman.

———. 2001. *Grave Undertakings: An Archaeology of Roger Williams and the Narragansett Indians.* Washington, D.C.: Smithsonian Institution Press.

———. 2008a. "Engaging Monuments, Memories, and Archaeology." In *Archaeologies of Placemaking: Monuments, Memories, and Engagement in Native North America,* ed. Patricia E. Rubertone, pp. 1–33. Walnut Creek, Calif.: Left Coast.

———. 2008b. "Memorializing the Narragansett: Place-Making and Memory-Keeping in the Aftermath of Detribalization." In *Archaeologies of Placemaking: Monuments, Memories, and Engagement in Native North America,* ed. Patricia E. Rubertone. Walnut Creek, Calif.: Left Coast.

Russell, Lyent W. 1942. "The Menunketisuck Site, Westbrook, Connecticut." *Bulletin of the Archaeological Society of Connecticut* 14:3–55.

———. 1995. "A Description of Some Interesting Artifacts." *Bulletin of the Archaeological Society of Connecticut* 58:1–12.

Russo, Paul. 1994. "Summary Report Prehistoric Archaeological Inventory East-Central Killingly." Unpublished report submitted to the Town of Killingly by the Public Archaeology Laboratory, Inc., of Pawtucket, R.I. . PAL, Inc., Report No. 536.

Rutsch, Edward S. 1970. "An Analysis of the Lithic Materials Used in the Manufacture of Projectile Points in Coastal New York." *Bulletin of the New York State Archaeological Association* 49:1–12.

Salisbury, Neal. 1981. "Squanto: Last of the Patuxets." In *Struggle and Survival in Colonial America,* ed. David G. Sweet and Gary B. Nash, pp. 228–246. Berkeley: University of California Press.

Salwen, Bert. 1966. "European Trade Goods and the Chronology of the Fort Shantok Site." *Bulletin of the Archaeological Society of Connecticut* 34:5–38.

———. 1968. "Muskeeta Cove 2: A Stratified Woodland Site on Long Island." *American Antiquity* 33(3):322–340.

———. 1969. "A Tentative 'In Situ' Solution to the Mohegan-Pequot Problem." In

*The Connecticut Valley Indian: An Introduction to Their Archaeology and History,* ed. William R. Young. Springfield, Mass.: Springfield Museum of Science.

———. 1970. "Cultural Inferences from Faunal Remains: Examples from Three Northeastern Coastal Sites." *Pennsylvania Archaeologist* 40(1):1–8.

———. 1975. "Post-Glacial Environments and Cultural Change in the Hudson River Basin." *Man in the Northeast* 10:43–70.

———. 1978. "Indians of Southern New England and Long Island: Early Period." In *Handbook of North American Indians,* vol. 15, *The Northeast,* ed. Bruce G. Trigger, pp. 160–176. Washington, D.C.: Smithsonian Institution.

Salwen, Bert, and Sandra Mayer. 1978. "Indian Archaeology in Rhode Island." *Archaeology* 31:5758.

Salwen, Bert, and Ann Ottesen. 1972. "Radiocarbon Dates for a Windsor Occupation at the Shantok Cove Site, New London County, Connecticut." *Man in the Northeast* 3:8–19.

Sanders, John E., and Charles V. Ellis. 1961. "Geological Aspects of Connecticut's Coastal Marshes." *The Connecticut Arboretum Bulletin* 12:16–20.

Sanger, David. 1986. "An Introduction to the Prehistory of the Passamaquoddy Bay Region. *American Review of Canadian Studies* 16(2):139–159.

Sargent, Howard. 1952. "A Preliminary Report on the Excavations at Grannis Island." *Bulletin of the Archaeological Society of Connecticut* 26:30–50.

Sassaman, Kenneth E. 2008. "The New Archaic, It Ain't What It Used to Be." *The SAA Archaeological Record* 8(5):6–8.

Satz, Ronald N. 2002. *American Indian Policy in the Jacksonian Era.* Norman: University of Oklahoma Press.

Saunders, Ellen. 2004. "It Took Two Generations." *Mammoth Trumpet* 19(3):6–7.

Schindler, Debra L., James W. Hatch, Conran A. Hay, and Richard C. Bradt. 1982. "Aboriginal Thermal Alteration of a Central Pennsylvania Jasper: Analytical and Behavioral Implications." *American Antiquity* 47(3):526–544.

Sedgwick, Charles F. 1877. *General History of the Town of Sharon, Litchfield County, Conn.* Amenia, N.Y.: C. Walsh.

Semenov, S. 1963. *Prehistoric Technology.* London: Cory, Adams & MacKay.

Sempowski, Martha L. 1989. "Fluctuations Through Time in the Use of Marine Shell at Seneca Iroquois Sites." In *Proceedings of the 1986 Shell Bead Conference: Selected Papers,* gen. ed. Charles F. Hayes III, Research records 20, pp. 81–96. Rochester, N.Y.: Research Division, Rochester Museum and Science Center.

Sgarlata, Cosimo. 2006. "The Archaeology of West Rock: The Importance of Trap-Rock Ridges in Connecticut Prehistory." *Bulletin of the Archaeological Society of Connecticut* 68:11–27.

Shaw, John, and Orson van de Plassche. 1991. "Palynology of Late Wisconsinan/Early Holocene Lake and Marsh Deposits, Hammock River Marsh, Connecticut." *Journal of Coastal Research* 11:85–104.

Shepard, James. 1893. "The Stone Age of Connecticut." *New England Journal,* November 1893, pp. 327–343.

Silliman, Stephen W. 2008. *Collaborating at the Trowel's Edge: Teaching and Learning in Indigenous Archaeology.* Tucson: University of Arizona Press.

———. 2009. "Change and Continuity, Practice and Memory: Native American Persistence in Colonial New England." *American Antiquity* 74(2):211–230.

Silverman, David J. 2003. "'We Chuse to Be Bounded': Native American Animal Husbandry in Colonial New England." *William and Mary Quarterly* 60(3):511–548.

———. 2005. *Faith and Boundaries: Colonists, Christianity, and Community Among the Wampanoag Indians of Martha's Vineyard, 1600–1871.* Cambridge: Cambridge University Press.

———. 2011. *Red Brethren: The Brothertown and Stockbridge Indians and the Problem of Race in Early America.* Ithaca: Cornell University Press.

Simmons, William S. 1970. *Cautantowwit's House: An Indian Burial Ground on the Island of Conanicut in Narragansett Bay.* Providence, R.I.: Brown University Press.

———. 1986. *Spirit of the New England Tribes: Indian History and Folklore, 1620–1984.* Hanover, N.H.: University Press of New England.

Smith, Bruce D. 1989. "Origins of Agriculture in Eastern North America." *Science* 246:1566–1571.

Smith, Carlyle S. 1950. "The Archaeology of Coastal New York." *Anthropological Papers of the American Museum of Natural History* 43(2):94–200.

Smith, Chard P. 1946. *The Housatonic: Puritan River.* New York: Rinehart.

Smith, Claude C. 1985. *Quarter Acre of Heartache.* Blacksburg, Va.: Pocahontas.

Smith, Donald A. 2011. "The Carpenter Brook Site: Social Setting and Early Late Woodland Ceramic Vessel Variation in Central New York." In *Current Research in New York Archaeology: A.D. 700–1300,* ed. Christina B. Rieth and John P. Hart, pp. 7–25. New York State Museum Record 2. Albany: University of the State of New York, State Education Department.

Smith, Jane T. Hills. 1916. *The Last of the Nehantics.* East Lyme, Conn.: East Lyme Historical Society.

Smith, John. 1624. "The Generalle Historie of Virginia, New-England, and the Summer Isles. The Sixth Booke: The Generall History of New England." Reprinted in *Forerunners and Competitors of the Pilgrims and Puritans,* ed. Charles H. Levermore, pp. 650–753. Vol. 2. Brooklyn, Conn.: New England Society of Brooklyn, 1912.

Snow, Dean. 1980. *The Archaeology of New England.* New York: Academic.

Solecki, Ralph. 1950. "The Archaeological Position of Historic Fort Corchaug, L.I., and Its Relation to Contemporary Forts." *Bulletin of the Archaeological Society of Connecticut* 24:3–40.

———. 1992–1993. "Indian Forts of the Mid-17th Century in the Southern New England–New York Coastal Area." In *From Prehistory to the Present: Studies in Northeastern Archaeology in Honor of Bert Salwen,* ed. N. A. Rothschild and D. Wall. Special issue, *Northeast Historical Archaeology* 21–22:64–78.

———. 2006. "The Archaeology of Fort Neck and Vicinity, Massapequa, Long Island, New York." In *Native Forts of the Long Island Sound Area,* ed. Gaynell Stone, pp. 143–224. Stony Brook, N.Y.: Suffolk County Archaeological Association.

Soulsby, Mary G., Robert R. Gradie, and Kevin A. McBride. 1981. "Phase 2 Archaeological Survey, U.S. Navy Housing Project, Groton, Connecticut." Public Archaeology Survey Team, Inc. Submitted to the U.S. Department of the Navy. On file, State Historic Preservation Office, Hartford, Conn.

Speck, Frank G. 1903. "Notes on Scattacook Indians," in Speck's field notebook, August 15, 1903. In Speck's Papers, on file at the American Philosophical Society, Philadelphia, box 14, call no. 572.97.

———. 1909a. "Notes on the Mohegan and Niantic Indians." *Anthropological Papers of the American Museum of Natural History* 3:183–210.

———. 1909b. "The Scaticook Indians." *Anthropological Papers of the American Museum of Natural History* 3:205–207.

———. 1915. *Decorative Art of Indian Tribes of Connecticut.* Anthropological Series, Memoir 75, No. 10. Ottawa: Canada Department of Mines.

———. 1931. *The Delaware Indian Big House Ceremony: In Native Text Dictated by Witapanoxwe.* Harrisburg: Pennsylvania Historical Commission.

———. 1940. *Penobscot Man: The Life History of a Forest Tribe in Maine.* Orono: University of Maine Press.

———. 1945. "The Memorial Brush Heap in Delaware and Elsewhere." *Bulletin of the Archaeological Society of Delaware* 4:17–23.

———. 1947. *Eastern Algonkian Block-Stamp Decoration: A New World Original or an Acculturated Art.* Trenton: Archaeological Society of New Jersey.

Spencer, Linda S. 1993. *Eastern Uplands: Historical and Architectural Overview and Management Guide. Historical Preservation in Connecticut.* Vol. 2. Hartford, Conn.: Connecticut Historical Commission and State Historic Preservation Office.

Spiess, Arthur E., and Bruce D. Spiess. 1987. "New England Pandemic of 1616–1622: Causes and Archaeological Implications." *Man in the Northeast* 34:71–83.

Spiess, A. G., M. L. Curran, and J. R. Grimes. 1985. "Caribou (*Rangifer tarandus L.*) Bones from New England Paleo-Indian Sites." *North American Archaeologist* 6(2):145–159.

Spiess, Matthias, and Hayden L. Griswold. 1930. "Map of Connecticut, Circa 1625, Indian Trails, Villages, Sachemdoms." Compiled by Mathias Spiess and drawn by Hayden L. Griswold. Scale ca. 1:350,000, 38 by 50 cm. Published by the Colonial Dames of America Connecticut Society. Map and Geographic Information Center, University of Connecticut Libraries, Storrs.

Starbuck, David. R. 1980. "The Middle Archaic in Central Connecticut: The Excavation of the Lewis-Walpole Site." In *Early and Middle Archaic Cultures in the Northeast,* ed. David R. Starbuck and Charles E. Bolian, pp. 5–37. Occasional Publications in Northeastern Anthropology 7. Rindge, N.H.: Department of Anthropology, Franklin Pierce College.

———. 1992. "The Lewis-Walpole Site (6-HT-15)." *The New Hampshire Archaeologist* 33:73–86.

Steever, E. Z. 1972. "Productivity and Vegetation Studies of a Tidal Salt Marsh in Stonington, Connecticut: Cottrell Marsh." Master's thesis, Connecticut College, New London, Conn.

Stefferud, Alfred, ed. 1949. *Trees, Yearbook of Agriculture, 1949*. Washington, D.C.: U.S. Department of Agriculture, U.S. Government Printing Office.

Steiner, Bernard Christian. ed. 1897. "A History of the Plantation of Menunkatuck and the Original Town of Guilford, Connecticut, Comprising the Present Towns of Guilford and Madison: written largely from the manuscripts of the Hon. Ralph Dunning Smyth." Baltimore, Md.: published by the author.

Stewart, R. Michael. 1982. "The Middle Woodland of the Abbott Farm: Summary and Hypotheses." In *Practicing Environmental Archaeology: Methods and Interpretations*, ed. R. Moeller, pp. 19–28. Vol. 3. Occasional Papers of the American Indian Archaeological Institute. Washington, Conn.: American Indian Archaeological Institute.

Stewart, R. Michael, Chris Hummer, and Jay F. Custer. 1986. "Late Woodland Cultures of the Upper Delmarva Peninsula and the Lower and Middle Delaware River Valley." In *Late Woodland Cultures of the Middle Atlantic Region*, ed. Jay F. Custer, pp. 58–89. Newark: University of Delaware Press.

Stiles, Ezra. Papers. General Collection, Beinecke Rare Book and Manuscript Library, Yale University.

———. 1783. "Discourse IX: Dr. Stiles's Election Sermon, 1783." In *The Pulpit of the American Revolution: or, The Political Sermons of the Period of 1776*, ed. John Wingate Thornton, pp. 399–520. Boston: Gould and Lincoln, 1860.

———. 1794. *A History of the Three Judges of King Charles I*. Hartford: Elisha Babcock.

———. 1916. *Extracts from the Itineraries and Other Miscellanies of Ezra Stiles, D.D., L.L.D., 1755–1794, with a Selection from His Correspondence*, ed. Franklin B. Baxter. New Haven: Yale University Press.

Stoltman, James B. 1966. "New Radiocarbon Dates for Southeastern Fiber-Tempered Pottery." *American Antiquity* 31:872–874.

———. 1991. *New Perspectives on Cahokia: Views from the Periphery*. Madison, Wisc.: Prehistory.

Stone, Janet Radway, John P. Schafer, Elizabeth Haley London, Mary L. DiGiacomo-Cohen, Ralph S. Lewis, and Woodrow B. Thompson. 2005. *Quaternary Geological Map of Connecticut and Long Island Sound Basin*. Scientific Investigations Map 2784 with explanations. U.S. Department of the Interior, U.S. Geological Survey; http://pubs.usgs.gov/sim/2005/2784/index.html.

Storck, Peter. 1983. "Commentary on AENA's Compilation of Fluted Points in Eastern North America." *Archaeology of Eastern North America* 11:34–36.

Strahler, Arthur N. 1966. *A Geologist's View of Cape Cod*. Garden City, N.Y.: Natural History.

Strauss, Alan E. 1989. "Narragansett Basin Argillite: Lithology, Chronology, and Prehistoric Tool Manufacture." *North American Archaeologist* 10(1):25–37.

———. 1992. "Jack's Reef Corner Notched Points in New England: Site Distribution, Raw Material Preference, and Implications for Trade." *North American Archaeologist* 13(4):333–350.

Struever, Stuart, and G. L. Houart. 1972. "An Analysis of the Hopewell Interaction Sphere." In *Social Exchange and Interaction*, ed. E. Wilmsen, pp. 47–80. Anthropological Papers of the University of Michigan Museum of Anthropology 46. Ann Arbor: University of Michigan.

Strong, John A. 1985. "Late Woodland Dog Ceremonialism on Long Island in Comparative and Temporal Perspective." *The Bulletin and Journal of Archaeology for New York State* 91:32–38.

Sturtevant, William C. 1975. "Two 1761 Wigwams at Niantic, Connecticut." *American Antiquity* 40(4):437–444.

Suggs, Robert C. 1958. "The Manakaway Site, Greenwich, Connecticut." *Bulletin of the Archaeological Society of Connecticut* 29:21–47.

"Sunday in Great Barrington, 131 Years Ago." *Berkshire Courier,* November 15, 1866. Cited in Bernard A. Drew. 2009. *Faded Tracks on Monument Mountain.* Great Barrington: Attic Revivals, p. 42.

Swan, James G. 1870. *The Indians of Cape Flattery, at the Entrance to the Straight of Fuca, Washington Territory.* Washington, D.C.: Smithsonian Institution.

Swigart, Edmund K. 1973. The Kirby Brook Site (6-LF-2): An Interim Report. *Bulletin of the Archaeological Society of Connecticut* 38:40–76.

———. 1974. *The Prehistory of the Indians of Western Connecticut: Part 1, 9,000–1,000 B.C.* Research Report of the American Indian Archaeological Institute 1. Washington, Conn.: American Indian Archaeological Institute.

———. 1975. "Connecticut Indian Prehistory. Part 5." *Artifacts* 4(2):5–8.

———. 1977. "The Ecological Placement of Western Connecticut Sites." *Archaeology of North America* 5:61–73.

———. 1987. "The Woodruff Rockshelter Site—6LF126 an Interim Report—Faunal Analysis as a Means to Evaluate Environment and Culture." *Bulletin of the Archaeological Society of Connecticut* 50:43–76.

Tantaquidgeon, Gladys. 1977. *Folk Medicine of the Delaware and Related Algonkian Indians.* Harrisburg: Pennsylvania Historical and Museum Commission.

Tantaquidgeon, Gladys, and Jayne Fawcett. 1987. "Symbolic Motifs on Painted Baskets of the Mohegan-Pequot." In *Rooted Like the Ash Trees: New England Indians and the Land,* ed. Richard G. Carlson, pp. 50–51. Naugatuck, Conn.: Eagle Wing.

Taylor, Charlotte C. 2006. "The History and Archaeology of Fort Ninigret, a 17th-Century Eastern Niantic Site in Charlestown, Rhode Island." In *Native Forts of the Long Island Sound Area,* ed. Gaynell Stone, pp. 277–286. Stony Brook, N.Y.: Suffolk County Archaeological Association.

Thomas, David H. 1978. "Arrowheads and Atlatl Darts: How the Stones Got the Shaft." *American Antiquity* 43(3):461–472.

Thompson, David H. 1969. "The Binette Site, Naugatuck, Connecticut." *Eastern States Archaeological Federation Bulletin* 27–28:14–15.

———. 1973. "Preliminary Excavations at the Hopkins Site (6LF1), Warren, Connecticut." *Bulletin of the Archaeological Society of Connecticut* 38:5–24.

———. 1975. "The Hansel Site (6-LF-15): A Rockshelter in Litchfield County." *Bulletin of the Archaeological Society of Connecticut* 39:35–48.

———. 1989. "The Susquehanna Horizon as Seen from the Summit of Rye Hill (6LF100),

Woodbury, Connecticut." *Bulletin of the Archaeological Society of Connecticut* 52:17–54.

———. 1995. "Turkey-Tails as a Measure of Marginality and Economic Exchange." *Bulletin of the Archaeological Society of Connecticut* 58:71–82.

Thompson, Nora Dean. 1983. "The Spiritual World of the Lenape or Delaware Indians." In *Many Trails: Indians of the Lower Hudson Valley* (exhibition catalog). Katonah, N.Y.: The Katonah Gallery.

Thomas, Peter A. 1978. "Indian Subsistence and Settlement Patterns in Noncoastal Regions: Early Historic Massachusetts." In *Conservation Archaeology in the Northeast: Toward Research Orientation,* ed. Arthur E. Speiss, pp. 17–26. Peabody Museum Bulletin 3, Cambridge, Mass.: Peabody Museum of Archaeology and Ethnology, Harvard University.

Thorbahn, Peter F. 1988. "Where Are the Late Woodland Villages in Southern New England?" *Bulletin of the Massachusetts Archaeological Society* 49(2):46–57.

Thwaites, Reuben Gold, ed. 1897. *The Jesuit Relations and Allied Documents: Travels and Explorations of the Jesuit Missionaries in New France, 1610–1791.* Volume 10, Hurons: 1636. Cleveland: Burrows Bros. Reprinted, New York: Pageant, 1959.

Toensing, Gale C. 2004. "Salisbury Gives Schaghticoke an Earful." *Waterbury Republican-American,* June 2, 2004.

———. 2005. "Schaghticoke Status Attacked." *Indian Country Today,* April 29, 2005.

———. 2006. "Blumenthal Seeks Intervener Status in Schaghticoke Appeal." *Indian Country Today,* March 27, 2006.

———. 2007. "Eastern Pequots Anticipate Traditional Gathering." *Indian Country Today,* May 30, 2007.

———. 2011. "Schaghticoke Tribal Nation Seeks to Regain Rightful Status." *Indian Country Today,* May 31, 2011.

Toner, Mike. 2006. "Impossibly Old America?" *Archaeology* 59(3):40–45.

Torrey, E. F. 1986. *Witchdoctors and Psychiatrists: The Common Roots of Psychotherapy and Its Future.* New York: Harper and Row.

Townshend, Charles H. 1893. "The Quinnipiac Indians and Their Reservation." *Connecticut Papers of the New Haven Colony Historical Society* 6:151–219.

Trelease, Allen W. 1960. *Indian Affairs in Colonial New York: The Seventeenth Century.* Ithaca: Cornell University Press.

Trigger, Bruce G. 1971. "The Mohawk-Mahican War (1624–1628): The Establishment of a Pattern." *Canadian Historical Review* 52(3):276–286.

Truex, James. 1983. "The Livingston Pond Site." *Suffolk County Archaeological Association Newsletter* 9(3):3–6.

Trumbull, J. Hammond, comp. 1852. *The Public Records of the Colony of Connecticut from 1665–1677.* Hartford, Conn.: Case, F. A. Brown.

Trumbull, J. Hammond, and Charles Hoadley, eds. 1881. *The Public Records of the Colony of Connecticut.* Hartford, Conn.: Case, Lockwood and Brainard.

Truncer, James. 2004a. "Steatite Vessel Age and Occurrence in Temperate Eastern North America." *American Antiquity* 69(3):487–513.

———. 2004b. *Steatite Vessel Manufacture in Eastern North America*. British Archaeological Reports International Series 1326. Oxford: Archaeopress.

Tryon, Christian A., and Anthony R. Philpotts. 1997. "Possible Source of Mylonite and Hornfels Debitage from the Cooper Site, Lyme, Connecticut." *Bulletin of the Archaeological Society of Connecticut* 60:3–12.

Turgeon, Laurier. 1998. "French Fishers, Fur Traders, and Amerindians During the Sixteenth Century: History and Archaeology." *William and Mary Quarterly* 55(4), 3rd series:585–610.

Underhill, John. 1638. *Newes from America*. Reprint, New York: Underhill Society of America, 1902.

Van Laer, A. J. F. 1908. *Van Rensselaer Bowier Manuscripts, being the letters of Kiliaen Van Rensselaer, 1630–1643, and other documents relating to the colony of Rensselaerswyck*. Trans. and ed. Mrs. Alan H. Strong. Albany: University of the State of New York.

Vara, Theresa 2008. "Walled-in Shoes in Roxbury." *A.S.C. News* 216(January):8–9.

Vaughan, Alden T. 1965. *New England Frontier Puritans and Indians, 1620–1675*. Boston: Little, Brown.

———. 1977. "Introduction." In *New England's Prospect* (1634), by William Wood, ed. Alden Vaughan. Amherst, Mass.: University of Massachusetts Press.

Vescelius, Gary. 1952. "Excavated Material from Pine Orchard, Branford, Connecticut." *Bulletin of the Archaeological Society of Connecticut* 26:51–53.

Vila, Carlos, P. Savolainene, J. E. Maldonado, I. R. Amorim, J. E. Rice, R. L. Honeycutt, K. A. Crandall, J. Lundeberg, R. K. Wayne. 1997. "Multiple and Ancient Origins of the Domestic Dog." *Science* 276(5319):1687–1689.

Visel, Timothy C., A. Dusla, S. Weber, and P. Russell. 2006. "The First Shad Fishery." Connecticut River Museum Shad Program, Essex, Conn., lecture presented May 20, 2006. Illustrations by Alicia Cook. New Haven: Adult Education Program, The Sound School Regional Vocational Aquaculture Center; www.soundschool.com /firstshad.pdf.

Visel, Timothy C., Susan Weber, and Alex Disla. 2009. "The History of Madison's Finfish and Shellfish Industries. The Bauer Lecture Series, February 21, 2009. Native American Fisheries of the Connecticut Shoreline." New Haven: Adult Education and Outreach Programs, The Sound School Regional Vocational Aquaculture Center; www .soundschool.com/madifinfish.pdf.

Volmar, Michael A. 1992. "The Conundrum of Effigy Pestles." Master's thesis, University of Massachusetts, Amherst.

———. 1996. "Maugua the Bear in Northeastern Indian Mythology and Archaeology." *Bulletin of the Massachusetts Archaeological Society* 57(2):37–45.

Von Gernet, Alexander, and Peter Timmons. 1987. "Pipes and Parakeets: Constructing Meaning in an Early Iroquoian Context." In *Archaeology as Long-Term History*, ed. Ian Hodder, pp. 31–42. Cambridge: Cambridge University Press.

Wadleigh, William. 1981. "Settlement and Subsistence Patterns in the Northeastern Highlands of Connecticut." *Man in the Northeast* 2:67–85.

Wall, Suzanne. 2003. "Aboriginal Soapstone Workshops at the Skug River II Site, Essex County, MA." *Bulletin of the Massachusetts Archaeological Society* 64(2):30–36.

Wallace, Anthony F. C. 1993. *The Long, Bitter Trail: Andrew Jackson and the Indians*. New York: Hill and Wang.

Walling, Richard S. 1999. *Death in the Bronx*. Hudson, N.Y.: Native American Institute, Columbia-Greene Community College.

Walwer, Gregory F. 1996. *Survey of Native American Burials and Cemeteries East of the Connecticut River*. Guilford, Conn.: Archaeological Consulting Services for the Connecticut Historical Commission.

Washburn, Wilcomb E. 1978. "Seventeenth-Century Indian Wars." In *Handbook of North American Indians*, vol. 15, *The Northeast*, ed. Bruce G. Trigger, pp. 90–100. Washington, D.C.: Smithsonian Institution.

Watrous, Louise E. 1939. "Madison: 1645–1938." On file at the E. C. Scranton Memorial Library, Madison, Conn.

Webb, William. 1952. "The Archaic Cultures and the Adena People." *Ohio History* 61(2):173–181.

Weinstein, Laurie. 1994. "Samson Occom: A Charismatic Eighteenth-Century Mohegan Leader." In *Enduring Traditions: The Native Peoples of New England*, ed. Laurie Weinstein, pp. 91–102. Westport, Conn.: Bergin and Garvey.

———. 2011. "Who Were Danbury's First Peoples? The Pahquioque." *Danbury News Times*, March 5, 2011; www.newstimes.com (accessed March 7, 2011).

Weinstein, Laurie, and Desiree Heme. 2005. "Oh Wither Weantinock: Deeds and Their Interpretations." *Northeast Anthropology* 70:49–66.

Weslager, C. A. 1974. "Delaware Indian Name Giving and Modern Practice," as written for A Delaware Indian Symposium, paper presented at Seton Hall University, May 6, 1972. In *A Delaware Indian Symposium*, ed. Herbert C. Kraft; proceedings. Anthropological Series No. 4. Harrisburg: Pennsylvania Historical and Museum Commission.

West, Lee. 2005. Editorial commentary. *ASC News* 208.

Whipple, Chandler. 1974. *First Encounter: The Indian and the White Man in Massachusetts and Rhode Island*. Stockbridge: Berkshire Traveler.

Wiegand, Ernest A. 1978. "The Athena Site." *Bulletin of the New York State Archaeological Association* 74:10–25.

———. 1979. "The Lake Kitchawan Mastodon Dig." *Artifacts* 7(4):4.

———. 1980. "Rockrimmon Rockshelter." *Bulletin of the Archaeological Society of Connecticut* 42:15–28.

———. 1983. *Rockshelters of Southwestern Connecticut: Their Prehistoric Occupation and Use*. Norwalk, Conn.: Norwalk Community College Press.

Wilbur, C. K. 1978. *The New England Indians*. Chester, Conn.: Globe Pequot.

Wilcox, U. Vincent. 1967. "The Lewis-Walpole Site in Farmington, Connecticut: A Preliminary Report." *Bulletin of the Archaeological Society of Connecticut* 35:5–48.

Willey, Gordon R., and Philip Phillips. 1958. *Method and Theory in American Archaeology*. Chicago: University of Chicago Press.

Williams, Frederick H. 1897. "Prehistoric Remains of the Tunxis Valley." *Connecticut Quarterly* 3(2):150–165, (3):403–423.

Williams, Lorraine E. 1972. *Fort Shantok and Fort Corchaug: A Comparative Study of Seven-*

*teenth Century Culture Contact in the Long Island Sound Area.* Ann Arbor, Mich.: University Microfilms International.

Williams, Lorraine E., Kevin A. McBride, and Robert S. Grumet. 1997. "Fort Shantok National Historic Landmark." *Bulletin of the Archaeological Society of Connecticut* 60:29–42.

Williams, Mary Beth, and Jeffrey Bendremer. 1997. "The Archaeology of Maize, Pots, and Seashells: Gender Dynamics in Late Woodland and Contact Period New England." In *Women in Prehistory: North America and Mesoamerica,* ed. Cheryl Claassen and Rosemary A. Joyce, pp. 136–152. Philadelphia: University of Pennsylvania Press.

Williams, Roger. 1643. *A Key into the Language of America,* ed. John J. Teunissen and Evelyn J. Hinz. Detroit: Wayne State University Press, 1973.

Williamson, Lynne. 1989. "The Interior Landscapes of Algonkian Artists." *Artifacts* 17(4):12–18.

Williamson, Lynne, and Trudie Lamb Richmond. 1991. "I Was Brought Up Mohegan. . . . We Were Always Known as Mohegan." Courtland Fowler. *Artifacts* 19(2):6–7.

Willoughby, Charles C. 1935. *Antiquities of the New England Indians.* Cambridge, Mass.: Peabody Museum of American Archaeology and Ethnology, Harvard University.

Winslow, Edward. 1624. "Winslow's Relation [Good Newes from New England]." In *Chronicles of the Pilgrim Fathers of the Colony of Plymouth from 1602–1625,* ed. Alexander Young, pp. 269–373. Boston: Little and Brown.

Winters, Howard D. 1969. *The Riverton Culture.* Reports of Investigation. 13, Monograph. 1. Springfield: Illinois State Museum; Illinois Archaeological Survey.

Winthrop, John, Jr. 1908. *Winthrop's Journal: History of New England, 1630–1649,* ed. James K. Hosmer. New York: Charles Scribner and Sons.

Winthrop Papers. 1678. *Collections of the Massachusetts Historical Society* 8 (5th series). Boston: Published by the Society, 1872.

Wiseman, Frederick M. 2005. *Reclaiming the Ancestors, Decolonizing a Taken Prehistory of the Far Northeast.* Toronto: University Press of New England.

Witek, John C. 1990. "An Outline of the Aboriginal Archaeology of Shelter Island, New York." *Bulletin of the Archaeological Society of Connecticut* 53:39–57.

Witthoft, John. 1953. "Broad Spearpoints and the Transitional Period Cultures. *Pennsylvania Archaeologist* 23(1):4–31.

Wobst, H. M., 1977. "Stylistic Behavior and Information Exchange." In *For the Director: Research Essays in Honor of James B. Griffen,* ed. E. H. Cleland, pp. 317–342. Anthropological Papers 61. Ann Arbor: Museum of Anthropology, University of Michigan.

Wojciechowski, Franz L. 1985. *The Paugussett Tribes: An Ethnohistorical Study of the Tribal Interrelationships of the Indians in the Lower Housatonic River Area.* Nijmegen, The Netherlands: Department of Cultural and Social Anthropology, Catholic University of Nijmegen.

Wood, William. 1634. *New England's Prospect,* ed. Alden Vaughan. Amherst, Mass.: University of Massachusetts Press, 1977.

Woodruff, Mary R., comp. 1949. *History of Orange, North Milford, Connecticut, 1639–1949.* New Haven: Payne and Lane Builders of Books.

Wright, Gary. 1967. "Some Aspects of Early and Mid-17th Century Exchange Networks in the Western Great Lakes. *Michigan Archaeologist* 13(4):81–197.

Wright, Henry T. 1973. *An Archeological Sequence in the Middle Chesapeake, Maryland.* Maryland Geological Survey Archeological Studies 1. Washington, D.C.: Maryland Geological Survey.

Wrong, G. M., ed., trans. 1939. *The Long Journey to the Country of the Hurons, by Father Gabriel Sagard.* Toronto: Champlain Society.

Wroth, Lawrence C. 1970. *The Voyages of Giovanni da Verrazzano, 1524–1528.* New Haven: Published for the Pierpont Morgan Library by Yale University Press.

Wyatt, Ronald. 1977. "The Archaic on Long Island." *Annals of the New York Academy of Sciences* 288:400–410.

Wymer, Dee Anne. 1987. "The Middle Woodland–Late Woodland Interface in Central Ohio: Subsistence Continuity amid Cultural Change." In *Emergent Horticultural Economies of the Eastern Woodlands,* ed. William F. Keegan, pp. 201–216. Occasional Paper 7. Carbondale: Southern Illinois University, Center for Archaeological Investigations.

———. 1992. "Trends and Disparities: The Woodford Paleoethnobotanical Record in the Mid-Ohio Valley." In *Cultural Variability in Context: Woodland Settlements of the Mid-Ohio Valley,* ed. Mark Seeman, pp. 65–76. Kent, Ohio: Kent State University Press.

Young, Alexander, ed. 1841. "Winslow's Relation [Good Newes from New England]." In *Chronicles of the Pilgrim Fathers of the Colony of Plymouth from 1602–1625,* pp. 269–373, Boston: Little and Brown. Originally published London, 1624.

Young, Bilione W., and Melvin L. Fowler. 1999. *Cahokia: The Great Native American Metropolis.* Urbana: University of Illinois Press.

Zarrillo, Sonia, Deborah M. Pearsall, J. Scott Raymond, Mary Ann Tisdale, and Dugane Quon. 2008. "Directly Dated Starch Residues Document Early Formative Maize (*Zea mays* L.) in Tropical Ecuador." *Proceedings of the National Academy of Sciences* 105(13):5006–5011.

Zax, David. 2007. "Daringly Different." *Smithsonian Magazine,* September 2007:37, 40.

Ziac, Delancy C., and John E. Pfeiffer. 1989. "Dry Bone Cremations from Five Sites in New England." *Bulletin of the Archaeological Society of Connecticut* 53:55–60.

Zielbauer, Paul. 2001. "Attorney General Sues to Halt U.S. Recognition of 2 Tribes." *New York Times,* January 19, 2001.

———. 2002. "Bill to Brake Recognition of Tribes Dies in Senate." *New York Times,* September 24, 2002.

# Figure Credits

page 4  Images of Yale Individuals RU 684. Manuscripts and Archives, Yale University Library.

page 7  YPM.ANTSS.011433, Division of Anthropology, Peabody Museum of Natural History, Yale University.

page 8  YPM.ANTPPP.001271, Division of Anthropology, Peabody Museum of Natural History, Yale University.

page 9  (top) Courtesy of the Department of Anthropology, Yale University. (bottom) YPM.ANTPPP.001391, Division of Anthropology, Peabody Museum of Natural History, Yale University.

page 10, 14  Division of Anthropology Archives, Peabody Museum of Natural History, Yale University.

page 13  YPM.ANTPPP.006257, Division of Anthropology, Peabody Museum of Natural History, Yale University.

pages 15, 16, 80  Courtesy of the Lewis Walpole Library, Yale University.

pages 17, 20 (right), 21 (middle right), 22 (top), 30 (bottom), 31 (top left), 93, 94, 100 (top), 108, 126 (bottom), 137, 261  Courtesy of David H. Thompson.

pages 19, 43, 149, 213  Courtesy of the Institute for American Indian Studies.

page 21 (top)  Courtesy of New York University.

pages 21 (middle left), 22 (bottom), 23 (right)  Courtesy of Nicholas F. Bellantoni.

page 23 (left)  Courtesy of Norwalk Community College Archaeology as an Avocation Program.

pages 27, 112, 140, 182 (left and bottom)  Photograph by Marc Banks.

page 32  *American Journal of Science:* Radiocarbon Supplement, May 1959, Volume 1, edited by R. F. Flint and E. S. Deevey.

page 34  Courtesy of Lucinda J. McWeeney, Ph.D.

page 37  U.S. Geological Survey. Adapted from Stone et al. 2005.

page 39  *The Age of Mammals,* a mural by Rudolph F. Zallinger. © 1966, 1975, 1989, 1991, 2000 Peabody Museum of Natural History, Yale University.

page 40  YPM.VP.011985, Division of Vertebrate Paleontology, Peabody Museum of Natural History, Yale University.

page 41  Adapted from McWeeney 1994, 157, table 5.1, 159, fig. 5.5.

page 42  Modified from Forrest et al. 2006, fig. 2.

page 44  (top) IAIS 82-2-1/18.25.2.3. (bottom) IAIS 82-2-1/17.1.3.5. Courtesy of the Institute for American Indian Studies.

pages 45 (top), 59, 145, 320, 349  Peabody Museum of Natural History, Yale University.

page 75  (left to right) IAIS 00-2-99/555 and 00-2-99/589 (no provenience for the gouge). Courtesy of the Institute for American Indian Studies.

pages 76, 237  © Jeanne MORNINGSTAR Kent; www.morningstarstudio9.com.

page 78  Courtesy of the Mashantucket Pequot Museum and Research Center.

page 81  From Wilcox 1967, 38, fig. 1, 39, fig. 2. Illustrations by Joan McGoran. Courtesy of the Archaeological Society of Connecticut.

page 82  From Wilcox 1967, 40, fig. 3, 41, fig. 4. Illustrations by Joan McGoran. Courtesy of the Archaeological Society of Connecticut.

page 83 (top)  Detail from *Coastal Region,* Hall of Southern New England dioramas, Peabody Museum of Natural History, Yale University; painting by J. Perry Wilson, foreground by Ralph C. Morrill. © 2003 Peabody Museum of Natural History, Yale University.

page 83 (lower left) YPM.CBS.029265. (lower right) YPM.YU.048286. Yale Herbarium/Division of Botany, Peabody Museum of Natural History, Yale University.

page 89 (left) YPM.YU.055751. (right) YPM.CBS.029666. Yale Herbarium/Division of Botany, Peabody Museum of Natural History, Yale University.

page 91 YPM.CBS.017621. Division of Botany/Yale Herbarium, Peabody Museum of Natural History, Yale University.

pages 92, 127, 128 (top), 172 (inset), 347 (right), 350 (top, bottom)  Courtesy of K. L. Feder, photographer.

page 95 (left) YPM.ANT.010358. (right) YPM.ANT.014707. Division of Anthropology, Peabody Museum of Natural History, Yale University.

page 96  YPM.ANTPPP.000955, Division of Anthropology, Peabody Museum of Natural History, Yale University.

page 97  Division of Anthropology, Peabody Museum of Natural History, Yale University. (right) YPM.ANT.005166A.

page 99 (right) IAIS 00-2-99. Courtesy of the Institute for American Indian Studies.

page 101  Courtesy of John Pfeiffer.

page 104  From Pfeiffer 1984, fig. 1. Courtesy of the Archaeological Society of Connecticut.

page 110  Visel et al., 2006. © 2006 Alicia Cook and Timothy C. Visel. Used with permission.

page 111  From Parkos 1991, 55, fig. 1. Courtesy of the Archaeological Society of Connecticut.

page 113  (bottom left, left to right) IAIS 76-1-729/4, 3; 76-1-730/1 and 3079; 76-1-718/246; and 76-1-730/6. Courtesy of the Institute for American Indian Studies. (two-part hook, far right) YPM.ANT.010191, Division of Anthropology, Peabody Museum of Natural History, Yale University.

page 115  IAIS 1991-1-1/1. © 2005 Institute for American Indian Studies. Photograph by Lisa Piastuch.

page 119 (left) YPM.ANT.002042. (center) YPM.ANT.010375. (right) YPM.ANT .188630 and YPM.ANT.001532, Division of Anthropology, Peabody Museum of Natural History, Yale University.

pages 127 (bottom), 170  Courtesy of Andrea Rand.

page 130 (clockwise from left) IAIS 76-1-531/1; 76-1-639/002; 76-1-763/1; 76-1-504/6 and 76-1-454/4; 76-1-370/1; and (center) 76-1-356/1. Courtesy of the Institute for American Indian Studies.

page 131 From the collections of the Institute for American Indian Studies.

page 133 From Pagoulatos 1990, 66, fig. 4. Courtesy of the Archaeological Society of Connecticut.

page 134 From Swigart 1973, 65, fig. 15; 77, fig. 22. Courtesy of the Archaeological Society of Connecticut.

pages 138, 249 Photograph by John Spaulding.

page 139 YPM.ANT.001526, Division of Anthropology, Peabody Museum of Natural History, Yale University.

page 146 YPM.ANT.029224 and YPM.ANT.019986, Division of Anthropology, Peabody Museum of Natural History, Yale University.

page 148 Original illustrations by Armand Morgan, with illustrations by David Kiphuth modified from Lavin 1984, 32, fig. 3. Illustration of reconstructed Niantic Incised vessel by Marina Mozzi from Lavin, Gudrian, and Miroff 1993, 77, fig. 2. Courtesy of the Archaeological Society of Connecticut.

page 154 (top) Norris L. Bull Collection, University of Connecticut Museum of Natural History. From Calogero and Philpotts 2006, 65, fig. 14. Courtesy of the Archaeological Society of Connecticut.

page 154 (bottom) From Calogero and Philpotts 2006, 59, fig. 4. Courtesy of the Archaeological Society of Connecticut.

page 155 Bourn Collection. From Calogero and Philpotts 2006, 68, fig. 19. Courtesy of the Archaeological Society of Connecticut.

page 158 (top, left) YPM.ANT.005984, Division of Anthropology, Peabody Museum of Natural History, Yale University. (right) From Lavin 1984, 33, fig. 4. Illustration by David Kiphuth. Courtesy of the Archaeological Society of Connecticut.

pages 158 (bottom), 160 Photograph by Dave Cooke.

page 161 (top) IAIS 81-26-21/4. (center) IAIS 76-1-750/1. (bottom) IAIS 76-1-830/1. Courtesy of the Institute for American Indian Studies.

page 164 From Nadeau and Bellantoni 2004, figs. 3, 4. Courtesy of the Archaeological Society of Connecticut.

page 169 Courtesy of Bruce T. Kulas.

page 172 (bottom) From Calogero and Philpotts 2006, 56, fig. 1. Courtesy of the Archaeological Society of Connecticut.

page 174 IAIS 76-1-403/1, 3, 4, 6, E. H. Rogers Collection. Courtesy of the Institute for American Indian Studies.

page 176 Private collection. Courtesy of the Institute for American Indian Studies.

pages 178, 236 (right), 243 © Institute for American Indian Studies. Photographs by Lillia McEnaney.

page 182 (upper right) Lavin and Banks 2007.

page 184 From Lavin 1985a, 16–17. Illustrations by David Kiphuth.

page 185 (top) © 1985 Peabody Museum of Natural History, Yale University. Illustration by David Kiphuth. (bottom) Ezra Stiles Papers. Courtesy of the Beinecke Rare Book and Manuscript Library, Yale University.

page 186   (top) Photograph by John Pfeiffer. (bottom) Photograph by Harold Juli.

page 187   Detail from *Coastal Region,* Hall of Southern New England dioramas, Peabody Museum of Natural History, Yale University; painting by J. Perry Wilson, foreground by Ralph C. Morrill. © 2003 Peabody Museum of Natural History, Yale University.

page 188   YPM.ANT.229361, YPM.ANT.242586, Division of Anthropology, Peabody Museum of Natural History, Yale University.

page 189   YPM.ANT.002885, Division of Anthropology, Peabody Museum of Natural History, Yale University.

page 195   1842.44.1. Gift of William C. Gilman, Connecticut Historical Society Collections, Hartford, Connecticut.

page 199   IAIS 85-14-2/1. Courtesy of the Institute for American Indian Studies.

page 201   From the American Geographical Society Library, University of Wisconsin–Milwaukee Libraries.

page 202   YPM.CBS.016029, Division of Botany/Yale Herbarium, Peabody Museum of Natural History, Yale University.

page 211   Tim MacSweeney (2008). From "Return to the Mortar/Turtle (Part One)," Rock Piles blog, posted September 30, 2008; http://rockpiles.blogspot.com/2008/09/return-to-mortarturtle-part-one.html.

page 215   (top left) IAIS 76-1-529/1. Courtesy of the Institute for American Indian Studies. Other artifacts from the collections of Division of Anthropology, Peabody Museum of Natural History, Yale University. (bottom) YPM.ANT.0101428.

page 216   (left) YPM.ANT.006068. Gift of John C. Booth, Division of Anthropology, Peabody Museum of Natural History, Yale University. (right) Howell Walker/National Geographic Stock.

page 217   From McBride 1984b, 192, fig. 4.25. Courtesy of Kevin A. McBride.

page 218   IAIS 76-1-724/1. Courtesy of the Institute for American Indian Studies.

page 219   © Gerry Biron; www.gerrybiron.com. Used with permission.

page 224   (top) YPM.ANT.010988. (bottom) YPM.ANT.148200. Division of Anthropology, Peabody Museum of Natural History, Yale University.

page 225   IAIS 83-4-1/1. Courtesy of the Institute for American Indian Studies.

page 226   YPM.ANTPPP.000842, Division of Anthropology, Peabody Museum of Natural History, Yale University.

page 232   A: IAIS 76-1-729/299, 13. B: IAIS 76-1-729/278, 20, 299, 18. C: IAIS 76-1-729/296. D: IAIS 76-1-729/7, 6. E: IAIS 76-1-729/15, 18. F: IAIS 76-1-729/295. Courtesy of the Institute for American Indian Studies. Other artifacts from the collections of the Division of Anthropology, Peabody Museum of Natural History, Yale University.

page 236   © Institute for American Indian Studies. (left) Photograph by Matthew B. Barr.

page 238   Courtesy of Strong Eagle Daly. © Institute for American Indian Studies. Photograph by Matthew B. Barr.

page 245   American, oil on canvas. Gift of Mr. Robert Winthrop 48.246. Photograph by

Erik Gould, courtesy of the Museum of Art, Rhode Island School of Design, Providence.

pages 247, 251 (bottom), 280 (bottom)  Photograph by Susan DiPiazza and L. Lavin.

page 251  (top) From McBride 1984b, 191, fig. 4.24; Courtesy of Kevin A. McBride.

page 254  IAIS 84-3-1/1. Courtesy of the Institute for American Indian Studies.

page 255  (right) Library and Archives Canada, Acc. No. 1977-35-1. Acquired with a special grant from the Canadian Government in 1977.

page 257  IAIS 76-1-403/15 and 76-1-403/16. Courtesy of the Institute for American Indian Studies.

page 259  Courtesy of Riverside Rescue, Riverside, California.

page 264  IAIS 812-63-5/15. Courtesy of the Institute for American Indian Studies.

page 265  (left) YPM.ANT.014767 and YPM.ANT.008931, Division of Anthropology, Peabody Museum of Natural History, Yale University. Illustrations by David Kiphuth, from Lavin 1984, 33, fig. 4; courtesy of the Archaeological Society of Connecticut.

page 265  IAIS 76-1-749/1. Courtesy of the Institute for American Indian Studies.

page 266  From the collections of the Division of Anthropology, Peabody Museum of Natural History, Yale University. Illustrations by David Kiphuth, from Lavin 1984, 33, fig. 4; courtesy of the Archaeological Society of Connecticut.

page 271  From Langton and Ganong 1922.

page 279  (top left) IAIS 79-7-3/2. (top right) IAIS 79-7-1/4. (bottom left) IAIS 79-7-1/4. (bottom right) IAIS 79-7-1/3. Courtesy of the Institute for American Indian Studies.

page 280  (top) IAIS 76-1-729/241. Courtesy of the Institute for American Indian Studies. Photograph by Lisa Piastuch.

pages 287, 312  General Collection, Beinecke Rare Book and Manuscript Library, Yale University.

page 288  See Butler 1946, 2, fig. 1. Courtesy of the Archaeological Society of Connecticut.

page 289  Glynn 1973, 86–77, figs. 3, 4, 5. Courtesy of the Archaeological Society of Connecticut.

page 291  From the collection of Michael Hellwinkle. Photograph by L. Lavin.

page 293  "The 'Old Indian God.' Further Facts Concerning the Relic Recently Unearthed," New York Times, published Sunday, September 24, 1893, p. 5. General Collection, Beinecke Rare Book and Manuscript Library, Yale University.

page 297  Courtesy of Bob DeFosses/DeFosses Photo.

page 301  Fort Shantok Collection, Division of Anthropology, Peabody Museum of Natural History, Yale University.

page 302  Anonymous. Gift of Mr. David Ross McCord (M1913). © McCord Museum of Canadian History.

page 306–7  Compiled by Mathias Spiess and created by Haydon Griswold in 1930 for the Connecticut Society of the Colonial Dames of America. University of Connecticut Libraries Map and Geographic Information Center.

page 311  (top right) YPM.ANT.059014. (bottom) YPM.ANT.189140–189143. Division of Anthropology, Peabody Museum of Natural History, Yale University.

page 326  YPM. ANTPPP.000912, Division of Anthropology, Peabody Museum of Natural History, Yale University.

page 328  By John Underhill in his *Newes from America*. Courtesy of the John Carter Brown Library at Brown University.

page 329  Courtesy of Marian K. O'Keefe.

page 330  Norris L. Bull Collection, Connecticut Archaeology Center, University of Connecticut Museum of Natural History. Courtesy of the Office of State Archaeology, University of Connecticut, and Mashantucket Pequot Museum and Research Center.

pages 332, 333  Salwen 1966, 6, fig. 1; 8, fig. 2. Courtesy of the Archaeological Society of Connecticut.

page 334  (top) IAIS 76-1-719/145; 76-1-729/235, 236, 238; 76-1-719/146; Collections of the University of Connecticut Museum of Natural History; IAIS 76-1-430/2, 76-1-694/1, 76-1-721/239; IAIS 76-1-553/2; Collections of the University of Connecticut Museum of Natural History. (bottom) IAIS 76-1-702/1; 76-1-729/23 and 76-1-505/11; 76-1-721/240; 76-1-687/1; 76-1-702/2; 76-1-719/149; 76-1-504/9; 76-1-704/1. Courtesy of the Institute for American Indian Studies.

page 338  Joseph P. Tustin Papers, Special Collections, Harvey A. Andruss Library, Bloomsburg University of Pennsylvania.

page 340  From Naumec 2008b. Cogswell Family Photographs, courtesy of the Schaghticoke Tribal Nation.

page 341  Courtesy of Faith Damon Davison.

page 342  (top) IAIS 83-3-3/1. Courtesy of the Institute for American Indian Studies. (center and bottom) YPM.ANT.148197 and YPM.ANT.010997, Division of Anthropology, Peabody Museum of Natural History, Yale University.

page 343  (left) Smithsonian Institution National Anthropological Archives.

pages 343 (right), 345, 346, 354, 356 (bottom)  Courtesy of the Schaghticoke Tribal Nation.

page 347  (left) Courtesy of the New Hartford Historical Society, New Hartford, Connecticut.

page 352  From Woodruff 1949, 13. Courtesy of the Orange Historical Society Archives.

page 353  Cogswell family Photographs, courtesy of the Schaghticoke Tribal Nation.

page 356  (top) YPM.ANTPPP.001863, Division of Anthropology, Yale Peabody Museum of Natural History.

page 357  © 1994 Steve Kelley, San Diego Union-Tribune/Copley News Service. By permission of Steve Kelley and Creators Syndicate, Inc.

page 359  Courtesy of the Institute for American Indian Studies. Photograph of Dale Carson by Matthew B. Barr. Photograph of Erin Lamb Meeches by Kimberly Parent.

page 361  Courtesy of Kevin A. McBride.

## COLOR PLATES

atlatl weights  (top) Collections of the Division of Anthropology, Peabody Museum of Natural History, Yale University. (bottom) IAIS 76-1-425/1. Courtesy of the Institute for American Indian Studies.

incised atlatl weight  IAIS 76-1-639/002. Courtesy of the Institute for American Indian Studies.

steatite bowl  Courtesy of the Institute for American Indian Studies.

Otter Creek points  Collections of the Division of Anthropology, Peabody Museum of Natural History, Yale University.

jasper blades  IAIS 76-1-403/1, 3, 4, 6. © Institute for American Indian Studies.

birchbark basket  Private collection.

woodsplint baskets  (top) YPM.ANT.148197.  (bottom) YPM.ANT.010997. Division of Anthropology, Peabody Museum of Natural History, Yale University.

stamped and painted baskets  (top) YPM.ANT.010988.  (bottom) YPM.ANT.148200. Division of Anthropology, Peabody Museum of Natural History, Yale University.

baby rattle  IAIS 83-3-3/1. Courtesy of the Institute for American Indian Studies.

stone hoes  (top) Collections of the University of Connecticut State Museum of Natural History. (bottom) Courtesy of the Institute for American Indian Studies.

Eastern Woodlands arrow  Private collection. Courtesy of the Institute for American Indian Studies. (right) Collections of the Division of Anthropology, Peabody Museum of Natural History, Yale University.

ball clubs  (center) IAIS 84-3-1/1.  (top) IAIS 82-1-14/11.  (bottom) IAIS 06-6-1/1. Institute for American Indian Studies.

monolithic axe  Norris L. Bull Collection, Connecticut Archaeology Center, University of Connecticut Museum of Natural History. Courtesy of the Office of State Archaeology, University of Connecticut, and Mashantucket Pequot Museum and Research Center.

boatstone and birdstones  (left) Collections of the University of Connecticut Museum of Natural History.  (right, top to bottom) IAIS 81-26-21/4, 76-1-750/1, and 76-1-830/1. Courtesy of the Institute for American Indian Studies.

maskette  Photograph by John Spaulding.

soapstone bowl  YPM.ANT.001526, Division of Anthropology, Peabody Museum of Natural History, Yale University.

rock carving  From the collection of Michael Hellwinkle. Photograph by L. Lavin.

pottery from Kent Furnace  Courtesy of the Institute for American Indian Studies.

pottery from Lovers Leap  Courtesy of the Institute for American Indian Studies.

Sebonac pot  IAIS 85-14-21/1. Courtesy of the Institute for American Indian Studies.

North Beach Net-marked pot  Courtesy of the Institute for American Indian Studies.

pots from Tubbs Shell Heap  (left) IAIS 1976-1-729/239.  (right) IAIS 76-1-729/256.  (front) IAIS 1976-1-718/260. Courtesy of the Institute for American Indian Studies.

Bowman's Brook Incised pot  IAIS 3484. Courtesy of the Institute for American Indian Studies.

Niantic Stamped pot  IAIS 3681. Courtesy of the Institute for American Indian Studies.

pot restored from fragments  YPM.ANT.005942, Division of Anthropology, Peabody Museum of Natural History, Yale University.

Windsor Cord-marked pot  YPM.ANT.002885, Division of Anthropology, Peabody Museum of Natural History, Yale University.

herringbone pattern  IAIS 3982. Courtesy of the Institute for American Indian Studies.

charcoal baskets  IAIS 2011-7-1/1. From the collection of David H. Thompson. Courtesy of the Institute for American Indian Studies.

yohicake bag  1842.44.1. Gift of William C. Gilman, Connecticut Historical Society Collections, Hartford, Connecticut.

birchbark containers  IAIS 79-7-1/4, 79-7-3/2, 1 and (bottom right) 79-7-1/3. Courtesy of the Institute for American Indian Studies.

beaded bags  © Gerry Biron; www.gerrybiron.com. Used with permission.

game pieces  © Institute for American Indian Studies. Photograph by Lillia McEnaney.

wooden flute  Courtesy of Strong Eagle Daly. © Institute for American Indian Studies. Photograph by Matthew B. Barr.

Native American artists  Courtesy of Allen Hazard, Sr., and Craig Spears, Sr. © Institute for American Indian Studies. Photograph by Matthew B. Barr.

dugout canoe  Courtesy of the Mashantucket Pequot Museum and Research Center.

stone sources  Adapted from the *Connecticut Native Americans* exhibition at the Peabody Museum of Natural History, Yale University.

projectile point types  From a display at the Institute for American Indian Studies. Used with permission.

# Index

Abbott complex, 190

Abbott Farm (Trenton, N.J.), 190

Abenaki people, 212, 242, 275, 299

accelerator mass spectroscopy (AMS), 29, 193, 196

Achterberg, Jeanne, 220

Adena culture: blocked-end tube pipes, 157; burial practices, 162–165; Meadowood points, 153; mound building, 151, 152, 156; and trade, 156, 166, 167, 191, 193, 361

Afghanistan conflict, 337

Africa, 50

Africans in America, 3

African slave trade, 335–336, 337, 396n67

Aganstata, Mikki, 85

Agawam lunar calendar, 286, 295

agriculture, horticulture distinguished from, 203

Alaska, 95, 174

Albert Morgan Archaeological Society, 21, 25, 206

alcohol, and trade, 315–316

Algonkian language, 81, 103, 104, 165, 255

Algonquian peoples: and beadwork, 219; and dolls, 241–242; and gift exchanges, 322; Great Lakes Algonquian people, 105, 263; and indigenous conflict, 298, 299; and Munsee people, 248; music and dance, 240; place names of, 389n36; social organization of, 249; and wampum trade, 392n160

Allegheny River, 250

Allen's Meadows site (Wilton), 41, 52

Alling, Dwight, 352

Alling, Mrs. Dwight, 352

Alling, Theron, 352

Alphonsce, Jehan, 271, 313

Alvord, J. D., 3

American Anthropological Association, 6

American Association for the Advancement of Science, 6

American Cultural Specialists, 27, 28, 140, 182, 268

American culture, Native American contributions to, 304–305

American Indian Archaeological Institute (AIAI), 18, 19, 29, 39, 43

American Indian Day (Connecticut), 354

American Indian Religious Freedom Act (1978), 318

*American Journal of Science,* 6, 32

American Museum of Natural History (New York), 162

American Revolution, 337, 338–339

American School of Prehistoric Research (Paris), 6, 7, 8

Ames Rock Shelter (Old Lyme), 98, 100

Andastogehronnon people, 298

Andrew, Fields, 352

Andrew, Mrs. Fields, 352

Andrew, Mrs. Leonard, 352

Annasnappet Pond (Massachusetts), 52

anthropology, as scientific discipline, 5

Antiquities Act (1906), 6

antler implements, 25, 91; Early Archaic period, 61; Late Archaic period, 107, 111, 117; Late Woodland period, 193, 205, 209, 227, 229, 230, 231–232, 233, 234, 237, 242, 246; Middle Archaic period, 79; Middle Woodland period, 177; Paleo-Indian period, 42, 45, 52; Post-Contact period, 342, 361

April, Kathleen, 351–352

Arawak people, 193

Arbucci site (Old Lyme), 98

archaeobotany, 33–34, 38, 139

Archaeological and Historical Services, Inc., 20

Archaeological and Historic Preservation Act (1974), 19

archaeological research: development of archaeological theory, 23, 24; geo-archaeology, 32–33; maritime, 71; professional methods, 5, 12–13, 16–17, 23, 25–34. *See also* Connecticut archaeology

Archaeological Research Specialists, 30

archaeological sites: archaeological investigation of, 27–28; destruction of, 5, 6, 11, 12; excavation of, 7–8, 9, 12, 25–27; plant remains from, 33; preservation of, 27

Archaeological Society of Connecticut (ASC), 12, 16, 17, 18

Archaeological Society of Southeastern Connecticut, 186

Archaic period
—Early Archaic, 1, 57; climate, 57, 60; clothing and ornamentation, 64–69, 70; diversity of groups, 60, 69, 71; economic activities, 58, 62, 64, 69, 70; known Archaic sites, 59; mixed pine-hardwood forest environment, 59–60, 71; projectile points, 57, 58, 61, 62, 63–64, 71, 81; settlement patterns, 57, 58, 62
—Middle Archaic, 1, 57; atlatls, 52; climate, 72, 84; dugout canoes, 74–76, 77, 78; economic activities, 84; food and dietary remains, 84; grasslands, 72; Laurentian sites, 119; Narrow